Extraterritoriality Around the Globe

Analysing different political and policy drivers of extraterritoriality in various social, cultural, and economic settings, this book assesses the value of politics within the context of the law and practice of extraterritoriality.

Extraterritoriality is one of the most complex and multifaceted concepts in international law, shaped by a dynamic interplay of legal, political, and practical factors. This book discusses the challenges of understanding extraterritoriality in the context of evolving international relations, the political forces behind state practices, and why international law matters in a field that, at first glance, may seem primarily national in scope. To address these issues, this book includes 12 case studies that explore extraterritoriality from a national perspective, offering both thematic and geographic breadth. It analyses the political drivers of extraterritoriality among similar countries to assess and prove their value. By examining states' extraterritorial behaviour, the book provides a more nuanced, empirical perspective on extraterritoriality, highlighting emerging trends and offering insights into its role in shaping global, legal, and political landscapes in the 21st century.

This book will be of interest to researchers and practitioners in the field of extraterritoriality, law, and politics.

Lucia Leontiev is a Max Weber fellow at the European University Institute, Department of Law. Before joining the EUI, she was a postdoctoral fellow at the Berlin Potsdam Research Group "International Rule of Law-Rise or Decline?", Germany. Lucia received her PhD in International Law from the University of Maastricht and Sant'Anna School of Advanced Studies of Pisa (double doctoral degree) with a dissertation that addresses the jurisdiction of territorial non-state entities in international law. She is an alumna of The Hague Academy of International Law and of the International Law Seminar organised by the UNOG in connection with the annual session of the International Law Commission (ILC). Her research focuses on the law of statehood, jurisdiction, human rights, the interaction between national and international legal orders, as well as the role of geopolitics in a changing international legal order; topics on which she has also extensively published.

Manuel José Segovia González holds a PhD (Law) from the University of Luxembourg. He is a qualified lawyer in Mexico, where he practices as an international legal consultant. He is an Adjunct Lecturer of Private International Law at the University of Luxembourg and was a Visiting Scholar at the Max Planck Institute for Comparative Public Law and International Law. He also served as Deputy Director of International Law at the Office of the Legal Adviser of the Ministry of Foreign Affairs of Mexico. He is a Full Member of the *Asociación Americana de Derecho Internacional Privado* (ASADIP) and a Member of The European Association of Private International Law (EAPIL) Young Research Network. He has carried research stays at the Max Planck Institute Luxembourg for International, European, and Regulatory Procedural Law, the European University Institute, and The Hague Academy of International Law. He is a former National Researcher Candidate in Social Sciences (CONAHCYT, Mexico). He has published on a variety of topics of private international law, public international law, international dispute settlement and arbitration, and comparative law.

Extraterritoriality Around the Globe

Multiform Approaches in a Multipolar World

Edited by Lucia Leontiev and
Manuel José Segovia González

Routledge
Taylor & Francis Group
LONDON AND NEW YORK

First published 2026
by Routledge
4 Park Square, Milton Park, Abingdon, Oxon OX14 4RN

and by Routledge
605 Third Avenue, New York, NY 10158

Routledge is an imprint of the Taylor & Francis Group, an informa business

British Library Cataloguing-in-Publication Data
A catalogue record for this book is available from the British Library

ISBN: 978-1-032-51589-2 (hbk)
ISBN: 978-1-032-51590-8 (pbk)
ISBN: 978-1-003-40297-8 (ebk)

DOI: 10.4324/9781003402978

Typeset in Sabon
by Apex CoVantage, LLC

We would like to express our deepest gratitude to our families and dedicate this work to our mothers. Para mi mamá, María Magdalena González. Pentru mama, cu multă dragoste!

Contents

Contributors

Marjolaine Abada-Fasquelle holds a doctorate in law, with her thesis focusing on the extraterritorial application of economic sanctions in international trade. After working for the French Committee of the International Chamber of Commerce (ICC France), she has taught courses, first as a temporary assistant lecturer at the Sorbonne Law School and, since January 2024, as a temporary teaching and research assistant at the University of Caen Normandie.

Paul Arnell is Associate Professor in Law within the Law School, Robert Gordon University, Aberdeen, Scotland. He has degrees from Canada, England, and Scotland, graduating with a PhD in international law from the University of Hull in 1999. Dr. Arnell's research falls within the areas of criminal jurisdiction, extradition, and human rights. His monograph, *Law Across Borders*, was published by Routledge in 2012. He has published over 100 articles on his areas of expertise. His work has been published in a range of outlets, including the International and Comparative Law Quarterly, Journal of Criminal Law, Scots Law Times, International Journal of Human Rights, the Juridical Review, and the Scotsman.

Pouria Askary is Associate Professor of International Law at Allameh Tabataba'i University of Iran (ATU). His expertise spans International Human Rights Law, International Humanitarian Law, and the International Law of Foreign Investment. He serves as Secretary-General and board member of the Iranian Association for UN Studies (IAUNS). He is also a member of the Executive Council of the Asian Society of International Law (ASIANSIL).

Francesca Capone is Associate Professor of International Law at Sant'Anna School of Advanced Studies in Pisa. Prior to being appointed as Associate Professor in 2021, she served as Assistant Professor (tenure track), Senior Research Fellow, and Coordinator of the Master in Human Rights and Conflict Management at the same academic institution (2014–2021). From 2012–2013, she worked as Research Fellow in public international law at the British Institute of International and Comparative Law in London,

UK. She holds a joint PhD in international law from Sant'Anna School of Advanced Studies and Tilburg University, which she earned in 2013. She has been a visiting fellow and a guest lecturer at several academic institutions across Europe, including Leiden University, Tilburg University, and the Max Planck Institute for Comparative Public Law and International Law and beyond Europe. She has undertaken research on a wide range of topics, focusing in particular on international humanitarian law and counterterrorism. She co-edited, together with Dr. Christophe Paulussen and Prof. Andrea de Guttry, the volume *Foreign Fighters under International Law and Beyond* (T.M.C. Asser Press/Springer 2016), as well as the follow-up volume *Returning Foreign Fighters: Responses, Legal Challenges and Ways Forward* (T.M.C. Asser Press/Springer 2023), co-edited with Dr. Christophe Paulussen and Dr Rebecca Mignot-Mahdavi. Both volumes have been well received, becoming pivotal academic contributions in the field. Prof. Capone's book *Reparations for Child Victims of Armed Conflict: State of the Field and Current Challenges* (Intersentia 2017) won the 2018 Ciardi Prize for the best book in the field of international humanitarian law.

Rishi Gulati is Associate Professor in International Law at the University of East Anglia, United Kingdom, and Barrister, Victorian Bar, Australia. He researches, teaches, and practices in all areas of public and private international law. Rishi has a PhD from King's College London, which he undertook as a Dickson Poon Scholar of Law, Advanced Masters in Public International Law from Leiden University, and a Bachelor of Laws (Honours) from the Australian National University. He has previously held positions at Freie Universität Berlin in the context of the interdisciplinary Berlin Potsdam Research Group "International Rule of Law – Rise or Decline?", as Assistant Professor at the Dublin City University, Fellow at the London School of Economics and Political Science, and has been a Laureate Research Fellow at the University of New South Wales. Rishi is the author or co-editor of several books and articles, including *Access to Justice and International Organisations* (Cambridge University Press, 2022), *Elgar Companion on the Hague Conference on Private International Law* (Edward Elgar, 2020), *Elgar Companion on the United Nations Commission on International Trade Law* (Edward Elgar, 2023), and *The Elgar Companion on the Institute for the Unification of Private Law* (Edward Elgar, 2024). Rishi has also worked as an international lawyer for the Australian Government, as a Judge's Associate at the Federal Court of Australia, appears as counsel before international and national courts, and has consulted for several UN agencies.

Liliya Khasanova is a postdoctoral fellow at the Hitachi Center for Technology and International Relations at the Fletcher School of Law and Diplomacy, Tufts University. She specialises in international public law and governance, with a particular focus on the international law of cyberspace. Her current research explores national and cultural perspectives on governing information and communication technologies (ICTs), global and regional data governance, and the impact of ICTs on the international legal order. Liliya earned her PhD from Kazan Federal University in Russia (2019) and held several doctoral and postdoctoral positions at the Nanterre Center for International Law (CEDIN) in France, Center for International Law and Justice in Sweden, Fribourg University in Switzerland and the Berlin Potsdam Research Group "International Rule of Law – Rise or Decline?" in Germany. She also served as a graduate research fellow with the Negotiation Program at Harvard Law School (2017) and was selected as a Women, Peace, and Security (WIIS) Next Generation Fellow (2021).

Sarah McGibbon (LLB (UP), LLM (Cantab), PhD (UM)) is Lecturer in the Foundations of Law department at Maastricht University, Netherlands. She previously held the position of Lecturer in International Peace and Security at Durham University, UK, where she was also Deputy Director of the interdisciplinary Durham Global Security Institute. Sarah has written on a range of topics, including non-state effective territorial entities, extraterritoriality, secession, use of force, statehood, and various constitutional law topics. She previously practised as a constitutional law and human rights attorney in her native South Africa.

Matthew Nelson is an Australian lawyer with more than a decade of experience in practice as a government solicitor and prosecutor. He lectures in criminal law and evidence and international law in the Faculty of Law and Justice at the University of New South Wales in Sydney, Australia. Matthew was based in London for several years, where he assisted in prosecutions of international crimes in domestic and international courts. He holds a Master of Laws in International Law from University College London, where he attended as the Sir John Salmond Scholar, as well as holding a Bachelor of Laws with Honours and a Bachelor of Social Science from the University of New South Wales.

Sudipta Purkayastha is an associate with Withers LLP in the international arbitration and public international law teams. She is a dual-qualified lawyer in England and Wales and India. Prior to joining Withers, Sudipta worked with a senior barrister on cases before international criminal tribunals in The Hague, The Netherlands. She also previously worked as a Legal Adviser with a non-profit organisation on matters related to public international law, international criminal law, international humanitarian law, international human rights, as well as business and human rights (corporate accountability in relation to violations of international law).

Aniruddha Rajput is a distinguished professor of Law at National Law University, Delhi. He is a barrister and practices as a consultant with Withers LLP in London. He was a Member of the United Nations International Law Commission (2017–22), where he served as the Chairperson of the Drafting Committee of the International Law Commission at its 69th Session in 2017. He advises and appears on behalf of States and private entities before international courts and tribunals. His areas of teaching, research, and writing span across general international law and various specialised areas such as the law of the sea, boundary disputes, use of force, international trade and investment law, etc. He is currently a member of the Panel of Experts constituted by the UNIDROIT to draft principles of international investment contracts.

Yaël Ronen is a professor and a senior research fellow at the Minerva Center for Human Rights at the Hebrew University of Jerusalem and the academic editor of the Israel Law Review (CUP), a journal of human rights, public and international law. In recent years, she has been directing the Digest of Israeli Practice in International Law project. Yaël's scholarship and teaching focus on the intersection between issues of territorial status and other areas of international law, particularly human rights. Her book publications include, with David Kretzmer and Yaël Ronen, *The Occupation of Justice* (2nd, expanded edition, Oxford University Press 2021). Yaël received her LLB and LLM from the Hebrew University of Jerusalem and her PhD from the University of Cambridge, England. Prior to embarking on an academic career, she was a career diplomat and lawyer in the Ministry of Foreign Affairs and was a member of the Israeli team in the negotiations over the Israel-Palestinian Interim Agreement (the Oslo Accord).

Nailia Savenkova holds a LLB in International Law from Kazan Federal University and an LLM in International Human Rights and Humanitarian Law from European University Viadrina (2018). For the past six years, she has been working for various international humanitarian organisations as a legal adviser.

Kamila Shaibakova holds a degree in Criminal Law and Criminology from Kazan Federal University and an LLM in Human Rights Law and Human Rights Research from Maastricht University. In 2020, she earned her PhD from Kazan Federal University, focusing on extradition and human rights. She has conducted research at the Stockholm Centre for International Law and Justice, Leipzig University, and the Human Rights Center at Kazan Federal University. Currently, she serves as a Programme Officer at an international human rights organisation in Sweden.

Juan Ignacio Stampalija is Associate Professor and Deputy Director of the LLM in International Arbitration, Litigation, and Contracts at Austral University Law School (Buenos Aires, Argentina). He has an LLM in International Legal Studies from New York University, where he was an Arthur T. Vanderbilt Scholar. He also has an LLM from Hong Kong University.

Emre Turkut is an affiliated researcher at the Ghent Rolin-Jaequemyns International Law Institute (GRILI) and a non-resident research fellow at the European Center for Populism Studies (ECPS). His research covers a variety of fields within the domain(s) of public international law, international human rights law, and comparative constitutional law, including states of emergency, derogations, emergency powers, counterterrorism, self-determination movements, international law in domestic courts, transnational judicial dialogue and judicial politics in authoritarian regimes. His research outputs have appeared in top-tier journals and received several scholarly awards and prizes, including an honorable mention for the American Society of Comparative Law's prestigious Colin B. Picker Prize in Comparative Law in 2020. Emre previously served as a Lecturer in International Law at the Anglo-American University in Prague and a postdoctoral researcher at Hertie School's Centre for Fundamental Rights. He also held a Swedish Institute fellowship at Uppsala University (2018–19), a DAAD fellowship at Hertie School (2019–20), and a *re:constitution* fellowship at the Max Planck Institute for Comparative Public Law and International Law and the European Court of Human Rights (2021–22). Along with his academic work, Emre is frequently contacted by NGOs and global media platforms to give expert opinions on issues of human rights, international law, and Turkish law. He also serves as a legal consultant and expert witness on Turkish law to several private entities.

Hassan Vakilian is an associate professor of Public Law at Allameh Tabataba'i University of Iran (ATU). His expertise lies in Constitutional Law, Comparative Constitutional Law, and Legislative Studies.

Alina Veneziano is an attorney, CPA, and PhD Candidate at King's College London, writing her dissertation on extraterritoriality and blockchain technology. She received her JD at Georgetown University Law Center and LLM at New York University School of Law. Alina is a Partner at Oberheiden, P.C., a nationally recognised law firm in the United States focusing on federal defense, litigation, and compliance. The firm's practice areas encompass white-collar criminal defense, securities litigation, and corporate compliance. At Oberheiden, P.C., Alina advises clients on compliance with SEC rules and regulations, defending against SEC enforcement actions and DOJ investigations, navigating IRS audits, and providing advice and guidance on emerging technologies such as cryptocurrencies and blockchain technology.

Foreword

It is my great pleasure to introduce this insightful compilation of approaches addressing the issue of extraterritorial jurisdiction of states in public international law. *Extraterritoriality Around the Globe: Multiform Approaches in a Multipolar World*, thoughtfully structured and meticulously edited, explores how selected states address the delicate topic of exercising extraterritorial jurisdiction. This book arrives at a timely moment, as instances of state jurisdiction being exercised beyond national borders – once considered illegitimate – are increasingly receiving (tacit) acknowledgement from the international community. As the title suggests, and bearing in mind that international law cannot be viewed *in abstracto* without considering foreign affairs, the editors wisely decided to explore non-legal factors that may help explain this shift.

Each chapter begins by acknowledging that contemporary academic discourse treats the principle of territoriality as a cornerstone of jurisdiction in international law. Thus, the authors do not attempt to challenge the fact that, in Kuhnian terms, public international law's dominant paradigm of state jurisdiction is based on the territorial principle. However, they constructively argue that the increasing interdependence of global actors and markets – two essentially non-legal considerations – has led to a growing recognition of the need for extraterritorial measures to ensure effective legal regulation. As a result, there is a trend towards a broader acceptance of extraterritoriality, particularly in areas such as human rights, environmental protection, and global commerce.

From a methodological standpoint, this book stands out for its detailed and comprehensive overview of the approaches followed by selected states. The chapters, engaging in a sort of dialogue with one another, transcend traditional political dichotomies, such as those based on divisions along East-West or Global South-Global North lines. Instead, they reveal that states from diverse regions – each with varying legal traditions, economic policies, and political directions – often exhibit similar tendencies in their extraterritorial jurisdiction practices. In addition to challenging the conservative view, this nuanced perspective allows readers to track recent developments in this field of international law.

These developments, when approached as case studies, raise another important question about the state of this field: Can we speak of an emerging new state practice of extraterritorial jurisdiction? If so, it could trigger a domino effect of questions, eventually leading to a plausible claim for a change in the customary international law of state jurisdiction. As such, these examples subtly suggest that the paradigm in this area of international law may be on the brink of change. The book, therefore, lays a solid foundation – both methodologically and theoretically – for future research and scholarly debate.

This book's content deserves equal praise. It deepens our understanding of global legal practices by shedding light on previously under-researched questions. With chapters that cover a diverse range of examples – such as marriage law developments in Israel and Argentina's aspirations for universal criminal jurisdiction – the authors address multiple research gaps in the respective academic sub-fields. The accessible writing style, paired with contemporary examples, ensures that this book will be a valuable resource not only for scholars but also for undergraduate students seeking to understand the complexities of extraterritorial jurisdiction in their own states and beyond.

In conclusion, rather than offering a classical comparison of jurisdictions within each chapter, this book allows readers to see the broader picture of how different states (il)legitimately exercise extraterritorial jurisdiction and draw their own conclusions. This approach minimises academic bias and provides ample food for thought, encouraging constructive engagement with the arguments presented. Moreover, the authors and editors convey a clear message to their readers: non-legal considerations often not only play a role in shaping international legal practices but also directly influence them. While prompting discussions about a potential Kuhnian scientific revolution in the approach to state jurisdiction within public international law, this book does not seek to initiate it – rather, it provides indications that such a shift might already be underway.

Prof. Dr. **Diana Sârcu**
Judge at the European Court of Human Rights
Strasbourg, 31 January 2025

Acknowledgements

We would like to express our sincere gratitude to **Serena D'Elia,** who served as an editorial assistant during the preparation of this volume. Her thoughtful assistance in revising the manuscript was truly appreciated and made a valuable contribution to the process.

1 The Global Stretch

Untangling the Complexities of Extraterritoriality

Lucia Leontiev and Manuel José Segovia González

1 Introduction

Extraterritoriality is one of the most complex legal concepts. The difficulties traditionally associated with it obey a combination of factors. First, one must be conscious of the extremely dynamic and diverse realities that extraterritoriality covers. The interests that states may want to regulate beyond their borders are numerous and change constantly according to the specific necessities of the time. Second, the concept has evolved in tandem with the various legal disciplines that address the different interests of states abroad. What started as the justification of diplomatic immunity of ambassadors and embassies back in the 16th and 17th centuries,[1] based on the legal fiction that considered them direct emanations of the sending state and physically present in its territory,[2] in modern days – extraterritoriality – rises as a tool for the regulation of state interests such as data flows and cybersecurity, among other contemporary applications. Within this spectrum, a wide variety of legal fields (essentially of a public law nature) have served states as platforms to extend their jurisdiction extraterritorially. Third, while there is countless scholarship on the effects of extraterritoriality in light of the different fields, works of a transversal nature providing a broader view of the concept are much less common. This piecemeal and disciplinary evolution of extraterritoriality results in a protean or chameleonic concept, always in transformation, as some scholars call it.[3]

With more states concentrating significant power in the world scene,[4] there is an increasing need to expand empirical research on the concept

1 Momchil Milanov, "L'extraterritorialité avant la territorialisation de l'Etat: essai sur le développement historique d'un concept protéen," in *Extraterritoriality*, eds. Hannah L. Buxbaum and Thibaut Fleury Graff (Leiden/Boston: Brill | Nijhoff, 2022), 130–131, 143–145.

2 The same legal fiction through which a ship in the high seas was considered a floating part of state territory in the 19th century and after.

3 Milanov, "L'extraterritorialité avant la territorialisation de l'Etat," 131.

4 Emma Ashford and Evan Cooper, "Yes, the World Is Multipolar. And That Isn't Bad News for the United States," *Foreign Policy*. Accessed 22 February 2025. https://foreignpolicy.com/2023/10/05/usa-china-multipolar-bipolar-unipolar/.

DOI: 10.4324/9781003402978-1

of extraterritoriality across the different national practices around the world, irrespective of legal fields. The heavy disciplinary research orientation in the field has cast the attention away from other objects and fields of extraterritoriality that, although underresearched, deserve equal attention, at least if a more comprehensive understanding of extraterritoriality is sought. To construct, sometimes it is necessary to deconstruct. The turnaround consists of looking directly at the state practices without any prejudice in order to explore and discover general trends that inform the concept of extraterritoriality from a variety of national perspectives. As it will be referred to in this chapter, this exercise and methodology exist, but much more is needed.

Extraterritoriality is a concept that outruns legal science to an important extent. In practical terms, the world is no *terra nullius*, so the extension of the power of a state beyond its borders necessarily encounters other state power, at least in a dormant form. States being sovereign and equal, there is no natural law that can serve as the basis of extraterritoriality. As such, extraterritoriality incorporates a legal void that can only be filled by understanding the forces of another nature that are involved. Considering that extraterritoriality is largely motivated by national interests and that states are relatively free in this respect *vis-à-vis* international law, it is quite easy to observe that one of the most, if not the most important of such forces is politics. However, legal scholarship has paid very little attention to the political nature of extraterritoriality.[5] What is important is not the study of the politics of extraterritoriality, a task that corresponds to other areas of social studies, but how politics inform the legal concept of extraterritoriality. In this context, politics is understood in a broad sense, covering the essential characteristics and circumstances of states that motivate them to make decisions as political communities in the international arena.

The present volume puts together twelve carefully selected case studies addressing extraterritoriality at a national level, with the intention to provide the transversal, wider (both in substance and geographic breadth), and interdisciplinary approaches needed for a more comprehensive understanding of one of the most convoluted, yet compelling international law and international relations concepts of the 21st century. In this introductory chapter, we intend to clear the way by addressing the complexities of extraterritoriality from epistemological and international law perspectives. We then present the methodological approach of the book and the rationale of the case study selection. This

5 Some exceptions, although of a hybrid nature with other fields of social sciences, include: Daniel S. Margolies, Umut Özsu, Maïa Pal and Ntina Tzouvala, eds., *The Extraterritoriality of Law. History, Theory, Politics* (Abingdon/New York: Routledge, 2019); Maïa Pal, *The Politics of Extraterritoriality: A Historical Sociology of Public International Law* (Sussex: University of Sussex, 2013); Paul B. Stephan, "The Political Economy of Extraterritoriality," *Politics and Governance* 1 (2013): 92–101.

chapter concludes with an overview of the structure of the book, mapping the national trends and approaches detected among the selected states.

2 Epistemology of Extraterritoriality

Epistemology is the theory or philosophy of knowledge. In contrast to ontology, or theory of being, epistemology is not concerned with what is in the world but rather with how – indeed whether – we can know it.[6] As one of the most elusive legal concepts, extraterritoriality presents a strong epistemological interest, starting with the terminology. Indeed, the prefix *extra* denotes a concept that refers to a situation that occurs outside common or accepted canons, or at least that goes beyond the ordinary. Another terminological concern is the generalised use of the terms 'extraterritoriality' and 'extraterritorial jurisdiction' interchangeably. While both terms refer to the same situation in essence, it is important to distinguish them in order to provide the conceptual basis that facilitates the comprehension of the phenomenon – even if this book unavoidably incurs in the same practice. As an adjective, extraterritorial jurisdiction relates to the juridical character of the power of the state exercised abroad. The word 'jurisdiction' thus designates the legal vehicle through which state power is conducted beyond the territory of the state. As a noun, extraterritoriality is a neutral term that only captures situations indicating that states are involved in exercising their power beyond their borders, whichever means, juridical, political, or other. Simply put, extraterritoriality only describes the attitudes and conducts of a state with respect to its power abroad. Some authors suggest that it even "means subjects, items and events located outside [a sovereign] territorial power of a given state; also beyond geographical and legal borders of a given state".[7]

There is also a more substantial feeling of despair among scholars with respect to the concept of extraterritoriality. Some consider that looking for a definition is a hopeless[8] and impossible task.[9] Some attribute to it even a mysterious character.[10] These feelings exacerbate in proportion to the efforts to apprehend the concept from a technical perspective. For instance, scholars tend to look for a definition in the different legal areas that have animated

6 Jonathan Joseph, "Epistemology," in *A Concise Oxford Dictionary of Politics and International Relations*, eds. Garrett W. Brown, Iain McLean and Alistair McMillan (Oxford: Oxford University Press, 2018).

7 Krzystof Zalucki, "Extraterritorial Jurisdiction in International Law," *International Community Law Review* 17 (2015): 407.

8 Hannah L. Buxbaum, "The Practice(s) of Extraterritoriality," in *Extraterritoriality*, eds. Buxbaum and Fleury Graff, 3.

9 Thibaut Fleury Graff, "(Il)licéités et (dé)mesures de l'extraterritorialité," in *Extraterritoriality*, eds. Buxbaum and Fleury Graff, 51.

10 Horatia Muir Watt, Lucia Bíziková, Agatha Brandão de Oliveira, Diego P. Fernández Arroyo and Megan Ma, eds., *Le tournant global en droit international privé* (Paris: Pedone, 2020), 363.

extraterritoriality through time, or invest themselves in seemingly philosophical legal debates in order to elucidate if it is an institution or just a situation, a state competence or just the reach of a given statute.[11]

This preliminary assessment shows that there is a need to explore what we know about the concept of extraterritoriality and the ways that may lead to a better understanding of it. The task should start by acknowledging that extraterritoriality is mainly a legal construct, not an illegal or prohibited action – even if extraterritoriality has been used as a concept to condemn state attitudes and conduct in the international domain. In our opinion, the main complexity around the concept of extraterritoriality has to do with the contradictory and fragmented reality in which it operates. As a legal construct, extraterritoriality mainly supposes the existence of state interests beyond territorial borders, which they are entitled to pursue. However, in the real world, this possibility is pretty much hypothetical, as the exercise of extraterritorial jurisdiction clashes with the interests of other states, which are equally important, starting with territorial sovereignty. Such a level of tension hinders the development of legal rules of extraterritoriality and, as a consequence, the configuration and consolidation of extraterritoriality as a legal concept.

Legal scholarship must transcend the dichotomy of power and constraint that embraces extraterritoriality, and the way to do it is to look at the many and varied legal and non-legal elements orbiting around it.

2.1 *Metalegal Aspects of Extraterritoriality*

Extraterritoriality is a concept that strives to provide juridical content to a reality that is pretty much transcended by non-legal factors. Inevitably influenced by state equality, the relationships of power between states are deeply immersed both in a factual and a political reality. In a factual reality because the exercise and effects of extraterritorial jurisdiction are often conditioned to some physical relationship of contact between the state and the targeted object. More importantly, because the extension of the power of a state frequently confronts the power of another, generating situations of concurrent jurisdiction for which there is no legal solution. In a political reality because extraterritorial jurisdiction strongly responds to the structures of politics, including schemes of identification, belonging, and community aspirations, among others.

2.1.1 *The Factual Nature of Extraterritoriality*

Traditionally, state jurisdiction is theorised as a right. It is defined as the right of the state to regulate the conduct of persons, both natural and legal, property, and the consequences of events.[12] In his general course at The

11 Cf. Thibaut Fleury Graff, "(Il)licéités et (dé)mesures de l'extraterritorialité," 52.
12 *Banković and Others v Belgium and Others 2001-XII 333, (2007) EHRR SE5, paras 59 and 60.*

Hague Academy, Frederick A. Mann explains that "jurisdiction involves both the right to exercise it within the limits of the State's sovereignty and the duty to recognize the same right of other States".[13] However, the definition suggests a strong unilateral character: states only recognise jurisdiction as their own right and duty, but there is no indication of complementary duties and rights. Positive philosophers such as Jeremy Bentham and John Austin argued that the binomial 'rights and duties' is a single and simultaneous phenomenon.[14] In private international law, where jurisdiction is considered the object of a legal relationship between states and individuals, normally, it is not theorised as a right. The reason is that domestic law already comprises mechanisms that guarantee the right of the parties to be heard – which is the most essential function of jurisdiction from this perspective – while a hierarchical system of norms is still pretty much lacking in public international law.[15]

In (public) international law, state jurisdiction is the object of a legal relationship, basically in two situations only. First, with respect to territory, where state jurisdiction "extends to everybody and everything".[16] In the *Lotus* case of 1927, which constitutes the landmark international law judgement on jurisdiction, the Permanent Court of International Justice (PCIJ) declared that a state "may not exercise its power in any form in the territory of another state".[17] The absolute right that accrues to states within their territories naturally results in a universal obligation to respect territorial sovereignty. The second revolves around the exclusive jurisdiction of states, the so-called *domaine réservé*. In terms of Article 2(7) of the United Nations Charter, exclusive jurisdiction refers to those "matters which are essentially within the domestic jurisdiction of any state". Addressed extensively by scholars, as well as in different fora since it appeared in the Covenant of the League of Nations of 1919, including the PCIJ's Advisory Opinion on the *Nationality Decrees Issued in Tunis and Morocco* of 1923,[18] the notion of exclusive or domestic jurisdiction plays as a sort of wall of containment

13 Frederick A. Mann, *The Doctrine of International Jurisdiction Revisited after Twenty Years* (The Hague: Collected Courses, 1984), 20.

14 Guillaume Tusseau, "Les contraintes intellectuelles de la construction des notions juridiques. L'exemple du concept de pouvoir chez Jeremy Bentham et John Austin," in *Les notions juridiques*, ed. Guillaume Tusseau (Paris: Economica, 2009), 69.

15 Although some scholars defend the idea of a hierarchical international legal order reflected by *jus cogens* norms, *erga omnes* obligations, as well as certain human rights which could be put at the top of the pyramid of international legal norms. See Jure Vidmar, "Norm Conflicts and Hierarchy in International Law: Towards a Vertical International Legal System?" in *Hierarchy in International Law. The Place of Human Rights*, eds. Erika de Wet and Jure Vidmar (Oxford: Oxford University Press, 2012), 13–41.

16 Mann, *The Doctrine of International Jurisdiction*, 20, citing Max Huber and Joseph Story.

17 *SS Lotus (France v Turkey)*, PCIJ Series A No. 10, 18.

18 *Nationality Decrees Issued in Tunis and Morocco*, Advisory Opinion, [1923] PCIJ Series B, No. 4.

against the permanent expansion of the international legal order, reserving the relationships between legal (private and public) and natural persons of municipal law to the sole power of states.[19] The underlying idea is that essentially national matters, alien to international relations *strictu sensu*, remain within the domestic realm.[20] Matters such as the form of government and national defence are thus associated with the idea of exclusive jurisdiction.[21] Naturally flexible according to the evolution of interstate relationships,[22] the concept of exclusive jurisdiction remains an important element in the demarcation of power in the international arena. It mainly prevents the political organs of the international community from intervening in those matters. International organisations are thus obligated towards states which hold the right of exclusive jurisdiction. The concept of exclusive jurisdiction has also contributed to the delimitation of direct interstate legal relationships by providing the principle of non-intervention with some of its concrete substance.[23]

State jurisdiction is even further from supposing a legal relationship in the extraterritorial domain. In the *Lotus*, the PCIJ also declared that

> Far from laying down a general prohibition to the effect that States may not extend the application of their laws and the jurisdiction of their courts to persons, property and acts outside their territory, [international law] leaves them in this respect a wide measure of discretion which is only limited in certain cases by prohibitive rules.[24]

The *Lotus* thus completes the foundations of the system of jurisdiction in the field of international law and international relations. First, by enshrining the principle of territorial sovereignty, the Court recognises the exclusive right of states to exercise their power in their territories in whichever form. In this famous passage, the Court acknowledges that states are also entitled to exercise their prescriptive and adjudicatory jurisdiction extraterritorially. In the end, the *Lotus* endorses a system of concurrent jurisdiction.[25] The possibility that the prescriptive jurisdiction of a state coincides with the territorial jurisdiction of another is virtually always present, and no preference

19 Gaetano Arangio-Ruiz, *Le domaine réservé. L'Organisation internationale et le rapport entre droit international et droit interne* (The Hague: Collected Courses, 1990), 31, 35, 138.
20 *Ibid.*, 136.
21 *Ibid.*, 40.
22 Areas once considered as belonging to the exclusive jurisdiction of states that can no longer be characterised as such are human rights, fascist regimes, the emancipation of peoples from colonial domination, and racial discrimination. Arangio-Ruiz, *Le domaine réservé*, 39–40.
23 *Ibid.*, 1–2, 428 *et seq.*
24 *SS Lotus (France v Turkey)*, 19.
25 *Ibid.*, 30–31.

can be established as long as the horizontal nature of international relations prevails.[26]

The most common situations driving states to extend the application of their laws beyond their borders show that concurrent jurisdiction is practically an intrinsic part of extraterritorial jurisdiction. One of the best and simplest examples is the repression of crime committed by or against the nationals of the state. In the case of the repression of nationals, the chances of concurrent jurisdiction are quite high as the national state and the state where the crime is committed appear equally interested in regulating it. The case of the repression of crime against nationals arguably admits an assessment of the interests at stake. This is why, in this situation, states subject their relevant provisions to principles such as double criminality and *ne bis in idem* and may apply the lower penalty. While these mechanisms reduce the number of concurrent jurisdiction cases and may attenuate their effects, they do not eradicate them. For instance, with respect to the *ne bis in idem* principle, concurrent jurisdiction persists until and in particular cases even after there is a judgment in the foreign country.

States assert their universal jurisdiction to repress serious criminal conduct, driven by public policy and moral grounds, irrespective of the national origin of the perpetrator or the place of commission. The progression of international criminal law, both through treaties and the establishment of specialised tribunals, has extended the catalogue of conducts that justify universal jurisdiction while contributing to the unification of the applicability criteria. The principle of universal jurisdiction thus emerges as an indicator of the general acknowledgement of the international community with respect to the heinous character of an array of crimes. Many states, however, claim universal jurisdiction through their own laws according to their own understanding of public policy or the heinous character of a given crime. The result of this uneven regulation is a variety of grounds to exercise universal jurisdiction across the world. The scene is again set to concurrent jurisdiction. The universal jurisdiction of a given state may easily encounter the territorial jurisdiction of a state that criminalises the given conduct only under ordinary law. In her chapter, among the constitutional values and imperatives for extraterritorial jurisdiction of South Africa, Sarah McGibbon indicates that there is an obligation to exercise universal jurisdiction in relation to the crime of torture, arguing that, in so doing, it goes even further than international law, specifically the Rome Statute.

Another neat example of concurrent jurisdiction in the criminal context arises in the field of the fight against corruption. It is widely accepted that corruption is a plague that affects the world economy and that acts of corruption frequently spread across borders. Led by the United States, some

26 Cedric Ryngaert, *Jurisdiction in International Law* (Oxford: Oxford University Press, 2015), 143.

of the wealthiest countries, whose economies are the most affected by these practices, have enacted legislation to sanction corruption abroad, at its source, through slight, and sometimes very slight grounds of jurisdiction.[27] While the unilateral efforts of wealthy states obey to a lack of enforcement worldwide, as pointed out by Marjolaine Abada-Fasquelle in her chapter on France, the states where the acts of corruption take place can exercise their territorial jurisdiction to repress the conduct, as well as their jurisdiction based on nationality to impose an administrative penalty to the responsible authorities.

An important element of the fight against corruption, unaddressed until recently, is the criminalisation of the conduct of foreign authorities. Establishing jurisdiction over the acts of foreign authorities unilaterally may be disrespectful towards foreign states and even amount to a violation of the principle of non-intervention. With forty-six and 191 state parties, respectively, the OECD Convention on Combating Bribery of Foreign Public Officials in International Business Transactions of 1997 and the United Nations Convention Against Corruption of 2003, solve pretty much the issue. However, they also create a space of concurrent jurisdiction that equals their size. Both conventions grant jurisdiction to punish the acts of corruption of foreign public officials and acknowledge the jurisdiction of the parties to prosecute their national authorities for offences committed abroad.[28]

The navigation of ships is another area particularly prone to concurrent jurisdiction. Vessels are artefacts registered in a single state, the laws of which regulate different aspects in connection to their purpose, like administrative, technical, and social issues. Thus, flag state jurisdiction, which is equivalent to nationality jurisdiction, determines the responsibility for a ship, and it is pretty much exclusive on the high seas. Vessels also carry passengers of different nationalities and merchandises of different origins across the globe, constantly docking in foreign territories. The daily life and activity that takes place within inevitably takes place also in the territory of other states. The view that a ship is a floating part of state territory has long fallen into disrepute;[29] hence, the exercise of jurisdiction of the flag state in a foreign port presents an extraterritorial character. When a ship enters a port, there are no

27 On more than one occasion, the US have been blamed for exercising jurisdiction on the basis that the relevant transaction was made in dollars or that the clearing operation was performed by a financial institution located in the US.

28 OECD Convention, Article 4(1) and (2). The UN Convention provides for territorial jurisdiction in Article 42(1). Concerning offences committed abroad, according to Article 42(2) of this Convention, jurisdiction is granted only to the state the national of which commits the offence or is offended. Thus, concurrent jurisdiction may arise only between two states (except in cases of multiple nationality), contrary to the OECD convention, in the context of which more than two countries may end up exercising jurisdiction.

29 James R. Crawford, *Brownlie's Principles of Public International Law* (Oxford: Oxford University Press, 2012), 464.

limits to the local criminal jurisdiction over it, provided that action is taken with regard only to breaches of local law.[30] But if the crime is committed by or against a national of the flag state, in most cases, nothing will impede that state from exercising its jurisdiction, too. In the regulatory sphere, state port jurisdiction and flag state jurisdiction may also be encountered. Article 218 of the UN Convention on the Law of the Sea (UNCLOS) grants port states the right to institute proceedings or impose monetary penalties for illegal discharges that occur outside their territorial sea and Exclusive Economic Zone (EEZ). Also, according to Article 23 of the Straddling Stocks Agreement, a port state has the duty to take certain steps to combat illegal fishing, such as inspecting documents, fishing gear, and the catch. However, these provisions do not impede the flag state from imposing its own sanctions on the ships upon their return.

Aniruddha Rajput and Sudipta Purkayastha show that India's global aspirations to maintain a safe, open, and stable Indian Ocean region leads it to exercise its jurisdiction in ways that it competes with that of other states, particularly in areas where state jurisdiction remains somewhat uncertain, like the EEZ. The authors address the *"Enrica Lexie" Incident*, at the occasion of which Italian marines were arrested in Kochi following the shooting and killing of Indian fishermen in India's contiguous zone. India's allegations before a UNCLOS Annex VII arbitral tribunal were based on nationality and territorial jurisdiction. The tribunal held that the marines were entitled to sovereign immunity, but it did not find that India's jurisdiction was illegal.

In the case of aircraft, for instance, Article 3(1) of the Convention on Offences and Certain Other Acts Committed on Board Aircraft (Tokyo Convention) of 1963 provides that the state of registration is competent to exercise jurisdiction over offences and acts committed on board, while Article 3(3) provides that criminal jurisdiction exercised in accordance with national law is not excluded.

Concurrent jurisdiction also arises beyond territorial and nationality jurisdiction. Political struggles between states are another important source. The interplay between unilateral economic sanctions adopted by countries like the US in their quest to prevent trade with nationals from states, the politics of which they oppose, and the 'blocking statutes' enacted by several states to counter these measures are good examples. Blocking statutes basically prohibit compliance with the sanctioning laws, failing which prosecution can be initiated by the 'blocking' states against the offenders.[31] As pointed out by Marjolaine Abada-Fasquelle, commercial operators are trapped in the crossfire, as they risk prosecution if they do and do not comply with the sanctioning laws. Such (secondary) unilateral sanctions are disconnected

30 Cf. Crawford, *Brownlie's Principles*, 464–465.

31 Seyed Y. Ziaee, "Jurisdictional Countermeasures *Versus* Extraterritoriality in International Law," *Russian Law Journal* 4 (2016): 27–45.

from territory or nationality, and some blocking statutes may also be. For instance, the European Union's blocking statute prohibits European operators from complying with US extraterritorial sanctions.[32] As such, it is not based on nationality.

2.1.2 *The Political Nature of Extraterritoriality*

Situations of concurrent jurisdiction may be resolved by deference. It is plausible since states may not accord the same importance to the basis of their jurisdiction in a given case. It may also be that a state considers exercising jurisdiction is not worth it in terms of material possibilities and chances of success.[33] However, when states are equally interested in exercising their jurisdiction, the reality is that, absent legal mechanisms, the state with more leverage will impose over the other. Extraterritorial jurisdiction thus involves an element of pure or factual power, just like politics. While legal theorists such as Karl Olivecrona, Hans Kelsen, and Alf Ross refer to the law as a system of rules about force, the power that comes in support of the realisation of the law is the power of politics in the form of "assistance from outside".[34] Political power is a factual force inherent to political institutions, which is not the result of a construction of technical and hierarchical rules of organisation, like legal power.

Different instances show that pure state power is decisive in the exercise of extraterritorial jurisdiction and its outcome. Historically, extraterritorial jurisdiction is related to the use of power by powerful states. The first contemporary practice to which the notion of extraterritorial jurisdiction is associated is the application by the Western Powers of their laws to their nationals living in Asian countries between the 18th and the early 19th centuries. Their weaker position in the trade scene of the time led Eastern states to accept what has been referred to as "unfair" treaties.[35] Through these treaties, Asian countries waived the application of their laws, accepting the law of the Western Powers in the form of consular jurisdiction.[36]

The state with more leverage is the state that presents a closer territorial connection with the specific case at hand. In criminal cases, for instance,

32 Council Regulation (EC) No 2271/96 of 22 November 1996 protecting against the effects of the extra-territorial application of legislation adopted by a third country, and actions based thereon or resulting therefrom.

33 As an example, see section 4.3 in Chapter 9 (Australia), in the context of the investigation and prosecution of transnational crime.

34 Miro Cerar, "The Relationship between Law and Politics," *Annual Survey of International Law & Comparative Law* 15 (2009): 28.

35 See generally Douglas Howland, "The Japan House Tax Case, 1899–1905: Leases in Perpetuity and the Myth of International Equality," *Zeitschrift für ausländisches öffentliches Recht und Völkerrecht* 75 (2015): 413–434.

36 Milanov, "L'extraterritorialité avant la territorialisation de l'Etat," 163–169.

the jurisdiction of the state in the territory of which the offender lives or is located probably will prevail over any other. On the occasion of the *"Enrica Lexie" Incident*, for instance, India was able to exercise its jurisdiction over the marines because they had docked in the oil port of Kochi. Territorial connections are also decisive in cases involving sanctions and blocking statutes. Against the impossibility of complying with contradicting laws, persons in this situation likely will decide to comply with the law of the state in the territory of which they have their residence or the centre of their main interests. The United States is the best illustration of the relationship between factual power and territorial connections. The US is able to realise its diverse interests abroad through its extraterritorial arsenal mainly because, as the most powerful state of the world, it entertains more relationships and, thus, more territorial connections with the world than any other state.

Negotiation and cooperation are other essential characteristics of political activity that describe the practice of extraterritorial jurisdiction. Contrary to the law, politics can take into account value-normative spheres other than legal norms.[37] The field of the fight against corruption offers neat examples of state cooperation and negotiation that are as flexible as in politics. The UN convention commends that states exercising their jurisdiction over the same conduct consult with each other with a view to coordinating their actions, while the OECD convention refers to consultations for the determination of the most appropriate jurisdiction for prosecution. Their wording suggests that state parties maintain some level of discretion on whether they implement cooperation or not.[38] States also cooperate to build compromise-based solutions to prevent concurrent jurisdiction. In her chapter, Marjolaine Abada-Fasquelle explains how, instead of opposing the *Foreign Account Tax Compliance Act*, a US statute designed to combat tax evasion of US citizens with no meaningful ties with the US, notably by requiring foreign financial institutions to communicate information concerning these persons, France incorporated it into its own national law, eliminating the potential concurrent jurisdiction instances that could have resulted.

Politics also involves a constant balance between competing interests. Political power is thus relative, different from the law, which is self-contained.

37 Cerar, "The Relationship between Law and Politics," 33.

38 Article 42(5) of the UN Convention provides: "If a State Party exercising its jurisdiction under paragraph 1 or 2 of this article has been notified, or has otherwise learned, that any other States Parties are conducting an investigation, prosecution or judicial proceeding in respect of the same conduct, the competent authorities of those States Parties shall, as appropriate, consult one another with a view to coordinating their actions". Article 4(3) of the OECD Convention provides: "When more than one Party has jurisdiction over an alleged offence described in this Convention, the Parties involved shall, at the request of one of them, consult with a view to determining the most appropriate jurisdiction for prosecution".

In absolutist regimes, the competition between the people and the ruler never disappears, so much so that it eventually leads to a change of regime. This competing character is inherent to democratic regimes. Some manifestations are the separation of powers, the system of checks and balances, the large bureaucratic apparatuses within all powers, and the federal constitutions. Extraterritorial jurisdiction obeys the same kind of complex processes of balancing and amalgamation of competing interests. In her chapter, Alina Veneziano explains in detail that in the United States, where there is a presumption against extraterritoriality as a matter of principle, requiring that no extraterritorial effect to any law is given unless sufficient evidence shows a clear intention from Congress to the contrary, the US judiciary frequently takes the stage as the primary actor in articulating new standards and establishing trends by inferring and discerning congressional intent. In their chapter on Australia, Rishi Gulati and Matthew Nelson argue that strongly independent functions traditionally spared from external oversight, such as the investigation and prosecution of transnational crime, need to be made more transparent and articulated with other branches or offices of the executive withholding relevant information for the sake of efficiency and effectiveness.

Interest balancing is particularly acute regarding the repression of crime. As pointed out by our Australian authors, states always face the dichotomy of whether to prosecute their nationals or see them prosecuted by a foreign state. In the case of the United Kingdom, for instance, as explained by Paul Arnell in his chapter, the crime of conspiracy to murder was introduced in 1861 in order to address criticism from France over conspiracies by persons within the UK to murder persons abroad. In cases where their own nationals are victims abroad, some states will refrain from exercising their jurisdiction only after making sure that the law was appropriately enforced by the foreign country, irrespective of the traditionally applicable principles of double criminality, *ne bis in idem*, and the lower penalty. It is the case of Israel with respect to the Jewish nation around the world, as revealed by Yaël Ronen in her chapter.

While expressed in individualising provisions applicable to specific cases, following the most conventional legal technique, extraterritorial jurisdiction is also driven by a political sense of belonging and community aspirations. One of the most evocative cases within this volume is Israel, where Jewishness appears as the link for extraterritorial jurisdiction for different purposes. Another example worth mentioning is Iran. In their chapter, Pouria Askari and Hassan Vakilian explain how the domination of the British and Russian Empires over Iran during the 19th century, including a couple of 'unfair' treaties, influenced the Revolution and the Constitution of 1979. They underscore that the Iranian Constitution enshrines freedom and independence as the cornerstones of the principle of non-intervention and builds on them to support the defence of the rights of all Muslims. They indicate that the Constitution couples individual freedom with responsibility before God. The sense of political community and belonging may lead not only to extraterritorial projects of a defensive or protective character but also to progressive projects. As Sarah McGibbon suggests, South Africa's progressive approach towards universal jurisdiction, and more generally, its commitment to international justice and accountability, is motivated to some extent by its desire to break from the shadows of its authoritarian past and become an equal and leading member of the international community.

The political character of extraterritorial jurisdiction definitely finds an expression in positive law. In acknowledging the extraterritorial use of prescriptive and adjudicatory jurisdiction in the *Lotus*, the PCIJ must have taken into account the nature of nation-states as political communities whose development necessarily extends beyond their territories and the fact that, as this happens, they inevitably take with them their identities and common interests. This is the only possible explanation of the legality of extraterritorial jurisdiction in a system dominated by territorial sovereignty. This construction goes in line with the protection of political freedom in the jurisprudence of the International Court of Justice (ICJ) in the name of non-intervention and self-determination.[39]

2.2 *Paralegal Aspects of Extraterritoriality*

Concerning the legal regime of extraterritoriality, it is important to conduct an analysis of the different elements at stake and, in particular, of their interaction. The actual law of extraterritoriality is a mosaic of domestic and international provisions in their different forms. The most important illustration of the pluralism of extraterritoriality is the well-known principles of extraterritorial jurisdiction. It is equally important to analyse their specific significance in light of their varied influences.

2.2.1 *Striking a Balance Between Territorial Sovereignty, Jurisdiction, and State Power*

The absolute prohibition in the *Lotus* regarding the use of state power in the territory of another has led to thinking that any state act, including acts taken under dubious regimes and even outside any legal regime, is extraterritorial. Some of these acts include abductions, espionage, targeted killings, and even military interventions.[40] This creates the confusion that extraterritoriality is a concept that serves to condemn these acts in legal terms, when

39 *Military and Paramilitary Activities in and against Nicaragua (Nicaragua v United States of America)* ICJ Reports 1986, 133.

40 Cf. Menno T. Kamminga, "Extraterritoriality," in *Max Plank Encyclopedia of Public International Law* (Oxford: Oxford University Press, 2015), para. 22 *et seq.*

they are already illegal as a matter of *jus cogens* under the principle of territorial sovereignty and several other international law principles. Extraterritoriality already has a negative connotation, given that states may apply their laws beyond their territories unilaterally. Associating these acts with the concept of extraterritoriality adds a good amount to it. It is true that extraterritoriality exists in opposition to territory or, more precisely, to territorial sovereignty.[41] However, extraterritoriality is basically a functional concept. It represents nothing more than a sort of compromise between the need to regulate the activity or interests of states in spaces that lie beyond their sovereign territories and the territorial sovereignty of states where those activities and interests are located. If extraterritoriality is construed in such an open-ended way, it will then apply to any use of state power, legal, illegal, and merely factual. Excluding the case of extraterritorial obligations, which arise when there is effective overall control of an area,[42] the legal concept of extraterritoriality does not take any advantage of a criteria based on pure power. As Mann puts it: "No State may exercise enforcement jurisdiction outside its own territory in the absence of its own legislature authorizing it to do so, that is to say, in the absence of legislative jurisdiction".[43] The *Lotus* dicta also constitutes a warning against such conceptual miscue. After declaring that a state "may not exercise its power in any form in the territory of another state", the PCIJ specifies that "jurisdiction is certainly territorial".[44] By associating the term 'in any form' with jurisdiction, the Court seemingly targets any of the ways in which states formalise and legalise their power domestically.

Some of the chapters within this volume suggest that the principle of territorial sovereignty, while inseparable from the concept of extraterritoriality, should not overshadow jurisdiction, understood as the way in which states organise their power domestically. As explained by our authors writing on Iran and Israel, fundamental laws in these countries may allow action in the territories of foreign states in order to support, respectively, "the just struggles of the freedom fighters against the oppression in every corner of the globe", and "to secure the welfare of members of the Jewish People and of its citizens, who are in straits and in captivity, due to their Jewishness or due to their citizenship". India and Turkey, for their part, as our authors working on these chapters explain, have conducted actions such as surgical strikes and broader military operations abroad to combat organisations that supposes a threat to them. It does not seem that these actions are taken under

41 Buxbaum, "The Practice(s) of Extraterritoriality," 4.

42 Marko Milanović, "From Compromise to Principle: Clarifying the Concept of State Jurisdiction in Human Rights Treaties," *Human Rights Law Review* 8 (2008): 423.

43 Mann, *The Doctrine of International Jurisdiction*, 34.

44 *SS Lotus (France v Turkey)*, 18.

pre-established legal norms, but they are official and may be justified under the principle of self-defence.

Still, such actions might transgress the principle of territorial sovereignty. However, this should not exclude such state activity from the debate around the concept of extraterritoriality. The PCIJ finishes its dictum declaring that the prohibition upon states to exercise their jurisdiction outside their territory can be waived "by virtue of a permissive rule derived from international custom or from a convention".[45] Exercises of jurisdiction typically mentioned under this exception include consular jurisdiction of states over their nationals abroad or jurisdiction over military personnel in overseas bases, both of which have their basis in the consent of the territorial state.[46] The automatic exclusion of these forms of jurisdiction elides the possibility of them being contemplated in the international discussions and fora that accompany the process of materialisation of customary international law. These are only four examples, but all of them correspond to states that share similar geopolitical characteristics and protection concerns. It would be interesting to extend the survey to more states from the region and see whether elements for the formation of a regional customary international law exist. Also, leaving these state actions outside of the debate may result in them being categorised as illegal *per se*, with the necessary unfortunate consequences.

The prevalence of territorial sovereignty over jurisdiction seems incompatible also with the ongoing shift from a state-centred to an individual-centred international legal system. This shift implies the rise of jurisdiction and a proportional downgrade of the corollaries of sovereignty, including territorial sovereignty. The importance of territory is displaced by the more functional concept of jurisdiction in front of a greater exigency of protection for individuals in the context of a globalised world. Indeed, it is argued, precisely in the context of the protection of individuals at home and abroad, that the concept of responsibility to protect (R2P) can displace some of the most important corollaries of sovereignty, such as the principle of non-intervention.[47] Let us not forget that jurisdiction is the link through which obligations are imposed on states on an extraterritorial basis to assure the protection of human rights.

45 *Ibid.*, 19.

46 Buxbaum, "The Practice(s) of Extraterritoriality," 10–11; Milanović, "From Compromise to Principle," 420.

47 Anne Peters, "Humanity as the *A* and Ω of Sovereignty," *European Journal of International Law* 20 (2009): 533–543. The author argues that "the new concept of *sovereignty as responsibility to protect* infuses external sovereignty with elements of internal sovereignty, because it conditions non-intervention (a consequence or corollary of external sovereignty) on the capability properly to discharge the internal functions of a sovereign, and postulates the sovereign's accountability *vis-à-vis* the population," 517.

Just as the territorial aspect of extraterritoriality should not overshadow jurisdiction, focusing excessively on jurisdiction does not do justice to the concept of extraterritoriality. Jurisdiction is a broad concept that captures the legal meaning and basis of state power. In theory, there can be as many forms of jurisdiction as there are forms of organisation within a state. However, the traditional tripartite separation of powers strongly influences scholarly constructions of extraterritoriality. It is understandable since such a way of state organisation is pretty much a universal axiom, and the relations between states are normally forged through these channels. Focusing excessively on jurisdiction leads to a formalist approach to extraterritoriality, which erodes its functional nature. Concerning adjudicative jurisdiction, for instance, scholars focus on whether the tribunal of a state may sit in the territory of another[48] when what really counts is if there is enough connection between the adjudicative state and the case at hand. A formalist approach inevitably leads to assimilating extraterritoriality with physical power. Taking in consideration that the executive is in charge of enforcing the mandates of the two other powers as well as its own directives, the *Lotus* prohibition is easily related to acts taken by it only.

The use of physical power by a state in the territory of another certainly constitutes the most radical interference with the principles of territorial sovereignty and integrity, but other exercises of jurisdiction produce an equally undesirable extraterritorial effect of coercion without supposing the use of physical force. In their chapter on Russia, Lilya Khasanova, Nailia Savenkova, and Kamila Shaibakova explain that data protection of Russian nationals is subject to a 'territorialisation' process through localisation provisions that impose certain obligations on data operators with and without a physical presence in Russia, including recording, storing and processing data. This supposes an act of coercion on those operators, as they would need to make the necessary arrangements at home to move the data into Russia in order to prevent being sanctioned in the terms of the law.

The case *United States v Microsoft*[49] illustrates the extraterritorial coercive character of the law in the digital sphere, as well as the debate around it. The case arose from an investigation initiated under the *Store Communication Act (SCA)*. Microsoft was ordered to transfer to the US authorities the content of communications stored in Ireland of an individual as part of a criminal investigation. Microsoft argued that the order implied the extraterritorial execution of US law since the American authorities would obtain evidence abroad through it without the consent of local authorities. The American authorities, for their part, argued that

48 Cf. Kamminga, "Extraterritoriality," para. 20.
49 *United States v Microsoft Corp.*, 584 U.S. (2018).

the order was addressed to a US company to transfer information within the US territory, regardless of the fact that the data must previously be transferred from abroad since it only supposed a simple electronic operation that did not require an action in foreign territory. Following a long litigation that reached the Supreme Court, the US Congress enacted the *Clarifying Lawful Overseas Use of Data Act (Cloud Act),* basically investing American authorities with the contested power.[50] Nevertheless, the act also creates a clearer judicial remedy for data operators, both in substance and procedure.

Other more typical forms of extraterritorial coercion include discovery procedures and economic sanctions. In the first case, the sanctions to which the parties to civil proceedings may be subject to for failing to comply with the provisions of disclosure contained in Rule 26 of the US Federal Rules of Civil Procedure, like criminal sanctions resulting from an eventual contempt of court, force them to communicate information that may be located in foreign countries. In the case of economic sanctions, the embargo resulting from the trade prohibition is one of the most powerful acts of extraterritorial coercion that could exist.

A formalist approach to extraterritoriality does not help the development of a concept still under construction. For instance, secondary economic sanctions are often characterised as extraterritorial given that the sanctioning mechanism is based neither on territorial nor on personal jurisdiction,[51] while in reality, their coercive effects suffice to condemn them. Ultimately, the concept and the phenomenon of extraterritoriality itself are not vacated by the concept of jurisdiction. Excluding extraterritoriality only because it results from enforcement jurisdiction is as simplistic as accepting it only because it results from prescriptive jurisdiction. In the end, there is nothing in the *Lotus* suggesting such a statement. While the PCIJ expressly refers to the concept of jurisdiction, it must be read essentially beyond its domestic meaning and reach, as international law is not concerned with the internal organisation of the state.[52]

Finally, the reference to the exercise of power "*in* the territory of another state" should not be construed as meaning acts taken in foreign territory.

50 The *Cloud Act* considers the possible violation of a foreign law that may result from the transmission of information by the operators only with respect to states with which the US has concluded executive agreements of cooperation in the field of data access (Sec. 2703 *(h)* (2), USC). By the way, the solution is an example of the back and forth between the US Congress and the judiciary with respect to the construction and application of extraterritorial laws, and the frequent reforms frequently ensuing from these processes, as detailed by Alina Veneziano in her chapter.

51 Julia Schmidt, "The Legality of Unilateral Extra-Territorial Sanctions under International Law," *Journal of Conflict & Security Law* 27 (2022): 61–69.

52 Jean-Denis Mouton, "La notion d'État et le droit international public," *Droits* 16 (1992): 57.

As seen, prescriptive jurisdiction may produce an equally harmful effect in foreign territories as the use of *in situ* physical force.

2.2.2 *Decoding the Significance of the Principles of Extraterritorial Jurisdiction*

The grounds of extraterritorial jurisdiction are commonly referred to, and considered as principles by scholars,[53] national[54] and international adjudicative bodies,[55] as well as international organisations.[56] This characterisation alone suggests certain international recognition. The recognition of states about the value of an international practice supposes the existence of a concept that depends as much on domestic law as it does on international law. Ontologically, it could not be different because states conceive their extraterritorial power according to their own conceptions, and at the same time, their extraterritorial power exists in relation to other states. The process that conducts principles of domestic law into the realm of international customary law does not change this observation. Given the inherent subjectivity of extraterritorial jurisdiction, even in the case when these principles are recognised as a general practice accepted as law by the international community, the sense of legal obligation (*opinio juris*) leading to such acknowledgment would need to be construed mainly from the perspective of domestic law.

The relationship between domestic and international law is stronger with respect to those principles in which the state appears directly implicated, *i.e.*, the territorial principle, on the basis of which a state exercises its power upon acts that occur in its territory, and the nationality principle, on the basis of which a state exercises its power upon acts undertaken by its nationals wherever they are committed (*active personality*). Territory and nationality are legal constructs determined entirely by the domestic legal order. Indeed, nationality is one of the most representative areas within the *domaine réservé*. While international law does not influence the substance of these legal constructs, it validates their formal existence whenever a state enters the international community. In these areas, there is a relationship of complementarity and smooth coordination between domestic and international law. Thus, if states enjoy complete freedom to determine what nationality is in the field of jurisdiction they are equally free to regulate it, even in the

53 An early and illustrative example is the *Harvard Research Draft Convention on Jurisdiction with Respect to Crime* of 1935.

54 UK examples of the protective principle include *Naim Molvan v AG for Palestine* [1948]; *Giles v Tumminello* (1969) 38 ILR 120.

55 *Arrest Warrant*, ICJ Report 2002, 76–77 (with respect to the passive personality principle), 37 and 92 (with respect to the protective principle); *SS Lotus (France v Turkey)*, 20, 23 (with respect to the principle of territoriality).

56 For instance, the *Report of the International Law Commission on the Work of Its Fifty-Eighth Session* (2006), Annex V, 230–232.

extraterritorial domain. One should note that states are not only repressing or regulating conduct but also regulating nationhood. The fact that nationality is the only completely uncontested principle of extraterritorial jurisdiction can be explained by its intimate relationship with the state.

The principles that focus on a particular situation or event abroad that affects the state enjoy less acceptance. Their legitimacy lies in the existence of some harm in the territory (*objective territoriality*) or against the people (*passive personality*) of the state. In other words, their legitimacy is measured in objective terms. However, if one considers that each state determines harm unilaterally, these principles also include a heavy dose of subjectivity. What is clear is that their origin is found in the domestic legal order. In the *Lotus*, the PCIJ found that the prosecution of the officer of the watch of the French ship by Turkey for colliding with the *Boz-Kourt* on the high seas was not contrary to international law, referring precisely to the advanced development of state practice with respect to the effects of an offence in a foreign territory. At the end of World War II, the principle of objective territoriality expanded to what became known as the effects doctrine in the United States, basically to cover economic harm. The effects doctrine has also gained some acceptance in the European Union, but its international recognition stops pretty much there. This is not surprising considering the difficulties that suppose the extension of jurisdiction upon natural and legal persons of foreign states based on a unilateral determination of economic harm. Regarding passive personality, while many laws enshrining the principle refer to specific offences, many are open provisions precisely because the essence of the principle is the protection of nationals abroad.[57] As such, the door to subjectivity remains quite wide.[58] For its part, international law performs its unifying and codifying missions as it measures the relevance of these principles among the international community.

Domestic and international law do converge on the necessity of states of exercising their jurisdiction extraterritorially to protect their fundamental national interests (*protective principle*) as well as those of the international community with respect to the most heinous crimes (*universal jurisdiction*). While there is a convergence between the legal orders as to the motivations

57 Like Article 6 of the Turkish Penal Code, Law No. 765 of March 1st, 1926, upon which the Turkish criminal court apparently claimed jurisdiction in the *Lotus*. That provision states: "Any foreigner who, apart from the cases contemplated by Article 4, commits an offence abroad to the prejudice of Turkey or of a Turkish subject, for which offence Turkish law prescribes a penalty involving loss of freedom for a minimum period of no less than one year, shall be punished in accordance with the Turkish Penal Code provided that he is arrested in Turkey". The PCIJ declined to assess whether the provision was a comprehensive exercise of passive personality jurisdiction; it only focused on whether the specific factual situation fell within Turkish jurisdiction or not.

58 There is, however, something approaching a consensus on the use of passive personality in certain cases, often linked to international terrorism. Also, many criminal law treaties authorise it as between state parties. Crawford, *Brownlie's Principles*, 460.

behind these principles, as well as to the fact that they are not based on a territorial or a personal connection with the state, their base is so broad that they leave a large room for subjectivity. It is thus hard to argue that the specific interests invoked by states, both with respect to the protective principle and universal jurisdiction, will receive the same acceptance.[59] Some of the chapters within this volume illustrate that their implementation may obey very particular and not necessarily consonant interests. In the UK, the protective principle is related to a heightened concern about espionage driven by technological developments; in Israel, to the protection of the Jewish nation around the world; and in Iran, among other offences, it targets actions against the regime and the independence of the Islamic Republic. With respect to universal jurisdiction in Argentina, as explained by Juan Ignacio Stampalija in his chapter, while there is a strong tradition to prosecute violations of human rights and crimes against humanity, the efforts have been strongly driven by the personal agendas and interests of human rights organisations and federal courts.

It should be noted that the source of extraterritorial jurisdiction may also be found in a more intimate relationship between the state and the individual. Paul Arnell explains that in the UK, citizenship is also the basis of extraterritorial criminal jurisdiction. He notes that citizenship is a larger concept than nationality as it involves a connection between individuals, and not only between an individual and a state. In other words, citizenship denotes a stronger sense of belonging rather than a mere exclusive juridical link. Actually, the current law of nationality of ancient empires such as the UK evokes much larger and more intimate belonging.[60] As a concept, citizenship is in line with international law inasmuch as it has the potential to explain better the relationship between state/individual in the context of challenging international trends and phenomena such as the multiplication of multiple nationalities, migration, statelessness, and the internationalisation of human rights, among others.[61] Additionally, Paul Arnell considers that the term personal jurisdiction is more suitable than nationality-based jurisdiction as it reflects better the range of relevant relationships that states may rely upon in extending their jurisdiction.

Ultimately, the principles of state jurisdiction are formulated to justify the extraterritorial power of the state in a context of territorial sovereignty and state equality. The result is the configuration of principles of jurisdiction

59 With respect to the former, there is also some consensus as regards immigration and currency offences. Crawford, *Brownlie's Principles*, 460.

60 Alioune Badara Thiam, "Citoyenneté et nationalité dans le *Commonwealth*," in *The Concept of Citizenship in International Law*, eds. Jean-Denis Mouton and Péter Kovács (Leiden/Boston: Brill | Nijhoff, 2018), 461–488; Manuel José Segovia González, "Nationalité, double nationalité et citoyenneté dans la communauté hispanique," in *The Concept of Citizenship*, eds. Mouton and Kovács, 531–569.

61 *The Concept of Citizenship*, eds. Mouton and Kovács.

intending more to regulate a dichotomy than solving specific situations. While the principles suppose a link between the state and the different objects being regulated, they incarnate a rather abstract method, easily leading to different results for the same kind of situation. As seen, the different principles have strong similarities; some of them are even considered special applications of others, and in practice, they often interweave.[62] The fact that their application is almost a synonym of concurrent jurisdiction exemplifies their large breadth. However, there is hope that the law of extraterritorial jurisdiction will become more objective and can yield more satisfactory results. This will happen as states abandon the prevailing territorial approach and substitute for it a flexible method based upon the degree of connection of facts with the relevant state and not of a state with a given situation in light of the different principles. The method of the genuine or strong link, as scholars call it, is one of a close and not closest connection, and as such, still admits concurrent jurisdiction.[63] Yet, it excludes the idiosyncrasies of states or judges, as well as mere political, economic, commercial, or social interests as relevant factors to determine a sufficient connection.[64] It results in a closer, more substantial, direct, and weighty connection between a given state and a set of facts in such a way that the applicable legislation is in harmony with international law and its various aspects, including the practice of states, the principles of non-interference and reciprocity (comity), and the demands of interdependence.[65] Actually, the genuine connection is more than just a hope: it has already been applied in cases of dual nationality by the ICJ to decide diplomatic claims,[66] as well as investment arbitration tribunals with regard to the exercise of protection.[67] The case studies within this volume and their diversity are good parameters for the analysis of this method in its way to its consolidation as a principle.

3 The Entanglement and Enchantment of Extraterritorial Jurisdiction in International Law

Extraterritorial jurisdiction both entangles and enchants. State jurisdiction and extraterritoriality are created and constrained by both domestic and international law. The intertwined relationship between these two legal regimes – called here 'entanglement' – frames the normativity of extraterritoriality. However, international law transcends this binary framework. It

62 James Crawford, *Brownlie's Principles of International Law* (Oxford: Oxford University Press, 9th ed., 2019), 477.
63 Frederick A. Mann, *The Doctrine of Jurisdiction in International Law* (The Hague: Collected Courses, 1964), 46, 49.
64 *Ibid.*, 46, 49.
65 *Ibid.*, 49.
66 *Nottebohm*, ICJ Reports 1955, 22.
67 Ian Brownlie, *Principles of Public International Law* (Oxford: Oxford University Press, 2008), 400.

offers tools for states to exercise extraterritorial jurisdiction in specific cases where, theoretically, there is no jurisdictional link to justify a state's exercise of jurisdiction. This is what we refer to here as the 'enchantment' of extraterritorial jurisdiction in international law. These two perspectives – entanglement and enchantment – of extraterritorial jurisdiction in international law are explored in this section.

3.1 *The Entanglement of Extraterritorial Jurisdiction in International Law*

International law conceives of jurisdiction as a state prerogative. States, as an expression of their sovereign authority, have jurisdiction over their territories and the populations within them.[68] In other words, a state has absolute and exclusive authority to prescribe, adjudicate, and enforce its laws on its territory and population. While territory is commonly accepted as the uncontested link of jurisdiction, jurisdiction is not solely territorially bound; it can also be extraterritorial. Scholars agree that, nowadays, extraterritoriality is seen as a starting point for exercising jurisdiction rather than an exception.[69] It is important to note that, in general, a genuine link understood as a legitimate relationship of closeness between the state and the object under regulation, must exist for a state to exercise extraterritorial jurisdiction.[70] In most cases, states seek a territorial linkage to assert jurisdiction, including extraterritorially. Thus, it is unsurprising that jurisdiction is a central institution in domestic law. But the story does not end here.

State jurisdiction is also a central institution in international law. State jurisdiction and its extraterritorial manifestations are inherently constituted and constrained by international law. The starting point of this assertion is that international law, in general, is created by states and for states, with states being the primary subjects of its legal norms.[71] This means that both domestic and international law determine the same state authority and jurisdiction. Therefore, jurisdiction – including extraterritoriality – represents an institution that best captures the entanglement of domestic law and international law.

The argument is simple. Jurisdiction is both constructed and constrained by domestic and international law.[72] Domestically, the rules on jurisdiction

68 Malcolm N. Shaw, *International Law* (Cambridge: Cambridge University Press, 9th ed., 2021); Crawford, *Brownlie's Principles*.

69 Stephen Allen et al., "Introduction: Defining State Jurisdiction and Jurisdiction in International Law," in *The Oxford Handbook of Jurisdiction in International Law*, eds. Stephen Allen et al. (Oxford: Oxford University Press, 2019), 8.

70 Crawford, *Brownlie's Principles*, 442–443; Andrea Bianchi, "Comment: Jurisdictional Rules in Customary International Law," in *Extraterritorial Jurisdiction in Theory and Practice*, ed. Karl M. Meessen (Brill | Nijhoff, 1996), 74, 87.

71 Samantha Besson, "The Authority of International Law – Lifting the State Veil," *Sydney Law Review* 31(3) (2009): 343.

72 Samantha Besson, "Why and What (State) Jurisdiction: Legal Plurality, Individual Equality and Territorial Legitimacy," in *The Challenge of Inter-Legality*, eds. Jan Klabbers and Gianluigi Palombella (Cambridge: Cambridge University Press, 2019), 99.

and extraterritoriality are embodied in national legislation. International law norms shape a state's jurisdiction from the outside. It is argued here that international law plays a pivotal role in constructing and constraining state jurisdiction, including extraterritoriality. This binomial relationship entails, on the one hand, that international law constitutes state jurisdiction through the principle of equity and independence.[73] On the other hand, international law also constrains state jurisdiction by limiting it in relation to other states – the principle of non-intervention[74] – and in its domestic scope and exercise, such as through human rights law and criminal law.[75] International law also determines – as a constraint of state jurisdiction –[76] the concept of *domaine réservé*,[77] discussed previously.

To better understand the exercise of state jurisdiction in the extraterritorial domain and the role international law plays in framing extraterritoriality, the following sections explore how state extraterritorial jurisdiction relates to international law and why international law matters in a field that, *prima facie*, might seem primarily a domestic affair.

3.1.1 On the Construction of State Extraterritorial Jurisdiction

As discussed and exemplified in this book, states have the right to prescribe, adjudicate, and enforce laws in their territory; they may also prescribe extraterritorial laws. This reflects states' rights, often referred to as independence. In *Island of Palmas,* it was stated that "sovereignty in the relations between states signifies independence. Independence in regard to a portion of the globe is the right to exercise therein, to the exclusion of any other State, the functions of a State".[78] However, states also have the duty to exercise jurisdiction in order to address global issues through international law and procedures. One may consider duties to exercise jurisdiction under environmental law, international criminal law, or international human rights law.[79] By addressing global concerns and exercising universal jurisdiction, state actions enter the extraterritorial domain. In short, states' responsibilities under international law may require them to adopt and enforce laws beyond their territorial limits.

73 *SS Wimbledon (United Kingdom and Others v Germany)*, Judgment, [1923] PCIJ Series A, No. 1, 21–22.
74 *Military and Paramilitary Activities in and against Nicaragua*, paras. 202–209.
75 Besson, "Why and What (State) Jurisdiction," 96.
76 *Ibid.*, 108.
77 On Article 2(7) of the UN Charter, see *e.g.*, Kawser Ahmed, "The Domestic Jurisdiction Clause in the United Nations Charter: A Historical View," *Singapore Year Book of International Law* 10 (2006): 175–197.
78 *Island of Palmas (Netherlands v United States of America)*, Arbitral Award, 4 April 1928, Reports of International Arbitral Awards Vol. II, 829–871, page 838.
79 *Catan and Others v Moldova and Russia*, Application Nos. 43370/04, 8252/05 and 18454/06, ECtHR [GC] Judgment, 19 October 2012.

Despite a general understanding of what extraterritorial jurisdiction is and when a state may assert its jurisdiction extraterritorially, reaching widely accepted rules on extraterritorial jurisdiction remains a difficult challenge. This is primarily because states operate under different legal systems, many areas of substantive law have developed independently, and for some states, extraterritorial jurisdiction remains a highly politicised subject.[80] As Omri Sender and Michael Wood explain, "a number of attempts have been made to codify the international law on extraterritorial jurisdiction," and "while some have not been without influence, none has led to a widely accepted set of rules, let alone an international convention. Some attempts were abandoned without concrete results".[81]

Thus, attention turns to customary law. According to the International Law Commission's *Draft Conclusions on Identification of Customary International Law,* "to determine the existence and content of a rule of customary international law, it is necessary to ascertain whether there is a general practice that is accepted as law (*opinion juris*)".[82] In the context of extraterritorial jurisdiction, as William S. Dodge argues, "there is ample state practice supporting each of the traditional bases for jurisdiction to prescribe".[83]

Different sets of international law rules govern extraterritorial jurisdiction. Customary international law rules that regulate the jurisdiction to prescribe differ from the international law rules governing the jurisdiction to enforce, which, as a rule, is prohibited extraterritorially. As the *Lotus* judgement states, extraterritorial jurisdiction can only be prescriptive. This implies that the exercise of an enforcement-based extraterritorial jurisdiction is generally prohibited. Despite existing critiques,[84] the *Lotus* judgment summarises the main points regarding state jurisdiction: prohibitive – outside its territory, a state cannot exercise its power in any form unless an international treaty or customary law permits it.[85] An example of this is the Agreement

80 Omri Sender and Michael Wood, "Extraterritorial Jurisdiction and the Limits of Customary International Law," in *Research Handbook on Extraterritoriality in International Law*, eds. Cedric Ryngaert and Austen Parrish (Cheltenham: Edward Elgar Publishing, 2023), 39.

81 For a comprehensive overview of the attempts to codify the rules of extraterritorial jurisdiction in international law, see Sender and Wood, "Extraterritorial Jurisdiction," 35–41.

82 Conclusion 2 of the Draft Conclusions on Identification of Customary International Law, *Yearbook of the International Law Commission*, 2018, vol. II, Part Two.

83 The author makes reference to the reporters' notes to Sections 408–413 of the Restatement (Fourth) of Foreign Relations Law. See William S. Dodge, "Extraterritoriality and Self-Determination," *Transnational Litigation Blog*, 26 November 2024. Accessed 20 December 2024. https://tlblog.org/extraterritoriality-and-self-determination/.

84 Hersch Lauterpacht, *The Function of the Law in the International Community* (Cambridge: Cambridge University Press, 2011), 102–104; Alex Mills, "Rethinking Jurisdiction in International Law," *British Yearbook of International Law* 84 (2014): 192–194.

85 *SS Lotus* (*France v Turkey*), para. 45. "Now the first and foremost restriction imposed by international law upon a State is that – failing the existence of a permissive rule to the contrary – it may not exercise its power in any form in the territory of another State. In this sense jurisdiction is certainly territorial; it cannot be exercised by a State outside its territory except by virtue of a permissive rule derived from international custom or from a convention".

between the UK and the Netherlands, through which the UK obtained the consent of the Netherlands to prosecute two Libyans accused in the Lockerbie bombing, with the trial being conducted by a Scottish court sitting in the Netherlands.[86] Permissive – within its territory, a state may freely exercise its jurisdiction,[87] even if no specific rule of international law permits it.[88] This suggests that states have a broad measure of discretion, limited only by the prohibitive rules of international law. In other words, a state may exercise its jurisdiction based on the principle of personal jurisdiction, the protective principle, or universal jurisdiction. Under customary international law, these are the generally accepted bases on which a state may exercise extraterritorial jurisdiction.[89]

The bases of extraterritorial jurisdiction are defined by reference to territorial jurisdiction, which serves as the primary connection between a state and its people. As Samantha Besson mentions, the tendency is to prioritise the bases of extraterritorial jurisdiction that are closest to territory, as illustrated by the 'effects doctrine'.[90] In the case of a cross-border event where the wrongful act of a state causes damage in another state, both states have jurisdiction: the state where the act occurred has subjective territorial jurisdiction, and the state where the damage occurred has objective territorial jurisdiction. The use and expansion of 'effects'-based jurisdiction can be observed in the case of the US. As Alina Veneziano argues in her chapter, courts in various areas of the law, such as anti-trust regulation or

86 Agreement Between the Government of the Kingdom of the Netherlands and the Government of the United Kingdom of Great Britain and Northern Ireland Concerning a Scottish Trial in the Netherlands, 18 September 1998, *International Legal Materials* 38(4) (1999): 926–936.

87 Despite the permissibility of prescriptive extraterritorial jurisdiction and established practice, recently extraterritorial prescriptive jurisdiction was grounded or 'territorialised' by the International Tribunal for the Law of the Sea (ITLOS) in the *MV Norstar* case. The Tribunal, by referencing the *Lotus* case dictum and connecting it with UNCLOS Article 92, stated that in the absence of territorial sovereignty over the high seas, the prohibition of extraterritoriality extends not only to enforcement but also to prescriptive jurisdiction. See *MV Norstar Case* (*Panama v Italy*), Case No. 25, ITLOS Judgment, 10 April 2019, ITLOS Reports 2018–2019, para. 225.

88 *SS Lotus* (*France v Turkey*), paras. 46–47. In the PCIJ words, "It does not, however, follow that international law prohibits a state from exercising jurisdiction in its own territory, in respect of any case which relates to acts which have taken place abroad, and in which it cannot rely on some permissive rule of international law . . . . Far from laying down a general prohibition to the effect that states may not extend the application of their laws and the jurisdiction of their courts to persons, property and acts outside their territory, it leaves them in this respect a wide measure of discretion, which is only limited in certain cases by prohibitive rules; as regards other cases, every state remains free to adopt the principles which it regards as best and most suitable".

89 Gunther Handl, "Extra-Territoriality and Transnational Legal Authority," in *Beyond Territoriality – Transnational Legal Authority in an Age of Globalization*, eds. Peer Zumbansen, Gunther Handl and Joachim Zekoll (Brill | Nijhoff, 2012), 4.

90 Besson, "Why and What (State) Jurisdiction," 107.

security regulation, may invoke the 'effects' doctrine, though acknowledging its controversial nature, as it permits extraterritorial jurisdiction without necessarily any conduct by the foreign company, for effects that may be arguably unintentional.

States have also shaped the form and scope of their jurisdictional powers through treaty design. In respect to the principle of cooperation, which requires states to solve conflicts relating to extraterritorial jurisdiction peacefully and in good faith, over time, various jurisdictional possibilities have been enshrined in treaties, placing obligations on states.[91] There are more than a dozen criminal law enforcement treaties,[92] all of which impose jurisdictional obligations on states. These treaties require states to criminalise specific offences based on customary heads of the jurisdiction (territoriality and nationality) and allow states to exercise prescriptive jurisdiction under more controversial heads, such as passive personality,[93] or even impose an obligation to exercise universal jurisdiction with respect to certain crimes. As Matthew Nelson and Rishi Gulati argue, this highlights the need for extraterritorial jurisdiction as a key tool in combating transnational criminal conduct.

Despite its regulatory framework, the exercise of jurisdiction in international law is discretionary. In matters not explicitly regulated by international law, the use of state discretion is restricted by the obligations undertaken towards other states. Therefore, state jurisdiction is limited by the rules of

91 Rosalyn Higgins, *Problems and Process: International Law and How We Use It* (Oxford: Oxford University Press, 1994), 78; For example, the League of Nations Convention to Suppress the Slave Trade and Slavery from 1926 provides that High Contracting Parties undertook, "each in respect of the territories placed under its sovereignty, jurisdiction, protection, suzerainty or tutelage, so far as they have not already taken the necessary steps: (a) to prevent and suppress the slave trade; (b) to bring about, progressively and as soon as possible, the complete abolition of slavery in all its forms". See Mahmoud Cherif Bassiouni, "Enslavement: Slavery, Slave-Related Practices, and Trafficking in Persons for Sexual Exploitation," in *International Criminal Law, I: Sources, Subjects, and Contents*, ed. Mahmoud Cherif Bassiouni (Brill | Nijhoff, 3rd ed., 2008), 535, 545.

92 Agreement on Mutual Legal Assistance Between the United States of America and the European Union (2003), OJ 34 (2006); and the Treaty Between the United States of America and Ireland on Mutual Legal Assistance in Criminal Matters (2001), Treaty Doc. No. 107–109 (2002). For an analysis of information sharing practice in the investigation and prosecution of transnational crimes with a focus on Australia, see Chapter 9 of this book.

93 Kimberley N. Trapp, "Jurisdiction and State Responsibility," in *The Oxford Handbook of Jurisdiction in International Law*, eds. Stephen Allen et al. (Oxford: Oxford University Press, 2019), 358.

international law.[94] The discretionary nature of jurisdiction[95] has led states to adopt common practices, and customary principles have emerged from domestic, public international law, and private international law,[96] such as comity,[97] equity,[98] and reciprocity.[99] Concerns over these principles – united around concepts such as respect, fairness, and cooperation – guide states' exercise of extraterritorial jurisdiction, particularly as a matter of restraint. As Aniruddha Rajput and Sudipta Purkayastha explain in their chapter, equality of states and comity form the basis of India's approach to the exercise of jurisdiction. In the words of the Indian Supreme Court, the legislative power

> does not assert or assume jurisdiction which goes beyond the limits established by the common consent of nations, and statutes are to be interpreted, provided that their language permits, so as not to be inconsistent with the comity of nations or with the established principles of International Law.[100]

Similar views are expressed in the chapters discussing extraterritoriality in the UK, US, or Australia, where, as Matthew Nelson and Rishi Gulati inform, courts hold that the extraterritorial reach of one state's criminal law is contrary to the comity of nations and an intrusion into the territorial sovereignty of other states.

In criminal matters, the principle of reciprocity is especially relevant, whether framed in a bilateral or multilateral treaty or as a duty to assist

94 *Nationality Decrees Issued in Tunis and Morocco*, page 24. The Court notes that "it may well happen that, in a matter which, . . . is not, in principle, regulated by international law, the right of a state to use its discretion is nevertheless restricted by obligations which it may have undertaken towards other states. In such a case, jurisdiction which, in principle, belongs solely to the state, is limited by rules of international law".

95 The PCIJ referred to 'discretion' – what it regarded as the "wide measure of discretion" – "left to States by international law [which] explains the great variety of rules which they have been able to adopt without objections or complaints on the part of other States" and of the various efforts "for many years past . . . to prepare conventions the effect of which would be precisely to limit the discretion at present left to states in this respect by international law, thus making good the existing lacunae arising from the diversity of the principles adopted by the various states." See *SS Lotus* (*France v Turkey*), 18–19. Also, Mills, "Rethinking Jurisdiction," 182, 183.

96 Ryngaert, *Jurisdiction in International Law*, Chapter 6.

97 Frequently used in conflict of laws cases, comity encompasses an attitude of respect by a domestic legal system toward the actions and interests of foreign states. See Kerry Sun, "International Comity and the Construction of the Charter's Limits: Hape Revisited," *Queen's Law Journal* 45(1) (2019): 115.

98 Margaret White, "Equity-A General Principle of Law Recognised by Civilised Nations?" *Queensland University of Technology Law and Justice Journal* 4(1) (2004): 103–116.

99 In international law, reciprocity means the right to equality and mutual respect between states.

100 *V/O Tractor Export, Moscow v M/S. Tarapore & Company & Anr*, 1971 AIR 1; *Gramophone Company of India Ltd v Birendra Bahadur Pandey & Ors*, 1984 AIR 667.

based on international cooperation, mutual assistance, and solidarity. In their chapter on Russia, Liliya Khasanova, Nailia Savenkova, and Kamila Shaibakova highlight the need to ensure reciprocity in extradition matters to effectively enforce criminal law, particularly in cases involving extraterritorial jurisdiction. However, as they argue, due to the political implications of extradition, the duty to assist in a non-treaty framework is often not respected. For example, the absence of an extradition treaty between the United States and Russia, compounded by their complex diplomatic relations, hampers mutual assistance in criminal law matters. This leads to tolerance and reliance on illegal practices such as extraterritorial abductions and luring.

All this explains the pivotal role that international law plays in constructing extraterritorial jurisdiction through normative and procedural means. But, international law is also crucial as a constraint on the exercise of extraterritorial jurisdiction. In this sense, international law serves as a benchmark for assessing the legality of the exercise of extraterritorial jurisdiction, as observed in most of the case studies discussed in this book.

3.1.2 On the Constraint of State Extraterritorial Jurisdiction

From the perspective of international law, the *Lotus* case remains a key reference when addressing the constraints on a state's exercise of extraterritorial jurisdiction. As has been discussed at length in this introductory chapter, the PCIJ confirmed that a state "may not exercise its power in any form in the territory of another state", except where there is "a permissive rule derived from international custom or a convention".[101]

Extraterritorial enforcement jurisdiction – generally prohibited – refers to a state's authority to ensure compliance with its regulations concerning actions committed abroad. As Robert J. Curries notes, "for the time being states are still committed to a 'Westphalian-bound model' that prohibits extraterritorial enforcement jurisdiction".[102] This aligns with how Pouria Askary and Hassan Vakilian, in their chapter, characterise Iran as a state that advocates for the illegality of most forms of extraterritorial jurisdiction. Being primarily territorial, the exercise of jurisdiction in the extraterritorial domain raises questions of legality and legitimacy under international law.

If the exercise of extraterritorial prescriptive jurisdiction does not raise many questions of legality – it is generally accepted – the exercise of

101 An Hertogen, "Letting Lotus Bloom," *European Journal of International Law* 26 (2016): 901, 902.

102 Robert J. Currie, "Cross-Border Evidence Gathering in Transnational Criminal Investigation: Is the Microsoft Ireland Case the Next Frontier?" *Canadian Yearbook of International Law* 54 (2016): 97.

extraterritorial enforcement jurisdiction is considered illegal because it violates fundamental principles that underpin the stability of the global legal and political order.[103] This includes the principle of *sovereign equality* of states in international law, which asserts that all states are equal in international law,[104] occupying the same position in the international legal order and possessing identical rights and duties.[105] Compliance with the principle of reciprocity is essential for ensuring respect for sovereign equality.[106] When viewed in the context of extraterritorial jurisdiction, a state that exercises its jurisdiction in a non-permissive manner violates or threatens this principle, as evidenced in the *Arrest Warrant* case.[107] The ICJ found that Belgium violated its obligation to the Congo, "it failed to respect the immunity of the incumbent Minister for Foreign Affairs of the Congo and, more particularly, infringed the immunity from criminal jurisdiction and inviolability then enjoyed by him under international law"[108] by issuing an international arrest warrant. This sustains Congo's first final submission that Belgium's actions constituted a "violation of the rule of customary international law concerning absolute inviolability and immunity from criminal process of incumbent foreign ministers," a

> violation of the principle that a state may not exercise its authority on the territory of another state and of the principle of sovereign equality among all Members of the United Nations, as laid down in Article 2, paragraph 1, of the Charter of the United Nations.[109]

The exercise of extraterritorial jurisdiction may violate the principle of *territorial integrity*. Historically, this principle was seen as a safeguard against military aggression and threats to state territory. Today, however, it is broadly understood as protecting a state's *domaine réservé* within its territory, preventing other states from exercising authority over it.[110] An extraterritorial law may violate this principle by challenging the *domaine réservé* of the state over its territory. Legal scholarship is divided on this matter. Some scholars

103 Lucia Leontiev, "Conceptualising Extraterritoriality. Public International Law and Private International Law Considerations," *Global Jurist* 24(2) (2024): 119–155.

104 Peters, "Humanity as the A and Ω of Sovereignty," 528.

105 Sergio M. Carbone and Lorenzo Schiano di Pepe, "Fundamental Rights and Duties of States," in *Max Planck Encyclopaedia of Public International Law*, ed. Rüdiger Wolfrum (Oxford: Oxford University Press, 2019), 25.

106 *Reparations for Injuries Suffered in the Service of the United Nations*, Advisory Opinion, [1949] ICJ Reports 174, 177–178.

107 *Arrest Warrant*, 3.

108 *Ibid.*, paras. 62–71.

109 See *Arrest Warrant*, para. 17, 62.

110 Oliver Dörr, "Prohibition of Use of Force," in *Max Planck Encyclopaedia of Public International Law*, ed. Rüdiger.

argue that any act by another state could undermine territorial integrity.[111] In contrast, the majority contends that safeguarding a state's territorial integrity from foreign authoritative acts involves a physical dimension.[112] So, the exercise of enforcement jurisdiction (*e.g.*, arrests, seizure) may endanger territorial integrity due to its physical component, whereas prescriptive jurisdiction poses no such threat. This view was also confirmed by the ICJ in the *Certain Criminal Proceedings in France*[113] and *Corfu Channel*[114] cases, where the Court held that a state's territorial integrity could be violated by physical acts carried out on foreign territory but not by initiating proceedings without the use of physical force.[115]

The *principle of non-intervention* becomes particularly relevant in cases of the use of force and other forms of interference by one state in the domestic affairs of another. Its violation, especially in the form of extraterritorial enforcement jurisdiction, affects a state's *domaine réservé* – its jurisdiction over its sovereign territory, people, property, and events within it, as well as its political, economic, social, and cultural systems, and foreign policy.[116] Thus, when an issue falls within a state's *domaine réservé*, the non-intervention principle can be invoked to limit another state's extraterritorial jurisdiction. However, not all the acts that may *prima facie* interfere with a state's *domaine réservé* are necessarily illegal. In the ICJ's view, coercion defines and constitutes the essence of prohibited intervention.[117] Coercion can take the form of military, political, economic, or other forms of pressure; it must be forcible and dictatorial to qualify as intervention. Indirect support for

111 Oliver Dörr and Albrecht Randelzhofer, "Article 2 (4)," in *The Charter of the United Nations: A Commentary*, Vol. I, eds. Bruno Simma et al. (Oxford: Oxford University Press, 3rd ed., 2012), 208.

112 Prosper Weil, "International Limitations on State Jurisdiction," in *Extraterritorial Application of Laws and Responses Thereto*, ed. Cecil J. Olmstead (Oxford: International Law Association in association with ESC Publishing Ltd., 1984), 32–42; Steven R. Ratner, *The Thin Justice of International Law: A Moral Reckoning of the Law of Nations* (Oxford: Oxford University Press, 2015), 105; Alexander Orakhelashvili, *Akehurst's Modern Introduction to International Law* (London: Routledge, 8th ed., 2019), 213–216.

113 *Certain Criminal Proceedings in France* (*Democratic Republic of Congo v France*), 110–111, the Court rejected Congo's request to suspend French proceedings against several Congolese officials for grave human rights violations, holding that Congo's territorial integrity had not been violated.

114 In *Corfu Channel* (*United Kingdom v Albania*), the Court declared that the United Kingdom's acts of minesweeping Albanian waters violated Albania's sovereignty, emphasising that between independent states, respect for territorial sovereignty is an essential foundation of international relations. See *The Corfu Channel Case* (*United Kingdom v Albania*), Judgment, [1949] ICJ Reports 244, page 35.

115 Charlotte E. Blattner, *Protecting Animals Within and Across Borders* (Oxford: Oxford University Press, 2019), 388.

116 *Corfu Channel*, 35; *Military and Paramilitary Activities in and against Nicaragua*, 108.

117 *Military and Paramilitary Activities in and against Nicaragua*, para. 205, "Intervention is wrongful when it uses methods of coercion . . . . The element of coercion . . . defines, and indeed forms the very essence of prohibited intervention".

subversive or terrorist activities in another state,[118] as well as securing evidence in another state's territory,[119] are also seen as forms of forced intervention. A violation of the non-intervention principle may occur if a state calls for the laws of another state to be violated or if a foreign state enacts extraterritorial laws with the aim of undermining the jurisdiction of another state or destabilising its regime.[120] As discussed in the chapters on Russia and Iran, unilateral economic sanctions (secondary sanctions) are extraterritorial in nature and violate the principles of non-intervention and sovereign equality of states. The principle of non-intervention is explicitly articulated in the 1979 Constitution of Iran. As Askary and Vakilian argue, this reflects Iran's stance that many current applications of extraterritorial jurisdiction fundamentally contradict the principle of non-intervention.

International law principles limit not only enforcement jurisdiction but also adjudicative jurisdiction. Of particular relevance here is the principle of the *immunity of states* from foreign jurisdiction. Jurisdiction and immunity act like communicating vessels: on the one hand, any grant of immunity implies a refusal to exercise jurisdiction, while on the other hand, a denial of immunity leads to the assertion of jurisdiction.[121]

The customary international law principle of state immunity is often seen as an obstacle to domestic judicial scrutiny over international wrongful acts and accountability of states before the national judiciaries.[122] This reflects the nature of international law, where states are the creators and original subjects, all equal and enjoying absolute sovereignty and immunity (*par in parem non habet imprerium*). Current international law on state immunity consists of a general presumption of immunity – the coercive measures to a state and its properties are absolute (a*cta iure imperii*), and specified exceptions exclusively in the context of commercial and trading activities (*acta iure gestionis*).[123] States enjoy absolute immunity with regard to criminal proceedings.[124] It is important

118 *Ibid.*

119 *Corfu Channel*, 35.

120 *Asylum Case (Colombia v Peru)*, Judgment, [1950] ICJ Reports 266, 286.

121 Paul Gragl, "Jurisdictional Immunities of the State in International Law," in *The Oxford Handbook of Jurisdiction in International Law*, eds. Stephen Allen et al. (Oxford: Oxford University Press, 2019), 229; Alexander Orakhelashvili, "State Immunity from Jurisdiction Between Law, Comity, and Ideology," in *Jurisdiction and Immunities in International Law*, ed. Alexander Orakhelashvili (Cheltenham: Edward Elgar Publishing, 2015), 151.

122 Paola Gaeta, "Immunity of States and State Officials: A Major Stumbling Block to Judicial Scrutiny?" in *Realizing Utopia: The Future of International Law*, ed. Antonio Cassese (Oxford: Oxford University Press, 2012), 229.

123 Xiaodong Yang, *State Immunity in International Law* (Cambridge: Cambridge University Press, 2012), 426; Gragl, "Jurisdictional Immunities," 231.

124 Report of the Commission to the General Assembly on the Work of its Forty-Third Session, *Yearbook of the International Law Commission*, A/CN.4/SER.A/1991/Add.1 (Part 2), p. 12 at 14, commentary to Art. 2, para. (2); Report of the Ad Hoc Committee, 2003, A/58/22, Annex II, p. 15; Report of the Ad Hoc Committee, 2004, A/59/22, p. 3 and 4, paras. 11 and 14; Resolution A/RES/59/38, 2 December 2004, para. 2.

to recall that in international law, there is no concept of a crime committed by a state,[125] although individual criminal responsibility is regulated.

The ICJ in the *Jurisdictional Immunities* case (*Germany v Italy*) confirmed both the absolute and procedural nature of state immunity. Since the development of state immunity largely occurred within national judiciaries, one could argue that there are currently various attempts to 'relativise' the absolute nature of state immunity at the domestic level. The circumstances under which a domestic court might exercise its jurisdiction to consider a claim involving the application of domestic law to the acts of a foreign sovereign remain controversial.

Italian judiciaries may be considered trendsetters[126] in advancing the doctrine of limited immunity for *acta delicta imperii* in cases involving human rights violations. As Francesca Capone explains in her chapter, the Court of Cassation in the *Ferrini* case and the Italian Constitutional Court in *Sentenza* n. 238/2014 held that granting immunity to a state that violated *jus cogens* norms of international law was incompatible with the fundamental rights enshrined in the Italian Constitution. Therefore, the absolute nature of the customary rule on state immunity, as conveyed by the ICJ, could not be incorporated into the Italian legal system.[127]

The ICJ confirmed that "under customary international law as it presently stands, a state is not deprived of immunity by reason of the fact that it is accused of serious violations of international human rights law or the international law of armed conflict".[128] The Court denied any normative conflict, stating that "the rules of state immunity are procedural in character" and "do not bear upon the question whether or not the conduct in respect of which the proceedings are brought was lawful or unlawful".[129] The Court's decision is by no means progressive; rather, it reflects a traditional, positivist approach to international law, which unsurprisingly has drawn criticism for

125 See *International Law Commission Draft Articles on State Responsibility*, 2001.

126 Supreme Court of Brazil judgment of 2021 that condemned Germany for the killing of fishermen by Nazi officers in 1943 in the *Changri-La* case; District Court of Seoul decision of 2020 against Japan in the so-called 'comfort women' case. These judgments are largely built on the doctrine of limited immunity for *delicta imperi* put forward by the Italian Supreme Court and further elaborated by the Italian Constitutional Court in the well-known *Sentenza* 238/2014.

127 Recent trends that emerged in domestic courts on the interpretation of the customary rule on state immunity in cases of historical injustices, namely, of serious violations of international law perpetrated by states during war or war-like situations that have left victims without an effective remedy. See Eleonora Branca, "'Yet, It Moves . . .': The Dynamic Evolution of State Immunity in the 'Comfort Women case'," *EJIL:Talk!*, 7 April 2021. Accessed 20 December 2024. https://www.ejiltalk.org/yet-it-moves-the-dynamic-evolution-of-state-immunity-in-the-comfort-women-case/.

128 *Jurisdictional Immunities of the State* (*Germany v Italy: Greece intervening*), Judgment, [2012] ICJ Reports 99, para. 91.

129 *Ibid.*, para. 93.

obstructing the development of new customary international rules. Critics question whether substantive norms – *jus cogens* norms – should take precedence over the procedural law of state immunity.[130]

It is important to emphasise that the *jus cogens* argument is used by domestic courts in two ways: first, as a norm of higher hierarchical status (*e.g.*, prohibition of torture) that overrides inferior norms, and second, as a basis for waiving immunity before national courts.[131] However, this approach is not supported by state practice. In those cases where domestic courts have referred to *jus cogens* norms as overriding or waiving state immunity, the argument has typically been used to reinforce traditional grounds of jurisdiction, such as territoriality. For example, in *Distomo Massacre Case*, the Greek Court based its jurisdiction on the existence of territorial jurisdiction rather than on a *jus cogens* norm prohibiting the killing of a civilian population when stating that Germany had impliedly waived its immunity when its soldiers engaged in a massacre in a Greek village during the Second World War.[132]

Immunity essentially means exemption from an otherwise applicable and exercisable jurisdiction. State immunity typically arises within the context of territorial jurisdiction, and its projection into the extraterritorial domain presents significant challenges. Therefore, in the context of human rights violations, the central issue lies in the exercise of extraterritorial jurisdiction on one hand and its exemption on the other. If a violation occurs outside the forum state, jurisdiction should be established on the grounds of illegality and in accordance with international law, which permits the exercise of extraterritorial jurisdiction.[133]

Given the discrepancy between international human rights law and the law of state immunity, the exercise of extraterritorial jurisdiction – contemplated by international human rights law – cannot easily serve as a viable basis for denying immunity.[134] As Xiaodong Yang points out, "[T]here is a significant incongruity between the urgent need for international protection of human rights and the lack of clear rules and precedents concerning the issue of state immunity in cases involving human rights violations".[135]

Despite existing international law and practice regarding state immunity, states may adopt national regulations that provide further exceptions to

130 Gragl, "Jurisdictional Immunities," 241–242.

131 Yang, *State Immunity*, 429.

132 *Distomo Massacre Case*, Greece (2000) 129 ILR 513; *Ferrini v Germany*, Italy (2004) 128 ILR 658, 670–671, para. 10, the Italian Court of Cassation in the *Ferrini* case relied likewise on the territorial jurisdiction (the plaintiff had been captured in Italy by the German occupation forces and deported to Germany for forced labour during the Second World War).

133 Yang, *State Immunity*, 426.

134 *Ibid.*

135 *Ibid.*, 428.

state immunity. This is the case with Canada[136] and the US,[137] both of which explicitly recognise a 'terrorist exception' to state immunity. Iran brought a case before the ICJ, claiming that Canada violated its immunity from jurisdiction and enforcement. Iran also contested that Canada violated its immunity by "adopting sections 6.1 and 12 (l)(d) of the SIA, and enlisting Iran . . . as so-called supporter of terrorism", actions which are of a legislative and executive nature. Numerous lawsuits and enforcement procedures have been successful in Canadian courts, Iranian government being accused of acts of terrorism,[138] thus overruling the principle of state immunity. The outcome of the case before the ICJ remains to be seen, and it is uncertain whether the ICJ will assert its jurisdiction and rule on the merits. However, it is clear that, as international law currently stands, there is no 'terrorist exception' to the customary rule on state immunity, and state practice regarding such exceptions is neither widespread nor consistent.

Francesca Capone argues in her chapter that Italy's stance reads as a progressivist view of the law of state immunity. This approach allows for a dilution of the absolute nature of state immunity in cases of the most serious human rights violations.[139] On the other hand, our Iranian contributors, aligning with the decision in the *Jurisdictional Immunities* case, assert that any 'relativisation' of the absolute nature of state immunity contradicts the customary international law rule on state immunity. While customary international law evolves and national courts play a crucial role in the development of international law – especially in the area of state immunity[140] – one might question whether applying international law based on domestic law, as the Italian Constitutional Court has done, is the correct approach.

136 State Immunity Act (SIA), Section 6.1(1): "A foreign state that is set out on the list . . . is not immune from the jurisdiction of a court in proceedings against it for its support of terrorism". Regarding immunity from execution, Section 12(1)(d) SIA provides the corresponding exception. Canada, through an executive action, placed Iran on the list of state supporters of terrorism. For an analysis, see Valentin von Stosch and Felix Herbert, "Jurisdictional Immunities, All Over Again?" *EJIL:Talk!*, 7 July 2023. Accessed 20 December 2024. https://www.ejiltalk.org/jurisdictional-immunities-all-over-again/.

137 Foreign Sovereign Immunities Act precludes immunity in §1605A (a) (1) "in any case . . . in which money damages are sought against a foreign state for personal injury or death that was caused by an act of torture, extrajudicial killing, aircraft sabotage, hostage taking, or the provision of material support or resources for such an act".

138 von Stosch and Herbert, "Jurisdictional Immunities."

139 *Jurisdictional Immunities of the State*, paras. 55–61.

140 Being subsidiary means for the determination of the law in the sense of Article 38 (1)(d) of the ICJ Statute, the role of domestic courts is especially important in State immunity cases since "customary international law on the subject of State immunities has grown principally and essentially out of the judicial practice of States on the matter". Preliminary Report by Sompong Sucharitkul, Special Rapporteur on the topic of jurisdictional immunities of States and their property, UN Doc. A/CN.4/323 (1979), para. 23.

Furthermore, one might wonder whether these judgments, deeply tied to unresolved historical grievances, genuinely reflect the evolution of the law of state immunity or are merely the product of specific geopolitical situations that will not alter international law.

3.2 *The Enchantment of Extraterritorial Jurisdiction in International Law*

States should exercise their extraterritorial jurisdiction within the legal framework established by international law. Moreover, international law also provides avenues for states to exercise extraterritorial jurisdiction in specific cases where, theoretically, no jurisdictional link to justify such an exercise exists. One such avenue is universal jurisdiction. Furthermore, international law may impose extraterritorial obligations to states for human rights violations.

3.2.1 *Universal Criminal Jurisdiction and Extraterritoriality in the Common Interest*

Universal jurisdiction is one of the most contentious jurisdictional principles. The debates around its controversial nature revolve around its 'universality' in terms of substance and assertion. Despite the 'universality' of universal jurisdiction, which presumes that every state has jurisdiction in cases where the interests of the international community as a whole are affected and the most heinous crimes are committed, the questions that arise are: which state and based on which jurisdictional link, can assert universal jurisdiction. The lack of straightforward answers to these questions often results in the absence of universal jurisdiction. As Eugene Kontorovich and Steven E. Art argue, "perhaps the most obvious reason for the lack of universal jurisdiction is the fact that it is universal".[141] In other words, the belief that other states should also bear the enforcement burden leads to no state taking action.[142] This may explain why relying on a jurisdictional link remains relevant for states in assuming their responsibility.

In practice, the general rule is that states will abstain from exercising universal jurisdiction if there is no jurisdictional link. With a jurisdictional link present, allocating jurisdictional authority and encouraging action in the common interest becomes easier (the principle of subsidiarity).[143] However,

141 Eugene Kontorovich and Steven E. Art, "An Empirical Examination of Universal Jurisdiction for Pirates," *American Journal of International Law* 104 (2010): 453.

142 Frédéric Mégret, "The 'Elephant in the Room' in Debates about Universal Jurisdiction: Diasporas, Duties of Hospitality, and the Constitution of the Political," *Transnational Legal Theory* 6 (2015): 95.

143 Cedric Ryngaert, "Cosmopolitan Jurisdiction and the National Interest," in *The Oxford Handbook of Jurisdiction in International Law*, eds. Stephen Allen et al. (Oxford: Oxford University Press, 2019), 212.

this does not mean that the state with the strongest jurisdictional link will necessarily exercise its 'cosmopolitan' – to quote Cedric Ryngaert – jurisdiction. In the end, jurisdiction in international law is discretionary; jurisdictional deference by one state does not imply the assumption of jurisdiction by another.

However, theoretically, universal jurisdiction does not operate based on a connecting factor linking to a state's interests. It is solely based on the international nature of the (criminal) act committed. In the words of the Court of Appeals of Argentina, "the exercise of universal jurisdiction in the country . . . does not require any link with the state where the facts took place".[144] Under international law, the prosecution and arrest of pirates serve as the classic example of universal jurisdiction, which any state can exercise since pirates threaten the community of states at large. The fact that anti-piracy courts, sponsored by the international community, operate in Kenya is reflective of this.[145]

Judge ad hoc Van den Wyngaert, in her dissenting opinion in the *Arrest Warrant* case, explored the principle of universal jurisdiction, specifically referencing the *Lotus* principle. In the Judge's words,

> [I]t follows from the 'Lotus' case that a state has the right to provide extraterritorial jurisdiction on its territory unless there is a prohibition under international law. I believe there is no prohibition under international law to enact legislation allowing it to investigate and prosecute war crimes and crimes against humanity abroad.[146]

Indeed, international law does not prohibit states from adopting laws with extraterritorial reach, including rules enacting universal jurisdiction. For example, as Juan Ignacio Stampalija informs, the concept of universal jurisdiction was present in the Argentine Constitution as early as 1853. Moreover, states may have international obligations to prosecute and investigate heinous crimes through multilateral treaties, such as the International Criminal Court (ICC) Statute. States' willingness to embrace universal criminal jurisdiction and therefore extend their jurisdiction to acts committed abroad is also confirmed in some of the chapters of this book. As has been said, Sarah McGibbon argues that South Africa not only implemented the Rome Statute but also found itself obligated (where appropriate) to exercise universal jurisdiction over the crime of torture.

144 Stampalija, Chapter 13 of this book.

145 Dapo Akande, "Anti-Piracy Court Opens in Kenya," *EJIL:Talk!*, 28 June 2010. Accessed 20 December 2024. https://www.ejiltalk.org/anti-piracy-court-opens-in-kenya/.

146 *Arrest Warrant*, 169, Dissenting Opinion of Judge ad hoc Van den Wyngaert, para. 51.

Criminal justice requires a forum for its administration, and in this regard, if the ICC lacks jurisdiction, domestic courts play a crucial role in investigating and prosecuting heinous crimes. Nowadays, there is a surge in cases where national courts are called upon to adjudicate based on universal jurisdiction.[147] In 1998, Spain set a significant precedent by indicting former Chilean dictator Pinochet,[148] sending the message that governments should prosecute those responsible for international crimes.

However, according to customary international law, acting heads of state cannot be prosecuted before the national judiciaries. Yet, heads of state are not immune before international criminal tribunals because, as the ICC explained, the international courts do not act on behalf of a particular state in the same way national courts do. Thus, the principle of sovereign equality of states, which underpins the international rules on immunities, does not apply to international criminal courts. This implies that personal immunity does not bar prosecution before an international criminal court, although it does prevent such prosecutions in domestic courts.

Yet, states seem to be enchanted with extraterritorial jurisdiction, and, much like in the case of state immunity, they tend to 'relativise' international law principles to extend their jurisdiction. In 2023, acknowledging that Syrian authorities were unable or unwilling to prosecute President Bashar al-Assad, the French judiciary issued an arrest warrant for him due to his role as an accomplice in the crimes against humanity and war crimes committed during the chemical attacks in Eastern Ghouta, Syria.[149] To reach this decision, the court separated the prohibition on the use of chemical weapons – which is a customary international law norm of *jus cogens* nature from the head of state functions tied to sovereignty. In other words, it used the *jus cogens* argument to 'relativise' the absolute nature of state immunity for acting heads of state. Naturally, such a decision has faced criticism, as it challenges the well-established customary international law principle of personal jurisdictional immunity for acting heads of state. Moreover, while exceptions may be accepted by some states (notably

147 In the European Union see "New Investigations on Core International Crimes Increase by 44% Since 2016," *Press Release European Union Agency for Criminal Justice Cooperation*, 23 May 2022. Accessed 20 December 2024. https://www.eurojust.europa.eu/news/new-investigations-core-international-crimes-increase; Globally, see "Universal Jurisdiction Annual Review," *TRIAL International*, 2024. Accessed 20 December 2024. https://trialinternational.org/wp-content/uploads/2024/04/UJAR-2024_digital.pdf.

148 More on the case *see* Richard J. Wilson, "Prosecuting Pinochet: International Crimes in Spanish Domestic Law," *Human Rights Quarterly* 21(4) (1999).

149 Appeal Court of Paris, "Press Release on the Decision of the Chamber of Instruction Regarding the Regularity of the Arrest Warrant Against the Syrian President Bachar al-Assad," 26 June 2024. Accessed 20 December 2024. https://www.cours-appel.justice.fr/sites/default/files/2024-06/Communiqu%C3%A9%20de%20presse-mandat%20d%27arr%C3%AAt%20Bachar%20AL%20ASSAD.pdf.

Western) for the functional immunity of state officials, no state practice supports an exception under international law to the immunity *ratione personae* of acting state officials.

It is also worth noting that the probability of enforcing jurisdiction based on the principle of universality is minimal. Practically, the perpetrator is absent and cannot be brought before the enforcement institutions of the foreign state. Abduction on foreign state territory is prohibited as well. The abduction of an individual in State B's territory by agents of State A constitutes an internationally wrongful exercise of extraterritorial enforcement jurisdiction, as well as a breach of the UN Charter and international human rights law.[150] The legality of the subsequent exercise of territorial enforcement jurisdiction against the abductee is also contested. For Latin American states, this question was open enough to prompt a request for an Advisory Opinion from the International Court of Justice.[151]

So, one may wonder when and why states might exercise universal jurisdiction. The answer does not lie so much in the existence of a jurisdictional link but rather in the presence of a national interest or goal.[152] Domestic courts may resort to creative reasoning to establish an unorthodox jurisdictional link. An example of this is the ruling by the South African Constitutional Court in the *Zimbabwe* case, where it stated that "[g]iven the international and heinous nature of the crime of torture, South Africa has a substantial connection to it".[153] This reading implies that international crimes are connected to every state and that the interests of the international community are considered a national interest. As McGibbon argues in her chapter, this

150 Hersch Lauterpacht, ed., *Oppenheim's International Law* (London: Longman, 8th ed., 1955), 295; Question Relating to the Case of Adolf Eichmann, Resolution 138 (1960) [S/4349]: "the violation of the sovereignty of a Member State is incompatible with the Charter of the United Nations". The HRC, applying the ICCPR, held that the abduction of a Uruguayan national from Argentina (by Uruguayan security forces) amounted to an arbitrary arrest and detention in breach of Art. 9(1) of the Covenant (applying the ICCPR extraterritorially on the basis of a personal approach to 'jurisdiction' as the trigger for human rights obligations). See *Sergio Euben López Burgos v Uruguay*, HRC, 29 July 1981, UN Doc. A/36/40 (1981) 176, paras. 12–14.

151 Request for an Advisory Opinion from the International Court of Justice (by way of letter from Argentina, Bolivia, Brazil, Chile, Colombia, Costa Rica, Cuba, Dominican Republic, Ecuador, El Salvador, Guatemala, Honduras, Mexico, Nicaragua, Panama, Paraguay, Peru, Portugal, Spain, Uruguay, and Venezuela to the United Nations addressed to the Secretary-General, requesting that the item be placed on the Sixth Committee's agenda), UN Doc. A/47/249, 17 November 1992, Annex.

152 Michael Farbiarz, "Extraterritorial Criminal Jurisdiction," *Michigan Law Review* 114 (2016): 508.

153 *National Commissioner of The South African Police Service v Southern African Human Rights Litigation Centre and Another* (CCT 02/14), [2014] ZACC 30, para. 78.

represents the most progressive domestic case on international criminal law not only in South Africa but arguably across Africa.

In the al-Bashir case discussed previously, the message that the French judiciary aimed to convey is most likely that it is in the interest of every state to ensure that justice is administered for international crimes, as these crimes affect the international community and all its members.[154] The French case may also be a testament to the fact that when states have had a strong influence on the creation of international law, the likelihood of domestic enforcement of international law in the interest of the international community is higher in such states.[155]

Some states exercise universal jurisdiction as a means of atoning for domestic historical injustices or laying the foundations for the domestic or extraterritorial prosecution of these injustices. Spain's prosecutions of Latin American human rights violators, informed by universal jurisdiction, are instructive in this regard.[156] A similar motivation can be observed in Argentine's case. As Stampalija notes, Argentina's human rights tradition shaped its stance as an active participant in universal jurisdiction cases. This tradition is closely tied to the resistance and the fight for justice regarding the crimes against humanity committed during the military junta's rule from 1976 to 1982.

The existence of universal criminal justice over core crimes against international law is a sign of jurisdictional solidarity, which may extend to other offences in the long run.[157] Despite its role in filling enforcement gaps in international law, universal jurisdiction faces significant political and legal backlash. The cases over which a state exercises its universal criminal jurisdiction are often politically sensitive, frequently involving former political leaders of foreign states. There is also the risk of strained diplomatic relations. Some states exercise universal jurisdiction when "the stakes are not very high – for example, over lower-ranking perpetrators, in which case

154 Ryngaert, "Cosmopolitan Jurisdiction," 221.

155 Lisa Conant, "Whose Agents? The Interpretation of International Law in Domestic Courts," in *Interdisciplinary Perspectives on International Law and International Relations: The State of the Art*, eds. Jeffrey L. Dunoff and Mark A. Pollack (Cambridge: Cambridge University Press, 2012), 411–412.

156 Spain's own problems regarding its failure to achieve justice for violations, the lack of accountability for crimes committed under Franco, and the persistence of silence and impunity. See Amy Ross, "The Ríos Montt Case and Universal Jurisdiction," *Journal of Genocide Research* 18 (2016): 367. This political background – Spain's failure to come to terms with its own past – was brought into even starker relief after the adoption of a Historical Memory Law in 2007, which failed to fully break official silence on the crimes committed by the Franco regime. See *Ley de Memoria Histórica por la que se reconocen y amplían derechos y se establecen medidas en favor de quienes padecieron persecución o violencia durante la Guerra Civil*, Law 52/2007 of 16 December.

157 Ryngaert, "Cosmopolitan Jurisdiction," 211.

the risk of upsetting foreign nations is limited".[158] Other states deliberately shield certain states, while some may abusively use universal criminal jurisdiction. It is crucial for states to avoid abusing this principle and using it as part of geopolitical rivalries. States should strive to maintain a 'healthy' balance between state sovereignty and the interests of the international community as a whole.[159]

3.2.2 Extraterritorial Human Rights Obligations

Scholars argue that "the real purpose of international law . . . in the international realm is not the protection of sovereign states but the protection of the populations committed to their charge".[160] This may explain the enchantment of extraterritorial jurisdiction in international law in the field of human rights. In addition to the previously discussed practice of states 'relativising' international law principles of an absolute nature in the name of human rights, international law also imposes extraterritorial human rights obligations on states. As Mark Gibney frames it,

> [W]hile international law regulates the (horizontal) relationship between sovereign states, and international human rights law regulates the (vertical) relationship between a state and its own citizens – extraterritorial obligations are concerned with the 'diagonal' relationship between a state and individuals living in other countries.[161]

The territorial construct of international law is also evident in human rights law. Human rights treaties themselves refer to states' territory or jurisdiction as a means of enshrining their human rights obligations.[162] However,

158 Máximo Langer, "The Diplomacy of Universal Jurisdiction: The Political Branches and the Transnational Prosecution of International Crimes," *American Journal of International Law* 105(1) (2011): 1–49.

159 Lucia Leontiev, "On the Rise of Universal Criminal Justice," *Policy Brief No. 167*, Torkel Opsahl Academic EPublisher (2025). Accessed 27 February 2025. https://www.legal-tools.org/doc/riacv20o/pdf.

160 Jeremy Waldron, "Are Sovereigns Entitled to the Benefit of the International Rule of Law?" *European Journal of International Law* 22(2) (2011): 325.

161 Mark Gibney, "The Historical Development of Extraterritorial Obligations," in *The Routledge Handbook on Extraterritorial Human Rights Obligations*, eds. Mark Gibney et al. (London: Routledge, 2021), 13.

162 Article 2(1) of the International Covenant on Civil and Political Rights (ICCPR) provides: "Each State Party to the present Covenant undertakes to respect and to ensure to all individuals within its territory and subject to its jurisdiction the rights recognised in the present Covenant". Article 2(1) of the Torture Convention employs similar language: "Each State Party shall take effective legislative, administrative, judicial or other measures to prevent acts of torture in any territory under its jurisdiction". Article 1 of the European Convention on Human Rights stipulates that "The High Contracting Parties shall secure to everyone within their jurisdiction the rights and freedoms defined in . . . this Convention".

this has not impeded human rights bodies from considering the applicability of human rights treaties in the extraterritorial domain for actions taken by states on foreign territories, such as military operations.[163]

The extraterritorial applicability of human rights treaties is limited to situations where states exercise jurisdiction. In human rights law, jurisdiction serves as a "test for when the extraterritorial obligations would be triggered".[164] The European Court of Human Rights (ECtHR) takes the position that there is a connection between traditional jurisdiction rules and 'jurisdiction' as defined in Article 1 of the European Convention on Human Rights (ECHR), according to which "The High Contracting Parties shall secure to everyone within their jurisdiction the rights and freedoms defined in Section I of this Convention". Jurisdiction, therefore, relates primarily to territorial application, with certain categories for extraterritorial application. It can be defined as the link between the state and individuals' human rights, the factual control and authority a state exercises over a territory, individual or situation.[165] Extraterritorially, two instances should be mentioned: (1) effective control over territory (spatial model) and (2) physical power or control over persons (personal model).[166] The basic idea is that states have extraterritorial obligations, at least when they have sufficient control over territories or individuals. Emre Turkut aptly exemplifies this in his chapter, where he discusses how Turkey's geopolitical agenda and conduct challenge its international legal obligations, especially in the human rights field, as noted by the ECtHR.

The UN human rights treaty-based bodies have gone further, stating that not only the effective control exercised by a state but also its authority constitutes jurisdiction.[167] In other words, if a state exercises functions that directly and reasonably impact the human rights of individuals, those individuals fall within the state's jurisdiction. This broad approach implies that, in

163 Human Rights Committee (HRC) in its General Comment 31 (2004) on the scope of the ICCPR states that "a state party must respect and ensure the rights laid down in the Covenant to anyone within the power or effective control of that state Party, even if not situated within the territory of the state Party". ECtHR in *Loizidou* stated that "the concept of jurisdiction under Article 1 ECHR is not restricted to the national territory of the Contracting States. Accordingly, the responsibility of Contracting States . . . could arise when as a consequence of military action – whether lawful or unlawful – it exercises effective control of an area outside its national territory". *Loizidou v Turkey*, Application No. 15318/89, ECtHR Judgment, 18 December 1996, para. 52.

164 Ralph Wilde, "Dilemmas in Promoting Global Economic Justice through Human Rights Law," in *The Frontiers of Human Rights: Extraterritoriality and Its Challenges*, ed. Nehal Bhuta (Oxford: Oxford University Press, 2016), 130.

165 Antal Berkes, *International Human Rights Law Beyond Territorial Control* (Cambridge: Cambridge University Press, 2021), 21.

166 *Al-Skeini and Others v The United Kingdom*, Application No. 55721/07, ECtHR [GC] Judgment, 7 July 2011, paras. 130–142.

167 Berkes, *International Human Rights Law*, 52.

principle, extraterritorial obligations may arise for all negative and positive human rights obligations. This echoes the Maastricht Principles on Extraterritorial Obligations, which clearly articulate that under current international law, all states have extraterritorial obligations. This means that "states have obligations to respect, protect and fulfil human rights, including civil, cultural, economic, political and social rights, both within their territories and extraterritorially".[168] Indeed, as the ICJ observed in *Construction of a Wall*, Israel has the duty to respect the rights of people in the Palestinian territories; notably, it "is under an obligation not to raise any obstacle to the exercise of such rights in those fields where competence has been transferred to Palestinian authorities".[169] The court also specified that, as a duty to prevent genocide, for instance, states are expected "to employ all means reasonably available to them, so as to prevent genocide as far as possible".[170]

In determining state responsibility in the extraterritorial domain for its indirect actions through local proxies, the ICJ also resorts to the 'effective control' test, although with a high threshold. In *Nicaragua v United States*, the ICJ stated that for such a responsibility to arise, the US would need to have exercised effective control over paramilitary groups (para 106), meaning control over virtually every activity of these groups. This very high threshold of 'effective control' was maintained by the court in *Bosnia v Serbia*, where it found that no Serbian responsibility for human rights atrocities following the fall of Srebrenica existed, as the 'effective control' test was not met. For its part, however, the Tribunal for the Former Yugoslavia described the ICJ's 'effective control' test as inconsistent with the "very logic of the entire system of state responsibility" and "at variance with judicial and state practice", thus endorsing the 'overall control' test.[171]

While the territorial confines of international law are far from being abandoned, all this is proof that states' obligations extend extraterritorially, and that state responsibility in the name of human rights does too.

4 Study Delimitation and Methodology

4.1 Scope and Methodological Approach

States vary significantly, both physically and politically, in terms of their populations and the entities that compose them. Thus, states are influenced

168 Maastricht Principles on Extraterritorial Obligations of States in the Area of Economic, Social and Cultural Rights, September 2011, General Principle 3.

169 *Legal Consequences of the Construction of a Wall in the Occupied Palestinian Territory*, Advisory Opinion, [2004] ICJ Reports 136, para. 112, also paras. 133–134.

170 *Case Concerning Application of the Convention on the Prevention and Punishment of the Crime of Genocide (Bosnia and Herzegovina v Serbia and Montenegro)*, Judgment, [2007] ICJ Reports 43, para. 430.

171 *Prosecutor v Dusko Tadic*, Appeal Judgment, [1999] ICTY, Case No IT-94-1-A, para. 131.

by their particular nature when deciding whether to exercise extraterritorial jurisdiction to regulate their diverse interests abroad.

As discussed, extraterritoriality is governed by both domestic and international law. International law, in particular, establishes the limits within which states can regulate and exercise their extraterritorial jurisdiction. Ultimately, any exercise of extraterritoriality must be lawful.

However, this does not imply that the exercise of extraterritoriality is a linear process. As the chapters of this book demonstrate, different states have different interests and engage with extraterritoriality in distinct ways. Some states, for instance, interpret international law in a traditionalist, positivist manner, finding it difficult to detach jurisdiction from territoriality (*e.g.*, Russia). Others embrace a progressivist reading of international law, which at times leads them to 'relativise' international law principles that are typically seen as absolute (*e.g.*, Italy).

This book examines how different legal and policy drivers influence the law and practice of extraterritoriality in selected states. The contributors to this edited volume were asked to provide a 'radiography' of their respective state's approach to extraterritoriality and reflect on how international law shapes this approach. This exercise involves analysing various factors and policies that shape, affect, and determine the exercise of extraterritoriality among nations.

In methodological terms, this research endeavour naturally adopts a comparative international law perspective. Comparative international law

> utilises insights and methods from comparative law in order to identify, analyse, and explain similarities and differences in how international law is understood, interpreted, applied, and approached by different national and international actors.[172]

Indeed, despite claims of universality, international law often presents different outlooks in diverse settings. As Bhupinder S. Chimni argues, for international law, "location matters, be it in terms of the issues that are addressed or the ways in which these are approached".[173]

This book offers a fresh appraisal of how extraterritoriality is addressed and approached in different states. In this sense, the benchmark for comparison is the international rule itself – extraterritoriality – as it is common to the legal systems under study. Comparative international law scholarship argues that single-country studies qualify as comparative work due to the fact that

172 Anthea Roberts et al., "Conceptualising Comparative International Law," in *Comparative International Law*, eds. Anthea Roberts et al. (Oxford: Oxford University Press, 2018), 4.

173 Bhupinder S. Chimni, "The World of TWAIL: Introduction to the Special Issue," *Trade Law and Development* 3(1) (2011): 22.

international law provides a benchmark for comparison,[174] a view that we fully endorse and apply in this book.

As part of the comparative international law exercise, the contributors to this book were encouraged to go beyond traditional descriptive research and present arguments that explain the similarities and differences in how extraterritoriality is understood, interpreted, applied, and approached. It is noteworthy that for some states (*e.g.*, the UK, the US, and Australia), their belonging to the common law tradition significantly influences the law and practice of extraterritoriality. For France, among other factors, its membership in the EU helps explain its approach to extraterritoriality. In other cases (*e.g.*, Argentina and South Africa), the human rights tradition has shaped their active participation in universal jurisdiction cases. In Turkey's case, geopolitics plays an important role in framing extraterritoriality. These are just a few examples of the similarities and differences in how extraterritoriality is approached in the various states examined in this book.

The comparative method is complemented by an interdisciplinary analysis of extraterritoriality. Given the politico-legal nature of extraterritoriality, it is not surprising that the contributors to this book often draw from politics and policies to explain states' extraterritorial regulations and practices. For example, Emre Turkut examines Turkey's approach to extraterritorial jurisdiction through the lens of geopolitics, highlighting how the state's geopolitical agenda influences its exercise of extraterritoriality and challenges its international legal obligations.

This methodological approach allows us to observe how states legally construct and exercise extraterritoriality. As Hannah L. Buxbaum once noted, " 'territoriality' and 'extraterritoriality' . . . are legal constructs".[175] The chapters of this book indeed illustrate "claims of authority, or of resistance to authority, [are] made by particular actors with particular substantive interests to promote".[176] In other words, a state's approach to extraterritoriality is shaped by various factors, which ultimately translate into legal terms. Understanding the similarities and differences in how extraterritoriality is approached helps to better understand international law and its role at the domestic level. This is particularly relevant given the current metamorphosis of the international order as it transitions from a unipolar to a multipolar world.

4.2 *Case Studies Selection*

Explaining similarities and differences in a legal construct or institution around the world is not an easy task, and such purpose is the *raison d'être* of comparative legal sciences. When the object of comparison is influenced by

174 Roberts et al., "Conceptualising," 14.

175 Hannah L. Buxbaum, "Territory, Territoriality, and the Resolution of Jurisdictional Conflict," *American Journal of Comparative Law* 57(2) (2009): 635.

176 *Ibid.*

other social forces that transcend legal frameworks, like extraterritoriality, the task becomes more complex. The main comparative output of this volume is the case studies selection that it offers, as it provides the reader with a door into the broadest possible view with respect to extraterritoriality in its politico-legal dimension.

The comparative methodology behind this volume is thus based on a twofold approach: breadth and orientation. Considering that extraterritoriality concerns the international community as a whole, as well as its individual members, the volume is guided by the necessity of covering as much ground as possible. Likewise, in order to offer the intended view of extraterritoriality, the volume directs its efforts efficiently across the broad spectrum. Geography, law, and culture, widely understood as the essential national idiosyncrasies that shape the character of states, both in their political and economic dimensions, constitute the main points of reference for conducting this study.

Geographically, the volume comprises twelve countries: Argentina, Australia, France, India, Iran, Israel, Italy, Russia, South Africa, Turkey, the United Kingdom and the United States of America. Geographical breadth is important given the unique and intimate relationship between extraterritoriality and a given state, and more generally because law and politics spread across the world in uneven ways. These countries represent the five continents, three important world regions (North America, Latin America, Middle East), two subcontinents (Australia, India), the most populated country in the world (India), other four top twenty most populated countries (US, Russia, Iran, Turkey), and the largest country on earth (Russia) – something that is important considering that territory constitutes the *A* and Ω of extraterritoriality. In this sense, the case studies on Argentina, Australia, India, Iran, and the US are also significant as they are among the top twenty largest countries. Other works based on a comparable methodology exist, but they are limited to a handful of Asian states and to criminal law,[177] which, although an important field of extraterritoriality, constitutes only one among its numerous expressions.

Legally, this volume takes pride in including countries belonging to at least three legal systems, four if South Africa is also considered under its traditional law dimension. As civil law countries, the volume includes Argentina, France, Italy, Russia, and Turkey. As common law countries, the volume includes the UK, the US, and Australia. As countries of mixed origin, resulting from a blend of one or both of the main legal families – like South Africa – and a religious system, the volume includes India, Iran, and Israel. Perhaps, except from the common law and the religious states, the volume

177 *Extraterritoriality in East Asia. Extraterritorial Criminal Jurisdiction in China, Japan, and South Korea*, ed. Danielle Ireland-Piper (Cheltenham: Edward Elgar, 2021); Danielle Ireland-Piper, *Accountability in Extraterritoriality. A Comparative and International Law Perspective* (Cheltenham: Edward Elgar, 2017).

does not expressly attach specific characteristics to extraterritoriality based on the legal systems. Nevertheless, the vigilant reader will detect important variances and similarities under these classifications. It is not a coincidence that the structure of the volume, as presented hereinafter, reflects the legal systems to some extent. Other works of a comparable legal breadth exist, but their scope is rather disciplinary in the form of national reports.[178]

Culturally, the volume includes several Western democracies from different latitudes (Argentina, Australia, France, Italy, South Africa, the UK, and the US), the most important representative of the Eastern Bloc (Russia), three of the most powerful Middle Eastern states (Israel, Iran, and Turkey), and one of the most important representatives of the Third World (non-aligned): India. Neither is it a coincidence that the structure of the volume reflects this division of the world to some extent. Other works containing regional perspectives of extraterritoriality exist, but their breadth is shorter and softens in the sense that they condense the topic basically into continental case studies, while extraterritoriality mainly develops in national contexts, except from the European Union, to some extent.[179]

5 Book Structure: Mapping the Existing Trends

Understanding state practices in asserting extraterritorial jurisdiction is essential to uncover the factors influencing extraterritorial behaviour and emerging trends. This volume identifies three distinct attitudes toward extraterritoriality: reactive, transitive, and progressive.

5.1 Reactive Approaches

By 'reactive', we refer to a state's tendency to pragmatically use extraterritorial jurisdiction when it aligns with its national interests and is influenced by geopolitical considerations. This attitude could also be described as protective or defensive to some extent. While many states claim to adhere to the principles of territoriality of jurisdiction and non-intervention, opposing extraterritoriality in principle, in practice, things are not so clear-cut. As reflected in this book, in certain instances, states embrace extraterritoriality, shifting from a passive to an active role in asserting extraterritorial jurisdiction. Moreover, some states use extraterritorial jurisdiction as a tool to project their geopolitical influence. This is not surprising, as many states are often caught between their international legal obligations and their geopolitical aspirations and national interests.

178 *Extraterritoriality in Comparative Perspective*, ed. Hannah L. Buxbaum (Leiden/Boston: Brill | Nijhoff, 2025).

179 *Research Handbook on Extraterritoriality in International Law*, eds. Parrish and Ryngaert.

A markedly reactive approach to extraterritoriality, going from a general restraint to an active attitude, can be observed in the case of France (Chapter 2). Marjolaine Abada-Fasquelle argues that, although France has consistently opposed extraterritorial jurisdiction, a shift has occurred in its approach – moving away from complete opposition toward a more open stance. As the author explains, foreign extraterritorial jurisdiction, particularly that of the US, has acted as a political driver of change. The concerns surrounding extraterritorial jurisdiction are now less about the legal basis invoked and more about the policy objectives it serves.

In the case of India (Chapter 3), as Aniruddha Rajput and Sudipta Purkayastha explain, despite its commitment to the principles of comity and state sovereignty and its general reluctance to apply domestic laws beyond its territorial boundaries, India has carved out exceptions for exercising extraterritorial jurisdiction when national security and national interests are at stake. As the authors note, with India's rising political and economic influence, its global engagement has expanded, and its interests have diversified. Consequently, the number of factors justifying the exercise of extraterritorial jurisdiction has inevitably increased.

A similar evolution can be observed in Russia's approach to extraterritoriality (Chapter 4). By examining Russia's defensive and offensive strategies against sanctions, its efforts to reinforce sovereignty in a 'borderless' domain such as the information space in the name of national interest, and its reliance on alternatives to extradition for prosecution purposes, Liliya Khasanova, Nailia Savenkova, and Kamila Shaibakova argue that Russia's approach to extraterritoriality has shifted from a strong commitment to the principles of sovereignty and non-intervention to a more pragmatic stance. Influenced by a complex geopolitical context, Russia has become more active in implementing extraterritorial legal and policy measures. The authors further suggest that its growing geopolitical interests, national security concerns, and ambition to play a significant regulatory role in the global economy are key factors driving Russia's turn toward extraterritoriality.

National security issues and spatial military interests have been central to Turkey's (Chapter 5) geopolitical expansionist agenda. By analysing Turkey's military actions in Syria and Iraq, the author contends that the exercise of extraterritoriality has played a significant role in shaping Turkey's geopolitical identity, evolving as part of its broader projection of national power. The chapter also examines Turkey's extraterritorial human rights obligations as a consequence of its geopolitical agenda.

Caught in the 'Great Game', geopolitics has historically played an important role in shaping Iran's approach to extraterritoriality (Chapter 6). Due to its eventful history, as Pouria Askary and Hassan Vakilian argue, Iran advocates for the illegality of most forms of extraterritorial jurisdiction and strongly adheres to the principle of non-intervention. At the same time, Iran's Constitution mandates that its authorities support – while scrupulously refraining from interference in the internal affairs of other nations – Muslims against dominating powers, based on the concept of the *Umma*, or the universal community of Muslims; this 'support' could entail extraterritorial actions. As with other states, Iran may assert its jurisdiction outside its territory when the most essential national interests are at stake.

In the case of Israel (Chapter 7), the projection of its jurisdiction in the extraterritorial domain is closely tied to Israel's self-perception as the state of the Jewish people. As Yaël Ronen argues, Israel asserts extraterritorial jurisdiction in certain matters based on the Jewishness of the individuals involved. Israeli legislative instruments convey the message that Jews around the world, whether as individuals or communities, are, to some extent, Israel's concern because they are, in this context, "an expression of Israel being the state of the Jewish people". As the author notes, the appropriation of world Jewry by Israel, along with its commitment to protect foreigners – even those kin to the majority and hegemonic population – raises significant concerns. In other words, such legislative provisions push the limits of commonly practised and internationally accepted standards of extraterritorial jurisdiction.

5.2 *Transitive Approaches*

A transition from a strong adherence to territorial sovereignty regarding prescriptive jurisdiction to very sophisticated systems of prescriptive extraterritoriality is a strong trend among the selected common law states. In these states, a particularly strong link between law and territory (territoriality of the law), reinforced by an acute sense of comity (reciprocity in civil law terms), excludes, in principle, any extraterritorial application of the law. Common law courts are thus traditionally neither called upon nor entitled to correct conduct occurring abroad.

It is in this context that the prominent common law principle of the *presumption against extraterritoriality* appears, both within the legislature and the judiciary. The transition starts within the judiciary. Coupled with the essential unwritten law characteristic of the common law, and the strong statutory interpretation powers of the judiciary, the realities of modern conduct in a globalised world have led to the transformation of the presumption from a principle to a rather narrow and strictly circumscribed exception.

In the United Kingdom (Chapter 8), transnational fraud, inchoate crimes, and even sexual offences have been important catalysts in 'stretching' the territory into a more general and inclusionary approach to the particular connection to territory required by the law. In the case of Australia (Chapter 9), international obligations contained in treaties, as well as a significant increase in transnational crime, have shaped the geographical reach of this country's criminal law. In the case of the United States (Chapter 10), its exponential growth relative to other foreign powers in the 20th century and the global connections ensuing thereof has led to what may arguably be called the most sophisticated and far-reaching extraterritorial system, especially in an array of economic areas of the law. Nevertheless, the United States is also the theatre of a tug-of-war between the legislative and the judiciary with respect to the scope and interpretation of the principle of the *presumption against extraterritoriality*.

5.3 Progressive Approaches

A progressive approach to extraterritorial jurisdiction refers to an extensive use of states' jurisdiction, even in cases where no substantive jurisdictional link exists. Some states – due to specific reasons such as their historical context, political considerations, or national interests – may willingly exercise jurisdiction even in the absence of a jurisdictional link. The substantive argument behind this jurisdictional behaviour is that it serves the interests of all states, protects human rights, and ensures that justice is administered for international crimes, as they affect the entire international community. In other words, states assert extraterritorial jurisdiction in the name of human rights and the international community's interests.

Francesca Capone's analysis of Italy's approach to extraterritoriality (Chapter 11) shows that by prioritising the protection of fundamental rights and rejecting the absolute nature of sovereign immunity in cases involving violations of *jus cogens* norms, Italian courts extend the reach of their jurisdiction beyond national borders. This position implicitly challenges the traditional understanding of state immunity as a procedural bar that shields foreign states from the legal processes of other jurisdictions, regardless of the nature of the conduct. Instead, Italian jurisprudence asserts that where serious breaches of peremptory norms are at issue, immunity cannot be sustained without contravening constitutional and international human rights commitments. In rejecting the interpretation endorsed by the International Court of Justice in the *Jurisdictional Immunities* case, Italy adopts a progressivist stance that reconfigures the relationship between immunity and jurisdiction. It thus affirms the role of domestic courts as agents of international accountability, capable of adjudicating serious human rights violations irrespective of the territorial or sovereign boundaries traditionally imposed by international law.

In the case of South Africa (Chapter 12), as Sarah McGibbon argues, South Africa's commitment to being an equal member of the international community has led to its active participation in the movement toward international criminal accountability. By grounding its approach to extraterritoriality in constitutional mandates and values, South Africa positions itself as a leader in the global arena of human rights protection and views itself as obligated (where appropriate) to exercise universal jurisdiction over the crime of torture. These values have served as key policy drivers in shaping South Africa's relatively expansive approach to extraterritoriality.

Argentina's human rights tradition (Chapter 13) has shaped its stance as an active participant in universal jurisdiction cases. Juan Ignacio Stampalija argues that this tradition is deeply connected to the resistance and the fight for justice concerning the crimes against humanity committed during the military junta that ruled the country from 1976 to 1982.

References

Allen, Stephen et al., eds. *The Oxford Handbook of Jurisdiction in International Law*. Oxford: Oxford University Press, 2019.

Berkes, Antal. *International Human Rights Law Beyond Territorial Control*. Cambridge: Cambridge University Press, 2021.

Besson, Samantha. "Why and What (State) Jurisdiction: Legal Plurality, Individual Equality and Territorial Legitimacy." In *The Challenge of Inter-Legality*, edited by Jan Klabbers and Gianluigi Palombella. Cambridge: Cambridge University Press, 2019.

Buxbaum, Hannah et al., eds. *Extraterritoriality*. Leiden/Boston: Brill | Nijhoff, 2022.

Cerar, Miro. "The Relationship between Law and Politics." *Annual Survey of International Law & Comparative Law* 15 (2009).

Crawford, James R. *Brownlie's Principles of Public International Law*. Oxford: Oxford University Press, 2012.

Gibney, Mark et al., eds. *The Routledge Handbook on Extraterritorial Human Rights Obligations*. London: Routledge, 2021.

Kamminga, Meno T. "Extraterritoriality," In *Max Plank Encyclopedia of Public International Law*. Oxford University Press, 2015.

Mann, Frederick A. *The Doctrine of International Jurisdiction Revisited after Twenty Years*. The Hague: Collected Courses, 1984.

Milanović, Marko. "From Compromise to Principle: Clarifying the Concept of State Jurisdiction in Human Rights Treaties." *Human Rights Law Review* 8 (2008).

Mills, Alex. "Rethinking Jurisdiction in International Law." *British Yearbook of International Law* 84 (2014).

Orakhelashvili, Alexander, ed. *Jurisdiction and Immunities in International Law*. Cheltenham: Edward Elgar Publishing, 2015.

Parrish, Austen, and Cedric Ryngaert. *Research Handbook on Extraterritoriality in International Law*. Cheltenham: Edward Elgar Publishing, 2023.

Peters, Anne. "Humanity as the *A* and Ω of Sovereignty." *The European Journal of International Law* 20 (2009).

Roberts, Anthea et al., eds. *Comparative International Law*. Oxford: Oxford University Press, 2018.

Ryngaert, Cedric. *Jurisdiction in International Law*. Oxford: Oxford University Press, 2nd edition, 2015.

Schmidt, Julia. "The Legality of Unilateral Extra-Territorial Sanctions under International Law." *Journal of Conflict & Security Law* 27 (2022).

Yang, Xiaodong. *State Immunity in International Law*. Cambridge: Cambridge University Press, 2012.

Part I

Reactive Approaches

2 The Progression of French Approaches to Extraterritoriality

In Between a Traditional Reluctance and a Quest for Legitimacy

Marjolaine Abada-Fasquelle

1 Introduction

Andreas Lowenfeld introduced the notion of extraterritoriality in its course at The Hague Academy of International Law in 1994, as follows:

> The search for a satisfactory definition of extraterritorial jurisdiction . . . is doomed to failure: 'extraterritorial jurisdiction', like 'bureaucratic', is a term that could never be rescued from its unattractive reputation.[1]

Thirty years later, this assessment remains profoundly accurate, encapsulating the ongoing debates surrounding extraterritoriality. Even though this topic is far from novel – as extraterritorial jurisdiction has been the subject of abundant scholarship[2] – it continues to evolve.

For instance, the effects doctrine, which once caused international tension between the United States and the European Union, was initially regarded as

1 Andreas F. Lowenfeld, "International Litigation and the Quest for Reasonableness," *Collected Courses of the Hague Academy of International Law* 245 (1994): 44.

2 See notably Marie-France Labouz, ed., *L'application extraterritoriale du droit économique* (Paris: Montchrestien, 1987); Brigitte Stern, "Une tentative d'élucidation du concept d'application extraterritoriale," *Revue québécoise de droit international* 3 (1986): 49–78; Brigitte Stern, "Quelques observations sur les règles internationales relatives à l'application extraterritoriale du droit," *Annuaire français de droit international* 32 (1986): 7–52; Brigitte Stern, "L'extra-territorialité 'revisitée': où il est question des affaires *Alvarez-Machain, Pâte de Bois* et de quelques autres . . .," *Annuaire français de droit international* 38 (1992): 239–313; Albane Geslin, "La position de la France en matière d'extraterritorialité du droit économique national," *Revue juridique de l'Ouest* 4 (1997): 411–467; Mathias Audit and Etienne Pataut, eds., *L'Extraterritorialité* (Paris: Pedone, 2020); Alina Miron and Bérangère Taxil, eds., *Extraterritorialités et droit international* (Paris: Pedone, 2020); Edouard Dubout, Francesco Martucci and Fabrice Picod, eds., *L'Extraterritorialité en droit de l'Union européenne* (Bruxelles: Bruylant, 2021); Hannah L. Buxbaum and Thibault Fleury-Graff, eds., *Extraterritoriality/L'Extraterritorialité* (Leiden/Boston: Brill/Nijhoff, 2022); Alan Hervé and Cécile Rapoport, eds., *L'Union européenne et l'extraterritorialité: Acteurs, fonctions, réactions* (Rennes: PUR, 2023).

DOI: 10.4324/9781003402978-3

an impermissible exercise of extraterritorial jurisdiction.[3] However, it is now well-established and widely applied in competition law on both sides of the Atlantic. Currently, discussions on extraterritoriality have taken on a new dimension, primarily due to advancements in digital data and dematerialised activities, which necessitate state action beyond national borders.[4] Intrinsically linked to globalisation and the evolution of digital technology, extraterritoriality is now considered "one of the major contemporary developments in economic law".[5] Accordingly, new forms of jurisdiction have emerged to address these changes.

In France, extraterritoriality has garnered renewed attention following the *Alstom* and *BNP Paribas* cases, evolving into a highly sensitive political topic. These cases represent a turning point in France's approach to extraterritoriality, shifting from outright opposition to a more nuanced stance.[6] Initially, US practices provoked vehement criticism. Unlike the United States, however, France – and the European Union more broadly – does not operate under a 'presumption against extraterritoriality'. Nevertheless, France has historically exhibited reluctance towards extraterritorial jurisdiction – or at least towards certain foreign exercises of extraterritoriality.

It is worth mentioning that, in 1927, the Permanent Court of International Justice (PCIJ) adjudicated the first – and only – case[7] directly addressing extraterritorial jurisdiction. France, in this case, challenged the extraterritorial exercise of jurisdiction, underscoring its longstanding opposition to such practices. France argued that

> according to international law . . ., a state is not entitled, apart from express or implicit special agreements, to extend the criminal jurisdiction of its courts to include a crime or offence committed by a foreigner abroad solely in consequence of the fact that one of its nationals has been a victim of the crime or offence.[8]

It could be argued that France's position has remained largely unchanged since then.

3 The effects doctrine originated in the US with the *Alcoa* case (*United States v Aluminum Co. of America*, 148 F.2d 416 (2d Cir. 1945)). At the time, it was strongly criticised. See, for instance, Najeeb Samie, "The Doctrine of 'Effects' and the Extraterritorial Application of Antitrust Laws," *University of Miami Inter-American Law Review* 14 (1982): 27 *et seq.*

4 Thibaut Fleury Graff, "(Il)licéités et (dé)mesures de l'extraterritorialité," in *Extraterritoriality/L'Extraterritorialité*, eds. Hannah L. Buxbaum and Thibault Fleury Graff (Leiden/Boston: Brill/Nijhoff, 2022), 62.

5 Mathias Audit, "L'extraterritorialité est partout!" *Echanges internationaux* 112 (2018): 20.

6 See *infra* 66 *et seq.*

7 *SS Lotus (France v Turkey)*, 1927 PCIJ (ser. A) No. 10 (Sept. 7).

8 *Ibid.*, 7.

Before addressing the core discussion, it is essential to outline some methodological considerations. In France, most discussions on extraterritoriality have focused on US practice, and the definition of this concept has been shaped accordingly. Although this chapter examines the French approach to extraterritorial jurisdiction, a discussion of US extraterritoriality is unavoidable and will be used as a comparative reference.

Similarly, France is a member state of the European Union. Any analysis of the French approach cannot be entirely disentangled from that of the EU, given that many laws and policies are formulated at the European level and that EU regulations are "directly applicable in all Member States".[9] However, to accurately reflect France's perspective, this chapter primarily relies on national legislation as the principal source of analysis. Moreover, it draws – though not exclusively – on research conducted by French scholars.

Finally, the following discussion is primarily confined to economic legislation, broadly construed. After defining the concept of extraterritoriality and outlining the associated challenges, the discussion will examine France's historical opposition to certain forms of extraterritoriality. It will then illustrate how the *BNP Paribas* and *Alstom* cases marked a political milestone, leading to a new understanding of extraterritoriality that extends beyond the sole issue of jurisdiction.

2 Defining the Notion: The Legal Aspects of Extraterritoriality

The scope of the concept of extraterritoriality varies depending on whether it is construed around the theory of jurisdiction or the lack of a genuine connection.

2.1 *The Theory of Jurisdiction*

There is no consensus among French scholars regarding the notion of extraterritoriality. As a result, legal scholars have favoured the plural form, 'extraterritorialities', to emphasise the diversity of situations it encompasses.[10] *Stricto sensu*, extraterritoriality refers to a 'situation in which state powers (legislative, executive, or judicial) govern legal relations situated outside the state's territory'.[11] Defined in this way, extraterritoriality is simultaneously "everywhere and nowhere".[12]

9 Article 288 of the Treaty on the Functioning of the European Union.

10 The French Society for International Law (*Société française pour le droit international* – SFDI) has chosen to pluralise this concept for its symposium, which was held in Angers in 2019. Miron and Taxil, eds., *Extraterritorialités et droit international*. See also Fleury Graff, "(Il)licéités et (dé)mesures," 87; Régis Bismuth, "Regards croisés sur l'extraterritorialité du droit," *Cahiers de droit de l'entreprise* 4 (2018): 19.

11 "Extraterritorialité," in *Dictionnaire de droit international public*, ed. Jean Salmon (Bruxelles: Bruylant, 2001), 491 [translation from Hervé Ascencio, *Extraterritoriality as an instrument*, Contribution to the work of the UN Secretary General's Special Representative on human rights and transnational corporations and other businesses, 2010, 1].

12 Fleury Graff, "(Il)licéités et (dé)mesures," 52.

Indeed, according to this definition, the distinction between territoriality and extraterritoriality is based solely on a binary opposition. Although this dichotomy is historically well established,[13] it no longer appears to align with the contemporary usage of this term. Extraterritoriality today carries the implication of exceptionality – that is, a deviation from the norm – thus conferring upon it a derogatory character.[14] In the French legal community, such a neutral conception of extraterritoriality is therefore often regarded as outdated, particularly in a globalised and digitised world where, by definition, "extraterritoriality is omnipresent".[15] As a result, much of the legal doctrine has questioned the very concept of extraterritoriality, arguing that it may have become inappropriate, if not entirely obsolete.[16]

The debates surrounding the relevance – or irrelevance – of extraterritoriality stem primarily from its classical opposition to territoriality. Since extraterritoriality, thus defined, is no longer (if it ever was) truly 'exceptional', its conceptual utility has been called into question. Moreover, from the perspective of public international law, territoriality is no longer the sole recognised basis for the exercise of jurisdiction. Extraterritoriality, in fact, concerns the exercise of a state's jurisdiction beyond its territory without relying on any other established jurisdictional basis under international law – specifically, the recognised permissive principles that justify a state's exercise of jurisdiction. That said, there is no international convention explicitly defining the limits of a state's jurisdictional authority. Consequently, this issue falls under the domain of customary international law.[17]

13 Following the Treaties of Westphalia of 1648, contemporary public international law was founded on the principle of sovereign equality, which notably entails that States have exclusive jurisdiction within their respective territories. Territoriality is thus a central concept in this field of study.

14 Stéphanie Francq, *L'Applicabilité du droit communautaire dérivé au regard des méthodes de droit international privé* (Bruxelles/Paris: Bruylant/LGDJ, 2005), 71–72; Alina Miron and Bérangère Taxil, "Les extraterritorialités, entre unilatéralisme et multilatéralisme. L'*imperium* sans le *dominum*?" in *Extraterritorialités et droit international*, eds. Alina Miron and Bérangère Taxil (Paris: Pedone, 2020), 16; Fleury Graff, "(Il)licéités et (dé)mesures," 54.

15 Louis d'Avout, "L'extraterritorialité vue de Sirius (où il est question d'extraterritorialité 'régulatoire', entre autres difficultés actuelles d'un droit mondial des affaires peu coordonné)," *Revue de droit bancaire et financier* 6 (2015): 2.

16 See, notably, Alain Pellet, "Conclusion," in *Sanctions unilatérales, mondialisation du commerce et ordre juridique international. A propos des lois Helms-Burton et d'Amato-Kennedy*, eds. Habib Ghérari and Sandra Szurek (Paris: Montchrestien, 1998), 321–334; Mathias Audit and Etienne Pataut, "Ouverture," in *L'Extraterritorialité*, eds. Mathias Audit and Etienne Pataut (Paris: Pedone, 2020), 6; Louis d'Avout, "L'extraterritorialité du droit dans les relations d'affaires," *La semaine juridique édition générale* 42 (2015): 1875; Régis Bismuth, "Au-delà de l'extraterritorialité, une compétence économique," in *Extraterritorialités et droit international*, eds. Alina Miron and Bérangère Taxil (Paris: Pedone, 2020), 113.

17 Cedric Ryngaert, *Jurisdiction in International Law* (Oxford: Oxford University Press, 2008), 8; Alejandro Chehtman, "Jurisdiction," in *The Oxford Handbook of Criminal Law*, eds. Markus D. Dubber and Tatjana Hörnle (Oxford: Oxford University Press, 2014), 402.

According to the dictum of the *Lotus* case, extraterritorial enforcement jurisdiction is prohibited unless explicitly permitted, whereas extraterritorial prescriptive jurisdiction is allowed unless expressly forbidden.[18] For example, in the aforementioned *BNP Paribas* and *Alstom* cases, there was no formal enforcement on French territory, as both companies settled with US authorities. From this perspective, the imposition of fines for breaches of US extraterritorial legislation did not constitute an exercise of genuine imperium:[19] there was no direct exercise of enforcement jurisdiction by the United States. Consequently, the distinction between different forms of state jurisdiction may, in practice, appear obsolete.

With regard to prescriptive jurisdiction, legal scholars generally acknowledge three principles – personality, protection, and universality – that serve as recognised jurisdictional grounds under public international law beyond territoriality. Under the personality principle,[20] states may exercise jurisdiction over their nationals, whether natural or legal persons. The protection principle permits a state to prosecute offences that threaten its fundamental interests, such as national security, territorial integrity, sovereignty, or other vital governmental functions.[21] However, its application is limited to specific criminal offences, including espionage and counterfeiting of state currency or official documents. In France, such jurisdiction is established under Article 113–10 of the Criminal Code.

Finally, the universality principle grants states jurisdiction over certain crimes of exceptional gravity, such as piracy, genocide, and crimes against humanity. Unlike the personality or protection principles, universality does not require any direct connection between the offence and the prosecuting

18 *SS Lotus* (*France v Turkey*), Judgment, [1927] PCIJ Rep Series A, No. 10, paras. 18–19: "Now the first and foremost restriction imposed by international law upon a State is that – failing the existence of a permissive rule to the contrary – it may not exercise its power in any form in the territory of another State. . . . Far from laying down a general prohibition to the effect that States may not extend the application of their laws and the jurisdiction of their courts to persons, property and acts outside their territory, it [international public law] leaves them in this respect a wide measure of discretion which is only limited in certain cases by prohibitive rules; as regards other cases, every State remains free to adopt the principles which it regards as best and most suitable".

19 Régis Bismuth, "Pour une appréhension nuancée de l'extraterritorialité du droit américain – Quelques réflexions autour des procédures et sanctions visant Alstom et BNP Paribas," *Annuaire français de droit international* 61 (2015): 806.

20 Legal doctrine traditionally differentiates between the active personality and the passive personality principles. In accordance with the active personality principle, a State may exercise its jurisdiction over its nationals if they are the perpetrator of an offence (in criminal matters) or the applicant (in civil matters). Conversely, based on the passive personality principle, a State may exercise its jurisdiction over its nationals where they are the victim of the offence (in criminal matters) or the respondent (in civil matters). Nevertheless, the passive personality principle is much more debated – especially in civil matters – as it may result in legal uncertainty.

21 Chehtman, "Jurisdiction," 410.

state. However, it is similarly limited to specific categories of criminal offences. Under French law, universal jurisdiction is provided for in Article 689–11 of the Code of Criminal Procedure. Nonetheless, for prosecution to be possible, the suspect must "habitually reside on the territory of the French Republic". In other words, the existence of a territorial link is required, which substantially limits the scope of the provision.

Although these jurisdictional bases are not as universally accepted as territoriality, they are not considered derogatory under public international law. Extraterritoriality, therefore, may be more accurately characterised as the absence of a genuine connection between the regulating state and the conduct in question.

2.2 *The Lack of a Genuine Connection*

Scholars have contended that, according to the theory of jurisdiction, "states are *not* authorised to exercise their jurisdiction, unless they could rely on such permissive principles as the territoriality, personality, protective, and universality principles".[22] However, this restrictive interpretation, which presupposes the existence of a permissive rule, does not account for all situations encompassed by the concept of extraterritoriality.

Indeed, in an increasingly globalised world, there are few, if any, instances in which no nexus exists whatsoever.[23] From this perspective, extraterritorial jurisdiction appears to refer not to a complete absence of connection with the enacting state but rather to the absence of a 'substantial connection'. Most, if not all, grounds of jurisdiction regarded as extraterritorial are not entirely disconnected from the traditional bases of jurisdiction mentioned previously; rather, they represent broader or more expansive interpretations of these bases. The underlying issue, therefore, lies in the tenuous nature of the nexus invoked, which may be insufficient to properly assert jurisdiction under public international law.

This suggests that limits exist on the exercise of state jurisdiction, even when it falls within the categories established by the theory of jurisdiction. It is widely accepted that the assertion of jurisdiction should be reasonable and should not infringe upon another state's sovereignty.

In France, extraterritoriality is generally understood as the absence of a 'genuine connection' between the enacting state and the regulated situation.

22 Ryngaert, *Jurisdiction*, 21 [original emphasis].

23 Mathias Audit and Yann Kerbrat, "Regards croisés sur l'extraterritorialité droit international public/droit international privé," in *Extraterritorialités et droit international*, eds. Alina Miron and Bérangère Taxil (Paris: Pedone, 2020), 67; Edouard Dubout, Francesco Martucci and Fabrice Picod, "Introduction," in *L'Extraterritorialité en droit de l'Union européenne*, eds. Edouard Dubout, Francesco Martucci and Fabrice Picod (Bruxelles: Bruylant, 2021), 11; Hervé Synvet, "Conclusion – Les actes du colloque de l'association droit & affaires," *Revue droit et affaires* 16 (2019): 175.

Extraterritorial jurisdiction may thus involve extended territoriality[24] or, in the case of nationality, an "extended exercise of personal jurisdiction".[25] This means that the regulating state applies an overly broad interpretation of the principles recognised under public international law – interpretations that are often perceived as unreasonable. However, while scholars have argued that there is a shared understanding within French legal doctrine of the necessity for a 'genuine connection' between the jurisdictional basis invoked and the situation to be governed,[26] no clear international consensus exists regarding the precise nature of such a connection or what constitutes a 'reasonable' exercise of jurisdiction. Consequently, some authors distinguish between jurisdictional titles and the connections that justify their application.[27] According to Thibaut Fleury Graff, public international law clearly defines the former, whereas the latter remains somewhat ambiguous.[28]

3 A Historical Perspective: The Opposition to Foreign Unilateral Extraterritorial Claims

In France, certain extraterritorial assertions of jurisdiction have been perceived as an overreach and have consequently provoked opposition.

3.1 A Jurisdictional Overreach

Extraterritoriality commonly carries negative connotations,[29] as it implies that a state is exercising its jurisdiction in a manner inconsistent with public international law. Beyond the mere fact that the regulated conduct occurs outside the enacting state's territory, it is the "legitimacy of the criterion used"[30] that may be subject to criticism. For instance, in the context of economic sanctions, the Directorate-General for External Policies of the European

24 Georges Affaki, "Regards bancaires sur l'extraterritorialité," *Cahiers de droit de l'entreprise* 4 (2018): 33 [original emphasis].

25 Bernard Audit, "Rapport de synthèse," *Revue de droit bancaire et financier* 6 (2015): 2.

26 Miron and Taxil, "L'*imperium* sans le *dominum*?" 29.

27 *Ibid.*, 17–18; also Fleury Graff, "(Il)licéités et (dé)mesures," 71–72.

28 Fleury Graff, "(Il)licéités et (dé)mesures," 71–72.

29 See Susan Emmenegger, "Extraterritorial Economic Sanctions and Their Foundation in International Law," *Arizona Journal of International and Comparative Law* 3 (2016): 637; Ryngaert, *Jurisdiction*, 8; Lowenfeld, "International Litigation," 43–44; Audit and Kerbrat, "Regards croisés," 64; Cécile Rapoport, "A la recherche des frontières de l'extraterritorialité du droit de l'Union européenne: essai d'identification des manifestations d'un phénomène nébuleux," in *L'Extraterritorialité en droit de l'Union européenne*, eds. Edouard Dubout, Francesco Martucci and Fabrice Picod (Bruxelles: Bruylant, 2021), 17.

30 Mathias Audit, "Les lois extraterritoriales américaines comme facteur d'accélération de la compliance," in *Compliance: l'entreprise, le régulateur et le juge*, eds. Nicolas Borga, Jean-Claude Marin and Jean-Christophe Roda (Paris: Dalloz, 2018), 47 [original emphasis].

Parliament has stated that "US economic sanctions are often characterised as 'extraterritorial' to signify their incompatibility with international law".[31]

However, in the absence of precisely defined international rules, the extraterritorial application of a state's prescriptive jurisdiction cannot be categorically deemed lawful or unlawful.[32] Moreover, the "wide measure of discretion", articulated in the *Lotus* case, does not imply that a state's prescriptive jurisdiction is unlimited. While extraterritoriality is not generally prohibited, certain grounds of jurisdiction may nonetheless contravene customary international rule. As the International Law Commission has explained:

> The assertion of extraterritorial jurisdiction by a state is entitled to recognition by other states to the extent that it is consistent with international law. In the event that one state exercises extraterritorial jurisdiction that another state judges excessive, the other state may oppose such an exercise of jurisdiction in a number of different ways.[33]

Assessing the legality of the extraterritorial application of a national law necessarily requires a case-by-case analysis, depending on the jurisdictional basis invoked. For example, French law contains jurisdictional provisions that have been criticised by foreign states, such as Article 14 of the Civil Code, which allows French plaintiffs to bring actions against foreign defendants who have undertaken obligations outside French territory.[34] In 1964, Frederick Mann strongly criticised this provision, arguing that it exceeded the limits of state jurisdiction, even going so far as to describe it as indefensible.[35] At the EU level, this provision has also been contentious, leading to its exclusion under certain regulations, such as Brussels I bis.[36] As a result, Article 14 of the Civil

31 Directorate-General for External Policies of the Union, "Extraterritorial Sanctions on Trade and Investments and European Responses," PE 653.618 (2020): 51.

32 Fleury Graff, "(Il)licéités et (dé)mesures," 86.

33 International Law Commission, "Annex V – Extraterritorial Jurisdiction," Document A/61/10, Report of the ILC on the work of its fifty-eighth session (1 May–9 June and 3 July–11 August 2006), in *Yearbook of International Law Commission 2006*, Vol. II, A/CN.4/SER.A/2006/Add.l (Part 2), 234, §28.

34 Article 14 of the Civil Code states what follows: "An alien, even if not residing in France, may be cited before French courts for the performance of obligations contracted by him in France with a French person; he may be brought before the courts of France for obligations contracted by him in a foreign country towards French persons". Translation from David Gruning, Alain R. Levasseur, John R. Trahan, et al., *Traduction du code civil français en anglais. Version bilingue* (2015). Accessed 28 May 2024. https://shs.hal.science/halshs-01385107/document.

35 Frederick A. Mann, "The Doctrine of Jurisdiction in International Law," *Collected Courses of the Hague Academy of International Law* 111 (1964): 80.

36 Regulation (EU) No. 1215/2012 of the European Parliament and of the Council of 12 December 2012 on Jurisdiction and the Recognition and Enforcement of Judgments in Civil and Commercial Matters (recast), 2012 O.J. (L351) 1, Article 5§2.

Code now serves only a subsidiary function, applying solely in cases where no international convention or EU regulation is applicable.[37]

Extraterritoriality is also frequently associated with unilateralism, particularly when employed to advance domestic interests.[38] As such, it may be seen as contradicting the principle of equal sovereignty, given that one sovereign state should not ordinarily be subject to the legal system of another.[39] A negative interpretation of the principle of sovereign equality suggests that the sovereignty of one state is necessarily constrained by the sovereignty of others.[40] In this sense, sovereignty is not absolute but rather delimited by the equal sovereignty of all states. Using a well-known adage, one author has explained that "the freedom of the state ends where the freedom of other states begins".[41] Accordingly, a state is free to exercise its jurisdiction only to the extent that it does not infringe upon another state's right to exercise its own jurisdiction.

Additionally, the principle of non-intervention and non-interference in the internal and external affairs of other states may also be relevant.[42] Even if one were to accept that there are no absolute limits on state jurisdiction under the theory of jurisdiction, constraints would still arise from the requirement not to violate another state's sovereignty. From this perspective, the issue is less about the jurisdictional basis itself and more about the implications of extraterritoriality – particularly its unilateral dimension. It is within this context that certain foreign extraterritorial claims have provoked opposition in France.

3.2 *Opposing Certain Unilateral Extraterritorial Claims*

France has expressed its opposition to extraterritorial jurisdiction through various measures, including the so-called 'blocking statutes'. Blocking statutes refer to legislative provisions designed primarily to prevent nationals from complying with certain foreign extraterritorial laws. Two such statutes are currently in force in France: a French law enacted in 1968[43] and a European regulation adopted in 1996.[44] While both seek to counter specific exercises of extraterritorial jurisdiction, they operate differently and apply to distinct areas.

37 Cass. civ. 1, 19 Novembre 1985, No. 84–16.001, *Soc. Cognacs and Brandies.*
38 Fleury Graff, "(Il)licéités et (dé)mesures," 88 *et seq.*
39 Jean Combacau and Serge Sur, *Droit international public* (Paris: LGDJ, 2019), 273.
40 Julian Fernandez, *Relations internationales* (Paris: Dalloz, 2021), para. 112.
41 Emmanuelle Tourme-Jouannet, *Le droit international* (Paris: PUF, 2016), 12.
42 Stern, "Quelques observations," 49.
43 Law No. 68–678, 26 July 1968.
44 Council Regulation (EC) No. 2271/96 of 22 November 1996 Protecting Against the Effects of the Extraterritorial Application of Legislation Adopted by a Third Country, and Actions Based Thereon or Resulting Therefrom, 1996 O.J. (L309) 1.

The French blocking statute was introduced in response to the extensive use of discovery procedures by US authorities, particularly in antitrust law. Discovery procedures allow US authorities to obtain evidence, including documents located within the territory of another state. Initially limited to the maritime transport sector, the French law of 1968 was broadened in 1980[45] to cover all economic activities.[46] It prohibits the transfer of documents abroad, notably outside the framework established by the 1970 Hague Convention on the Taking of Evidence Abroad in Civil or Commercial Matters.[47] Violations of this statute may result in criminal penalties, including imprisonment.[48]

Some authors, however, argue that referring to it as a 'blocking' statute is misleading, as it formally establishes a 'screening' mechanism rather than an outright prohibition.[49] The purpose of the law is not to prevent all document transfers but to introduce a filtering process: before any documents can be transmitted abroad, they must first be submitted to French authorities for review, after which they may be forwarded to the relevant foreign authorities.

In 2022, the law was amended[50] due to concerns over its lack of enforcement in France.[51] Although the changes were relatively limited,[52] they indicate that France remains committed to its approach to extraterritoriality – namely, that extraterritorial jurisdiction should not be exercised outside of international agreements or without the consent of the territorial state. Finally, it is noteworthy that while the French statute was enacted in response to perceived US overreach in extraterritorial jurisdiction, the US Supreme Court, in

45 Law No. 80–538, 16 July 1980.

46 Emmanuel Caradec, "3 questions – Loi de blocage: pourquoi une réforme est-elle nécessaire?" *La semaine juridique entreprise et affaires* 39 (2015): 7.

47 Law No. 80–538, 16 July 1980, Article 1.

48 *Ibid.*, Article 3.

49 Raphaël Gauvain (interviewed by Miren Lartigue), "*Legal privilege*: 'mettre la France au même niveau que ses partenaires européens et américains'," *Gazette du Palais* 24 (2019): 12; Noëlle Lenoir, "Le commissaire, artisan de l'entraide civile ou commerciale internationale et du respect de la loi Preuves improprement dite 'loi de blocage'," *La semaine juridique edition générale* 48 (2020): 2115 *et seq.*

50 Decree No. 2022–207, 18 February 2022; Order of 7 March 2022.

51 The French blocking statute has only been applied once (Cass. crim., 12 Dec. 2007, No. 07–83.228). In this instance, a French lawyer, correspondent of a US lawyer, had provided the latter with information pertaining to the board of directors of a French company in the context of proceedings before a federal court in the State of California. He was convicted and fined 10,000 euros. For more information on this case, see notably Marie Danis, "Sanction de la communication illicite de renseignements à une autorité judiciaire étrangère," *La semaine juridique entreprise et affaires* 35 (2008): 2016; Caradec, "Loi de blocage," 7.

52 Authors notably advocated a significant increase of the criminal penalties in case of infringement, which was not included in the revision of the statute. See Raphaël Gauvain, "Rétablir la souveraineté de la France et de l'Europe et protéger nos entreprises des lois et mesures à portée extraterritoriale," *Report commissioned by the French Prime Minister Edouard Philippe*, 26 June 2019, 69.

the landmark *Aerospatiale* case, characterised it as "an extraordinary exercise of legislative jurisdiction by the Republic of France".[53] This emphasises how extraterritoriality can lead to the clashing of legal systems and hence sovereignties.

The European blocking statute was enacted to counter certain US sanctions. Broadly speaking, these sanctions constitute coercive measures imposed on states or their nationals in response to their relations with targeted states. The EU has taken the position that "by their extra-territorial application such laws, regulations and other legislative instruments violate international law".[54] The blocking regulation prohibits European operators from complying with US extraterritorial sanctions listed in its annex,[55] specifically those imposed under US sanctions programmes against Cuba and Iran. Additionally, it bars recognition and enforcement of judgments and administrative decisions that give effect to such legislation.[56] Finally, it establishes a legal basis for European operators to seek compensation for damages incurred as a result of the application of specified extraterritorial legislation – commonly referred to as the 'claw back clause'.[57]

Interestingly, France initially considered adopting a national law incorporating these provisions but ultimately abandoned the initiative in favour of coordinated action at the European Communities level.[58] At the time of its adoption, a French official described the blocking regulation as a "political success for European diplomacy".[59] Indeed, one could argue that the European Communities enacted this regulation not only as a protective measure but also as a strategic tool to prompt dialogue with the United States and achieve a negotiated resolution – which they ultimately did.[60] This aligns

53 *Société nationale industrielle aérospatiale v US District Court*, 482 US 522 (1987), note 29. In this instance, two French companies (Société nationale industrielle aérospatiale, an entity owned by the French Government, and its wholly-owned subsidiary, Société de construction d'avions de tourisme) invoked the Hague Convention – to which both France and the US are parties – and the French blocking statute to justify their inability to provide the documents requested in discovery proceedings. They argued that complying with such a request would lead them to breach the blocking statute and expose them to criminal penalties in France. The US Supreme Court relied on the interests balancing test and the comity principle to justify its decision not to consider the French blocking statute.

54 Council Regulation (EC) No. 2271/96, Preamble.

55 *Ibid.*, Article 5.

56 *Ibid.*, Article 4.

57 *Ibid.*, Article 6.

58 Geslin, "La position de la France en matière d'extraterritorialité," 465.

59 Denys Wibaux, "Un point de vue étatique – Le Gouvernement français et les lois américaines," in *Sanctions unilatérales, mondialisation du commerce et ordre juridique international. A propos des lois Helms-Burton et d'Amato-Kennedy*, eds. Habib Ghérari and Sandra Szurek (Paris: Montchrestien, 1998), 154.

60 Besides the enactment of the blocking regulation, the European Communities also filed a complaint against the US before the Dispute Settlement Body of the World Trade Organization (WTO). Both parties found an agreement, and the dispute was eventually dropped.

with the French approach, which holds that while extraterritoriality can lead to jurisdictional conflicts, such disputes can be resolved through diplomatic negotiations between the states concerned.

However, the regulation's ineffectiveness in shielding EU operators from US extraterritorial sanctions is now widely acknowledged. Critics argue that, rather than offering protection, it has placed European operators in a legal dilemma, subjecting them to contradictory obligations: on the one hand, they risk prosecution if they fail to comply with US sanctions; on the other, they face penalties under the EU blocking regulation if they do comply.[61] This exemplifies how extraterritoriality can give rise to conflicting mandatory rules.

The EU reactivated the blocking regulation in 2018[62] following the unilateral withdrawal of the United States from the Joint Comprehensive Plan of Action (JCPoA).[63] By reinstating its secondary sanctions – *i.e.*, extraterritorial sanctions – against Iran, the US effectively barred European operators from maintaining commercial activities in the Islamic Republic despite prior commitments under the JCPoA.[64] Recognising the shortcomings of the block-

61 See Marjolaine Abada-Fasquelle and Jan Dunin-Wasowicz, under the supervision of Mathias Audit, Etienne Pataut and George Bermann, "The Impact of Extraterritorial Application of National Legal Norms on International Business Transactions: A Transatlantic View," *Sorbonne Student Law Review* 3 (2020): 94–95; Pierre-Emmanuel Dupont, "Impact des sanctions internationales sur la documentation de financement: enjeux," *La semaine juridique entreprise et affaires* 45 (2018): 29–30; Emmanuel Breen and Régis Bismuth, "L'extraterritorialité des sanctions économiques américaines," *JEM* special issue on "compliance" (2021): 61–62; Tom Ruys and Cedric Ryngaert, "Secondary Sanctions: A Weapon Out of Control? The International Legality of, and European Responses to, US Secondary Sanctions," *British Yearbook of International Law* 89 (2020): 85–86.

62 Commission Delegated Regulation 2018/1100 of 6 June 2018 amending the Annex to Council Regulation (EC) No. 2271/96 protecting against the effects of extraterritorial application of legislation adopted by a third country, and actions based thereon or resulting therefrom, 2018 O.J. (L199I) 11.

63 The JCPoA is an international agreement signed in Vienna between Iran, the five permanent members of the United Nations Security Council, Germany, and the European Union. It was adopted on 14 July 2015 and approved by the United Nations Security Council Resolution 2231 (2015) (document S/RES/2231 (2015), 20 July 2015). It became effective on 16 January 2016, after the International Atomic Energy Agency (IAEA) confirmed Iran had satisfied its obligations under the agreement. Specifically, it called for a gradual removal of international sanctions against Iran, with the aim of eventually removing all such sanctions. While the Trump Administration has terminated the agreement, it remains active in principle among the other signatory countries.

64 On the US unilateral withdrawal from the JCPoA, see notably Dominique Perben and Louis de Gaulle, eds., "Le retrait des États-Unis de l'accord de Vienne sur le programme nucléaire iranien: une situation juridique contrastée," *Report of the ad hoc Commission of the Club des juristes*, July 2018. See also a special feature under the supervision of Régis Bismuth, *Revue internationale des services financiers* 4 (2018): 5–23: Régis Bismuth, "La réactivation des sanctions extraterritoriales américaines contre l'Iran et le secteur financier," 5–6; Ryan Fayhee, Olivier Dorgans, Tyler Grove et al., "The Re-imposition of US Secondary Sanctions on Iran and the European Union Response," 7–10; Marjolaine Abada-Fasquelle, "Le secteur

ing regulation, the EU initiated a reform process; however, this effort now appears to have been placed on hold.[65]

It should be noted that these legislative measures are designed to block only specific extraterritorial claims – namely, those related to discovery procedures and economic sanctions – rather than extraterritoriality as a whole. These measures are intended to counter foreign extraterritorial assertions perceived as mechanisms for advancing domestic interests. Indeed, the reception of foreign extraterritoriality varies depending on the legal domain in question. Extraterritorial jurisdiction carries distinct meanings and implications across different areas of law, including competition law, anti-corruption law, securities regulation, data protection, and economic sanctions. While extraterritorial sanctions are often regarded as infringements upon sovereign equality[66] and unlawful interferences in a state's internal affairs, the same concerns do not necessarily apply to the extraterritorial enforcement of competition or anti-corruption laws. In this regard, the legality of extraterritorial sanctions under public international law remains the most widely contested. At the very least, such sanctions are significantly less accepted than other forms of extraterritorial jurisdiction.[67]

Certain extraterritorial claims are thus perceived as instruments employed by economically and politically powerful states to advance their own interests. Conversely, other extraterritorial assertions do not provoke the same

---

financier européen confronté au rétablissement des sanctions américaines contre l'Iran," 11–14; Ryan Fayhee, Olivier Dorgans, Tyler Grove et al., "Lawful Transactions with Iran Continue But Face Significant Hurdles," 15–17; Daniel Ventura, "Les effets de l'ordonnance de la Cour internationale de justice du 3 octobre 2018 sur les opérateurs économiques et financiers," 18–23.

65 The Commission's adoption of the new text was originally scheduled for the second quarter of 2022. No new date has been announced. As of 5 January 2024, the European Commission website still states that adoption is planned for the second quarter of 2022, but no additional information has been provided. See European Commission, "Unlawful Extra-Territorial Sanctions – A Stronger EU Response (amendment of the Blocking Statute)." Accessed 28 May 2024. https://ec.europa.eu/info/law/better-regulation/have-your-say/initiatives/13129-Reponse-plus-ferme-de-lUE-aux-sanctions-extraterritoriales-illegales-modification-de-la-loi-de-blocage-_fr.

66 This analysis has been circumstantiated by the United Nations General Assembly, which has stated to be "*gravely concerned* over the continued application of unilateral extraterritorial coercive measures whose effects have an impact on the sovereignty of other States and the legitimate interests of their entities and individuals in violation of the norms of international law and the purposes and principles of the United Nations." Resolution 57/5, 16 October 2002, Elimination of unilateral extraterritorial coercive economic measures as a means of political and economic compulsion, document A/RES/57/5 [original emphasis].

67 Jan Wouters and Nicolas Pineau, "L'extraterritorialité du droit de l'Union européenne au regard du droit international public," in *L'Extraterritorialité en droit de l'Union européenne*, eds. Edouard Dubout, Francesco Martucci and Fabrice Picod (Bruxelles: Bruylant, 2021), 68; Charlotte Beaucillon, "Panorama de la pratique contemporaine des sanctions extraterritoriales," in *Extraterritorialités et droit international*, eds. Alina Miron and Bérangère Taxil (Paris: Pedone, 2020), 75–76.

level of opposition. In this regard, the Foreign Account Tax Compliance Act (FATCA) provides a noteworthy example.[68] Enacted by the United States in 2010, FATCA was designed to combat tax evasion by requiring non-US financial institutions to report to the US administration all relevant information concerning individuals presenting indications of 'Americanity'. This led to the emergence of so-called 'accidental Americans' – individuals who, despite having formally acquired US citizenship, retain no substantive ties to the United States.[69] To mitigate the practical difficulties arising from this law, the United States eventually negotiated bilateral agreements with various states, including France,[70] whereby these countries agreed to implement FATCA provisions within their own legal frameworks.

By incorporating FATCA's provisions into its national law, France effectively resolved potential issues related to the statute's extraterritorial reach.[71] This demonstrates, once again, that concerns surrounding foreign extraterritorial claims – particularly their unilateral dimension – can be addressed through interstate negotiations. Furthermore, a report from the French Senate underscores that, unlike the scenario that would have prevailed had FATCA remained a purely unilateral mechanism, the agreement signed between France and the United States includes safeguards that provide French authorities, financial institutions, and their clients with a degree of legal certainty.[72] In this instance, France's approach appears pragmatic: rather than resisting FATCA outright, it sought to secure advantageous terms through negotiation. Ultimately, the French perspective suggests that the fundamental issue with extraterritoriality is not necessarily its cross-border application but rather its unilateral nature. Accordingly, the challenges associated with extraterritorial jurisdiction can, in many cases, be mitigated or resolved through international agreements.

4 A Political Milestone: The *BNP Paribas* and *Alstom* Cases

The *BNP Paribas* and *Alstom* cases have raised significant political concerns in France, but they also mark a turning point in France's attitude towards extraterritoriality.

68 Public Law 111–147.

69 See Régis Bismuth, "L'extraterritorialité du FATCA et le problème des 'Américains accidentels'," *Journal du droit international (Clunet)* 4 (2017): 1197–1261.

70 Agreement Between the Government of the United States of America and the Government of the French Republic to Improve International Tax Compliance and to Implement FATCA, signed in Paris on 14 November 2013.

71 Bismuth, "Une compétence économique," 125.

72 Michèle André, "Le projet de loi autorisant l'approbation de l'accord entre le Gouvernement de la République française et le Gouvernement des États-Unis d'Amérique en vue d'améliorer le respect des obligations fiscales à l'échelle internationale et de mettre en œuvre la loi relative au respect des obligations fiscales concernant les comptes étrangers (dite 'loi FATCA')," *Report No. 751* of the French Senate, filed with the Presidency of the Senate on 17 July 2014, 17.

4.1 *The Promotion of Domestic Interests*

In 2014, Alstom entered into a Deferred Prosecution Agreement (DPA) for violating the Foreign Corrupt Practices Act of 1977 (FCPA)[73] and agreed to pay a $772 million fine. At the time, this was, according to the US Department of Justice (DOJ), the "largest-ever foreign bribery resolution with the Department of Justice".[74] The same year, BNP Paribas also pleaded guilty under a similar procedure for violating several US sanctions programmes against Cuba, Iran, and Sudan.[75] BNP Paribas and several US authorities reached a settlement of $8.974 billion, which remains the largest penalty ever imposed on a European bank by the US administration for sanctions violations.[76] In both cases, the conduct that led the French companies to infringe US law occurred outside of US territory. Between 2016 and 2019, three congressional reports solely dedicated to extraterritoriality, and more specifically, US extraterritorial jurisdiction, were published in France.[77] This underscores the growing political significance of this issue within France, particularly in the aftermath of the *Alstom* and *BNP Paribas* cases. The reports largely condemned US practices, and their primary objective was to propose solutions to counter what was perceived as an abusive exercise of extraterritorial jurisdiction.

These reports specifically criticised the exercise of so-called 'dollar-based jurisdiction'. However, contrary to an oversimplified interpretation, US authorities did not formally rely solely on the use of the dollar to substantiate their jurisdiction. Rather, they based it on the clearing operation – an essential step in virtually all transactions in US dollars[78] – which was conducted by a financial institution located within US territory.[79] As a result, the US generally

73 Public Law 95–213.

74 See DOJ, "Alstom Pleads Guilty and Agrees to Pay $772 Million Criminal Penalty to Resolve Foreign Bribery Charges," *Press Release*, 22 December 2014. Accessed 28 May 2024. https://www.justice.gov/opa/pr/alstom-pleads-guilty-and-agrees-pay-772-million-criminal-penalty-resolve-foreign-bribery.

75 On the different types of settlements in the US, see *infra* note 117.

76 See *United States of America v BNP Paribas, S.A.*, Statement of Facts, 30 June 2014. Accessed 28 May 2024. https://www.justice.gov/sites/default/files/opa/legacy/2014/06/30/statement-of-facts.pdf.

77 Pierre Lellouche and Karine Berger, "L'extraterritorialité de la législation américaine," *Information Report No. 4082* of the French National Assembly, filed with the Presidency of the National Assembly on 5 October 2016; Philippe Bonnecarrère, "L'extraterritorialité des sanctions américaines," *Senate Information Report No. 17*, filed with the Presidency of the Senate on 4 October 2018; Gauvain, Report.

78 Large-value transactions are cleared through the Federal Reserve's Fedwire system or the Clearing House Interbank Payments System (CHIPS). The justification for US jurisdiction is attributed to these clearing operations, which are conducted on US soil despite the main payment transaction taking place between two non-US banks.

79 Juliette Morel-Maroger, "La compliance financière, les enseignements de l'affaire BNP Paribas," in *Compliance: l'entreprise, le régulateur et le juge*, eds. Nicolas Borga, Jean-Claude Marin and Jean-Christophe Roda (Paris: Dalloz, 2018), 72; Emmanuel Breen, "La

denies the extraterritorial nature of this jurisdictional ground, arguing that because clearing operations occur within the United States, the jurisdiction asserted remains territorial rather than extraterritorial. However, France considered this definition of territorial jurisdiction to be excessively broad.

The concept of dollar-based jurisdiction has been described as a 'weaponisation of the dollar'[80] or a 'dollar unilateralism',[81] a policy constructed around the US currency to primarily safeguard US interests, including national security. From this perspective, the United States leverages the dollar's global economic dominance to extend the reach of its sanctions programs to all entities conducting transactions in US dollars. Interestingly, from a political standpoint, France has long been critical of the power inherent in the US currency – a concern dating back to 1964, when Valéry Giscard d'Estaing, then Minister of Finance (later President), referred to the "exorbitant privilege" of the dollar.

However, it is important to note that the controversy surrounding these cases stemmed not only from the jurisdictional basis but also from the size of the financial penalties imposed.[82] For instance, the fine paid by BNP Paribas had macroeconomic consequences, leading to a €4.3 billion reduction in France's current account balance.[83] This economic impact explains some of the political concerns, as extraterritoriality often has underlying economic dimensions. In this regard, despite its immediate effects on private actors, extraterritorial jurisdiction is largely perceived as a matter of state-to-state relations.[84] Indeed, the exercise of extraterritorial jurisdiction entails a projection of power[85] and has been characterised as a means of exerting a form of legal imperialism.[86] Beyond its legal implications, extraterritoriality is primarily a political phenomenon, reflecting a state's political, economic, and cultural influence, as well as its capacity to extend its sphere of authority

---

compétence américaine fondée sur le dollar: réalité juridique ou construction politique?" *Revue européenne du droit* 1 (2020): 55; Régis Bismuth, "Fantasmes et réalités autour de l'extraterritorialité du droit américain," *Revue Lamy droit des affaires* 157 (2020): 36.

80 Ruys and Ryngaert, "Secondary Sanctions," 23; Ellie Geranmayeh et Manuel Lafont Rapnouil, "Meeting the Challenge of Secondary Sanctions," *ECFR Policy Brief No. 289*, June 2019, 2. Another author speaks of 'weaponized dollar'. Joshua P. Zoffer, "The Dollar and the United States' Exorbitant Power to Sanction," *American Journal of International Law Unbound* 113 (2019): 153.

81 Suzanne Katzenstein, "Dollar Unilateralism: The New Frontline of National Security," *Indiana Law Journal* 90 (2015): 293–351.

82 For instance, Mathias Audit argued that if the penalties associated with the infringement of extraterritorial norms were less severe, the debate over the extraterritoriality of their scope would not be as heated. Mathias Audit, "L'arbitrage international confronté à l'extraterritorialité du droit," *Revue de l'arbitrage* 4 (2015): para. 18.

83 See Lellouche and Berger, Report No. 4082, 35.

84 Audit and Kerbrat, "Regards croisés," 64.

85 Miron and Taxil, "L'*imperium* sans le *dominum*?" 54; Fleury Graff, "(Il)licéités et (dé) mesures," 88 *et seq.*

86 Audit and Kerbrat, "Regards croisés," 61.

beyond its own borders. In this sense, this type of jurisdiction is less about extraterritoriality *per se* and more about economic jurisdiction.[87] Scholars have even questioned whether extraterritoriality is anything more than the legal manifestation of economic globalisation.[88] This perspective also helps explain why legal efforts to resist foreign extraterritorial jurisdiction have largely been ineffective.[89]

The same jurisdictional basis can be perceived as detrimental when used to advance specific domestic interests yet beneficial when applied to serve a more widely accepted cause. Thus, there is no universal approach to determining the legitimacy of extraterritorial jurisdiction. In this regard, one scholar has distinguished between 'good' and 'bad' extraterritoriality.[90]

US extraterritorial sanctions are frequently challenged on the grounds that they stem from politically motivated extraterritoriality. By contrast, the *Alstom* case did not provoke the same level of criticism. Unlike unilateral sanctions, which are inherently tied to national foreign policy objectives, anti-corruption efforts enjoy widespread international support and are reinforced by multilateral agreements.[91] For example, Article 4 of the OECD Convention[92] grants signatory states broad jurisdiction, which has been interpreted as authorising the extraterritorial enforcement of national anti-bribery

87 Bismuth, "Une compétence économique," 113–127.

88 Miron and Taxil, "L'*imperium* sans le *dominum*?" 15.

89 As extraterritorial exercises of jurisdiction are based on economic considerations, several authors have suggested to resort to economic solutions, such as using the euro to avoid dollar-based jurisdiction. See Lellouche and Berger, *Report No. 4082*, 122; Bonnecarrère, *Report No. 17*, 25–26; Florence Roussel, "Les stratégies des pouvoirs publics face aux sanctions extraterritoriales américaines," in *Extraterritorialités et droit international*, eds. Alina Miron and Bérangère Taxil (Paris: Pedone, 2020), 109–110; Ruys and Ryngaert, "Secondary Sanctions," 100 *et seq.*

90 Patrick Jacob, "Peut-on être mondial sans être extraterritorial? Réflexions à partir du régime européen de sanctions des violations des droits de l'homme," in *L'Union européenne et l'extraterritorialité: Acteurs, fonctions, réactions*, eds. Alan Hervé et Cécile Rapoport (Rennes: PUR, 2023), 169 *et seq.*

91 OECD Convention on Combating Bribery of Foreign Public Officials in International Business Transactions, signed on 17 December 1997; United Nations Convention against Corruption (the 'Merida Convention'), adopted through a resolution of the United Nations General Assembly (Resolution 58/4, 31 October 2003, United Nations Convention against Corruption, document A/RES/58/4).

92 Article 4 of the OECD Convention states: "1. Each Party shall take such measures as may be necessary to establish its jurisdiction over the bribery of a foreign public official when the offence is committed in whole or in part in its territory. 2. Each Party which has jurisdiction to prosecute its nationals for offences committed abroad shall take such measures as may be necessary to establish its jurisdiction to do so in respect of the bribery of a foreign public official, according to the same principles. 3. When more than one Party has jurisdiction over an alleged offence described in this Convention, the Parties involved shall, at the request of one of them, consult with a view to determining the most appropriate jurisdiction for prosecution. 4. Each Party shall review whether its current basis for jurisdiction is effective in the fight against the bribery of foreign public officials and, if it is not, shall take remedial steps".

laws.[93] From this perspective, the exercise of extraterritorial jurisdiction may be viewed simply as an implementation of the convention's obligations.

Nevertheless, the *Alstom* case has not been exempt from criticism. Notably, it was not the extraterritorial enforcement itself that was primarily condemned by French scholars, but rather the perception that it served interests beyond those ostensibly justifying it.[94] In other words, while the United States had a legitimate jurisdictional basis under the OECD Convention, the prevailing French view was that it exploited this framework to advance its own economic interests. As a result, French authors have equated US extraterritoriality with economic warfare[95] – although the validity of this assertion remains unproven.

Even in areas of broad international consensus, extraterritorial jurisdiction may still provoke controversy. While the subject matter of an international treaty significantly influences how other states perceive the extraterritorial application of national laws, it does not necessarily eliminate all opposition to such assertions of jurisdiction.

In the wake of the *BNP Paribas* and *Alstom* cases, France has gradually moved towards a greater acceptance of extraterritoriality. With regard to dollar-based jurisdiction, some French scholars now contend that if a transaction prohibited under US law passes through US territory via the clearing mechanism, jurisdiction exercised on this basis cannot be deemed inherently unreasonable under the principle of territoriality.[96] This view is further reinforced by the notable absence of opposition from the home states of the affected companies and banks. Scholars have observed, for instance, that when French President François Hollande wrote to his US counterpart, Barack Obama, regarding the *BNP Paribas* case, he did not primarily contest the legitimacy of the extraterritorial jurisdictional claim but rather criticised the disproportionate nature of the financial penalty imposed.[97] Ultimately,

93 Nicola Bonucci, "La définition internationale d'une compétence extraterritoriale en matière de corruption et de détournement de fonds publics," in *Extraterritorialités et droit international*, eds. Alina Miron and Bérangère Taxil (Paris: Pedone, 2020), 188–189; Fleury Graff, "(Il)licéités et (dé)mesures," 97–98; Ruys and Ryngaert, "Secondary Sanctions," 28–29.

94 Patrick Jacob, "L'élargissement des compétences des Etats en matière de lutte contre la corruption," in *Extraterritorialités et droit international*, eds. Alina Miron and Bérangère Taxil (Paris: Pedone, 2020), 178.

95 Ali Laïdi, *Le Droit, nouvelle arme de guerre économique. Comment les États-Unis déstabilisent les entreprises européennes* (Arles: Actes Sud, 2019).

96 Bismuth, "Une compétence économique," 121; Yann Kerbrat, "Unilateral/Extraterritorial Sanctions as a Challenge to the Theory of Jurisdiction," in *Research Handbook on Unilateral and Extraterritorial Sanctions*, ed. Charlotte Beaucillon (Cheltenham: Edward Elgar Publishing, 2021), 176.

97 Mirko Sossai, "Legality of Extraterritorial Sanctions," in *Economic Sanctions in International Law and Practice*, ed. Masahiko Asada (London: Routledge, 2020), 70; Ruys and Ryngaert, "Secondary Sanctions," 23; Régis Bismuth and Pierre-Emmanuel Dupont, "The Doubtful Legality of US Extraterritorial Sanctions Applied to European Financial Institutions," *Revue internationale des services financiers* 1 (2015): 108.

these two high-profile cases have catalysed a shift in France's perception of extraterritoriality – from a mechanism viewed solely as a tool for advancing domestic interests to one increasingly recognised as a legitimate and valuable means of enforcement.

4.2 *A Valuable Means of Enforcement*

Some authors increasingly regard extraterritoriality as a beneficial mechanism capable of addressing issues that would otherwise remain unregulated[98] – particularly in areas such as human rights and environmental protection. It has been argued that extraterritoriality could help combat impunity among multinational corporations and corporate groups, which, exploiting the absence of a 'global' legal personality,[99] use subsidiaries to evade responsibility through a form of normative dumping.[100]

Historically, France has lacked a strong culture of legal enforcement, particularly in relation to white-collar crime. Despite the existence of relevant legislation, enforcement efforts have often been insufficient. This is reflected in the fact that there is no precise French equivalent for the term 'enforcement', underscoring how foreign the concept remains to France's traditional justice system.[101] In contrast, the role of law in the United States is markedly different; Americans tend to approach law and the justice system in a fundamentally distinct manner compared to France.[102] The *Alstom* case highlighted deficiencies in the French legal system's approach to anti-corruption enforcement, ultimately prompting the enactment of the Sapin II law.[103] The first French statute explicitly aimed at preventing corruption was

98 Meriem Ouassini Sahli, *La Responsabilité de la société mère du fait de ses filiales*, PhD thesis (University Paris-Dauphine, 2014), 278 *et seq.*; Lisa Aerts, "L'extraterritorialité dans le contexte de la globalisation: l'exception deviendrait-elle la règle? L'exemple des Principes directeurs de l'OCDE à l'intention des entreprises multinationales et des accords-cadres internationaux," in *L'Extraterritorialité*, eds. Mathias Audit and Etienne Pataut (Paris: Pedone, 2020), 123 *et seq.*; Marie Nioche, "Responsabilité sociétale des entreprises et compétence civile extraterritoriale," in *Extraterritorialités et droit international*, eds. Alina Miron and Bérangère Taxil (Paris: Pedone, 2020), 233 *et seq.*; Nicolas Maziau, "L'extraterritorialité du droit entre souveraineté et mondialisation des droits," *La semaine juridique entreprise et affaires* 28 (2015): 1343 *et seq.*

99 Multinational companies or corporate groups have no legal personality. Each entity has its own legal personality, hence nationality, depending on where it was constituted and on national laws.

100 Aerts, "L'extraterritorialité dans le contexte de la globalisation," 124.

101 Antoine Garapon, "Une justice 'très' négociée," in *Deals de justice. Le Marché de l'obéissance mondialisée*, eds. Antoine Garapon and Pierre Servan-Schreiber (Paris: PUF, 2013), 126.

102 Elisabeth Zoller, *Le Droit des Etats-Unis* (Paris: PUF, 2014), 1–2. Accessed 28 May 2024. http://www.u-paris2.fr/1396864022103/0/fiche___article/&RH=CDPC-ETUDES.

103 See *infra* note 114.

enacted in 1993,[104] yet it undeniably suffered from a lack of enforcement. A 2012 OECD report criticised France's low number of corruption-related convictions,[105] noting that "only one company ha[d] been convicted, at first instance, for foreign bribery since the entry into force of the [OECD] Convention in France".[106] The United States has justified its interventions in this area by pointing to insufficient enforcement efforts in other jurisdictions.

A similar lack of enforcement is evident with French and European economic sanctions – referred to as 'restrictive measures' – which are imposed on states, entities, or individuals in response to alleged breaches of international law. Although such sanctions are adopted at the EU level, their enforcement remains the responsibility of individual Member States. In this regard, one scholar noted that between 2011 and 2021, the French administrative authority responsible for enforcing asset freezes – the ACPR *(Autorité de contrôle prudentiel et de résolution)* – imposed penalties only twenty-seven times.[107] By comparison, in 2019 alone, the US Office of Foreign Assets Control (OFAC) handled twenty-six cases.[108] Regarding criminal penalties, there have been no convictions for breaches of French or European economic sanctions, and few prosecutions have been pursued on these grounds.[109]

To address these shortcomings, some scholars have proposed the creation of an autonomous extraterritorial system in France and the EU.[110] The rationale for such a system would be twofold. First, it would enhance enforcement efforts, thereby reducing the perceived need for other states to exercise extraterritorial jurisdiction. The underlying premise is that if the EU and its Member States effectively prosecute violations, there would be less justification for foreign states to do so. Second, this approach could establish

104 Law No. 93–122, 29 January 1993.

105 OECD Working Group on Bribery, "Phase 3 Report on Implementing the OECD Anti-Bribery Convention in France," October 2012. Accessed 28 May 2024. https://web-archive.oecd.org/2012-10-23/214311-oecdseriouslyconcernedatlackofforeignbriberyconvictionsinfrancebutrecognisesrecenteffortstoensureindependenceofprosecutors.htm.

106 *Ibid.*, 21.

107 Fadma Bouharchich, "Le renforcement progressif des exigences en matière de gel des avoirs dans un contexte marqué par une augmentation du risque terroriste," *Revue internationale de la compliance et de l'éthique des affaires* 5 (2022): 23.

108 David Mortlock, Britt Mosman, Nikki Cronin et al., "US Sanctions Enforcement by OFAC and the DOJ," in *The Guide to Sanctions*, eds. Rachel Barnes KC, Paul Feldberg, Anna Bradshaw et al. (London: Law Business Research, 2023), 135.

109 In this respect, it should be noted that the Ministry of the Economy has taken legal action against the French company Lafarge for violating, among other things, the arms embargo against Syria. This case is unprecedented as charges for complicity in a crime against humanity have been brought for the first time against a company. Stéphane de Navacelle, Julie Zorrilla, and Juliette Musso, "Practical Applications of International Sanctions and Export Controls in France," in *The Guide to Sanctions*, eds. Rachel Barnes KC, Paul Feldberg, Anna Bradshaw et al. (London: Law Business Research, 2023), 281.

110 Marie-Hélène Bérard, Farid Fatah, Pascal Lamy et al., "L'Europe face aux sanctions américaines, quelle souveraineté ?" *Institut Jacques Delors Policy Paper No. 232* (2018): 4.

a system of reciprocity:[111] if third countries impose extraterritorial penalties on European operators, the EU would respond in kind by imposing similar measures on foreign entities. It is worth noting that, in this second scenario, extraterritoriality would function as a retaliatory measure, essentially countering extraterritoriality with extraterritoriality.

The *BNP Paribas* and *Alstom* cases illustrated that extraterritoriality can enhance legal effectiveness by ensuring that legislation is widely enforced. France has come to recognise that extending the spatial scope of its legislation strengthens its enforcement mechanisms.

France's perspective on extraterritoriality is thus evolving. There is growing recognition that extraterritorial jurisdiction can serve as a crucial safeguard in combatting certain illicit practices – provided its use remains reasonable. Consequently, extraterritoriality can be perceived both as an excessive assertion of jurisdiction and as a valuable tool for ensuring compliance with legal norms.

5 Beyond the Jurisdictional Aspects: The New Approach to Extraterritoriality

France is now using extraterritoriality to extend the scope of the application of certain laws. This may result in resolving the previous debates surrounding extraterritorial exercises of jurisdiction.

5.1 A Soft Extraterritorial Application of Legislations

It is now widely accepted that the central issue with extraterritorial jurisdiction lies in the objective that a given norm seeks to achieve. The same jurisdictional connection may be regarded as legitimate when its purpose is to protect fundamental or broadly shared values, yet illegitimate when used to advance domestic political and economic interests. From this perspective, it is not so much the jurisdictional basis itself that is problematic; rather, the content and purpose of the norm.[112] As Yann Kerbrat explains, "[I]t is perfectly acceptable for the scope of the legislative jurisdiction to vary according to the purpose of the regulation".[113] The same jurisdictional ground may, therefore, be admissible in certain legal domains and inadmissible in others. As a result, the debate has shifted from the legitimacy of the jurisdictional basis to the legitimacy of the norm itself. The concerns surrounding extraterritorial jurisdiction are now less about the legal basis invoked and more about the policy objectives it serves. Thus,

111 Noëlle Lenoir, "L'extraterritorialité, nouvelle donne de la mondialisation," *Echanges internationaux* 112 (2018): 19.
112 See Bismuth, "Une compétence économique," 118; Audit and Kerbrat, "Regards croisés," 68; Kerbrat, "A Challenge to the Theory of Jurisdiction," 175.
113 Kerbrat, "A Challenge to the Theory of Jurisdiction," 175.

any discussion of extraterritoriality cannot overlook the substantive content of the norm in question.

France has embraced this new approach to extraterritorial jurisdiction. For example, in order to strengthen its anti-corruption policy, France enacted the Sapin II law,[114] which includes enhanced extraterritorial provisions. Under this law, its provisions apply to any person conducting all or part of their economic activity within French territory.[115] After years of criticising US extraterritorial claims, France ultimately chose to implement a similar system rather than oppose it.[116] It has even adopted the US model of settlement agreements,[117] creating the Judicial Public Interest Convention *(convention judiciaire d'intérêt public)*.[118] In this sense, the unilateral extraterritoriality practised by the United States in the field of anti-corruption can be seen as a catalyst for the emergence of a global legal framework.[119] In this context, foreign extraterritorial jurisdiction has acted as a political driver for the development of French extraterritorial norms.

However, the Sapin II law has not yet been enforced in a particularly extraterritorial manner, given that all companies prosecuted under this law thus far have been French. The former Director of Legal Affairs at the OECD described the legislation as "real extraterritoriality" but "essentially virtual extraterritoriality",[120] suggesting that while the provisions are extraterritorial in

114 Law No. 2016–1691, 9 December 2016.

115 Art. 435–11–2 of the Criminal Code.

116 Jacob, "L'élargissement des compétences," 180.

117 In the US, there are three types of settlements in criminal matters: Non-Prosecution Agreements (NPAs), Deferred Prosecution Agreements (DPAs), and guilty pleas. Such settlement agreements necessitate that the offending companies, in addition to paying a fine, enter into undertakings and agree to comply with certain obligations (in particular the implementation of a compliance programme under the supervision of a monitor) for a specified period of time. In return, the prosecuting authorities will reduce the penalties to a greater or lesser extent, taking into account the circumstances of the case, which may be mitigating or, on the contrary, aggravating. In contrast to guilty pleas, which result in a conviction, NPAs and DPAs (which form what are known as "pretrial diversions") permit the avoidance of a formal indictment and ultimate criminal conviction. The primary distinction between NPAs and DPAs is that in the former, there is no prosecution, whereas in the latter, prosecution is immediately suspended.

118 Art. 41-1-2 of the Code of Criminal Procedure. Introduced into French law by the 'Sapin II' law, the CJIP is similar to the US DPA. However, it is only accessible to legal entities and only in relation to specific offences, including bribery, trading in influence, tax fraud, and tax laundering, as well as related offences. The agreement stipulates that the individual or entity subject to prosecution must (i) pay a fine of up to 30% of its annual turnover, (ii) implement a compliance programme lasting a maximum of three years, and (iii) compensate the victim if the latter is known. For more details, see notably Guillaume de Rancourt, and Caroline Hailey, "La transaction pénale à la française: un premier bilan," *Echanges internationaux* 115 (2020): 29; Alexia Artigas and Pauline Barbier, "Les conventions judiciaires d'intérêt public," *Cahiers de droit de l'entreprise* 1 (2020): 27–31.

119 Bismuth, "Fantasmes et réalités," 38.

120 Bonucci, "La définition internationale," 190.

scope, they have not been applied as such. This distinction can be framed as the difference between possessing an extraterritorial reach (the potential to apply beyond national borders) and actively enforcing the law extraterritorially.

Significant differences, therefore, remain between the French and US approaches. The United States typically employs a double-trigger mechanism in its use of extraterritoriality – combining a broad scope of application with an expansive interpretation of jurisdiction by US authorities.[121]

Moreover, European States, including France, "have adopted a broad vision of the personal connection in areas other than sanctions".[122] In other words, they have engaged in extended exercises of personal jurisdiction. Following the Rana Plaza disaster,[123] France enacted a law on duty of vigilance (*loi relative au devoir de vigilance des sociétés mères et des entreprises donneuses d'ordre*),[124] which is regarded as having extraterritorial components.[125] Under this law, a company's legal obligations extend not only to the activities of the parent company but also to those of its subsidiaries and entities it directly or indirectly controls.[126] In this way, France applies the same control theory[127] that has faced criticism in relation to US sanctions programmes targeting Iran and Cuba.

The issue, therefore, is not the decision to establish jurisdiction based on corporate control in order to expand the geographical scope of the law but rather the nature of the law itself and the implications of such an extension. More critically, it has been suggested that within the EU, "what is controversial is, above all, the extraterritoriality of others".[128]

121 Bismuth, "Pour une appréhension nuancée de l'extraterritorialité du droit américain," 789.

122 Kerbrat, "A Challenge to the Theory of Jurisdiction," 175.

123 On 24 April 2013, the Rana Plaza – a building housing garment factories for international clothing brands, located in Dhaka, Bangladesh – collapsed, claiming the lives of over 1,000 people. This tragedy, caused notably by negligence, rekindled the debate on corporate liability of multinational companies in terms of Human Rights and the environment.

124 Law No. 2017–399, 27 March 2017.

125 See, for instance Aude-Solveig Epstein, "Devoir de vigilance – La portée extraterritoriale du devoir de vigilance des sociétés mères et entreprises donneuses d'ordre," *Cahiers de droit de l'entreprise* 4 (2018): 47–51; Jean-Baptiste Racine, "Le déploiement du devoir de vigilance dans un contexte transnational," *La semaine juridique entreprise et affaires* 31–35 (2023): paras. 13–19.

126 Art. L225-102-4 of the Code of Commerce.

127 According to the control theory, the nationality of a company is determined by the persons who own or control it. In international law, the principle is the independence of legal persons. This means that each entity within a group of companies or a multinational enterprise has its own legal personality, hence its own nationality. The question at hand is whether the criterion of control can be used to attribute nationality and whether a State can claim jurisdiction on this basis.

128 Régis Bismuth, "The European Union Experience of Extraterritoriality: When a (Willing) Victim Has Become a (Soft) Perpetrator," in *Research Handbook on Extraterritoriality in International Law*, eds. Austen Parrish and Cedric Ryngaert (Cheltenham: Edward Elgar Publishing, 2021), 131.

The French law on the duty of vigilance was one of the first of its kind globally and inspired the EU to adopt a directive at the European level.[129] France thus played a leading role in promoting the use of extraterritoriality in this domain. However, similar to the Sapin II law, the duty of vigilance law has not been applied extraterritorially, despite its extraterritorial reach.

In a recent case, the Judicial Tribunal of Paris acknowledged the law's potential extraterritorial effects. The judges stated that legislation addressing global supply chains inevitably has extraterritorial consequences but that such laws remain compatible with a particular interpretation of a state's responsibility to ensure that third parties respect human rights.[130] Given that international law does not prohibit a state from enacting legislation with extraterritorial scope for companies operating within its jurisdiction, the law was deemed legitimate.[131] While the alleged misconduct occurred outside French borders, all companies brought before French courts under this law have been French. For instance, in the aforementioned case, TotalEnergies was sued over projects in Uganda and Tanzania. Another ongoing case involves BNP Paribas, which faces allegations of financing beef production linked to deforestation in the Amazon.[132] In both cases, the facts relate to activities outside French territory, yet jurisdiction is established under the personality principle, given that the companies in question are French.

5.2 *Towards the End of the Debates Surrounding Extraterritoriality?*

Extraterritorial unilateral claims are fundamentally incompatible with multilateralism and contradict the values upheld by the Union and its member states, including France. The EU is a strong advocate of free trade and, more broadly, of multilateralism, making the core of the issue easily understandable. Furthermore, the use of power to influence the policies of other states contradicts the principles upon which the EU was founded, especially given its historical context. Multilateralism is a defining feature of the EU's identity, as enshrined in its founding treaties. For instance, Article 21 of the Treaty on the European Union stipulates that the Union "shall promote multilateral solutions" and support "an international system based on stronger multilateral cooperation". This would explain why the EU's legal tradition is to "multilateralise its law rather than unilaterally project it".[133]

129 Proposal for a Directive of the European Parliament and of the Council on Corporate Sustainability Due Diligence and amending Directive (EU) No. 2019/1937, Brussels, 23/02/2022, COM(2022) 71 final.
130 The Judicial Tribunal previously mentioned the "Guiding Principles on Business and Human Rights and those of the OECD." Judicial Tribunal of Paris, 28 February 2023, No. 22/53942.
131 Judicial Tribunal of Paris, 28 Feb. 2023, No. 22/53942.
132 Racine, "Le déploiement du devoir de vigilance," para. 16.
133 Jacob, "Peut-on être mondial sans être extraterritorial?" 162–163.

This multilateralisation has been described as the "*de jure* Brussels effect".[134] It is notably illustrated by the adoption of legislation by third countries that closely mirrors EU law. For instance, the requirement to obtain an adequacy decision for the transfer of personal data from the EU[135] has led nearly 120 third countries to adopt legislation in this area, often directly inspired by the General Data Protection Regulation (GDPR).[136] More generally, the adoption of national laws incorporating EU legal standards is frequently formalised through international treaties. In this respect, the EU's practice of extraterritoriality aligns perfectly with the French approach: extraterritorial jurisdiction should be negotiated between states.

The current legal landscape is likely to continue evolving. Despite its longstanding policy[137] and initial opposition, the EU has recently introduced its first extraterritorial economic sanctions (known as 'restrictive measures' in EU law) through an anti-circumvention mechanism,[138] which is directly applicable in France. Although not yet implemented, these sanctions are designed – mutatis mutandis – to function in the same manner as the US secondary sanctions that the EU sought to oppose with its blocking regulation. Secondary sanctions can take different forms, but they primarily function as "economic restrictions designed to deter third-country actors from supporting a primary target of unilateral sanctions".[139] Similarly, the anti-circumvention instrument enables the EU to impose sanctions on entities and individuals

134 Anu Bradford, *The Brussels Effect. How the European Union Rules the World* (Oxford: Oxford University Press, 2020).

135 Regulation (EU) No. 2016/679 of the European Parliament and of the Council of 27 April 2016 on the protection of natural persons with regard to the processing of personal data and on the free movement of such data, and repealing Directive 95/46/EC (General Data Protection Regulation), O.J. 2016 (L119) 1, art. 45.

136 Adeline Jeauneau, "Bibliographie – The Brussels Effect. How the European Union Rules the World, par Anu Bradford: New York, Oxford University Press, 2020, 404 pages," *Revue critique de droit internatinal privé* 2 (2021): 526.

137 Pursuant to the EU Guidelines on restrictive measures, "EU restrictive measures should only apply in situations where links exist with the EU," which means that "the EU will refrain from adopting legislative instruments having extra-territorial application in breach of international law". Council of the EU, *Guidelines on Implementation and Evaluation of Restrictive Measures (Sanctions) in the Framework of the EU Common Foreign and Security Policy*, 4 May 2018, doc. 15598/17, paras. 51–52.

138 Council of the EU, "Russia's War of Aggression Against Ukraine: EU Adopts 11th Package of Economic and Individual Sanctions," *Press Release*, 23 June 2023. Accessed 28 May 2024. https://www.consilium.europa.eu/en/press/press-releases/2023/06/23/russia-s-war-of-aggression-against-ukraine-eu-adopts-11th-package-of-economic-and-individual-sanctions/; Council Decision (CFSP) No. 2023/1217 of 23 June 2023 amending Decision No. 2014/512/CFSP concerning restrictive measures in view of Russia's actions destabilising the situation in Ukraine, O.J. (LI 159) 451; Council Regulation (EU) No. 2023/1214 of 23 June 2023 amending Regulation (EU) No. 833/2014 concerning restrictive measures in view of Russia's actions destabilising the situation in Ukraine, 2023 O.J. (LI 159) 1.

139 Jeffrey A. Meyer, "Second Thoughts on Secondary Sanctions," *University of Pennsylvania Journal of International Law* 30 (2009): 906.

from third countries that fail to comply with European restrictive measures against Russia, thereby strengthening Russia's ability to wage war.[140] By implementing this mechanism, the EU seeks to align third-country policies with its own sanctions regime.[141] In this regard, the new European restrictive measures closely resemble US extraterritorial sanctions, both in terms of their operational framework and underlying rationale.

For decades, Western strategies on economic sanctions have diverged significantly: the EU has favoured multilateralisation, whereas the US has relied on extraterritoriality.[142] The EU's adoption of a form of secondary sanctions challenges this established approach and may signal a significant policy shift. However, this initiative may not be as drastic as it initially appears. Notably, the Council of the EU itself has emphasised that these sanctions should be regarded as "exceptional, last-resort measures".[143] Furthermore, it appears that the EU has structured the mechanism to comply with the conditions set out in the international legal framework on countermeasures. This could suggest that the EU is maintaining its traditional position that such measures are generally inconsistent with public international law but seeks to justify their legality under countermeasures.

Nevertheless, this development raises an issue of consistency,[144] and does little to clarify the EU's stance on the legitimate exercise of extraterritorial jurisdiction. Maintaining the European blocking regulation in this context may become increasingly difficult to justify. If the EU continues on this trajectory, it is highly likely that the planned reform of the blocking regulation – intended to address its lack of effectiveness – will be abandoned. Following this shift in perspective, the longstanding debates surrounding extraterritorial jurisdiction may ultimately fade away.

140 Council Regulation (EU) No. 2023/1214, para. 13: "To that effect, Decision (CSFP) 2023/1217 has introduced the possibility to take exceptional, last-resort measures restricting the sale, supply, transfer or export of sensitive dual-use goods and technology, or goods and technology that might contribute to the enhancement of Russia's military, technological or industrial capacities or to the development of Russia's defence and security sector, in a way that strengthens its ability to wage war, and whose export to Russia is prohibited under Regulation (EU) No. 833/2014 to third countries whose jurisdiction is demonstrated to be at a continuing and particularly high risk of being used for circumvention".

141 Régis Bismuth, "Les nouvelles frontières des sanctions européennes et les zones grises du droit international," *Revue européenne du droit* 5 (2023): 11.

142 Charlotte Beaucillon, "Aspects globaux – Les sanctions internationales au soutien de l'intégrité territoriale de l'Ukraine: leur effectivité," *Revue française de droit administratif* 4 (2022): 596 *et seq*.

143 Council of the EU, "Russia's War of Aggression Against Ukraine," *Press Release*.

144 Bismuth, "Les nouvelles frontières des sanctions européennes," 12.

6 Conclusion

France has historically opposed foreign unilateral extraterritorial claims, viewing them as a potential jurisdictional overreach. However, when negotiated solutions are reached, concerns surrounding extraterritoriality tend to dissipate. This suggests that the fundamental issue with extraterritoriality may not lie in the extraterritorial exercise of jurisdiction itself. The enactment of France's and the EU's own extraterritorial laws has led to the emergence of a new interpretative framework.

There is a clear distinction between what is perceived as illegitimate extraterritoriality and what is regarded as legitimate, depending on a combination of factors. In this regard, the challenges appear to stem less from the jurisdictional basis itself and more from the underlying purpose and content of the law, its effects, and the rationale for its extraterritorial application – that is, the political motivations driving its enforcement. The line between a legitimate and an illegitimate exercise of jurisdiction remains fluid and is likely to continue evolving.

References

Abada-Fasquelle, Marjolaine. "Le secteur financier européen confronté au rétablissement des sanctions américaines contre l'Iran." *Revue internationale des services financiers* 4 (2018): 11–14.

Abada-Fasquelle, Marjolaine, and Jan Dunin-Wasowicz, under the supervision of Mathias Audit, Etienne Pataut and George Bermann. "The Impact of Extraterritorial Application of National Legal Norms on International Business Transactions: A Transatlantic View." *Sorbonne Student Law Review* 3 (2020): 63–101.

Affaki, Georges. "Regards bancaires sur l'extraterritorialité." *Cahiers de droit de l'entreprise* 4 (2018): 30–34.

André, Michèle. "Le projet de loi autorisant l'approbation de l'accord entre le Gouvernement de la République française et le Gouvernement des États-Unis d'Amérique en vue d'améliorer le respect des obligations fiscales à l'échelle internationale et de mettre en œuvre la loi relative au respect des obligations fiscales concernant les comptes étrangers (dite 'loi FATCA')." *Report No. 751* of the French Senate, filed with the Presidency of the Senate on 17 July 2014.

Artigas, Alexia, and Pauline Barbier. "Les conventions judiciaires d'intérêt public." *Cahiers de droit de l'entreprise* 1 (2020): 27–31.

Audit, Bernard. "Rapport de synthèse." *Revue de droit bancaire et financier* 6 (2015): 1–4.

Audit, Mathias. "L'arbitrage International confronté à l'extraterritorialité du droit." *Revue de l'arbitrage* 4 (2015): 1001–1035.

Audit, Mathias. "L'extraterritorialité est partout!" *Echanges internationaux* 112 (2018): 20.

Audit, Mathias, and Etienne Pataut, eds. *L'Extraterritorialité*. Paris: Pedone, 2020.

Avout, Louis d'. "L'extraterritorialité du droit dans les relations d'affaires." *La semaine juridique edition générale* 42 (2015): 1875–1884.

Avout, Louis d'. "L'extraterritorialité vue de Sirius (où il est question d'extraterritorialité 'régulatoire', entre autres difficultés actuelles d'un droit mondial des affaires peu coordonné)." *Revue de droit bancaire et financier* 6 (2015): 1–5.

Barnes KC, Rachel, Paul Feldberg, Anna Bradshaw, et al. *The Guide to Sanctions*. London: Law Business Research, 2023.

Beaucillon, Charlotte. "Aspects globaux – Les sanctions internationales au soutien de l'intégrité territoriale de l'Ukraine: leur effectivité." *Revue française de droit administratif* 4 (2022): 596–605.

Bérard, Marie Hélène, Farid Fatah, Pascal Lamy, et al. "L'Europe face aux Sanctions américaines, quelle souveraineté?" *Institut Jacques Delors Policy Paper No. 232* (2018).

Bismuth, Régis. "Pour une appréhension nuancée de l'extraterritorialité du droit américain – Quelques réflexions autour des procédures et sanctions visant Alstom et BNP Paribas." *Annuaire français de droit international* 61 (2015): 785–807.

Bismuth, Régis. "L'extraterritorialité du FATCA et le problème des 'Américains accidentels'." *Journal du droit international (Clunet)* 144(4) (2017): 1197–1261.

Bismuth, Régis. "La réactivation des sanctions extraterritoriales américaines contre l'Iran et le secteur financier." *Revue internationale des services financiers* 4 (2018): 5–6.

Bismuth, Régis. "Regards croisés sur l'extraterritorialité du droit." *Cahiers de droit de l'entreprise* 4 (2018): 19–20.

Bismuth, Régis. "Fantasmes et réalités autour de l'extraterritorialité du droit américain." *Revue Lamy droit des affaires* 157 (2020): 35–39.

Bismuth, Régis. "The European Union Experience of Extraterritoriality: When a (Willing) Victim Has become a (Soft) Perpetrator." In *Research Handbook on Extraterritoriality in International Law*, edited by Austen Parrish and Cedric Ryngaert, 118–132. Cheltenham: Edward Elgar Publishing, 2021.

Bismuth, Régis. "Les nouvelles frontières des sanctions européennes et les zones grises du droit international." *Revue européenne du droit* 5 (2023): 8–14.

Bismuth, Régis, and Pierre-Emmanuel Dupont. "The Doubtful Legality of US Extraterritorial Sanctions Applied to European Financial Institutions." *Revue internationale des services financiers* 1 (2015): 104–108.

Bonnecarrère, Philippe. "L'extraterritorialité des sanctions américaines." *Senate Information Report No. 17*, filed with the Presidency of the Senate on 4 October 2018.

Borga, Nicolas, Jean-Claude Marin, and Jean-Christophe Roda, eds. *Compliance: l'entreprise, le régulateur et le juge*. Paris: Dalloz, 2018.

Bouharchich, Fadma. "Le renforcement progressif des exigences en matière de gel des avoirs dans un contexte marqué par une augmentation du risque terroriste." *Revue internationale de la compliance et de l'éthique des affaires* 5 (2022): 20–23.

Bradford, Anu. *The Brussels Effect. How the European Union Rules the World*. Oxford: Oxford University Press, 2020.

Breen, Emmanuel. "La compétence américaine fondée sur le dollar: réalité juridique ou construction politique?" *Revue européenne du droit* 1 (2020): 55–61.

Breen, Emmanuel, and Régis Bismuth. "L'extraterritorialité des sanctions économiques américaines." *JEM* special issue on "compliance" (2021): 58–62.

Buxbaum, Hannah L., and Thibault Fleury-Graff, eds. *Extraterritoriality/L'Extraterritorialité*. Leiden/Boston: Brill/Nijhoff, 2022.

Caradec, Emmanuel. "3 questions – Loi de blocage: pourquoi une réforme est-elle nécessaire?" *La semaine juridique entreprise et affaires* 39 (2015): 7–8.

Chehtman, Alejandro. "Jurisdiction". In *The Oxford Handbook of Criminal Law*, edited by Markus D. Dubber and Tatjana Hörnle, 399–421. Oxford: Oxford University Press, 2014.

Combacau, Jean, and Serge Sur. *Droit international public*. Paris: LGDJ, 2019.

Council of the EU. "Russia's War of Aggression against Ukraine: EU Adopts 11th Package of Economic and Individual Sanctions." *Press Release*, Brussels, 23 June 2023. Accessed 28 May 2024. https://www.consilium.europa.eu/en/press/press-releases/2023/06/23/russia-s-war-of-aggression-against-ukraine-eu-adopts-11th-package-of-economic-and-individual-sanctions/.

Danis, Marie. "Sanction de la communication illicite de renseignements à une autorité judiciaire étrangère." *La semaine juridique entreprise et affaires* 35 (2008): 2016.

Directorate General for External Policies of the Union. *Extraterritorial Sanctions on Trade and Investments and European Responses*. PE 653.618 (2020).

Dubout, Edouard, Francesco Martucci, and Fabrice Picod, eds. *L'Extraterritorialité en droit de l'Union européenne*. Bruxelles: Bruylant, 2021.

Dupont, Pierre-Emmanuel. "Impact des sanctions internationales sur la documentation de financement: enjeux." *La semaine juridique entreprise et affaires* 45 (2018): 24–30.

Emmeneger, Susan. "Extraterritorial Economic Sanctions and their Foundation in International Law." *Arizona Journal of International and Comparative Law* 3 (2016): 631–60.

Epstein, Aude-Solveig. "Devoir de vigilance – La portée extraterritoriale du devoir de vigilance des sociétés mères et entreprises donneuses d'ordre." *Cahiers de droit de l'entreprise* 4 (2018): 47–51.

European Commission. "Unlawful Extra-Territorial Sanctions – a Stronger EU Response (Amendment of the Blocking Statute)." Accessed 28 May 2024. https://ec.europa.eu/info/law/better-regulation/have-your-say/initiatives/13129-Reponse-plus-ferme-de-lUE-aux-sanctions-extraterritoriales-illegales-modification-de-la-loi-de-blocage-_fr.

Fayhee, Ryan, Olivier Dorgans, Tyler Grove, et al. "Lawful Transactions with Iran Continue but Face Significant Hurdles." *Revue internationale des services financiers* 4 (2018): 15–17.

Fayhee, Ryan, Olivier Dorgans, Tyler Grove, et al. "The Re-Imposition of US Secondary Sanctions on Iran and the European Union Response." *Revue internationale des services financiers* 4 (2018): 7–10.

Fernandez, Julian. *Relations internationales*. Paris: Dalloz, 2021.

Francq, Stéphanie. *L'Applicabilité du droit communautaire dérivé au regard des méthodes de droit international privé*. Bruxelles/Paris: Bruylant/LGDJ, 2005.

Garapon, Antoine. "Une justice 'très' négociée." In *Deals de justice. Le Marché de l'obéissance mondialisée*, edited by Antoine Garapon et Pierre Servan-Schreiber, 117–44. Paris: PUF, 2013.

Gauvain, Raphaël (interviewed by Miren Lartigue). "*Legal privilege*: 'mettre la France au même niveau que ses partenaires européens et américains'." *Gazette du Palais* 24 (2019): 12.

Gauvain, Raphaël. "Rétablir la souveraineté de la France et de l'Europe et protéger nos entreprises des lois et mesures à portée extraterritoriale." *Report commissioned by the French Prime Minister Edouard Philippe*, 26 June 2019.

Geranmayeh, Ellie, and Manuel Lafont Rapnouil. "Meeting the Challenge of Secondary Sanctions." *ECFR Policy Brief No. 289*, June 2019.

Geslin, Albane. "La position de la France en matière d'extraterritorialité du droit économique national." *Revue juridique de l'Ouest* 4 (1997): 411–67.

Ghérari, Habib, and Sandra Szurek, eds. *Sanctions unilatérales, mondialisation du commerce et ordre juridique international. A propos des lois Helms-Burton et d'Amato-Kennedy*. Paris: Montchrestien, 1998.

Gruning, David, Alain R. Levasseur, John R. Trahan, et al. *Traduction du code civil français en anglais. Version bilingue*. 2015. Accessed 28 May 2024. https://shs.hal.science/halshs-01385107/document.

Hervé, Alan, and Cécile Rapoport, eds. *L'Union européenne et l'extraterritorialité: Acteurs, fonctions, réactions*. Rennes: PUR, 2023.

International Law Commission. "Annex V – Extraterritorial Jurisdiction." Document A/61/10, Report of the ILC on the work of its fifty-eighth session (1 May-9 June and 3 July-11 August 2006). In *Yearbook of International Law Commission 2006*, Vol. II, A/CN.4/SER.A/2006/Add.l (Part 2), 229–39.

Jeauneau, Adeline. "Bibliographie – The Brussels Effect. How the European Union Rules the World, par Anu Bradford: New York, Oxford University Press, 2020, 404 pages." *Revue critique de droit internatinal privé* 2 (2021): 525–528.
Katzenstein, Suzanne. "Dollar Unilateralism: The New Frontline of National Security." *Indiana Law Journal* 90 (2015): 293–351.
Kerbrat, Yann. "Unilateral/Extraterritorial Sanctions as a Challenge to the Theory of Jurisdiction." In *Research Handbook on Unilateral and Extraterritorial Sanctions*, edited by Charlotte Beaucillon, 164–184. Cheltenham: Edward Elgar Publishing, 2021.
Labouz, Marie-France, ed. *L'Application extraterritoriale du droit économique*. Paris: Montchrestien, 1987.
Laïdi, Ali. *Le Droit, nouvelle arme de guerre économique. Comment les États-Unis déstabilisent les entreprises européennes*. Arles: Actes Sud, 2019.
Lellouche, Pierre, and Karine Berger. "L'extraterritorialité de la législation américaine." *Information Report No. 4082* of the French National Assembly, filed with the Presidency of the National Assembly on, 5 October 2016.
Lenoir, Noëlle. "L'extraterritorialité, nouvelle donne de la mondialisation." *Echanges internationaux* 112 (2018): 19.
Lenoir, Noëlle. "Le commissaire, artisan de l'entraide civile ou commerciale internationale et du respect de la loi Preuves improprement dite 'loi de blocage'." *La semaine juridique édition générale* 48 (2020): 2115–2121.
Lowenfeld, Andreas F. "International Litigation and the Quest for Reasonableness." *Collected Courses of the Hague Academy of International Law* 245 (1994): 9–319.
Mann, Frederick A. "The Doctrine of Jurisdiction in International Law." *Collected Courses of the Hague Academy of International Law* 111 (1964): 9–162.
Maziau, Nicolas. "L'extraterritorialité du droit entre souveraineté et mondialisation des droits." *La semaine juridique entreprise et affaires* 28 (2015): 23–32.
Meyer, Jeffrey A. "Second Thoughts on Secondary Sanctions." *University of Pennsylvania Journal of International Law* 30 (2009): 905–968.
Miron, Alina, and Bérangère Taxil, eds. *Extraterritorialités et droit international*. Paris: Pedone, 2020.
OECD Working Group on Bribery. "Phase 3 Report on Implementing the OECD Anti-Bribery Convention in France." October 2012. Accessed 28 May 2024. https://web-archive.oecd.org/2012-10-23/214311-oecdseriouslyconcernedatlackofforeignbriberyconvictionsinfrancebutrecognisesrecenteffortstoensureindependenceofprosecutors.htm.
Ouassini Sahli, Meriem. *La Responsabilité de la société mère du fait de ses filiales*. PhD Thesis, University Paris-Dauphine, 2014.
Perben, Dominique, and Louis de Gaulle, eds. "Le retrait des États-Unis de l'accord de Vienne sur le programme nucléaire iranien: une situation juridique contrastée." *Report of the* ad hoc *Commission of the Club des Juristes*, July 2018.
Racine, Jean-Baptiste. "Le déploiement du devoir de vigilance dans un contexte transnational." *La semaine juridique entreprise et affaires* 31–35 (2023): 29–34.
Rancourt, Guillaume de, and Caroline Hailey. "La transaction pénale à la française: un premier bilan." *Echanges internationaux* 115 (2020): 29.
Ruys, Tom, and Cedric Ryngaert. "Secondary Sanctions: A Weapon out of Control? The International Legality of, and European Responses to, US Secondary Sanctions." *British Yearbook of International Law* 89 (2020): 1–116.
Ryngaert, Cedric. *Jurisdiction in International Law*. Oxford: Oxford University Press, 2008.
Salmon, Jean, ed. *Dictionnaire de droit international public*. Bruxelles: Bruylant, 2001.
Samie, Najeeb. "The Doctrine of 'Effects' and the Extraterritorial Application of Antitrust Laws." *University of Miami Inter-American Law Review* 14 (1982): 23–59.

Sossai, Mirko. "Legality of Extraterritorial Sanctions". In *Economic Sanctions in International Law and Practice*, edited by Masahiko Asada, 62–79. London: Routledge, 2020.

Stern, Brigitte. "Quelques observations sur les règles internationales relatives à l'application extraterritoriale du droit." *Annuaire français de droit international* 32 (1986): 7–52.

Stern, Brigitte. "Une tentative d'élucidation du concept d'application extraterritoriale." *Revue québécoise de droit international* 3 (1986): 49–78.

Stern, Brigitte. "L'extra-territorialité 'revisitée': où il est question des affaires *Alvarez-Machain*, *Pâte de Bois* et de quelques autres . . ." *Annuaire français de droit international* 38 (1992): 239–313.

Synvet, Hervé. "Conclusion – Les actes du colloque de l'association droit & affaires." *Revue droit et affaires* 16 (2019): 171–77.

Tourme-Jouannet, Emmanuelle. *Le droit international.* Paris: PUF, 2016.

Ventura, Daniel. "Les effets de l'ordonnance de la Cour internationale de justice du 3 octobre 2018 sur les opérateurs économiques et financiers." *Revue internationale des services financiers* 4 (2018): 18–23.

Zoffer, Joshua P. "The Dollar and the United States' Exorbitant Power to Sanction." *American Journal of International Law Unbound* 113 (2019): 152–156.

Zoller, Elisabeth. *Le Droit des Etats-Unis.* Paris: PUF, 2014. Accessed 28 May 2024. http://www.u-paris2.fr/1396864022103/0/fiche___article/&RH=CDPC-ETUDES.

3 India's Approach to Extraterritorial Jurisdiction

Evolving Practice Amidst Evolving Global Aspirations

Aniruddha Rajput and Sudipta Purkayastha

1 Introduction

Jurisdiction is the authority of a state to regulate affairs within its borders. Extraterritorial jurisdiction is the instance where a state exercises that power beyond its borders. Such an exercise of power, in most cases, inevitably involves a conflict since it results in an encroachment on the jurisdiction of another state. In the extraterritorial exercise of jurisdiction on matters regulated by public international law, there is greater scope for conflict and confrontation since there is often no agreement as to such exercises, hence no semblance of reciprocity.

Equality of states and comity have constituted the bedrock of India's approach towards the exercise of jurisdiction. These principles are well-respected and usually automatically enforced by all the branches of the state: the judiciary, legislature, and the executive. However, these are not absolute rules without allowable departures. Based on the urgency of the time and the subject matter, exceptions have been identified and developed to allow the exercise of jurisdiction beyond borders, as will be detailed in this chapter.

As India's global influence has increased, so has its ability to shape international law.[1] This shift has enhanced India's confidence and, consequently, its willingness to exercise extraterritorial jurisdiction, as well as to expand the areas in which it would exercise it. This contribution aims to assess this transformation based on the evolving Indian practice.

It does so by first providing a description of the general framework setting out the Indian legal system's approach towards extraterritorial jurisdiction. It then examines the exercise of extraterritorial jurisdiction based on domestic law by analysing India's practice in specific areas such as criminal

1 See, generally, Aniruddha Rajput, "BRICS as 'Rising Powers' and the Future of International Law," in *International Rule of Law: Rise or Decline?*, eds. Heike Krieger et al. (Oxford: Oxford University Press, 2019); Aniruddha Rajput, "India's Contribution to the Making of International Law at the United Nations," in *Advancing Reformed Multilateralism in the Changing World*, eds. Nutan Kapoor Mahwar and Deepika Sawaswat (Noida: Macmillan Education, 2022).

DOI: 10.4324/9781003402978-4

law, competition and securities law, taxation, and anti-suit injunctions. Lastly, the chapter analyses the complex and controversial exercise of extraterritorial jurisdiction under public international law based on the enforcement of jurisdiction beyond 12 nm in the sea, pre-emptive self-defence, and security concerns aboard.

2 India's General Framework on Extraterritorial Jurisdiction

The starting point for assessing the state of the law on extraterritorial jurisdiction for a constitutional democracy is the constitution itself. The Constitution of India expressly protects extraterritorial jurisdiction exercised through legislation. Article 245(2) of the Constitution specifically states: "No law made by Parliament shall be deemed to be invalid on the ground that it would have extraterritorial operation". The power of the executive branch of the Government of India is concomitant with that of Parliament, and it can exercise further powers beyond those provided under Indian domestic laws by virtue of international agreements or treaties signed by the government.[2] If not a binding commitment, the government is bound to promote international peace and security through a set of guidelines.[3] National security and public order seem to be an undercurrent, if not on the surface, since they can be an exception to fundamental rights, which are the most basic and inalienable rights of people.[4] Since the government is responsible for ensuring compliance, extraterritorial actions may often be defended as steps taken towards the protection of fundamental rights, especially the right to life.[5] As noted by the Supreme Court, "the first duty of a State is to survive. To do so it has got to deal with enemies both overt and covert whether they be inside the country or outside".[6] Thus, silence may be considered as a permission and may need to be resolved through extraterritorial actions.

Nevertheless, the issue of extraterritorial jurisdiction has arisen only in specific instances in the past; a general prescription has not yet been raised or tested either in the courts or in the legislative or executive actions. For reasonable and justifiable grounds, there may be obstacles to the exercise of extraterritorial jurisdiction, even where permitted by the constitutional architecture.

Judicial practice is of particular relevance in this regard since it is a vocal expression of the approach based on reason, unlike an executive action, which often may not be in the public domain and may not contain detailed explications. Additionally, the decisions of the Supreme Court constitute a source of binding law due to the common law rule of precedent and are thus

2 Constitution of India, Article 73.
3 *Ibid.*, Article 51.
4 *Ibid.*, Article 19(2).
5 *Ibid.*, Article 21.
6 *G. B. Singh v Govt. of India*, 1973 AIR 2667.

an integral part of the legal architecture;[7] of course, they also constitute additional material forming state practice.[8]

As a starting point, the understanding is that the power to exercise jurisdiction is limited to a certain territorial area (often even more restrictively to certain matters and causes within such area) and that such power is detailed and granted under the Indian Constitution or other legislation.[9] The principle of comity has long been engrained in the Indian legal system. The Supreme Court has confirmed that there is a presumption that the Indian Parliament

> does not assert or assume jurisdiction which goes beyond the limits established by the common consent of nations, and statutes are to be interpreted, provided that their language permits, so as not to be inconsistent with the comity of nations or with the established principles of International Law.[10]

Similarly, the Indian judiciary has also long recognised international comity as precluding jurisdiction over foreign persons or property[11] and considered that India may not extend its jurisdiction beyond its own territorial limits to subject either persons or property to its judicial decisions, except by virtue of a permissive rule derived from international custom or from a convention.[12]

A legislation with extraterritorial application must have both some "impact on or nexus with India" and be "beneficial to India" in order to find protection under the Constitution.[13] The requirements of sufficient nexus and benefit to India demonstrate respect for state sovereignty, foster respect for international and treaty obligations, and facilitate India's maintenance of just and honourable relations with other sovereign states.[14] International peace and security have been recognised as vital for the interests of India.[15]

The application of these principles shows that Indian courts have long performed a careful balancing act between refraining from exercising extraterritorial jurisdiction out of respect for international comity and protecting the domestic interests of India.

7 Constitution of India, Article 141.

8 International Law Commission, "Draft Conclusions on the Identification of Customary International Law," *Yearbook of the International Law Commission* II(2) 2018, Conclusions 5, 6, 10, 13 (special significance).

9 *Dayabhai Poonambhai Patel v The Regional Transport Authority*, 1951 CriLJ 1305.

10 *V/O Tractor Export, Moscow v M/S. Tarapore & Company & Anr*, 1971 AIR 1; *Gramophone Company of India Ltd v Birendra Bahadur Pandey & Ors*, 1984 AIR 667.

11 *Kessowji Damodar Jairam v Khimji Jairam*, 1888 ILR 12 Bom 507.

12 *K.T.M.S. Abdul Cader and Ors. v The Union of India*, 1977 CriLJ 1708.

13 *GVK Industries v Income Tax Officer*, 2011 4 SCC 36. See also *Anil Kumar v Roop Kumar Sharma & Anr*, 2019 ACJ 381, where the Punjab and Haryana High Court has assessed the Article 245 criteria through a 'causes and effects' lens.

14 *GVK Industries v Income Tax Officer*, 2011 4 SCC 36.

15 *Ibid.*

3 Extraterritorial Jurisdiction Based on Domestic Law

A general trend across various subject matters and fields of respect for foreign state sovereignty forms the foundational protective layer in deciding the exercise of extraterritorial jurisdiction; however, also embedded in this layer are various structures facilitating exceptional exercises of such jurisdiction.

Most critical is the application of the 'effects doctrine', which can be a basis for the exercise of jurisdiction where: (1) an extraterritorial offence causes some harmful effect to the state exercising jurisdiction, even when the offence does not actually meet the criteria of territorial jurisdiction; or (2) the issue represents an interest sufficiently vital to the internal or external security of the state in question to justify invoking the protective principle.[16]

3.1 *Criminal Laws*

The exercise of extraterritorial jurisdiction is well-established in the realm of criminal law. The statutory basis for such an exercise is Section 4 of the Indian Penal Code (IPC), read with Section 188 of the Code of Criminal Procedure (CrPC). These provisions allow the extraterritorial application of the IPC to any citizen of India in any place outside and beyond India; any person on any ship or aircraft registered in India, wherever it may be; or any person in any place outside India committing an offence targeting a computer resource located in India. Indian courts have exercised jurisdiction over Indian citizens outside Indian territorial bounds as if the crime had been committed by them at any place within India, including investigating, inquiring into, passing detention and extradition orders, and even holding trials against such individuals.[17] The CrPC allows Indian courts to exercise jurisdiction for offences committed outside India. The text of Section 188 reads as follows:

> When an offence is committed outside India
>
> a. by a citizen of India, whether on the high seas or elsewhere; or
> b. by a person, not being such citizen, on any ship or aircraft registered in India, he may be dealt with in respect of such offence as if it had been committed at any place within India at which he may be found: Provided that, notwithstanding anything in any of the preceding sections of this Chapter, no such offence shall be inquired into or tried in India except with the previous sanction of the Central Government.

16 James Crawford, *Brownlie's Principles of Public International Law* (Oxford: Oxford University Press, 2019), 447.

17 See *Muhammed Sajeed K. v The State Of Kerala*, 1995 CriLJ 3313; *Gour Gopal Mukherjee v Chief Secretary to the Govt. of West Bengal and Others*, AIR 1953 Cal 81; *Remla v S.P.*, 1993 (1) KLT 412; *Mohammed Shameer Ali v State of Kerala and Another*, 2019 (3) KLT 1034.

For exercising criminal jurisdiction over non-citizens, the Indian courts have considered that the "protective" or "security" principle can be used.[18] In *Gautam Sarma v Sanyukta Baruah*, the Gauhati High Court was confronted with questions of whether a crime under the IPC, which had been committed either wholly or partly outside India, could be investigated by Indian police and tried before Indian courts. The court noted that Sections 3 and 4 of the IPC embodied the protective or security principle:

> The protective principle is based on the nature of interest of the country injured rather than of the country, where the offence has taken place. Irrespective of the fact as to whether an offence has been committed abroad by a citizen or an alien, when the offence affects, or is likely to affect, the security or integrity of another State, the State, which is affected, must be able to take punitive action against the offender regardless of the 'principle of territoriality', which is commonly known as *locus delecti*. This principle of extraterritorial jurisdiction can be traced to the right of self-defence in the United Nations Charter.[19]

India has generally sought to maintain its respect for comity and reciprocity with other states when trying foreign citizens outside the territory of India by entering into extradition treaties with third states, usually providing for extraterritorial jurisdiction over non-citizens for crimes committed by them outside India.[20] The Extradition Act of 1962, as amended by the Extradition Amendment Act of 1993, allows extradition of persons who have committed a "composite offence", *i.e.*, where

> an act or conduct of a person occurred, wholly or in part, in a foreign state or in India, but its effects or intended effects, taken as a whole, would constitute an extradition offence in India or in a foreign state, as the case may be.[21]

Furthermore, while political offences are generally excluded from the scope of an extraditable offence,[22] the Extradition Act enumerates a list of offences which cannot be justified as political, such as terrorism, murder, crimes against internationally protected persons, including diplomatic agents, and the taking of hostages.[23]

18 See *T. Mohammed v State and Others*, 1994 (1) KLT 464.
19 *Gautam Sarma and Anr. v Sanyukta Baruah*, 2009 (3) GLT 1.
20 *Daya Singh Lahoria v Union of India*, 2001 4 SCC 516.
21 The Extradition Act 1962, S. 2(a); The Extradition (Amendment) Act 1993, S. 4(a).
22 See The Extradition Act 1962, S. 29.
23 *Ibid.*, The Schedule. The other crimes excluded are other serious crimes such as hurt or grievous hurt by a dangerous weapon or means, wrongful restraint, and wrongful confinement.

In *Marie-Emmanuelle Verhoeven v Union of India*, the Supreme Court of India considered a case where a French national was sought to be extradited from India by the Republic of Chile for the assassination of a Chilean Senator while she was in India on a holiday.[24] The Supreme Court found that an extradition treaty existed between Chile and India since 1897 but noted that even in the absence of an extradition treaty, extradition could be requested on the basis of the principle of reciprocity. It further considered the principles of reciprocity and comity, as well as the obligation of a state to extradite or prosecute, to find that an extradition could be ordered if all conditions were fulfilled. The case was then forwarded to a lower magistrate's court for a decision on extradition. However, the Government of India eventually withdrew its extradition inquiry into the accused on "health and humanitarian grounds" and allowed the accused to return to France.[25]

The case showed that while India is willing to respect the principle of reciprocity and comity to extradite fugitives in support of the international community's fight against impunity, the assessment of whether such an exercise of extraterritorial jurisdiction is warranted would be decided on a case-by-case basis, taking into account factors such as political reasons of extradition or human rights issues.

3.2 *Competition and Securities Laws*

The effects doctrine has been used to exercise extraterritorial jurisdiction in competition and securities laws.

The Supreme Court in 2015 declared that the erstwhile competent regulatory authority – the Monopolies and Restrictive Trade Practices Commission (MRTP) Commission – had jurisdiction over transactions executed outside India where "the effect of restrictive trade practices came to be felt in India because of a part of the trade practice being implemented in India",[26] further declaring:

> This 'effects doctrine' will clothe the MRTP Commission with jurisdiction to pass an appropriate order even though a transaction, for example, which results in exporting goods to India at predatory price, which was in effect a restrictive trade practice, had been carried out outside

24 *Marie-Emmanuelle Verhoeven v Union of India*, AIR 2016 SC (Criminal) 776.

25 "Wanted in Chile for Allegedly Killing Senator, French Woman Will Return Home," *Indian Express*, 28 July 2017. Accessed 20 September 2023. https://indianexpress.com/article/cities/delhi/wanted-in-chile-for-allegedly-killing-senator-french-woman-will-return-home-4770658/; Ministerio de Relaciones Exteriores de Chile, "The Government of Chile Regrets the Refusal of the Indian Government to Extradite Marie Emmanuelle Verhoeven," 26 July 2017. Accessed 20 September 2023. https://minrel.gob.cl/the-government-of-chile-regrets-the-refusal-of-the-indian-government-to/minrel_old/2017-07-26/161629.html.

26 *Haridas Exports v All India Float Glass Manufacturers Association*, 2002 6 SCC 600.

> the territory of India if the effect of that had resulted in a restrictive trade practice in India. If power is not given to the MRTP Commission to have jurisdiction with regard to that part of trade practice in India which is restrictive in nature then it will mean that persons outside India can continue to indulge in such practices whose adverse effect is felt in India with impugnity [sic]. A competition law like the MRTP Act is a mechanism to counter cross border economic terrorism. Therefore, even though such an agreement may enter into outside the territorial jurisdiction of the Commission but if it results in a restrictive trade practice in India then the Commission will have jurisdiction . . . to pass appropriate orders in respect of such restrictive trade practice.

The decision dealt with provisions of the MRTP Act, which has now been repealed and replaced by the Competition Act; however, these principles in the decision have been confirmed under the Competition Act regime.

Section 32 of the Competition Act of India expressly provides that even where any agreement, party, abuse of dominant position, or a combination thereof exists entirely outside of India, competent authorities in India (the Competition Commission of India) will have the power to inquire into, initiate investigation into, and pass any relevant orders on such an agreement, abuse of dominant position, or combination if any of these factors has, or is likely to have, an "appreciable adverse effect on competition" in the relevant market in India.[27] The types of orders that can be passed in such scenarios are regulated by other provisions of the Competition Act, such as Sections 31 and 42, which allow the Commission to pass orders seeking modification of a combination having an adverse effect on competition in India, imposing penalties, or even declaring any acquisition, merger, or amalgamation as not having taken place.[28]

With regards to securities law, again, the Supreme Court used the 'impact on or nexus with India' test and held that the Securities and Exchange Board of India (SEBI) Act 1992 contains sufficient provisions for proceeding against 'any person' who engages in a fraudulent activity that affects the interests of Indian investors. Further, it was held that the SEBI has the statutory mandate to proceed against persons who are not corporally present within Indian territory if the acts committed affect the legitimate interests of India.[29]

3.3 Taxation Laws

The general rule in taxation in India has been that the Indian Taxation Act 1961 is restricted to the territory of India, and no extraterritorial application of the

27 Competition Act 2002, S. 32, read with Ss. 19, 20, 26, 29 and 30.
28 *Ibid.*, Ss. 31, 42.
29 *SEBI v Pan Asia Advisors*, AIR 2015 SC 2782.

Act is allowed.[30] In the case of *McDermott International Inc. v Union of India and Ors.*, the Bombay High Court determined, for instance, that taxation could not be charged for income accrued in the high seas or waters beyond the territorial sovereignty of India (12 nautical miles from the Indian shore).[31]

However, certain provisions of the Indian Taxation Act do allow the exercise of extraterritorial jurisdiction. As held by the Calcutta High Court in the case of *Commr. Of Income Tax, New Delhi v M/s Eli Lilly & Co. (India) P. Ltd.*,

> the general concept as to the scope of income-tax is that, given a sufficient territorial connection or nexus between the person sought to be charged and the country seeking to tax him, income-tax may extend to that person in respect of his foreign income. The connection can be based on the residence of the person or business connection within the territory of the taxing state; and the situation within the state of the money or property from which the taxable income is derived.[32]

This is a common exercise of extraterritorial jurisdiction by most states, yet again the Indian legal framework confirms that exceptions to the general rule of non-exercise of extraterritorial jurisdiction exist where the interests of India are affected.

In relation to recovery of customs duties, Section 1 of the Customs Act 1962 was amended by way of Section 57 of the Finance Act 2018,[33] as a result of which the application of the Act also extends to "any offence or contravention thereunder committed outside India by any person".[34] This implies that any person who commits one of the offences under the Customs Act outside India, such as making a false declaration or submitting false documentation, may be subjected to criminal proceedings in India.[35]

3.4 *Anti-Suit Injunctions*

An important avenue through which Indian courts exercise extraterritorial jurisdiction in civil dispute resolution cases is the issuance of anti-suit injunctions. These are injunctions in the form of orders issued by Indian courts prohibiting foreign courts or arbitration proceedings taking place outside India.

Although exercised rarely, the Supreme Court has confirmed that they can exercise this jurisdiction. The Supreme Court has affirmed the principle

30 See Income Tax Act 1961, S. 1(2); *Satellite Television Asian Region Ltd. v Deputy Commissioner of Income Tax*, 2006 99 ITD 91 Mum.

31 *McDermott International Inc. v Union of India and Ors.*, 1988 173 ITR 155 Bom.

32 *Commr. of Income Tax, New Delhi vs. M/s Eli Lilly & Co. (India) P. Ltd.*, 312 ITR 225 (SC).

33 The Finance Act, 2018, S. 57.

34 *Ibid.*

35 See Customs Act, 1962, Chapter XVI, Ss. 132, 137(1).

that an anti-suit injunction, having an impact on a foreign jurisdiction, can be granted so long as the parties are subject to *in personam* jurisdiction (*i.e.*, they are present in Indian territory). However, even such power will be exercised sparingly, keeping in mind the principle of comity and respect for another court's jurisdiction. Indian courts are courts of both law and equity, like in England, and hence can issue an equitable remedy in the form of injunctions. An anti-suit injunction may only be granted as an exceptional remedy, particularly based on principles arising from conflict of laws, where it is in the interest of justice since it would compromise the principle of comity.[36]

The Supreme Court cautioned that anti-suit injunctions should not be granted routinely and should only be granted sparingly.[37] The Delhi High Court, relying on the principles laid down by the Supreme Court, held that if a "party endeavours to invoke the jurisdiction of a foreign court to a cause of action already being prosecuted in the national forum, it would amount to vexatious or oppressive litigation, which can be injuncted by the Indian courts".[38] The Gujarat High Court categorically stated two essential conditions that would govern the grant or refusal of anti-suit injunctions in respect of proceedings pending in a foreign court:

> First, that the defendant, who is sought to be injuncted, is amenable to the jurisdiction of the Indian Court issuing the injunction, and secondly, that refusal of the prayer for injunction would result in defeating the ends of justice and perpetuating injustice. The relief, fundamentally, has to be equitable in nature.[39]

Moreover, in one case, the Bombay High Court refused to grant an anti-suit injunction on the grounds that the party would not suffer grave injustice if the court refused to grant such an injunction.[40] Again, Indian courts have made it clear that respect for the comity of courts and conflict of laws must be carefully balanced against national security, national integrity, and threats to sovereignty.[41]

4 Extraterritorial Jurisdiction Based on Public International Law

The application of principles in international law for the exercise of extraterritorial jurisdiction in the Indian context is discussed in this section.

36 *Modi Entertainment Network and Another v W.S.G. Cricket PTE Ltd*, 2003 4 SCC 341.
37 *Dinesh Singh Thakur v Sonal Thakur*, 2018 17 SCC 12.
38 *Essel Sports (P) Ltd. v Board of Control for Cricket in India*, 2011 SCC OnLine Del 1629.
39 *Mashreq Bank PSC v Indian Overseas Bank*, 2021 SCC OnLine Guj 2678.
40 *Milind Ashok Kalamkar v Sheetal Milind Kalamkar Nee*, 2021 SCC OnLine Bom 2370.
41 *Swami Ramdev & Anr. v Facebook, Inc. & Ors*, 2019 263 DLT 689.

4.1 *Pre-Emptive Self-Defence*

Although the exercise of authorisation under public international law would not be considered an illegal extraterritorial exercise of jurisdiction, pre-emptive self-defence exercised by India on foreign soil can be treated as a *de facto* extraterritorial jurisdiction. In the past, India's practice was muted when it came to matters of pre-emptive use of force against territories in foreign countries. India has, however, consistently raised serious concerns about terrorism, which it has faced for decades, much of which is sponsored and originates abroad, specifically in Pakistan. Between 2000 and 2015 alone, terrorist attacks by organisations based in Pakistan caused 7,835 deaths in India,[42] adversely affected India's growth rate and exports,[43] and disrupted its securities market and foreign investment.[44]

For the first time, in September 2016, the Indian Army conducted 'surgical strikes' at launch pads of terrorist organisations (mostly Pakistan-based terrorist organisation *Jaish-e-Mohammad* (JeM)) based along the Line of Control in Pakistani territory, where they had positioned themselves "with an aim to carry out infiltration and terrorist strikes in Jammu & Kashmir and in various other metros' in India".[45] In a joint briefing by the Indian Ministry of External Affairs and the Ministry of Defence, the Director General of Military Operations of India declared that while India respected the maintenance of peace and tranquillity in the region, it would "certainly not allow the terrorists to operate across the Line of Control with impunity and attack the citizens of our country".[46] Hence, pre-emptive self-defence was used for the protection of its internal peace and security, prioritising internal stability over the maintenance of regional harmony.

42 Institute of Economics and Peace, *Global Terrorism Index: Measuring and Understanding the Impact of Terrorism* (2016). Accessed 10 October 2023. http://economicsandpeace.org/wp-content/uploads/2016/11/Global-Terrorism-Index-2016.2.pdf.

43 "Terrorist Attacks Will Further Weaken a Slowing Indian Economy," *Knowledge@Wharton*, 11 December 2008. Accessed 10 October 2023. https://knowledge.wharton.upenn.edu/article/terrorist-attacks-will-further-weaken-a-slowing-indian-economy/; Subhayu Bandyopadhyay, "Trade and Terror: The Impact of Terrorism on Developing Countries," *Federal Reserve Bank of St. Louis*, 11 December 2017. Accessed 10 October 2023. www.stlouisfed.org/publications/regional-economist/fourth-quarter-2017/impact-terrorism-developing-countries.

44 Imlak Shaikh, "The Impact of Terrorism on Indian Securities Market," *Economic Research-Ekonomska Istraživanja* 32 (2019): 1.

45 Ministry of External Affairs, "Transcript of Joint Briefing by MEA and MoD (29 September 2016)," last modified 29 September 2016. Accessed 10 October 2023. https://www.mea.govin/media-briefings.htm?dtl/27446/Transcript_of_Joi. See also "Surgical Strike Day: Here's How the 2016 Operation Was Carried Out," *Hindustan Times*, 29 September 2021. Accessed 10 October 2023 https://www.hindustantimes.com/india-news/surgical-strike-day-here-s-how-the-2016-operation-was-carried-out-101632882272993.html.

46 Transcript of Joint Briefing by MEA and MoD, 29 September 2016.

The second set of surgical strikes occurred on 14 February 2019. Another statement was released, this time by the Foreign Secretary of India, declaring that India had conducted the strikes on Balakot, Pakistan, in response to a suicide terror attack conducted by JeM, which killed 40 members of the Indian Central Reserve Police Force (CRPF). India claimed that JeM was "attempting another suicide attack" and *fidayeen jihadis* were being trained for this purpose. These fidayeen were largely eliminated in the attack, while India attempted to avoid civilian casualties.[47] India clearly characterised the surgical strike as "non-military pre-emptive action . . . specifically targeted at the JeM camp".[48] It is noted that since the surgical strike was conducted in Indian territories under Pakistani occupation, the legal regime governing those actions was of belligerent occupation rather than the use of force as pre-emptive self-defence on 26 February 2019.[49]

India has relied on the principle of pre-emptive self-defence to exercise its jurisdiction over non-state actors in its neighbouring states. Most importantly, statements backing the effort were made to set out clearly India's position on its willingness to exercise extraterritorial jurisdiction over non-state actors. India relied on the customary international law on self-defence, which allows a state to use pre-emptive self-defence against non-state actors on a third state's territory to neutralise an imminent threat to the state, provided the 'Caroline Test' of 1837 is met.[50]

The 'Caroline Test' was developed in relation to the case of attacks by British forces against a merchant vessel 'Caroline', which was used illegally by Canadian rebels and their supporters in the United States to carry out attacks in Canada against the British (who had colonised Canada). The vessel was sunk, and both Canadian and US nationals were killed. According to the 'Caroline Test', a state may use force if there is "a necessity of self-defence, instant, overwhelming, leaving no choice of means and no moment

47 Ministry of Foreign Affairs, "Statement by Foreign Secretary on 26 February 2019 on the Strike on JeM Training Camp at Balakot," last modified 26 February 2019. Accessed 30 October 2023. https://www.mea.govin/press-releases.htm?dtl/31091/Statement_by_Foreign_Secretary_on_26_February_2019_on_the_Strike_on_JeM_training_camp_at_Balakot.

48 Statement by Foreign Secretary on 26 February 2019 on the Strike on JeM training camp at Balakot.

49 Yoram Dinstein, *War, Aggression and Self-Defence* (Cambridge: Cambridge University Press, 2001), 202; Anthony Aust, *Handbook of International Law* (Cambridge: Cambridge University Press, 2010), 211.

50 Elizabeth Wilmshurst, "The Chatham House Principles of International Law on the Use of Force in Self-Defence," *International and Comparative Law Quarterly* 55 (2006): 963, 964–965; Nico Schrijver and Larissa van den Herik, "Leiden Policy Recommendations on Counter-Terrorism and International Law," *Netherlands International Law Review* 57(3) (2010): 42–43.

for deliberation".[51] The 'Caroline Test' was applied by the International Military Tribunals at Nuremberg[52] and Tokyo[53] and has been confirmed by state practice,[54] thereby solidifying its position under customary international law.

The requisites for the exercise of pre-emptive self-defence, referred to in the 'Caroline incident' are that the attack is "imminent", and the response is "necessary and proportionate".[55]

The assessment of whether an armed attack is "imminent" is based on various factors, including:

a. the nature and immediacy of the threat,
b. the probability of an attack,
c. whether the anticipated attack is part of a concerted pattern of continuing armed activity,
d. the likely scale of the attack and the injury, loss, or damage likely to result therefrom in the absence of mitigating action, and
e. the likelihood that there will be other opportunities to undertake effective action in self-defence that may be expected to cause less serious collateral injury, loss, or damage.[56]

Force may be used if "any further delay would result in an inability by the threatened state to effectively defend against or avert the attack".[57] Where the threat of an attack emanates from non-state actors and specific terrorist outfits possessing the intention and capability to conduct repeated attacks on a state, the use of force in self-defence is, therefore, justified.[58]

51 "The Caroline Case," *Yale Law School's The Avalon Project*. Accessed 30 October 2023. https://avalon.law.yale.edu/19th_century/br-1842d.asp.
52 "Nuremberg Judgment, France and Ors v Göring (Hermann) and Ors, Judgment and Sentence," *American Journal of International Law* 41(1947): 172, 205.
53 See Leon Friedman, ed., "International Military Tribunal at Tokyo (1948)," in *The Law of War: A Documentary History* (Greenwood Pub Group, 1972), 1029, 1157–1159.
54 For examples of state practice, see Thomas M. Franck, *Recourse to Force: State Action Against Threats and Armed Attacks* (Cambridge: Cambridge University Press, 2002). For a survey of the pre-emptive right of self-defense see Noam Lubell, *Extraterritorial Use of Force Against Non-State Actors* (Oxford: Oxford University Press, 2010), 57–59.
55 *Legality of the Threat or Use of Nuclear Weapons* (Advisory Opinion) [1996] ICJ Rep 226, 263 [41]; Yoram Dinstein, *War, Aggression and Self-Defense* (Cambridge: Cambridge University Press, 5th ed., 2011), 209. See also United Nations General Assembly, "A More Secure World: Our Shared Responsibility, Report of the High Level Panel on Threats, Challenges and Change," UN Doc A/59/565 (2 December 2004), [188].
56 Daniel Bethlehem, "Self-Defence Against an Imminent or Actual Armed Attack by Nonstate Actors," *American Journal of International Law* 106(4) (2012): 772, principle 8.
57 Wilmshurst, "The Chatham House Principles of International Law on the Use of Force in Self-Defence," 967.
58 For example, Security Council Resolutions 1368(2001), 1373(2001) and 2249 (2015) support the view that self-defence is available to avert large-scale terrorist attacks. See also

As for the tests of "necessity and proportionality", the requirement of necessity would be satisfied where the source of the attack is real and continues to pose a threat,[59] whereas the requirement of proportionality is not to be determined in isolation but in relation to the type of force required to end the threat of attack.[60] For example, if a state suffers a series of successive and different acts of armed attack from another state, "the requirement of proportionality will certainly not mean that the victim state is not free to undertake a single armed action on a much larger scale in order to put an end to this escalating succession of attacks".[61]

The attacks from terrorist groups based in Pakistan, especially JeM, have had a degree of continuity over decades. Pakistan was informed repeatedly and requested to take measures to stop such activities, but it failed to do so. Apart from this continuity, there was credible information that the terrorists were undergoing training and preparing to conduct attacks in India. These situations are sufficient to satisfy the requirements of imminence from different perspectives.

Force may be used in self-defence to avert an imminent attack.[62] All peaceful means to end or avert the attack should have been exhausted or unavailable.[63] The past experience shows that these means were exhausted and

---

for examples of State practice, the UK: Hansard (21 April 2004), vols. 370–1, and France: "Identical letters dated 8 September 2015 from the Permanent Representative of France to the United Nations addressed to the Secretary-General and the President of the Security Council," UN Doc S/2015/745, 9 September 2015; United Nations Security Council, "7589th meeting of the Security Council," UN Doc S/PV7589, 18 December 2015.

59 Judith Gardam, *Necessity, Proportionality and the Use of Force by States* (Cambridge: Cambridge University Press, 2004), 148–153.

60 Franklin Berman et al., *Principles of International Law on the Use of Force by States in Self-Defense*, ed. Elizabeth Wilmshurst (The Royal Institute of International Affairs, Chatham House, October 2005), 52, 53, 55; 57. According to Ago: "It would be mistaken, however, to think that there must be proportionality between the conduct constituting the armed attack and the opposing conduct. The action needed to halt and repulse the attack may well have to assume dimensions disproportionate to those of the attack suffered. What matters in this respect is the result to be achieved by the 'defensive' action, and not the forms, substance and strength of the action itself": Roberto Ago, "The Internationally Wrongful Act of the State, Source of International Responsibility (part 1): Addendum to the 8th Report on State Responsibility by the Special Rapporteur," *Yearbook of the International Law Commission* II(1) (1980): 121.

61 Ago, "The Internationally Wrongful Act of the State, Source of International Responsibility (part 1): Addendum to the 8th Report on State Responsibility by the Special Rapporteur," 121; also see Norman M. Feder, "Reading the UN Charter Connotatively: Toward a New Definition of Armed Attack," *New York University Journal of International Law and Politics* 19 (1987): 395, 414–418.

62 Wilmshurst, "The Chatham House Principles of International Law on the Use of Force in Self-Defence," 966.

63 *Ibid.*, 967; Bethlehem, "Self-Defence Against an Imminent or Actual Armed Attack by Non-State Actors," principles 11 and 12.

unavailable. Had Pakistan been informed, it would have taken steps to alert the terrorist groups and facilitate the relocation of training camps.

JeM is designated as a terrorist organisation by the Security Council and is responsible for carrying out a series of terrorist attacks in India, including the one on the Indian Parliament and the Pathankot airbase in January 2016.[64] Information regarding the location of training camps in Pakistan was provided to Pakistan repeatedly; however, Pakistan denied their existence. India considered that the "existence of such massive training facilities, capable of training hundreds of *jihadis*, could not have functioned without the knowledge of Pakistan authorities".[65] India has been repeatedly urging Pakistan to take action against JeM to prevent *jihadis* from being trained and armed inside Pakistan. Yet Pakistan did not take any concrete action. Further, "credible intelligence" was received that JeM was "attempting another suicide attack", and *fidayeen jihadis* were being trained for this purpose. Due to this "imminent danger, a pre-emptive strike became absolutely necessary".[66] Moreover, the "non-military pre-emptive action was specifically targeted at the JeM camp" to "avoid civilian casualties". The training facility was located in a thick forest on a hilltop, far away from any civilian presence, to ensure that the attack was proportional.[67]

Reaffirming its stance on pre-emptive self-defence, in 2021, India attended the UNSC Arria Formula meeting hosted by Mexico, where it declared:

> [A] state would be compelled to undertake a pre-emptive strike when it is confronted by an imminent armed attack from a non-state actor operating in a third state. This state of affairs exonerates the affected state from the duty to respect, vis-a-vis the aggressor, the general obligation to refrain from the use of force. In fact, Security Council resolutions 1368(2001) and 1373(2001) have formally endorsed the view that self-defense is available to avert terrorist attacks such as in the case of the 9/11 attacks.[68]

The Indian representative at the UN meeting noted that non-state actors such as terrorist groups often attack states from remote locations within

64 Ministry of Foreign Affairs, "Statement by Foreign Secretary on 26 February 2019 on the Strike on JeM training camp at Balakot."

65 *Ibid.*

66 *Ibid.*

67 *Ibid.*

68 Ambassador K. Nagaraj Naidu, "Upholding the Collective Security System of the UN Charter: The Use of Force in International Law, Non-State Actors and Legitimate Self-Defence," *UNSC Arria Formula Meeting*, 24 February 2021. Accessed 5 November 2023. https://pminewyork.govin/IndiaatUNSC?id=NDE3Nw.

other states, using the sovereignty of that host state as a "smokescreen".[69] India's indirect reference to Pakistan was clear: it highlighted as examples the numerous "proxy, cross-border and relentless state-supported terrorist attacks from [its] neighbourhood", such as the 1993 Mumbai bombings, the 2008 Mumbai terrorist killings, and more recently, the attacks in Pathankot and Pulwama.[70]

India's recent aggressive stance towards self-defence is attributable to the criticism it previously received for not appropriately employing its military power against Pakistan following the 2001 attack on the Indian Parliament and the Mumbai attacks in 2008.[71] Further, where India had previously refrained due to Pakistan's nuclear capabilities, there is now a growing sentiment that escalation into a full nuclear attack is unlikely – perhaps now further strengthened by the absence of such escalation following the two air strikes.[72]

Pakistan's 'proxy war', involving the support of non-state actors like terrorist groups through "training, financing, intelligence and weapons to logistics and recruitment facilitation" "evade international censure".[73] In response, India's cross-border military strikes are considered a viable measure to send a strong message to Pakistan that it would face attacks unless it dismantles its terror network.[74] These are extraterritorial measures undertaken as an act of self-defence to neutralise terrorist armed groups that pose a threat to India's security.

4.2 *Enforcement Jurisdiction in the Sea Beyond 12 Nautical Miles*

Having one of the largest coastlines, India inevitably has an interest in the seas surrounding it, particularly in the Indian Ocean region. Critically, the Indian Ocean – from the Eastern coast of Africa to the Andaman Sea – is of strategic importance to India, both from an internal security perspective and from a naval and maritime perspective, as India's own trade and energy

69 Nagaraj Naidu, "Upholding the Collective Security System of the UN Charter: The Use of Force in International Law, Non-State Actors and Legitimate Self-Defence."

70 *Ibid.* See also "Would Be Compelled to Take Pre-emptive Strike When Confronted: India at UN," *The Economic Times*, 25 February 2021. Accessed 5 November 2023. https://economictimes.indiatimes.com/news/defence/would-be-compelled-to-take-pre-emptive-strike-when-confronted-by-imminent-attack-from-non-state-actor-operating-in-third-state-india-at-un/articleshow/81207144.cms?from=mdr.

71 Lt. Gen. Deependra Singh Hooda (Retd.), "Three Years After Balakot: Reckoning with Two Claims of Victory, Stimson," *Stimson*, 28 February 2022. Accessed 5 November 2023. https://www.stimson.org/2022/three-years-after-balakot-reckoning-with-two-claims-of-victory/.

72 *Ibid.*

73 Naidu, "Upholding the Collective Security System of the UN Charter."

74 See Lt. Gen. Deependra Singh Hooda (Retd.), "Three Years After Balakot."

activities depend on a safe, open and stable Indian Ocean region.[75] It may seem natural for India to aspire to be a net security provider in the region, taking on the responsibility of ensuring safety in the region.[76] These interests are multi-fold and especially security-related. India has been active in the suppression of piracy and is one of the most active contributors to suppressing piracy off the coast of Somalia.[77] Matters on activities of naval warships on the high seas are outside the coverage of the United Nations Convention on the Law of the Sea (UNCLOS), and the rules of customary international law remain unclear or imprecise. This lacuna of law has been the basis for states with strong naval forces to conduct policing and security-related activities on the high seas.

Accordingly, the security-related activities conducted in the region by India are extensive and may constitute a form of extraterritorial jurisdiction. This jurisdiction is primarily enforcement jurisdiction (the use of executive, administrative, judicial, police, or other non-judicial action to enforce or compel compliance or to punish non-compliance with domestic laws or regulations), not prescriptive (making domestic law applicable to persons or entities through legislation, executive acts or regulation, or determination by a court) or adjudicative jurisdiction (subjecting persons or things to the process of its criminal or civil courts or administrative tribunals).[78] Enforcement jurisdiction is generally considered prohibited under international law unless permitted by international custom or treaty law, following the Permanent Court of International Justice (PCIJ) decision in *SS Lotus*.[79]

75 Giulia Nicoloso, "The Strategic Importance of the Indian Ocean: International Maritime Actors in the Region," *Critical Maritime Routes Programme*, 20 July 2022. Accessed 5 November 2023. https://rusieurope.eu/wp-content/uploads/2023/03/The-strategic-importance-of-the-Indian-Ocean-international-maritime-actors-in-the-region-doc.pdf; Darshana M. Baruah, et al., *Mapping the Indian Ocean Region* (Carnegie Endowment for International Peace, 2023), 3, https://carnegieendowment.org/files/Baruah_IO_final_6-28.pdf.

76 "India Well Positioned to Become a Net Provider of Security: Manmohan Singh," *The Hindu*, 23 May 2013. Accessed 5 November 2023. https://www.thehindu.com/news/national/india-well-positioned-to-become-a-net-provider-of-security-manmohan-singh/article4742337.ece; "PM Modi Outlines Five-Point Framework for Maritime Security Debate at UNSC," *The Hindu*, 9 August 2021. Accessed 5 November 2023. https://www.thehindu.com/news/national/prime-minister-narendra-modi-chairs-high-level-open-debate-at-united-nations-security-council/article61432009.ece; Harsh V. Pant, *Indian Foreign Policy: An Overview* (Oxford: Oxford University Press, 2016), 197.

77 Aniruddha Rajput, "South Asia's Cultural Influence on the Law of the Sea," in *Cultural Influence on the Law of the Sea*, ed. James Kraska and Hayoun Jessie Ryou-Ellison (Oxford: Oxford University Press, 2025, forthcoming).

78 See Cedric Ryngaert, "The Concept of Jurisdiction in International Law," in *Research Handbook on Jurisdiction and Immunities in International Law*, ed. Alexander Orakhelashvili (Cheltenham: Edward Elgar Publishing, 2015), 54–55, 57–58, using Restatement (Third) of US Foreign Relations Law, Ss 401(a)-(c).

79 *The Case of the SS Lotus*, (1927) PCIJ Reports, Series A, No. 10, 18–19.

The UNCLOS permits the exercise of criminal jurisdiction over a foreign vessel passing through a country's territorial sea if the consequences of that crime are felt within its territory or if the crime has the ability to disturb the peace of the country or good order within the territorial sea.[80] There is no comparable provision in relation to the exercise of jurisdiction in the exclusive economic zone (EEZ) or the continental shelf; only the duty of 'due regard' applies.[81] There is some degree of uncertainty about the nature of the exercise of jurisdiction in these areas, and the exercise of jurisdiction, particularly criminal jurisdiction, which may constitute an extraterritorial exercise of jurisdiction, seems to be frequent and controversial.

Additionally, two instances are prominent in this regard. In January 2015, approximately 365 km (around 197 nm) off the coast of India, the Indian Coast Guard intercepted a suspicious Pakistani fishing vessel. The vessel contained explosives, and those on board detonated the explosives immediately.[82] This instance represents the willingness of the Indian Coast Guard or naval forces to intercept and exercise jurisdiction over activities beyond the territorial sea that may pose a threat to the security and integrity of India. This is particularly essential due to the large coastline and constant threat of terrorist attacks posed from the sea, especially due to Pakistan's promotion and protection of terrorists.

The second incident was the *Enrica Lexie* case, which "illustrates the complexities that arise in managing jurisdictional conflicts and deciphering the relationship between international and domestic law".[83] On 15 February 2012, an Italian-flagged commercial ship "Enrica Lexie" , with six armed personnel onboard and heading towards Djibouti, encountered an Indian fishing boat, 'St. Anthony', off the coast of Kerala. While at 22.5nm from the Indian baseline, two of the armed guards on board the "Enrica Lexie" fired at 11 fishermen on board the 'St. Anthony', killing two of the fishermen. The incident took place in the contiguous zone of India (CZ), which extends from 12nm to 24nm from the baseline.[84] The jurisdiction in the contiguous zone is limited to "infringement of its customs, fiscal, immigration or sanitary laws and

80 United Nations Convention on the Law of the Sea, Article 27.

81 *Ibid.*, Arts. 56(2), 58(2),

82 Rajat Pandit, "Coast Guard Foils 26/11-Type Attack, Intruder Boat Blows Itself Up," *Times of India*, 3 January 2015. Accessed 5 November 2023. https://timesofindia.indiatimes.com/india/Coast-Guard-foils-26/11-type-attack-intruder-boat-blows-itself-up/articleshow/45737506.cms.

83 Danielle Ireland-Piper, "The Enrica Lexie and St Antony: A Voyage into Jurisdictional Conflict," *QUT Law Review* 14(2) (2014): 75.

84 India's sovereignty extends to a distance of 12 nautical miles from the baseline, while the Contiguous Zone (CZ) is an additional 12 nautical miles, *i.e.*, a total of 24 nautical miles; the Exclusive Economic Zone (EEZ) is 200 nautical miles from the baseline, therefore the incident was pegged to fall within the CZ and the EEZ of India. See *Massimilano Latorre v Union of India*, 2012 252 Kerala LR 794.

regulations within its territory or territorial sea", but criminal jurisdiction is not expressly included.[85]

The two Italian marines were apprehended by the local police forces and were first remanded to police custody and later to judicial custody. The two Italian officers and the government of Italy filed writ petitions before the Kerala High Court. They sought to be released, contending *inter alia* that India could not exercise criminal jurisdiction in the contiguous zone and that the Italian marines were covered by sovereign immunity.[86] All of these arguments were rejected by the Kerala High Court, which stated:

1. The Permanent Court of International Justice (PCIJ) decision in *SS Lotus*,[87] which set out the basis of the 'Effects Doctrine', would apply over Article 97 of the UNCLOS, which mandates jurisdiction of the flag state in cases of collisions or incidents of navigation. Section 179 of the CrPC allows the exercise of jurisdiction in the territory where the consequences of a criminal act have ensued;
2. Section 3 of the IPC applied, which allows, in certain situations if provided under Indian law, for the IPC to apply to crimes committed outside India as if they had been committed in India. Section 7 of the Territorial Waters Act 1976 also allowed the Central Government to issue notification regarding the application of Indian Law to the EEZ, and in the exercise of this power, the Government of India issued a notification on 27 August 1981, which extended the application of the IPC to the EEZ;
3. While India respected sovereign immunity, the extent of immunity depends upon the circumstances in which the forces are admitted by the territorial State, and in particular, upon the absence or presence of any express agreement between the host and the sending State regulating the terms and conditions governing the entry of forces in the coastal territory.[88] According to the court, "a merciless attack of gunshots at fishermen, while passing through the CZ/EEZ of India", was not in alignment with such conditions of granting sovereign immunity.[89]

The Italian Government approached the Supreme Court of India in an appeal in September 2012.[90] The Supreme Court, in January 2013, dismissed these arguments on the same grounds as the Kerala High Court. However, it determined that the Kerala High Court did not have any

85 United Nations Convention on the Law of the Sea, Article 33.
86 *Massimilano Latorre v Union of India*, 2012 252 Kerala LR 794.
87 *Ibid.*
88 *Ibid.*
89 *Ibid.*
90 *Republic of Italy Thr. Ambassador v Union of India & Ors*, 2013 9 SC 89.

jurisdiction over the crimes charged[91] as the crimes had not been committed in Kerala but in the EEZ, over which only the central government of India could exercise jurisdiction.[92] Accordingly, the Supreme Court ordered the central government to establish a special court to try the Italian marines under the provisions of the Maritime Zones Act 1976, the Indian Penal Code, the Code of Criminal Procedure, and most importantly, the provisions of UNCLOS 1982.[93]

Relations between India and Italy – two otherwise friendly states – were further strained when the Italian Foreign Ministry, reneging on the Italian Ambassador's written undertaking to the court that the marines would temporarily travel to Italy to cast votes in an election and subsequently return to India for the trial, declared in March 2013 that the marines would not return.[94] As a result, the Indian Supreme Court ordered the Italian Ambassador not to leave the country pending the return of the marines, setting aside his diplomatic immunity owing to the breach of his undertaking to the court.[95] Since the Italian Ambassador had participated in court proceedings, his diplomatic immunity was waived.[96] The Indian Government termed Italy's refusal to send back the marines as "unacceptable",[97] and warned that "there [would] be consequences" unless Italy returned the marines. Finally, following diplomatic intervention, Italy decided to send the marines back to India.[98]

To conclude, the Indian government extended, and the Indian courts applied, the extension of India's jurisdiction over criminal acts committed in the CZ (*i.e.*, beyond the territorial limits of India) as if they had been committed within India.

91 The Italian marines were charged under Sections 302 (murder), 307 (attempt to commit murder), 427 (commission of mischief) read with Section 34 (criminal conspiracy) of the Indian Penal Code and Section 3 (offences against ship, fixed platform, cargo of a ship, maritime navigational facilities) of the Suppression of Unlawful Acts against Safety of Maritime Navigation and Fixed Platforms on Continental Shelf Act, 2002.

92 *Republic of Italy Thr. Ambassador v Union of India & Ors*, 2013 9 SC 89.

93 *Ibid.*

94 "Italy Marines Will Not Return to India Over Killings," *Reuters*, 11 March 2013. Accessed 20 November 2023. https://www.reuters.com/article/uk-india-italy-marines/italy-marines-will-not-return-to-india-over-killings-idUKBRE92A0RN20130311.

95 "Italian Ambassador Can't Claim Immunity: Supreme Court," *The Economic Times*, 19 March 2023. Accessed 20 November 2023. https://economictimes.indiatimes.com/news/politics-and-nation/italian-ambassador-cant-claim-immunity-supreme-court/articleshow/19049801.cms?from=mdr.

96 Vienna Convention on Diplomatic Relations 1961, Article 32(3).

97 See "India Orders Italy Ambassador Mancini Not to Leave," *BBC*, 14 March 2013. Accessed 20 November 2023. https://www.bbc.co.uk/news/world-asia-india-21781993.

98 "Italy to Return Marines to India for Trial," *Al Jazeera*, 21 March 2013. https://www.aljazeera.com/news/2013/3/21/italy-to-return-marines-to-india-for-trial#:~:text=Two%20Italian%20marines%20who%20skipped,be%20sent%20back%20to%20India.&text=Two%20Italian%20marines%20accused%20of,them%20back%20to%20face%20trial.

The Indian courts also declared that they had jurisdiction based on the rule of effects (or the "Objective Territorial Principle") as well as passive personality.[99] Since the wrong was suffered by an Indian national and the ultimate act was completed on an Indian vessel, which is deemed to be Indian territory, there was thus a basis for India to exercise jurisdiction. The incident could hardly be called a navigational incident under Article 97 of UNCLOS since there was no collision or similar accident, and thus, there was no basis to say that the flag state would have jurisdiction due to Article 97.

Eventually, in proceedings before an arbitral tribunal constituted under Annex VII of UNCLOS, India did not refer to the Territorial Waters Act 1976 or the 1981 Notification as the basis of its jurisdiction, relying solely on arguments of territorial and passive personality principles.[100] The tribunal did not find that Articles 92 and 97 of the UNCLOS had been breached by India's exercise of adjudicative jurisdiction or that India had been shown to exercise enforcement jurisdiction.[101] In the end, the tribunal decided that the marines were entitled to immunity in relation to their acts against the Indian fishermen since they were state officials acting in their official capacity in an area that was not part of the Indian territory. The tribunal also ordered India to cease exercising its criminal jurisdiction over the Italian marines.[102] The tribunal further ordered Italy to pay the families of the Indian victims INR 100 million as reparations.[103]

In compliance with the tribunal's order, the Indian government filed an application before the Indian Supreme Court to dispose of the proceedings in conformity with the award, and the Supreme Court finally dismissed the criminal charges against the Italian marines on 15 June 2021.[104]

This case represents India's uncompromising attempt at exercising jurisdiction over foreign marines. The exponential increase in the number of commercial ships carrying people from different nationalities, as well as the rise in mining and exploration activities near coasts indicate legitimate interests of the coastal state in protecting itself against and exercising jurisdiction over crimes.[105] India's strong protective stance on the protection of its nationals and vessels registered in India was clearly displayed in this incident.

99 Crawford, *Brownlie's Principles of Public International Law*, 440.

100 *The Italian Republic v The Republic of India* ("The 'Enrica Lexie' Incident"), PCA Case No. 2015-28, Award, 21 May 2020, paras 359, 361.

101 *Ibid.*, para 1094(B).

102 *Ibid.*, paras 873, 888, 1094.

103 *Massimilano Latorre v Union of India*, Special Leave Petition (Civil) No. 20370 of 2012, Order, 15 June 2021.

104 *Ibid.*

105 See V. S. Mani, "It's Our Boat, Our Courts," *The Hindu*, 23 March 2013. Accessed 20 November 2023. https://www.thehindu.com/opinion/lead/its-our-boat-our-courts/article4538854.ece.

Although Indian fishermen had previously been killed by anti-piracy forces since 2008, this particular case saw India take a particularly tough position towards the incident, despite traditionally having good relations with Italy, in not bowing down to the diplomatic efforts of and matching the strong stance of Italy.[106]

4.3 Security Concerns Originating Abroad

Taking its active stance in the interests of national security a step further, in 2019, India asserted its extraterritorial powers through the National Investigation Agency (NIA) in tackling crimes affecting its national security. The NIA was constituted in 2008 to investigate certain 'Scheduled Offences', which mostly relate to acts of terrorism, waging war against India, and counterfeiting currency notes.[107] The 2008 NIA Act also allowed the Indian government to constitute 'Special Courts', which would have criminal jurisdiction over the 'Scheduled Offences'.[108]

In 2019, an amendment was passed to extend the jurisdiction of the NIA, initially covering the entire territory of India and citizens of India (both inside and outside India), to now also cover persons who commit a 'Scheduled Offence' beyond India against an Indian citizen or affecting the interest of India.[109] Therefore, extraterritorial power and jurisdiction were given to the NIA to investigate any 'Scheduled Offence' under the Act committed outside India by a non-citizen and thereafter prosecute the case before a Special Court. Further, the 2019 Amendment removed the extra step of constituting Special Courts to try offences under the NIA Act, allowing the existing Courts of Sessions (district courts) to be designated as Special Courts to try such offences.[110]

India's rationale for this amendment, as expressed in the legislative debates for the passing of the NIA (Amendment) Bill 2019 in the Parliament, was clear: "When it comes to national security, [the Indian Parliament] must stand together to tell the world in one voice that we stand united against any corruption or any national security issue".[111]

106 See Ireland-Piper, "The Enrica Lexie and St Antony: A Voyage into Jurisdictional Conflict," 77.

107 The National Investigation Agency Act 2008, S. 3 and The Schedule.

108 *Ibid.*, Ss. 11, 13, 14, 16.

109 The National Investigation Agency (Amendment) Act 2019, S. 1(2)(d). See also The National Investigation Agency Act 2008, S. 1(2).

110 The National Investigation Agency (Amendment) Act 2019, S. 11.

111 "Discussion on Motion for Consideration of the National Investigation Agency (Amendment) Bill, 2019 (Discussion Concluded and Bill Passed)," *17th Lok Sabha Debate*, 15 July 2019, 99. Accessed 20 November 2023. https://loksabhadocs.nic.in/Synop/17/I/Syn-15-07-2019.pdf.

The Indian Parliament noted that since 2008, a series of events affecting the national security of India could not be prosecuted by Indian courts owing to the absence of legislation allowing the exercise of extraterritorial jurisdiction: the 2008 Mumbai terrorist attack case (where India had to rely on the United States to prosecute connected terrorist David Headley under its own legislation), the 2008 attack on the Indian embassy in Afghanistan, which killed 41 people, and the killings of Indians in bomb blasts in Sri Lanka.[112]

India has, therefore, made clear through its various approaches to terrorism and other threats to its sovereignty or its citizens that it will not hesitate to exercise extraterritorial powers to maintain internal security.

5 Conclusion

The philosophy of seeking ways to extend jurisdiction has not guided Indian policy. Despite its greater willingness to exercise extraterritorial jurisdiction, it would be an error to think that India is moving towards a trajectory of an orientation that seeks to expand this power. As India's global engagement has expanded and its interests have diversified, the number of items forming the basis for the exercise of extraterritorial jurisdiction has inevitably grown. These are the results of a country's rising political and economic influence. India also feels less insecure and worried about international reactions to its extraterritorial exercise of jurisdiction compared to the past.

However, there are reasons to believe that India will not transform into a state that asserts extraterritorial jurisdiction overly. Considering its large size and the interests of its nationals and legal entities aboard, there will always be concerns about foreign states' reactions to India's assertive exercise of extraterritorial jurisdiction. India's large diaspora abroad adds to these concerns, as it is aware of the potential backlash its people may have to face due to the state's involvement in sensitive extraterritorial political activities. An assertive exercise of jurisdiction on political and other sensitive matters has its own costs and consequences. These factors call for a careful balance of security interests abroad and the reciprocal consequences of its assertive extraterritorial jurisdiction.

112 *Ibid.* See also "41 Killed in Indian Embassy Bombing in Kabul," *PBS News*, 7 July 2008. Accessed 20 November 2023. https://www.pbs.org/newshour/world/asia-july-dec08-kabulbomb_07-07; US Department of Justice Office of Public Affairs, "David Coleman Headley Sentenced to 35 Years in Prison for Role in India and Denmark Terror Plots," 24 January 2013. Accessed 20 November 2023. https://www.justice.gov/opa/pr/david-coleman-headley-sentenced-35-years-prison-role-india-and-denmark-terror-plots; "Sri Lanka Blasts: 3 Indians Among 27," *Times of India*, 22 April 2019. Accessed 20 November 2023. https://timesofindia.indiatimes.com/world/south-asia/sri-lanka-blasts-3-indians-among-27-foreigners-dead-13-suspects-arrested/articleshow/68982316.cms.

India is rapidly rising politically and economically. However, it is neither a single dominating hegemonic power in world affairs nor one of the two competing global superpowers. If it reaches either stage, India may choose to exercise extraterritorial jurisdiction more freely and assertively – not just as a legal tool but, most importantly, as an assertion of its political presence and influence. The more interesting question would be: When it reaches such a position, what will its approach be? Will it adopt the traditional Western approach of power and hegemony, or will it uphold the traditional Indian approach of *dharma* – value-based relations?

References

"41 Killed in Indian Embassy Bombing in Kabul." *PBS News*, 7 July 2008. https://www.pbs.org/newshour/world/asia-july-dec08-kabulbomb_07–07

Ago, Roberto. "The Internationally Wrongful Act of the State, Source of International Responsibility (part 1): Addendum to the 8th Report on State Responsibility by the Special Rapporteur." *Yearbook of the International Law Commission* II(1) (1980).

Aust, Anthony. *Handbook of International Law*. Cambridge: Cambridge University Press, 2010.

Bandyopadhyay, Subhayu. "Trade and Terror: The Impact of Terrorism on Developing Countries." *Federal Reserve Bank of St. Louis*, 11 December 2017. www.stlouisfed.org/publications/regional-economist/fourth-quarter-2017/impact-terrorism-developing-countries.

Baruah, Darshana M., Nitya Labh, and Jessica Greely. *Mapping the Indian Ocean Region*. Washington, DC: Carnegie Endowment for International Peace, 2023. https://carnegieendowment.org/files/Baruah_IO_final_6–28.pdf.

Berman, Franklin, et al. In *Principles of International Law on the Use of Force by States in Self-Defense*, edited by Elizabeth Wilmshurst. The Royal Institute of International Affairs, Chatham House, October 2005.

Bethlehem, Daniel. "Self-Defence Against an Imminent or Actual Armed Attack by Non-state Actors." *American Journal of International Law* 106(4) (2012): 769–777.

"The Caroline Case." *Yale Law School's The Avalon Project*. https://avalon.law.yale.edu/19th_century/br-1842d.asp.

Crawford, James. *Brownlie's Principles of Public International Law*. Oxford: Oxford University Press, 2019.

Dinstein, Yoram. *War, Aggression and Self-Defence*. Cambridge: Cambridge University Press, 2001.

"Discussion on Motion for Consideration of the National Investigation Agency (Amendment) Bill, 2019 (Discussion concluded and Bill Passed)." *17th Lok Sabha Debate*, 15 July 2019. https://loksabhadocs.nic.in/Synop/17/I/Syn-15-07-2019.pdf.

Feder, Norman. "Reading the UN Charter Connotatively: Toward a New Definition of Armed Attack." *New York University Journal of International Law and Politics* 19 (1987): 395–432.

Franck, Thomas. *Recourse to Force: State Action Against Threats and Armed Attacks*. Cambridge: Cambridge University Press, 2002.

Friedman, Leon. "International Military Tribunal at Tokyo (1948)." In *The Law of War: A Documentary History*. Greenwood Pub Group, 1972.
Gardam, Judith. *Necessity, Proportionality and the Use of Force by States*. Cambridge: Cambridge University Press, 2004.
Hansard. 21 April 2004. vols. 370–371. https://hansard.parliament.uk/about
Hooda, Lt. Gen. Deependra Singh (Retd.). "Three Years After Balakot: Reckoning with Two Claims of Victory, Stimson." *Stimson*, 28 February 2022. https://www.stimson.org/2022/three-years-after-balakot-reckoning-with-two-claims-of-victory/.
"Identical letters dated 8 September 2015 from the Permanent Representative of France to the United Nations addressed to the Secretary-General and the President of the Security Council." UN Doc S/2015/745, 9 September 2015.
ILC, "Draft Conclusions on the Identification of Customary International Law," *Yearbook of the International Law Commission* II(2) (2018).
"India Orders Italy Ambassador Mancini Not to Leave." *BBC*, 14 March 2013. https://www.bbc.co.uk/news/world-asia-india–21781993.
"India Well Positioned to Become a Net Provider of Security: Manmohan Singh." *The Hindu*, 23 May 2013. https://www.thehindu.com/news/national/india-well-positioned-to-become-a-net-provider-of-security-manmohan-singh/article4742337.ece
Institute of Economics and Peace. *Global Terrorism Index: Measuring and Understanding the Impact of Terrorism*, 2016. http://economicsandpeace.org/wp-content/uploads/2016/11/Global-Terrorism-Index–2016.2.pdf.
Ireland-Piper, Danielle. "The Enrica Lexie and St Antony: A Voyage into Jurisdictional Conflict." *QUT Law Review* 14(2) (2014): 74–89.
"Italian Ambassador Can't Claim Immunity: Supreme Court." *The Economic Times*, 19 March 2023. https://economictimes.indiatimes.com/news/politics-and-nation/italian-ambassador-cant-claim-immunity-supreme-court/articleshow/19049801.cms?from=mdr.
"Italy Marines Will Not Return to India Over Killings." *Reuters*, 11 March 2013. https://www.reuters.com/article/uk-india-italy-marines/italy-marines-will-not-return-to-india-over-killings-idUKBRE92A0RN20130311.
"Italy to Return Marines to India for Trial." *Al Jazeera*, 21 March 2013. https://www.aljazeera.com/news/2013/3/21/italy-to-return-marines-to-india-for-trial#:~:text=Two%20Italian%20marines%20who%20skipped,be%20sent%20back%20to%20India.&text=Two%20Italian%20marines%20accused%20of,them%20back%20to%20face%20trial.
Lubell, Noam. *Extraterritorial Use of Force Against Non-State Actors*. Oxford: Oxford University Press, 2010.
Mani, V S., "It's Our Boat, Our Courts." *The Hindu*, 23 March 2013. https://www.thehindu.com/opinion/lead/its-our-boat-our-courts/article4538854.ece.
Ministerio de Relaciones Exteriores de Chile. "The Government of Chile Regrets the Refusal of the Indian Government to Extradite Marie Emmanuelle Verhoeven." 26 July 2017. https://minrel.gob.cl/the-government-of-chile-regrets-the-refusal-of-the-indian-government-to/minrel_old/2017-07-26/161629.html.
Ministry of External Affairs. "Transcript of Joint Briefing by MEA and MoD (29 September 2016)." https://www.mea.govin/media-briefings.htm?dtl/27446/Transcript_of_Joi.
Ministry of Foreign Affairs. "Statement by Foreign Secretary on 26 February 2019 on the Strike on JeM training camp at Balakot." https://www.mea.govin/press-releases.htm?dtl/31091/Statement_by_Foreign_Secretary_on_26_February_2019_on_the_Strike_on_JeM_training_camp_at_Balakot.

Naidu, Ambassdor K. Nagaraj. "Upholding the Collective Security System of the UN Charter: the Use of Force in International Law, Non-State Actors and Legitimate Self-Defense." *UNSC Arria Formula Meeting*, 24 February 2021. https://pminewyork.govin/IndiaatUNSC?id=NDE3Nw.
Nicoloso, Giulia. "The Strategic Importance of the Indian Ocean: International Maritime Actors in the Region." *Critical Maritime Routes Programme*, 20 July 2022. https://rusieurope.eu/wp-content/uploads/2023/03/The-strategic-importance-of-the-Indian-Ocean-international-maritime-actors-in-the-region-doc.pdf.
Pandit, Rajat. "Coast Guard Foils 26/11-type Attack, Intruder Boat Blows Itself Up." *Times of India*, 3 January 2015. https://timesofindia.indiatimes.com/india/Coast-Guard-foils-26/11-type-attack-intruder-boat-blows-itself-up/articleshow/45737506.cms.
Pant, Harsh V. *Indian Foreign Policy: An Overview*. Oxford: Oxford University Press, 2016.
"PM Modi Outlines Five-Point Framework for Maritime Security Debate at UNSC." *The Hindu*, 9 August 2021. https://www.thehindu.com/news/national/prime-minister-narendra-modi-chairs-high-level-open-debate-at-united-nations-security-council/article61432009.ece
Rajput, Aniruddha. "BRICS as 'Rising Powers' and the Future of International Law." In *International Rule of Law: Rise or Decline?*, edited by Heike Krieger, Georg Nolte, and Andreas Zimmermann, 105–124. Oxford: Oxford University Press, 2019.
Rajput, Aniruddha. "India's Contribution to the Making of International Law at the United Nations." In *Advancing Reformed Multilateralism in the Changing World*, edited by Nutan Kapoor Mahwar and Deepika Sawaswat. Noida: Macmillan Education, 2022.
Rajput, Aniruddha. "South Asia's Cultural Influence on the Law of the Sea." In *Cultural Influence on the Law of the Sea*, edited by James Kraska and Hayoun Jessie Ryou-Ellison. Oxford: Oxford University Press, 2025.
Ryngaert, Cedric. "The Concept of Jurisdiction in International Law." In *Research Handbook on Jurisdiction and Immunities in International Law*, edited by Alexander Orakhelashvili, 50–75. Edward Elgar Publishing, 2015.
Schrijver, Nico and Larissa van den Herik. "Leiden Policy Recommendations on Counter-Terrorism and International Law." *Netherlands International Law Review* 57(3) 2010: 531–550.
Shaikh, Imlak. "The Impact of Terrorism on Indian Securities Market," *Economic Research-Ekonomska Istraživanja* 32 (2019): 1.
"Sri Lanka Blasts: 3 Indians among 27." *Times of India*, 22 April 2019. https://timesofindia.indiatimes.com/world/south-asia/sri-lanka-blasts-3-indians-among-27-foreigners-dead-13-suspects-arrested/articleshow/68982316.cms.
"Surgical Strike Day: Here's How the 2016 Operation was Carried Out." *Hindustan Times*, 29 September 2021. https://www.hindustantimes.com/india-news/surgical-strike-day-here-s-how-the-2016-operation-was-carried-out-101632882272993.html.
"Terrorist Attacks Will Further Weaken a Slowing Indian Economy." *Knowledge@Wharton*, 11 December 2008. https://knowledge.wharton.upenn.edu/article/terrorist-attacks-will-further-weaken-a-slowing-indian-economy/
United Nations General Assembly. "A More Secure World: Our Shared Responsibility, Report of the High Level Panel on Threats, Challenges and Change." UN Doc A/59/565, 2 December 2004.
US Department of Justice Office of Public Affairs. "David Coleman Headley Sentenced to 35 Years in Prison for Role in India and Denmark Terror Plots." 24

January 2013. https://www.justice.gov/opa/pr/david-coleman-headley-sentenced-35-years-prison-role-india-and-denmark-terror-plots

United Nations Security Council. "7589th Meeting of the Security Council." UN Doc S/PV7589, 18 December 2015.

"Wanted in Chile for Allegedly Killing Senator, French Woman Will Return Home." *Indian Express*, 28 July 2017. https://indianexpress.com/article/cities/delhi/wanted-in-chile-for-allegedly-killing-senator-french-woman-will-return-home-4770658/.

Wilmshurst, Elizabeth. "The Chatham House Principles of International Law on the Use of Force in Self-Defence." *International and Comparative Law Quarterly* 55 (2006): 963–972.

"Would be Compelled to Take Pre-emptive Strike when Confronted: India at UN," *The Economic Times*, 25 February 2021. https://economictimes.indiatimes.com/news/defence/would-be-compelled-to-take-pre-emptive-strike-when-confronted-by-imminent-attack-from-non-state-actor-operating-in-third-state-india-at-un/articleshow/81207144.cms?from=mdr.

4 The Extraterritoriality of Russia in the Digital, Economic Sanctions and Criminal Prosecution Spheres

Liliya Khasanova, Nailia Savenkova and Kamila Shaibakova

1 Introduction

Russia's traditional standpoint firmly opposes the application of foreign laws beyond national borders, considering it as a violation of state sovereignty and a tool of political coercion. This perspective on extraterritorial jurisdiction is shaped by a fundamental criticism of some Western unilateral practices.

Russian scholars approach extraterritorial jurisdiction from various angles. A common position among these studies runs across sovereignty-based arguments.[1] There is an emphasis on territorial limitations of state jurisdiction[2] and the principle of non-interference in internal affairs.[3] Two terms frequently appear in discussions in Russian legal scholarship: 'extra-territoriality' and 'exterritoriality'. While some scholars use these terms interchangeably,[4] others distinguish them relying on linguistic analysis. Some scholars argue that 'extraterritoriality' reflects the perspective of the receiving state, which perceives this exercise of jurisdiction as an over-reach. Conversely, it is suggested that the state extending its jurisdiction may be more receptive with respect to the term 'exterritoriality'.[5] This chapter uses the term 'extraterritoriality' without delving into terminological debates.

Despite following a traditional stance, Russia's approach to extraterritoriality is increasingly pragmatic, influenced by (geo)political considerations. This chapter examines how this 'reactive' discourse and extraterritorial

1 Ludmila Terentieva, "Extraterritorial Jurisdictions of State and Perception Transformation of Its Spatial Boundaries," *Pravo. Zhurnal Vysshey shkoly ekonomiki* 3 (2019): 162.
2 Alfiia Kayumova, *Criminal Jurisdiction in International Law* (Tsentr innovatsionnykh tekhnologiy, 2016): 14, 29; Lyudmila Terenteeva, "Territorial Aspect of State Jurisdiction and Sovereignty in Cyberspace," *Lex Russia* 4(149) (2019): 141.
3 Anatoly Kapustin and Bulat Khabriev, "Unilateral Sanctions – A Vestige of a Unipolar World: The Conceptualization of the Legal Position of the BRICS Countries," *BRICS Law Journal* 6(4) (2019): 67–94.
4 Vladislav Tolstykh, *Course of International Law: Textbook* (Wolters Kluwer, 2009), 347.
5 Yevgeniy Zinkov, "Specific Features of Legal Space," *Obschestvo i pravo* 3 (2012): 20.

DOI: 10.4324/9781003402978-5

practice is reflected in three key spheres: digital, economic sanctions and criminal prosecution.

We begin with the digital domain, where sovereignty is asserted both nationally and internationally, sometimes impacting actors and practices beyond Russia's borders. We then analyse Russia's response to extraterritorial economic sanctions and the comparable countermeasures it has adopted. Finally, we examine criminal prosecution, focusing on the expansion of alternative measures to extradition.

2 Translating Sovereignty to the Information Space

Information space presents a domain where Russia is not only re-evaluating its approach to extraterritoriality but also propagating it in international norm-making settings. The rapid development of Information and Communication Technologies (ICT) and the rise of the Internet have raised significant questions about traditional conceptions of state sovereignty and territorial jurisdiction, particularly in a domain once seen as borderless.[6] Contrary to past predictions that globalisation and global cooperation would reduce the focus on state sovereignty, it has become an even more prominent feature of government narratives surrounding the Internet. Over the past two decades, Russian legal and diplomatic positions reflect a broader strategy of cyber sovereignty, where it seeks to protect the informational space within its territory while challenging foreign interference in its space. This assertive approach, however, has led to diverse and sometimes conflicting practices in the exercise of extraterritorial jurisdiction in the cyber domain.

2.1 *Evolution of Key Domestic Policies*

Russian normative proposals and legal academic literature at the end of the 1990s and early 2000s still perceived information space as a global domain that primarily facilitates international communication and the limitation of information flows as a violation of the right to information. However, in the face of increasing interdependence, surveillance scandals, the growing economic value of data and the power of social media to consolidate civil unrest, the 'territorialisation' of the information space with a traditional vision of territorial sovereignty became firmly integrated into broader national security initiatives.[7] Thus, in the past two decades, several waves of legal developments and policies have led to systemic changes in extraterritorial jurisdiction through the expansion of institutional powers in controlling information movement and its content. These developments were largely driven by the

6 Georg Glasze et al., "Contested Spatialities of Digital Sovereignty," *Geopolitics* (2022): 1–40.

7 Lincoln Pigman, "Russia's Vision of Cyberspace: A Danger to Regime Security, Public Safety, and Societal Norms and Cohesion," *Journal of Cyber Policy* 4 (2019): 22–34.

broad conception of national security, as well as social stability considerations. According to Lincoln Pigman, the regime's security was also one of the underlying factors in light of colour revolutions in Georgia and Ukraine.[8]

Before describing key developments, it is important to clarify that the Russian understanding of 'information space' today is much broader conceptually than what is perceived as 'cyberspace' in some Western countries.[9] The object of regulation in this case (under the jurisdiction) encompasses not only the physical and non-physical components that store, modify and exchange data using computer networks,[10] but also the production, use and movement of the information. The Doctrine of Information Security (2016) defines the information sphere[11] as both physical infrastructure and information handling within the *territory* of the Russian Federation. The Sovereign Internet Law (2019)[12] manifested territorial regulation and control over the infrastructure and Internet traffic. The National Security Strategy (2021)[13] introduces the notion of 'information security', which aims to ensure the country's sovereignty in information space by securing critical data and infrastructure, as well as preventing the monopoly of foreign corporations in the information domain. Such understanding of the scope of the domain, coupled with the strong notion of sovereignty and territorial integrity, informs a particular approach to prescriptive jurisdiction over information flows.

2.2 *Sovereignty in Information Space and Extraterritorial Jurisdiction*

Two key practices have been leading the discourse in Russia when it comes to extraterritorial jurisdiction in a 'borderless' domain. Firstly, the regulations and policies around data localisation and the cross-border flow of data

8 Pigman, "Russia's Vision of Cyberspace," 22–34.

9 Liliya Khasanova, "Conceptual Discrepancies in Russian and Western Approaches to International Regulation of Cyber [Information] Space," *Baltic Yearbook of International Law* 22 (2023): 3–21.

10 Michael N. Schmitt, ed., *Tallinn Manual 2.0 on the International Law Applicable to Cyber Operations: Prepared by the International Groups of Experts at the Invitation of the NATO Cooperative Cyber Defence Centre of Excellence* (Cambridge: Cambridge University Press, 2017).

11 The Doctrine of Information Security (2016) provides the following definition of the 'information sphere': "combination of information, informatisation objects, information systems and websites within the internet, communications networks, information technologies, entities involved in generating and processing information, developing and using the above technologies, and ensuring information security, as well as a set of mechanisms regulating public relations in the sphere".

12 Russian Federation, Federal Law No. 90-FZ "On Amendments to the Federal Law 'On Communications' and to the Federal Law 'On Information, Information Technologies and on the Protection of Information'" of 1 May 2019.

13 Russian Federation, Decree of the President of the Russian Federation No. 400 "On the National Security Strategy of the Russian Federation" of 2 July 2021.

of Russian citizens. Secondly, law enforcement practices that are related to cross-border access to data when dealing with cybercrimes.

2.2.1 *Regulation of Cross-Border Data Flows*

Regulation of cross-border data flows is key to translating a territory-based understanding of sovereignty into cyberspace. This entails the growing practices of keeping the data 'within' a state's territory (data localisation) and allowing it to 'exit' contingent on certain requirements (cross-border transfers). There are various underlying logics to the expansion of data localisation regulations.

The core red line among all the data localisation laws is an information security concern as an integral part of national security.[14] According to the Russian national security strategy (2021), 'information security' aims to reinforce the sovereignty of Russia in a broader information space, where it is in the national interest to protect Russian citizens and their personal data from foreign surveillance and from 'destructive influence' by means of manipulated information provided by transnational corporations.[15] Looking beyond the rhetoric of information security and data protection, there is an undercurrent of 'regime security' concerns that seems to have driven the extensive amendments in 2014 and 2015 after the protest movements related to former presidential elections[16] and the latest amendments to cross-border data rules in 2022 after the escalation of the Russian-Ukrainian conflict. In this sense, localisation keeps data within easier jurisdictional reach for law enforcement purposes because information stored in a foreign jurisdiction can be harder to access through legal channels.

Several major sets of rules on cross-border data flows were introduced in the past ten years that influenced the territorialisation of data.[17] The initial data localisation provisions appeared in the banking sphere in 2013, requiring *a copy* of the financial data to be stored on Russian territory,[18] and then evolved into a broader set of amendments to the Federal Law No. 149-FZ On Information, Information Technologies and Protection

14 Liliya Khasanova and Katharin Tai, "Shades of Authoritarian Approach to Digital Sovereignty: Russian and Chinese Data Localization Models," *Journal of Cyber Policy* (2024): 8.

15 Russian Federation, "Strategiia Natsionalnoi Bezopasnosti Rossiiskoi Federatsii," 2 July 2021.

16 Alexander Savelyev, "Russia's New Personal Data Localization Regulations: A Step Forward or a Self-Imposed Sanction?" *Computer Law & Security Review* 32 (2016): 128–145; Pigman, "Russia's Vision of Cyberspace," 22–34.

17 Khasanova and Tai, "Shades of Authoritarian Approach," 5.

18 The Central Bank of Russia, "Maintenance and Database Storage on Electronic Media No. 397-P," 2013.

of Information in 2014[19] and the Federal Law 152-FZ On Personal Data in 2015.[20] In short, the major requirement was introduced for all data operators having a physical presence in Russia to record, store and process any personal data of Russian individuals in a database located in Russia starting from 1 September 2015. These changes forced many companies to resort to third-party data centres located in Russia within one year of the enactment of the law to ensure compliance. According to the head of Roskomnadzor,[21] at least 600 foreign companies notified the government of their intentions to move their data processing and storage to Russian territory.[22] A violation of data localisation provisions resulted in access to LinkedIn being fully restricted in Russia.[23] Several rounds of administrative charges have been imposed on Facebook, Twitter, WhatsApp, Zoom and other foreign companies for violating data localisation requirements.[24] According to a spokesperson from Roskomnadzor, in 2021, forty-six companies were found to be in breach of localisation requirements.[25] From 1 September 2022, with another set of amendments to the personal data law, this requirement also applies to foreign entities and individuals even if they don't have a physical presence in Russia in case they process the personal data of Russian data subjects through their websites or apps. Only data of Russian citizens should be localised, and it is on data controllers (companies) to decide how they determine individuals' citizenship. This is quite an extensive extraterritorial application of personal data regulation, which makes companies worldwide liable if they engage with Russian citizens' personal data. Such broad application of law makes it difficult to enforce; however, it opens up the possibility for selective enforcement against companies.

19 Russian Federation, Federal Law No. 97-FZ "On Amendments to the Federal Statute 'On Information, Information Technologies and on the Protection of Information' and Specific Legal Acts of the Russian Federation on the Issues of Regulation of Information Exchange with the Use of Telecommunication Networks" of 5 May 2014.

20 Russian Federation, Federal Law No. 242-FZ "On Amendments to Certain Legislative Acts of the Russian Federation for Clarification of Personal Data Processing in Information and Telecommunications Networks" of 21 July 2014.

21 Roskomnadzor is short for The Federal Service for Supervision of Communications, Information Technology and Mass Media.

22 Daria Chebakova and Anna Balashova, "Vlasti Napravili Inostrannym Kompanijam Zaprosy o Hranenii Dannyh Rossijan," *RBC*, 29 June 2021. Accessed 10 February 2025. https://www.rbc.ru/technology_and_media/28/06/2021/60d6d5cb9a7947e0a57257a2.

23 The Moscow City Court, No. 33–38783/16, 10 November 2016.

24 "Russia – Data Protection Overview," last modified on 2 December 2022. Accessed 10 February 2025. https://www.dataguidance.com/notes/russia-data-protection-overview-0.

25 "Shtrafy IT-Kompanij Za Neobespechenie Lokalizacii Baz Dannyh Sostavili 48,5 Mln Rublej," *TASS*, 22 January 2022. Accessed 10 February 2025. https://tass.ru/ekonomika/13555931.

2.2.2 *Cybercrimes*

By pursuing a sovereignty-focused approach in cyberspace, Russia takes an active role in influencing international norm-making related to cybercrime and extraterritorial access to data for law enforcement purposes.

Cross-border access to data as part of a criminal investigation without host state authorisation was one of the main stumbling blocks in the Council of Europe's Budapest Convention on Cybercrime (2001), which Russia publicly opposed. Along with China, it argued that Article 32b of the Convention, which permits state parties to unilaterally access electronic evidence located beyond their territories, violates the principle of state sovereignty. The article states:

> A Party may, without the authorization of another Party: . . . b) access or receive, through a computer system in its territory, stored computer data located in another Party, if the Party obtains the lawful and voluntary consent of the person who has the lawful authority to disclose the data to the Party through that computer system.

In this case, it is not the mere act of extraterritorial access that is troublesome *per se* but the host state's authorisation of such access. Russia's stance reflects a strong emphasis on bilateral or multilateral agreements that prevent foreign agencies from bypassing Russian jurisdiction or accessing Russian data without direct cooperation.[26] Russia has channelled that vision through the proposition of the UN convention countering crimes in the information space.[27] After several years of negotiations under UN auspices, a highly controversial text has been unanimously proposed in August 2024 for adoption by the UNGA by the end of the year.[28] The Convention departs from

26 "Russia's Comments for the Seventh Meeting of the Open-Ended Intergovernmental Expert Group on Cybercrime," last modified 8 April 2021. Accessed 10 February 2025. https://www.unodc.org/documents/organized-crime/cybercrime/Cybercrime-April-2021/Comments/Additional-comments/Russian_Federation.pdf.

27 Draft Convention on Cooperation in Combating Information Crimes, last modified 29 June 2021. Accessed 10 February 2025. https://www.unodc.org/documents/Cybercrime/AdHocCommittee/Comments/RF_28_July_2021_-_E.pdf.

28 Proposed Text of the Cybercrime Convention, last modified 24 December 2024. Accessed 10 February 2025. https://www.unodc.org/unodc/en/cybercrime/convention/home.html; Oleg Shakirov, "Sostav kiberprestupleniia: chto zhdat' ot novoi konventsii OON po bor'be s khakerami," *Forbes.ru*, 14 August 2024. Accessed 10 February 2025. https://www.forbes.ru/mneniya/518976-sostav-kiberprestuplenia-cto-zdat-ot-novoj-konvencii-oon-po-bor-be-s-hakerami; Eli Scher-Zagier, "The New UN Cybercrime Treaty Is a Bigger Deal Than Even Its Critics Realise," *Lawfare*, 2 October 2024. Accessed 10 February 2025. https://www.lawfaremedia.org/article/the-new-un-cybercrime-treaty-is-a-bigger-deal-than-even-its-critics-realize; Maggie Miller, "White House Agonises Over UN Cybercrime Treaty," *POLITICO*, 27 September 2024. Accessed 10 February 2025. https://www.politico.com/news/2024/09/26/un-cybercrime-treaty-white-house-russia-00181271.

the Budapest Convention approach by emphasising state sovereignty[29] and requiring *mutual consent* between the two sovereign jurisdictions to conduct cross-border investigations.[30]

This vision of sovereignty and cybercrime was manifested by Russia in a range of bilateral and regional agreements in the past twenty years through the Commonwealth of Independent States (CIS),[31] the Shanghai Cooperation Organization (SCO)[32] and The Collective Security Treaty Organization (CSTO). The CSTO's Parliamentary Assembly approved model laws on information security (2021),[33] critical infrastructure security (2023) and the protection of information and cybersecurity (2023)[34] – all reflecting a strong sovereignty approach and underlying the non-intervention principle.

Through bilateral and regional agreements, as well as active international norm-making, Russia is quite clear and outspoken on its approach to extraterritorial jurisdiction in information space related to cybercrimes. In that framework, cross-border access to data is only possible through mutual cooperation. Otherwise, it would be regarded by the state as an infringement of sovereignty.

In summary, Russia enforces sovereignty and non-intervention principles over physical and logical components of information space by opposing any non-consensual exercise of extraterritorial jurisdiction. Over the past two decades, several waves of legal developments and policies in Russia have brought systemic changes to extraterritorial jurisdiction by expanding institutional powers to control the movement of data. To prevent cross-border access to data, Russia has implemented data localisation requirements and restricted cross-border transfers of personal data. In its approach to cybercrime enforcement, Russia continues to resist unilateral extraterritorial data

29 Proposed Text of the Cybercrime Convention, Articles 5, 48.

30 *Ibid.*, Article 22.

31 Agreement on Cooperation of the Member States of the Commonwealth of Independent States in Combating Computer Information Offenses (Minsk, 2001); Agreement on Cooperation of the Member States of the Commonwealth of Independent States in Combating Computer Information Offenses (Dushanbe, 2018); "Predstaviteli Parlamentov Stran SNG Odobrili Model'nyy Zakon "O Protivodeystvii Kiberprestupnosti," *IACIS*, last modified 25 June 2024. Accessed 10 February 2025. http://iacis.ru:80/media-tcentr/fotogalereya/predstaviteli_parlamentov_stran_sng_odobrili_modelnij_zakon_o_protivodejstvii_kiberprestupnosti.

32 Agreement between the Governments of the Member States of the Shanghai Cooperation Organization on Cooperation in the Field of International Information Security (Yekaterinburg, 2009).

33 Model Law on Information Security, last modified 29 November 2021. Accessed 10 February 2025. https://paodkb.org/documents/modelnyy-zakon-odkb-ob-informatsionnoy-bezopasnosti?ysclid=lvdraams22984283281.

34 "PA ODKB Podderzhala Model'nyj Zakon o Bezopasnosti Kriticheskoj IT-Infrastruktury," *TASS*, 19 December 2023. Accessed 10 February 2025. https://tass.ru/mezhdunarodnaya-panorama/19575759.

access, allowing access to data only through mutual assistance agreements with the respective governments.

3 Responding to Extraterritorial Sanctions

Similar to its approach in the information sphere, Russia has long maintained a strong stance on sovereignty and non-intervention in the field of economic regulation, viewing extraterritorial economic measures with scepticism, especially those enacted outside the UN Security Council framework. However, over the past decade, several key factors have shaped Russia's approach to extraterritoriality in this field. Among them are Russia's ambition to play a significant regulatory role in the global economy, as well as being the most sanctioned country in the world today.[35] While Russia continues to rhetorically oppose extraterritorial economic measures, in practice, it has adopted its own extraterritorial instruments. To illustrate Russia's current stance, this section provides a general position on unilateral sanctions and then examines specific examples of legal mechanisms it has developed to counter them.

3.1 Unilateral Sanctions

Scholars rightfully point out that international law does not provide for a one-size-fits-all answer to the question of the lawfulness of unilateral sanctions.[36] Russia's stance on sanctions is nuanced and complex as well. The usage of the term 'sanctions' is already disputable from Russia's perspective. While the term typically refers to the non-armed coercive measures adopted by a state or organisation to induce a change in behaviour of another state, group of states or a non-state target,[37] Russia questions the use of it outside the scope of the measures adopted under the auspices of the UN Security Council. Indeed, adherents of this approach argue that the term 'unilateral sanctions' does not correspond to sanctions under the typical meaning of international law.

Russia also challenges the legality of unilateral sanctions. Along with some other states, it claims that sanctions are only legitimate when authorised by the UN Security Council. Russia raises concerns that unilateral measures beyond the UN framework are generally incompatible with the principles

35 Alexandra Prokopenko, "How Sanctions Have Changed Russian Economic Policy," *Carnegie Politica*, 9 May 2023. Accessed 10 February 2025. https://carnegieendowment.org/russia-eurasia/politika/2023/04/how-sanctions-have-changed-russian-economic-policy?lang=en.

36 Charlotte Beaucillon, "An Introduction to Unilateral and Extraterritorial Sanctions: Definitions, State of Practice and Contemporary Challenges," in *Research Handbook on Unilateral and Extraterritorial Sanctions*, ed. Charlotte Beaucillon (Cheltenham: Edward Elgar Publishing Limited, 2021), 7.

37 *Ibid.*, 2.

of sovereign equality, non-interference in internal affairs and international cooperation and hence violate international law.[38] However, the states adopting such measures justify them as countermeasures in reaction to serious breaches of *erga omnes* obligations committed by the sanctioned state.[39] Although European Union and United States sanctions taken outside the UN Security Council have gained some legitimacy in Western literature,[40] the lawfulness of sanctions has not been confirmed by any international judicial mechanisms. Moreover, unilateral sanctions have a big drawback compared to collective measures adopted by the UN Security Council: their scope of application is as limited as the scope of jurisdiction of the state (or a group of states) that adopts them.[41]

3.2 Measures to Counter Sanctions

Russia has been condemning the use of unilateral restrictive measures with extraterritorial effects for years.[42] The current Russian Concept of Foreign Policy criticises unilateral restrictive measures and the abuse by certain states of their dominant position.[43] However, while being targeted with multilateral sanctions over the past decade, Russia not only has formally declared its readiness to "use symmetrical or asymmetrical measures to suppress such unfriendly acts and . . . prevent them from recurring in

38 "Statement by Permanent Representative Vassily Nebenzia at an informal Arria Formula meeting on Humanitarian Impact of Unilateral Coercive Measures." Accessed 25 November 2024. https://russiaun.ru/en/news/arria_sanctions_251124; Beaucillon, "An Introduction to Unilateral and Extraterritorial Sanctions," 8; Ivan Timofeev, Vladimir Morozov and Yulia Timofeeva, "UCM-Study on the Notion, Characteristics, Legal Status and Targets of Unilateral Sanctions. Russia's submission on the UN Special Rapporteur Call." Accessed 30 January 2025. https://www.google.com/url?sa=t&rct=j&q=&esrc=s&source=web&cd=&cad=rja&uact=8&ved=2ahUKEwjGz4aivZ2LAxUb0AIHHbAnNeIQFnoECBcQAQ&url=https%3A%2F%2Fwww.ohchr.org%2Fsites%2Fdefault%2Ffiles%2FDocuments%2FIssues%2FUCM%2FReportHRC48%2FStates%2Fsubmission-russia.docx&usg=AOvVaw3GdOpLyOmM1c9bbkVlrjq5&opi=89978449.

39 Mirko Sossai, "Sanctioning Russia: Questions on the Legality and the Legitimacy of the Measures Imposed Against the Invasion of Ukraine," *Roma Tre Law Review* (2022): 163.

40 Sossai, "Sanctioning Russia," 164.

41 Beaucillon, "An Introduction to Unilateral and Extraterritorial Sanctions," 5.

42 See "Statement by Mr. Peter Iliichev, Deputy Permanent Representative of the Russian Federation to the United Nations at the Security Council Meeting on Non-Proliferation," last modified 15 July 2013. Accessed 10 February 2025. https://russiaun.ru/en/news/sc_res1737; "Joint Statement by Bolivia, China, Cuba, Iran, Nicaragua, Syria, Venezuela, Zimbabwe and Russia at the 2019 ECOSOC Forum on Financing for Development Follow-Up," last modified 15 April 2019. Accessed 10 February 2025. https://russiaun.ru/en/news/develop150419; "Statement by Deputy Permanent Representative Gennady Kuzmin at UNSC Briefing," last modified 16 July 2021. Accessed 10 February 2025. https://russiaun.ru/en/news/civil16072021.

43 "The Concept of the Foreign Policy of the Russian Federation – the Ministry of Foreign Affairs of the Russian Federation," para. 10, last modified 31 March 2023. Accessed 10 February 2025. https://mid.ru/en/foreign_policy/fundamental_documents/1860586/.

the future"[44] but also practically demonstrated its position mirroring the measures of its 'unfriendly' partners and finding its own innovative instruments to counter the sanctions. Hence, Russia considers its own unilateral restrictive measures as legitimate reciprocal measures in accordance with international law.[45]

While it is commonly accepted that foreign sanctions against Russia have an extraterritorial effect,[46] it should be noted that many of the Russian counter-sanction measures are extraterritorial as well. This section focuses on personal sanctions and commercial arbitration related measures.

3.2.1 Personal Sanctions

As a response to unilateral (secondary) sanctions,[47] Russia created its own sanctions mechanisms to target specific individuals and entities: Federal Law No. 127-FZ On Measures of Influence (Countermeasures) in Response to the Unfriendly Actions of the United States of America and Other Foreign States of 2018, and Federal Law No. 281-FZ On Special Economic Measures and Coercive Measures, adopted in 2006 and largely amended since then.

Among other relevant ministries and agencies, the Ministry of Foreign Affairs is in charge of the implementation of personal sanctions. In May 2022, the Ministry published a 'stop list' of US citizens against whom personal sanctions were introduced, including a permanent ban on entry to Russia. As of 28 August 2024, the list included 2,170 persons.[48] Russia stated

44 "The Concept of the Foreign Policy of the Russian Federation," paras 14, 26.

45 Timofeev, Morozov, and Timofeeva, "UCM-Study on the Notion, Characteristics, Legal Status and Targets of Unilateral Sanctions."

46 Nicole Erb et al., "Sanctions Extraterritoriality and Overlapping Jurisdictions: New Horizons in US, EU and UK Law," *Global Investigations Review*, 20 June 2024. Accessed 10 February 2025. https://globalinvestigationsreview.com/guide/the-guide-sanctions/fifth-edition/article/sanctions-extraterritoriality-and-overlapping-jurisdictions-new-horizons-in-us-eu-and-uk-law; Carolina Dackö, "When Economic Sanctions Lead to Conflict of Laws and Real Risks for Businesses," in *Regulation of Risk: Transport, Trade and Environment in Perspective*, eds. Abhinayan Basu Bal et al. (Boston: Brill Nijhoff, 2023), 105.

47 Primary sanctions apply to persons located on the territory or bearing the nationality of the state or group of states imposing the unilateral sanctions. As such, these sanctions do not imply any controversial extraterritorial reach. Secondary sanctions are designed to constrain individuals and entities located in or having the nationality of a third state to adhere to unilateral sanctions, even if they are not directly subject to the jurisdiction of the sanctioning state. These sanctions specifically target foreign individuals and businesses that engage in transactions with those subjects who have been unilaterally sanctioned. Seeking to regulate activities that lie outside the reach of the law of the sanctioning state, secondary sanctions are extraterritorial in nature.

48 "US Citizens Subject to Personal Sanctions, Including a Ban on Entry into the Russian Federation," [In Russian] last modified 28 August 2024. Accessed 10 February 2025. https://www.mid.ru/ru/maps/us/1814243.

that its countermeasures are forced and defensive in nature, as their aim is to influence the American regime to reconsider its stance towards a rules-based world order.[49]

The US, EU and now Russian personal sanctions are extraterritorial in nature. Indeed, Russian countersanctions affect non-Russian persons active outside Russian territory.[50] Their broad rationale is an alleged engagement of the targeted persons in certain sanctionable conduct, *i.e.*, unfriendly actions against Russia, Russian citizens and entities.[51]

However, there is a significant difference between Russia's personal countersanctions and many of the sanctions that target Russian persons. The implementation of Russian sanctions is mandatory for Russian state bodies, local authorities, Russian citizens and legal entities under the jurisdiction of the Russian Federation, as well as for branches of foreign legal entities carrying out activities on the territory of Russia.[52] Thus, Russia's personal countersanctions could be classified as primary sanctions to some extent. For their part, many of the anti-Russian sanctions imposed by the US are clearly secondary as they constrain individuals and entities located in or having the nationality of a third state from engaging with a primary sanctions target.[53]

3.2.2 Sanctions and Commercial Arbitration

Russian law has introduced several so-called "resilience-increasing measures" in the field of commercial arbitration to safeguard national trade interests.[54] Following the 2020 amendment to the Arbitration Code (Federal Law No. 171-FZ), Russian commercial courts were granted exclusive jurisdiction over disputes involving sanctions or sanctioned entities. Initially, this jurisdiction

49 "Foreign Ministry Statement on the Publication of the List of American Citizens Included in the 'Stop List'," [In Russian] last modified 21 May 2022. Accessed 10 February 2025. https://www.mid.ru/ru/foreign_policy/news/1814248.

50 "Foreign Ministry Statement on New Personal Sanctions on US Citizens," [In Russian] last modified 19 May 2023. Accessed 10 February 2025. https://mid.ru/ru/foreign_policy/news/1871495.

51 Russian Federation, Federal Law No. 127-FZ "On Measures of Influence (Countermeasures) in Response to the Unfriendly Actions of the United States of America and Other Foreign States" of 4 June 2018 (with amendments and additions), Article 1(2).

52 *Ibid.*, Article 1(4).

53 For a view on US secondary sanctions against foreign financial institutions linked to Russia's military economy, see "Russia-related Designations; Publication of Russia-related Determination; Issuance of Russia-related General Licenses and Frequently Asked Questions," last modified 12 June 2024. Accessed 10 February 2025. https://ofac.treasury.gov/recent-actions/20240612.

54 Ivan N. Timofeev, "Unilateral and Extraterritorial Sanctions Policy: The Russian Dimension," in *Research Handbook on Unilateral and Extraterritorial Sanctions*, ed. Beaucillon, 107.

was conditional: applicants had to demonstrate that sanctions represented a barrier to fair adjudication and access to justice.

The Supreme Court of the Russian Federation applied the law as soon as 2021 in the case *Ural Transport Machinery Construction Company JSC* (Russian company, hereinafter 'Uraltransmash') *v Pojazdy Szynowe PESA Bydgoszcz Spolka Akcyjna* (Polish company, hereinafter 'PESA'). The dispute arose from contractual obligations between Uraltransmash and PESA. The parties had agreed that disputes regarding the performance of their contract were to be resolved by the Arbitration Institute of the Stockholm Chamber of Commerce. Uraltransmash appealed to Russia's Supreme Court, asking to prevent PESA from pursuing arbitration proceedings outside the territory of the Russian Federation. The Supreme Court rejected the application because the proceedings in Stockholm had already concluded. As a result, the application was deemed meaningless. However, the Court found that the existence of sanctions was sufficient to invalidate arbitration agreements.[55]

This regime gained particular relevance in 2022 when the sanctions pressure on Russia significantly increased. In June 2023, the Arbitrazh Court of St Petersburg held in *Linde v. RusChemAlliance* that arbitral institutions in non-sanctioning states may be considered non-neutral under the law.[56] RusChemAlliance and Linde entered into an engineering, procurement construction (EPC) contract for a gas processing plant and other facilities. The contract provided for dispute resolution at the Hong Kong International Arbitration Centre (HKIAC). Although HKIAC does not operate under the jurisdiction of a sanctioning state, the Arbitrazh Court of St Petersburg considered that China operates under the political and legal concept of "one country – two systems" and, as such, Hong Kong's political, legal and economic systems are largely based on the United Kingdom system. It also found that judges from the UK and the EU are part of the Hong Kong Supreme Court of Appeal, and by virtue of their citizenship, they are obliged to comply with sanctions imposed by the UK and the EU. Third, since English is one of the official languages of Hong Kong, it found that the dispute could not be impartially and independently treated in a territory under the significant

55 Supreme Court of the Russian Federation, Ruling No. 309-ЭС21-6955, Case No. A60–36897/2020, *JSC Uraltransmash v PESA* [In Russian], 9 December 2021. Accessed 10 February 2025. https://kad.arbitr.ru/Document/Pdf/99ce7aa2-7f06-4615-baa5-94473b980771/1f0d228b-cefb-435f-a5f1-8950060144da/A60-36897-2020_20211209_Opredelenie.pdf?isAddStamp=True.

56 Arbitrazh Court of St. Petersburg and Leningrad Region, Ruling, Case No. A56–129797/2022, *RusChemAlliance v Linde GmbH* [In Russian], 8 June 2023. Accessed 10 February 2025. https://kad.arbitr.ru/Document/Pdf/6047cdd9-1247-4d04-b76b-bb6f14579d6a/bb4d3370-be86-4e2c-9dae-67ea8deb2ee2/A56-129797-2022_20230608_Opredelenie.pdf?isAddStamp=True.

influence of a state unfriendly to Russia. Based on this, the Court asserted jurisdiction over the dispute.

In January 2025, the Arbitrazh Court of St Petersburg took its exclusive jurisdiction further in *RusChemAlliance v. Bayerische Landesbank*.[57] The case involved bank guarantees that Bayerische Landesbank issued in favour of RusChemAlliance in 2021. The parties included an arbitration clause with an explicit reference to the International Court of Arbitration of the International Chamber of Commerce (ICC Arbitration). In 2023, RusChemAlliance filed a case against Bayerische Landesbank in the Arbitrazh Court of St Petersburg to recover payments under the bank guarantees. In turn, Bayerische Landesbank initiated arbitration at the ICC, challenging the jurisdiction of the Russian court. It also commenced proceedings in the High Court of Justice of England and Wales, seeking to prohibit RusChemAlliance from continuing its legal action in Russia by means of an anti-suit injunction. However, the Arbitrazh Court of St Petersburg accepted to consider the dispute and satisfied RusChemAlliance's claim. RusChemAlliance did not stop there; it filed another claim requesting the court to prevent Bayerische Landesbank from continuing any ongoing proceedings in France and the UK, as well as initiating any new arbitration and judicial proceedings related to the dispute, except in the Russian courts. Again, the Arbitrazh Court of St Petersburg satisfied the claim. If the ban is violated, Bayerische Landesbank will be ordered to pay € 272.6 million in penalties.[58]

It should be noted that the status of sanctioned persons, whose interests Russia seeks to protect through this regime, may prevent them from participating in legal proceedings abroad. This could, in turn, hinder fair arbitration proceedings and potentially violate the principle of equal treatment of the parties. Considering that Russia "lands" in its territory cases that should otherwise be adjudicated abroad, Russia's use of administrative resources and lack of enforcement of foreign arbitration clauses constitutes an example of prescriptive and adjudicative extraterritorial jurisdiction. However there are concerns that the Russian regulations open the door for sanctioned persons to abuse as they force their counterparts to go to arbitration in Russia.[59]

57 Arbitrazh Court of St. Petersburg and Leningrad Region, Ruling, Case No. A56–90987/2024, *RusChemAlliance v Bayerische Landesbank* [In Russian], 27 January 2025. Accessed 10 February 2025. https://kad.arbitr.ru/Document/Pdf/d068b1b6-fd0a-4ab9-8a48-f8f-5724b5a2e/e640a91f-eab4-4a0f-bc1d-d4b62c98c4bd/A56-90987-2024_20250127_Opredelenie.pdf?isAddStamp=True.

58 Arbitrazh Court of St. Petersburg and Leningrad Region, Ruling, Case No. A56–90987/2024, *RusChemAlliance v Bayerische Landesbank* [In Russian], 27 January 2025. Accessed 10 February 2025. https://kad.arbitr.ru/Document/Pdf/d068b1b6-fd0a-4ab9-8a48-f8f-5724b5a2e/e640a91f-eab4-4a0f-bc1d-d4b62c98c4bd/A56-90987-2024_20250127_Opredelenie.pdf?isAddStamp=True.

59 Timofeev, "Unilateral and Extraterritorial Sanctions Policy," 107.

4 Criminal Prosecution: Extradition and Alternative Practices

Extradition plays a crucial role in facilitating the exercise of extraterritorial jurisdiction by allowing a state to obtain legal assistance to enforce its criminal law. It bridges the gap between a state's need to address crimes with extraterritorial implications and the territorial limits of its law enforcement authority. However, in the recent past, Russia has relied to an important extent on alternatives to extradition as a means to enforce its prosecution interests abroad.

4.1 Extradition and Extraterritoriality

Russian legal scholarship contrasts extraterritorial jurisdiction with the territoriality principle[60] and frequently describes it as "limited".[61] This means that states may only exercise full jurisdiction within their sovereign borders and can extend it abroad only with respect to their citizens and legal persons.[62]

Article 12 of the Criminal Code of the Russian Federation provides the legal framework of extraterritorial criminal jurisdiction. It allows the prosecution of Russian citizens and permanent residents for crimes committed abroad, thus reflecting the active personality principle. Section 3.1 of the Code incorporates other important extraterritorial principles, including the passive personality principle (for crimes against Russian nationals), the protective principle (for crimes against Russia's interests) and universal jurisdiction (for crimes covered by international treaties).

The legal provisions governing extradition are contained in the Russian Constitution,[63] the Criminal Procedure Code,[64] the Criminal Code[65] and various regional extradition conventions[66] and bilateral treaties.[67] As a member of the international community, Russia is also bound by general principles

60 Terentieva, "Extraterritorial Jurisdictions of State," 163.

61 Yurii Klyuchnikov, "Principles of Prescriptive Jurisdiction," *Mezhdunarodnoe publichnoe i chastnoe pravo* (2002): 11–17.

62 Igor Lukaschuk and Anatoliy Naumov, *Extradition of Defendants and Convicts under International Criminal Law* (Moscow: Yurist, 1998), 39.

63 Articles 61 and 63.

64 Articles 460 to 468.

65 Article 13.

66 European Convention on Extradition, Paris. 1957; Convention on Legal Assistance and Legal Relations in Civil, Family and Criminal Matters, Minsk, 1993; Convention on Legal Assistance and Legal Relations in Civil, Family and Criminal Matters, Chisinau, 2002.

67 For example, bilateral agreements on legal assistance in civil, family and criminal cases between the USSR/Russia and Azerbaijan, Brazil and India. The full list: "The list of officially published bilateral international treaties of the Russian Federation concerning extradition issues" [in Russian], last modified 3 March 2015. Accessed 10 February 2025. https://www.consultant.ru/document/cons_doc_LAW_131317/7b2ba4d36a85652c535f3c6f12ea165e4b614b12/.

of law, as well as customary international law. For instance, a common basis for refusing extradition or deportation is the principle of *non-refoulement*, which prohibits transferring individuals to a state where they face a real risk of torture or other forms of ill-treatment.[68] Recognised as a *jus cogens* norm in international human rights law,[69] the principle reflects the absolute prohibition of torture and other cruel, inhuman or degrading treatment.[70] There is also the prohibition against extraditing individuals persecuted for political reasons or accused of political offences, which is considered to be a generally accepted principle.[71]

Russia's approach to extradition remains largely influenced by certain legal and political challenges. For instance, with respect to the United States, in addition to the complex diplomatic relations, the lack of an extradition agreement hampers mutual assistance. Another issue is the inconsistency in interpreting the state's margin of appreciation with respect to "political offences".[72] These challenges often lead Russia to explore alternative methods, such as luring and extraterritorial abductions.[73]

4.2 *Alternatives to Extradition*

Extraterritorial abduction involves forcibly removing a fugitive from the territory of a state by agents of another, which obviously raises serious human rights and sovereignty concerns.[74] The extent of the sovereignty violation depends on whether the host state was complicit. Abductions may occur with explicit approval, tacit consent and also without any involvement from the host state.[75] In this case, it is difficult to determine whether the host state was aware of the operation or failed to act to prevent it.

68 Mahmoud Cherif Bassiouni, *International Extradition: United States Law and Practice* (New York: Oxford University Press, 2001), 198.

69 Jean Allain, "The *Jus Cogens* Nature of Non-Refoulement," *International Journal of Refugee Law* 13 (2001): 534–538.

70 Universal Declaration of Human Rights, Article 5; Geneva Convention, Article 3; European Convention on Human Rights, International Covenant on Civil and Political Rights, Article 7; Inter-American Convention on Human Rights, Article 5; African Charter on Human and People's Rights, Article 5; General Comment N20, Committee on Civil and Political Rights, para. 3; *Prosecutor v Furundžija*, Case No. IT-95-17/1-T, Judgment of 10 December 1998, paras. 153–154.

71 Christine van den Wyngaert, *The Political Offence Exception to Extradition* (Kluwer Academic Publishers, 1980), 1.

72 *Abdulazhon Isakov v Russia*, Application No. 14049/08, ECtHR Judgment, 8 July 2010, para. 110; *Ermakov v Russia*, Application No. 43165/10, ECtHR Judgment, 7 November 2013, paras. 126–127.

73 David A. Sadoff, *Bringing International Fugitives to Justice: Extradition and Its Alternatives* (New York: Cambridge University Press, 2016), 454.

74 Ivan Shearer, *Extradition in International Law* (Manchester: Manchester University Press, 1971), 72–26.

75 Shearer, *Extradition in International Law*, 72–26.

When examining cases like these, the European Court of Human Rights (ECtHR) considers, *inter alia*, whether the host state conducted an effective investigation.[76] The absence of such an investigation, or an ineffective investigation, may indicate the level of involvement of a state in the unlawful transfer. Regardless of the circumstances, extraterritorial abductions are highly contentious due to their blatant disregard for territorial sovereignty and individual rights.[77]

A state may not exercise its enforcement jurisdiction on the territory of another state without its explicit consent.[78] However, cases before the ECtHR often reveal evidence of passive or active cooperation between states in such abductions.[79] When there is cooperation, the issue of sovereignty breaches is often excluded from the discussion. In *Abdulkhakov v Russia*, however, the ECtHR emphasised that any extrajudicial transfer, by deliberately violating due process, constitutes a fundamental denial of the rule of law and the values upheld by the ECHR.[80]

Luring occurs when a state persuades, deceives or coerces an individual to leave a jurisdiction where extradition is not possible.[81] This often involves a third state, where the person travels believing it is safe, only to be extradited from there. This is less problematic since the individual leaves voluntarily, but the use of deception always raises concerns. Luring methods include calls, messages and influence from friends or family, with motives ranging from economic incentives to personal reasons, like invitations to visit a sick relative.[82]

Some legal experts claim that "abducting a person from a foreign country or enticing a person under false pretences to leave another country to subject them to arrest and criminal prosecution is contrary to public international law".[83] One of the most well-known cases of luring is *Öcalan v Turkey*. In this case, the ECtHR ruled that authorities transferring an individual must provide proof, through concordant inferences, that they did not act

76 *K.J. and Others v Russia*, Applications Nos. 27584/20 and 39768/20, ECtHR Judgment, 19 March 2024, para. 80.

77 Geoff Gilbert, *Transnational Fugitive Offenders in International Law* (The Hague: Martinus Nijhoff Publishers, 1998), 60.

78 Marko Milanović, "From Compromise to Principle: Clarifying the Concept of State Jurisdiction in Human Rights Treaties," *Human Rights Law Review* 8(3) (2008): 421.

79 *Ermakov v Russia*, para. 220; *Savriddin Dzhurayev v Russia*, Application No. 71386/10, ECtHR Judgment, 25 April 2013, para. 198.

80 *Abdulkhakov v Russia*, Application No. 14743/11, ECtHR Judgment, 2 October 2012, para. 156.

81 Sadoff, *Bringing International Fugitives to Justice*, 55.

82 Alberto Costi, "Problems with Current International and National Practices Concerning Extraterritorial Abductions," *Yearbook of the New Zealand Association for Comparative Law* 8 (2002): 64.

83 "Mutual Assistance in Criminal Matters: XV Congress of International Penal Law Association Adopts Resolution," *International Enforcement Law Reporter* 10 (1994): 385.

extraterritorially in a way that violated the host state's sovereignty.[84] The Court took into account the Kenyan government's assessment that the transfer did not breach its sovereignty.[85] At the same time, it found that the detention followed "a procedure prescribed by law".[86]

4.3 Recent Developments in Alternative Practices

Prior to February 2022, Russia frequently appeared as a respondent state in ECtHR cases involving individuals removed from Russian territory.[87] These cases often concerned individuals from Central Asian countries, such as Uzbekistan and Turkmenistan,[88] and more recently, Belarusian nationals, following the mass protests of 2020.[89] The ECtHR frequently held Russia accountable under Articles 3 and 5 of the ECHR. Specifically, it found that Russian authorities bore responsibility by acquiescing in or failing to prevent irregular detention, even when carried out by private persons.[90] Evidence often showed that Russian authorities cooperated with Central Asian law enforcement agencies to facilitate transfers outside legal channels.[91]

Given that Russia is no longer a party to the ECHR since 16 September 2022, individuals can no longer file complaints against the Russian Federation for events occurring after that date. Although Russia is no longer a respondent state before the ECtHR, it may still be implicated in cases where an individual is extradited or abducted from the territory of a state that remains a party to the ECHR. Claims against Russia may still be brought before the UN Committees. Despite the fact that there is no comparable jurisprudence with respect to the ECtHR, *non-refoulement* cases are in line with the Court's position.[92] However, UN mechanisms face significant limitations that discourage many from using them. These include case backlogs,

84 *Öcalan v Turkey*, Application No. 46221/99, ECtHR Judgment, 12 May 2005, para. 90.
85 *Ibid.*, para. 95.
86 *Ibid.*, para. 99.
87 *Abdulkhakov v Russia*; *Iskandarov v Russia*, Application No. 17185/05, ECtHR Judgment, 23 September 2010, para. 115.
88 *Garabayev v. Russia*, Application No. 38411/02, ECtHR Judgement, 30 January 2008; *Ryabikin v. Russia*, Application No. 8320/04, ECtHR Judgement, 19 June 2008; *Kolesnik v. Russia*, Application No. 26876/08, ECtHR Judgement, 17 June 2010; *Garayev v. Azerbaijan*, Application No. 53688/08, ECtHR Judgement, 10 June 2010.
89 "How Belarusians Are Being 'Squeezed Out' of Russia," last modified 9 September 2021. Accessed 10 February 2025. https://www.mhg.ru/kak-iz-rossii-vydavlivayut-belorusov.
90 *Medova v Russia*, Application No. 25385/04, ECtHR Judgment, 15 January 2009, paras. 123–25; *Rantsev v Cyprus and Russia*, Application No. 25965/04, ECtHR Judgment, 7 January 2010, paras. 319–321; *Razvozzhayev v Russia and Ukraine and Udaltsov v Russia*, Applications Nos. 75734/12, ECtHR Judgment, 19 February 2020, para. 169.
91 *Savriddin Dzhurayev v Russia*, para. 134.
92 For example, CAT, Decision adopted by the Committee at its fifty-fifth session (27 July–14 August 2015), communication No. 554/2013, para. 12.4.

lengthy review processes and the absence of compensation for victims. For instance, in 2024, different UN committees considered cases communicated to them in 2017 and 2018.[93] More fundamentally, UN mechanisms lack enforcement power. They rely on diplomatic pressure and "naming and shaming" tactics. While symbolic, these methods can still have some impact in certain contexts.

Following the escalation of the Russia-Ukraine conflict, Russia started to engage more actively in forcible returns of its citizens abroad. Many of them had protested Russia's actions in Ukraine or fled the country to avoid mandatory conscription. Recent cases include those of Rafail Shepelev in Georgia, Lev Skoryakin in Kyrgyzstan and Kamil Kasimov in Kazakhstan.[94] These cases are brought primarily before local courts – often with minimal public information and limited transparency regarding the transfer processes. Before the escalation of the conflict Russia often facilitated and assisted neighbouring countries in returning foreign alleged fugitives from its territory. Human rights defenders and activists are now more vigilant of this rather recent trend. Indeed, understanding these developments is crucial for relocation and legal protection purposes.

Lev Skoryakin had fled to Kyrgyzstan to avoid sentencing in Russia. Following the initiation of extradition proceedings by Russia, a court in Bishkek placed Skoryakin under extradition detention while awaiting a decision. Skoryakin sought political asylum in Kyrgyzstan, which should have taken precedence over any extradition process according to international law.[95] Skoryakin was reportedly released from detention in September 2023 and transferred to Russia allegedly by Kyrgyz authorities. The Kyrgyz Prosecutor General's Office denied the accusation, informing the press that the extradition request had been denied and that there was no further information on Skoryakin's whereabouts.[96]

93 See, for example, Human Rights Committee, Views adopted by the Committee under Article 5 (4) of the Optional Protocol, concerning communications No. 2943/2017, No. 2953/2017 and No. 2954/2017; CEDAW, Views adopted by the Committee under Article 7 (3) of the Optional Protocol, concerning communication No. 129/2018.

94 Amalia Zatari, " 'We're Handing You Over to Russia, Just Don't Cry.' Why Political Emigrants Are in Danger in Kazakhstan, Kyrgyzstan, and Armenia and Who's Helping Them Leave," *BBC News*, 25 April 2024. Accessed 10 February 2025. https://www.bbc.com/russian/articles/cv263dxyl0yo; "Russian Security Forces Kidnapped a Deserter from Russia in Astana; Kazakh Authorities Have Not Made a Decision on His Extradition or Deportation," *Mediazona*, 24 September 2024. Accessed 10 February 2025. https://zona.media/news/2024/09/24/kasimov; Vlad Gagin, "They Called a Driver and Took Him to a Military Base'. On the Abduction of Russians in Post-Soviet Countries," *Lavamedia*, 3 October 2024. Accessed 10 February 2025. https://www.lavamedia.am/2024/10/0",76689/.

95 "UNHCR Comments to the Council of Europe's Committee of Experts on the Operation of European Conventions on Co-operation in Criminal Matters (PC-OC) On the Replies to the Questionnaire on the relationship between asylum procedures and extradition procedures," United Nations High Commissioner for Refugees, last modified April 2009. Accessed 10 February 2025. https://rm.coe.int/168058f749.

96 Zatari, "We're Handing You Over to Russia."

For its part, the Shepelev case suggests limited local involvement. Shepelev was reportedly lured from Georgia to a location where Russian agents allegedly detained him, but there is no clear evidence of the participation of Georgian authorities.[97]

In the case of Kamil Kasimov, no formal extradition or deportation request was submitted to Kazakhstan. According to a reported response from the Astana Police Department to a request by the Kazakhstan International Bureau for Human Rights, officials from the regional department of the Russian Ministry of Internal Affairs travelled to Kazakhstan on a ten-day business trip to detain him.[98] Upon his transfer, Kasimov was sentenced to six years of imprisonment in Russia.[99]

Another frequently used method for effecting returns to Russia is through Interpol's red notices. A red notice is a request to law enforcement agencies worldwide to locate and detain individuals pending legal actions. According to Interpol's website, as of January 2024, Russia accounted for 47% of the 6,843 active red notices.[100] These numbers raise concerns about the political use of this instrument in politically sensitive cases concerning individuals who confront persecution due to political beliefs, activism or minority status.

While many states are aware of the potential misuse and have pledged caution, recent cases suggest ongoing reliance on red notices. After February 2022, Poland and Romania reportedly responded to Russian red notices either denying entry to or initiating extradition against asylum seekers. Interestingly, red notices seem to be less successful and effective between Russia and its "unfriendly" states.[101]

5 Conclusion

Over the past two decades, Russia's official stance on extraterritoriality has remained largely consistent, reflecting a strong commitment to the principles of sovereignty and non-interference. A relevant illustration is Russia's

97 Olga Lebedeva, "Russian Activist Who Went Missing in Georgia Found in Russian Pretrial Detention Center," *DW*, 5 December 2023. Accessed 10 February 2025. https://www.dw.com/ru/pravozasitniki-propavsij-v-gruzii-aktivist-iz-rf-nahoditsa-v-sizo-v-niznem-tagile/a-67635759.

98 "Russian Security Forces Kidnapped a Deserter from Russia in Astana".

99 *Ibid.*

100 "Interpol: View and Search Public Red Notices for Wanted Persons," last modified 23 January 2025. Accessed 10 February 2025. https://www.interpol.int/en/How-we-work/Notices/View-Red-Notices#.

101 The list of "unfriendly" states is included in the Order of the Government of the Russian Federation, 5 March 2022 No. 430-r; "unfriendly" states become so when they impose economic or political sanctions against the Russian Federation, its citizens or legal entities; commit an action that threatens the territorial integrity of the Russian Federation; commit an action aiming at destabilising the Russian Federation economically or politically.

approach to the enforcement of cybercrime, where it continues to resist extraterritorial data access, allowing access only through mutual assistance agreements with the respective governments. Furthermore, Russia has consistently denounced the application of unilateral economic restrictive measures that carry extraterritorial effects, arguing that such practices contravene international law.

Nonetheless, Russia has implemented certain legal and policy measures it claimed were a rational response to Western sanctions and political pressures. In the digital domain, Russia has expanded its institutional powers regarding control of data flows, introducing data localisation laws that are applicable to all foreign entities dealing with Russian audiences. In the economic sphere, Russia has developed a series of practical measures aimed at countering the restrictive measures imposed by European Union and United States legislators, many of which exhibit extraterritorial implications. The criminal prosecution examples and practices illustrate that since February 2022, Russia has relied on alternatives to extradition to an important extent, playing an active role in bringing individuals to its territory while expanding the list of individuals sought through the red notices system.

The driving forces behind Russia's extraterritorial legal and policy measures are multifaceted, rooted in both global dynamics and internal considerations. These include a complex international and internal political landscape that has led to extraordinary prosecutorial actions alongside an economic situation which is increasingly strained by ongoing sanctions.

Bibliography

Bassiouni, M. Cherif. *International Extradition: United States Law and Practice*. Oxford: Oxford University Press, 2014.

Beaucillon, Charlotte. "An Introduction to Unilateral and Extraterritorial Sanctions: Definitions, State of Practice and Contemporary Challenges." In *Research Handbook on Unilateral and Extraterritorial Sanctions*, edited by Charlotte Beaucillon, 1–17. Cheltenham: Edward Elgar Publishing Limited, 2021.

Costi, Alberto. "Problems with Current International and National Practices Concerning Extraterritorial Abductions." *Yearbook of the New Zealand Association for Comparative Law* 8 (2002): 57–99.

Council of Europe Newsroom. "Russia ceases to be a party to the European Convention on Human Rights." Accessed 10 February 2025. https://www.coe.int/en/web/portal/-/russia-ceases-to-be-party-to-the-european-convention-on-human-rights

Dackö, Carolina. "When Economic Sanctions Lead to Conflict of Laws and Real Risks for Businesses." In *Regulation of Risk: Transport, Trade and Environment in Perspective*, edited by Abhinayan Basu Bal, Trisha Rajput, Gabriela Argüello, and David Langlet, 211–235. Boston: Brill Nijhoff, 2023.

Data Guidance. "Russia – Data Protection Overview." Accessed 10 February 2025. https://www.dataguidance.com/notes/russia-data-protection-overview-0.

Erb, Nicole, Cristina Brayton Lewis, Genevra Forwood, Sara Nordin, Peter Chessick, and Chris Thomas. "Sanctions Extraterritoriality and Overlapping Jurisdictions: New Horizons in US, EU and UK Law." *Global Investigations Review*, 20 June 2024. Accessed 10 February 2025. https://globalinvestigationsreview.com/guide/the-guide-sanctions/fifth-edition/article/sanctions-extraterritoriality-and-overlapping-jurisdictions-new-horizons-in-us-eu-and-uk-law.

Gagin, Vlad. "They Called a Driver and Took Him to a Military Base.' On the abduction of Russians in post-Soviet countries." *Lavamedia*, 3 October 2024. Accessed 10 February 2025. https://www.lavamedia.am/2024/10/03/76689/

Gilbert, Geoff. *Transnational Fugitive Offenders in International Law*. The Hague: Martinus Nijhoff Publishers, 1998.

Glasze, Georg, Amaël Cattaruzza, Frédérick Douzet, Finn Dammann, Marie-Gabrielle Bertran, Clotilde Bômont, Matthias Braun, et al. "Contested Spatialities of Digital Sovereignty." *Geopolitics* (2022): 1–40.

IACIS. "Predstaviteli Parlamentov Stran SNG Odobrili Model'nyy Zakon 'O Protivodeystvii Kiberprestupnosti'." Accessed 10 February 2025. http://iacis.ru:80/mediatcentr/fotogalereya/predstaviteli_parlamentov_stran_sng_odobrili_modelnij_zakon_o_protivodejstvii_kiberprestupnosti.

Interpol. "View and search public Red Notices for wanted persons." Accessed 10 February 2025. https://www.interpol.int/en/How-we-work/Notices/View-Red-Notices#

Kapustin, Anatoly and Bulat Khabriev. "Unilateral Sanctions – A Vestige of a Unipolar World: The Conceptualization of the Legal Position of the BRICS Countries." *BRICS Law Journal* VI(4) (2019): 67–94.

Kayumova, Alfiia. *Criminal Jurisdiction in International Law*. Kazan: Tsentr innovatsionnykh tekhnologiy, 2016.

Khasanova, Liliya. "Conceptual Discrepancies in Russian and Western Approaches to International Regulation of Cyber [Information] Space." *Baltic Yearbook of International Law* 22 (2023): 3–21.

Khasanova, Liliya, and Katharin Tai. "Shades of Authoritarian Approach to Digital Sovereignty: Russian and Chinese Data Localization Models." *Journal of Cyber Policy* 9(1) (2024): 70–94.

Klyuchnikov, Yurii. "Principles of Prescriptive Jurisdiction." *Mezhdunarodnoe publichnoe i chastnoe pravo* (2002): 11–17.

Lebedeva, Olga. "Russian Activist Who Went Missing in Georgia Found in Russian Pretrial Detention Center." *DW*, 5 December 2023. Accessed 10 February 2025. https://www.dw.com/ru/pravozasitniki-propavsij-v-gruzii-aktivist-iz-rf-nahoditsa-v-sizo-v-niznem-tagile/a-67635759

Milanović, Marko. "From Compromise to Principle: Clarifying the Concept of State Jurisdiction in Human Rights Treaties." *Human Rights Law Review* 8 (2008): 411–448.

Ministry of Foreign Affairs of the Russian Federation. "Foreign Ministry Statement on New Personal Sanctions on US citizens." [In Russian] Accessed 10 February 2025. https://mid.ru/ru/foreign_policy/news/1871495/.

Ministry of Foreign Affairs of the Russian Federation. "Foreign Ministry Statement on the Publication of the List of American Citizens Included in the 'Stop List'." [In Russian] Accessed 10 February 2025. https://www.mid.ru/ru/foreign_policy/news/1814248/.

Ministry of Foreign Affairs of the Russian Federation. "US Citizens Subject to Personal Sanctions, Including a Ban on Entry into the Russian Federation." [In Russian] Accessed 10 February 2025. https://www.mid.ru/ru/maps/us/1814243.

Igor Lukaschuk, and Anatoliy Naumov. *Extradition of Defendants and Convicts under International Criminal Law*. Moscow: Yurist, 1998.

"PA ODKB Podderzhala Model'nyj Zakon o Bezopasnosti Kriticheskoj IT-Infrastruktury." *TASS*, December 19, 2023. https://tass.ru/mezhdunarodnaya-panorama/19575759.

Permanent Mission of the Russian Federation to the United Nations. "Joint Statement by Bolivia, China, Cuba, Iran, Nicaragua, Syria, Venezuela, Zimbabwe and Russia at the 2019 ECOSOC Forum on Financing for Development Follow-Up." Accessed 10 February 2025. https://russiaun.ru/en/news/develop150419.

Permanent Mission of the Russian Federation to the United Nations. "Statement by Deputy Permanent Representative Gennady Kuzmin at UNSC Briefing." Accessed 10 February 2025. https://russiaun.ru/en/news/civil16072021.

Permanent Mission of the Russian Federation to the United Nations. "Statement by Permanent Representative Vassily Nebenzia at an informal Arria Formula meeting on Humanitarian Impact of Unilateral Coercive Measures." Accessed 10 February 2025. https://russiaun.ru/en/news/arria_sanctions_251124.

Permanent Mission of the Russian Federation to the United Nations. "Statement by Mr. Peter Iliichev, Deputy Permanent Representative of the Russian Federation to the United Nations at the Security Council Meeting on Non-Proliferation." Accessed 10 February 2025. https://russiaun.ru/en/news/sc_res1737.

Pigman, Lincoln. "Russia's Vision of Cyberspace: A Danger to Regime Security, Public Safety, and Societal Norms and Cohesion." *Journal of Cyber Policy* 4, 1 (2019): 22–34.

Prokopenko, Alexandra. "How Sanctions Have Changed Russian Economic Policy." *Carnegie Politica*, 9 May 2023. Accessed 10 February 2025. https://carnegieendowment.org/russia-eurasia/politika/2023/04/how-sanctions-have-changed-russian-economic-policy?lang=en.

"Russian Security Forces Kidnapped a Deserter from Russia in Astana; Kazakh Authorities Have not Made a Decision on His Extradition or Deportation." *Mediazona*, 24 September 2024. Accessed 10 February 2025. https://zona.media/news/2024/09/24/kasimov.

Sadoff, David A. *Bringing International Fugitives to Justice: Extradition and Its Alternatives*. New York: Cambridge University Press, 2016.

Savelyev, Alexander. "Russia's New Personal Data Localization Regulations: A Step Forward or a Self-Imposed Sanction?" *Computer Law & Security Review*, 32 (2016): 128–145.

Schmitt, Michael N., ed. *Tallinn Manual 2.0 on the International Law Applicable to Cyber Operations: Prepared by the International Groups of Experts at the Invitation of the NATO Cooperative Cyber Defence Centre of Excellence*. Cambridge: Cambridge University Press, 2nd edition, 2017.

Shakirov, Oleg. "Sostav kiberprestupleniia: chto zhdat- ot novoi konventsii OON po bor-be s khakerami." *Forbes.ru*, 14 August 2024. Accessed 10 February 2025. https://www.forbes.ru/mneniya/518976-sostav-kiberprestuplenia-cto-zdat-ot-novoj-konvencii-oon-po-bor-be-s-hakerami.

Shearer, Ivan. *Extradition in International Law*. Manchester: Manchester University Press, 1971.

"Shtrafy IT-Kompanij Za Neobespechenie Lokalizacii Baz Dannyh Sostavili 48,5 Mln Rublej." *TASS*, 22 January 2022. Accessed 10 February 2025. https://tass.ru/ekonomika/13555931.

Sossai, Mirko. "Sanctioning Russia: Questions on the Legality and the Legitimacy of the Measures Imposed Against the Invasion of Ukraine." *Roma Tre Law Review* (2022): 157–166.

Terentieva, Lyudmila. "Extraterritorial Jurisdictions of State and Perception Transformation of its Spatial Boundaries." *Pravo. Zhurnal Vysshey shkoly ekonomiki* 3 (2019): 160–180.

Terenteeva, Lyudmila. "Territorial Aspect of State Jurisdiction and Sovereignty in Cyberspace." *Lex Russia* 4 (2019): 139–150.

Timofeev, Ivan N. "Unilateral and Extraterritorial Sanctions Policy: The Russian Dimension." In *Research Handbook on Unilateral and Extraterritorial Sanctions*, edited by Charlotte Beaucillon, 90–109. Cheltenham: Edward Elgar Publishing Limited, 2021.

Timofeev, Ivan, Vladimir Morozov, and Yulia Timofeeva. "UCM-Study on the Notion, Characteristics, Legal Status and Targets of Unilateral Sanctions. Russia's submission on the UN Special Rapporteur Call." Accessed 10 February 2025. https://www.google.com/url?sa=t&rct=j&q=&esrc=s&source=web&cd=&cad=rja&uact=8&ved=2ahUKEwjGz4aivZ2LAxUb0AIHHbAnNeIQFnoECBcQAQ&url=https%3A%2F%2Fwww.ohchr.org%2Fsites%2Fdefault%2Ffiles%2FDocuments%2FIssues%2FUCM%2FReportHRC48%2FStates%2Fsubmission-russia.docx&usg=AOvVaw3GdOpLyOmM1c9bbkVlrjq5&opi=89978449.

Tolstykh, Vladislav. *Course of International Law: Textbook*. [In Russian] Wolters Kluwer, 2009.

U.S. Department of the Treasury, Office of Foreign Control. "Russia-related Designations; Publication of Russia-related Determination; Issuance of Russia-related General Licenses and Frequently Asked Questions." Accessed 10 February 2025. https://ofac.treasury.gov/recent-actions/20240612.

"Vlasti Napravili Inostrannym Kompanijam Zaprosy o Hranenii Dannyh Rossijan." *RBC*, 29 June 2021. Accessed 10 February 2025. https://www.rbc.ru/technology_and_media/28/06/2021/60d6d5cb9a7947e0a57257a2.

Wyngaert, Christine van den. *The Political Offence Exception to Extradition*. Kluwer Academic Publishers, 1980.

Zatari, Amaliya. "'We're Handing You Over to Russia, Just Don't Cry.' Why Political Emigrants Are in Danger in Kazakhstan, Kyrgyzstan, and Armenia and Who's Helping Them Leave." *BBC News*, 25 April 2024. Accessed 10 February 2025. https://www.bbc.com/russian/articles/cv263dxyl0yo.

5 Turkey's Political Expansionism and the Geopolitics of Extraterritoriality under International Law

Emre Turkut

1 Introduction: Geopolitics of Extraterritoriality Under International Law

Geopolitics generally refers to the influence of geographic factors on international politics and relations. Over the past decade, scholars have consistently argued that global politics has undergone a swift and profound transformation, accompanied by a redistribution of power in the international legal system. Dominant major powers, including the United States of America and Europe, are increasingly taking a back seat in steering the international system.[1] While a wealth of scholarly works in international relations explored the implications of this power shift,[2] there has been a noticeable lack of examination within the realm of international law regarding how this evolving power landscape will reshape and transform both the procedural mechanisms and foundational principles of international law.[3]

This oversight is not entirely surprising, given the longstanding tendency of traditional or mainstream international law scholarship to focus on positive law while largely disregarding the influential role of power in international legal processes. This tendency is particularly evident in specific fields

1 Ziya Öniş and Mustafa Kutlay, "Rising Powers in a Changing Global Order: The Political Economy of Turkey in the Age of BRICS," *Third World Quarterly* 38(4) (2013): 1409–1426; Andrew Hurrell, "Beyond the BRICS: Power, Pluralism, and the Future of Global Order," *Ethics & International Affairs* 32(1) (2018): 89–101.

2 Enrico Fels, "Power Shift? Power in International Relations and the Allegiance of Middle Powers," in *Power in the 21st Century: International Security and International Political Economy in a Changing World*, eds. Enrico Fels, Jan-Frederik Kremer and Katharina Kronenberg (Berlin: Springer, 2012), 3–28; Leslie Armijo and Cynthia Roberts, "The Emerging Powers and Global Governance: Why the BRICS Matter," in *Handbook of Emerging Economies*, ed. Robert E. Looney (London: Routledge, 2014), 503–520.

3 For a handful of notable exceptions, see Nico Krisch, "International Law in Times of Hegemony: Unequal Power and the Shaping of the International Legal Order," *European Journal of International Law* 16(3) (2005): 369–408; William Burke-White, "Power Shifts in International Law: Structural Realignment and Substantive Pluralism," *Harvard International Law Journal* 56(1) (2015): 1, and Anne Orford, "Regional Orders, Geopolitics, and the Future of International Law," *Current Legal Problems* 74(1) (2021): 149–194.

DOI: 10.4324/9781003402978-6

of international law, such as jurisdiction, where explanations often lack historical, political, and social context, thereby overlooking the pivotal role of power dynamics in their formulation and interpretation.[4]

Against this backdrop, this chapter examines the interplay between geopolitics and extraterritoriality, investigating how geopolitical power projection and spatial interests or strategies influence the exercise and regulation of extraterritorial jurisdiction. For the purposes of this chapter, the geopolitics of extraterritoriality is defined as the strategic use of a state's legal, military, and economic powers beyond its territorial boundaries to influence global political dynamics. This includes how states assert jurisdiction and project power in foreign territories to pursue national interests, navigate international relations, and manage conflicts. Such actions frequently result in complex interactions involving sovereignty, international law, and geopolitical strategy.

The chapter argues that Turkey provides a compelling case study for exploring the relationship between this type of geopolitics of extraterritoriality and international law. To this end, it examines various facets of Turkey's geopolitical expansionism in relation to its adherence to international law. At a broader level, the exercise of extraterritoriality has consistently played a prominent role in Turkey's geopolitical identity and spatial military interests, evolving as part of its expansionist projection of national power.

While international law imposes structural limits and obligations on state power and its geographically related interests – conditioning these actions on respect the principles for such as sovereign territorial equality, the laws of war (*jus ad bellum*), and human rights – geopolitics nonetheless allows states certain leeway to deviate from such obligations.

Overall, the chapter concludes that Turkey's expansionist extraterritorial actions, initiated through a geopolitical lens and occurring within an authoritarian political and social context, have broader implications for the international legal regime governing extraterritorial jurisdiction and international law as a whole.

2 Turkey's Geopolitical Identity and Political Expansionism

Extraterritoriality plays a central role in Turkey's discursive, policy, and legal landscape. Traditionally, the Turkish state employs geopolitics as a tool to justify and explain its pursuit of specific power-politics agendas, particularly those related to political spatial expansion and the strategic responses elicited by such expansion from other nations.[5] Situated at a

4 Michael Byers, *Custom, Power and the Power of Rules: International Relations and Customary International Law* (Cambridge: Cambridge University Press, 1999), 53–126.

5 Geoffrey Parker, "Globalization and Geopolitical World Orders," in *Globalization: Theory and Practice*, eds. Eleonore Kofman and Gillian Youngs (London: Continuum, 2nd ed., 2003), 237.

unique geopolitical crossroads – where Europe, Asia, and the Middle East converge – Turkey's political leadership, including its founder Mustafa Kemal Atatürk, has long recognised that this position offers both advantages and disadvantages.

The advantages lie in the potential to attract allies rather than adversaries and to grant Turkey an influential voice on the international stage.[6] Following its establishment as a republic in 1923, Turkey aligned itself with the Western bloc, forging close economic and military ties, including joining NATO in 1952, as part of its vision of becoming a modern, secular nation.[7] The country also sought to secure full sovereignty and diplomatic recognition, foster economic independence, and pursue a policy of neutrality and non-alignment in regional and international conflicts.[8]

However, this geopolitical location also presents significant disadvantages. As a relatively young state situated at the intersection of multiple geopolitical fault lines, Turkey finds it challenging to avoid confrontations with major and regional powers.[9] Cognisant of this reality, Turkish leaders have consistently emphasised the importance of being prepared to defend the nation's rights and interests through both diplomatic and military means.

Against this backdrop, national security issues and spatial military interests have been key pillars of Turkey's geopolitical expansionist agenda.[10] In this context, the Turkish invasion of Cyprus in 1974 serves as a striking example of its conventional approach of projecting power and influence beyond its national borders while safeguarding its geopolitical interests through assertive military action. Although the Turkish state justified the 1974 invasion by citing its commitment to protecting the Turkish minority (approximately 18 percent of the total population), there is a consensus among scholars and policymakers that the primary objective was to restore the balance of power in Cyprus. This involved occupying one-third of the island to prevent a Greek-Cypriot axis from dominating the eastern Mediterranean and aiming for long-term strategic control of the island.[11]

6 Leonard Stone, "Turkish Foreign Policy: Four Pillars of Tradition," *Perceptions: Journal of International Affairs* 6(2) (2001): 1, 3.

7 Şuhnaz Yılmaz, "Turkey's Quest for NATO Membership: The Institutionalization of the Turkish – American Alliance," *Southeast European and Black Sea Studies* 12(4) (2012): 481, 484.

8 Nicholas Danforth, "Ideology and Pragmatism in Turkish Foreign Policy: From Atatürk to the AKP," *Turkish Policy Quarterly* 7(3) (2008): 83–95.

9 Selim Deringil, *Turkish Foreign Policy during the Second World War: An 'Active' Neutrality* (Cambridge University Press, 2004), 1–2.

10 Mustafa Aydin, "Determinants of Turkish Foreign Policy: Changing Patterns and Conjunctures during the Cold War," *Middle Eastern Studies* 36(1) (2000): 103, 117.

11 John Sakkas and Nataliya Zhukova, "The Soviet Union, Turkey and the Cyprus Problem 1967–1974," *Les Cahiers Irice* 2 (2012): 123–135; Suha Bolukbasi, *The Superpowers and the Third World: Turkish-American Relations and Cyprus* (Lanham, MD: University Press of America, 1988), 188–189.

The Turkish invasion persisted until 1983, after which the Turkish-held northern part declared itself the Turkish Republic of Northern Cyprus (TRNC). The TRNC has been officially recognised only by Turkey, and no other country acknowledges it as a sovereign state. At the same time, the Cyprus issue persists as one of the primary obstacles to Turkey's full accession to the European Union.[12]

Despite the considerable costs of the Cyprus conflict, Turkey perceives Cyprus as an extension of its territory, as reflected in the enduring rhetoric that "Turkey's defence starts from Cyprus".[13] Consequently, the Cyprus question has been of eminent relevance to Turkey's foreign and domestic political agenda.[14] The TRNC, due to its international isolation and the embargo on its ports, heavily depends on Turkish military and economic support. As such, the TRNC embodies a sphere of interest and influence where Turkey exerts substantial economic, political, and military control influence economically, political, and military control.[15]

Inevitably tethered to Turkey, scholars categorise the TRNC (and other de facto states under international law) as a 'proto-state' or, more aptly, an 'aporetic state' – existing in reality but remaining unrecognised by other states due to complex and unresolved political situations.[16]

A more expansionist foreign policy marked by extraterritorial military interventions, territorial claims, and cross-border zones of influence has become evident over the past two decades during the AKP (Justice and Development Party) era under President Erdoğan's leadership.[17] These expansionist policies have been shaped by a complex interplay of external and internal challenges – what may appear to be 'irrational' or 'incoherent' state policies have been critical to sustaining Erdoğan's rule domestically and enhancing his influence internationally.[18]

12 Meltem Müftüler-Bac and Aylin Güney, "The European Union and the Cyprus Problem 1961–2003," *Middle Eastern Studies* 41(2) (2005): 281–293.

13 Nathalie Tocci, "Cyprus and the European Union Accession Process: Inspiration for Peace or Incentive for Crisis?" *Turkish Studies* 3(3) (2002): 113.

14 Hansjörg Brey, "Turkey and the Cyprus Question," *The International Spectator* 34(1) (1999): 111–121; Ayşe Çelenk, "The Restructuring of Turkey's Policy Towards Cyprus: The Justice and Development Party's Struggle for Power," *Turkish Studies* 8(3) (2007): 349–363.

15 Spheres of influence in international relations refer to regions or areas where a major power exerts significant political, economic, or military influence, often at the expense of other nations' autonomy and power. See Susanna Hast, *Spheres of Influence in International Relations: History, Theory and Politics* (London: Routledge, 2016), 1–44.

16 Rebecca Bryant and Mete Hatay, *Sovereignty Suspended: Building the So-Called State* (Philadelphia: University of Pennsylvania Press, 2020), 190–236.

17 Burak Bilgehan Özpek and Nebahat Tanriverdi Yaşar, "Populism and Foreign Policy in Turkey under the AKP Rule," in *Islamism, Populism, and Turkish Foreign Policy*, eds. Burak Bilgehan Özpek and Bill Park (London: Routledge, 2020), 30–48.

18 Eren Duzgun and Can Cemgil, "Class, State and Geopolitics: Explaining Erdoğan's Turkey," *Socialist Register* 60 (2024): 2.

For one, the global economic downturn and Turkey's increasingly dire economic situation have made it more difficult for the AKP and President Erdoğan to manage the economy through financialised and rules-based approaches. On the political economy and domestic governance fronts, the AKP has faced mounting difficulties over the past decade in maintaining electoral support and addressing growing social contradictions. Domestically, since the 2010s, the AKP has tightened its grip on the country by curtailing judicial independence, subverting political pluralism and civil society, and dismantling key checks and balances.[19] The failed military coup in 2016 marked a new phase of escalating authoritarianism. The ensuing state of emergency and the accompanying measures enabled the Turkish government to crack down further on perceived political opponents and stifle dissent through mass detentions, collective dismissals, institutional closures, and minority suppression measures.[20]

More fundamentally, with the rule of law effectively suspended, the President Erdoğan government, using vast emergency powers, implemented controversial policies to consolidate political authority. These actions have led commentators to assert that they now operate under an authoritarian political regime.[21]

In this context, a political ideology labelled as 'Neo-Ottomanism' emerged as a new method of assertive foreign policy strategy. Neo-Ottomanism has increasingly been used by Turkey observers as an overarching term "to signal the gradual Islamicisation of domestic politics and the growing presence of Islamic irredentism in foreign policy".[22] On the foreign policy front, the AKP has established a more assertive geopolitical paradigm, which scholars have termed "geopolitical adventurism".[23]

19 Alina Polyakova et al., "The Anatomy of Illiberal States: Assessing and Responding to Democratic Decline in Turkey and Central Europe," *Foreign Policy*, 2019. Accessed 27 September 2024. https://www.brookings.edu/wp-content/uploads/2019/02/illiberal-states-web.pdf.

20 Tom Ruys and Emre Turkut, "Turkey's Post-coup 'Purification Process': Collective Dismissals of Public Servants under the European Convention on Human Rights," *Human Rights Law Review* 18(3) (2018): 539–565; Emre Turkut and Thomas Phillips, "Non-discrimination, Minority Rights and Self-determination: Turkey's Post-coup State of Emergency and the Position of Turkey's Kurds," in *Human Rights in Turkey: Assaults on Human Dignity*, eds. Hasan Aydin and Winston Langley (Cham: Springer, 2021): 109–129, and Emre Turkut and Sabina Garahan, "The 'Reasonable Suspicion' Test of Turkey's Post-coup Emergency Rule under the European Convention on Human Rights," *Netherlands Quarterly of Human Rights* 38(4) (2020): 264–282.

21 Koray Çalışkan, "Toward a New Political Regime in Turkey: From Competitive Toward Full Authoritarianism," *New Perspectives on Turkey* 58 (2018): 5, 6.

22 M. Hakan Yavuz, *Nostalgia for the Empire: The Politics of Neo-Ottomanism* (Oxford: Oxford University Press, 2020), 179.

23 Eren Duzgun and Can Cemgil, "Class, State and Geopolitics: Explaining Erdoğan's Turkey," *Socialist Register* 60 (2024): 13. Other scholars have adopted a more balanced approach explaining it by the concept of 'strategic autonomy': Marc Pierini, "Turkey's Geopolitical

Turkey actively engages in high-risk situations across Europe, the Middle East, and beyond, as exemplified by its involvement in Russia's illegal invasion of Ukraine, the Nagorno-Karabakh conflict, the Cyprus issue, the Libya intervention, and hostilities in the Kurdish-ruled areas of Iraq and Syria.[24] Moreover, Turkey actively seeks to increase its soft power through capacity- and institution-building initiatives in regions such as Africa[25] and the Balkans,[26] often carried out by publicly funded civic and humanitarian organisations.[27]

As a result of this geopolitical agenda, Turkey has gained significant economic and political advantages, including knowledge transfers, business and investment deals,[28] arms and drone sales,[29] and the expansion of its embassy network.[30] However, in recent years, there has been a discernible shift, with the tangible and prospective costs of Turkey's geopolitical initiatives increasingly outweighing the political and economic advantages.

3 Turkey's Extraterritorial Use of Force and Spatial Military Interests in Northern Iraq and Syria

Turkey's extraterritorial use of force and regional militarisation policy in Northern Iraq and Syria constitute the most important theatre of Turkey's geopolitical power projection. The Turkish government has argued that these military operations are necessary to counter 'separatist terror organisations', including the PKK (Kurdistan Workers' Party – *Partiya Karkerên Kurdistanê*) and its affiliates, such as the Kurdish Democratic Union Party (PYD) and its military wing, the People's Protection Units (YPG). These efforts aim to purge terrorism

Role. Between National Ambitions, Western Anchors and Russian Sway," *IEMed: Mediterranean Yearbook* (2023): 124–130.

24 Gencer Özcan, "The Changing Role of Turkey's Military in Foreign Policy Making," *Revista UNISCI* (2010): 23–45.

25 Jense Heibach and Hakki Taş, "Beyond the Soft Power Tradition," *Journal of Balkan and Near Eastern Studies* 6(2) (2001): 1–16.

26 Basak Alpan and Ahmet Öztürk, "Turkish Foreign Policy in the Balkans Amidst 'Soft Power' and 'De-Europeanisation'," *Southeast European and Black Sea Studies* 22(1) (2022): 45–63.

27 Ozge Zihnioglu, "The Limits of Civil Society Geopolitics in Turkey," in *Global Civil Society in a Geopolitical Age: How Civic Activism Is Being Reshaped by Great Power Competition*, ed. Richard Youngs (Washington, DC: Carnegie Endowment for International Peace, 2022), 31–32.

28 Kemal Kirişçi, "The Transformation of Turkish Foreign Policy: The Rise of the Trading State," *New Perspectives on Turkey* 40 (2009): 29–56.

29 Digdem Soyaltin-Colell and Tolga Demiryol, "Unusual Middle Power Activism and Regime Survival: Turkey's Drone Warfare and Its Regime-Boosting Effects," *Third World Quarterly* 44(4) (2023): 724–743.

30 Ali Tepecikliоğlu, Elem Tepecikliоğlu and Can Karabıyık, "(Exploring) the Impact of Turkey's Embassies on Trade with Sub-Saharan Africa," *Journal of Balkan and Near Eastern Studies* 26(3) (2024): 360–377.

from Turkey's southern borders. Since the PKK began its armed struggle in the early 1980s, security concerns – particularly the Kurdish issue – have been crucial in shaping the Turkish state's domestic and geopolitical strategies.[31] Domestically, from the early days of the modern Republic, the Turkish state has wielded arbitrary and sweeping powers against the Kurdish population, resulting in pervasive human rights violations, including torture, kidnapping, disappearances, extrajudicial killings, and the destruction of homes.[32]

On an extraterritorial basis, Turkey has a history of cross-border operations into Iraqi territory dating back to the 1980s in response to PKK attacks originating from south-eastern Turkey and the Qandil mountains in Northern Iraq. To address similar PKK-related security concerns, Turkey signed bilateral treaties with Syria, starting with the Adana Security Agreement[33] and later the Joint Cooperation Agreement in 2010.[34] These agreements reflected a joint commitment to specific military goals, primarily focusing on combatting and eliminating the threat by PKK and its affiliates. Meanwhile, Turkey also leveraged the threat posed by the Islamic State threat in Syria as an opportunity to expand operations against the PKK, YPG, and PYD.[35] Scholars broadly agree that Turkey's military interventions violate both these bilateral treaties and the principle of self-defence enshrined in Article 51 of the UN Charter.[36] Specifically, Turkey's prolonged military presence in Syria constitutes a breach of Syria's territorial integrity, disregarding the legitimate authority of the Syrian government within its borders.

Since 2012, the self-proclaimed politically autonomous Kurdish regions, such as the Rojava cantons in Northern Iraq and Syria, have been viewed by Turkey as a significant national security concern.[37] This concern likely explains Turkey's primary motivation for its military interventions: a fear

31 Michael Gunter, "The Kurdish Factor in Turkish Foreign Policy," *Journal of Third World Studies* 11(2) (1994): 440–472.

32 For an excellent analysis on these systematic violations in the context of ECHR, see Onder Bakircioglu and Brice Dickson, "The European Convention in Conflicted Societies: The Experience of Northern Ireland and Turkey," *International & Comparative Law Quarterly* 66(2) (2017): 263–294.

33 Adana Security Agreement, signed by Turkey and Syria, Adana, 20 October 1998, Voltaire Network. Accessed 27 September 2024. https://www.voltairenet.org/article208057.html.

34 Joint Cooperation Agreement on Counterterrorism between the Republic of Turkey and the Syrian Arab Republic, 21 December 2010. Accessed 27 September 2024. https://www.resmigazete.gov.tr/eskiler/2011/07/20110705M1-12-1.pdf.

35 In a letter to the UN Security Council, Turkey invoked its inherent right of self-defence against ISIS due to Syria's unwillingness or inability to fight ISIS, which posed a threat to Turkey's national security. Accessed 27 September 2024. https://documents-dds-ny.un.org/doc/UNDOC/GEN/N18/017/57/PDF/N1801757.pdf?OpenElement.

36 Saeed Bagheri, "Turkey's Extraterritorial Use of Force against Armed Non-State Actors," *Israel Law Review* 56(2) (2023): 143–170.

37 Loqman Radpey, "Assessing International Law on Self-Determination and Extraterritorial Use of Force in Rojava," *Lawfare*, 2020. Accessed 27 September 2024. https://www.lawfaremedia.org/article/assessing-international-law-self-determination-and-extraterritorial-use-force-rojava.

that YPG-controlled areas could eventually integrate into a future Kurdish state. Through these operations, Turkey has capitalised on the cross-border nature of the Kurdish issue, transforming it into a geopolitical instrument for expansion. Since the Syrian civil war began in 2011, Turkey has openly pursued the dual objectives of maintaining spatial control and creating a buffer zone along its borders with Syria and Iraq. These goals appear to have been realised, as Turkey now controls large areas of territory in Northern Syria[38] and maintains an extensive network of military bases and operational posts in Iraq, effectively establishing secure zones free of conflict.[39]

In addition to its military presence, Turkey has undertaken state-building activities in these regions through civic and humanitarian organisations, providing education, healthcare, security, and essential services.[40] In 2020, the Turkish lira was introduced as an alternative currency to the Syrian pound.[41] Furthermore, the administration of these regions is overseen by seven Turkish government-appointed representatives operating under the directives of the governors of three Turkish borders: Hatay, Gaziantep, and Şanlıurfa.[42] These combined measures have led commentators to argue that Turkey is systemically pursuing a policy of Turkification in the areas under its control.[43]

Turkey's expansive policies in these regions have been facilitated by the declining role of major global powers in managing regional geopolitics. In most cases, Turkey's actions in Syria and Iraq have only elicited weak responses from the United States, Russia, and Iran. Turkey's relationship with both Russia and the US, as well as its European partners, is precarious, requiring careful balancing. At the onset of the Syrian civil war, however, Turkey and Russia pursued conflicting geopolitical goals, culminating in Turkey's

38 "Turkish-Syrian Rapprochement: Rhetoric and Motivations," *Middle East Directions Programme Blog*, 7 October 2022. Accessed 27 September 2024. https://blogs.eui.eu/medirections/turkish-syrian-rapprochement-rhetoric-and-motivations/.

39 Salim Cevik, "Turkey's Military Operations in Syria and Iraq," *SWP Comment* 2022/C 37, 30 May 2022. Accessed 27 September 2024. https://www.swp-berlin.org/10.18449/2022C37/.

40 Al Ghandura, "Turkey Kicks Off Syria Housing Project for Refugee Returns," *France 24*, 25 May 2023. Accessed 27 September 2024. https://www.france24.com/en/live-news/20230525-turkey-kicks-off-syria-housing-project-for-refugee-returns.

41 Hadia Al Mansour, "The Devastating Domino Effect of Turkey's Currency Crisis on Northwest Syria," *The New Arab*, 26 May 2023. Accessed 27 September 2024. https://www.newarab.com/features/turkeys-currency-crisis-having-domino-effect-nw-syria.

42 In August 2023, the Turkish government proposed a new 'single governor administrative system' to manage its 'safe zones', intending to replace the existing mechanism. At the time of writing, this plan has not yet been implemented. See Al Tareek, "Turkey to Appoint Single Governor for 'Safe Zones' in Syria," 23 August 2023. Accessed 27 September 2024. https://syrianobserver.com/news/84700/turkey-to-appoint-single-governor-for-safe-zones-in-syria.html.

43 Rauf Baker, "Turkish Imperialism: When Will Turkey Annex Northern Syria?" *Middle East Quarterly*, 28(4) (2021). Accessed 28 September 2024. https://www.meforum.org/62607/when-will-turkey-annex-northern-syria.

shooting down of a Russian military plane.[44] More recently, however, mutual understanding and direct coordination between the two countries have developed, even if this does not fully explain the broader complexities of their relationship. At the same time, Ankara seeks to maintain strong ties with Western powers. These efforts can be understood as forms of "geopolitical rentierism",[45] whereby Turkey exploits its geographical advantage, playing major powers against each other to enhance its influence and capitalise on its unique geostrategic location.

Overall, Syria and Northern Iraq are of considerable importance to Turkey's geopolitical strategy and spatial military interests, serving what it asserts is a stabilising function. While Turkey claims its objective in these areas is to mitigate conflict and eliminate threats to its security, the systematic pursuit of complete military control raises concerns about potential annexation in the long term.[46]

4 Geopolitics of Extraterritoriality, Jurisdiction, and International Law

International law aims to respond to such geostrategic military agendas by pronouncing the illegality of interventions.[47] However, it must be emphasised that an international court decision to that effect would fall short of addressing the intricate and multifaceted implications embedded within the broader political and strategic interests motivating a state's actions. For instance, the International Court of Justice (ICJ) has long faced criticism as having for its limited influence and capacity to control state behaviour, largely due to its consent-based and arguably flawed jurisdictional architecture – this despite possessing the broadest jurisdictional reach of any international court.[48] Substantial evidence suggests that states are increasingly hesitant to consent *ex ante* to the adjudication of conflicts by the ICJ, particularly where significant political issues are involved.[49] Notably, only slightly over one-third (74 out of 193) of UN member states have submitted an optional

44 Doug Bandow, "Turkey Downs Russian Plane, Shows Is No Friend of West," *Policy Commons*, 30 November 2015. Accessed 28 September 2024. https://policycommons.net/artifacts/1307658/turkey-downs-russian-plane-shows-is-no-friend-of-west/1910949/.

45 Clemens Hoffmann and Can Cemgil, "The (Un)Making of the Pax Turca in the Middle East: Understanding the Social-Historical Roots of Foreign Policy," *Cambridge Review of International Affairs* 29(4) (2016): 1279–1302.

46 Ryan Bohl, "A Final Term for Turkey's Erdoğan in the Age of Annexation," *Stratfor*, 8 June 2023. Accessed 27 September 2024. https://worldview.stratfor.com/article/final-term-turkeys-erdogan-age-annexation.

47 Alexander Orakhelashvili, "International Law and Geopolitics: One Object, Conflicting Legitimacies?" *Netherlands Yearbook of International Law* 39 (2008): 155–204.

48 Karen Alter, "The International Court of Justice in Comparison: Understanding the Court's Limited Influence," *Melbourne Journal of International Law* 21(3) (2021): 676, 687.

49 Onuma Yasuaki, "Is the International Court of Justice an Emperor without Clothes?" *International Legal Theory* 8(1) (2002): 1, 2.

declaration under Article 36(2) of the ICJ Statute, recognising the Court's compulsory jurisdiction.[50] The activation of the ICJ's consent-based jurisdiction is further complicated by the Court's own approach, wherein it has asserted jurisdiction even in cases lacking explicit textual delegation.[51] This ambiguity is widely perceived as posing significant risks of non-compliance with ICJ decisions.[52]

Beyond procedural jurisdictional issues, it can nonetheless be argued that fundamental international legal norms – such as the principles of sovereign equality, non-intervention, and self-determination – offer significant avenues for international law to address complex geopolitical agendas, such as Turkey's. Sovereign equality, a foundational principle of international law, entails that all states possess inherent rights of full sovereignty, including the inviolability of their territorial integrity and political independence.[53] The International Court of Justice, for its part, has upheld this principle by applying the *Lotus* doctrine in several cases, including the *Nicaragua* case, stating that "respect for territorial sovereignty is an essential foundation of international relations" and that "international law requires political integrity to also be respected".[54]

While there is a scholarly consensus regarding acts likely to infringe a state's sovereignty (and the relatively low threshold for attribution),[55] a cur-

50 "Declarations Recognizing the Jurisdiction of the Court as Compulsory," *ICJ*, https://www.icj-cij.org/en/declarations.

51 *Maritime Delimitation and Territorial Questions between Qatar and Bahrain (Qatar v Bahrain)*, Jurisdiction and Admissibility, [1994] ICJ Reports, 112.

52 Scholars who contested this assertion can be categorised into two groups: The first group argues that the decisions of the ICJ have achieved substantial, albeit imperfect, compliance (see Aloysius Llamzon, "Jurisdiction and Compliance in Recent Decisions of the International Court of Justice," *European Journal of International Law* 18(5) (2007): 815–852). The second group, at a more general level, notes that compliance is an inadequate metric for assessing the influence of international institutions (see Jana von Stein, "The Engines of Compliance," in *Interdisciplinary Perspectives on International Law and International Relations: The State of the Art*, eds. Jeffrey L. Dunoff and Mark A. Pollack (Cambridge: Cambridge University Press, 2013), 477–502 and Robert Howse and Ruti Teitel, "Beyond Compliance: Rethinking Why International Law Really Matters," *Global Policy* 1(2) (2010): 127–136.

53 Article 2(1) of the UN Charter and the Declaration on Principles of International Law concerning Friendly Relations and Cooperation among States in accordance with the UN Charter, UNGA Res 2625 (XXV), 24 October 1970, 124.

54 *Military and Paramilitary Activities in and against Nicaragua (Nicaragua v United States of America)*, Merits, [1986] ICJ, para. 202; *Corfu Channel Case (United Kingdom v Albania)*, Merits, [1949] ICJ, para. 35.

55 Examples include sending State officials into foreign territory in contravention of immigration policy (Michael Akehurst, "Jurisdiction in International Law," *British Year Book of International Law* 45 (1972): 145–150) and to conduct clandestine operations (Robert Jennings and Arthur Watts, *Oppenheim's International Law*, vol. 1 (Oxford: Oxford University Press, 1996), paras. 117, 382).

sory review reveals that the ICJ imposes a high threshold of attribution[56] and strict standards of evidence[57] to hold states accountable for wrongful acts – namely, requiring 'effective control' by the intervening state over the offending conduct. Although these standards did not prevent the ICJ from declaring certain US actions illegal in the *Nicaragua* case, it is clear that they are unlikely to be met in cases such as Turkey's extraterritorial use of force in Northern Iraq and Syria. Additionally, ruling on the illegality of such interventions risks opening a Pandora's box on the international stage.

The principles of non-intervention and self-determination are arguably even more relevant in this context than territorial sovereignty. The principle of non-intervention is designed to safeguard a state's "inalienable right to choose its political, economic, social and cultural systems, without interference in any form by another State".[58] This inalienable right is equally protected under the principle of self-determination, which ensures that all peoples have the right to "freely determine their political status and freely pursue their economic, social and cultural development".[59] Conceptually, the two principles share common ground, as evidenced by the *travaux préparatoires* of the Friendly Relations Declaration.[60]

At the intersection of these two principles – and central to their violation – lies external coercion by the intervening state. As the ICJ has consistently held, coercion "defines, and indeed forms the very essence of, prohibited intervention".[61] Yet the ICJ case law does not encompass all forms of coercion, focusing instead on limited instances of direct (military action) and indirect (support for armed activities) use of force. Similarly, the International Law Commission established an exceptionally high threshold for coercion under Article 18 of the Draft Articles on State Responsibility for Internationally Wrongful Acts (ARSIWA):

> Nothing less than conduct which forces the will of the coerced State will suffice, giving it no effective choice but to comply with the wishes of the coercing State. It is not sufficient that compliance with the obligation is made more difficult or onerous.[62]

56 In addition to the *Nicaragua* case, paras. 61–62; see also *Application of the Genocide Convention (Bosnia v Serbia)*, [2007] ICJ, paras. 393–395.

57 *Case Concerning the Armed Activities on the Territory of the Congo (Democratic Republic of the Congo v Uganda)*, Judgment, [2005] ICJ, paras. 168 et seq.

58 UNGA, *The Friendly Relations Declaration*, *supra* footnote 53.

59 Common Article 1 of the International Covenant on Civil and Political Rights (ICCPR) and the International Covenant on Economic, Social and Cultural Rights (ICESCR).

60 Report of the Special Committee on Principles of International Law concerning Friendly Relations and Co-operation among States, Rapporteur: W. Riphagen (Netherlands), 27 June 1966, UN Doc A/6230, para. 480.

61 *Nicaragua* case, para. 205.

62 See Article 18 (on 'Coercion of another State') of the 'Draft Articles on Responsibility of States for Internationally Wrongful Acts: Text,' in International Law Commission, *Draft Articles on Responsibility of States for Internationally Wrongful Acts*, Supplement No. 10 (A/56/10), chp. IV.E.1, November 2001.

Considering Turkey's extraterritorial use of force in Syria, executed through a seemingly bilateral approach and alternatively justified under the self-defence provision of Article 51 of the UN Charter, the potential added value of any judicial pronouncement in this specific case appears minimal, if not altogether uncertain. Moreover, while these principles underscore the importance of respecting the core tenets of international law, the complex and ever-changing nature of geopolitics introduces a degree of flexibility that allows states to navigate – and at times deviate from – these legal constraints. This flexibility becomes particularly evident in circumstances where states perceive a pressing need to secure their geopolitical interests, leading them to prioritise strategic and military concerns over strict adherence to international law.

5 Human Rights Implications of Turkey's Exercise of Extraterritoriality

Geopolitics, driven by state interests, power dynamics, and strategic considerations, can frequently clash with the principles of human rights. States often prioritise their geopolitical agendas, leading to instances where human rights are compromised in the pursuit of perceived national interests. The tension arises when the principles of sovereignty and non-interference similarly conflict with the imperative to uphold the rights and dignity of individuals, especially in regions marked by political instability or conflict.

The 1974 Turkish invasion of Cyprus has become a characteristic case due to the alleged flagrant and widespread violations of human rights that were brought before the Strasbourg bodies, in particular, the European Court of Human Rights (ECtHR). A central theme in these cases has understandably been the extraterritorial obligations of Turkey and the corresponding extraterritorial reach of the European Convention on Human Rights (ECHR). The ECtHR developed and deployed its earlier jurisdictional model (the effective control over territory) in this line of cases. A particularly important case is *Loizidou v Turkey*, in which a Cypriot citizen complained that her property rights had been breached as a result of Turkey's control over Northern Cyprus, which prevented her from accessing her home and other properties.[63] In *Loizidou*, the ECtHR highlighted that

> the concept of jurisdiction under Article 1 ECHR is not restricted to the national territory of the Contracting States. Accordingly the responsibility of Contracting States . . . could arise when as a consequence of military action – whether lawful or unlawful – it exercises effective control of an area outside its national territory.[64]

63 *Loizidou v Turkey*, Application No. 15318/89, ECtHR Judgment, 18 December 1996.
64 *Ibid.*, para. 52.

This 'effective control test' was reaffirmed in *Cyprus v Turkey*, a rare inter-state application brought by the government of Cyprus alleging numerous violations under the ECHR arising from Turkey's occupation of Northern Cyprus.[65] By referencing the earlier *Loizidou* case, the ECtHR Grand Chamber ruled that "having effective overall control over northern Cyprus", Turkey had responsibility not only for "to the acts of its own soldiers or officials in northern Cyprus but also . . . by virtue of the acts of the local administration which survives by virtue of Turkish military and other support".[66] The Grand Chamber eventually concluded that Greek Cypriots in northern Cyprus *en masse* were subjected to widespread violations of fundamental human rights under the ECHR.

On its face, these cases provide clear evidence of how Turkey's geopolitical agenda and conduct, justified under the guise of projecting and safeguarding national power, challenge its international legal obligations.

Another interesting case that sits at the intersection of extraterritorial jurisdiction, Turkish geopolitical thinking, and the protection of human rights is *Öcalan v Turkey* by the ECtHR.[67] Since the 1980s, the PKK, under the leadership of Abdullah Öcalan, has been responsible for numerous armed attacks that have resulted in tens of thousands of casualties in Turkey.[68] Following his expulsion from Syria in 1998, Öcalan sought refuge in Kenya, initially finding shelter at the Greek embassy with the assistance of Greek diplomats. Subsequently, the Kenyan government demanded Öcalan's departure from the country, leading to his apprehension by Turkish security officers at Nairobi airport. Öcalan was then arrested, flown to Turkey, and subsequently tried and convicted. In response to his extradition, Öcalan submitted an application to the ECtHR, contending that Turkey's actions were severely flawed, resembling kidnapping. Additionally, he alleged that his treatment by Turkish security officials during the plane journey back to Turkey amounted to cruel, inhuman, and degrading treatment.

In the *Öcalan* case, although the ECtHR Grand Chamber ultimately concluded that Öcalan's abduction and treatment during the plane journey from Kenya to Turkey did not violate the ECtHR, the Court asserted its jurisdiction over these matters. It acknowledged jurisdiction despite the involvement of Turkish security officials abroad and in a context where Turkey lacked effective control over any part of Kenyan territory. The Grand Chamber's key assertion was based on the notion that, immediately after being transferred

65 *Cyprus v Turkey*, Application No. 25781/94, ECtHR Judgment, 10 May 2001.

66 *Ibid.*, para. 77.

67 *Öcalan v Turkey*, Application No. 46221/99, App No 46221/99, ECtHR [GC] Judgment, 12 May 2005, paras. 13–60.

68 A Turkish Parliament report in 2013 found that the PKK conflict in Turkey is commonly estimated to have killed 35,576 people. See Turkish Parliament's Human Rights Inquiry Committee, *Report on the Violations of the Right to Life in Terror and Violence Activities* (Ankara: Turkish Parliament, 2013), 78.

to Turkish officials by Kenyan authorities and at the moment of his arrest, Öcalan fell under the effective authority of Turkey. Therefore, he was deemed within the 'jurisdiction' of Turkey according to Article 1 of the ECHR, even though Turkey exercised its authority outside its own territory.

The *Öcalan* case is among the initial cases in which the ECtHR invoked its other jurisdictional test: control over individuals, which is largely based on active nationality. Put simply, as first established in *M. v Denmark,*[69] the ECtHR held that a state exercises jurisdiction over a specific individual or population under its control, including, first and foremost, its state agents. On the surface, *Öcalan* seemed to suggest a more expansive interpretation and broader reach of the ECHR, implying the possibility of establishing jurisdiction whenever a state exercises effective control over a person beyond its borders. However, the ECtHR Grand Chamber later rejected this argument in the *Banković* case, which introduced a 'grey zone' in delineating the circumstances that would activate states' obligations to uphold human rights protections under the ECHR concerning extraterritorial activities.[70]

Nevertheless, as is evident from the *Öcalan* case, the ECtHR has largely neglected to address the numerous human rights violations that could have resulted from the extrajudicial abduction of Öcalan. Put bluntly, while the ECtHR, in a series of cases arising out of Turkey's Kurdish issue, found Turkey violating core rights under the ECHR,[71] the cross-border legal implications of Turkey's handling of the Kurdish people and the corresponding extraterritorial human rights obligations of Turkey have largely gone unaddressed. To give a salient example, in the case of *Issa v Turkey*, which concerns the alleged extrajudicial killings of Iraqi Kurds by Turkish security forces in Northern Iraq,[72] the ECtHR seems to have contributed to the conflation in the evaluative activity of interpreting jurisdiction against the backdrop of the concepts of power and control. In particular, the Court limited its decision to the available evidence, focusing instead on particular actions and omissions

69 The case concerns the removal of an East German citizen from the premises of the Danish embassy in East Berlin in 1988. See *M v Denmark*, Application No. 17392/90, ECtHR Judgment, 14 October 1992.

70 Kerem Altiparmak, "Bankovic: An Obstacle to the Application of the European Convention on Human Rights in Iraq?" *Journal of Conflict and Security Law* 9(2) (2004): 213–251.

71 The ECtHR cases concerning the actions of the Turkish security forces are bundled into four groups of cases: Aksoy group of cases (287 cases), Batı group of cases (117), Erdoğan and Kasa group of cases (30). Also relevant is the Ataman group of cases (46 cases) that involve excessive force used during public demonstrations, most of which also concerned the issue of ineffectiveness of investigations under Articles 2, 3, and 13 of the ECHR. See Interim Resolution CM/ResDH (2008) 69, Committee of Ministers, Council of Europe, 18 September 2008.

72 *Issa and Others v Turkey*, Application No. 31821/96, ECtHR Judgment, 16 November 2004. For a jurisdictional analysis on the Issa case, see Tarik Abdel-Monem, "The Long Arm of the European Convention on Human Rights and the Recent Development of Issa v Turkey," *Human Rights Brief* 12(2) (2005): 9–11.

of the Turkish state agents only to the extent that these are backed up by the evidence provided (Turkish state power *over* its state forces rather than Turkish power *to* carry out its own authority and/or control – borrowing from Pamela Pansardi's concepts of 'power-to' and 'power-over').[73] Consequently, the Court found that it is not satisfied that the case falls within Turkish jurisdiction for the purposes of Article 1 ECHR.

However, a more principled approach would involve assessing the capacity of the Turkish state to influence specific outcomes, considering its authority and control. Regrettably, the ECtHR, in its jurisprudence, has traditionally approached jurisdiction through a narrow lens, primarily focusing on the concept of 'power-over'.[74]

Turning back to the case of *Öcalan*, the Court, in line with its conventionally narrow approach, failed to address crucial questions regarding how the power of potential duty bearers (*i.e.*, Turkish state agents) shapes their relationship with right holders (*i.e.*, individuals within its jurisdiction, or more generally, under its 'power' in the Weberian sense).[75] It also failed to explore the impact of state institutions (*i.e.*, Turkish authorities such as the military and potentially domestic courts in the cases of human rights and laws-of-war violations) on the lives and interests of individuals. A comprehensive analysis, therefore, should involve delving into the dynamics of power and control, elucidating the influence of state actors on the relationship between duty bearers and right holders.

Understanding the mechanisms through which institutions shape the actions and omissions of individuals within a territory is crucial for a nuanced assessment of jurisdiction. In light of these considerations, a more robust examination of the broader context of state power and its impact on human lives and interests is essential for a principled application of jurisdiction under Article 1 of the ECHR. By broadening the focus to encompass the power of the state to bring about specific outcomes, the ECtHR could contribute to a more comprehensive understanding of jurisdiction at the crossroads of power projection and enhance the effectiveness of its role in upholding human rights standards.[76]

73 Pamela Pansardi, "Power to and Power Over: Two Distinct Concepts of Power?" *Journal of Political Power* 5(1) (2012): 73, 74–77.

74 For a detailed analysis on the ECtHR's approach to jurisdiction, see Lea Raible, *Human Rights Unbound: A Theory of Extraterritoriality* (Oxford: Oxford University Press, 2020), 41–72.

75 Max Weber defines this type of *social* power as "the probability that one actor within a social relationship will be in a position to carry out his own will despite resistance, regardless of the basis on which this probability rests". See Max Weber, "Power, Domination and Legitimacy," in *Power in Modern Societies*, eds. Terhi Rantanen, Margaret Olsen and Carolina Fonseca (London: Routledge, 2019), 37–47.

76 For a similar, yet more developed, account on how the ECtHR should improve its approach to jurisdiction, see Raible, *A Theory of Extraterritoriality*, 74–101.

In this context, several pending cases originating from Turkey present a crucial opportunity for the ECtHR to refine its jurisprudence in this field. Although viewed through a different lens, these cases are similar to the *Öcalan* case and concern extraterritorial renditions and state-sponsored abductions of Turkish citizens, most of whom are alleged members of the Gülen Movement.[77] In two noteworthy cases that give rise to similar issues, namely *Senturk v Azerbaijan*,[78] and *Özdil v Turkey*,[79] the ECtHR found that the detention and rendition of Turkish citizens violated their core rights, including Article 3 of the ECHR (due to a denial of effective guarantees against arbitrary *refoulement*), Article 5 (due to unlawful detention as part of an extra-legal transfer), and Article 8 (due to the impact on the right to respect for privacy in expulsion cases). It is essential to note that these countries are parties to the ECHR, and the applicability of the Convention in their territories is undisputed.

The ECtHR is currently reviewing another case involving the detention and extra-legal transfer of six Turkish citizens from Kosovo to Turkey.[80] Despite Kosovo not being a state party to the ECHR, this case is almost identical to the *Ozdil* and *Senturk* cases. In the *Ozdil* case, for example, the Court determined that meticulous planning and swift execution, including the transfer of individuals to Turkey on a chartered plane, indicated a premeditated plan to catch them completely off guard.[81] The ECtHR viewed this strategic approach as an effort to prevent the individuals from making use of available legal mechanisms, which would minimise if not completely remove, the potential for any attempt to impede or thwart their extradition to Turkey. It was this 'element of bad faith or deception' on the part of Turkish state authorities that led the ECtHR to conclude that the transfer of detainees from Moldova to Turkey "circumvented all guarantees offered to them by domestic and international law".[82]

The Kosovan abduction case unfolded in an almost identical manner to the *Ozdil* case, involving individuals brought back to Turkey via a private jet, with the Kosovan intelligence agency being aware of Turkey's rendition

77 For a proper analysis on these extraterritorial abductions, see Yasir Gökçe, "The Legality of the Extraterritorial Abductions by the Erdoğan Regime under International Law," *Blog of the Berkeley Journal of International Law*, 28 October 2018. Accessed 27 September 2024. https://www.berkeleyjournalofinternationallaw.com/post/the-legality-of-the-extraterritorial-abductions-by-the-erdogan-regime-under-international-law.

78 *Senturk and Others v Azerbaijan*, Application No 41326/17, ECtHR Judgment, 10 March 2022.

79 *Ozdil and Others v Moldova*, Application No 42305/18, ECtHR Judgment, 11 June 2019, paras. 54–55.

80 Stockholm Centre for Freedom, "International Human Rights Bodies Slam Abduction of 6 Turkish Nationals in Kosovo," 31 March 2018. Accessed 28 September 2024. https://stockholmcf.org/intl-human-rights-bodies-slam-abduction-of-6-turkish-nationals-in-kosovo/.

81 *Ozdil and Others v Moldova*, paras. 54–55.

82 *Ibid.*, para. 57.

plans.[83] These abductions triggered a governmental crisis, resulting in the dismissal of the Minister of Internal Affairs and the Intelligence Chief.[84] In the application lodged by these individuals, the UN Working Group on Arbitrary Detention (UN WGAD) found Turkey responsible for their arrest, detention, abduction, and deportation, which circumvented the guarantees offered by multiple provisions under the ICCPR – to which Turkey is a state party – while also highlighting the responsibility of Kosovo under the Universal Declaration of Human Rights (as Kosovo is not a state party to the ICCPR).[85]

There is certainly a strong case to be made that the ECtHR should apply its *Ozdil* approach to the Kosovan abduction case while also drawing inspiration from the UN WGAD decision in this case. Such a holistic approach would not only enhance the understanding of jurisdiction, particularly at the intersection of power projection and human rights but also has the potential to strengthen the safeguarding of human rights under the ECHR. This could shed significant light on the complexities surrounding extraterritorial state actions and their implications for human rights.

5 Conclusion

This chapter has aimed to explore the interplay between geopolitics, extraterritoriality, and international law while surveying different facets of Turkey's geopolitical expansionism against its international legal obligations. Turkey's geopolitical stance revolves around strategic alliances and assertive military actions, as exemplified by the 1974 invasion of Cyprus and its recent military interventions in Northern Iraq and Syria. While Turkey frames these actions as responses to security threats, its pursuit of strategic goals with the aim of exerting long-term territorial influence reflects a complex interplay of geopolitics and spatial military interests.

Addressing such geopolitical complexity through international law is a formidable task. While the ICJ may declare such interventions illegal, its limited influence and consent-based jurisdiction, compounded by states' reluctance to submit to its adjudication, hinder its effectiveness. Fundamental international legal norms like sovereign equality, the principle of non-intervention, and self-determination may provide avenues for addressing these issues. However, the

83 For the facts of the case, see UN WGAD, Opinion No. 47/2020 concerning Kahraman Demirez, Mustafa Erdem, Hasan Hüseyin Günakan, Yusuf Karabina, Osman Karakaya and Cihan Özkan (Turkey and Kosovo), 25 September 2020.

84 The Ombudsperson Institution of Kosovo, *Annual Report in 2018*. Accessed 28 September 2024. https://www.theioi.org/downloads/cvjtu/Kosovo_OM_Annual%20Report_2018_EN.pdf.

85 The UNWGAD found Kosovo and Turkey in contravention of Articles 2, 3, 8, 9, 10, and 19 of the Universal Declaration of Human Rights. Moreover, it found Turkey's state conduct is arbitrary under Articles 2 (1) and (3), 9, 14, 19, and 26 of the ICCPR. Commonly, these violations fell within categories I, II, III and V. See UN WGAD, Opinion No. 47/2020, para. 83.

high threshold of attribution and stringent evidentiary standards required by the ICJ makes it unlikely to hold states accountable for wrongful acts, particularly in cases like Turkey's extraterritorial use of force in Syria.

The principles of non-intervention and self-determination, though crucial, are often inadequate in dealing with the complex and evolving nature of geopolitics, where states may prioritise strategic and military concerns over strict adherence to international law. The exercise of extraterritoriality by Turkey presents additional challenges at the intersection of geopolitics and human rights.

The ECtHR has grappled with cases involving alleged human rights violations resulting from Turkey's actions beyond its borders. While the Court applied clear jurisdictional tests, including effective control over territory and individuals, its narrow focus on the concept of jurisdiction ('power-over' rather than 'power-to') has limited its ability to examine broader dynamics. A more comprehensive understanding of jurisdiction, encompassing the state's power to influence outcomes, could enhance the ECtHR's role in upholding human rights standards within the complex landscape of extraterritorial state actions.

Overall, as the Turkish case clearly shows, states are constantly navigating between their international legal obligations (which seek to impose constraints) and their geopolitical interests (which drive their foreign policy decisions). In essence, while international law attempts to set limits on the geopolitical agenda, the inherent leeway for geopolitical considerations remains a fundamental aspect, with state interests serving as the primary explanatory factor in the complex tapestry of international relations.

References

Al Mansour, Hadia. "The Devastating Domino Effect of Turkey's Currency Crisis on Northwest Syria." *The New Arab*, 26 May 2023. Accessed 20 September 2024. https://www.newarab.com/features/turkeys-currency-crisis-having-domino-effect-nw-syria.

Alpan, Basak, and Ahmet Öztürk. "Turkish Foreign Policy in the Balkans amidst 'Soft Power' and 'De-Europeanisation'." *Southeast European and Black Sea Studies* 22(1) (2022): 45–63.

Armijo, Leslie, and Cynthia Roberts. "The Emerging Powers and Global Governance: Why the BRICS Matter." In *Handbook of Emerging Economies*, edited by Robert E. Looney. London: Routledge, 2014.

Aydin, Mustafa. "Determinants of Turkish Foreign Policy: Changing Patterns and Conjunctures during the Cold War." *Middle Eastern Studies* 36(1) (2000): 103–139.

Bagheri, Saeed. "Turkey's Extraterritorial Use of Force against Armed Non-State Actors." *Israel Law Review* 56(2) (2023): 143–170.

Baker, Rauf. "Turkish Imperialism: When Will Turkey Annex Northern Syria?" *Middle East Quarterly* 28(4) (2021). Accessed 20 September 2024. https://www.meforum.org/62607/when-will-turkey-annex-northern-syria.

Bandow, Doug. "Turkey Downs Russian Plane, Shows It Is No Friend of the West." *Policy Commons*, 30 November 2015. Accessed 20 September 2024. https://policycommons.net/artifacts/1307658/turkey-downs-russian-plane-shows-is-no-friend-of-west/1910949/

Bryant, Rebecca, and Mete Hatay. *Sovereignty Suspended: Building the So-Called State*. Philadelphia: University of Pennsylvania Press, 2020.

Byers, Michael. *Custom, Power and the Power of Rules: International Relations and Customary International Law*. Cambridge: Cambridge University Press, 1999.

Çalışkan, Koray. "Toward a New Political Regime in Turkey: From Competitive Toward Full Authoritarianism." *New Perspectives on Turkey* 58 (2018): 5–33.

Deringil, Selim. *Turkish Foreign Policy during the Second World War: An 'Active' Neutrality*. Cambridge: Cambridge University Press, 2004.

European Court of Human Rights (ECtHR). *Loizidou v Turkey*, App No 15318/89, 18 December 1996.

Fels, Enrico. "Power Shift? Power in International Relations and the Allegiance of Middle Powers." In *Power in the 21st Century: International Security and International Political Economy in a Changing World*, edited by Enrico Fels, Jan-Frederik Kremer, and Katharina Kronenberg. Berlin: Springer, 2012.

Hast, Susanna. *Spheres of Influence in International Relations: History, Theory and Politics*. London: Routledge, 2016.

Hurrell, Andrew. "Beyond the BRICS: Power, Pluralism, and the Future of Global Order." *Ethics & International Affairs* 32(1) (2018): 89–101.

International Court of Justice (ICJ). *Case Concerning Military and Paramilitary Activities in and against Nicaragua (Nicaragua v United States of America)*, Merits, 27 June 1986.

Jennings, Robert Y., and Arthur Watts. *Oppenheim's International Law*, Vol. 1. Oxford: Oxford University Press, 1996.

Müftüler-Bac, Meltem, and Aylin Güney. "The European Union and the Cyprus Problem 1961–2003." *Middle Eastern Studies* 41(2) (2005): 281–293.

Öniş, Ziya, and Mustafa Kutlay. "Rising Powers in a Changing Global Order: The Political Economy of Turkey in the Age of BRICS." *Third World Quarterly* 38(4) (2013): 1409–1426.

Özpek, Burak, and Nebahat Yaşar. "Populism and Foreign Policy in Turkey under the AKP Rule." In *Islamism, Populism, and Turkish Foreign Policy*, edited by Burak Bilgehan Özpek and Bill Park. Routledge, 2020.

Pierini, Marc. "Turkey's Geopolitical Role: Between National Ambitions, Western Anchors and Russian Sway." *IEMed: Mediterranean Yearbook* (2023): 124–130.

Raible, Lea. *Human Rights Unbound: A Theory of Extraterritoriality*. Oxford: Oxford University Press, 2020.

Soyaltin-Colell, Digdem, and Tolga Demiryol. "Unusual Middle Power Activism and Regime Survival: Turkey's Drone Warfare and Its Regime-Boosting Effects." *Third World Quarterly* 44(4) (2023): 724–743.

Turkut, Emre, and Sabina Garahan. "The 'Reasonable Suspicion' Test of Turkey's Post-coup Emergency Rule under the European Convention on Human Rights." *Netherlands Quarterly of Human Rights* 38(4) (2020): 264–282.

UN WGAD. Opinion No. 47/2020 concerning Kahraman Demirez, Mustafa Erdem, Hasan Hüseyin Günakan, Yusuf Karabina, Osman Karakaya, and Cihan Özkan (Turkey and Kosovo), 25 September 2020.

Yavuz, M. Hakan. *Nostalgia for the Empire: The Politics of Neo-Ottomanism*. Oxford: Oxford University Press, 2020.

Zihnioglu, Ozge. "The Limits of Civil Society Geopolitics in Turkey." In *Global Civil Society in a Geopolitical Age: How Civic Activism Is Being Reshaped by Great Power Competition*, edited by Richard Youngs. Washington, DC: Carnegie Endowment for International Peace, 2022.

6 Bridging Concepts

Iran's Approach to Extraterritorial Jurisdiction Within the Framework of the Non-Intervention Principle

Pouria Askary and Hassan Vakilian

1 Introduction

Aligned with the Iranian Constitution, the Islamic Republic of Iran is committed to refraining from any form of intervention in other nations' internal affairs. Iran interprets this commitment as a cornerstone of international law, which generally prohibits most forms of intervention in other states' sovereignty. With this understanding of sovereignty and political independence, Iran perceives that the majority of current forms of application of extraterritorial jurisdiction fundamentally contradict the principle of non-intervention. As a result, extraterritorial jurisdiction is scarcely reflected in Iranian laws and regulations, with exceptions for criminal cases as stipulated in Articles 5–8 of the Islamic Penal Code. Furthermore, as an emerging power in the Islamic world, the Constitution mandates the Islamic Republic to lay the groundwork for the continuation of the Islamic Revolution both domestically and internationally. In line with this mandate, since 1979, Iran has played a pivotal role in supporting Shia uprisings across the Middle East, championing the struggles of the oppressed against the oppressors.[1] This political strategy, in certain instances, has resulted in conflicts with the West, primarily the United States of America (US). Consequently, for nearly the past four decades, Iran has consistently been under the US sanctions regime.

This chapter first delves into the relationship between the principle of non-intervention and the application of extraterritorial jurisdiction. Following a study of the Constitution and other laws and regulations in Iran, it then discusses Iran's practical approach towards the legality of extraterritorial application of national laws and jurisdiction and its limitations due to the principle of non-intervention.

1 See the discussion later on about the Constitution of the Islamic Republic of Iran.

DOI: 10.4324/9781003402978-7

2 Extraterritorial Jurisdiction and the Principle of Non-Intervention

Extraterritorial jurisdiction empowers states to unilaterally regulate persons, conduct, or property beyond their borders.[2] While jurisdiction, in essence, is governed by domestic law, the application of one state's jurisdiction outside its territory must be governed by the rules and principles of international law. This is because when a state exercises extraterritorial jurisdiction, it is essentially asserting its sovereignty in another sovereign's territory. As Cedric Ryngaert highlights, sovereignty is inherently tied to territory, making territoriality the fundamental principle of jurisdictional law in the current international legal order.[3]

Having said that, it is important to distinguish between prescriptive jurisdiction and enforcement jurisdiction. The Permanent Court of International Justice (PCIJ), in the renowned 1927 *Lotus* case, adopted a permissive approach to prescriptive jurisdiction but emphasised that the enforcement of extraterritorial jurisdiction is not permissible.[4] According to the Court:

> Now the first and foremost restriction imposed by international law upon a State is that – failing the existence of a permissive rule to the contrary – it may not exercise its power in any form in the territory of another State. In this sense, jurisdiction is certainly territorial; it cannot be exercised by a State outside its territory except by virtue of a permissive rule derived from international custom or from a convention.[5]

It is worth noting that even in 1927, the 12 judges of the Court were evenly split, and the case was ultimately decided by the President of the PCIJ's casting vote. Nearly a century has passed since the Court's ruling, yet the division among states and lawyers on the issue of extraterritorial jurisdiction remains, and the ambiguity surrounding restrictions on its application has yet to be resolved. This may explain why all attempts to reach an international agreement have failed.

2 Omri Sender and Michael Wood, "Extraterritorial Jurisdiction and the Limits of Customary International Law," in *Research Handbook on Extraterritoriality in International Law*, eds. Austen Parrish and Cedric Ryngaert (Cheltenham: Edward Elgar Publishing, 2023), 31.

3 Cedric Ryngaert, "International Jurisdiction Law," in *Research Handbook on Extraterritoriality in International Law*, eds. Austen Parrish and Cedric Ryngaert (Cheltenham: Edward Elgar Publishing, 2023), 13.

4 *SS Lotus* (*France v Turkey*), Judgment, [1927] PCIJ Rep Series A, No. 10, 19: "Far from laying down a general prohibition to the effect that States may not extend the application of their laws and the jurisdiction of their courts to persons, property and acts outside their territory, it leaves them in this respect a wide measure of discretion which is only limited in certain cases by prohibitive rules".

5 *Ibid.*, 18–19.

In their enlightening article, Omri Sender and Michael Wood provide a comprehensive overview of all governmental and private efforts made since 1925 to codify the rules of international law governing extraterritorial jurisdiction.[6] Interestingly, this issue has faced obstacles from both political and legal perspectives since its inception. As they discuss, following a report prepared by J. L. Brierly and Charles De Visscher, the Committee of Experts of the League of Nations declared that "international regulation of these questions by way of a general convention, although desirable, would encounter grave political and other obstacles".[7] Similarly, after 18 years of work, the *Institut de droit international* admitted defeat.[8] In the concluding debate, Ian Sinclair remarked that "this topic has failed to yield a consensus in any forum in which it has been presented, and that the *Institut* is in this regard no exception".[9] This finding remains relevant today, and as Sender and Wood note, it is likely the reason why the UN International Law Commission (ILC) has not included this issue on its current working agenda.[10]

After examining the failed efforts to codify the rules of international law on extraterritorial jurisdiction, Sender and Wood turn their attention to whether there are any customary international law rules regulating this matter.[11] Wood, who was previously the ILC special rapporteur on identifying customary international law,[12] perfectly knows the sensitivity and division among states on this issue. Therefore, before exploring the existence and content of possible customary rules of international law on extraterritorial jurisdiction, they caution that any study on this matter must be conducted with careful consideration of the principles of sovereign equality of states and territorial sovereignty.[13] In their words:

> Extraterritorial jurisdiction may represent a departure from these underlying principles, and this tension ought to be taken into account. This applies both to claimed rules that contain an obligation to adopt extraterritorial jurisdiction and to permissive rules providing for a right of the State to exercise such jurisdiction if it so chooses.[14]

6 Sender and Wood, "Extraterritorial Jurisdiction," 35–41.

7 James Leslie Brierly, "Criminal Competence of States in Respect of Offences Committed Outside Their Territory," *American Journal of International Law Supp.* 20(S5) (1926): 252.

8 Yearbook of the Institute of International Law, Vol. 69 (2001), Session of Vancouver, Preparatory Work and Deliberations of the Institute 92, 116–117.

9 *Ibid.*, 115.

10 Sender and Wood, "Extraterritorial Jurisdiction," 39. While in 2006 the Commission included the topic on its long-term programme of work, there is no indication that it will take it up any time soon. See YILC (2006) Vol II Part Two, Annex V, para. 34.

11 *Ibid.*, 41–44.

12 See the final outcome of the work of the ILC on identification of customary international law (2018), https://legal.un.org/ilc/texts/instruments/english/draft_articles/1_13_2018.pdf.

13 Sender and Wood, "Extraterritorial Jurisdiction," 41.

14 *Ibid.*

In this regard, it is noteworthy to mention that in a recent UN General Assembly Resolution on the pending issue of democratic and equitable international order, the concern of the states is raised with regard to "continued abuse by Member States of the extraterritorial application of their national legislation in a manner that affects the sovereignty of other States, the legitimate interests of entities or persons under their jurisdiction and the full enjoyment of human rights".[15] This resolution was adopted by 125 votes in favour, 55 against, and eight abstentions.

These kinds of strong statements against the application of extraterritorial jurisdiction make it difficult for legal scholars to conclude that there is an *opinio juris* among states regarding the permissibility of such jurisdiction when it comes to the sovereignty of other states. This is because international law, as it currently stands (*lex lata*), upholds the principle of non-intervention, which does not authorise states to unilaterally apply their national laws to regulate foreigners and their activities in the territory of other states.[16] Austen Parrish provides further insight into this matter:

> [R]ejecting colonial practices, modern international law seeks to recognise even more distinctly the right of States and their citizens to be free from foreign interferences, ... The most aggressive forms of unilateral extraterritorial regulation of non-citizens are disfavoured, if not sometimes prohibited, under public international law precisely because that kind of regulation can interfere with the rights of individuals and the prerogatives of other States, and is the kind of interference likely to lead to conflict.[17]

He goes further and states that "those advocating unilateral extraterritorial approaches should at least recognise that doing so circumvents and undermines existing public international law".[18]

It is important to emphasise that the rules and regulations of international law are designed to govern the contemporary relations between all actors in the international community. They cannot remain unchanged when confronted with the needs of today's international life, which require both states

15 UN Doc. A/RES/75/178, 16 December 2020, preamble, 2.

16 One of the authors of this chapter has recently discussed the way principle of non-intervention is interpreted in the current international legal order, see Pouria Askari, "The Principle of Non-Intervention and the Dilemma of the Legality of the Unilateral Coercive Measures," in *The Routledge Handbook of the Political Economy of Sanctions*, ed. Ksenia Kirkham (London: Routledge, 2023), 318–329.

17 Austen Parrish, "Sovereignty, Self-Determination, and the Duty to Cooperate: Public International Law's Limits on Unilateral Extraterritorial Regulation of Non-Citizens," in *Research Handbook on Extraterritoriality in International Law*, eds. Austen Parrish and Cedric Ryngaert (Cheltenham: Edward Elgar Publishing, 2023), 45.

18 *Ibid.*, 46.

and non-state entities to engage in extraterritorial interactions. These types of interactions are subject to numerous international law instruments that not only endorse them but also ensure their proper application. Furthermore, established principles of human rights law modify the traditional view of international law regarding matters solely within the domain of states. Based on this, no state can justify its mistreatment of individuals under its jurisdiction as a matter of national policy or discretion.[19] However, these developments in various domains of international law do not overshadow the sovereign rights of states, including those attached to the principle of non-intervention, which generally prohibits states from regulating foreigners in foreign states without a genuine connection to the regulating state.[20]

The aforementioned interpretation of how the principle of non-intervention, as a core principle of international law, may limit the application of extraterritorial jurisdiction aligns with the authors' comprehension of Iran's approach towards the application of extraterritorial jurisdiction. The subsequent sections of the chapter will assess this understanding by delving into Iran's legal and operational practices.

3 Extraterritorial Jurisdiction and the Principle of Non-Intervention in Iran's Legal System

As previously stated, the concept of extraterritorial jurisdiction is primarily embodied in Iran's criminal laws. Therefore, this section initially explores this manifestation. Subsequently, it will elucidate the connection between the principle of non-intervention and extraterritorial jurisdiction within Iran's constitutional legal order.

3.1 Manifestation of Extraterritorial Jurisdiction in the Criminal Code of Iran

Within Iran's legal system, as is the case with numerous other legal systems, different forms of extraterritorial jurisdiction in criminal law are articulated. These include the principles of active personality, protective, and passive personality, which are outlined in Chapter 2 of the first section of the Criminal Code (Articles 3–9). As observed by one author, the principle of passive personality has been gradually acknowledged by many Asian countries.[21] Iran

19 For further reading, see Yoram Dinstein, "The *Erga Omnes* Applicability of Human Rights," *Archiv des Völkerrechts* 30(1) (1992): 16–21.

20 Ian Brownlie, *Principles of Public International Law* (Oxford: Oxford University Press, 4th ed., 1990).

21 Mari Takeuchi, "Asian Experience with Extraterritoriality," in *Research Handbook on Extraterritoriality in International Law*, eds. Austen Parrish and Cedric Ryngaert (Cheltenham: Edward Elgar Publishing, 2023), 165–166.

is also recognised as one of the countries that have recently integrated this principle into its Criminal Code.

The territoriality principle is stated in Chapter 2, Article 3 of the Criminal Code: "Iran's criminal laws shall apply to all persons who commit a crime within the territorial, maritime, and airspace jurisdiction of the Islamic Republic of Iran". Also, according to Article 4, "whenever part of an offence or its result occurred inside Iranian territory, the offence shall be deemed as having been committed inside the Islamic Republic of Iran".

Obviously, according to these provisions, which reflect the territorial principle, Iranian courts have jurisdiction to address such crimes, whether significant or insignificant, and whether committed by Iranian nationals or foreign nationals. Article 5 extends the jurisdiction of Iranian criminal courts beyond national borders. This expansion aims to protect the country from crimes that may jeopardise its vital interests. According to this Article:

> [A]ny Iranian or non-Iranian person who commits one of the following offences, or offences which are prescribed in specific laws, *outside Iran's jurisdiction*, shall be tried and punished in accordance with the laws of the Islamic Republic of Iran, . . .
>
> a. Acting against the regime, and the internal and external security, and territorial integrity or independence of the Islamic Republic of Iran.
> b. Forging a stamp, signature, decree, order, or handwriting of the Leader or using them.
> c. Forging the official stamp, signature, decree, order, or handwriting of the President, Head of Judiciary, Speaker and Members of Parliament, Chairperson of Experts Assembly, Head of Supreme Court, Attorney General, Members of Guardian Council, Chairperson and Members of the Expediency Council, any of Ministers or Vice Presidents, or using them.
> d. Forging decisions or writs of judicial authorities or legal bodies, or using them.
> e. Fabricating Iranian current banknotes or bank's biding documents and also forging treasury bills, bonds issued or guaranteed by the government, or fabricating coins and distributing fabricated current domestic coins.

The *raison d'etre* of these provisions is the fact that states typically cannot rely on other states' measures to protect their essential interests. Consequently, they often criminalise such conduct in their national laws, resorting to extraterritorial jurisdiction to protect these crucial interests.

Article 7 of the Iranian Criminal Code embodies the active personality principle. According to this, if an Iranian national perpetrates a crime overseas and is either located in Iran or extradited to Iran, they will be subjected to trial and punishment under the laws of the Islamic Republic of Iran, provided certain conditions are met. A significant condition for the enforcement of this article is that the offender has not been previously tried and acquitted for the same offence. Furthermore, in the event of a trial, the punishment must not have been fully or partially carried out against the individual.

Article 8 of the Iranian Criminal Code, last revised in April 2013, addresses one of the most contentious topics in criminal and international criminal law, namely the passive personality principle. This article stipulates the following:

> [I]f a non-Iranian person commits a crime other than those mentioned in previous articles against an Iranian person or the Iranian State and is found in, or extradited to Iran, his crime shall be dealt with in accordance with the criminal laws of Islamic Republic of Iran, only if:
>
> a. In the case of crimes punishable by *Tazir*,[22] the accused person is not tried and acquitted in the place of commission of the crime, or in the case of conviction, the punishment is not wholly or partially, carried out against him.
> b. In the case of crimes punishable by *Tazir*, the committed conduct is deemed an offence under the law of the Islamic Republic of Iran and the law of the place of the commission.

It is important to highlight that the acknowledgment of the passive personality principle is a novel development. This principle was introduced for the first time in the Iranian Criminal Code of 2013. This article signifies a fresh perspective of the Iranian legislature towards the extraterritorial jurisdiction of national courts based on the nationality of the victims. This concept had never been mentioned in the Iranian Criminal Codes prior to and following the Revolution of 1979. This article stipulates that the perpetrator must necessarily be non-Iranian, the victim must be Iranian, and the crime must have occurred outside the borders of Iran's territory. The provision encompasses all

22 For further reading, see Oxford Reference: *Tazir*. Accessed 29 September 2023. https://www.oxfordreference.com/view/10.1093/oi/authority.20110803102745701. The Iranian Criminal Code, based on Sharia rules, outlines four types of punishments. First, Hadd is a punishment whose degree and type are specified in Sharia. Second, Qisas or retaliation is defined as a punishment for a crime which God has prescribed for murder or bodily harm. Third, Diya is a financial compensation paid to a victim or the heirs of a victim in cases of unintentional murder or bodily harm. Fourth, Tazir is a type of punishment left to the discretion of the judge, and its degree and type are not identified in Sharia. See Mohammad Hashim Kamali, *Crime and Punishment in Islamic Law* (Oxford: Oxford University Press, 2019), 21, 201, 213.

crimes committed against Iranians abroad by non-Iranians.[23] However, in specific types of crimes where their punishments are *Tazirs*, the application of this article is subject to the existence of the conditions mentioned in the last part.

3.2 *Iran's Constitutional Legal Order: The Back-and-forth Between Non-Intervention and Extraterritoriality Concepts*

The initial Constitution of Iran, along with its supplement, was ratified in 1906 and 1907, respectively, following the Iranian Constitutional Revolution.[24] During the 19th century, specifically in the *Qajar* era, Iran found itself caught in the 'Great Game', a policy of geopolitical rivalry between the Russian Empire and the British Empire, both vying for influence over Central Asia. As reflected in *Encyclopedia Iranica*, "Iran's geographical position on the borders of Russia, India, and the Persian Gulf, turned it into a natural target in the political struggle between Russia and Britain".[25] Although Iran was under political pressure of these rival powers, nothing was mentioned in the Constitution about the non-intervention principle. The only provision that implicitly referred to this principle was Article 24. According to it, the National Consultative Assembly must approve the conclusion of treaties, covenants, and the granting of concessions in various sectors such as commerce, industry, and agriculture. This applies to both Persian and foreign subjects, except for treaties that need to be kept secret for the benefit of the state and the public. However, Article 52 of the supplement of the Iranian Constitution ratified in 1907, creates additional responsibility for the King in this respect. In accordance with this Article, the treaties mentioned in Article 24 of the Constitution must be communicated to the National Consultative Assembly and the Senate by the King, with necessary explanations, after the removal of secrecy reasons and if they serve national interests.[26]

Undoubtedly, the two Articles mentioned in the Constitution and its supplement have been influenced by historical events. These include the signing of treaties such as *Golestan* (1813) and *Turkmenchay* (1828) between *Qajar* Iran and the Russian Empire and the granting of detrimental privileges to

23 Hassan Purbaferani, "Foundations and Evolution of Nationality-Based Jurisdiction," *Pajohesh Hoghogh Keifari* 17 (2017): 14.

24 For further reading, see Encyclopedia Iranica. n.d. "Constitutional Revolution," *Iranicaonline.org*. Accessed 29 September 2023. https://www.iranicaonline.org/articles/constitutional-revolution-index.

25 Encyclopedia Iranica, "Russia i. Russo-Iranian Relations up to the Bolshevik Revolution," *Iranicaonline.org*. Accessed 28 December 2023. https://www.iranicaonline.org/articles/russia-i-relations.

26 Article 52: "The treaties which, according to article 24 of the Constitution promulgated on December 30, 1906, must remain secret, shall be communicated by the king, with the necessary explanations, to the National Consultative Assembly and the Senate after the disappearance of the reasons which necessitated such secrecy, as soon as the public interest shall require it".

foreign nations like the Tobacco Concession given by Naser al-Din Shah to the United Kingdom in 1890. The one-sided relations with and interventions by the Russian and British Empires were not confined to the 19th century; they continued into the *Pahlavi* era in the 20th century. For instance, the Anglo-Soviet invasion of Iran in 1941[27] and the *coup d'état* against Prime Minister Mohammad Mussaddiq in 1953,[28] with the involvement of Britain and the United States,[29] had a significant impact on the anti-imperialist tone of the Constitution of 1979. As will be detailed in the subsequent section, these events have resulted in numerous references to the principle of non-intervention in the Constitution of the Islamic Republic.

Unlike the Constitution of 1906–07, the principle of non-intervention is explicitly articulated in the preamble and the body of the 1979 Constitution, which was established following the Islamic Revolution in Iran. The Islamic Revolution of 1979, akin to many other revolutions, encompasses a multitude of objective and subjective factors, both internal and external. However, the emphasis of this chapter is on the impact of the external factor, namely the interference of foreign powers and their influence on Iran's 1979 Revolution. In this regard, as one author posits, "the Shah was seriously compromised by his close and subservient association with the United States; and the American military and economic presence and the presence of a large European workforce acted as a major stimulus to mass mobilisation".[30] There are extensive discussions regarding the role of foreign countries in the advent of the Iranian Islamic Revolution. However, what remains indisputable is that during that period, the Iranian populace viewed the Shah as being reliant on foreigners. This sentiment was so profound that it was echoed in the central slogans of the Iranian people during their demonstrations against the Shah.[31]

One of the most famous slogans of the demonstrators on the eve of the Islamic Revolution of 1979 was 'Independence, Freedom, and the Islamic Republic'. The demands for 'independence' displayed the deep-seated resentment of the Iranian people of the foreign powers' interference in Iran, especially during the *Qajar* dynasty in the 19th century.[32] This concern is reflected in different parts of the 1979 Constitution as the term 'independence' is

27 For further reading, see F. Eshraghi, "Anglo-Soviet Occupation of Iran in August 1941," *Middle Eastern Studies* 20(1) (1984): 27–52.

28 For further reading, see Homa Katouzian, *Musaddiq and the Struggle for Power in Iran* (New York: I.B. Tauris, 1999).

29 For further reading, see Ervand Abrahamian, *Iran between Two Revolutions* (Princeton: Princeton University Press, 1982).

30 Said Amir Arjomand, *The Turban for the Crown, the Islamic Revolution in Iran* (Oxford: Oxford University Press, 1988), 91.

31 Abrahamian, *Iran between Two Revolutions*, 515.

32 See, for example, Sirus Ghani, *Iran and the Rise of Reza Shah: From Qajar Collapse to Pahlavi Rule*, translated by Hassan Kamshad (Tehran: Nilofar Publications, 1998), 414.

repeated 15 times in the Constitution. For instance, in Article 9 it is stated that:

> In the Islamic Republic of Iran, the freedom, *independence*, unity, and territorial integrity of the country are inseparable from one another, and their preservation is the duty of the government and all individual citizens. No individual, group, or authority, has the right to infringe in the slightest way upon the political, cultural, economic, and military *independence* or the territorial integrity of Iran under the pretext of exercising freedom. Similarly, no authority has the right to abrogate legitimate freedoms, not even by enacting laws and regulations for that purpose, under the pretext of preserving the independence and territorial integrity of the country.
>
> (emphasis added)

The principle of non-intervention is more vividly stated in Article 152:

> The foreign policy of the Islamic Republic of Iran is based upon the rejection of all forms of domination, both the exertion of it and submission to it, the preservation of the independence of the country in all respects and its territorial integrity, the defence of the rights of all Muslims, non-alignment with respect to the hegemonic superpowers, and the maintenance of mutually peaceful relations with all non-belligerent States.

This article not only enunciates the principle of non-intervention but also requires the State of Iran to support Muslims against dominating powers. The question then arises as to the relationship between this provision and the application of extraterritorial jurisdiction, as well as the principle of non-intervention. Does this mean that the Constitution of the Islamic Republic recognised extraterritoriality and interference in the internal affairs of other countries? The answer to this question is plainly given in Article 154:

> The Islamic Republic of Iran has as its ideal human felicity throughout human society and considers the attainment of independence, freedom, and rule of justice and truth to be the right of all people of the world. Accordingly, *while scrupulously refraining from all forms of interference in the internal affairs of other nations,* it supports the just struggles of the freedom fighters against the oppressors in every corner of the globe.
>
> (emphasis added)

Here, there are some important points to consider: first, interference in the internal affairs of other nations is explicitly prohibited in this article. The same point is stated in Article 2(6)(c):

> The Islamic Republic is a system based on the faith in: . . . 6. The exalted dignity and value of man, and his freedom coupled with responsibility

> before God; in which equality, justice, political, economic, social and cultural independence, and national solidarity are secured by recourse to: . . . c. negation of all forms of oppression, both the infliction of and the submission to it, *and of dominance, both its imposition and its acceptance.*
>
> (emphasis added)

Clearly, this article is influenced by Iran's eventful history and incorporates religious and ethical principles in its denunciation of oppression and mistreatment. Moreover, the content of the Iranian Constitution of 1979, as well as that of many other countries, was evidently shaped by the prevailing anti-imperialist and leftist ideologies of that time. For example, Section C of Article 25 of the Constitution of Bangladesh, ratified in 1972, explicitly includes similar provisions.[33]

According to these provisions, the Islamic Republic of Iran supports the just struggle of the oppressed against their oppressors worldwide. The oppressed include both Muslims and non-Muslims who may be citizens of other countries. Unlike contemporary constitutions where the jurisdiction of states is determined solely based on the concept of the 'nation-state', in Islamic thought, the concept of the *Umma* or the universal community of Muslims is also crucial. *Umma* is an Arabic word meaning 'way' or 'main road'. While the *Umma* is the entity that follows, the entity that is followed is the *Imam*. Both etymologically and historically, as well as theoretically, an Imam signifies a book, a guide, one that is followed by a group of people: "And the Quran is the Imam of the Muslims".[34] Consequently, it can be asserted that the term *Umma* encompasses all adherents of the Islamic faith who follow the Quran, Prophet, and Imam, irrespective of their nationality, ethnicity, race, colour, and so forth. As articulated by H. E. Chehabi and Asghar Schirazi, the revolutionaries of 1979 perceived themselves as the forefront of a movement poised to influence the entire Muslim world, transcending the restricted concept of the nation-state.[35] This concept finds its way into the Constitution of the Islamic Republic. One can find it in the preamble and Articles 5, 11, 57, and 177. In the preamble, it is stated that: "The Constitution of the Islamic Republic of Iran sets forth the cultural,

33 This article stipulated that: "The State shall base its international relations on the principles of respect for national sovereignty and equality, non-interference in internal affairs of other countries, peaceful settlement of international disputes, and respect for international law and principles enunciated in the United Nation Charter, and on the basis of those principles shall [.] c. support oppressed peoples through the world waging a just struggle against imperialism, colonialism or racism".

34 Tamim Al-Barghouti, *The Umma and the Dawla, The Nation-State and the Arab Middle East* (London: Pluto Press, 2008), 38.

35 H. E. Chehabi and Asghar Schirazi, "The Islamic Republic of Iran," *Journal of Persianate Studies* 5 (2012): 183.

social, political, and economic institutions of Iranian society on the basis of Islamic principles and norms, which represent the earnest aspiration of the Islamic *Umma*".

However, the Constitution is not limited to the world Muslim community. The word 'oppressed', which covers Muslims and non-Muslims, also goes beyond Iran's national borders and links the Iranian Revolution to other popular movements:

> The Constitution provides the necessary basis for ensuring the Continuation of the Revolution at home and abroad. In particular, in the development of *international relations,* the Constitution will strive with other Islamic and popular movements to prepare the way for the formation of a single world *Umma.*
>
> (emphasis added)

Supporting the oppressed by the Islamic government is also justified religiously.[36] For example, there is a famous saying (*Hadith*) quoted from Prophet Mohammad, which says: "If a Muslim fails to assist someone in need who is oppressed, he is not truly a Muslim".[37] Now, an important question arises here: What obligations does the Islamic government have towards Muslims and the oppressed?

The key point here is that the commitment undertaken by the Islamic Republic towards Muslims and the oppressed is merely support, and support is different from intervention. There are two arguments for such an interpretation in favour of the non-intervention principle in this article. First, using the word 'support' after recognising the non-intervention principle cannot include intervention. In other words, this interpretation can be understood by reference to the words in the Constitution itself (literal interpretation of the Constitution). Second, setting aside the literal interpretation of the term 'support', the precedent of interpreting this article by the Guardian Council as an official body for the interpretation of the Constitution (Article 98) delineates the scope of the term 'support'. The Guardian Council, in the course of examining the chart of the Islamic Revolution Guard Corps (the IRGC) in 1983, has rejected draft Article 1 of the aforementioned chart due

36 For further reading, see "Support for the Oppressed in the Islamic Republic of Iran's Foreign Policy." Accessed 5 December 2023. https://english.khamenei.ir/news/8328/Support-for-the-oppressed-in-the-Islamic-Republic-of-Iran-s.

37 See at: https://makarem.ir/maaref/fa/article/index/406588/%c2%ab%d8%ad%d9%85%d8%a7%db%8c%d8%aa-%d8%a7%d8%b2-%d9%85%d8%b8%d9%84%d9%88%d9%85%c2%bb-%d8%af%d8%b1-%d8%b1%d9%88%d8%a7%db%8c%d8%a7%d8%aa-%d8%a7%d8%b3%d9%84%d8%a7%d9%85%db%8c.

to its incompatibility with the non-intervention principle.[38] According to draft Article 1:

> Islamic Revolution Guard Corps is an institution under the supreme command of the Supreme Leader, whose purpose is to safeguard the Islamic Revolution and its achievements, engage in *Jihad* for the sake of God and expand the rule of God's law in the world in accordance with the laws of the Islamic Republic of Iran. It also aims to strengthen the comprehensive defence structure of the Islamic Republic through cooperation with other armed forces, military training, and organising popular forces.[39]

The Guardian Council held that the generality of the statement "jihad for the sake of God, and expand the rule of God's law in the world which includes the war of aggression and attack on the non-belligerent States", is contrary to Article 154 of the Constitution, which prohibits interference in the internal affairs of other nations.[40] Considering the opinion of the Guardian Council, ultimately, the Parliament enacted Article 1 of IRGC's chart as follows:

> The Islamic Revolution Guard Corps, under the supreme command of the Supreme Leader, aims to safeguard the Islamic Revolution and its achievements, and continuously strive towards the realisation of divine ideals, as well as the expansion of God's sovereignty. This is achieved through collaboration with other armed forces, military training, and organising popular forces in accordance with the laws of the Islamic Republic.

Therefore, in the ultimate resolution, expressions that had the potential for interpretations beyond mere 'support', leading to a perception of interference in the affairs of other nations, were eliminated.

Hence, unlike the principle of extraterritoriality, which the Constitution does not address, there are provisions in the Constitution that cast doubt on the acceptance or rejection of the non-intervention principle. The interpretation by the Guardian Council clarifies that the Constitution of the Islamic Republic of Iran has acknowledged the non-intervention principle. Specifically, in contexts involving the concepts of the *Umma* and 'oppressed', the focus is on supporting them rather than intervening in the internal affairs of other countries.

38 Mohammad Salehi, "The Articles of the Constitution in the Light of the Guardian Council Interpretation: Article 151." Accessed 29 September 2023. https://ccri.ac.ir/files/fa/news_files/237618.pdf.

39 *Ibid.*

40 *Ibid.*

4 Extraterritoriality and Non-Intervention in the International Practice of Iran

As mentioned in the previous section, the Constitution of the Islamic Republic of Iran and its ordinary laws and regulations do not generally allow Iran to intervene in the domestic affairs of other states or exercise extraterritorial jurisdiction, excluding criminal cases. Therefore, except for the criminal code, there are no clear examples of extraterritorial application of Iranian laws or jurisdiction. However, the constitutional duty to support Muslims against dominant powers and the persistence of the Iranian government in backing the people of Palestine and other Islamic nations in the Middle East and beyond have caused serious tensions between Iran and the US, as well as some other Western powers who accuse Iran of interfering in the political independence of other countries. Iran has consistently denied these accusations and claims that its support is based on the requests of the people and the legitimate governments of those countries.[41] This political controversy is beyond the scope of this chapter. What is important to mention for our discussion is that Iran has not officially undermined the principle of non-intervention. Furthermore, it is important to note that no cases of extraterritorial application of Iranian laws or jurisdiction have been reported, even when Iranian commanders or troops were present on foreign soil. The caution in Iran's practice is also reflected in its official positions taken in different forums. In this section, the chapter examines these positions concerning the principle of non-intervention and extraterritoriality.

4.1 *Iran's Position Regarding the Principle of Non-Intervention*

Iran has expressed its adherence to the principle of non-intervention in several recent declarations. For instance, Article III of the 2020 Declaration of General Staff of the Armed Forces regarding International Law Applicable to Cyberspace states that Iran considers the principle of non-intervention as "an independent principle of customary international law".[42] Similarly,

41 For further reading, see Karine Bannelier-Christakis, "Military Interventions against ISIL in Iraq, Syria and Libya, and the Legal Basis of Consent," *Leiden Journal of International Law* 29(3) (2016): 743–775.

42 See "General Staff of Iranian Armed Forces Warns of Tough Reaction to Any Cyber Threat," *Nournews*, 18 August 2020. Accessed 23 September 2023. https://nournews.ir/En/News/53144/General-Staff-of-Iranian-Armed-Forces-Warns-of-Tough-Reaction-to-Any-Cyber-Threat. For further reading, see Michael N. Schmitt, "Noteworthy Releases of International Cyber Law Positions – PART II: Iran," *Articles of War-Lieber Institute West Point*, 27 August 2020. Accessed 23 September 2023. https://lieber.westpoint.edu/iran-international-cyber-law-positions/; "Iran Joins Discussions of Sovereignty and Non-Intervention in Cyberspace," *Just Security*, 3 September 2020. Accessed 20 January 2024. https://www.justsecurity.org/72181/iran-joins-discussions-of-sovereignty-and-non-intervention-in-cyberspace/.

paragraph 5 of the 2020 Declaration of the Islamic Republic of Iran and the Russian Federation on the Promotion of International Law declares that the two states regard any action or attempt to destabilise or undermine the stability of another state or its institutions as a violation of the principle of non-intervention.[43] Based on this, paragraph 6 condemns the extraterritorial application of national law by states not in conformity with international law as an example of violating the principle of non-intervention in the internal affairs of states.

These statements show how Iran interprets the principle of non-intervention in the realm of international law. It is worth noting that this conservative approach is not new in Iran's practice. For example, one can refer to Iran's verbal and written pleadings before the International Court of Justice (ICJ) in the Anglo-Iranian Oil Company Case.[44] Moreover, in the Oil Platforms Case against the US, Iran recognised compliance with this principle as "a *conditio sine qua non* of friendly relations amongst States".[45] This statement, though delivered as part of Iran's reasoning to prove that the respondent state has violated international law, clearly indicates that from Iran's point of view, friendly relations among states will be subject to controversy in case of intervention. In other words, Iran, like many other states of the Global South, considers the wording used in the 1970 UN Declaration on Friendly Relations among States as a manifestation of customary international law. In this resolution, the principle of non-intervention is declared as a principle of international law that provides that "no State or group of States has the right to intervene, directly or indirectly, in internal or external affairs of any other State".[46]

43 See "Iran, Russia Issue Declaration on Promotion of International Law," *Islamic Republic of Iran, Ministry of Foreign Affairs*, 17 June 2020. Accessed 20 January 2024. https://en.mfa.ir/portal/newsview/599243/iran-russia-issue-declaration-on-promotion-of-intl-law.

44 See, for example, ICJ *Case Concerning Anglo-Iranian Oil Co.* (*United Kingdom v Iran*), Communication from the Minister of Foreign Affairs of Iran to the President of the International Court of Justice, 29 June 1951. https://www.icj-cij.org/sites/default/files/case-related/16/8987.pdf, 4.

45 *Case Concerning Oil Platforms* (*Iran v The United States of America*), ICJ, Memorial submitted by Iran, 8 June 1993. https://www.icj-cij.org/sites/default/files/case-related/90/8622.pdf, 83. In discussing the relations between Iran and the USA, it is crucial to note that the General Declaration of 19 January 1981, which was reached following the mediation of the Algerian Government in the USA embassy hostage crisis in Tehran, prominently features the principle of non-intervention. Specifically, point (I)(1) states: "The United States pledges that it is, and from now on, will be the policy of the United States not to intervene, directly or indirectly, politically or militarily, in Iran's internal affairs". https://iusct.com/wp-content/uploads/2021/02/1-General-Declaration_.pdf.

46 UN General Assembly Declaration on Principles of International Law concerning Friendly Relations and Cooperation among States in accordance with the Charter of the United Nations. A/RES/2625(XXV), 24 October 1970.

4.2 *Iran's Position on Extraterritoriality (Mainly Secondary Sanctions)*

The UN Charter authorises the Security Council to impose sanctions to maintain international peace and security.[47] Some states and scholars believe that any other type of sanction is illegal under international law because it contradicts the Charter.[48] However, it is important to note that even those who do not consider all types of unilateral coercive measures (UCMs) as illegal mostly reject the legality of UCMs with negative human rights impacts or UCMs that apply extraterritorially.[49]

In its observations submitted to the UN concerning a questionnaire by the UN Special Rapporteur on the negative impact of the UCMs on the enjoyment of human rights, Iran stated: "extraterritorial sanctions disregard generally accepted rules of international law governing the jurisdiction of States under international law and consequently are unlawful".[50] This is the position of Iran, which has been repeated on many occasions in response to the US so-called 'secondary sanctions', *i.e.*, those UCMs that are extraterritorial and prohibit non-US nationals and companies from trading with and investing in the state under sanction. The term 'extraterritorial or secondary sanctions' refers mainly to those types of unilateral coercive measures with extraterritorial effects that target, or at least encompass, foreign actors completely outside the jurisdiction of the state imposing the sanctions.[51] As Tom Ruys and Cedric Ryngaert said, secondary sanctions seek to deter third-state nationals from certain economic relations with the target state, usually by conditioning access to economic privileges with the targeting state on third-state nationals' abstention from

47 For further reading, see Jeremy Matam Farrall, *United Nations Sanctions and the Rule of Law* (Cambridge: Cambridge University Press, 2007).

48 See, for example, Aytekin Kaan Kurtul, "The Evolving Qualification of Unilateral Coercive Measures: A Historical and Doctrinal Study," *Athena – Critical Inquiries in Law, Philosophy and Globalization* 2(1) (2022): 204–205.

49 See, for example, a recent Resolution of the General Assembly on the issue of human rights and UCM which provides that: "Strongly objects to the extraterritorial nature of those measures which, in addition, threaten the sovereignty of States, and in this context calls upon all Member States neither to recognize those measures nor to apply them, as well as to take administrative or legislative measures, as appropriate, to counteract the extraterritorial applications or effects of unilateral coercive measures". UN Doc. A/RES/78/202, 22 December 2023, para. 5.

50 Observations of the Islamic Republic of Iran Concerning "UCM-Study on the Notion, Characteristics, Legal Status and Targets of Unilateral Sanctions," 29 January 2021. https://www.ohchr.org/sites/default/files/Documents/Issues/UCM/ReportHRC48/States/submission-iran.pdf, 5.

51 Joshua Andresen, "U.S. Secondary Sanctions; Lawful After All?" in *The Routledge Handbook of the Political Economy of Sanctions*, ed. Ksenia Kirkham (London: Routledge, 2024), 305.

specified economic relations with the target state.[52] Ellie Gerqanmayeh and Manuel Lafont Rapnouil describe secondary sanctions as measures targeting foreign persons from third-party countries who have not conducted business activity with the sanctioning country and do not have a nexus to the sanctioning country.[53]

These measures, which are widely used by the US against Iran and Cuba, as described by Julia Schmidt,

> not only disregard the foreign policy choices of sovereign actors worldwide that do not want to limit trade with Iran and Cuba, but they aim to replace those foreign policy choices with US foreign policy preferences, and they put pressure on foreign actors to change their foreign policies towards both Iran and Cuba in line with US foreign policy goals through the medium of natural and legal persons that are constrained by the extra-territorial legislation.[54]

The 'foreign actors' referred to in the previous passage mostly include the European individuals and companies that have lost their trade relations with Iran and Cuba due to US-imposed UCMs.[55] Therefore, it is not surprising that the European Union

> has condemned the extraterritorial application of third country's legislation imposing restrictive measures which purports to regulate the activities of natural and legal persons under the jurisdiction of the Member States of the European Union, as being in violation of international law.[56]

52 Tom Ruys and Cedric Ryngaert, "Secondary Sanctions: A Weapon out of Control? The International Legality of, and European Responses to, U.S. Secondary Sanctions," *British Yearbook of International Law* (2020): 7.

53 Ellie Geranmayeh and Manuel Lafont Rapnouil, "Meeting the Challenge of Secondary Sanctions," *European Council on Foreign Relations*, 25 June 2019. Accessed 18 March 2024. https://ecfr.eu/publication/meeting_the_challenge_of_secondary_sanctions/. For further reading, see Christian Tietje and Cristina Lloyd, "Secondary Sanctions," in *Research Handbook on Extraterritoriality in International Law*, eds. Austin Parrish and Cedric Ryngaert (Cheltenham: Edward Elgar Publishing, 2023).

54 Julia Schmidt, "The Legality of Unilateral Extraterritorial Sanctions under International Law," *Journal of Conflict and Security Law* 27(1) (2022): 70.

55 For further reading, see Alan Cafruny, "The U.S. Sanctions Offensive: Implications for 'Third Parties' and the Transatlantic Relationship," in *The Routledge Handbook of the Political Economy of Sanctions*, ed. Ksenia Kirkham (London: Routledge, 2024), 223–233.

56 Report of the Special Rapporteur on the Negative Impact of Unilateral Coercive Measures on the Enjoyment of Human Rights on His Mission to the European Union, A/HRC/39/54/Add.1, 17 July 2018, https://www.undocs.org/Home/Mobile?FinalSymbol=A%2FHRC%2F39%2F54%2FAdd.1&Language=E&DeviceType=Desktop&LangRequested=False, footnote 31.

This is in line with the position of the UN Special Rapporteur, who declares that:

> Extraterritorial sanctions are not only contrary to international law, they also create adverse effects, to the extent that they seek to dissuade, often under threat of severe penalties, private parties of third countries from entering into trade or other dealings with the targeted State.[57]

In her report on over-compliance, the Special Rapporteur stipulates that "even sanctioning countries admit that the practice of extraterritoriality violates international law and that the concept of extraterritoriality with regards to sanctions raises questions of compatibility with international law, including international human rights law".[58]

Statements like these may support the case brought by Iran against the US to the International Court of Justice regarding the re-imposition of the latter's sanctions against Iran after withdrawing from the nuclear deal. Iran nuclear deal, or the Joint Comprehensive Plan of Action (JCPOA), was adopted on 14 July 2015 between China, France, Germany, the Russian Federation, the United Kingdom, and the United States of America, with the High Representative of the European Union for Foreign Affairs and Security Policy and the Islamic Republic of Iran, and was endorsed by the UN Security Council Resolution 2231 on 20 July 2015.[59] The declared purpose of that Plan was to ensure the exclusively peaceful nature of Iran's nuclear programme and to produce the comprehensive lifting of all UN Security Council sanctions as well as multilateral and national sanctions related to Iran's nuclear programme, including steps on access to areas of trade, technology, finance, and energy. Following the adoption of the JCPOA, President Barack Obama issued Executive Order 13716[60] revoking or amending a certain number of earlier executive orders on nuclear-related 'sanctions' imposed on Iran or Iranian nationals. After President Donald Trump took office, on 8 May 2018, he issued a National Security Presidential Memorandum announcing the end of the participation of the United States in the JCPOA and directing the re-imposition of sanctions lifted or waived in connection with the JCPOA. In the memorandum, the President of the United States indicated that "Iranian or Iran-backed forces have gone on the march

57 *Ibid.*, para. 35.
58 UN Doc. A/78/196, 4 September 2023, para. 60.
59 UN Doc. S/RES/2231, 20 July 2015, para. 1.
60 Executive Order 13716 – Revocation of Executive Orders 13574, 13590, 13622, and 13645 with Respect to Iran, Amendment of Executive Order 13628 with Respect to Iran, and Provision of Implementation Authorities for Aspects of Certain Statutory Sanctions Outside the Scope of US Commitments Under the Joint Comprehensive Plan of Action of 14 July 2015. Accessed 20 January 2024. https://www.presidency.ucsb.edu/documents/executive-order-13716-revocation-executive-orders-13574-13590-13622-and-13645-with-respect.

in Syria, Iraq, and Yemen, and continue to control parts of Lebanon and Gaza".[61] The memorandum further specified, *inter alia*, that the Secretary of State and the Secretary of the Treasury were to prepare any necessary executive actions to re-impose sanctions lifted by Executive Order 13716 of 16 January, 2016; to prepare to re-list persons removed, in connection with the JCPOA, from any relevant 'sanctions lists', as appropriate; to revise relevant 'sanctions regulations'; and to issue limited waivers during the wind-down period, as appropriate.

In the case before the World Court, Iran, with reference to rules and principles of international law, such as the illegality of extraterritorial sanctions, categorised the UCMs imposed by the US in many aspects as a violation of the 1955 Treaty of Amity between the two states.[62] This case is still pending, and the US has already claimed that the secondary sanctions or, in its words, 'third-country measures' should be disregarded from this case because the Treaty of Amity does not cover the relations that the US has with nationals of other states.[63] In its judgment on jurisdiction, the ICJ holds that

> the fact that some of the measures challenged whether or not they are 'the vast majority', as the United States maintains directly target third States or the nationals or companies of third States does not suffice for them to be automatically excluded from the ambit of the Treaty of Amity.[64]

On this basis, the Court unanimously rejected the objections raised by the US and held that it has jurisdiction to enter into this dispute.[65]

Apart from the details of this case, the oral and written statements by Iran demonstrate its negative position regarding exterritorial jurisdiction.

61 "President Donald J. Trump is Ending United States Participation in an Unacceptable Iran Deal," 8 May 2018. Accessed 20 January 2024. https://trumpwhitehouse.archives.gov/briefings-statements/president-donald-j-trump-ending-united-states-participation-unacceptable-iran-deal/.

62 *Alleged Violations of the 1955 Treaty of Amity, Economic Relations, and Consular Rights (Islamic Republic of Iran v United States of America)*, ICJ. Memorial of the Islamic Republic of Iran, 24 May 2019. Accessed 20 January 2024 https://www.icj-cij.org/sites/default/files/case-related/175/175-20190524-WRI-01-00-EN.pdf.

63 *Alleged Violations of the 1955 Treaty of Amity, Economic Relations, And Consular Rights (Iran v United States of America)*. Preliminary Objections Submitted by the United States of America, 23 August 2019. Accessed 20 January 2024. https://www.icj-cij.org/sites/default/files/case-related/175/175-20190823-WRI-01-00-EN.pdf, 94-118.

64 *Alleged Violations of the 1955 Treaty of Amity, Economic Relations, and Consular Rights (Iran v United States of America)*, Judgment of 3 February 2021 on Preliminary Objection, ICJ Reports 2021, p. 9, para. 81.

65 *Ibid.*, para. 114.

Moreover, Iran's submissions, in this case, which refer to the positions of other states and international organisations concerning extraterritoriality, can be used as a rich resource for further research on the topic. The potential benefits for the respondent state in relation to its arguments concerning 'third country measures' falling outside the protective scope of the Treaty of Amity are yet to be determined by the Court. However, the arguments put forth by the US offer an opportunity for the ICJ to address the permissibility of extraterritorial sanctions and examine the developments in international law regarding extraterritorial jurisdiction since the *Lotus* case.

5 Conclusion

The study conducted in this chapter indicates that Iran is in the category of countries that oppose extraterritorial jurisdiction and extraterritorial application of national laws. The Constitution of the Islamic Republic of Iran and some national laws and regulations, while emphasising the vital importance of the principle of non-intervention, obligate the State of Iran to support the oppressed of the world, and in practice, the Iranian officials have always adhered to this commitment, especially regarding the rights of the Palestinian people. The statements of Iranian authorities show that Iranian military forces were alongside Iraqi and Syrian forces in various operations, especially in the fight against ISIS terrorism. However, Iran's military presence has never led to extraterritorial application of Iran's jurisdiction or laws in these countries.

On the other hand, Iran is the target of the heaviest unilateral US sanctions, and these sanctions, especially when they are applied in the context of secondary sanctions, lead to the extraterritorial application of US jurisdiction and laws. In its legal objections to these sanctions, Iran always emphasises the illegality of extraterritorial application of jurisdiction and laws in the international legal system.

References

Abrahamian, Ervand. *Iran between Two Revolutions*. Princeton: Princeton University Press, 1982.

Al-Barghouti, Tami. *The Umma and the Dawla, The Nation-State and the Arab Middle East*, London: Pluto Press, 2008.

Amir Arjomand, Said. *The Turban for The Crown, The Islamic Revolution in Iran*. Oxford: Oxford University Press, 1988.

Andresen, Joshua. "U.S. Secondary Sanctions; Lawful After All?" In *The Routledge Handbook of the Political Economy of Sanctions*, edited by Ksenia Kirkham. London: Routledge, 2024.

Askari, Pouria. "The Principle of Non-Intervention and the Dilemma of the Legality of the Unilateral Coercive Measures." In *The Routledge Handbook of the Political Economy of Sanctions*, edited by Ksenia Kirkham. London: Routledge, 2024.

Bannelier-Christakis, Karine. "Military Interventions against ISIL in Iraq, Syria and Libya, and the Legal Basis of Consent." *Leiden Journal of International Law* 29(3) (2016): 743–775.
Brownlie, Ian. *Principles of Public International Law*. Oxford: Oxford University Press, 4th edition, 1990.
Cafruny, Alan. "The U.S. Sanctions Offensive: Implications for 'Third Parties' and the Transatlantic Relationship." In *The Routledge Handbook of the Political Economy of Sanctions*, edited by Ksenia Kirkham. London: Routledge, 2024.
Chehabi, Houchang, and Asghar Schirazi. "The Islamic Republic of Iran." *Journal of Persianate Studies* 5(2012): 175–204.
Dinstein, Yoram. "The *Erga Omnes* Applicability of Human Rights." *Archiv des Völkerrechts* 30(1) (1992): 16–21.
Elena Andreeva. "RUSSIA i. Russo-Iranian Relations up to the Bolshevik Revolution." *Encyclopedia Iranica*, online edition (2014). Accessed 10 September 2024. https://www.iranicaonline.org/articles/russia-i-relations.
Encyclopedia Iranica. "Constitutional Revolution." Vol. VI, Fasc. 2, 163–216. Accessed 10 September 2024. https://www.iranicaonline.org/articles/constitutional-revolution-index.
Eshraghi, F. "Anglo-Soviet Occupation of Iran in August 1941." *Middle Eastern Studies* 20(1) (1984): 27–52.
Farrall, Jeremy Matam. *United Nations Sanctions and the Rule of Law*. Cambridge: Cambridge University Press, 2007.
Geranmayeh, Ellie, and Manuel Lafont Rapnouil. "Meeting the Challenge of Secondary Sanctions." *European Council on Foreign Relations*, 25 June 2019. Accessed 10 September 2024. https://ecfr.eu/publication/meeting_the_challenge_of_secondary_sanctions/.
Ghani, Sirus. *Iran and the Rise of Reza Shah: From Qajar Collapse to Pahlavi Rule*. Translated by Hassan Kamshad. Tehran: Nilofar Publications, 1999.
Kamali, Mohammad Hashim. *Crime and Punishment in Islamic Law*. Oxford: Oxford University Press, 2019.
Katouzian, Homa. *Musaddiq and the Struggle for Power in Iran*. New York: I.B. Tauris, 1999.
Kurtul, Aytekin Kaan. "The Evolving Qualification of Unilateral Coercive Measures: A Historical and Doctrinal Study." *Athena – Critical Inquiries in Law, Philosophy and Globalization* 2(1) (2022): 204–253.
Parrish, Austen. "Sovereignty, Self-Determination, and the Duty to Cooperate: Public International Law's Limits on Unilateral Extraterritorial Regulation of Non-Citizens." In *Research Handbook on Extraterritoriality in International Law*, edited by Austen Parrish and Cedric Ryngaert, 45–56. Cheltenham: Edward Elgar Publishing, 2023.
Ruys, Tom, and Cedric Ryngaert. "Secondary Sanctions: A Weapon out of Control? The International Legality of, and European Responses to, U.S. Secondary Sanctions." *British Yearbook of International Law* (2020): 1–116.
Ryngaert, Cedric. "International Jurisdiction Law." In *Research Handbook on Extraterritoriality in International Law*, edited by Austin Parrish and Cedric Ryngaert. Cheltenham: Edward Elgar Publishing, 2023.
Salehi, Mohammad. "The Articles of the Constitution in the Light of the Guardian Council Interpretation: Article 151." Accessed 10 September 2024. https://ccri.ac.ir/files/fa/news_files/237618.pdf.
Schmidt, Julia. "The Legality of Unilateral Extraterritorial Sanctions under International Law." *Journal of Conflict and Security Law* 27(1) (2022): 53–81.

Sender, Omri, and Michael Wood. "Extraterritorial Jurisdiction and the Limits of Customary International Law." In *Research Handbook on Extraterritoriality in International Law*, edited by Austen Parrish and Cedric Ryngaert. Cheltenham: Edward Elgar Publishing, 2023.

Takeuchi, Mari. "Asian Experience with Extraterritoriality." In *Research Handbook on Extraterritoriality in International Law*, edited by Austen Parrish and Cedric Ryngaert. Cheltenham: Edward Elgar Publishing, 2023.

Tietje, Christian, and Cristina Lloyd. "Secondary Sanctions." In *Research Handbook on Extraterritoriality in International Law*, edited by Austen Parrish and Cedric Ryngaert. Cheltenham: Edward Elgar Publishing, 2023.

7 Owning and Owing

Israel's Law on Extraterritorial Jurisdiction Related to Jews

*Yaël Ronen**

1 Introduction

International law recognises the power of states to exercise jurisdiction extraterritorially, but not without limitations. The limitations are intended to protect interstate interests as well as individual rights. The primary form that these limitations take is the requirement of a genuine link between the legal dispute and the state exercising jurisdiction.[1] In criminal law, legitimate links for legislative or adjudicatory jurisdiction include the nationality of the individuals involved (as perpetrators or as victims) or the fact that the state itself is the victim of the offence. In civil matters, exceptional adjudicatory jurisdiction over foreign defendants rests on a connection between elements in the dispute and the territory of the forum state or on the choice of the parties. This contribution focuses on Israel's law that grants the state extraterritorial jurisdiction based on the Jewishness of the persons involved. This ethnic/national connection does not fall within the recognised links mentioned previously.

Israel's self-perception as the state of the Jewish people, enunciated in its Declaration of Independence in 1948, concerns not only a moral, historical, and political connection but also a legal one. This is reflected in the fact that in various contexts, Israel's domestic law extends the state's jurisdiction extraterritorially in matters relating to the Jewishness of individuals involved, even when they have no direct connection to the state. This contribution considers the law and, where such exists, practice relating to three Israeli legislative instruments which provide for such extraterritorial jurisdiction: The Penal Code 5773–1973 ('Penal Code'), which criminalises and grants Israel's courts' jurisdiction over acts committed outside Israel against the life, body, health, freedom, or property of a Jew as a Jew; Basic Law: Israel – Nation State of the Jewish People ('Basic Law: Nation State'), which establishes Israel's legal obligations towards Jews in the Diaspora and grants

* I am grateful to Mota Kremnitzer, David Kretzmer, Yoram Shachar and Celia Wasserstein-Fassberg for their helpful comments on earlier drafts; and to Nitzan Caspi-Shiloni for discussing certain nuances of Jewish law on marriage and divorce. Usual caveats apply.

1 Cedric Ryngaert, *Jurisdiction in International Law* (Oxford: Oxford University Press, 2008), 22.

DOI: 10.4324/9781003402978-8

the state executive jurisdiction when Jews are in 'in straits and in captivity' due to their Jewishness; and the Rabbinical Courts' Jurisdiction (Marriage and Divorce) Law, 5713–1953 ('Rabbinical Courts' Jurisdiction Law'), which grants rabbinical courts the jurisdiction to determine and compel the grant of divorce on recalcitrant Jewish husbands, even when neither of the disputing spouses has any real connection with Israel.

This contribution reviews each of these legislative instruments and places them in a legal and political context. It assesses the compatibility of Jewishness as the link for extraterritorial jurisdiction with the current law on jurisdiction in terms of both interstate relations and the rights of individuals. The contribution then explores the relationship between Israel and world Jewry, which is implied and perhaps shaped by the legislation.

2 The Penal Code

2.1 *The Law*

In 1994, the preliminary and general part of Israel's Penal Code underwent an overhaul, which included a systematic delineation of the extraterritorial reach of Israel's penal law. Chapter 2 of the Code concerns "foreign offences," namely offences (as defined under Israel's law) or their derivatives when committed entirely outside Israeli territory. Section 13 in this chapter is entitled "Offences against the State or against the Jewish people." This wording suggests a certain equivalence between the state and the Jewish people.

As the explanatory note to the code's bill indicated, it concerns the protective principle,[2] namely the right of states to exercise criminal jurisdiction over aliens who have committed acts abroad which are deemed prejudicial to the vital interests of the state.[3] Subsection 13(a) is a standard statement of this principle, dealing with the protection of national security, foreign relations, state secrets, form of government, orderly function of state authorities, and state property. Article 13(b) provides that:

(b) Israel penal laws shall also apply to foreign offenses against –

(1) the life, body, health, freedom or property of an Israel citizen, an Israel resident[4] or a public servant, in his capacity as such;
(2) the life, body, health, freedom or property of a Jew, as a Jew, or the property of a Jewish institution, because it is such.

Section 13(b) is followed by Section 14, entitled "offences against an Israel national or resident," which provides that "[t]he penal laws of Israel shall apply to foreign offences against the life, body, health or freedom of an Israel

2 Penal Code (Preliminary Part and General Part), 5752–1992, Statutory Bills 2098, 6 January 1992, 120.
3 Malcolm Shaw, *International Law* (Cambridge: Cambridge University Press, 6th ed., 2008), 666.
4 Hebrew uses the same word for 'residence' and 'domicile.'

citizen or of an Israel resident." Section 14 is a standard statement of the passive personality principle. It is exclusive to Israel's nationals and residents and does not mention Jews or the Jewish people.[5]

The differences between protective jurisdiction and passive personality jurisdiction are reflected in the differences between sections 13 and 14. Section 14 stipulates a subsidiary jurisdiction dependent on double criminality and subject to the *ne bis in idem* principle. It applies only to a specific set of crimes (a maximum sentence under Israel's law of at least one year) and applies the lower penalty. These stipulations are characteristic of jurisdiction based on the passive personality principle. In contrast, the protective jurisdiction under Section 13(b) is primary and has no prerequisites, as is common in the case of protective jurisdiction.[6] However, Section 13(b)(2) diverges from common practice in its assertion of jurisdiction when a Jewish person is targeted because of their Jewishness.[7] This protection of ethnic kin is exceptional. While many states offer preferential treatment to their kin groups who reside in other states (in which they are nationals),[8] including through legislation, Israel's legislation is quite unique in that it goes so far as to assert criminal jurisdiction over persons who harm persons belonging to its kin group.

The Penal Code's drafters defended the exceptional reach of Section 13(b)(2) on the grounds, among others, that the provision does not grant executive power to enforce the law extraterritorially.[9] This view overlooks the consequences of extraterritorial jurisdiction, adjudicatory and even more so legislative, both for interstate relations and for individual rights. These consequences are discussed below.

2.2 *Compatibility with the Law on Extraterritorial Jurisdiction: The Principle of Legality and Extraterritorial Criminal Jurisdiction*

2.2.1 *State Interests*

Both legislative and adjudicatory extraterritorial jurisdictions signal distrust in the territorial state's criminal enforcement systems. To some extent, this distrust is regarded as legitimate, as evidenced by the acceptance, albeit still

5 On the link between the passive personality principle and the protective principle when applied to the state see Kenneth S. Gallant, *International Criminal Jurisdiction: Whose Law Must We Obey?* (Oxford: Oxford University Press, 2022), 446; Alejandro Chehtman, *The Philosophical Foundations of Extraterritorial Punishment* (Oxford: Oxford University Press, 2010), 69.

6 Gallant, *Whose Law*, 415.

7 *Ibid.*, 451.

8 Venice Commission, Report on the Preferential Treatment of National Minorities by Their Kin-State (Venice, 19–20 October 2001).

9 Shneur-Zalman Feller and Mordechai Kremnitzer, "Reply to the Article 'Against Extra-Territorial Application of Criminal Law on National Grounds' by Professor Y. Shachar," *Plilim* 5 (1996): 67.

controversially, of the passive personality jurisdiction. Seen in this light, Section 13(b)(2) can be regarded as a response to other states' failure to protect Jews in the broadest sense, namely from physical harm and from violation of their right to remedy. But the signal embodied in Section 13(b)(2) is stronger than that reflected in the passive personality principle, since the assertion of jurisdiction under Section 13(b)(2) eschews the constraints normally associated with that jurisdiction, namely the requirements of double criminality, the *ne bis in idem* principle, and the principle of applying the lower penalty.

Ultimately, the evaluation of whether Israel's law goes too far into second-guessing the domestic matters of territorial states by arrogating jurisdiction over crimes causing harm to Jews would depend on practice rather than formal law. When the territorial state exercises its own criminal jurisdiction (and the acts prohibited by Section 13(b)(2) are likely to be prohibited under the law of any state[10]), there is little justification for Israel to exercise its own jurisdiction. Indeed, it is also unlikely that it will. But one might conceive of a different scenario in which the territorial state does not enforce the law (or enforces it disingenuously) because of institutional bias – antisemitism. In such a case, where the lack of trust (underlying the standard passive personality principle) is vindicated, the exercise of jurisdiction by Israel would not seem to raise particular difficulties in terms of interstate relations (provided the perpetrator reaches its territory). It would be difficult to maintain that Israel interferes in the domestic matters of the territorial state, since a failure to enforce international human rights law is not a domestic matter.

2.2.2 *Individual Rights: The Principle of Legality*

A harder question, not addressed by the Penal Code's drafters, is whether reliance on Article 13(b)(2) complies with international human rights law and with individual rights in the criminal process. One aspect of the latter is the *ne bis in idem* principle. Section 13(b)(2) does not mention it, and indeed, it is not clear that the principle necessarily applies in transnational situations. As noted previously, if the territorial state exercises its jurisdiction in practice, it is unlikely that Israel would apply its own. The more complicated scenario, to which the following analysis is dedicated, is one in which the territorial state does not enforce the law because of institutional antisemitism. Under these circumstances, the *ne bis in idem* principle would not be an obstacle to Israel's exercise of its own jurisdiction. However, attention should be paid to the principle of legality in criminal law (*nullum crimen sine lege*) recognised

10 Perhaps with the exception of the protection of property, as its definition may vary widely. The categories 'life, body, health, freedom, and property' are not strictly defined in the Penal Code, but the Code does contain chapters on harm to body (causing death, endangering of life and health, and harm to freedom) and harm to property.

as an international human right.[11] The principle holds that to be punishable legitimately an act must be criminalised under the law that was legitimately applicable at the time and in the circumstances of the act's commission.

Two issues must be addressed. First, whether the extraterritorial reach under Article 13(b)(2), namely based on the victim's identity, can be said to be 'legitimately applicable'; the other, whether extraterritorial jurisdiction is legitimate given the perpetrator's expectation of impunity (based on the institutional antisemitism) in the territorial state.

The first issue, namely whether the principle of legality allows extraterritorial exercise of jurisdiction, is not unique to Section 13(b)(2), since, in reality, perpetrators do not usually expect prosecution in states other than those in which they commit the crimes, and may not even know the connection of those states to their conduct. This challenge to the principle of legality is usually addressed by attributing to the perpetrator knowledge of the law despite the transnational element. This doctrinal response in the context of protective jurisdiction is somewhat contrived; moreover, it does not apply where Section 13(b)(2) is concerned.

When protective jurisdiction is exercised, the concern over the principle of legality is addressed by the construct that individuals can generally recognise that they are committing an act that violates the interests of a state, and, specifically, the state whose detriment they are pursuing. On this basis, it is argued that the exercise of jurisdiction by the injured state, both legislative and adjudicatory, cannot honestly be said to be unexpected. This construct has its limitations: it may be acceptable with respect to a limited group of offences that are directly related to vital state interests. Correspondingly, traditional protective jurisdiction is narrowly circumscribed.[12] In contrast, the protection that Section 13(b)(2) provides for individuals of a particular ethnic group that is not formally associated with the state, is not considered narrow and circumscribed conduct that is easily recognisable as harming the state's vital interests (even if it is vital according to that state's self-perception). Thus, the ordinary basis for attributing knowledge of the law to the perpetrator does not apply.

At the same time, it could be argued that, for the purpose of the principle of legality, Section 13(b)(2) is a specific manifestation of the passive personality jurisdiction. With regard to this jurisdiction, no constructive notice of a circumstantial element – the victim's citizenship in the adjudicatory state – is attributed to the perpetrator. The lack of notice is mitigated by the requirements of double criminality and lower punishment. As noted previously, in practice, double criminality is likely to be fulfilled when Section 13(b)(2) is

11 International Covenant on Civil and Political Rights (ICCPR), United Nations Treaty Series 999: 171, Article 15.

12 Including, usually, causing harm to the state's national security or state secrets, counterfeiting money, and espionage. Gallant, *Whose Law*, 415, 418.

applied.[13] Arguably, if double criminality and lower punishment are enough to mitigate the lack of notice under the passive personality principle when the link to the adjudicatory state is not an element of the crime,[14] then *a fortiori* lack of notice is not a bar to jurisdiction by the victim's state of ethnicity/nationality when that ethnicity/nationality *is* an element of the crime and is undoubtedly known to the perpetrator (since it is the motive for the crime). Thus, the extraterritorial reach of Section 13(b)(2) might not, in itself, violate the principle of legality.

The second issue is whether extraterritorial jurisdiction is legitimate when the perpetrator has an expectation of impunity (based on institutional antisemitism) in the territorial state. This issue might be viewed as a compounded version of an issue that has been considered in practice: that of the compatibility with the principle of legality of holding a person to account for crimes committed under a regime in which, under the law and for all practical purposes, there was no prohibition on the act. What is added here is the extraterritorial element.

The question of whether holding a person to account for crimes committed under a regime of impunity violates the principle of legality arose in German courts, both in the Nazi criminals' trials following World War II and in post-1990 trials of East German border guards. Defendants argued that their acts of violence against life and limb, while formally in contravention of state criminal law, were condoned and even required under the law applicable at the time. They claimed that they should, therefore, not have been prosecuted for those acts. In a number of cases, the German courts rejected the defendants' claims. In part, they did so by relying on the 'Radbruch formula.'[15] Radbruch, a German legal philosopher who had been Germany's Minister of Justice under the Weimar Republic, formulated in 1946 a legal theory that held that law that constituted an unbearable violation of fundamental principles of justice and humanity which must be respected by any state, was null and void. In the post-World War II cases, the court did not elaborate on what those fundamental principles were; however, in the post-1990 border guard cases, the German Court of Appeal related these 'fundamental principles' to international human rights law.[16]

13 As for a lower penalty: not only is it not guaranteed under Article 13(b)(2), but Israeli law regards racist motivation as an aggravating circumstance justifying a doubled penalty for certain offences, Penal Code, Article 144F.

14 In fact, the passive personality jurisdiction is subject to criticism precisely on this ground, with the exception being when the offense is in fact linked to the citizenship of the victim, as in the case of terrorism. Cedric Ryngaert, "International Jurisdiction Law," in *Research Handbook on Extraterritoriality in International Law*, eds. Austin Parish and Cedric Ryngaert (Cheltenham: Edward Elgar Publishing, 2023), 20.

15 Gustav Radbruch, Bonnie Litschewski Paulson and Stanley L. Paulson, "Statutory Lawlessness and Supra-Statutory Law (1946)," *Oxford Journal of Legal Studies* 26 (2006).

16 For example, BGH 5 StR 111/94, 20 March 1995 (LG Berlin). For a discussion, see Rudolf Geiger, "The German Border Guard Cases and International Human Rights," *European Journal of International Law* 9 (1998): 545.

Can the 'Radbruch formula' assist in the present context? The formula concerns the legitimacy of the substantive law, not of the adjudicating forum. It does not purport to grant states extraterritorial jurisdiction that they would not otherwise possess.[17] Its extension to procedural issues thus seems excessive. Moreover, the Radbruch formula appeals to universal principles of justice and humanity. Section 13(b)(2) does not purport to offset all discriminatory biases but is restricted to the protection of individuals only from a particular ethnicity/nationality. It is, therefore, difficult to justify it directly on the basis of universal principles.

At the same time, in a scenario in which crimes motivated by antisemitism are under-enforced as a result of institutional antisemitism, the exercise of jurisdiction by Israel is not only the only means of achieving the goals of criminal law but a response to a violation of the universal prohibition on racial discrimination.[18] When under-enforcement of criminal law motivated by antisemitism is a policy, it may even amount to persecution as a crime against humanity.[19] Israel's extraterritorial jurisdiction under Section 13(b)(2) does not extend to the crime of persecution itself (committed by law enforcement officials in the territorial state), but it is a response to the consequences of persecution. It is grounded not in universal principles but in a particular value of the State of Israel, namely its special affinity with the

17 If the acts in question constitute international crimes under customary law, the principle of legality might be satisfied under ICCPR Article 15(2) ("Nothing in this article shall prejudice the trial and punishment of any person for any act or omission which, at the time when it was committed, was criminal according to the general principles of law recognised by the community of nations"). However, most hate crimes do not, in themselves, constitute international crimes (hate speech calling for physical violence possibly being an exception, for example, ICTR, *Nahimana et al. v Prosecutor* (Media case), ICTR-99-52-A, 28 November 2007, paras. 502, 986–988, https://ucr.irmct.org/LegalRef/CMSDocStore/Public/English/Judgement/NotIndexable/ICTR-99-52/MSC31299R0000555179.PDF. For the relevance of ICCPR Article 15(2) for the border guard cases, see Geiger, "German Border Guard Cases," 543.

18 International Convention on the Elimination of All Forms of Racial Discrimination (CERD), 21 December 1965, United Nations Treaty Series 660, 195, Articles 2(1)(d) ("Each State Party shall prohibit and bring to an end, by all appropriate means, including legislation as required by circumstances, racial discrimination by any persons, group or organization"), 5(a) ("The right to equal treatment before the tribunals and all other organs administering justice"), 5(b) ("The right to security of person and protection by the State against violence or bodily harm, whether inflicted by government officials or by any individual group or institution"), 6 ("States Parties shall assure to everyone within their jurisdiction effective protection and remedies, through the competent national tribunals and other State institutions, against any acts of racial discrimination which violate his human rights and fundamental freedoms contrary to this Convention, as well as the right to seek from such tribunals just and adequate reparation or satisfaction for any damage suffered as a result of such discrimination"). For a successful judicial response to state failure to take antisemitic motive into account see *Allouche v France*, Application 81249/17, ECtHR, Merits and Just Satisfaction, 11 April 2024.

19 ICC Statute, Article 7(2)(g). Another element of crimes against humanity is that they are committed multiply. Whether that is the case or not would depend on the specific circumstances.

Jewish people. Is there any fault in countering the effects of a human rights violation, and possibly an international crime, on non-universal principles? States ought to be free to determine their prosecutorial priorities and policies so long as those are not discriminatory. The singling out by Israel of Jews for protection from persecution seems to qualify as a special measure permitted under international law, namely one taken

> for the sole purpose of securing adequate advancement of certain racial or ethnic groups or individuals requiring such protection as may be necessary in order to ensure such groups or individuals' equal enjoyment or exercise of human rights and fundamental freedoms.[20]

In conclusion, the formal scope of Section 13(b)(2) is broad and goes beyond the limits of existing permissive rules on the exercise of extraterritorial jurisdiction. There is no published case law in which the provision was implemented, and in practice, it is likely to be superfluous. However, should extreme circumstances arise in which the territorial state does not exercise jurisdiction over antisemitic crimes due to institutional antisemitism, and Israel's jurisdiction is the only one available to bring the perpetrator to justice (one the latter is in Israel), the exercise of that jurisdiction does not seem to raise undue difficulties.

3 Basic Law: Nation State

3.1 The Law

Basic Law: Israel – Nation State of the Jewish People states that "[t]he Land of Israel is the historical homeland of the Jewish People, in which the State of Israel was established"; that "[t]he State of Israel is the nation state of the Jewish People in which it realises its natural, cultural, religious and historical right to self-determination," and that the realisation of the right to self-determination in the State of Israel is exclusive to the Jewish people. The Basic Law determines the symbols of the state and more. Importantly, for present purposes, Section 6 proclaims the relations with the Diaspora:

a. The State shall strive to secure the welfare of members of the Jewish People and of its citizens, who are in straits and in captivity, due to their Jewishness or due to their citizenship.
b. The State shall act in the Diaspora, to strengthen the affinity between the State and members of the Jewish People.
c. The State shall act to preserve the cultural, historical, and religious heritage of the Jewish People among Jews of the Diaspora.

20 CERD, Article 1(4).

Section 6(b) is the only provision which explicitly mentions extraterritorial action. However, such conduct is implicit also in the other two sections, of which 6(a) is of particular interest.

The origin of the phrase "in straits and in captivity" is a Jewish morning prayer, and this provenance of the law's wording was repeatedly mentioned during the drafting process.[21] The prayer refers to salvation from the Heavens; its material, worldly implementation was restricted to financial assistance that community treasurers were expected to collect when members of the community were in debt or had been kidnapped for ransom. The Basic Law, in contrast, imposes a legal obligation upon the state.[22] Most proponents of the Basic Law probably saw this wording as a marginal and symbolic expression of a traditional Jewish deed.[23] But the drafters of the Basic Law attached a much broader meaning to the phrases 'secure the welfare,' and 'in straits and in captivity' than did the traditional text.[24] They imbued the words with a military undertone, in part on the understanding that the purpose was to ensure that 'never again.'[25] During the drafting negotiations, mention was made by the drafters of activities such as providing security services to Jews and Jewish institutions abroad and facilitating the relocation of Jews to Israel.[26] Yet Israel's past practice in the latter regard indicates its willingness to act on the territories of other states to assist Jews to leave for Israel was not restricted to instances where the danger to those persons' lives was because of their Jewishness.[27] Putting together that practice with the Basic Law's exhortations, Yoram Shachar warns that the expansive interpretations preferred by the drafters for the various components of Section 6(a) may create a constitutional obligation for the State of Israel to use force in the territory of other states in order to protect Jews suffering from various hardships, even if their connection to the State of Israel or to the Jewish people is tenuous and the cause of their distress is barely related to their identity.[28]

21 Yoram Shachar, "Article 6(a): 'The State Shall Strive to Secure the Welfare of Members of the Jewish People and of Its Citizens, Who Are in Straits and in Captivity, Due to Their Jewishness or Due to Their Citizenship'," in *Commentary on the Basic Law: Israel – the Nation-state of the Jewish People*, eds. Yuval Shany and Yedidia Z. Stern (Jerusalem: Israel Democracy Institute, 2023), 478.

22 *Ibid.*, 479.

23 There is a broader question of whether the Basic Law in its entirety is operational or merely symbolic, that has yet to be resolved, with the Supreme Court reserving judgment on the issue. HCJ 5555/18 *Hasson v The Knesset* (July 8, 2021), opinion of Justice Hayut, paras. 12, 48, 49. For views from the legislature and executive see Shachar, "Article 6(a)," 481–486.

24 Shachar, "Article 6(a)," 489–492.

25 A slogan associated with the lessons of the holocaust. Shachar, "Article 6(a)," 500.

26 Shachar, "Article 6(a)," 496–498.

27 For example, from Ethiopia in 1984 and 1991.

28 Shachar, "Article 6(a)," 474. For an example of an expansive interpretation of 'strait and captivity,' see Civil Case (Jerusalem) 2287/00 *Chaser estate v Zidan*, Decision 4 November

3.2 Compatibility with the Law on Extraterritorial Jurisdiction

Basic Law: Nation State problematically establishes extraterritorial executive jurisdiction for which there are no permissive rules under international law. Extraterritorial action may be lawful only if it is carried out with the territorial state's consent and within the limits of that state's laws;[29] or if permitted directly under international law, irrespective of domestic jurisdictional issues. The Basic Law does not preclude the possibility that Israel would obtain the territorial state's consent for a particular instance or as a general practice, but it does not require such consent as a condition for the exercise of extraterritorial executive jurisdiction. Article 6, in its entirety, therefore raises jurisdictional concerns.

Sections 6(b) and 6(c) are not exceptional in the goals that they set, namely to maintain the state's connection with its ethnic diaspora. Various states, especially in Central and Eastern Europe, have constitutional 'diaspora provisions.' However, the provisions of the Basic Law stand out in that they empower the state to act extraterritorially, whereas diaspora laws in Central and Eastern Europe are limited – except in rare instances such as Hungarian law – to granting benefits to kin foreigners when they are in the territory of the state itself[30] or to the standard provision of consular services.[31] According to the Venice Commission, extraterritorial activities, even in seemingly bureaucratic matters, could constitute unlawful intervention in another state if they go beyond the generally practised and accepted conduct of consulates.[32]

Article 6(a) is unique. It is not a diaspora law concerned with the continuous institutional maintenance of connections between Israel and world Jewry. Rather, it is an authorisation for the benefit of specific individuals, be they few or many. These measures could range from lawful provision of legal services for the defence in case of criminal proceedings[33] to emergency medical evacuation, which would likely receive the territorial state's consent; to military intervention, which would ordinarily not receive consent and be unlawful.

2018, a case in which victims of a terrorist act sued the Palestinian Authority. District judge Drori held that since the state failed in guaranteeing the welfare of the plaintiffs (alluding to the Basic Law), it must facilitate and assist them in exacting the maximum compensation available under Israeli law, para. 151.

29 Venice Commission, *Report*, 16. Such laws may raise other types of concern, such as regarding the prohibition on discrimination, primarily between ethnic communities within the state.

30 *Ibid.*, 15.

31 *Ibid.*, 18.

32 *Ibid.*

33 Compare with Russia's Federal Law on the State Policy of the Russian Federation in respect of compatriots abroad (adopted by the State Duma 5 March 1999, approved by the Federation Council 17 March 1999), as presented by Foreign Ministry Spokeswoman Maria Zakharova's comment on the EU's decision to include the Foundation for Supporting and Protecting the Rights of Compatriots Living Abroad on the sanctions list, 21 August 2023. Accessed 19 November 2023. https://mid.ru/en/foreign_policy/news/1901097/.

Under Israel's law, the presumption of harmonious interpretation demands that domestic law be interpreted under the assumption that the legislature intended to comply with the state's obligations under international law – namely, in this case, stopping short of permitting unilateral action in the territory of other states.[34] Yet the preparatory work on subsection 6(a) indicates that the intent of the drafters was specifically the opposite, namely to allow unilateral use of force outside state territory.[35] This hinders a harmonious interpretation, according to which the Basic Law establishes the authority to act outside state territory only when the action is carried out with the consent of the territorial state. However, since in some circumstances, activities such as those mentioned previously may be lawful under international law even without consent by the territorial state, a harmonious interpretation could be that the Basic Law grants authority to use force unilaterally in situations when the lives of Jewish citizens of a foreign state are in danger, in a manner engaging the responsibility to protect.[36]

4 Rabbinical Courts (Marriage and Divorce) Jurisdiction Law

4.1 The Law

Alongside the civil court system in Israel, there exists a system of religious courts that are competent to adjudicate in matters of personal status affecting members of their respective religious communities – in some cases exclusively, in others in parallel with the civil courts. In matters of marriage and divorce of Jews who are citizens or residents of Israel, the rabbinical courts have exclusive jurisdiction.[37] Traditionally, the religious courts adjudicate exclusively according to their religious law.[38] Accordingly, Jewishness for the purpose of marriage and divorce, as well as other matters in the jurisdiction of rabbinical courts, is determined by religious law.[39]

Under Jewish law, divorce consists of a bill of divorce (*get*) being voluntarily granted by the husband to his wife. It should not be forced on the wife. Thus, either spouse can withhold the divorce from the other by refusing to give the *get* or to receive it. However, the hardship caused to a wife held

34 Shachar, "Article 6(a)," 475.

35 *Ibid.*, 489–492. It would be left to a court to determine whether to interpret the provision according to the legislature's subjective purpose when its language permits a narrower interpretation.

36 For different perspectives on the circumstances in which the right to protect is engaged, see Ramesh Thakur, *Reviewing the Responsibility to Protect: Origins, Implementation and Controversies* (London: Routledge, 2018).

37 Rabbinical Courts Jurisdiction Law, s. 1.

38 Menashe Shava, "The Rabbinical Courts in Israel: Jurisdiction Over Non-Jews?" *Journal of Church and State* 27 (1985): 101.

39 More specifically, state-endorsed religious institutions interpret Jewishness and Judaism exclusively in accordance with orthodox doctrine.

captive in a marriage because of a husband's refusal to grant the *get* is much more severe than the hardship to a husband whose wife refuses to receive a *get*. The husband can effectively overcome the wife's refusal by obtaining rabbinical permission to marry bigamously. Women do not have this option. Moreover, while a man's extramarital relations carry no consequences for him and are thus a practicable option in case of refusal, a woman who maintains an extramarital relationship is an 'adulteress.' She may lose financial entitlements in her relationship with her husband, and her children born to a man who is not her husband are considered 'bastards.' Among other things, this makes it impossible for them to marry Jews.

Although divorce must be granted freely, in rare circumstances a rabbinical court may order and even compel a recalcitrant spouse to deliver or receive a *get*. Under Jewish law, a rabbinical court has wide leeway in terms of compulsion measures. Because of the rabbinical courts' status as part of the state's judicial apparatus, explicit legislation authorises these measures, which include severe limitations on freedom of movement, partial denial of statutory social benefits, and even incarceration and isolation during incarceration.[40] In 2017, the Supreme Court confirmed the rabbinical courts' authority to impose certain additional sanctions not specified in Israel's law.[41] Elsewhere in the world, where rabbinical courts exist, they are simply private arbitration-like institutions. Not being state organs, their writs are often disregarded by recalcitrant spouses, although in some cases, such as in New York State, state authorities require that the religious marriage be brought to an end before granting a civil divorce.[42]

Until 2005, the rabbinical courts' exclusive jurisdiction over divorce was limited to couples consisting of two Jews who were each connected to Israel through citizenship or residence and who were present in Israel at the opening of proceedings – at least constructively.[43] This was in line with the prevalent practice that the state of residence ordinarily has primary jurisdiction over divorce proceedings. In 2005, this jurisdiction was expanded to encompass over half a dozen situations in which only one of the spouses had a connection with Israel.[44] This expansion was criticised by legal experts for

40 Religious Courts (Enforcement of Compliance), 5716–1956.

41 Ruth Levush, "Israel: Extrajudicial Sanctions Against Husbands Noncompliant with Rabbinical Divorce Rulings," *Law Library of Congress*, May 2017. Accessed 19 November 2023. https://tile.loc.gov/storage-services/service/ll/llglrd/2017299909/2017299909.pdf.

42 Lisa Zornberg, "Beyond the Constitution: Is the New York Get Legislation Good Law," *Pace Law Review* 15(3) (1995): 706.

43 Rabbinical Courts Jurisdiction Law, s. 1.

44 Adjudication in Matters of Dissolving Marriages (Special Cases and International Jurisdiction) (Legislative amendments), 5765–2005.

expanding the state's jurisdiction far beyond that of other states, the laws of which do not allow *all* those links as direct jurisdictional links.[45]

Another expansion, enacted provisionally in 2018 and definitively in 2021, grants the rabbinical courts the power to order and compel the granting of a divorce when requested by women, even when neither spouse has any link (such as residence or nationality) to Israel.[46] The purpose of this expansion was to assist Jewish women from around the world, married in accordance with Jewish law, especially those belonging to ultra-Orthodox Jewish communities, when they cannot obtain a *get* in their state of residence.[47] The underlying premise of the amendment was that, regardless of the formal personal status of these women under the law in their state of residence, without a *get* they cannot properly remain and function within their community.[48] The amendment concerns only recalcitrant husbands, rather than wives, because of the latter's dependence on obtaining a valid *get,* which is, as noted previously, especially significant.

In broad terms, the amendment provides that a rabbinical court may exercise jurisdiction in any of three situations: If there is no court before which a divorce can be granted according to Jewish law in either the husband's or wife's place of residence; if the wife submitted an application for divorce according to Jewish law in a rabbinical court outside Israel, and the husband did not appear before the court for a period of four months; or if a rabbinical court outside Israel has determined that the husband should grant a divorce to his wife, but despite a reasonable effort to compel the divorce through the legal and religious means that exist in that country, the divorce has not been granted within a period of six months. If any of these situations occur, the jurisdiction of the rabbinical court in Israel is dependent solely on the documents being served to the husband in Israel, namely on his presence in Israel. The time limits for the various stages in the proceedings are expedited in comparison with the equivalent proceedings for Israeli litigants in order to minimise the inconvenience for defendant husbands who are caught in the legal net while visiting Israel.

45 Celia Wasserstein Fassberg, "Comments to Rabbinical Courts Jurisdiction (Marriage and Divorce) (Amendment No. 4) (International Jurisdiction in a Divorce Suit), 5772–2018," 25 April 2018, para. 1.

46 Rabbinical Courts Jurisdiction (Marriage and divorce) (Amendment No. 4) (International Jurisdiction in a Divorce Suit), 5772–2018, Rabbinical Court Jurisdiction (Marriage and Divorce) (Amendment No. 5 and Temporary Order) Law, 5782–2021, https://perma.cc/HK6B-BV9R.

47 Rabbi David Malka, Director, High Rabbinical Court, speaking in Meeting of Constitution, Law and Justice Parliamentary Committee, 5 June 2018. Accessed 20 November 2023. https://oknesset.org/meetings/2/0/2070906.html.

48 Adv. Shimon Yaakobi, Legal Advisor, Rabbinical Courts, speaking in Meeting of Constitution, Law and Justice Parliamentary Committee, 23 November 2021. Accessed 20 November 2023. https://fs.knesset.gov.il/24/Committees/24_ptv_614244.doc.

In the latter two situations triggering jurisdiction, the implied premise of the amendment is that the rabbinical courts in Israel have greater powers of compulsion over the husband than foreign rabbinical courts.[49] While this may be true in terms of law, in practice, Israel's rabbinical courts are often criticised for failing to make use of the powers granted to them, even when both spouses reside in Israel. It has, therefore, been questioned whether the extension of those powers to cases in which neither spouse resides in Israel is meaningful.[50]

Reliance on the amendment in practice has been examined in the annual reports by the Directorate of Rabbinical Courts. Those indicate that from 2018 to 2020, 119 divorce requests were filed on the basis of the amendment.[51] In the following year, the number dropped to 14, probably due to COVID-19.[52] An analysis of the latter 14 revealed that in nine of them, the rabbinical court could exercise jurisdiction without recourse to the amendment and that in the other five cases, the requisites for the exercise of jurisdiction under the amendment had not been fulfilled.[53] Thus, no case actually proceeded on the basis of the amendment.[54] Indeed, it has been argued that the requirement of the husband's presence in Israel, which was intended to mitigate the otherwise unlimited expansion of jurisdiction, rendered the amendment ineffectual because it hinged on the presence in Israel of persons who, by definition, had

49 Radzyner finds that this assumption may be misplaced. Amihai Radzyner, "Gittin: Mitsvot Ha'Teluyot Ba'Aretz? Prenuptial Agreements for the Prevention of Divorce Refusal: Between America and Israel," *Mishpatim* 47 (2018).

50 Sharon Shakargy, "Comments to Rabbinical Courts Jurisdiction (Marriage and Divorce) (Amendment No. 4) (International Jurisdiction in a Divorce Suit), 5772–2018," 29 April 2018. MK Merav Michaeli, speaking in Meeting of Constitution, Law and Justice Parliamentary Committee, 5 June 2018. Accessed 20 November 2023. https://oknesset.org/meetings/2/0/2070906.html; Response by private beth din that annulled Zvia Gorodetky's marriage 2019, https://www.cwj.org.il/sites/default/files/%D7%AA%D7%92%D7%95%D7%91%D7%AA%20%D7%91%D7%99%D7%AA%20%D7%94%D7%93%D7%99%D7%9F%20%D7%94%D7%A4%D7%A8%D7%98%D7%99%20%D7%9C%D7%98%D7%A2%D7%A0%D7%95%D7%AA%20%D7%91%D7%99%D7%AA%20%D7%94%D7%93%D7%99%D7%9F%20%D7%94%D7%A8%D7%91%D7%A0%D7%99.pdf#page=8; suggested by Shakargy, "Comments."

51 Discussion in Constitution, Law and Justice Parliamentary Committee, 17 November 2021, 19–21. Accessed 20 November 2023. https://fs.knesset.gov.il/24/Committees/24_ptv_613480.doc.

52 Adv. Avraham Singer, speaking in Meeting of Constitution, Law and Justice Parliamentary Committee, 23 November 2021, 19. Accessed 20 November 2023. https://fs.knesset.gov.il/24/Committees/24_ptv_614244.doc.

53 Adv. Avraham Singer, speaking in Meeting of Constitution, Law and Justice Parliamentary Committee, 17 November 2021, 30. Accessed 20 November 2023. https://fs.knesset.gov.il/24/Committees/24_ptv_613480.doc.

54 Directorate of Rabbinical Courts, Powerpoint Presentation Prepared for 9 November Meeting. Accessed 20 November 2023. https://fs.knesset.gov.il/24/Committees/24_cs_bg_610980.pdf#page=9.

no genuine link to the state and were, therefore, unlikely to visit it.[55] A different view of the amendment's effectiveness is put forward by organisations that assist women in obtaining divorce bills, who claim that the amendment's effectiveness lies not in the number of cases heard by courts, but in its deterrent effect, since the risk of being caught in proceedings – and detained – in Israel incentivised recalcitrant husbands to grant *gets*.[56] However, there is no indication that recalcitrant husbands prefer to grant a divorce for fear of proceedings rather than simply refrain from visiting Israel.

4.2 *Compatibility with the Law on Extraterritorial Jurisdiction: International Jurisdiction in Matters of Divorce*

The Rabbinical Courts' Jurisdiction Law, in its current version, extends the rabbinical courts' jurisdiction to men who have no connection with Israel simply because they are Jewish (by religion) and refuse to divorce their wives. This invasive and non-consensual arrangement causes significant difficulties both in terms of comity among states and the individual rights of the persons involved.[57] The 2005 amendment already strained these two issues by adding bases for jurisdiction that are far more numerous than those in other states and that call for relatively weak connections to Israel. The more recent amendment is particularly injurious to individual rights.

During the drafting negotiations, it was noted that the legislation's reliance on a shared religion with that of the majority population of the state to extend jurisdiction territorially is unprecedented.[58] It should be noted, however, that in Israel, the Jewish religion is not only practised by the majority of the population but is also incorporated into state law. Thus, the Jewish religion not only characterises the majority of the population but is a legal characteristic of the state.[59]

55 For example, "private beth din initiated by the Center for Women's Justice annulled the *kidushin* of another *aguna*," 16 January 2020. Accessed 20 November 2023. https://www.cwj.org.il/news/601.

56 Moriya Dayan, Yad Laisha, speaking in Constitution, Law and Justice Parliamentary Committee, 17 November 2021, 33. Accessed 20 November 2023. https://fs.knesset.gov.il/24/Committees/24_ptv_613480.doc; David Malka, Director of Rabbinical Courts, speaking in Meeting of Constitution, Law and Justice Parliamentary Committee, 9 November 2021. Accessed 20 November 2023. https://oknesset.org/meetings/2/1/2164025.html.

57 Shakargy, "Comments."

58 Rabbi Uri Regev, General-Director, Hiddush, speaking in Meeting of Constitution, Law and Justice Parliamentary Committee, 9 November 2021. Accessed 20 November 2023. https://oknesset.org/meetings/2/1/2164025.html.

59 Israel self-defines as 'Jewish and democratic' state. In this context, the word 'Jewish' denotes ethnicity rather than religion. However, not only is the distinction between the two complicated and controversial, the law does contain incorporate religious norms (for example, legislative prohibitions relating to religious holidays).

The requirement of service of documents in Israel minimises the likelihood of jurisdiction under the amendment being exercised, but it does not detract from the conceptual overreach of the amendment. The reliance on the service of documents even exacerbates this overreach because the husband's presence in Israel will be, almost by definition, fortuitous. In ordinary civil procedures, fortuitous presence indeed establishes jurisdiction, but unless there is a significant connection to Israel, the *forum non conveniens* doctrine will inhibit the exercise of jurisdiction.[60] In matters of personal status, a strong connection with Israel is always required, and the service of documents is regarded as merely a means of notifying the defendant. The Rabbinical Courts' Jurisdiction Law turns this matter on its head.[61] It is premised on a non-rebuttable assumption that Israel is the *forum conveniens* and makes a fortuitous presence in it a sufficient basis for jurisdiction.

When arguments on the excessiveness of the amendment under private international law rules were made in court, they were rejected on dubious grounds. In a case heard in the Rabbinical Court of Appeal, the husband appealed the lower court's jurisdiction on the grounds that exercising jurisdiction over an American citizen who had never violated any Israeli law and was detained merely because he was Jewish would violate private international law rules. The judges incorrectly suggested that the appellant had mistakenly invoked rules of jurisdiction under public international law and rejected his argument on the grounds that, under Israel's law, domestic law prevails over contrary public international law.[62] While Israel's law does give precedence to domestic law over public international law when the two are irreconcilable, the Court could have exercised its discretion to avoid the conflict. In another case, the Supreme Court held that, in line with existing case law, the amendment should be interpreted broadly so as to enable the rabbinical courts to offer relief to women who are denied a *get*.[63] The

60 The *forum non conveniens* provides the court with discretionary power to decline to exercise jurisdiction when a different court (*forum*) exists that may exercise jurisdiction and, in the particular circumstances of the case, is a more appropriate venue.

61 Fassberg, "Comments."

62 Case 1381090/1 *A v A, High Rabbinical Court in Jerusalem*, 3 February 2023, para. 9. A woman sued her husband for divorce in the Jerusalem Rabbinical court. The Court had before it letters from two rabbinical courts in Lakewood, New Jersey. One rabbinical court recounted that the wife had been seeking divorce for many years, but the husband was obstinate. The other rabbinical court wrote that it had repeatedly summoned the husband, but the latter did not make any contact. When the husband arrived in Israel, the wife requested and obtained a stay of exit order. She also submitted a claim in a rabbinical court in Israel.

63 HCJ 2170/23, *A v Regional Rabbinical Court of Tel Aviv*, Supreme Court of Israel, 7 May 2023. Accessed 20 November 2023. The disputed couple, married in England under Jewish law as well as state law, had been separated since 2019. In November 2021, while the husband was visiting Israel, the wife submitted a financial support claim against her husband in the Tel Aviv rabbinical court and obtained a stay of exit order. This was 11 days before the amendment

Court disregarded the fact that the expansive case law concerned domestic situations and that in a transnational situation, there are other factors to be considered. The Court further held that the requirements of service of documents in Israel and the exhaustion of options abroad resolve the private international law jurisdictional hurdle because they prevent incursion into the jurisdiction of foreign rabbinical courts. Additionally, since the rabbinical court's jurisdiction is limited to religious rather than civil status, the amendment does not interfere with the civil jurisdiction of other states.[64] The Supreme Court disregarded the interests of the defendant that the rules on jurisdiction are supposed to protect such as the right to due process, which may be endangered, for example, when the defendant is detained in Israel.[65]

During the negotiations on the drafting of the amendment, it was often highlighted that the amendment was initiated by the European rabbinical leadership, making the point that the affected communities were consulted and were supportive of it. However, the rabbinical leadership in the US, where almost half of world Jewry resides, was not consulted.[66]

The notion that rabbinical courts in Israel may exercise jurisdiction in these extreme circumstances, despite the absence of traditionally recognised connections to Israel, evokes the idea of a 'forum of necessity' rule

---

came into force. Two months later, the wife submitted a divorce claim. Relying on communication from the Manchester rabbinical court on failed efforts to persuade the husband to give a divorce, and after finding that in England the wife had no prospect for security the divorce, the Tel Aviv rabbinical court held that it had jurisdiction to hear the divorce claim. The husband disputed the rabbinical court's jurisdiction on the grounds that the substantive requirements (that a divorce in England could not be obtained) had not been proven. The desirability of releasing women from legal captivity has led rabbinical courts to interpret their jurisdiction and powers very broadly in general. In the context of the amendment, the Great Rabbinical Court's went so far as to dismiss as inconsequential the fact that the requirement of a husband's failure to appear before the foreign rabbinical court was fulfilled because he had already been detained – without legal authority – in Israel.

64 HCJ 2170/23, para. 14.

65 Any infringement on human rights must fulfill various requirements, one of which is that it is the least injurious means of achieving the desired (and legitimate) goal. Shakargy proposes that at the least, the European Rabbis Council, which initiated the legislation, could order rabbis to condition the performance of marriages on the parties accepting the authority of the Rabbinical Court in Israel under the amendment law. This would create awareness, if not consent, of the parties to the arrangement, and would be more or less objectionable from a private international law perspective.

66 Rabbi Uri Regev, General-Director, Hiddush, speaking in Meeting of Constitution, Law and Justice Parliamentary Committee, 9 November 2021. Accessed 20 November 2023. https://oknesset.org/meetings/2/1/2164025.html; and in Meeting of Constitution, Law and Justice Parliamentary Committee, 23 November 2021, 25. Accessed 20 November 2023. https://fs.knesset.gov.il/24/Committees/24_ptv_614244.doc.

of jurisdiction,[67] according to which a court may hear a claim despite the absence of a traditional jurisdictional basis when no other forum is available to the claimant, potentially subject to conditions that establish the forum has some interest in the dispute.[68] However, it is questionable whether Israel is such a forum. First, scholars have noted a variety of ways in which the granting of religious divorce could be facilitated in foreign states despite its informality in terms of state law.[69] Second, as a conceptual matter, one might ask whether individuals who voluntarily enter into an unequal relationship under non-state law, knowing that state institutions cannot release them from that relationship because it is not regarded by the state's law as legally binding, can be said to be in need of a particular forum in another state, by virtue of the fact that – fortuitously from their perspective, since they have no real and prior connection to that state – in that other state's law, the relationship is legally binding.[70] Moreover, it is ironic that the response to the plight of women who voluntarily (in terms of state law, at least) entered into a marital relationship under a non-egalitarian normative system should be a unilateral expansion of the same non-egalitarian normative system through the jurisdiction of a state that imposes it as the exclusive route to marriage and divorce.

5 Jurisdiction as an Expression of the Relations Between Israel and the Jewish People

Israel asserts extraterritorial legislative, executive, and adjudicatory jurisdiction in certain matters where Jews are involved as such. Legislative jurisdiction is asserted in the Penal Code, adjudicatory jurisdiction is arrogated in the Rabbinical Courts' Jurisdiction Law, and Basic Law: Nation State's provisions constitute a case of executive jurisdiction. Whether Jewishness is perceived as a person's ethnicity/nationality (as in the Penal Code and Basic Law: Nation State) or strictly as a religion (as in the Rabbinical Courts' Jurisdiction Law), the relevant legislative provisions push the limits of commonly practised and internationally accepted standards of extraterritorial jurisdiction. What follows is a discussion of Israel's perception of its role *vis-à-vis* the Jewish people, as reflected in its legislation. The drafters of the Penal Code stated that this relationship is one of 'affinity' that is so 'self-evident' that it is difficult to

67 Adv. Tammy Sela, Legal Advisor, Constitution, Law and Justice Parliamentary Committee, speaking in Meeting of Constitution, Law and Justice Parliamentary Committee, 5 June 2018. Accessed 20 November 2023. https://oknesset.org/meetings/2/0/2070906.html.

68 Alex Mills, "Private Interests and Private Law Regulation in Public International Law Jurisdiction," in *The Oxford Handbook of Jurisdiction in International Law*, eds. Stephen Allen et al. (Oxford: Oxford University Press, 2019), 342.

69 Radzyner, "Gittin"; Shakargy, "Comments."

70 On non-state law see Ralf Michaels, "What Is Non-State Law?," in *Negotiating State and Non-State Law*, ed. Michael A. Helfand (Cambridge: Cambridge University Press, 2015).

give reasons for it.[71] But the legal implications of this affinity must still be considered. The three legislative instruments convey a similar message: Jews around the world, whether as individuals or as communities, are, to some extent, Israel's concern.

Section 13(b)(2) of the Penal Code can be understood in either of two ways. One is as a response to the fact that Jews are often associated with Israel and that Jewish individuals are, therefore, often targeted in order to harm the State of Israel. Another way of understanding Section 13(b)(2) is as a response to antisemitism that is not related to Israel. This latter interpretation appears to be the better one because the title of Section 13 indicates that the protection of the Jewish people is distinct from the protection of the state. A similar perception arises from Section 6(a) of Basic Law: Nation State. Shuki Friedman, who was involved in the drafting of Basic Law: Nation State, holds that the State of Israel regards itself as the guardian of Jewish existence and that Section 6(a) confers upon it the duty and power to protect Jews from antisemitism.[72] This view is an unabashed assertion of Israel's prerogative to act internationally for the benefit of the Jewish people, even when no direct interest of the state is involved.

The differentiation between the State of Israel and the Jewish people is nonetheless blurred in the explanatory note to the bill that introduced Section 13(b), which grounded the protective jurisdiction regarding harm to a Jew or a Jewish institution because they are such, as "an expression of Israel being the state of the Jewish people."[73] This explanation may be read as an undertaking of the State of Israel to protect Jews from antisemitism, but it could also be read as implying that Israel regards any harm to Jews as harm to the State of Israel itself because all Jews are necessarily connected to Israel as a political entity. Indeed, the drafters of the Penal Code argued that Israel's constitutional makeup, as expressed in the Declaration of Independence and as understood by the majority of the Jewish public in Israel, rendered every Jew an 'absentee' from Israel.[74] They went so far as to frame this notion in quasi-legal terms, noting that, given that under Israel's 1950 Law of Return, any Jew may settle in Israel (and under Israel's 1952 Nationality Law, any immigrant relying on the right of return may acquire Israeli nationality), all world Jewry are potential citizens.[75] Friedman, too, regards the Law of Return (which concerns the right to enter and reside in Israel) as rendering the Jewish people and Israel a single group of reference. He even laments

71 Feller and Kremnitzer, "Reply," 85–86.

72 Shuki Friedman, "The Constitutional Status of the Diaspora in Israel: From Declaration to Obligation," in *Commentary on the Basic Law: Israel – the Nation-state of the Jewish People*, eds. Yuval Shany and Yedidia Z. Stern (Jerusalem: Israel Democracy Institute, 2023), 445.

73 Penal Law (Preliminary Part and General Part, 5752–1992), Statutory Bills 2098, 6 January 1992, 120.

74 Feller and Kremnitzer, "Reply," 86.

75 *Ibid.*, 85.

the fact that many Jews around the world 'deny' their connection to Israel,[76] implying that such a connection is a matter of objective reality.

In a scholarly debate that took place soon after the enactment of the Penal Code, Shachar criticised the Penal Code's wording for implying that the State of Israel and the Jewish people are inseparable.[77] The drafters responded that it was not easy to discern whether a particular instance in which harm is caused to a Jew is motivated by antisemitism or by hatred of Israel.[78] It is true that, as a matter of *fact*, it may be difficult to ascertain whether a particular crime was motivated by antisemitism or anti-Israelism (often related to anti-Zionism but not necessarily). But this does not justify conflating the two as a matter of *law*. There is no necessary connection between antisemitism and anti-Israelism.[79] Antisemitism existed prior to the State of Israel's establishment in 1948 and continues to exist today without any connection to it; conversely, people may oppose Israel as a colonial state without being antisemitic.

As for the meaning of protection from antisemitism: It is undeniably true that Israel was created mainly because the Jewish people lacked protection in other countries. But the protection that its creation sought to provide was the establishment of a political entity to serve as a home to Jews who wished to reside in it, not the assertion of global enforcement power against antisemitism. Nonetheless, the Penal Code's drafters made this leap when they held that it was unacceptable that antisemitic conduct would not be unaccounted for in the state of the Jews.[80]

Moreover, the legislation – both the Penal Code and Basic Law: Nation State – empowers the state to take action for the protection of Jews, both as individuals (who have been criminally harmed) and as a group. By asserting authority to exercise power over third parties, whether by criminalising antisemitic conduct and enforcing the law on perpetrators or by other measures to ensure the welfare of Jews *vis-à-vis* third parties, the state makes a claim over these individuals. Yet Jews around the world may object to being appropriated in this manner, whether as individuals[81] or as a group.

76 Friedman, "Diaspora," 465.

77 Yoram Shachar, "Against Extra-Territorial Application of Criminal Law on National Grounds," *Plilim* 5 (1996): 19–20.

78 Feller and Kremnitzer, "Reply," 84–85.

79 Despite attempts to claim that the latter is a manifestation of the former, for example, Prime Minister Benjamin Netanyahu's reaction to the ICC's confirmation of the investigation of the Palestine situation Haller, "Netanyahu Accuses ICC of Anti-Semitism in Pursuit of War Crimes Probe," Reuters, Declaration. 23 December 2019. Accessed 19 November 2023. https://www.reuters.com/article/world/netanyahu-accuses-icc-of-anti-semitism-in-pursuit-of-war-crimes-probe-idUSKBN1YR07Y/.

80 Feller and Kremnitzer, "Reply," 87.

81 Shachar, "Against Extra-Territorial Application," 41.

Appropriation is also evident in the use of the term 'diaspora' in Basic Law: Nation State. The term 'diaspora' describes communities that are voluntarily or otherwise detached from a political entity, such as their homeland, because either they or state borders have moved. While the land of Israel is undoubtedly the historical and religious source of the Jewish communities worldwide, the use of the term 'diaspora' in Basic Law: Nation State implies that World Jewry is categorically connected to the political entity that is Israel. This implication was forcefully criticised during the drafting of the amendment to the Rabbinical Courts' Jurisdiction Law by the Director-General of Hiddush, an NGO working for religious freedom and equality, who described the amendment's message as: "because I am a Jewish state, I therefore have authority over all the Jews in the world," and labelled it "a very strange concept."[82] Whether Jewishness is understood in the religious or in the ethnic/national sense, the assumption of an undisputed affinity flies in the face of reality. There are entire Jewish communities, let alone individuals, that not only do not associate themselves with the State of Israel but even oppose it.

The appropriation of world Jewry by Israel is problematic in more than one sense. First, it imposes on a person a legal relationship with a state to which they have no voluntary link. Granted, most individuals' relationship with their state of citizenship or residence is fortuitous and not voluntary. However, that relationship may be severed by renunciation of citizenship or emigration. In contrast, the relationship with Israel under the legislation described previously is non-severable and contains a particular set of unilaterally determined powers and obligations. Another problematic aspect of this appropriation is that it creates an appearance of dual loyalty, which may put a strain on the relationship between the community and its state of citizenship or residence.[83] Indeed, concern over precisely such a strain led to the inclusion of a non-prejudice clause in the Balfour Declaration's (and later Palestine Mandate's) endorsement of establishing a home for the Jewish people in Palestine.[84] The current legislation, which involves a greater risk of perceived disloyalty because Israel is a fully established state, makes no concession towards this concern.

The drafters of the Penal Code maintained that Section 13(b)(2) should be understood not as appropriation but as an undertaking by the State of Israel to protect world Jewry.[85] The same sentiment was expressed by the legal

82 Rabbi Uri Regev, General Director, Hiddush, speaking in Meeting of Constitution, Law and Justice Parliamentary Committee, 9 November 2021. Accessed 20 November 2023. https://oknesset.org/meetings/2/1/2164025.html.

83 In the context of the Penal Code, see Shachar, "Against Extra-Territorial Application," 41.

84 Lord Arthur J. Balfour, "Balfour Declaration," 2 November 1917. Accessed 20 November 2023. https://ecf.org.il/media_items/297.

85 Feller and Kremnitzer, "Reply," 86.

advisor of the rabbinical courts, who justified the amendment to the Rabbinical Courts' Jurisdiction Law on the grounds that

> [t]he only thing that women throughout the Jewish world want is that if they married according to the Jewish religion, there would be a country that would save them, as it provides relief to all Jewish women and men around the world.[86]

Friedman attempted to ground this undertaking, with respect to Basic Law: Nation State, in international law terms, arguing that "realisation of the right to self-determination in the nation state contains the option and *perhaps the obligation* of the nation state to preserve the people."[87] However, the right to self-determination, as understood in international law, is a political right of a people in a territory to political independence or another voluntary political choice.[88] For international law purposes, a 'people' is identified by reference to a territory.[89] It is, therefore, meaningless to speak of the nation state as distinct from the people who enjoy the right of self-determination because the nation state *is* that people (as understood under international law).

A state's undertaking to protect foreigners – even kin of the majority and hegemonic population – raises its own difficulties. The legislative instruments reviewed previously stand in some conflict with the obligations of a liberal democracy committed to the equal protection of the rights of all its citizens (and residents) and to the prioritisation of interests of its citizens over those of foreigners. Under the Penal Code, both Jewish and Arab citizens of the state are protected through the protective jurisdiction; but only the kin of Jewish citizens are protected under that jurisdiction, while not the kin of Arab citizens. This is because the State of Israel's constitutional ethos distinguishes its Jewish citizens from its Arab citizens and the Jewish people from others. Basic Law: Nation State entrenches this distinction constitutionally, stating that the realisation of the right to national self-determination in the State of Israel is exclusive to the Jewish people. Also, under Basic Law: Nation State, the state is constitutionally required to invest in the interests of foreigners. Given the finiteness of resources, such investment cannot but come at the expense of the state's own population (both Jewish and Arab). This may not antagonise most Jewish citizens because it is their kin who stand to benefit, but it is another manifestation of the fact that Basic Law: Nation State is explicit that

86 Adv. Shimon Yaakobi, Legal Advisor, Rabbinical courts, speaking in Constitution, Law and Justice Parliamentary Committee, 17 November 2021, 37. Accessed 20 November 2023. https://fs.knesset.gov.il/24/Committees/24_ptv_613480.doc.

87 Friedman, "Diaspora," 461.

88 Declaration on the Granting of Independence to Colonial Countries and Peoples, General Assembly Resolution 1514 (XV), 14 December 1960.

89 Hurst Hannum, *Autonomy, Sovereignty, and Self-Determination: The Accommodation of Conflicting Rights* (Philadelphia: University of Pennsylvania Press, 2011), 36.

collective rights accrue in Israel only to Jews. With regard to the Rabbinical Courts' Jurisdiction Law, the problem is more directly related to material resources, which are diverted in favour of foreigners over Israel's (Jewish) nationals and residents. The rabbinical court system is already caving under the load of files. The amendment exacerbates the detriment of Israeli litigants, not only by increasing the caseload further but also by granting foreign cases expedited schedule.[90]

6 Conclusion

Commenting on Sections 6(b) and 6(c) of Basic Law: Nation State, Friedman acknowledged that they tilt the balance between Israel's Jewish character and its democratic character towards the former.[91] This observation applies also to the other legislative instruments discussed previously. But, the effect of these instruments goes further than shaping Israel's internal character. They not only defy the obligation to treat all citizens (or residents) equally but also challenge the notion that a state's primary commitment is to its own population.[92] Framed in international legal terms, they invite an examination of the link between government, population, and territory as the indispensable mortar connecting the building blocks of a state.

References

Adjudication in Matters of Dissolving Marriages (Special Cases and International Jurisdiction) (Legislative amendments), 5765–2005.

Amnesty International. "Human Rights in Iran." https://www.amnesty.org/en/location/middle-east-and-north-africa/iran/report-iran/

Balfour, Lord Arthur J. "Balfour Declaration." 2 November 1971. https://ecf.org.il/media_items/297.

Benvenisti, Eyal. "Sovereigns as Trustees of Humanity: On the Accountability of States to Foreign Stakeholders." *American Journal of International Law* 107 (2013): 295–333.

BGH 5 StR 111/94, 20 March 1995 (LG Berlin). https://www.hrr-strafrecht.de/hrr/5/94/5-111-94.php.

Case 1381090/1. *A v A*, High Rabbinical Court in Jerusalem. 3 February 2023.

90 Gali Etzion, Parliamentary Committee for the Status of Women, speaking in Meeting of Constitution, Law and Justice Parliamentary Committee, 5 June 2018. Accessed 20 November 2023. https://oknesset.org/meetings/2/0/2070906.html; MK Gilad Kariv, Chair of Constitution, Law and Justice Parliamentary Committee, speaking in *Knesset* Plenary, 30 November 2021, 28. Accessed 23 November 2023. https://fs.knesset.gov.il//24/Plenum/24_ptm_612751.doc.

91 Friedman, "Diaspora," 470.

92 For an argument to the expansion of states' obligations outwards, but in different contexts than those considered here, see Eyal Benvenisti, "Sovereigns as Trustees of Humanity: On the Accountability of States to Foreign Stakeholders," *American Journal of International Law* 107 (2013): 295.

Chehtman, Alejandro. *The Philosophical Foundations of Extraterritorial Punishment*. Oxford: Oxford University Press, 2010.

Declaration on the Granting of Independence to Colonial Countries and Peoples. General Assembly Resolution 1514 (XV), 14 December 1960.

Feller, S. Z., and Mordechai Kremnitzer. "Reply to the Article 'Against Extra-Territorial Application of Criminal Law on National Grounds' by Professor Y. Shachar." *Plilim* 5 (1996): 65–99.

Friedman, Shuki. "The Constitutional Status of the Diaspora in Israel: From Declaration to Obligation." In *Commentary on the Basic Law: Israel – the Nation-state of the Jewish People*, edited by Yuval Shany and Yedidia Z. Stern, 445–472. Jerusalem: Israel Democracy Institute, 2023.

Gallant, Kenneth S. *International Criminal Jurisdiction: Whose Law Must We Obey?* Oxford: Oxford University Press, 2022.

Geiger, Rudolf. "The German Border Guard Cases and International Human Rights." *European Journal of International Law* 9 (1998): 540–549.

HCJ 2170/23, *A v Regional Rabbinical Court of Tel Aviv*. Supreme Court of Israel, 7 May 2023, Summary. https://marriage-il.com/תקציר-בגצ-2170-23-פלוני-07-05-2023-בית-משפט-עליון-דחה/.

ICTR. *Nahimana et al. v Prosecutor* (Media case), ICTR-99–52-A, 28 November 2007, paras. 502, 986–988. https://ucr.irmct.org/LegalRef/CMSDocStore/Public/English/Judgement/NotIndexable/ICTR-99–52/MSC31299R0000555179.PDF

International Convention on the Elimination of All Forms of Racial Discrimination (CERD), 21 December 1965. United Nations Treaty Series 660: 195.

International Covenant on Civil and Political Rights (ICCPR). United Nations Treaty Series 999: 171.

Levush, Ruth. "Israel: Extrajudicial Sanctions Against Husbands Noncompliant with Rabbinical Divorce Rulings." *Law Library of Congress*, May 2017. https://tile.loc.gov/storage-services/service/ll/llglrd/2017299909/2017299909.pdf

Michaels, Ralf. "What Is Non-State Law?" In *Negotiating State and Non-State Law*, edited by Michael A. Helfand. Cambridge: Cambridge University Press, 2015.

Mills, Alex. "Private Interests and Private Law Regulation in Public International Law Jurisdiction." In *The Oxford Handbook of Jurisdiction in International Law*, edited by Stephen Allen et al. Oxford: Oxford University Press, 2019.

Penal Code, 5773–1973.

Rabbinical Courts Jurisdiction (Marriage and Divorce) Law, 5713–1953.

Radbruch, Gustav, Bonnie Litschewski Paulson and Stanley L. Paulson. "Statutory Lawlessness and Supra-Statutory Law (1946)." *Oxford Journal of Legal Studies* 26 (2006): 1–11.

Radzyner, Amihai. "Gittin: Mitsvot Ha'Teluyot Ba'Aretz? Prenuptial Agreements for the Prevention of Divorce Refusal: Between America and Israel." *Mishpatim* 47 (2018): 5–59.

Religious Courts (Enforcement of Compliance), 5716–1956.

Rome Statute of the International Criminal Court (ICC Statute). 2187 United Nations Treaty Series 2187: 90.

Ryngaert, Cedric. *Jurisdiction in International Law*. Oxford: Oxford University Press, 2008.

Ryngaert, Cedric. "International Jurisdiction Law." In *Research Handbook on Extraterritoriality in International Law*, edited by Austin Parish and Cedric Ryngaert. Cheltenham: Edward Elgar, 2023.

Shachar, Yoram. "Against Extra-Territorial Application of Criminal Law on National Grounds." *Plilim* 5 (1996): 5–64.

Shachar, Yoram. "Article 6(a): 'The State shall strive to secure the welfare of members of the Jewish People and of Its Citizens, Who Are in Straits and in Captivity, Due to

Their Jewishness or Due to Their Citizenship'." In *Commentary on the Basic Law: Israel – the Nation-state of the Jewish People*, edited by Yuval Shany and Yedidia Z. Stern. Jerusalem: Israel Democracy Institute, 2023.
Shakargy, Sharon. "Comments to Rabbinical Courts Jurisdiction (Marriage and Divorce) (Amendment No. 4) (International Jurisdiction in a Divorce Suit), 5772–2018." 29 April 2018.
Shava, Menashe. "The Rabbinical Courts in Israel: Jurisdiction over Non-Jews?" *Journal of Church and State* 27 (1985): 99–112.
Shaw, Malcolm. *International Law*. Cambridge: Cambridge University Press, 6th edition. 2008.
Thakur, Ramesh. *Reviewing the Responsibility to Protect: Origins, Implementation and Controversies*. London: Routledge, 2018.
Venice Commission, Report on the Preferential Treatment of National Minorities by their Kin-State. Venice, 19–20 October 2001.
Wasserstein Fassberg, Celia. "Comments to Rabbinical Courts Jurisdiction (Marriage and Divorce) (Amendment No. 4) (International Jurisdiction in a Divorce Suit), 5772–2018." 25 April 2018.
Zornberg, Lisa. "Beyond the Constitution: Is the New York Get Legislation Good Law." *Pace Law Review* 15 (1995): 703–786.

Part II

Transitive Approaches

8 The United Kingdom's Approach to Criminal Extraterritoriality

Political and Policy Drivers

Paul Arnell

1 Introduction

The political and policy drivers affecting the United Kingdom's approach to criminal extraterritoriality are multifaceted. They are historical and current and manifest in the common law and in statute. They are both domestic and international. They are largely, but not exclusively, self-serving in that they purportedly act to benefit the UK *per se* or a UK-related interest. Such is the nature of the varied political and policy drivers, or influences, upon the extraterritoriality of the UK's criminal law discerning coherency and unity in thought and approach impossible. There is simply no single theory, factor, or related set of factors that explain it. Indeed, in some cases, the drivers are contradictory. These facts make the subject piecemeal and disjointed. UK extraterritorial jurisdiction is, as to be expected, reflective of the country's history, including its approach to crime and those living within it. There are two general contextual factors that particularly affect the extraterritorial application of UK criminal law. It is necessary to consider them first.[1]

2 The Context

2.1 Geography

Geography is one of the two pre-eminent contextual factors affecting the UK's approach to criminal jurisdiction, including extraterritorial criminal jurisdiction. The second is the fact that the legal systems within it are generally founded on the common law.[2] As to geography, the UK, like all countries, has been existentially affected by its physical location in the world. It is arguably the pre-eminent influence upon its approach to extraterritoriality. Great Britain is, of course, an island nation. It is only in the last century that

1 This chapter is, in part, based on the author's work, Paul Arnell, *Law Across Borders: The Extraterritorial Application of United Kingdom Law* (London: Routledge, 2012).

2 Scots law stands apart from the other UK jurisdictions through its civil law influence. See William G. Gordon, "The Civil Law in Scotland," *Edinburgh Law Review* 5 (2001): 130.

DOI: 10.4324/9781003402978-10

the UK has had one contiguous neighbour, the Republic of Ireland.[3] The UK comprises four nations: England, Wales, Scotland, and Northern Ireland. This latter fact is relevant, in part, because they entail three differing legal jurisdictions and the possibility of distinct approaches to extraterritoriality being taken. Historically, a lack of land borders has played a major role in territoriality becoming a central jurisdictional principle or basis, discussed further later on. The constraints consequential to geography have, of course, greatly lessened over the years, with jurisdictional effects.[4] Immigration from former colonies, EU Member States, and elsewhere changed the UK's population demographic.[5] This is relevant to the extent that, in conjunction with technological and travel-related developments, increased mobility has created space for the commission of extraterritorial crimes. It has also contributed to changing conceptions of the personal relationship between those living in the UK and the state. Also relevant in recent years is the ability to commit crimes remotely via the internet. Indeed, some of the most high-profile extradition cases in the UK – where third states have attempted to assume a form of extraterritorial jurisdiction – have concerned remotely committed criminality. One example of this is the US extradition request for Julian Assange.[6] Overall, there is no doubt that geography has played a significant part in the development of the rules of criminal jurisdiction in the UK. There is also little doubt that its influence has waned in modern times.

2.2 *Common Law Jurisdictions*

The UK is made up of common law jurisdictions. This "unwritten law has the same force as statute [and] receives its binding power from long and immemorial usage and universal reception throughout the realm and its authenticity rests entirely upon reception and usage, as declared by the judges".[7] The

3 In 1921, the Anglo-Irish Treaty established the Irish Free State, creating a land border between it and the six counties in the North.

4 One such effect, following immigration to the UK of persons from diverse cultures, has been a broadening of the crimes subject to extraterritorial jurisdiction. Historically, 'regular' crimes could be committed whilst a UK national or subject was abroad, such as murder. In more recent years, what can be termed, from a UK perspective, culturally affected criminality, has come to be included. Amongst the latter category of crimes are those of so-called 'honour-abuse' and female genital mutilation (FGM), see Crown Prosecution Guidance, "So-called Honour-Based Abuse." Accessed 6 January 2025. https://www.cps.gov.uk/legal-guidance/so-called-honour-based-abuse. In UK law both are subject to extraterritorial jurisdiction.

5 Philip H. Rees, Pia Wohland and Paul Norman, et al., "Populations Projections by Ethnicity: Challenges and Solutions for the United Kingdom," in *The Frontiers of Applied Demography*, ed. David Swanson (London: Springer, 2017), Chapter 18.

6 See Paul Arnell and Clive Walker, "The Resurrection of the Political Offence Exception to Extradition in UK Law," *New Journal of European Criminal Law* 15 (2024): 412.

7 Daniel Greenberg, Jowitt's Dictionary of English Law, *Common Law* (London: Sweet and Maxwell, 6th ed., 2023).

common law is jurisdictionally relevant for at least two reasons. Firstly, it provides a jurisdictional presumption that the criminal law is territorial.[8] Secondly, with a number of crimes having their basis in the common law and with statutory crimes being interpreted by the courts, it is the judiciary that is not uncommonly responsible for the extension of the criminal law across the UK's borders. This can arise, for example, where an offence 'occurs' in more than one country, and a question arises over where exactly it was committed for the purposes of a UK court taking cognisance of the act.[9] Clearly, the common law is significant in coming to an understanding of extraterritoriality and, in particular, the role of political and policy drivers behind the law's extension. As will be seen below, the UK's approach to transnational and extraterritorial criminal jurisdiction is found in an admixture of judicial precedent and legislative enactment. Whilst the latter is directly and explicitly driven by political and policy considerations, the common law is less so. Accordingly, the nature and substance of the political and policy drivers of UK common law transnationality and extraterritoriality are more difficult to discern.

3 Territory in UK Criminal Jurisdiction

The starting point of a consideration of the political and policy drivers behind extraterritoriality in UK law and practice is, paradoxically, territory. This is because territory is the foundation stone of jurisdiction in the country. The position of territory is such that extraterritorial crimes are, traditionally at least, exceptional. Territory is also relevant because it has been interpreted or stretched such that it can extend to extraterritorial and transnational circumstances.

The extraterritorial and transnational application of UK criminal law is of considerable pedigree, including that linked in some way to UK territory.[10] Criminal law has evolved from a position where its territorial nature was near absolute to a situation where it is tenable to argue that territory as the basis of the law is anachronistic. This is a function of the increasing and considerable extensions and exceptions to territorial jurisdiction. There is no doubt, however, that the origins and basis of UK criminal law is territory. There is indubitable common law support for it in England and Wales and

8 Julian D. M. Lew, "The Extra-territorial Criminal Jurisdiction of English Courts," *International and Comparative Law Quarterly* 27 (1978): 168.

9 *Ibid.*, 169.

10 Note that 'UK criminal law' is inaccurate. England, Wales, Scotland, and Northern Ireland have their own criminal law. Jurisdictionally, however, they are kindred. See generally as to the history of the criminal law being applied extraterritorially, Michael Hirst, *Jurisdiction and the Ambit of the Criminal Law* (Oxford: Oxford University Press, 2003), especially Chapter 2, "Historical, International and Other Influences," 28–59.

Scotland.[11] That support sheds light on the reasons, the political and policy drivers, for that position. In the Scottish context, Lord Young in *H.M. Advocate v Hall* stated:

> The general rule is that criminal law is strictly territorial – so that a man is subject only to the criminal law of the country where he is, and that his conduct there, whether by acting, speaking, or writing, shall be judged of as criminal or not by that law and no other.[12]

The point made here is that the law and territory are inherently connected to the exclusion of the law of other countries and jurisdictions.

The consequence or corollary of the pre-eminence of territory was that extraterritoriality was generally untenable and only exceptionally operative. David Hume, the authoritative Scottish institutional writer, made that point at the beginning of the 19th century. He stated:

> A person domiciliated here, whether a Scotsman or a foreigner, for any crime he may have committed abroad, is not liable to be tried before our courts. They are not instituted to administer justice over the whole world, but in our country, or a particular district of it only; and, therefore, if the crime charged has been committed beyond those limits, they are neither called upon not entitled to step forward for its correction.[13]

David Hume here alludes to the competence of Scottish courts over a particular spatial area – within Scotland or an area of it.

The jurisdictional position of territory in England and Wales is similar to that in Scotland. In *Cox v Army Council,* it was stated that "apart from those exceptional cases in which specific provision is made in regard to acts committed abroad, the whole body of the criminal law of England deals only with acts committed in England".[14] This primacy of territory has been said to follow "criminal justice in the troublous days of the dawn of civilization in the British Isles [being] concerned so exclusively with the problem of keeping the peace".[15] More practically, territory as a basis of jurisdiction

11 Discussing the continental approach are Christopher L. Blakesley and Otto Lagodny, "Finding Harmony Amidst Disagreement Over Extradition, Jurisdiction, the Role of Human Rights, and Issues of Extraterritoriality Under International Criminal Law," *Vanderbilt Journal of Transnational Law* 24 (1991): 1.

12 (1881) 4 Couper 438.

13 David Hume, *Commentaries on the Law of Scotland, Respecting Crimes* ii (Edinburgh: Bell and Bradfute, 1819), 52.

14 [1963] A.C. 48, 67.

15 Rollin M. Perkins, "The Territorial Principle in Criminal Law," *Hastings Law Journal* 22 (1970–71): 1157.

was "based on the fiction that innocence or guilt was determined by the empanelment of a jury who had personal knowledge of the accused and his culpability".[16] Here, it is geography in a localised sense that was vital. It is of some note as regards the early political and policy drivers behind jurisdiction that the nationality or residence of the accused was not directly relevant.[17] In England, and indeed the whole of the UK, the general rule is that "offences committed by British subjects out of England are not punishable by the criminal law of this country".[18] Allegiance, citizenship, or nationality and residence were not, and are not, general bases of jurisdiction. There has never been a political or policy imperative such that general criminal liability is attached to classes of individuals with a close connection to the country.

An illustration of the position of territory in UK criminal law – and, again, its place in the common law – is found in the rule of statutory interpretation that presumes that statutory offences apply only within the territory of the UK. In *Air India v Wiggins,* Lord Diplock stated that

> in construing Acts of Parliament there is a well-established presumption that, in the absence of clear and specific words to the contrary, an 'offence-creating section' of an Act of Parliament . . . was not intended to make conduct taking place outside the territorial jurisdiction of the Crown an offence triable in an English criminal court.[19]

Interestingly, this presumption applies with greater force to non-nationals. As Lord Diplock stated:

> The presumption against a parliamentary intention to make acts done by foreigners abroad offences triable by English criminal courts is even stronger. As Lord Russell of Killowen C.J. said in *R v Jameson* "One other general canon of construction is this – that if any construction otherwise be possible, an Act will not be construed as applying to foreigners in respect to acts done by them outside the dominions of the sovereign power enacting".[20]

This position lends strong support to the prevalence of territoriality and militates against the extraterritorial application of the law. It also sheds light on

16 Lew, "The Extra-territorial Criminal Jurisdiction," 168.

17 Allegiance, rather than nationality and residence, was the form of personal connection between an accused and the British state that found a place in early extraterritorial criminal provisions, see further later on.

18 *R v Page*, [1953] 2 All ER 1355, 1356 per Lord Goddard CJ.

19 [1980] 1 WLR 815, 819.

20 [1896] 1 QB 425, 430.

what will be discussed later: the jurisdictional relevance of the relationship between nationals, others, and the UK.

3.1 The Origins of Territory – Political and Policy Drivers

Territory was, and arguably is, a critical, almost existential facet of UK criminal jurisdiction. A question is why? An underlying factor is that the lesser mobility of persons in previous centuries led to there being little need to conceive of the law in any other way. Neither Parliament nor the judiciary was commonly seized with the question of the criminal law's scope or, more relevantly, an actual or perceived need to criminalise extraterritorial behaviour. As Michael Hirst notes, the reason the law was not extended can be seen to lie in the fact that "until relatively recent times, there was little (if any) perceived need for widespread change . . . . Crime . . . was generally considered to be entirely a local or territorial concern".[21]

The sufficiency of territoriality as a basis of jurisdiction is only part of the explanation for its position. Supplementing that was the role of venue and that the common law, as noted, "generally required that any indictable offence – treason, felony, or misdemeanour – should be tried in the county in which the relevant acts were alleged to have occurred, by a jury drawn from the residents of that county".[22] Hirst continues "the fundamental point was that a jury drawn from the *vicenage* was more qualified than any other body to ascertain the facts at issue" and the "venue doctrine almost accidentally contributed to the principle of territoriality, under which events abroad were regarded as beyond the criminal law's concern".[23] Local knowledge and the jury system, therefore, played real roles. The policy underlying (local) territoriality was that it enhanced the effectiveness of the criminal law in keeping the peace in a defined, local, area.

Further supporting the view that the origins of criminal law are inherently entwined with territoriality is O'Brien, who notes:

> The United Kingdom has, from the 19th century, been a strong supporter of the territorial system: (a) because in criminal law matters it is for the people of the relevant territory to determine the rules they wish to live under; (b) it is practical in that English criminal procedure places considerable reliance on the testing of oral testimony by cross-examination. That is best achieved in the relevant territory.[24]

21 Hirst, *Jurisdiction and the Ambit*, 56.
22 *Ibid.*, 29.
23 *Ibid.*, 30–33.
24 John O'Brien, *International Law* (London: Cavendish Publishing, 2001), 237.

The evidential and procedural point was, and is, an important one. The political and policy drivers here are underlying and inherent in the law – geography, localisation, effectiveness and criminal procedure. They have conspired to place territory at the heart of criminal law. In doing so, they have led to extraterritorial and transnational criminal jurisdiction being exceptional.

3.2 *Territoriality Extended – Political and Policy Drivers*

In recent decades, the UK's jurisdictional attachment to territory has remained. Paradoxically, the law has also been increasingly applied to extraterritorial and transnational circumstances. In response to various political and policy drivers 'territory' has been stretched. There has not, however, been a root and branch consideration of the law's attachment to territory.[25] Instead, the law has evolved in a reactive and *ad hoc* way. Accordingly, there are no single overarching political and policy considerations that inform territorial, or indeed extraterritorial and transnational, jurisdiction.

Territory in a jurisdictional sense has been considered and applied in different ways in UK jurisprudence and legislation. Befitting the importance of the common law, academics over the years have sought coherence and commonalities within jurisdictional jurisprudence. Such writers include Glanville Williams,[26] Julian Lew,[27] and Michael Hirst.[28] This body of work is, of course, distinct from the numerous writers taking an international law perspective to the subject.[29] Intrinsic to both domestic and international analyses of territory is the fact that a territorial link between a country and a crime can take three forms. It can be complete, with the whole offence (acts and effect or result) occurring within one territory or jurisdiction. It can be partial, with a particular part or aspect of the crime, such as the initial or

25 There has been the influential English Law Commission Report, The Territorial and Extraterritorial Extent of the Criminal Law, Law Commission Number 91, 1978. It did not, however, lead to a general amendment to the criminal law *per se*. There is also the Home Office Steering Committee Report, Review of Extra-Territorial Jurisdiction, July 1996, Home Office Communication Directorate, 7/96.

26 Glanville Williams, "Venue and Ambit of the Criminal Law," *Law Quarterly Review* 81 (1965): 276.

27 Lew, "The Extra-territorial Criminal Jurisdiction."

28 Hirst, *Jurisdiction and the Ambit.*

29 See Cedric Ryngaert, *Jurisdiction in International Law* (Oxford: Oxford University Press, 2nd ed., 2015); Micheal Ó Floinn, Lindsay Farmer, Julia Hornle and David Ormerod, eds., *Transformations in Criminal Jurisdiction* (London: Hart Publishing, 2023); W. Michael Riesemann, ed., *Jurisdiction in International Law* (Brookfield: Ashgate, 1999); Michael Akehurst, "Jurisdiction in International Law," *British Yearbook of International Law* 46 (1972–73): 145; Paul Arnell, "Criminal Jurisdiction in International Law," *Juridical Review* (2000): 179, and the classic Harvard Research Group, "Draft Convention on Jurisdiction with Respect to Crime," *American Journal of International Law* 29 (1935) (Supp): 480.

last act, effect(s) or result, or gist of the offence occurring within a territory. Or it can be general, with a connection of a requisite degree taking place within that territory, whatever its particular nature. The latter two of these forms will be considered later, with the underlying political or policy drivers being evinced.

3.2.1 Common Law Territorial Jurisdiction

The meaning of territory in a jurisdictional sense has been affected over the years by UK case law. The initial extensions of territory in the common law, whilst applying the law transnationally, limited the ambit of the law on what can be perceived as technical grounds.[30] It was the terminatory theory or approach that was adopted in the relatively early jurisprudence.[31] It provides that where and when an offence was 'completed' was critical for the purpose of jurisdiction. This applied to both 'conduct' and 'result' crimes. Conduct crimes were justiciable where some of the proscribed conduct occurred within the country, and result crimes were where some of the proscribed results did.[32] In practice, this meant that courts have considered "an offence to be committed where it is completed".[33] An illuminative example is in *HMA v Witherington.*[34] In the case it was held that the courts had properly taken cognisance of crimes of falsehood, fraud, and wilful imposition even though the accused was outside Scotland during the relevant period. That view was challenged because the accused

> is an Englishman; that the only fraud or criminal act alleged against him was committed in England: that he was never was in Scotland, and is not subject to the criminal law or to the jurisdiction of the criminal Courts of Scotland; that criminal jurisdiction does not extend *extra territorium*, and that the true foundation of ordinary criminal jurisdiction is the *locus delicti.*[35]

30 Farmer writes, "One of the most striking features of the [territorial] doctrine is that questions of jurisdiction have been dealt with on a piecemeal basis, responding to particular problems as they arose, with the result that the mass of provisions that developed in this area were (and remain) extremely technical and complex," Lindsay Farmer, "Territorial Jurisdiction and Criminalisation," *The University of Toronto Law Journal* 63(2) (2013): 225, 241.

31 Farmer notes, "The English courts historically took the objective view – that a crime was committed where it was completed," *Ibid.*, 240.

32 See *The Secretary of State for Trade v Markus* [1975] I All ER 958, 965, per Lord Diplock.

33 Hirst, *Jurisdiction and the Ambit*, 119.

34 (1880–81) 8 SC (JC), 41.

35 *Ibid.*, 46.

The reply was,

> The argument is certainly plausible, and there is, at first sight, something startling and paradoxical in the proposition that a man may commit a crime in a place in which he was never personally present. This proposition is nevertheless technically or constructively, but actually, true.[36]

The political and policy driver behind the law applying on a terminatory basis is not difficult to discern – the prohibited act or conduct occurred within the territory and accordingly merits punishment.

The common law has evolved over the years. This has entailed a move to a more general and inclusionary approach to the particular connection to territory required by the law. In *R (Purdy) v DPP*,[37] Lord Hope commented, with reference to *Smith (Wallace Duncan) (No 4)*,[38] that that case "settled the law on the point" on the appropriate approach to territorial jurisdiction.[39] It supported a broader approach. Of some note is the criticism of *Smith (Wallace Duncan) (No 4)*. The Law Commission of England and Wales in 2007 noted that "A recent academic article has described *Smith (Wallace Duncan) (No 4)* as 'controversial' and based on 'policy rather than principle'".[40] That policy is noted by the academics in the article as founded upon an "anxiety . . . that in contemporary society where international financial activity is so commonplace the reach of English criminal law should not be unduly impeded by technicality".[41] Here, then, is a putative example of policy – the desire to counter transnational fraud – affecting the common law's approach to territory.

Inchoate crimes are of particular relevance in understanding the common law (and legislative) move away from overly restrictive approaches to territorial jurisdiction. As regards the situation where persons abroad conspire or attempt to commit a crime within the UK, common law has evolved. A leading authority here is the decision of the Privy Council in *Somchai Liangsiriprasert v Government of the United States*.[42] In it, Lord Griffiths stated:

> Unfortunately in this century crime has ceased to be largely local in origin and effect. Crime is now established on an international scale

36 *Ibid.*

37 [2010] 1 AC 345.

38 [2004] EWCA Crime 631.

39 [2009] UKHL 45, para. 23.

40 The Law Commission, "Participating in Crime," May 2007, LC307, 10 May 2007. https://lawcom.gov.uk/project/assisting-and-encouraging-crime-participating-in-crime/, referred to Tom Rees and David Ormerod, "Jurisdiction of English Courts – Obtaining by Deception," *Criminal Law Review* (2004): 951.

41 *Ibid.*, 953.

42 [1991] 1 AC, 225.

> and the common law must face this new reality. Their Lordships can find nothing in precedent, comity or good sense that should inhibit the common law from regarding as justiciable in England inchoate crimes committed abroad which are intended to result in the commission of criminal offences in England.[43]

This policy behind this development appears to be in line with that in *Smith (Wallace Duncan) (No 4)*. This is simply because, in the absence of such jurisdictional evolution, acts committed abroad which contemplate harm within the UK would not be justiciable. The realities of modern criminality, and the judicial desire to act against them, were recognised and acted upon. In the converse circumstances, where an accused acts within the UK with an intention to attempt, incite, *etcetera,* a criminal act abroad Parliament has legislated.

3.2.2 Legislative Territorial Jurisdiction

The legislative approach to territorial jurisdiction is distinct from that found in the common law. It is, of course, different in form, being found in statute, not precedent. It is also, to an extent, different in substance. An early example, in section 10 of the Offences Against the Person Act 1861, takes both an initiatory and terminatory approach. As regards the former, jurisdiction is provided for where an offence commences within the UK. Section 10 *inter alia* states:

> Where any person . . . being criminally stricken, poisoned, or otherwise hurt in any place in England or Ireland, shall die of such stroke, poisoning, or hurt upon the sea, or at any place out of England or Ireland, every offence committed in respect of any such case . . . may be dealt with, inquired of, tried, determined, and punished . . . in England and Ireland.[44]

Section 4 of the 1861 applied similarly to conspiracy and solicitation to murder.[45] The policy behind its enactment can be discerned from the Parliamentary debates on the Offences Against the Person Bill. It is stated:

> Conspiracy to murder, as recent and unhappy experience had shown us, was an offence which might, not improbably, be committed in this country, either by foreigners acting alone or by foreigners in concert with Englishmen; and considering the conclusions – at times not very charitable to our feelings and sense of justice – drawn by Continental Government from the large and wide hospitality we afforded

43 *Ibid.*, 252.
44 Note that this provision also provides for the converse situation.
45 The crime of conspiracy is no longer proscribed by section 4, see later.

> to refugees of every kind, it was worthy of consideration whether, when there could be no great or serious objection, we should not put our law in such a form as might relieve us from discreditable accusations.[46]

Interestingly, the policy behind extending territorial jurisdiction on an initiatory basis was driven by an attempt to address criticisms from a continental European government over conspiracies by persons within the UK, including foreign nationals, to murder persons abroad.[47]

Over 130 years later, a somewhat similar legislative provision was inserted into the Criminal Law Act 1977. Section 1A was included in 1998 by the Criminal Justice (Terrorism and Conspiracy) Act 1998 and amended in 2009. It makes it an offence under English law, under certain conditions, to conspire in England to commit an offence abroad (as well as in other parts of the UK – by the Coroners and Justice Act 2009).[48] Notably, the Act was passed in the wake of the terrorist bombing in Omagh, Northern Ireland, in 1998. It extended the rules in regard to the crime of conspiracy generally, not merely in relation to terrorist conspiracies. Broadly, the Act criminalises agreements made within England and Wales to commit offences outside of that territory where there is a link between the agreement and the UK.[49] This is subject to the requirement that the offence to which the conspiracy relates is recognised as such in the territory in which it is intended to come to fruition as well as England and Wales.[50]

An example of the conspiracy under the 1977 Act being applied is found in *R v Patel (Sophia)*.[51] Here, Patel and others were convicted or pled guilty under section 1A of conspiring to unlawfully take immigrants into the United States. As explained in the judgment:

> The plain purpose of that amendment was to give the English courts extra-territorial jurisdiction in relation to conspiracies which are formed or carried out, at least in part, in England and Wales and where the object is the commission of a foreign offence.[52]

46 House of Commons Hansard, 15 July 1861, vol. 164, col. 928, per R. Palmer, Attorney General.

47 That government appears to have been the French, see *Ibid.*, col. 930–931.

48 See generally Colm Campbell, "Two Steps Backwards: The Criminal Justice (Terrorism and Conspiracy) Act 1998," *Criminal Law Review* (1999): 941, and Hirst, 142–148.

49 Campbell, *Ibid.*, 955.

50 This is a form of the double criminality requirement. Also of considerable note is the Criminal Justice Act 1993, which substantially altered the jurisdictional rules surrounding the application of a number of crimes – broadly falling under the rubric of fraud and blackmail.

51 [2009] EWCA Crim 67. It should be noted that these rules on conspiracy apply only where the agreement at issue would not be otherwise criminal.

52 *Ibid.*, para. 6.

The political and policy drivers behind the enactment of section 1A of the 1977 Act are discerned from the House of Commons debates leading to it. Jack Straw MP said, after alluding to the bombing in Omagh in Northern Ireland, "We have to send the clearest message to international terrorist groups that we in the United Kingdom will not allow this country to be used as a base for plotting and supporting terrorist operations abroad".[53] The impetus for the extension of the law in this vein, then, were transnational conspiracies commencing within the UK with a view towards the commission of terrorism-related offences abroad.

The last example to be mentioned where territory has been 'stretched' by way of legislative enactment relates to sexual offences. It usefully highlights a political and policy driver distinct from that which led to section 1A of the 1977 Act. In England and Wales and Northern Ireland, the Sexual Offences (Conspiracy and Incitement) Act 1996 criminalises *inter alia* incitement to commit sexual acts against children outside the UK. In introducing the Bill that led to the 1996 Act, John Marshall MP referred to the "revolution in overseas travel", and then stated, "Other people use this new-found freedom to travel for far darker purposes. Paedophiles, or child molesters as they ought to be called, go to countries where child prostitution is rife in order sexually to abuse young children".[54] Giving light into the political driver, he stated, "One cannot find words sufficient to describe the contempt felt by us all for the disgusting, degrading behaviour of some individuals. Unfortunately, some of the perverts who visit other countries for such holidays are British".[55] Significantly, the possibility of sexual crimes going unpunished abroad, in part on account of failings of extradition, was discussed:

> Extradition can take place only at the request of another country. If the countries concerned want to enforce their laws, they may seek to extradite British citizens. If they do not want to enforce their laws, there is nothing that the British Government can do. We cannot extradite citizens unless the countries concerned produce the evidence and it is up to them to do so.[56]

The aim of the Bill, affected by these political and policy drivers, then, was to make it

> far more difficult for British citizens to indulge in those activities by making it an offence to incite people to go on those holidays, an offence

53 House of Commons Hansard, 2 September 1998, vol. 317, col. 736.
54 House of Commons Hansard, 2 February 1996, vol. 270, col. 1225.
55 *Ibid.*, at col. 1227.
56 *Ibid.*, at col. 1230.

to organise those holidays and an offence for rings of paedophiles to encourage others to go on those holidays.[57]

4 Relationship Between Accused and UK – Active Personality

The most commonly employed form of wholly extraterritorial criminal jurisdiction in the UK is active personality, founded upon the relationship that the accused has with the state. The political and policy drivers behind it differ somewhat from those behind stretched territorial jurisdiction. Consideration of active personality jurisdiction can usefully take two forms. These are the types or categories of persons that have been and are deemed to fall within it, as well as the criminal acts that have been and are subject to its application.

The categories of persons subjected to this form of jurisdiction in UK law are opaque and inconsistent. This point reflects, in part, the fact that this type of jurisdiction is not uncommonly termed both nationality-based jurisdiction and active personality jurisdiction.[58] The latter is more accurate. It reflects the range of relevant relationships relied upon by states, including the UK, in extending criminal law. Those relationships go beyond nationality or citizenship. Indeed, those relationships did not form the original basis of jurisdictional relationships in UK law. Today, there are a relatively large number of such relationships and descriptions and definitions thereof. As Hirst has written, amongst them are 'any subject of Her Majesty', 'a British subject', 'a British officer or subject', 'a citizen of the United Kingdom and colonies', 'a British citizen', 'a United Kingdom national, a United Kingdom resident or a person subject to United Kingdom service jurisdiction', 'resident in the United Kingdom', 'resident in the United Kingdom, the Isle of Man or any of the Channel Islands,' and 'a United Kingdom person'.[59] There are others mentioned later. These varied iterations and expressions detrimentally affect clarity and consistency, of course. They both evince and obscure the political and policy drivers behind active personality jurisdiction.

57 *Ibid.*, at col. 1232. It should be noted that the Sexual Offences Act 2003 in England, Wales, and Northern Ireland and the Sexual Offences Act 2009 in Scotland, criminalise a number of substantive crimes of a sexual nature committed abroad on the basis of nationality and residence – they will be discussed later, along with the political and policy drivers affecting their enactment.

58 The former was used by the present author in Paul Arnell, "The Case for Nationality Based Jurisdiction," *International and Comparative Law Quarterly* 50 (2001): 955, and the latter in the International Bar Association's Legal Practice Division, "Report of the Task Force on Extraterritorial Jurisdiction." Accessed 6 January 2025. https://www.ibanet.org/MediaHandler?id=ECF39839-A217-4B3D-8106-DAB716B34F1E.

59 Hirst, *Jurisdiction and the Ambit*, 204. For a discussion of residence in relation to the International Criminal Court Act 2001, see Robert Cryer and Paul D. Mora, "The Coroners and Justice Act 2009 and International Criminal Law: Backing into the Future?" *International and Comparative Law Quarterly* 59 (2010): 803.

Early designations, including 'any subject of Her Majesty' as in the Offences Against the Person Act 1861, reflect the point at which the particular legislation was enacted and the prevalent view of citizenship, nationality, and belonging more generally subsisting at that time.[60] Active personality jurisdiction has been affected by changes in that vein. An important alteration took place in the middle of the 20th century. It was largely an attempt to "ensure the uniformity of British subjecthood, the possession of identical rights and privileges by all British subjects in the Commonwealth and Empire".[61] A review of citizenship commissioned by the UK government, the Goldsmith review, notes that the concept of citizenship has undergone a massive change, especially over the last century. Peter Goldsmith writes that it has changed from being solely a relationship between "individuals and the state; it has become a basis of connection between individuals".[62] This entailed, in general terms, a move from subjecthood to citizenship.[63] Of note are the reasons put forward for the evolution:

> This change occurred for a number of reasons: the expansion of the franchise, which meant that the broadest range of individuals became equal to one another as political citizens; the growth of cities, where we live in close contact with people of different backgrounds and different means; and the wide sense of social solidarity created by conflict and sacrifice during the Second World War.[64]

As noted, this evolution is seen in the changes in the forms of relationship-based jurisdiction relied upon in UK legislation. In this vein, Goldsmith notes the blurring of citizenship, where the distinction between citizens and non-citizens, or aliens, became less clear. Non-nationals with indefinite leave to remain in the UK (permanent residents), for example, have entitlements akin to citizens. Goldsmith points out that a question arises in terms of loyalty, where "non-citizens may be the subject to the duty of allegiance".[65] There is little doubt, however, that citizenship-related changes have influenced the development of UK relationship-based jurisdiction.

60 The British Nationality Act 1948 "removed the status of 'subject of the King' as the basis of British Nationality . . . [it] thus brought about an immense constitutional revolution, an entire alteration of the basis of our subjecthood and nationality," Enoch Powell, House of Commons Hansard, 3 March 1953, vol. 512, col. 245.

61 Randall Hansen, "The Politics of Citizenship in 1940's Britain: The British Nationality Act," *Twentieth Century British History* 10(1) (1999): 69.

62 Peter Goldsmith, "Citizenship: Our Common Bond, Review of British Citizenship," *Department of Justice*, 2008, 10–11.

63 Hansen, "The Politics of Citizenship," 70.

64 Goldsmith, "Citizenship," 11.

65 *Ibid.* Treason in UK law is the paradigmatic crime founded on a betrayal of allegiance, discussed later.

Reflecting the evolution of citizenship is, in relatively recent times, increasing reference to 'UK nationals' in active personality provisions. Section 4(3) of the Cluster Munitions (Prohibition) Act 2010, for example, applies the offences created by the Act outside the UK where committed by UK nationals, Scottish partnerships, and bodies incorporated under the law of any part of the UK. Defining UK nationals is section 4(6). It provides, that for the purposes of the section, UK nationals means

> an individual who is (a) a British citizen, a British overseas territories citizen, a British National (Overseas) or a British Overseas citizen, (b) a person who under the British Nationality Act 1981 is a British subject, or (c) a British protected person within the meaning of that Act.

Whilst the offences subjected to relationship-based jurisdiction are discussed later, it is useful here to note that the genesis of the Cluster Munitions (Prohibition) Act 2010 was the Convention on Cluster Munitions 2008,[66] as the preamble to the 2010 Act explicitly provides.

Demonstrating further change in the scope of UK active personality jurisdiction is the Sexual Offences Act 2003. It extends certain sexual offences to acts abroad committed by UK nationals, UK residents, and those who, after the offence has been committed, become a UK national or resident by section 72. Today, those crimes apply to residents, although not nationals, only where double criminality is satisfied.[67] Originally, double criminality applied to both nationals and residents. It was removed from nationals under section 72 of the Criminal Justice and Immigration Act 2008. Following the change, Maria Eagle MP stated that it would be possible to prosecute "a British citizen for child sex offences committed overseas regardless of whether the acts are legal in the country in question".[68] Within the 2003 Act, the definition of 'United Kingdom resident' is found in section 72(9), and it tautologically states that a "United Kingdom resident means an individual who is resident in the United Kingdom".

A detailed and complex definition of UK resident for jurisdictional purposes was only inserted into the law in 2010. It is found in the International Criminal Court (Scotland) Act 2001 and the International Criminal

66 Interestingly, the Convention does not explicitly provide that crimes related to cluster munitions be extended extraterritorially on the basis of nationality. Article 9, instead, *inter alia*, provides that state parties shall take measures, including the imposition of penal sanctions, to prevent activity prohibited by it undertaken by a person under its jurisdiction or control.

67 In *R v DA* [2023] EWCA Crim 1428, it was held that the fact that prosecution had been barred in the country where it had occurred by the expiry of a limitation period did not prevent the accused resident's trial and conviction in England. The 2003 Act is mentioned further later on.

68 House of Commons Hansard, 1 July 2008, vol. 478 col. 689WA.

Court Act 2001.[69] The definition is similar in both statutes. Section 8A of the International Criminal Court (Scotland) Act 2001 *inter alia* provides that a UK resident means a person who is resident in the UK. It then lists a number of persons who are to be considered residents for the purposes of the Act. They include an individual who has indefinite leave to remain in the UK, any individual who has made an application for such leave who is in the United Kingdom, and an individual who has leave to enter or remain in the United Kingdom for the purposes of work or study and who is in the United Kingdom. The list is not exhaustive. This detailed iteration of residence in a criminal jurisdiction context in the UK is notable, in part, for reflecting the varied and complex immigration status of persons in the country.

The political and policy driver behind the inclusion of a detailed definition of residence in the International Criminal Court Act 2001 was the desire to enhance the effectiveness of the provisions in that Act. Along with providing for the retrospective application of the crimes in the UK, the inclusion of specific categories of persons deemed resident was designed to remove the opacity around that category of person and to expand the concept to include those who might not have been otherwise. In a House of Lords debate on the proposed changes to the 2001 Act, Lord Bach, for the Government, firstly discounted the possibility of extending jurisdiction to those merely present in the UK. He said:

> We are not persuaded that extending the law to those simply 'present' here would be right. Short-term visitors here are not seeking a safe haven in the UK and they should ideally be prosecuted in the country where they are resident. To cover them would be a significant increase in our jurisdiction over people with no connection to the UK, except for temporary presence.[70]

Universal jurisdiction, therefore, was rejected. Lord Bach said, "Our aim is not to become a policeman for the world".[71] Instead, the meaning of residence was clarified for the purposes of the 2001 Act. Of some note was the fact that the extradition and possible prosecution case of a number of Rwandan nationals in the UK was mentioned in the House of Lords debate. Their extradition to Rwanda had been barred by the UK courts, and they were not prosecuted

69 Section 32 of the Criminal Justice and Licensing (Scotland) 2010 Act inserted a new Section 8A into the International Criminal Court (Scotland) Act 2001, and Section 70(4) of the Coroners and Justice Act 2009 inserted a new Section 67A into the International Criminal Court Act 2001.

70 Lord Bach, Parliamentary Under-Secretary of State, Ministry of Justice, House of Lords Hansard, 7 July 2009, vol. 712, col. 659.

71 *Ibid.*

in the UK despite the serious allegations against them.[72] The individuals had come to the UK in the aftermath of the genocide and claimed asylum.

Joining private natural persons as entities that may commit offences outside the UK are corporations and other legal persons, crown servants, and members of the armed forces. As regards legal persons (as well as natural persons), the Bribery Act 2010 is an interesting example.[73] Section 7 of that Act criminalises the failure of commercial organisations to prevent bribery. A commercial organisation is *inter alia* defined as a body which is incorporated under the law of any part of the United Kingdom and which carries on a business (whether there or elsewhere). In the Guidance produced by the Ministry of Justice on the Act, the breadth of the policy motivating the offences in the Act is evident. It states, in part, that tackling bribery is a priority for "anyone who cares about the future of business, the developing world or international trade".[74] In a similar vein, "Bribery undermines democracy and the rule of law and poses very serious threats to sustained economic progress in developing and emerging economies and to the proper operation of free markets more generally".[75] Clearly, the political and policy drivers here are relatively broad and not limited to the UK's national interest.[76]

Distinct and unique classes of persons for the purposes of jurisdiction are crown servants and members of the armed forces. The criminal law *in toto* applies to them when they commit crimes in the course of their employment, unlike the *ad hoc* application of the law in the case of nationals and residents generally.[77] As regards crown servants, the Criminal Justice Act 1948 section 31 and the Criminal Jurisdiction Act 1802 section 1 generally govern the extraterritorial application of the criminal law. The rationale that led to section 31 of the 1948 Act was described in the debates leading to its enactment. The then Lord Chancellor said, after alluding to the "sort of case with which it is meant to deal",

> Suppose one of our citizens . . . is in Germany, working under the Control Commission. Suppose that man does some disgraceful or discreditable act against some German – robbery, rape or what you will – and

72 See The Independent, "Five Rwandan Genocide Suspects Living Freely in Britain 30 Years After Massacre," 6 April 2024.

73 See Paul Arnell and Nicola Evans, "The Effect of the Bribery Act 2010," *Juridical Review* (2015): 61.

74 Ministry of Justice, "The Bribery Act 2010 – Guidance about Procedures Which Relevant Commercial Organisations Can Put into Place to Prevent Persons Associated with Them from Bribing," March 2011, 2.

75 *Ibid.*, 8.

76 Also a relevant driver was the OECD Convention on Combatting Bribery of Foreign Public Officials in International Business Transactions, 1997. The UK ratified the treaty in December 1998.

77 See, for example, Hirst, *Jurisdiction and the Ambit*, 209–216.

> then comes over to this country. Extradition is not available, because there is no Treaty, and he cannot be tried at all.[78]

The policy behind the 1948 Act, then, was to prevent the criminal immunity of crown servants for certain acts abroad. Interestingly, an attempt to have a former Prime Minister prosecuted for administering a noxious substance contrary to section 23 of the Offences Against the Person Act 1861 was unsuccessful because, in part, as Prime Minister, he was an office holder, not an employee of Her Majesty's Government.[79]

The application of the law to members of the armed forces is governed by the Armed Forces Act 2006. The essence of the regime of service law is that the regular criminal law is applied to acts of members of the armed forces whilst abroad – in addition to a variety of specific offences and a separate system of prosecution.[80] Section 42 of the 2006 Act provides that a person subject to service law, or civilian service discipline, commits an offence if he does any act that is punishable by the law of England and Wales or, if done in England and Wales, would be so publishable. It is not the regular courts, however, that try crimes under service law. Rather, they are tried by court martial, a system which has been subject to criticism.[81] The political and policy drivers behind this extension of the law are longstanding, centring upon the requirement to maintain discipline where armed forces may be stationed around the globe.[82]

4.1 Types of Crimes Applied on Active Personality Basis in UK

A second approach to understanding the political and policy drivers behind UK active personality jurisdiction entails focusing on the crimes to which it is attached. Those crimes are generally one of three types: long-established crimes of indigenous origin, modern crimes – also of indigenous origin, and crimes having their origin in an international agreement or obligation. The paradigmatic example of the first type is treason. It is criminalised by the Treason Act 1351.[83] Further crimes of this type are found in the Offences Against the People Act 1861, viz. bigamy,[84] murder, and manslaughter. All of

78 House of Lords Hansard, 7 June 1948, vol. 156, col. 358, per Viscount Jowitt.

79 *R (on the application of Defending Christian Arabs) v Guilford Magistrates' Court*, [2020] EWHC 1850 (Admin).

80 See generally the Manual of Service Law 2021, Jurisdiction and Time Limits, vol. 1, Chapter 3.

81 See Lord Thomas, House of Lords Hansard, 23 November 2017, vol. 787 col. 387.

82 The Explanatory Notes to the 2006 Act refer to the law governing the armed forces as a 'discipline system'. This refers to specific offences, such as assisting an enemy, and the criminal law of England and Wales generally.

83 Only one section of the Act, section 2, remains in force. A notable example of the crime being extraterritorially applied is *Joyce v DPP*, [1946] AC 347.

84 See The Trial of *Earl Russell*, [1901] AC 446.

these crimes apply extraterritorially on the basis of the relationship between the accused and the UK. Specifically, what is required is for the accused to be a subject of His Majesty. In line with the previous discussion, the extension of these crimes is premised upon the notion that, in certain cases, at least, the allegiance of British subjects transcends the border and substantiates extraterritorial criminal liability.[85] Whilst true, this fact obscures the point that the interests protected by these crimes differ considerably. Whilst generally public, they include protecting the sanctity of the state and its leaders, the institution of marriage, and the probity of subjects. The political and policy drivers of this first group of active personality-based crimes centre upon the protection of disparate public domestic and exceptionally international interests.[86]

The second type of active personality crime in UK law, generally those of a more recent origin, differs somewhat from the original incarnation. This is through the interests protected being broader in scope, including private and non-UK public interests. A notable example is sex-related crimes. The Sexual Offences (Scotland) Act 2009 extends the scope of a number of 'listed offences' in Scotland on the basis of nationality and residence. The Sexual Offences Act 2003 provides similarly for England, Wales, and Northern Ireland. The policy or political motivation driver for the extension of these crimes is not a UK public interest alone, albeit it seemingly includes reducing the likelihood of intra-territorial recidivism. What appears to be the case is that international solidarity and a general abhorrence of certain acts are germane. Relatedly, actual and perceived inefficiencies within the criminal justice systems of third states and the failings or difficulties with extradition and criminal cooperation agreements are also relevant. The failure of third-country prosecution and punishment has spawned and supported a belief by UK legislators and others of the need to provide for the domestic possibility. Leading to the enactment of the Sexual Offences Act 2003, Lord Falconer of Thoroton in the House of Lords stated:

> The Government are committed to tackling the sexual exploitation of children wherever it occurs in the world. This includes where UK citizens go abroad with the intention of abusing children. We have already put in place a number of measures to deal with this problem, but the Sexual Offences Bill, currently before Parliament, provides us with an

85 This is not to suggest that all crimes of a relatively early pedigree so operated. Section 2 of the Explosive Substances Act 1883, which criminalised causing explosions, originally applied to all persons, but was limited to citizens of the UK and Colonies and persons in the Republic of Ireland by the Criminal Jurisdiction Act 1975.

86 Mentioned previously is a factor leading to the 1861 Act being the desire to respond to foreign government objections to conspiracy to murder taking place in England.

> opportunity to ensure that we are doing everything we can to deal with those who commit sexual offences overseas.[87]

If the exploitation of children by UK nationals and residents was addressed where committed, the purpose behind the extension of UK law would, to some extent at least, be met overseas.

The third type of UK active personality-based crime is distinguished by its treaty derivation. The UK is party to a number of conventions which oblige, or permit, state-parties to criminalise certain behaviour and to extend their jurisdiction in certain ways. An example of a statute consequent to a treaty is the Landmines Act 1998. It criminalises the use of an anti-personnel mine, the development or production of an anti-personnel mine, and the assistance, encouragement, and inducement of such conduct. Section 3(1) of the 1998 Act provides that those crimes "apply to conduct in the United Kingdom or elsewhere". Those covered are UK nationals, Scottish partnerships, and bodies incorporated under the law of a part of the United Kingdom.

The conventional origin of the Landmines Act 1998 is the Convention on the Prohibition of the Use, Stockpiling, Production and Transfer of Anti-Personnel Mines and on Their Destruction 1997. It provides, in Article 9, that

> Each State Party shall take all appropriate legal, administrative and other measures, including the imposition of penal sanctions, to prevent and suppress any activity prohibited to a State Party under this Convention undertaken by persons or on territory under its jurisdiction or control.

In introducing the Landmine Bill to the House of Commons, Robin Cook MP, said, "the Bill gives full effect to the terms of the Ottawa Convention. Clause 2 prohibits British service men, or any other British citizen, from . . . possessing or exporting a landmine".[88] It is of some note that the interpretation of persons "under its jurisdiction or control" was interpreted to include UK nationals whilst abroad. There are a considerable number of further examples of UK crimes extended on the basis of active personality pursuant to an international legal obligation.[89]

The political and policy drivers for these crimes naturally align with the purpose of the convention to which they relate. They also include a manifestation of the UK's support for the international rule of law. This latter point

87 House of Lords Hansard, Written Answers, 6 March 2003, col. WA 123.

88 House of Commons Hansard, 10 July 1998, vol. 315, col. 1347. Note, the debate included argument that the Bill had not fully or appropriately implemented the Convention, see *Ibid.*, at cols. 1353 et seq.

89 These include the Nuclear Explosions (Prohibition and Inspections) Act 1998.

is an important one. It goes beyond the direct and immediate political and policy drivers to deeper and underlying considerations. Evidencing this influence is Lord Hermer, the UK Attorney General, who said in October 2024 in a speech entitled The Rule of Law in an Age of Populism, "Historically, the UK has been a leader in developing and promoting international law and the institutions on which effectiveness depends".[90] He argued that the UK's role in that regard is "so essential in today's highly-connected, but highly fragmented, world".[91] As regards the Landmine Convention itself, the UK government in 2023 noted that it continues to call for its universalisation and the destruction of anti-personnel mines in areas under state parties' jurisdiction or control.[92]

An interesting and contrasting example of conventionally-mandated active personality jurisdiction in the UK is found in the Domestic Abuse Act 2021 and the changes that that Act made to other legislation. The relevant treaty is the Council of Europe's Convention on Preventing and Combatting Violence Against Women and Domestic Violence 2011 (the Istanbul Convention). The 2011 Convention *inter alia* obliges state parties to make provision on extraterritorial jurisdiction as regards a number of offences relating to violence against women and domestic abuse. As the Explanatory Notes to the 2021 Act provide, while UK law provided for such jurisdiction in regard to female genital mutilation (under s.4 of the Female Genital Mutilation Act 2003) and forced marriage (s 121 of the Anti-social Behaviour, Crime and Policing Act 2014) a number of offences in the Convention were not subject to it.[93] Those offences include psychological violence, stalking, and sexual violence, including rape.

Amongst the relevant provisions in the 2021 Act is section 72, which *inter alia* subjects to extraterritorial jurisdiction murder, manslaughter, offences relating to bodily harm or injury, administering poison, and child destruction.[94] By section 72(1), the crimes extraterritorially apply to nationals and habitual residents. Notably, the section includes a double criminality requirement. The desire to limit the law in this way required the UK to enter a reservation to the Convention on this point.[95] Section 74 and Part 1

90 Delivered in the Annual Bingham Lecture. Accessed 6 January 2025. https://www.gov.uk/government/speeches/attorney-generals-2024-bingham-lecture-on-the-rule-of-law.

91 *Ibid.*

92 See House of Commons Library Landmine Awareness and Mine Action, 6 April 2023, CDP–0084.

93 Explanatory Notes to the Domestic Abuse Act 2021, paras. 48–53.

94 As noted previously, murder and manslaughter are applied to subjects of His Majesty on an extraterritorial basis under the Offences Against the Person Act 1861. This provision extends those crimes to, inter alia, those habitually resident in the UK.

95 See House of Lords Library, Istanbul Convention: Preventing and Combatting Violence Against Women and Domestic Violence, 23 June 2022, section 2.1.

of Schedule 3 of the 2021 Act also extends on an extraterritorial basis, *inter alia*, stalking under the Protection of Harassment Act 1977, rape and sexual assault where the victim is over 18 years of age under the Sexual Offences Act 2003, and coercive and controlling behaviour under the Serious Crime Act 2015. This example of the extension of the criminal law in the UK jurisdictions is notable for its breadth.[96] The political and policy drivers encompass both the UK's international legal obligation as well as organic concern over domestic abuse. As to the latter, the Explanatory Notes to the 2021 Act state, "Domestic abuse remains one of the most prevalent crimes in England and Wales".[97]

5 Relationship Between Victim and UK – Passive Personality

The second form of relationship-based jurisdiction is the converse of active personality. It describes instances where the law is extended with reference to the victim of an alleged crime. Termed passive personality in international law, this form of relationship-based jurisdiction has not traditionally found favour within the UK. It only became a part of UK law in 2000, in the form of section 63C of the Terrorism Act 2000.[98] Entitled Terrorist attacks abroad on UK nationals, residents, diplomatic staff, etc.: jurisdiction it *inter alia* provides:

> (1) If (a) a person does anything outside the United Kingdom as an act of terrorism or for the purposes of terrorism, (b) his action is done to, or in relation to, a United Kingdom national, a United Kingdom resident or a protected person, and (c) his action, if done in any part of the United Kingdom, would have constituted an offence listed in subsection (2), he shall be guilty in that part of the United Kingdom of the offence.

There is a relatively long list of offences in subsection 2, including murder, rape, assault causing injury, kidnapping, abduction, and false imprisonment.

Important in the application of section 63C is, of course, the meaning of "an act of terrorism or for the purposes of terrorism". Section 1 of the Terrorism Act 2000 provides that 'terrorism' means the use or threat of action *inter alia* comprising serious violence against a person where the use or threat is designed to influence the government or to intimidate the public or a section of the public, and the use or threat is made for the purpose of advancing a political, religious racial or ideological cause. Notably, according with the third type of active personality crimes, section 63C was enacted to comply with an

96 Similar provision has been made as regards Scotland and Northern Ireland.
97 Explanatory Notes to the Domestic Abuse Act 2021, para. 11.
98 A second instance in UK law is found in s. 113A of the Anti-terrorism, Crime and Security Act 2001 relating to the use of noxious substances.

international instrument.[99] That being Article 9(1)(e) of the EU Framework Decision on Combating Terrorism 2002.[100] It *inter alia* states:

> Each Member State shall take the necessary measures to establish its jurisdiction over the offences referred to in Articles 1 to 4 where: . . . (e) the offence is committed against the institutions or people of the Member State in question or against an institution of the European Union or a body set up in accordance with the Treaty establishing the European Community or the Treaty on European Union and based in that Member State.[101]

The Explanatory Notes to the Crime (International Co-operation) Act 2003 state that Part 2 of that Act, which introduced into the Terrorism Act 2000 the sections extending the law, affected the implementation of the Framework Decision. The political and policy driver behind the UK's one reference to passive personality jurisdiction is clearly a European legal obligation. It, in turn, is founded upon the collective desire to counter acts of terrorism. The Minister introducing the Bill that ultimately led to the section 63C stated,

> The Bill . . . takes extra-territorial jurisdiction over terrorist offences committed overseas against UK nationals, diplomatic staff and diplomatic premises . . . . We supported that measure during its negotiation in Brussels and welcome this opportunity promptly to implement the changes needed to bring it into force.[102]

6 Relationship Between the Interest Affected and the UK – Protective Jurisdiction

The interests affected by a crime, particularly domestic interests, form the basis of a distinct form of jurisdiction. Here, the law applies in the absence of any other connection between the accused and the UK apart from a crime affecting a specified interest. Termed protective jurisdiction in international law, it has traditionally been applied by countries regarding immigration

99 In contrast, the provision relating to passive personality jurisdiction in the Istanbul Convention was not acted upon by the UK. Article 44(2) provides that parties "shall endeavour" to establish jurisdiction where a relevant offence is committed against their nationals and habitual residents.

100 The 2002 Framework Decision OJ L 164, 22/06/2002, was repealed and replaced by Directive (EU) 2017/541 of the European Parliament and of the Council of 15 March 2017 on combating terrorism. Of course, EU law is distinct from public international law.

101 *Ibid.*

102 House of Lords Hansard, Crime (International Co-Operation Bill), 1 April 2003, vol. 402, col. 803.

and currency offences.[103] The UK has generally eschewed this approach.[104] Of considerable note here, however, is the National Security Act 2023. In force from December 2023, the Act criminalises three acts under the heading espionage.[105] They are obtaining or disclosing protected information, obtaining or disclosing trade secrets, and assisting a foreign intelligence service under sections 1–3. Section 36 provides that offences under Part 1 of the Act (including those mentioned) committed through conduct occurring outside the UK can be committed whatever the individual's nationality and, where committed by a body corporate, regardless of it being recognised by a country or territory outside the UK. The section 1 offence is particularly relevant regarding this form of jurisdiction. The protective element of the offence is manifest by the condition that the conduct is carried out with the individual knowing, or ought to have reasonably known, that it is prejudicial to "the safety or interests of the United Kingdom".[106] Unlike the other two offences, it applies without further conditions or restrictions.[107] As such, the section 1 offence represents an unprecedented extension of the UK's criminal jurisdiction on a protective basis.

Indicating the policy behind the UK's assumption of protection jurisdiction under the National Security Act 2003 is the Factsheet produced by the Government to accompany the Act. It notes that new technologies have created opportunities for states to conduct espionage against the UK outside its territory.[108] Further, it quoted from a previous Integrated Review of Security, Defence, Development and Foreign Policy,[109] noting that "the distinction between economic and national security is increasingly redundant". The breadth of the jurisdictional provision in section 1, giving force to the policy to act in such circumstances, was criticised during the legislative process. The Joint Committee on Human Rights, when scrutinising

103 See Kenneth S. Gallant, *International Criminal Jurisdiction* (Oxford: Oxford University Press, 2022), chapter 6, and Iain Cameron, *The Protective Principle of International Criminal Jurisdiction* (Dartmouth: Dartmouth Publishing, 1994).

104 A case sometimes used as an example of the UK taking such an approach to the application of its law is *DPP v Joyce*, [1946] AC 347. Shaw suggests that this "seems to have been applied" in this case in Malcom Shaw, *International Law* (Cambridge: Cambridge University Press, 6th ed., 2008), 667, whilst Hirst, *Jurisdiction and the Ambit*, 49, discounts this by highlighting the fact that Joyce was a British passport holder and so the law could be applied on the basis of his relationship to the UK.

105 It repeals the previously applicable Official Secrets Acts 1911, 1920, and 1939.

106 Found in sections 1(b), and 3(4).

107 The offences under sections 2 and 3 are limited, where the relevant conduct wholly takes place outside of the UK, to 'UK persons' and Crown employees. UK persons are defined by section 2(6) and *inter alia* include a UK national and an individual who lives in the UK.

108 New Espionage Offences: Factsheet, 19 August 2024. Accessed 6 January 2025. https://www.gov.uk/government/publications/national-security-bill-factsheets/espionage-etc-national-security-bill-factsheet.

109 16 March 2021, CP 403.

the Bill leading to the Act, noted that it had particular concerns about the operative phrase in section 1, "safety or interests of the United Kingdom". It argued that this required to be defined as it entailed ambiguity and a subjective approach.[110] The Law Commission, on the other hand, recommended that the phrase be retained.[111] As seen, it found its way into the law. The UK now has unabashedly adopted law that squarely falls within the category of protective jurisdiction. The political and policy drivers behind its enactment included heightened concern about espionage in part driven by technological developments.

7 Relationship Between the Crime and the UK – Universal Jurisdiction

UK law contains a form of jurisdiction that turns on the nature of the crime itself. It does not require any other link between the UK and the accused, victim, or domestic interests. These crimes are, in the parlance of international law, applied on a universal basis.[112] The application of the law on a universal basis in the UK is exceptional because it is attached to relatively few crimes. Examples include piracy, crimes against aircraft and ships, torture, hostage-taking, and crimes against internationally protected persons and United Nations personnel. All these crimes have a basis in international law. Amongst them, piracy is notable for its longstanding nature and common-law basis. Highlighting the rationale behind international law criminalising piracy is Viscount Sankey, who stated:

> according to international law the criminal jurisdiction of municipal law is ordinarily restricted to crimes committed on its *terra firma* or territorial waters or its own ships, and to crimes by its own nationals wherever committed, it is also recognised as extending to piracy committed on the high seas by any national on any ship, because a person guilty of such piracy has placed himself beyond the protection of any

110 Joint Committee on Human Rights, Legislative Scrutiny: National Security Bill, Fifth Report of Session 2022–23, 12 October 2022, 3.

111 Law Commission, Protection of Official Data, HC 716, Law Commission No. 395, 1 September 2000, 33. The Law Commission also recommended that there be a jurisdictional connection between the individual's behaviour and the interests of the UK, that being a 'significant link', 53. That suggestion was not adopted.

112 Universal jurisdiction has been written to amount "the claim by a state to prosecute crimes in circumstances where none of the traditional links of territoriality, nationality, passive personality or the protective principle exists at the time of the commission of the alleged offence," in the *AU – EU Expert Report on the Principle of Universal Jurisdiction*, 16 April 2009, 7. Accessed 6 January 2025. https://reliefweb.int/report/sudan/au-eu-technical-ad-hoc-expert-group-principle-universal-jurisdiction-report.

> State. He is no longer a national, but "*hostis humani generis*" and as such he is justicable by any State anywhere.[113]

The origins of the policy behind piracy being subjected to universal jurisdiction in the UK, then, is originally found in the common law. It seeks to allow the prosecution of persons who are "enemies of mankind". Such is the nature of the UK's legal system; the international crime of piracy exists at, and only at, common law.[114] Its definition, however, is found in international law. Section 26 of the Merchant Shipping and Maritime Security Act 1997 provides that the definition of piracy is found in Article 101 of the Law of the Sea Convention 1982. That is replicated in Schedule 5 of the 1997 Act.[115]

The vast majority of instances of universal jurisdiction in UK law are statutory. They normally are a consequence of a treaty obligation.[116] For example, section 9(1) of the Aviation and Maritime Security Act 1990 prescribes the hijacking of ships, *inter alia* providing:

> (1) A person who unlawfully, by the use of force or by threats of any kind, seizes a ship or exercises control of it, commits the offence of hijacking a ship, whatever his nationality and whether the ship is in the United Kingdom or elsewhere.

Adopting the policy purposes of the underlying treaties, the preamble of the Aviation and Maritime Security Act 1990 *inter alia* provides that it is:

> An Act to give effect to the Protocol for the Suppression of Unlawful Acts of Violence at Airports Serving International Civil Aviation . . . to give effect to the Convention for the Suppression of Unlawful Acts against the Safety of Maritime Navigation.

A further example of statutory universal jurisdiction is found under section 134 of the Criminal Justice Act 1988, criminalising torture.[117] The

113 In *re Piracy Jure Gentium*, [1934] AC 586 at p. 589 per Viscount Sankey L.C., quoting from Grotius, *De Jure Belli ac Pacis*, vol. 2, cap. 20, § 40. Whilst piracy can only be committed on the high seas (and so outside the territory of all states), it is subject to universal jurisdiction by virtue of every country being lawfully able to take cognisance over it.

114 See *Cameron v HMA*, [1971] SLT 333.

115 Hirst calls piracy the 'doyenne' of extraterritorial offences under English law, stating it arose through the criminal jurisdiction of the Admiral following a civil or Roman law procedure, thus forgoing the limitations caused by the issue of venue. Hirst, 33.

116 Some may also be found in customary international law, such as war crimes and crimes against humanity.

117 Torture was at issue in the UK proceedings relating to Augusto Pinochet. They came to an end with his flight back to Chile on 2 March 2000. See generally Hazel Fox, Colin Warbrick and Dominic McGoldrick, "The Pinochet Case No. 3," *International and Comparative Law Quarterly* 48 (1999): 687.

relevant treaty here is the Convention Against Torture and Other Cruel Inhuman or Degrading Treatment or Punishment 1984. Regarding universal jurisdiction generally, then, the political and policy drivers align with the purposes behind the relevant treaties and the UK's approach to the international rule of law noted previously. In general terms, these fall under the desire to fight against transnational crime and seek the prosecution of the most heinous acts.

8 Conclusion

UK extraterritorial jurisdiction has developed in an *ad hoc* manner in reaction to particular political or policy drivers. It lacks coherency as a result. The consequences of such a situation are a body of jurisdictional rules lacking clarity and consistency and having lacunae. Lawyers, judges, and indeed possible offenders, cannot easily or readily discern the scope of the UK's criminal law, nor the reasons for its extension in one circumstance and not in another. Of course, criminal law should be clear, accessible, and precise. As regards its extraterritorial application in the UK, it is not. There has not been a political or policy driver of such weight that a general approach to transnational and extraterritorial jurisdiction has been adopted. Indeed, it is instead the strength of the attachment to territory that has, and still does, predominate. UK extraterritorial jurisdiction will almost certainly remain piecemeal and be affected by *ad hoc* political and policy drivers acted upon by governments and courts at a particular point in time.

References

Akehurst, Michael. "Jurisdiction in International Law." *British Yearbook of International Law* 46 (1972–1973): 145–257.

Arnell, Paul. "Criminal Jurisdiction in International Law." *Juridical Review* (2000): 179–189.

Arnell, Paul. "The Case for Nationality Based Jurisdiction." *International and Comparative Law Quarterly* 50 (2001): 955–961.

Arnell, Paul. *Law Across Borders: The Extraterritorial Application of United Kingdom Law*. London: Routledge, 2012.

Arnell, Paul, and Nicola Evans. "The Effect of the Bribery Act 2010." *Juridical Review* 2 (2015): 61–83.

Arnell, Paul, and Clive Walker. "The Resurrection of the Political Offence Exception to Extradition in UK Law." *New Journal of European Criminal Law* 15 (2024): 412–431.

Blakesley, Christopher L., and Otto Lagodny. "Finding Harmony Amidst Disagreement Over Extradition, Jurisdiction, the Role of Human Rights, and Issues of Extraterritoriality Under International Criminal Law." *Vanderbilt Journal of Transnational Law* 24 (1991): 1–73.

Cameron, Iain. *The Protective Principle of International Criminal Jurisdiction*. Dartmouth: Dartmouth Publishing, 1994.

Campbell, Colm. "Two Steps Backwards: The Criminal Justice (Terrorism and Conspiracy) Act 1998." *Criminal Law Review* (1999): 941–959.

Cryer, Robert, and Paul D. Mora. "The Coroners and Justice Act 2009 and International Criminal Law: Backing into the Future?" *International and Comparative Law Quarterly* 59 (2010): 803–813.
Farmer, Lindsay. "Territorial Jurisdiction and Criminalisation." *The University of Toronto Law Journal* 63(2) (2013): 225–246.
Fox, Hazel, Colin Warbrick, and Dominic McGoldrick. "The Pinochet Case No. 3." *International and Comparative Law Quarterly* 48 (1999): 687–702.
Gallant, Kenneth S. *International Criminal Jurisdiction*. Oxford: Oxford University Press, 2022.
Goldsmith, Peter. "Citizenship: Our Common Bond, Review of British Citizenship." *Department of Justice*, 2008. Accessed 6 January 2025. https://image.guardian.co.uk/sys-files/Politics/documents/2008/03/11/citizenship-report-full.pdf.
Gordon, William G. "The Civil Law in Scotland." *Edinburgh Law Review* 5 (2001): 130–144.
Greenberg, Daniel. "Common Law." In *Jowitt's Dictionary of English Law*. London: Sweet and Maxwell, 6th edition, 2023.
Hansen, Randall. "The Politics of Citizenship in 1940's Britain: The British Nationality Act." *Twentieth Century British History* 10(1) (1999): 69–95.
Hirst, Michael. *Jurisdiction and the Ambit of the Criminal Law*. Oxford: Oxford University Press, 2003.
Hume, David. *Commentaries on the Law of Scotland, Respecting Crimes* ii. Edinburgh: Bell and Bradfute, 1819.
International Bar Association's Legal Practice Division. "Report of the Task Force on Extraterritorial Jurisdiction 2009." Accessed 6 January 2025. https://www.ibanet.org/MediaHandler?id=ECF39839-A217–4B3D-8106-DAB716B34F1E.
Lew, Julian D. M. "The Extra-territorial Criminal Jurisdiction of English Courts." *International and Comparative Law Quarterly* 27 (1978): 168–214.
O'Brien, John. *International Law*. London: Cavendish Publishing, 2001.
Ó Floinn, Micheal, Lindsay Farmer, Julia Hornle, and David Ormerod, eds. *Transformations in Criminal Jurisdiction*. London: Hart Publishing, 2023.
Perkins, Rollin, M. "The Territorial Principle in Criminal Law." *Hastings Law Journal* 22 (1970–1971): 1157–1172.
Rees, Philip H., Pia Wohland, Paul Norman, et al. "Populations Projections by Ethnicity: Challenges and Solutions for the United Kingdom." In *The Frontiers of Applied Demography*, edited by David Swanson. London: Springer, 2017.
Rees, Tom, and David Ormerod. "Jurisdiction of English Courts – Obtaining by Deception." *Criminal Law Review* (2004): 951–954.
Riesemann, W. Micheal, ed. *Jurisdiction in International Law*. Brookfield: Ashgate, 1999.
Ryngaert, Cedric. *Jurisdiction in International Law*. Oxford: Oxford University Press, 2nd edition, 2015.
Shaw, Malcom. *International Law*. Cambridge: Cambridge University Press, 6th edition, 2008.
Williams, Glanville. "Venue and Ambit of the Criminal Law." *Law Quarterly Review* 81 (1965): 276–289.

9 The Exercise of Extraterritorial Jurisdiction in Transnational Criminal Cases

An Australian Perspective

Matthew Nelson and Rishi Gulati

1 Introduction

The use of extraterritorial criminal jurisdiction (*i.e.*, the exercise of jurisdiction by a state over persons and/or activities occurring outside its borders) to prosecute transnational criminal conduct has witnessed a marked increase, attracting much controversy.[1] As Deborah Senz and Hilary Charlesworth make clear, extraterritorial assertions of jurisdiction by states "continues to be the subject of international litigation, scholarly debate and bureaucratic consideration".[2] It goes without saying that it is important to consider how such jurisdiction is created and exercised, as well as the challenges posed. This chapter focuses on those very matters as they pertain to the law and practice in Australia.

First, the chapter outlines the manner in which Australia's criminal law is given extraterritorial effect. Australia has a federal structure comprising the Commonwealth, six states, and a number of territories, some of which are self-governing. This chapter focuses on the Commonwealth (federal) level only. Specifically, it examines the various features of the extraterritorial application of criminal law in Australia, including those in common with international law. It explores when Australia typically exercises that jurisdiction and the motivations underlying such action.

Second, instances where extraterritorial jurisdiction is exercised frequently require transnational cooperation among law enforcement agencies, prosecuting agencies, and even courts. This is because the effective investigation of criminal conduct that occurs outside Australia but is to be prosecuted in Australia often relies on obtaining information and evidence located overseas. In this regard, the chapter examines the necessary corollary of extraterritorial jurisdiction in criminal law: mutual legal assistance and other information-sharing schemes as well. It argues that despite their noble origins, the exercise of extraterritorial jurisdiction and use of mutual legal assistance and other

1 Deborah Senz and Hilary Charlesworth, "Building Blocks: Australia's Response to Foreign Extraterritorial Legislation," *Melbourne Journal of International Law* 2 (2001): 72.
2 *Ibid.*, 70.

DOI: 10.4324/9781003402978-11

information-sharing mechanisms remain vulnerable to politicisation, lack appropriate and transparent guidance, and are subject to inadequate oversight.

Third, the chapter considers the practicalities of the exercise of extraterritorial jurisdiction, noting the factors that are, and should be, taken into account when doing so. Finally, it concludes by arguing in favour of changes that may improve the efficient and fair exercise of extraterritorial jurisdiction in transnational criminal cases.

2 Australia and Extraterritorial Criminal Jurisdiction

Presently, the concern revolves around how criminal law in Australia may be applied extraterritorially. As discussed later, the need for the extraterritorial application of criminal law is fairly obvious. But, who in Australia may enact such laws, and where they may be found, are questions that need explaining.

2.1 *The Need for Extraterritorial Criminal Jurisdiction*

It is useful to briefly state why there is a need to exercise extraterritorial jurisdiction in the first place. This need arises when some feature of the criminal conduct or the offender is not entirely within or connected to Australian territory. For example, the relevant offending conduct may occur only partly within Australia's geographical limits, with some of the offending occurring outside its territory. This scope also includes circumstances in which Australian citizens or residents or entities, such as companies registered in Australia, engage in criminal conduct outside Australian territory.

Given that a significant amount of criminal activity now transcends international borders, the need for the exercise of extraterritorial jurisdiction is readily apparent.[3] In fact, more and more international treaties require states to investigate, prosecute, and punish transnational criminal conduct. Consequently, the exercise of extraterritorial jurisdiction has become a key tool in combating transnational criminal activity. By its very nature, transnational crime involves activities that are at least partly extraterritorial. As such, transnational crime has been a focal point of international and regional multilateral and bilateral agreements to which Australia is a signatory.[4]

3 See various reports prepared by the Australian Institute of Criminology of the incidence and costs of transnational crime in Australia, including Russell G. Smith and Amelia Hickman, "Estimating the Costs of Serious and Organised Crime in Australia, 2020–21," *Statistical Report No. 38* (2022).

4 See, for example, United Nations Convention against Transnational Organized Crime (so too its three Protocols, including the Protocol to Prevent, Suppress and Punish Trafficking in Persons, Especially Women and Children); United Nations Convention against Corruption; United Nations Convention against Illicit Traffic in Narcotic Drugs and Psychotropic Substances; International Convention for the Suppression of the Financing of Terrorism; Convention on Combating Bribery of Foreign Public Officials in International Business Transactions.

Australia's federal parliament has the power to make laws for the peace, order, and good government of the Commonwealth with respect to its external affairs,[5] which generally includes laws enacted to give effect to Australia's international legal obligations.[6] For example, many of the offences in Chapter 8 of Australia's federal Criminal Code ('Criminal Code' or 'Code') are enacted pursuant to this power, giving effect to Australia's treaty obligations under the Rome Statute, UN Convention Against Corruption, and others.

Thus, exercising extraterritorial criminal jurisdiction is increasingly becoming an important aspect of a state's compliance with its treaty obligations, making it even more important to study this phenomenon. Having clarified the need for extraterritorial criminal jurisdiction, the next step is to outline who may enact such laws in Australia.

2.2 *Responsibility for Enacting Extraterritorial Criminal Laws in Australia*

Australia has a federal structure. Thus, the federal parliament as well as state and territory parliaments have powers to make criminal laws, including those with extraterritorial application. We focus on the federal context only, noting that overlaps between regimes can arise from time to time. In particular, Australia's federal parliament can enact criminal laws with extraterritorial application within the scope of its legislative power as prescribed in the Australian Constitution.[7]

Before we turn to the key federal statute providing for extraterritorial criminal jurisdiction in Australia, it is necessary to highlight the importance of the common law (also known as judge-made law), which is also a source of law in Australia, whose legal tradition is historically founded on the English system. Common law informs how statutory provisions are to be interpreted. In general, whether or not a particular criminal law has such effect will almost always be a matter of interpreting the words used in the statute creating it and the context in which those words appear.[8] Thus, statutory interpretation becomes crucial in determining if and to what extent a particular law has extraterritorial application.

In this context, at common law, there is a rule of statutory interpretation providing for a presumption against the extraterritorial application of a criminal offence. This presumption provides, in effect, that in the absence of an

5 Commonwealth of Australia Constitution, section 51(xxix).

6 See *Commonwealth v Tasmania* (1983) 158 CLR 1.

7 Commonwealth of Australia Constitution, section 51. States may also refer powers with respect to certain subject matter on which the Commonwealth may make criminal laws with respect to.

8 *Federal Commissioner of Taxation v Consolidation Media Holdings Ltd* (2023) 250 CLR 503 at [39]. See also Perry Herzfeld and Thomas Prince, *Interpretation* (Lawbook Co., 2020), 9 [1.50].

indication to the contrary in the language of the enactment, the general words in the enactment should be read to be restricted in their operation to the territory of the jurisdiction enacting the legislation.[9] Such a presumption, now largely found in statutes governing the interpretation of legislation, arose out of necessity, as many legislative provisions were drafted as though they were not explicitly limited in their reach to matters outside the territory.[10]

The presumption is simply a rule of construction. It says nothing as to why states do not (or, as the case may be, do) legislate in respect of conduct occurring outside their territory. The rule can serve multiple purposes. As early post-Federation judgments of the High Court of Australia recognised, the legislature is presumed to intend only to pass laws that are within its legislative competence unless language to the contrary appears. By doing so, one avoids constant challenges to those laws on the grounds that they extend beyond the territorial application allowed under the powers of those who passed the law.

This legislative competence comes from the very laws creating the Commonwealth of Australia. For example, the legislation comprising the Australian Constitution provides that the Australian parliament cannot make laws in relation to other states.[11] Therefore, the courts construed statutes with this competence in mind, with the necessary consequence that those laws were confined in their territorial application.

Australian courts have also long recognised that the reasons for the presumption against extraterritorial effect stem from the view that the extraterritorial reach of the criminal law of one country is contrary to the comity among nations and constitutes an intrusion into the territorial sovereignty of other countries.[12]

A presumption is subject to a contrary intention. As we explore in this chapter, many of the criminal laws that apply extraterritorially do so because the relevant conduct originates within Australia but produces effects beyond its borders. Where the provisions comprising the criminal offence evince a contrary intention, what a court thinks of the comity of nations or whether the law intrudes into the territorial sovereignty of other countries is largely irrelevant.

9 See, for example, earlier indications of this presumption in *Jumbunna Coal Mine NL v Victorian Coal Miners' Association* (1908) 6 CLR 309 at 363 (O'Connor J) referred to in Herzfeld and Prince, *Interpretation*, 216–217 [9.250].

10 Justice O'Connor noted, "if [the general words of most statutes] were to be taken literally in their widest sense, [the statutes' provisions] would apply to the whole world": *Jumbunna Coal Mine NL v Victorian Coal Miners' Association* (1908) 6 CLR 309 at 363.

11 See Commonwealth of Australia Constitution, section 5, which provides (notes omitted): "This Act, and all laws made by the Parliament of the Commonwealth under the Constitution, shall be binding on the courts, judges, and people of every State and of every part of the Commonwealth, notwithstanding anything in the laws of any State; and the laws of the Commonwealth shall be in force on all British ships, the Queen's ships of war excepted, whose first port of clearance and whose port of destination are in the Commonwealth".

12 See, for example, *Ex parte Blain; in re Sawers* 12 Ch. Div. 522 at 526 (James LJ) cited in *Morgan v White* (1912) 15 CLR 1 at 5 (Barton J).

With a federal system, the extraterritorial reach of the laws of states within Australia, as well as those of internal and external territories, carries some unique challenges in so far as these laws apply outside the particular state or territory but wholly within Australia. Although it is beyond the scope of this chapter to examine this operation in detail, it is worth noting that, given the parliaments of most Australian states and territories are legislatively competent to pass criminal laws, the presumption applies equally to laws that could, at least on their face, appear to have application beyond the territorial limits of that state or territory.

It is undoubted, as a general proposition, that assertions of extraterritorial jurisdiction, not least in criminal law, are controversial.[13] Danielle Ireland-Piper highlights tensions between states arising particularly in cases where there are competing claims to jurisdiction over conduct that traverses one or more state boundaries.[14] In Australia, therefore, the common law presumption against extraterritoriality can act as a brake on the exercise of extraterritorial criminal jurisdiction. However, this presumption is not absolute. It can be overcome, and the Australian parliament regularly provides for the extraterritorial application of criminal laws, with the federal Criminal Code constituting the key statutory regime. We consider this regime in detail in the next subsection.

2.3 *The Rules on the Extraterritorial Application of Federal Criminal Law in Australia*

The federal Criminal Code is the logical starting point for an examination of the extraterritorial effect of Australia's criminal law. While it should be noted that not all federal crimes are contained in the Code,[15] offence provisions contained in other federal statutes are frequently expressed as subject to the geographical provisions[16] of the Code.[17] Additionally, other statutes that

13 Danielle Ireland-Piper, "Extraterritorial Criminal Jurisdiction: Does the Long Arm of the Law Undermine the Rule of Law?" *Melbourne Journal of International Law* 13 (2012): 125.

14 *Ibid.*

15 So much is clear from Criminal Code, section 1.1.

16 'Geographical' is a term used in the Criminal Code and is used here for convenience. The expression, used in this context, should be understood as analogous to territorial.

17 See, for example, *Bankruptcy Act 1966* (Cth) section 7A; *Customs Act 1901* (Cth) section 5AA. The latter provides, in part: (1) Subject to subsection (2), Chapter 2 of the Criminal Code applies to an offence against this Act. (2) For the purposes of a Customs prosecution: (a) Parts 2.1, 2.2 and 2.3 of the Criminal Code apply; and (b) Parts 2.4, 2.5 and 2.6 of the Criminal Code do not apply; and (c) a reference to criminal responsibility in Chapter 2 of the Criminal Code is taken to be a reference to responsibility. (3) This section is not to be interpreted as affecting in any way the nature of any offence under this Act, the nature of any prosecution or proceeding in relation to any such offence, or the way in which any such offence is prosecuted, heard or otherwise dealt with. (4) Without limiting the scope of subsection (3), this section is not to be interpreted as affecting in any way the standard or burden of proof for any offence under this Act that is the subject of a Customs prosecution.

contain criminal offences may have their own self-contained extraterritorial regime or may be otherwise silent on the issue.[18]

Given the breadth of federal criminal law, it is beyond the scope of this chapter to discuss each and every statutory provision in Australia providing for extraterritorial jurisdiction. However, a discussion of the federal Criminal Code provides a useful snapshot of the key aspects of the approach at the federal level in Australia. More specifically, the constituent elements of an offence must be understood and geographically located to determine issues relating to extraterritoriality.

2.3.1 *Elements of Federal Criminal Offences*

Each federal criminal offence comprises two or more 'elements'. As we will explore in the following section, significant emphasis is placed on the elements of an offence when determining the geographical reach of that offence. In particular, the Code prescribes physical elements and fault elements for each offence. A physical element can be conduct (whether an act or omission), a circumstance, or a result (also referred to as a 'consequence' or the 'result of conduct').

The extraterritorial reach of a criminal offence to which the Code applies is determined according to whether the relevant 'conduct' occurs either wholly or partly in Australia and/or whether any relevant 'result' of the conduct manifests in Australia. Therefore, the elements of an offence, and their classification as conduct, a circumstance, or a result, are crucial when it comes to determining any extended geographical reach of the offence provision. This is because the relevant conduct (such as an act) may be committed by a person overseas, but the result of that conduct may occur in Australia (for example, if it affects a person who is an Australian resident at the time the result materialises).

The extraterritorial regime under the Criminal Code is notable for its focus on conduct and results as elements of criminal offences, rather than the overall characterisation of a criminal offence, as the guiding determinant for the extended geographical application of the law.

With this brief outline of the elements of federal criminal offences, we now turn to consider the modalities for the geographic jurisdiction in respect of the conduct or result that constitutes the offence.

2.3.2 *Geographical Jurisdiction of Federal Crimes*

Part 2.7 of the Criminal Code addresses the geographical reach of offences contained within it, as well as those found in other federal legislation that is

18 See, for example, *Crimes (Taxation Offences) Act 1980* (Cth) section 3A, which provides: "This Act extends to every external Territory and to Australian installations".

expressed as subject to its provisions. The regime in the Code largely aligns with traditional understandings of extraterritorial jurisdiction, including those recognised under international law.

One such form of geographical jurisdiction under the Criminal Code reflects the 'active personality principle' in international law. Under this principle, a state – in this case, Australia – asserts jurisdiction over its nationals for conduct committed abroad and confers on its national courts criminal jurisdiction over such conduct. The geographical reach of federal criminal offences may be extended to cover acts by Australians overseas that result in harm to vulnerable persons. This principle appears to underlie the extended territorial reach of offences relating to child sex trafficking,[19] conspiracies with the intent to be carried out in Australia but initiated wholly or partly overseas, laundering of the proceeds of crime,[20] and Australians' involvement in foreign fighting.[21]

Further, the Criminal Code also contains a form of geographical jurisdiction that embodies the 'passive personality principle' whereby a state extends criminal jurisdiction over conduct perpetrated against its nationals overseas. The Code's provisions extending the geographical reach of federal criminal laws reflect this principle, asserting jurisdiction to safeguard Australians abroad. Examples include offences relating to the murder or grievous bodily harm of Australian citizens or residents in other countries.[22] The Code distinguishes between standard (a) and extended geographic jurisdiction (b).

STANDARD GEOGRAPHICAL JURISDICTION

Section 14.1 of the Criminal Code is commonly referred to as the 'standard geographical jurisdiction' of a criminal offence.[23] This provision can be said to largely reflect the fundamental basis of jurisdiction under international law: the principle of territoriality. It stipulates that an offence – to which it applies – is not committed unless the conduct occurs either wholly or partly in Australia, or the result of that conduct occurs in Australia.[24]

This approach to geographical jurisdiction under the Criminal Code largely aligns with prevailing international views, provided that the conduct elements of a crime (*i.e.*, the acts or omissions) and/or the result of the crime

19 Criminal Code, section 272.6.

20 *Ibid.*, section 400.15.

21 *Ibid.*, section 117.2, applying an extended form of geographical jurisdiction provided by section 15.4 of the Criminal Code.

22 *Ibid.*, part 5.4, division 114.

23 It is worth noting that the provision only applies to conduct (and offences) that took place after the section came into effect, on 24 May 2001, and does not have retrospective application.

24 Criminal Code, section 14.1(2)(b). Criminal Code section 16.2 defines, albeit non-exhaustively, when conduct is taken to occur partly in Australia, and includes when a person sends a thing to or from Australia.

(typically, the harmful effects of the conduct) occur within Australia. As discussed in 2.3.1, a criminal offence may consist of multiple elements, some of which may take place in Australia, while others may have an impact or be undertaken outside Australia. Furthermore, conduct constituting a criminal offence could involve multiple acts, only some of which occur in Australia. In this sense, the standard geographical jurisdiction reflects increasingly relaxed notions of territoriality under international law.[25]

It has also been observed that no principle of comity prevents Australia from criminalising conduct outside its borders where the results of that conduct manifest within Australian territory.[26] This perspective, derived from English common law,[27] was adopted because criminality in result-based offences lies in the effect of conduct rather than the conduct itself. Accordingly, the focus is placed on the location of the results of the conduct (in Australia) rather than the location of the conduct that caused the result (which took place overseas). For example, the position of common law established that the crime of murder is deemed to be committed where the death occurred rather than where the act or omission causing death took place, though the two may often coincide.[28] Given that much criminal law in Australia is now codified, such a perspective on comity is likely to prevail.

Notably, in relation to offences to which section 14.1 applies, there exists a defence stipulating that if the conduct occurs wholly in a foreign country, and there is no offence in that foreign country comparable to the offence-creating provision in Australia, then the Australian offence does not apply.[29] The defence, introduced into the Criminal Code in the early 2000s, aimed to provide individuals who engage in conduct overseas – where such conduct is not illegal – the benefit of a defence to a criminal offence in Australia, even where the result of their conduct has an impact in Australia.[30]

EXTENDED GEOGRAPHICAL JURISDICTION

There are four categories that expand geographical jurisdiction beyond the standard provisions under the Criminal Code. If a law explicitly states its

25 See further, Cedric Ryngaert, *Jurisdiction in International Law* (Oxford: Oxford University Press, 2015), 77–79.

26 *Thompson v The Queen* (1989) 169 CLR 1 at 24 (Brennan J), referred to in The Honourable Chief Justice Andrew Bell, "Extraterritoriality in Australian Law," *2023 Spiegelman Oration*, 27 April 2023.

27 See, in particular, *Director of Public Prosecutions v Stonehouse* [1978] AC 55 at 75 (Lord Edmund-Davie).

28 See *R v Coombes* (1785) 168 ER 296 and *Ward v The Queen* (1980) 142 CLR 308 cited in *Thompson v The Queen* (1989) 169 CLR 1 at 25 (Brennan J).

29 Criminal Code, section 14.1(3).

30 Section 14.1(3) was introduced by the *Criminal Code Amendment (Theft, Fraud, Bribery and Related Offences) Act 2000* (Cth). See also Senate Standing Committee for the Scrutiny of Bills, Second Report of 2001 (2001), 32–37.

applicability to any of these categories, then it has the broader geographical reach as defined (that is, beyond the geographical reach provided for by the standard geographical jurisdiction in section 14.1).[31] These four categories[32] largely correspond to several bases on which states typically assert extraterritorial criminal jurisdiction under international law, including the principles of nationality, territoriality, and universality. The four categories are:

- Category A: Jurisdiction extends to conduct that occurs wholly or partly in Australia, as well as the conduct of Australian citizens and bodies corporate for any offences that occur outside Australia (or within Australia), where the conduct results in a specific outcome in Australia, and where the conduct occurs wholly in a foreign country, and the defendant is not an Australian citizen or body corporate. However, in such cases, there is a defence based on the law of the foreign country in which the offending occurred.[33] This category of jurisdiction heavily relies on elements of territoriality, focusing on the occurrence of the result within Australian soil. Offences falling within this category include certain forms of child sexual abuse offences where the victim is located in Australia, such as grooming a child via the Internet or supplying a child with indecent material.[34]
- Category B: Jurisdiction extends to conduct that occurs wholly or partly in Australia, in addition to the conduct of Australian citizens, bodies corporate, and Australian residents committed outside Australia.[35] This category incorporates not only aspects of the territoriality principle and the nationality principle whereby Australia asserts criminal jurisdiction over its nationals outside its geographical territory. Examples of prosecutions relying on this extended jurisdiction include cases related to human trafficking,[36] where Australian citizens arrange for the trafficking of a child into Australia, and drug trafficking offences, such as where a consignment of prohibited substances is arranged to be sent from outside Australia to Australia or by an Australian national.[37]
- Category C: Jurisdiction extends to conduct that occurs wholly in a foreign country, where the defendant is not an Australian citizen or body corporate. However, a defence exists if the conduct is not illegal under the law of the foreign country.[38] This category embodies the principle of universality, though liability for the offence can be avoided if the defendant can demonstrate that they engaged in the conduct believing, correctly,

31 Criminal Code, section 14.1(1).
32 *Ibid.*, division 15.
33 *Ibid.*, section 15.1.
34 *Ibid.*, sections 471.30, 471.25A, 471.26.
35 *Ibid.*, section 15.2.
36 *Ibid.*, section 271.10.
37 *Ibid.*, section 300.3.
38 *Ibid.*, section 15.3.

that the conduct was not a crime in the location in which it was committed. Offences subject to this category include causing harm to Australian public officials,[39] postal offences (such as causing explosives to be carried by post),[40] as well as less severe offences compared to those falling under Category D (discussed later) in the context of international criminal law.[41]

- Category D: Jurisdiction extends without limitation, irrespective of the status of the person who committed the conduct and irrespective of whether the conduct occurred wholly or partly within or outside Australia.[42] Like Category C, this category also embodies the principle of universality but removes the defence available under that category. It is reserved for the most serious offences under Australian (and international) law, including genocide, crimes against humanity, war crimes,[43] slavery,[44] and torture.[45] Unlike other categories, the offences under this jurisdiction do not require a connection to Australia, such as occurring within its territory, being committed by an Australian national abroad, or having an impact on an Australian citizen.

Beyond Category D, the Criminal Code also contemplates a special case for prosecuting offences where Australia exercises extraterritorial criminal jurisdiction based on universality.[46] Thus, a prosecution can occur where conduct constituting an offence under the Criminal Code occurs wholly in a foreign country,[47] and the person alleged to have committed the conduct is neither an Australian citizen nor a body corporate.[48] Further, it is not required that the effects or results of the offending be felt in Australia for such a prosecution to occur. In this sense, there is no connection between the offending and Australia other than that which is ordinarily invoked when asserting criminal jurisdiction on universal grounds.[49]

In particular, the offences of genocide, war crimes, and crimes against humanity, among others enumerated in the Criminal Code, were introduced

39 *Ibid.*, section 147.3.
40 *Ibid.*, sections 471.9, 471.15(2).
41 *Ibid.*, section 268.117(2).
42 *Ibid.*, section 15.4.
43 *Ibid.*, section 268.117(1).
44 *Ibid.*, section 270.3A.
45 *Ibid.*, section 274.2(5).
46 *Ibid.*, section 16.1.
47 *Ibid.*, section 16.1(1)(b).
48 *Ibid.*, section 16.1(1)(c).
49 For a general discussion on the application of universal jurisdiction in Australia, see, among others, Luc Reydams, "Australia," in *Universal Jurisdiction: International and Municipal Legal Perspectives*, ed. Luc Reydams (Oxford: Oxford University Press, 2004), 86–92; Anna Hood and Monique Cormier, "Prosecuting International Crimes in Australia: The Case of the Sri Lankan President," *Melbourne Journal of International Law* 13 (2012).

to comply with Australia's obligations under the Rome Statute.[50] However, there existed predecessor offences to those in the Criminal Code. The assertion of universal jurisdiction in such legislation was resolved by Australian courts, specifically as a matter of Australian constitutional law. Australian courts are generally concerned with whether Parliament has the power to pass a law with such jurisdictional effect, particularly when that effect is explicit within the offence provisions. For example, the predecessor statute to the genocide and war crimes provisions in the Criminal Code, the War Crimes Act 1945 (Cth), purported to extend jurisdiction on the basis of universality. In a multifaceted challenge to the validity of that law, the Australian government of the time submitted before the High Court in *Polyukhovich*[51] that it had jurisdiction to prosecute certain crimes that occurred outside Australia against non-nationals as a matter of international law.[52] While the case was resolved by the majority of the Court on other grounds, one High Court Justice acknowledged that the law was an exercise of universal jurisdiction under international law and thus valid.[53]

Importantly, this provision pertains to the prosecution of such offences;[54] it does not, in itself, extend the geographical reach of any offence under the Criminal Code to extraterritorial conduct. That jurisdiction must be separately established. Given the rarity with which universal jurisdiction is recognised as a category under the Criminal Code, and the specific circumstances in which it is exercised in a given case, any trends in when and why Australia exercises such jurisdiction are very difficult to discern.

There are also specific offences in the Criminal Code and elsewhere in federal legislation that criminalise conduct committed abroad against an Australian citizen or resident. These offences embody the passive personality principle, where a country asserts jurisdiction over an individual outside its borders based on the victim's nationality.[55] Such offences are rare in Aus-

50 Rome Statute of the International Criminal Court 1998, opened for signature 17 July 1998, [2002] ATS 15 (entered into force 1 July 2002). See also the *International Criminal Court (Consequential Amendments) Act 2002* (Cth), which introduced division 268 into the Criminal Code, and the *International Criminal Court Act 2002* (Cth). For a background of the introduction of division 268, see Gillian Triggs, "Implementation of the Rome Statute for the International Criminal Court: A Quiet Revolution in Australian Law," *Sydney Law Review* 25(4) (2003).

51 *Polyukhovich v Commonwealth* (1991) 172 CLR 501.

52 See the discussion of Toohey J in *Polyukhovich v Commonwealth* (1991) 172 CLR 501 at 658.

53 See the extension discussion of these crimes by Toohey J in *Polyukhovich v Commonwealth* (1991) 172 CLR 501 at 658–677.

54 Where such a prosecution is to occur, the Attorney-General must consent before this can take place. In this sense, it is a procedural provision, see Criminal Code section 16.1(1).

55 See, generally, Kenneth S. Gallant, "The Passive Personality Principle," in *International Criminal Jurisdiction: Whose Law Must We Obey?*, ed. Kenneth S. Gallant (Oxford: Oxford University Press, 2022), 441.

tralia within the corpus of criminal law that attracts extended geographical jurisdiction. Further, these offences tend to be limited to serious crimes in so far as penalties are concerned. One example can be found in Division 115 of the Criminal Code, which extends geographical jurisdiction to conduct constituting murder, manslaughter, or causing serious harm (either intentionally or recklessly) committed overseas against an Australian citizen or resident.[56] The offences in this division were introduced in response to the killing of an Australian in Brunei in 1994.[57]

For completeness, it is also worth noting that the Criminal Code does not fully regulate the geographical reach of Australian criminal law. While many federal offences contained in legislation other than the Code are expressed as subject to the geographical jurisdiction provisions in the Code,[58] others contain separate provisions governing their extraterritorial application.[59] Thus, no general rule governing the extended geographical reach of Australian criminal law can be definitively established. Where a statutory criminal offence is involved, statutory interpretation plays a crucial role in determining the geographical reach of that law.

3 Information Sharing in the Investigation and Prosecution of Transnational Crimes

The absence of effective means to investigate and/or prosecute conduct that relies on the exercise of extraterritorial jurisdiction can hinder a state in meeting its international legal obligations to combat transnational crime. With the potential extraterritorial reach of Australia's criminal laws comes significant importance attached to obtaining or sharing information and evidence. This process is crucial not only for the successful prosecution of conduct constituting an offence under Australian criminal law that relies on extended geographical jurisdiction but also for Australia's relationships with the countries involved in these processes and Australia's broader international legal obligations.

Neil Boister describes transnational criminal law as laws aimed at the suppression of criminal activity with transboundary effects, whether or not these

56 Criminal Code, sections 115.1–115.4. Section 115.8 removes any doubt as to the geographical limits of such jurisdiction. Consent must be provided for the prosecution of such offences: section 115.6.

57 See the Second Reading Speech to the Crimes Legislation Amendment (Harming Australians) Bill 2015 (Cth), Parliamentary Debates, 12 November 2015, 8447 (George Brandis).

58 Criminal Code, part 2.7.

59 See, for example, *Crimes (Aviation) Act 1991* (Cth); *Crimes (Biological Weapons) Act 1976* (Cth); *Crimes (Currency) Act 1981* (Cth); *Crimes (Overseas) Act 1964* (Cth); *Crimes (Ships and Fixed Platforms) Act 1992* (Cth).

effects actually materialise.[60] It is well established that much criminal law falling under extended geographical jurisdiction within the Criminal Code is inherently transnational. However, many offences are transnational by nature, even if they are not necessarily viewed in this way. For example, many offences governing the importation of prohibited drugs into Australia criminalise international drug trafficking activities.

As highlighted in the previous discussion on the extraterritorial reach of federal criminal law, whether or not criminal conduct produces effects in Australia or against Australians is not always a bar to the exercise of jurisdiction. For example, Category A jurisdiction is the only category of extraterritorial criminal jurisdiction under the federal Criminal Code that requires that the result of conduct occur in Australia. The other categories extend jurisdiction to conduct or its results, which need not actually occur in Australia. Given this scope, greater clarity is needed to delineate when transnational policing by Australian law enforcement agencies[61] ought to be exercised to prevent unnecessary investigations by law enforcement bodies and subsequent prosecutions that could damage Australia's bilateral relations or jeopardise Australia's compliance with its international legal obligations relating to transnational crime. In this section, we examine the formalised processes for information and evidence sharing by Australian authorities.

Australian law enforcement agencies are well acquainted with the challenges presented by the cross-border nature of criminal law and its actors. However, significant challenges persist in streamlining their processes to ensure they operate efficiently, transparently, and fairly.[62] In this part, we are concerned with the investigation of criminal offences with the objective of prosecutions in Australian courts. Our focus here is on how Australian authorities request and obtain information – both in terms of acquisition and dissemination – for the purposes of investigations and prospective prosecutions in Australia. We argue that the effective exercise of extraterritorial criminal jurisdiction in Australia is largely dependent on the operation of these processes. The fact that Australia has the means to exercise extraterritorial criminal jurisdiction becomes meaningless without these mechanisms being efficiently utilised by investigating and prosecuting authorities in Australia.

In the following sections, we briefly set out some of the key evidence and information-sharing processes relied upon by Australian law enforcement and prosecution authorities in transnational criminal matters. These

60 Neil Boister, "Transnational Criminal Law?" *European Journal of International Law* 14 (2003): 953; Neil Boister, *An Introduction to Transnational Criminal Law* (Oxford: Oxford University Press, 2018).

61 On transnational policing more broadly, see Ben Bowling and James Sheptycki, "Global Policing and Transnational Rule of Law," *Transnational Legal Theory* 6 (2015).

62 For a discussion of some of these challenges, see Rick Brown, "Understanding Law Enforcement Information Sharing for Criminal Intelligence Purposes," *Trends and Issues in Crime and Criminal Justice* 566 (2018).

mechanisms include mutual legal assistance, agency-to-agency arrangements, and data-sharing arrangements.

3.1 Mutual Legal Assistance

The reasons why Australian law enforcement authorities would commence an investigation into alleged criminal conduct that may be transnational in nature are varied. For example, the alleged conduct may have some connection to Australia, such as a planned import of drugs into Australia that is directed or necessarily originating from another country. However, when alleged criminal conduct occurs outside Australia, it will often be necessary for Australian authorities to obtain evidence relating to that conduct from foreign jurisdictions.

The extended geographical reach of Australia's criminal laws does not, of course, entitle Australian law enforcement authorities to obtain evidence for the purposes of Australian criminal proceedings in other countries unilaterally, that is, without the involvement of the relevant foreign authorities. In addition to concerns regarding sovereignty, laws governing the admissibility of evidence in criminal proceedings in Australia may also pose challenges to such an approach to transnational policing. The collection of evidence must be done properly and lawfully in order for it to be used, subject to other exclusions,[63] in Australian courts. For example, evidence can be excluded (or its use is limited) in a criminal prosecution if it was obtained improperly, such as by subterfuge or entrapment.[64] Further, in many cases, evidence such as witness statements or testimony that is given by a witness overseas (because that witness cannot attend court in Australia) must also be taken in accordance with the laws governing such processes in the jurisdiction in which the evidence is given, in order for it to be admissible in Australian proceedings.[65]

The collection of information by law enforcement agencies for intelligence purposes, as distinct from the collection of evidence to be used in prospective prosecutions, involves distinct considerations. The means by which information that is not sought to be admitted as evidence in a prosecution is collected remains relevant in so far as the admissibility of evidence obtained using this information is concerned. Nonetheless, law enforcement and intelligence agencies may not similarly feel constrained in the way in which information is collected for intelligence purposes. That said, various laws govern how information can be obtained and shared lawfully by these agencies.[66]

63 See, for example, Uniform Evidence Law, sections 135, 136, 137.

64 *Ibid.*, section 138.

65 Rules governing procedures in individual courts will often govern how evidence must be taken from a person overseas in order for the evidence to be admissible.

66 See, for example, part III of the *Australian Security Intelligence Organisation Act 1979* (Cth) in relation to the sharing of intelligence collected by Australia's domestic spy agency.

Mutual legal assistance is defined as "the process countries use to obtain government-to-government assistance in criminal investigations and prosecutions".[67] It is a well-established mechanism by which countries obtain information and evidence from persons or entities in other countries. Australia has more than 30 bilateral mutual legal assistance agreements with other countries.[68] However, these are not the only sources of arrangements for mutual legal assistance under international law to which Australia is a party. Many multilateral treaties contemplate the sharing of information through requests in relation to the investigation and prosecution of conduct caught by the subject matter of the agreement. For example, Chapter IV of the United Nations Convention against Corruption, to which Australia is a party, details international cooperation obligations on signatories, including provisions related to the extradition of suspected persons and mutual legal assistance for the investigation and enforcement of criminal laws made by signatories that are passed pursuant to their obligations under the Convention.[69]

The Australian Attorney-General's Department, an arm of the executive branch of government, is Australia's central authority. This means that it is responsible for handling most requests to, and from, Australia for mutual legal assistance in criminal investigations, prosecutions, and court proceedings. Mutual legal assistance requests can be made to Australia pursuant to a number of arrangements, including bilateral treaty arrangements or multilateral agreements pursuant to which Australia has passed specific laws to meet its international obligations.

In the context of criminal law, what may be the subject of a mutual legal assistance request depends on the conduct being investigated. Importantly, mutual legal assistance requests are not necessarily predicated on the exercise of extraterritorial criminal jurisdiction. For example, a murder may have been committed in Australia by an Australian citizen against another Australian citizen, but a witness to that murder is now based outside Australia. Mutual legal assistance may be required in order to obtain evidence from that witness who is present in another country. Even procedural matters, such as serving a subpoena (an order compelling the provision of oral or documentary evidence) on that person to appear in Australian court proceedings, may require mutual legal assistance through these channels.

Ultimately, mutual legal assistance requests in criminal matters often arise due to the transnational nature of the conduct. Where Australia relies

67 "Mutual Assistance." Accessed 25 May 2024. https://www.ag.gov.au/international-relations/international-crime-cooperation-arrangements/mutual-assistance.

68 See, for example, the Treaty between The Government of Australia and the Government of Canada on Mutual Assistance in Criminal Matters done at Ottawa on 19 June 1989, being the schedule to the *Mutual Assistance in Criminal Matters (Canada) Regulations* (Cth). Others include treaties with Brazil, Luxembourg, Greece, Hong Kong, Ecuador, the Republic of Korea, Portugal, Thailand, the United Arab Emirates, and the United Kingdom.

69 See Article 46.

on extended geographical jurisdiction to prosecute that conduct, mutual legal assistance is more routinely relied on to obtain relevant evidence. In Australia, a mutual legal assistance request (that is, from Australia to another country) is governed by the Mutual Assistance in Criminal Matters Act 1987 (Cth), and a number of regulations made under that Act specific to mutual legal assistance arrangements that Australia has with particular countries or pursuant to treaties to which it is bound.[70] The purpose of these separate legislative instruments is to account for any specific arrangements Australia has pursuant to these bilateral or multilateral treaties or other arrangements.[71] It is important to acknowledge that mutual legal assistance requests relating to investigations and prosecutions of criminal offences are not exclusively governed by these mutual legal assistance instruments.[72]

Australia's mutual legal assistance regime covers requests by Australia for various acts to be done or information to be obtained in other countries, including for criminal matters,[73] the taking of evidence,[74] the production of documents,[75] search and seizure of a thing,[76] surveillance of a person or thing,[77] access to data,[78] removal of a person to give evidence in relation to Australian criminal proceedings or assistance in a criminal investigation,[79] forensic procedures (which includes an examination of the body, taking of samples of blood, genital swabs, dental impressions),[80] and the arrest of a person.[81] Various other forms of requests may also be made.

70 See, for example, *Mutual Assistance in Criminal Matters (Convention against Corruption) Regulations 2005* (Cth).

71 Sections 7(2) and (3) of the *Mutual Assistance in Criminal Matters 1987* (Cth) contemplates as much.

72 See, in particular, section 6 of the *Mutual Assistance in Criminal Matters 1987* (Cth), which provides that the Act "does not prevent the provision or obtaining of international assistance in criminal matters other than assistance of a kind that may be provided or obtained under this Act". See also section 10(2).

73 *Mutual Assistance in Criminal Matters 1987* (Cth) section 10. 'Criminal matter' is defined in section 3(1), and includes matters such as the freezing of assets, forfeiting and confiscating property, imposing penalties, etc.

74 *Ibid.*, section 12. See sections 13 and 26 in relation to requests made *to* Australia.

75 *Ibid.*, section 12. See section 13 in relation to requests made *to* Australia.

76 *Ibid.*, section 14.

77 *Ibid.*, section 15C. See section 15CA in relation to requests made *to* Australia.

78 Requests *to* Australia: *Mutual Assistance in Criminal Matters 1987* (Cth), sections 15CC, 15D.

79 *Ibid.*, section 16. See section 27 in relation to requests made *to* Australia.

80 *Ibid.*, section 28A; *Crimes Act 1914* (Cth) section 23WA (definitions of 'forensic procedure', 'intimate forensic procedure', 'non-intimate forensic procedure'). See sections 28B and 28C in relation to requests made to Australia.

81 *Mutual Assistance in Criminal Matters 1987* (Cth) part VIIA. See, in particular, section 38C.

3.2 *Agency-to-Agency Assistance*

Agency-to-agency assistance refers generally to informal requests made by a law enforcement agency to a government agency of a foreign country. In the context of criminal investigations, law enforcement agencies, such as police services, typically make these agency-to-agency requests for assistance. This is frequently referred to as police-to-police assistance.

In Australia, the functions of law enforcement agencies, as prescribed in the constituent legislation, include international cooperation.[82] Further, Australia has a number of international legal obligations implemented domestically that require cooperation with other signatories' law enforcement agencies in the investigation and prosecution of certain types of criminal conduct outside the formal mutual legal assistance framework. These obligations are typically based on bilateral and multilateral treaty arrangements, which govern the way in which assistance may be sought by Australian authorities from overseas counterparts in certain cases.

The regime under which any requests for assistance may be sought depends on the specific circumstances of each case. Important factors in the assessment of which regime applies include: the country to which the request is made; what is being sought through the request; any implications on the admissibility of evidence in Australian proceedings arising from the way it is requested and/or taken; the likelihood that the request will be accepted; the importance of any information obtained as a result of the request, and the time and cost associated with making the request.

There are a number of limitations to agency-to-agency assistance. The informal nature of the process can present problems in terms of the admissibility of evidence at later stages of proceedings. Where the collection of information is for intelligence purposes, the utility of the process is clear. However, more formal processes enhance the likelihood that the evidence will be obtained in a legally admissible form and thus accepted in any later criminal proceedings.

Public information about how Australian law enforcement agencies handle agency-to-agency requests is scarce. While this lack of transparency is understandable to some extent, particularly given the sensitivities in how information is shared between such agencies, the provenance of collected information can be crucial to challenges to its admissibility in criminal proceedings in Australian courts. The extent to which such information may assist in the investigation of criminal conduct – in the sense that the information serves as a source of intelligence or identifies further sources of information that may be used in subsequent prosecutions in Australian courts – can also have serious implications for the fairness of any subsequent prosecution

82 See, for example, *Australian Federal Police Act 1979* (Cth) section 8(1)(bh).

and raises concerns regarding what must be disclosed by Australian authorities to defendants in any later criminal proceeding.

Ensuring transparency in the obtaining of information that assists in the identification of criminal conduct and the obtaining of further evidence is crucial to ensuring a fair trial in later criminal prosecutions. The approach of Australian law enforcement agencies in relation to police-to-police assistance is equally critical for understanding how the potential reliance on extended geographical jurisdiction plays a role in the commencement and/or continuation of such investigations. Additionally, it is important to assess whether such factors present an impediment to any later potential prosecution. However, there is a notable lack of publicly available information regarding the practices of Australian law enforcement agencies in the use of police-to-police assistance.

3.3 Data Sharing Agreements

Finally, it is important to highlight an emerging mechanism for the sharing of information in the context of investigations into transnational criminal activity. An indispensable part of much transnational crime is the use of online platforms, such as encrypted communications networks and the dark web. Communications sent and received using encrypted communications networks that involve Australian actors are often held by companies overseas. Australian law enforcement and national security authorities have long highlighted the difficulties posed by the location of such data. Australia's Department of Home Affairs highlighted the transnational crime conundrum resulting from the location of such data in other jurisdictions and competing priorities for access to it, noting that many transnational criminal actors "store data in third party foreign jurisdictions", and such storage is likely to be subject to that jurisdiction's laws.[83] The Department has acknowledged that accessing this data under these conditions "significantly frustrates the ability for Australian agencies to combat crime, putting the Australian community at risk".[84]

Recourse to conventional mutual legal assistance arrangements to access data stored in third countries is often not viable due to the lengthy processing time required to meet such requests. Delays of this nature are well-known issues in mutual legal assistance processes. The Cybercrime Convention Committee for the Council of Europe Budapest Convention on Cybercrime reported in 2014 that inefficiencies in mutual legal assistance processes

83 Department of Home Affairs of the Australian Government, "Regulation Impact Statement of the Agreement between the Government of the United States of America and the Government of Australia on Access to Electronic Data for the Purpose of Countering Serious Crime," 2022. Accessed 25 May 2024. https://oia.pmc.gov.au/sites/default/files/posts/2022/02/CLOUD%20Act%20Agreement%20RIS.DOCX.

84 *Ibid.*

regularly lead to abandoned requests and investigations.[85] A working group of the Committee also reported in 2016 that while these processes suffer from general inefficiencies with respect to electronic data, the use of mutual legal assistance is not always a realistic solution for obtaining evidence when remotely stored data is involved.[86]

To address this issue, Australia has introduced legislation[87] that established a scheme intended to codify bilateral agreements that Australia enters into to facilitate access to data relevant to transnational criminal investigations.[88] The pressing need for this legal infrastructure has been in part due to the prolonged delays associated with mutual legal assistance requests take.[89] The introduction of this legislative scheme also gave renewed impetus as Australia entered into an agreement with the United States for reciprocal access to data held by companies in both jurisdictions.[90] This agreement complements existing arrangements under mutual legal assistance and is likely to be designated under the aforementioned legislative scheme.

More specifically, this scheme is incorporated within the Telecommunications (Interception and Access) Act 1979 (Cth),[91] and, similar to extradition and mutual legal assistance requests to and from Australia, requests under this scheme are managed by the Attorney-General's Department.[92]

85 Cybercrime Convention Committee, "T-CY Assessment Report: The Mutual Legal Assistance Provisions of the Budapest Convention on Cybercrime," 3 December 2014, 123 [5.1.1]. Accessed 25 May 2024. https://rm.coe.int/16802e726c.

86 Cybercrime Convention Committee Cloud Evidence Group, "Criminal Justice Access to Electronic Evidence in the Cloud: Recommendations for Consideration by the T-CY" (Council of Europe, 2016), 9, [2.4].

87 Now schedule 1 to the *Telecommunications (Interception and Access) Act 1979* (Cth).

88 See [2] of the Explanatory Memorandum to the Telecommunications Legislation Amendment (International Production Orders) Bill 2020 (Cth).

89 See [5] of the Explanatory Memorandum to the Telecommunications Legislation Amendment (International Production Orders) Bill 2020 (Cth). For a discussion of the experience of mutual legal assistance requests by Australian law enforcement and prosecution agencies, and the time taken to process such requests, see chapter 2 in Parliament of the Commonwealth of Australia, Parliamentary Joint Committee on Intelligence and Security, "Advisory Report on the Telecommunications Legislation Amendment (International Production Orders) Bill 2020" (2021).

90 Agreement between the Government of Australia and the Government of the United States of American on Access to Electronic Data for the Purpose of Countering Serious Crime (commonly referred to as the Australia-US Cloud Act Agreement).

91 See schedule 1.

92 Being the Australian Designated Authority under the scheme. The scheme facilitates the making of requests to communications providers in foreign countries for access to certain communications data. Australia must have in place an agreement with the foreign country in which the communications data sought to be accessed is located, for the scheme to be utilised. The scheme is limited to the investigation of more serious offences with lower limits on the maximum penalties: see the definitions of 'serious category 1 offence' and 'serious category 2 offence' (and section 5D) in clause 2 of schedule 1 to the *Telecommunications (Interception and Access) Act 1979* (Cth), which refer generally to offences that will carry five years' imprisonment or more as the penalty.

Delegating responsibility to the Department ensures continuity with existing processes for the sharing of information and evidence. Further, a two-part test applies to such requests. Both steps are designed to prevent any unintended encroachment on the sovereignty of other countries while still requiring at least some connection (or contemplated connection) to Australia.

First, there is a 'minimum contacts' test that requires at least one or more Australians using the service to be ordinarily resident in Australia.[93] The second criterion is a 'reasonableness' requirement that assesses whether the communications provider could reasonably be expected to have offered or provided services to Australians.[94] Here, this provision aims to exclude domestic service providers that restrict their services to local operators and have no intention of allowing Australians to access their services.[95] It is conceivable that offending might be carried out using overseas telecommunications providers' services by individuals other than Australian residents, over whom Australia can exercise criminal jurisdiction.

At least in the current arrangement, Australia and the United States reached a compromise on the precise links required before such requests are approved. It remains to be seen how this legislation will function in practice, but its significance should not be underestimated.

4 Rethinking the Framework for the Assertion of Extraterritorial Jurisdiction

It is one thing to have laws that create extraterritorial jurisdiction and to adopt arrangements that facilitate investigating and prosecuting transnational crimes, but it is yet another challenge to ensure that the process is predictable and effective. In Section 3, what has been presented is a relatively *ad hoc* array of means by which Australian law enforcement agencies address investigating transnational crime. Undoubtedly, Australian law enforcement agencies have well-established networks for police-to-police assistance, and prosecution agencies are familiar with processes related to mutual legal assistance as part of prosecuting transnational crimes, particularly where Australia relies on extraterritorial jurisdiction. However, what is less clear is the consideration given by these actors to the most appropriate forum for the investigation and prosecution of transnational crime that has some connection to Australia, such that extraterritorial jurisdiction could be effectively exercised to prosecute the conduct in Australian courts.

93 See page 79 of the Explanatory Memorandum to the Telecommunications Legislation Amendment (International Production Orders) Bill 2020.

94 *Ibid.*

95 *Ibid.*

Much has been written about the harms, both potential and realised, associated with transnational policing.[96] The extent to which Australia should rely on extraterritorial jurisdiction to prosecute certain types of criminal conduct must inform the way in which Australian law enforcement and prosecution agencies approach the investigation and prosecution of transnational criminal conduct. Clearer parameters are needed to define the conditions for the reliance on this type of jurisdiction. Transparency in this process will improve consistency in allocating public resources and in the decision-making of prosecution agencies. In the following sections, we highlight how, in practice, extraterritorial criminal jurisdiction is operationalised in Australia and what may drive such an exercise.

4.1 *The Exercise of Extraterritorial Criminal Jurisdiction in Australia*

There is little guidance available regarding the way in which extraterritorial criminal jurisdiction is actually exercised. Single-policy documents often govern high-level decision-making within prosecution agencies around Australia. Such documents, important as they are, appear to be ill-equipped to address this unique issue of exercising extraterritorial jurisdiction in transnational criminal matters. For example, the Prosecution Policy of the Commonwealth, prepared by the Commonwealth Director of Public Prosecutions,[97] does not provide guidance on the circumstances in which the use of this type of jurisdiction should or should not be relied on in any given case. While there are factors contained in this policy that necessarily bear upon such an assessment,[98] the absence of any such guidance raises concerns regarding the use of mutual legal assistance and other information-sharing regimes by investigators in later prosecutions, where the decision to prosecute is not informed by transparent guidelines relevant to whether or not Australia should prosecute particular transnational crimes in any given case.

Further, whether these decisions ought to be made by prosecution agencies when assessing whether or not to commence or continue a prosecution is a matter of debate. The transnational nature of many such crimes requires careful consideration beyond merely the prospects of a conviction and whether it

96 See, for example, on transnational policing more broadly, see Ben Bowling and James Sheptycki, "Global Policing and Transnational Rule of Law," *Transnational Legal Theory* 6 (2015).

97 The Commonwealth Director of Public Prosecutions is responsible for the prosecution of most federal crimes: see, in particular, the *Director of Public Prosecutions Act 1983* (Cth) sections 6(1)(a), (b), (d) and (e).

98 For example, some of the public interest considerations relevant to whether to commence or continue a prosecution under the Prosecution Policy of the Commonwealth, including "the likely length and expense of a trial" (see [2.10(q)], "the necessity to maintain public confidence in the rule of law and the administration of justice through the institutions of democratic governance including the Parliament and the Courts" (see [2.10(u)].

is in the public interest for the prosecution to commence or continue. As discussed in Section 4.2, international law considerations also play – or should play – an increasing role in prosecuting certain transnational crimes.

A corollary of the previous suggestion is the possibility that the decision whether or not to prosecute (or continue to prosecute) transnational criminal activity may be subject to interference, actual or perceived, from other parts of the Executive Government. A requirement to consider Australia's relations with other countries, for example, in the conduct of prosecutions of transnational criminal activity, necessarily involves political considerations. The independence of prosecution agencies is not only essential to the rule of law but is also facilitated by legislation.[99] A prosecution agency is obviously ill-equipped to make such decisions but must also be protected from interference by other sources when making decisions about whether to proceed with a prosecution.

Such concerns are not fanciful. Sally Kennedy and Ian Warren highlight the scope for exploitation of transnational crime infrastructure to secure the extradition of individuals in politically motivated investigations and prosecutions.[100] In particular, the authors cite the use of conspiracy charges in the prosecution of Huw Griffiths for extradition to the United States due to the flexibility such charges provide. It shifted the focus away from the source of the offending to procedural steps in the extradition process.

4.2 *The Relevance of Australia's International Legal Obligations to the Exercise of Extended Geographical Jurisdiction*

Before considering a fresh approach to the investigation of transnational criminal matters and the exercise of extraterritorial criminal jurisdiction in Australia, it is worth illustrating the international legal obligations that Australia has undertaken with respect to transnational crime. There are a myriad of international and regional treaties to which Australia is a signatory, obligating it to establish offences within its jurisdiction that criminalise certain conduct, as well as to have in place effective means for the investigation and prosecution of such conduct.

By way of example, the OECD Convention on Combating Bribery of Foreign Public Officials in International Business Transactions contains a framework for the criminalisation of certain forms of bribery in international trade

99 It is noted that while the Australian Attorney-General can give to the Commonwealth Director of Public Prosecutions directions or guidelines in the performance of the Director's functions under the *Director of Public Prosecutions Act 1983* (Cth), the Act itself serves to protect the decision-making functions of the Director from interference by the Executive, including to commence and discontinue prosecutions.

100 Sally Kennedy and Ian Warren, "Extraterritorial Offending, Extradition, and Australia's Case against Hew Griffiths," *International Journal of Comparative and Applied Criminal Justice* 47 (2023): 299.

and commerce and serves as a useful illustration of the difficulties involved in prosecuting crimes relying on extraterritorial jurisdiction in Australia. Australia became a signatory to the Convention on 7 December 1998. Similar frameworks exist in other treaties relating to bribery. For example, Article 16(1) of the United Nations Convention Against Corruption requires states parties to establish criminal offences for the promise, offering, or giving of an undue advantage to a foreign public official for the benefit of the official or another person, so that the official acts or refrains from acting in the exercise of their official duties, allowing the person promising, offering, or giving the bribe to obtain or retain business or another undue advantage in relation to the conduct of international business.

To fulfil its obligations under the OECD Convention,[101] Division 70 in Chapter 4 of the Criminal Code was enacted.[102] The key offence – bribing a foreign public official[103] – is subject to a specific extraterritorial requirement. Section 70.5 states that this offence is not committed unless the conduct constituting the offence occurs wholly or partly in Australia[104] or, if the conduct occurs wholly outside Australia, the person or entity engaging in the conduct must be an Australian citizen or resident or an Australian company.[105] This jurisdiction largely reflects what is required of states parties under the OECD Convention.[106]

The OECD Convention also allows state parties to extend jurisdiction over alleged offenders present in the state party's territory when another state party seeks extradition of that person for prosecution under its own laws passed pursuant to the OECD Convention. Under Australian law, the Attorney-General must consent to the commencement of a prosecution for such an offence if the conduct occurs wholly outside Australia *and* the person who engaged in the conduct is an Australian resident, as distinct from an Australian citizen or an Australian-incorporated company.[107] In other words, if the entirety of the conduct occurs *outside* Australia, and the only connection to Australia is that the person was an Australian resident at the time of the conduct, prosecution requires the Attorney-General's consent.

While guidance for deciding whether to consent to such a prosecution is not publicly available, it is clear that a more tenuous connection between Australia and the alleged conduct necessitates more careful consideration. This is undoubtedly tied to Australia's desire to maintain good relations with

101 Australian Parliament, House of Representatives, Parliamentary Debates (Hansard), 3 June 1999, 6044. See also Australian Parliament, Senate, Criminal Code Amendment (Bribery of Foreign Public Officials) Bill 1999, Explanatory Memorandum, 3.

102 See *Criminal Code Amendment (Bribery of Foreign Public Officials) Act 1999* (Cth).

103 *Criminal Code* (Cth) section 70.2.

104 *Ibid.*, section 70.5(1)(a)(i).

105 *Ibid.*, sections 70.5(1)(b)(i), (ii), (iii).

106 See, generally, Article 42.

107 *Criminal Code* (Cth) section 70.5(2). See also Criminal Code section 16.1.

other states, in line with international comity, when making decisions about prosecuting conduct that occurred entirely overseas and has only a limited connection to Australia. In all other cases, prosecutions fall under the Commonwealth Director of Public Prosecutions following the Prosecution Policy of the Commonwealth. As previously noted, this document provides no specific guidance on extraterritorial jurisdiction when considering whether to initiate or continue a prosecution. Matters of practicality appear to be the determining factor in prosecuting cases in circumstances where prosecutions rely on extraterritorial jurisdiction contemplated in Section 70.5. The same could arguably be said as to the prosecution of any offence where jurisdiction for the relevant alleged conduct relies on the extended forms of extraterritorial jurisdiction under any of the four categories set out in Division 15 of the Criminal Code.

Foreign bribery prosecutions in Australian courts have been relatively rare. Across OECD state parties, approximately 950 individuals, corporations, or other entities have been convicted or subjected to criminal sanctions for foreign bribery offences. A large number of ongoing investigations and criminal proceedings continue across multiple state parties.[108] Publicly available information about foreign bribery prosecutions in Australian courts[109] shows that they have predominantly involved Australian companies and citizens, but, as is typical of such offences, the alleged conduct and business activities occurred overseas.[110]

While there is no reason to question the appropriateness of these prosecution decisions, it is unclear whether an assessment was made as to why Australia was the most appropriate forum for prosecution. The mere existence of extraterritorial jurisdiction under the Criminal Code is unlikely to be a decisive factor. In other words, the fact that parliament extended Australia's jurisdiction to cover such conduct does not automatically justify prosecution. However, such laws create a dilemma for Australian prosecution agencies: either Australia prosecutes Australian companies or citizens, or these entities face prosecution (or no prosecution) in a foreign state.

108 OECD Working Group on Bribery, "2021 Enforcement of the OECD Anti-Bribery Convention. Investigations, Proceedings, and Sanctions," 20 December 2022. Accessed 25 May, 2024. https://www.oecd.org/content/dam/oecd/en/publications/reports/2022/12/enforcement-of-the-oecd-anti-bribery-convention-2021-data_9610fac0/13f29a2c-en.pdf.

109 Under the Criminal Code section 70.2.

110 See, for example, *R v Jacobs Group (Australia) Pty Ltd* [2021] NSWSC 657 (see also, in relation to an appeal, *R v Jacobs Group (Australia) Pty Ltd* [2022] NSWCCA 152, and an appeal of this judgment, *The King v Jacobs Group (Australia) Pty Ltd* [2023] HCA 23); *R v Jousif; R v I Elomar; R v M Elomar* [2017] NSWSC 1299 (see also, in relation to an appeal, *Elomar v R; Elomar v R* [2018] NSWCCA 224); *CDPP v Brady and ors* [2016] VSC 334; *The Queen v Christanto (Sentence)* [2013] VSC 521, *CDPP v Curtis* [2017] VSC 613, *CDPP v Boillot* [2018] VSC 739 and *The Queen v Note Printing Australia Limited & Anor (Sentence)* [2012] VSC 302.

If such an assessment did occur in prior foreign bribery cases, the considerations that shaped prosecution decisions – whether based on existing policies governing prosecutions or broader international legal concerns – remain unknown.

4.3 *Reasons for the Investigation and/or Prosecution of Transnational Crime in Australia*

Again, it is difficult to discern a coherent and consistent policy in the approach of Australian law enforcement and prosecution agencies in the investigation and prosecution of transnational crime, particularly where the prosecution relies on extraterritorial jurisdiction. There are a number of clear reasons why such investigations and/or prosecutions may not be pursued.

First, evidence relevant to proving the elements of an offence where extraterritorial jurisdiction is relied on may be located outside Australia. This is not, in itself, an impediment to an effective investigation or prosecution. However, the way in which evidence is collected by Australian authorities overseas can be cumbersome and resource-intensive. As discussed earlier in this chapter, mutual legal assistance arrangements that Australia has established with other countries involve substantial costs, both financial and in terms of time. The process requires consultation between multiple agencies, due diligence assessments where necessary, and communication through diplomatic channels, which can be time-consuming. Given the pressures on prosecution agencies to ensure timely and fair prosecutions, such processes are not often conducive to fulfilling this duty. Consequently, decisions on whether to investigate or prosecute – or to continue doing so – may turn on the expected timeframes, costs, and potential outcomes of such processes. Recent data-sharing agreements, noted earlier in this chapter, appear to be aimed – at least in part – at improving the efficiency of such processes.

Second, the location of potential offenders is critical to decisions about an investigation and any related prosecution. The nature of transnational crime is such that offenders may be located outside Australia, at least at the time when authorities attempt to secure their custody during the investigation stage. As a general principle, a person cannot be tried in Australia for a criminal offence in *absentia*.[111] Thus, the likelihood of successfully bringing a suspect to Australia to face prosecution is a significant factor in deciding whether to commence or continue an investigation. The more remote the prospects of securing the suspect's custody, the less likely a prosecution will proceed. Even if the prospects are reasonable, the financial and logistical

111 Such processes are typically in relation to minor offences, following notification to the defendant and their failure to attend with no reasonable explanation. See, for example, *Criminal Procedure Act 1986* (NSW) section 196.

challenges associated with securing custody through processes such as extradition must also be considered.

Further, the location of witnesses needed for an investigation and prosecution is also relevant when deciding whether to commence or continue proceedings. As noted earlier, mutual legal assistance agreements allow for evidence to be obtained from witnesses located overseas. This does not inherently present an obstacle to an effective investigation or a successful prosecution of transnational crimes. That said, once again, the costs and time constraints associated with such processes must be considered.

Third, the seriousness of the conduct is an unavoidable factor in deciding whether to investigate and prosecute transnational crimes. It is self-evident that many of the criminal offences in Australia that have a transnational character derive from international agreements. These agreements frequently include broad and aspirational commitments regarding the need for state parties to combat crimes covered under the agreements. Many also have entire sections dedicated to cooperation. For example, Chapter IV of the OECD Convention obliges states parties to afford mutual legal assistance in response to requests for assistance in investigating or prosecuting alleged offenders covered by the Convention.[112] Additionally, many agreements include provisions allowing for the transfer of criminal proceedings between state parties. For example, Article 47 of the OECD Convention states that states parties "consider the possibility of transferring to one another proceedings for the prosecution of an offence . . . in cases where such transfer is considered to be in the interests of the proper administration of justice".[113] In some agreements, there is particular emphasis on "concentrating the prosecution" in one jurisdiction.[114]

It remains unclear to what extent these considerations are taken into account in the independent decision-making process of prosecution agencies when deciding whether to commence and continue prosecutions of transnational crimes.

4.4 *Integrating an Assessment of Appropriate Forum in Decisions to Prosecute*

At the outset, in the context of the foregoing discussion about the roles of investigators and prosecutors in meeting Australia's international legal obligations regarding transnational crime, it is important to appreciate that the decision to prosecute (or continue to prosecute) is generally not a matter that attracts judicial or other independent oversight. While we do not suggest that, in the absence of independent oversight, no discretion ought

112 See, for example, Article 46.
113 Article 47.
114 See, for example, Article 47.

to be exercised, the criteria for asserting such jurisdiction in transnational criminal cases should be made more transparent through the publication of guidance for prosecutors and investigators. This includes tailored guidance on Australia's international legal obligations in relation to the prosecution of transnational crimes that have led to the creation of offences prosecuted in Australia.

As part of any decision to commence or continue a prosecution, it is essential to consider whether Australia is the – or at the very least, an – appropriate forum for the prosecution of alleged offending with transnational characteristics. This assessment must be conducted in a way that preserves the independence of the agencies involved. At the same time, such decisions should also take into account information held by other parts of the Executive Government that may be relevant but could also become a source of undue interference, particularly if such information is withheld.

We do not intend to exhaustively list considerations that must be at the forefront of investigators' and prosecutors' decision-making when determining whether to investigate and prosecute a transnational crime in Australian courts. Nor do we suggest that there are fixed criteria that must be considered in each case. However, we highlight a few key considerations that should be prioritised in this task.

When deciding whether to continue a prosecution, forum shifting must be incorporated into any such framework. In this context, forum shifting refers to Australian prosecution agencies assessing, depending on the stage of a particular criminal matter, whether the prosecution of the relevant conduct would be more effectively handled in another jurisdiction. Whether another jurisdiction presents a viable alternative to Australia for prosecution will depend on various factors. Even if another jurisdiction appears more suitable, this would not necessarily preclude the prosecution from proceeding in Australia.

Among such factors are the connection between the conduct or its result and the alternative jurisdiction; whether the legal framework in that jurisdiction allows for the exercise of criminal jurisdiction over the conduct, including the exercise of extraterritorial criminal jurisdiction; the stance of the relevant prosecution agency or agencies in that jurisdiction, particularly regarding their willingness and capacity to prosecute the criminal matter; the adequacy of available criminal offences and whether the penalties in that jurisdiction appropriately reflect the seriousness of the offending; and Australia's international legal obligations under any relevant international agreement, particularly in relation to Australia's duty to investigate and/or prosecute specific offences.

It is evident that Australian prosecution agencies may lack the necessary expertise or access to information needed to assess these considerations fully. However, they can seek advice from relevant departments within the Executive Government while ensuring that the ultimate prosecutorial decision remains independent. To mitigate risks of interference in transnational crime investigations and prosecutions, a structured framework for information-sharing must be established.

5 Conclusion

In the first section of this chapter, we outlined the manner in which Australian law creates extraterritorial criminal jurisdiction. We explored how Australia's framework for extraterritorial criminal jurisdiction largely reflects the various jurisdictional bases recognised under international law, including territoriality, active and passive nationality, and universality. We examined how Australian criminal law has adapted to these principles to align with its offence structures.

We then discussed the legal infrastructure that facilitates the prosecution of transnational crimes requiring cross-border information sharing. This includes mechanisms such as mutual legal assistance arrangements, agency-to-agency cooperation, and, increasingly, data-sharing agreements.

In the final sections, the chapter demonstrated how the prosecution of transnational crime is not merely a legal exercise but also a political one, particularly in the context of international law. In Australia, it is the Executive Government that holds the authority to enter into treaties and bind Australia, as a matter of international law, to certain obligations arising from those treaties. While many international agreements designed to combat transnational crime emphasise the role of domestic law enforcement and prosecution agencies in investigating and prosecuting such offences, it is evident that fulfilling these obligations also raises questions about interstate relations. Australian laws acknowledge this reality.[115]

However, law enforcement and prosecution agencies are not well-equipped to manage interstate relations. There remains an important advisory role for the Executive in this task. Nonetheless, it is crucial that investigating and prosecuting agencies develop or are provided with guidance to assist in determining when to initiate investigations and pursue prosecutions for transnational criminal activity. This guidance should ultimately help identify the most appropriate forum for such proceedings.

Given that the principles governing extraterritorial criminal jurisdiction under international law form the basis for Australia's jurisdiction over transnational criminal activity, these principles must be central to any such guidance.

115 Australian Parliament has chosen, on occasion, to require a member of the Executive Government, the Attorney-General, to consent to the commencement of an investigation and/or prosecution for certain types of offences, including those that rely on universal jurisdiction. It is for Parliament to prescribe the cases where it is appropriate for the Executive Government to lawfully interfere with the otherwise independent decision-making processes of law enforcement and prosecution agencies.

References

Bell, Andrew. "Extraterritoriality in Australian Law." *2023 Spiegelman Oration*, 27 April 2023.

Boister, Neil. "Transnational Criminal Law?" *European Journal of International Law* 14 (2003): 953–976.

Boister, Neil. *An Introduction to Transnational Criminal Law*. Oxford: Oxford University Press, 2018.

Bowling, Ben, and James Sheptycki. "Global Policing and Transnational Rule of Law." *Transnational Legal Theory* 6 (2015): 141–173.

Brown, Rick. "Understanding Law Enforcement Information Sharing for Criminal Intelligence Purposes." *Trends and Issues in Crime and Criminal Justice* 566 (2018): 1–15.

Gallant, Kenneth S. "The Passive Personality Principle." In *International Criminal Jurisdiction: Whose Law Must We Obey?*, edited by Kenneth S. Gallant, 441–460. Oxford: Oxford University Press, 2022.

Herzfeld, Perry, and Thomas Prince. *Interpretation*. Lawbook Co., 2020.

Hood, Anna, and Monique Cormier. "Prosecuting International Crimes in Australia: The Case of the Sri Lankan President." *Melbourne Journal of International Law* 13 (2012): 235–265.

Ireland-Piper, Danielle. "Extraterritorial Criminal Jurisdiction: Does the Long Arm of the Law Undermine the Rule of Law?" *Melbourne Journal of International Law* 13 (2023): 122–157.

Kennedy, Sally, and Ian Warren. "Extraterritorial Offending, Extradition, and Australia's Case against Hew Griffiths." *International Journal of Comparative and Applied Criminal Justice* 47 (2023): 299–315.

Reydams, Luc. "Australia." In *Universal Jurisdiction: International and Municipal Legal Perspectives*, edited by Luc Reydams, 86–92. Oxford: Oxford University Press, 2004.

Ryngaert, Cedric. *Jurisdiction in International Law*. Oxford: Oxford University Press, 2015.

Senz, Deborah, and Hilary Charlesworth. "Building Blocks: Australia's Response to Foreign Extraterritorial Legislation." *Melbourne Journal of International Law* 2 (2001): 69–121.

Smith, Russell G., and Amelia Hickman. "Estimating the Costs of Serious and Organised Crime in Australia, 2020–21." *Statistical Report No*. 38 (2022).

Triggs, Gillian. "Implementation of the Rome Statute for the International Criminal Court: A Quiet Revolution in Australian Law." *Sydney Law Review* 25 (2003): 507–534.

10 The Evolution of the United States' Use of Extraterritoriality as a Regulatory Tool

Alina Veneziano

1 Introduction

The territoriality principle is the basic principle of jurisdiction. Under certain circumstances, a state's laws can have extraterritorial application if they can be justified by one of the theories of extraterritorial jurisdiction under public international law.[1] Broadly, under public international law principles, extraterritorial jurisdiction refers to the competence of a state to apply its laws to individuals, property, or conduct beyond its territorial borders. In the United States, extraterritoriality is defined as "the application of federal and state law to conduct that takes place at least partially outside the territory of the United States".[2] It involves taking a US statute and applying its substantive provisions to either foreign individuals or foreign conduct. Under the Restatement (Fourth) of the Foreign Relations Law, international comity is a condition when deciding instances of concurrent prescriptive jurisdiction. It mandates consideration of the "legitimate interests of other nations".[3] However, some "source of federal power" is still needed.[4] Therefore, when a case comes before a US court that may involve the extraterritorial application of a statute, the court must determine whether it has the authority and power to apply that statutory provision to foreign conduct and/or foreign nationals.[5] This includes authorisation under the Constitution and any relevant statute.

1 Cedric Ryngaert, *Jurisdiction in International Law. Second Edition. Oxford Monographs in International Law* (Oxford: Oxford University Press, 2015), 101.
2 Curtis A. Bradley, *International Law in the US Legal System* (Oxford: Oxford University Press, 3rd ed., 2020), 169.
3 Restatement (Fourth) of the Foreign Relations Law of the United States §§ 402(2), 407 reporters' note 4 (Am. Law Inst. 2018). In the United States, Restatements of the Law are treatises that outline the rules and principles of specific areas of law. They are not primary law and are only commentary. That said, many courts assess and consider the Restatements in their analyses as very persuasive authority.
4 Gerald L. Neuman, "Extraterritoriality and the Interest of the United States in Regulating Its Own," *Cornell Law Review* 99(6) (2014): 1448.
5 Tonya L. Putnam, *Courts without Borders: Law, Politics, and US Extraterritoriality* (Cambridge: Cambridge University Press, 2016), 36.

DOI: 10.4324/9781003402978-12

The US Constitution gives Congress the explicit power "[t]o regulate Commerce with foreign Nations".[6] As a result, Congress has and often does pass statutes with explicit language for extraterritorial application in order to regulate individuals and conduct outside its borders – leading to a multitude of domestic and international implications.[7]

In an effort to curb the negative consequences resulting from excessive uses of extraterritoriality, the United States has developed safeguards, including the Charming Betsy Canon, the presumption against extraterritoriality, and comity considerations, to name a few. This is further reiterated in the Restatement (Fourth) of Foreign Relations. The Restatement (Fourth) discusses extraterritoriality in the context of six bases of jurisdiction to prescribe a rule. It notes that prescriptive jurisdiction must not exceed the authority granted in the Constitution and must consider the "legitimate interests of other nations as a matter of *prescriptive comity*".[8] Despite these purported safeguards, the United States has been at the "cutting edge" of utilising extraterritoriality compared to other nations.[9] It has exhibited different trends in utilising this regulatory tool. Particularly, the US judiciary has taken the stage as the primary actor in articulating new standards in cross-border cases utilising extraterritorial applications and establishing trends. These trends are heavily dependent on whether a private claimant or a public governmental authority initiates the lawsuit, whether the allegations involve civil or criminal violations and the specific text of the statutory provision at issue. Concerns for the interests of foreign sovereigns – comity considerations – have been considered with varying degrees of emphasis and intensity by the US courts.

The goal of this chapter is to illuminate the driving factors and influences behind US decision-making in terms of extraterritoriality. It explains the development of US extraterritorial jurisdiction and how the context and circumstances of the era have both prompted and necessitated changes to the United States' approach and utilisation of extraterritoriality. The chapter also discusses the differences in extraterritorial applications in different areas of the law, including antitrust law, securities laws, and employment law, as some examples. It also analyses the core changes that have occurred in the United States regarding extraterritoriality and why distinctions have been made in certain areas of law and for different claimants.

6 USCS Const. Article I, § 8, Cl 3.

7 Alina Veneziano, "A New Era in the Application of US Securities Law Abroad: Valuing the Presumption Against Extraterritoriality and Managing the Future with the Sustainable-Domestic-Integrity Standard," *Annual Survey of International and Comparative Law* 23(1) (2019): 81–82.

8 Restatement (Fourth) of Foreign Relations Law: Jurisdiction §§ 402, 403, pt. II, ch. 1 (Am. Law Inst., Tentative Draft No. 2, 2016) (emphasis added).

9 Derek Barella, "Checking the 'Trigger-Happy' Congress: The Extraterritorial Extension of Federal Employment Laws Requires Prudence," *Indiana Law Journal* 69(3) (1994): 890.

2 Tracing the Use of Extraterritoriality in the United States

The use and development of extraterritoriality in the United States is related to the notion of state sovereignty. This can be seen as early as the 1800s. In an 1804 opinion, the Supreme Court of the United States held that "an act of Congress ought never to be construed to violate the law of nations if any other possible construction remains".[10]

Going one step further, the Court added that "[t]he laws of no nation can justly extend beyond its own territories, except so far as regards its own citizens. They can have no force to control the sovereignty or rights of any other nation, within its own jurisdiction".[11] Thus, from the early 1800s to the beginning of the twentieth century, sovereignty was a core factor in judicial decisions. The reach of a nation's laws must be confined within its own borders; to do otherwise would be an infringement of sovereignty. The United States, as a fledging nation at the time, relied on this rationale for stability.

The nineteenth century's strict adherence to sovereignty and territorialism started to fade during the twentieth century. As the nation grew, international law considerations such as comity were considered. To deal with the repercussions of the Great Depression, the United States passed massive reforms and legislations – recognising that interaction with foreign nations would be forthcoming and feeling more confident with this inevitability as it grew exponentially relative to other foreign powers. This developed into a conflicts approach. The Supreme Court tackled this new trend early on in 1909 when deciding whether a US antitrust statute applies to conduct occurring in foreign countries.[12] In holding that the US law does not apply extraterritorially to conduct in other nations, the Supreme Court held that "[t]he general and almost universal rule is that the character of an act as lawful or unlawful must be determined wholly by the law of the country where the act is done".[13] Thus, by looking at the location where the conduct occurred, the Court adopted a conflict of laws approach.[14] At first glance, this trend was still heavily focused on sovereignty by refusing to interfere with the affairs of another nation and territorialism by articulating a bright-line rule that asked where the conduct occurred. However, this soon permitted the United States to regulate foreign nationals where the alleged conduct occurred within the United States. As a result, this weakened the notion of strict territorialism and sovereignty – the twentieth century's adherent focus on not pushing its own laws into other sovereigns' borders. In its place stood an approach focused

10 *Murray v The Schooner Charming Betsy*, 6 US 64, 118 (1804).
11 *Apollon*, 22 US 362, 370 (1824).
12 *American Banana Co. v United Fruit Co.*, 213 US 347, 356 (1909).
13 *Ibid.*, 356.
14 *Ibid.* (citing to conflicts sources such as Dicey, Conflict of Laws (2d ed.)).

more on international comity[15] considerations in US courts as a means of promoting healthy foreign relations.[16]

By the mid-twentieth century, courts officially invented and started making use of the *presumption against extraterritoriality*. In simplest terms, the Supreme Court provided that the presumption requires courts to start with the "presumption" that "Congress is primarily concerned with domestic conditions".[17] It also "serves to protect against unintended clashes between [US] laws and those of other nations which could result in international discord".[18] Because this is a *presumption*, it can be rebutted with evidence that Congress intended the statute to be applied extraterritorially. The Restatement (Fourth) of Foreign Relations provides that federal statutes are to apply only within the territory of the United States unless it is rebutted by congressional intent showing otherwise.[19] The 1990s further wheeled in a stronger emphasis on the presumption. The idea was that the United States was not the arbiter of all cases, nor meant to be. By the turn of the twenty-first century, comity considerations were more greatly emphasised in addition to statutory interpretation and congressional intent.

From international law to comity considerations, the present day involves a primary emphasis on statutory interpretation. Interestingly, even before the Fourth Restatement's date of publication, US courts started to curb its perceived excessive use of extraterritoriality. For instance, decisions at this time continued the statutory interpretation approach with an additional multi-part test that enquires into the 'focus' of the statute.[20] As will be discussed in greater

15 Putnam, *Courts without Borders*, 14. The doctrine of international comity pertains to a "voluntary deference to foreign sovereigns" by US courts in an effort to avoid jurisdictional clashes with foreign governments.

16 William S. Dodge, "International Comity in American Law," *Columbia Law Review* 114(8) (2015): 2095.

17 *Foley Bros., Inc. v Filardo*, 336 US 281, 285 (1949).

18 *EEOC v Arabian Am. Oil Co.*, 499 US 244, 248 (1991) (citing *McCulloch v Sociedad Nacional de Marineros de Honduras*, 372 US 10, 20–22 (1963)).

19 Restatement (Fourth) of Foreign Relations Law: Jurisdiction § 203, pt. II, ch. 1.

20 *Morrison v Nat'l Austl. Bank Ltd.*, 561 US 247 (2010); *RJR Nabisco, Inc. v European Cmty.*, 136 S. Ct. 2090, 2101 (2016). In *RJR Nabisco*, the Supreme Court articulated the two-step framework: "*Morrison* and *Kiobel* reflect a two-step framework for analyzing extraterritoriality issues. At the first step, we ask whether the presumption against extraterritoriality has been rebutted – that is, whether the statute gives a clear, affirmative indication that it applies extraterritorially. We must ask this question regardless of whether the statute in question regulates conduct, affords relief, or merely confers jurisdiction. If the statute is not extraterritorial, then at the second step we determine whether the case involves a domestic application of the statute, and we do this by looking to the statute's 'focus'. If the conduct relevant to the statute's focus occurred in the United States, then the case involves a permissible domestic application even if other conduct occurred abroad; but if the conduct relevant to the focus occurred in a foreign country, then the case involves an impermissible extraterritorial application regardless of any other conduct that occurred in US territory". *RJR Nabisco*, 579 US at 337.

detail later on, cases at the Supreme Court, including *Morrison*,[21] *Kiobel*,[22] and *RJR Nabisco*[23] stood for the proposition that private parties – including class actions – need to allege more domestic connection to the United States in cross-border cases compared to cases brought by public governmental authorities.

3 Extraterritoriality in Different Areas of the Law

Extraterritorial jurisdiction in the United States began with an emphasis on territorialism and sovereignty. This is largely consistent across all areas of law. As the United States grew as a world power and economic expansion met globalisation, effects-based jurisdiction provided courts with the justification to extend its laws to foreign conduct and foreign territory. Finally, the present-day approach of US courts with respect to extraterritorial jurisdiction looks primarily at statutory construction techniques and discerning congressional intent. This section discusses the intricacies of this approach in the following areas of law: antitrust regulation, federal securities regulation, white collar crime, employment law, defence cases, trade secrets cases, and jurisdiction statutes such as the Alien Tort Statute (ATS). As demonstrated later, some areas of law use the presumption against extraterritoriality more than others, while other areas have developed special tests and exceptions. Importantly, the way courts have been interpreting the 'focus' of the statutes within these areas of law will prove to be both inconsistent and further complicating harmonisation and actually frustrating the goal of reducing foreign friction.

3.1 Antitrust Regulation

In the United States, extraterritorial applications were more common with economic legislation and occurred earlier compared to non-economic regulation. Antitrust law, like securities laws, often involves "global consequences" that can easily cause effects within the United States as well as effects "realised worldwide"[24] due to the inherent nature of markets and trading in an interdependent and globalised economy. The massive pieces of legislation and reform passed in the United States in the 1930s spawned extensive opportunities to regulate foreign conduct and foreign nationals under the guise of protecting the US economy from anticompetitive conduct.[25]

21 *Morrison v Nat'l Austl. Bank Ltd.*, 561 US 247 (2010).

22 *Kiobel v Royal Dutch Petroleum Co.*, 569 US 108 (2013).

23 *RJR Nabisco, Inc. v European Cmty.*, 579 US 325 (2016).

24 Erica Seigmund, "Extraterritoriality and the Unique Analogy between Multinational Antitrust and Securities Fraud Claims Note," *Virginia Journal of International Law* 51(4) (2011): 1060.

25 Kal Raustiala, *Does the Constitution Follow the Flag?: The Evolution of Territoriality in American Law* (Oxford: Oxford University Press, 2009), 94, 177; Alina Veneziano, "The Eras of Extraterritoriality in the United States," *University of Bologna Law Review* 5(2) (2020): 248.

Cross-border antitrust cases started with notions of territorialism that forbade the regulation of foreign conduct and then slowly expanded to extraterritorial 'effects-based' jurisdiction. At the beginning of the twentieth century, in *American Banana*, the anticompetitive conduct occurred outside its borders, and the United States – heavily considering comity concerns – refused to apply its laws to foreign conduct.[26] However, a few decades later, effects-based jurisdiction became popular. In 1945, the Second Circuit in *Alcoa* concluded that it could regulate monopolistic conduct and actors outside its borders if such conduct had consequences within its borders.[27] In the early 1990s, the Supreme Court held that the antitrust law, the Sherman Act, applies extraterritoriality to foreign conduct and did not consider comity in its majority opinion.[28] But a decade later, in yet another antitrust law case, the Supreme Court emphasised prescriptive comity in holding that independent foreign harm is not covered by the Act.[29] Thus, comity considerations were given an ebb and flow-type consideration by the courts.

Recently, in mid-2023, the Supreme Court had to decide the extraterritorial application of two provisions of the Lanham Act, an antitrust statute that prohibits trademark infringement.[30] In this case, a US company sued six foreign parties (five foreign entities and one foreign national) for the unauthorised use and sale of its mark on products in commerce and for doing so in a way that is likely to cause confusion.[31] The Court applied the presumption and determined that neither provision contains an "express statement . . . or any other clear indication" that they apply abroad.[32] It then had to ascertain what the focus of the statute involved; in other words, the Court needed to identify what activity Congress intended to regulate. The Court determined that those provisions under the Lanham Act extend only to claims that allege that the infringing "use in commerce" is domestic.[33] This was the focus of the statute; here, however, the claims do not involve domestic applications of the statutes, and extraterritorial application would be impermissible.[34] The Court observed that to permit extraterritorial application every time there is an effect within the United States or an effect likely to occur in the United States would transform the presumption against extraterritoriality into "nothing more than a

26 *American Banana Co. v United Fruit Co.*, 213 US 347 (1909).

27 *United States v Aluminum Co. of America*, 148 F.2d 416, 421 (2d Cir. 1945) (*Alcoa*). This case involved a claim by the United States against Alcoa under the Sherman Act for illegally monopolising interstate and foreign commerce and making conspiracies in restraint of trade.

28 *Hartford Fire Ins. Co. v. Cal.*, 509 US 764 (1993).

29 *F. Hoffmann-La Roche Ltd v Empagran S.A.*, 542 US 155 (2004).

30 *Abitron Austria GmbH v Hetronic International, Inc.*, 216 L. Ed. 2d 1013, 1020–1022 (2023).

31 *Ibid.*, 1020.

32 *Ibid.*, 1023.

33 *Ibid.*, 1025, 1028–1029.

34 *Ibid.*, 1024–1026.

muzzled Chihuahua"[35] or a "craven watchdog".[36] Such an approach would only require a very tenuous connection to the United States and "threatens *international discord*".[37] Here, specifically, the use of a mark, even if it is limited to within one country will still "often have effects that radiate to any number of countries".[38] Requiring the judiciary to decide these matters when the broad effects test is used is the equivalent of the judiciary "navigating foreign policy disputes belong[ing] to the political branches".[39] Thus, in these cross-border trademark cases, adding that the infringement involves "use in commerce" that is domestic alleviates some of these concerns.

Importantly, the Court also noted that trademark law is territorial and has a "separate existence" in each nation for which it is registered or recognised.[40] As a result of this, the Court continued, each nation is therefore "empowered to grant trademark rights and police infringement within its borders", a principle which has been "enshrined in international law".[41] On this point, the Court made references to various international law agreements and viewpoints such as the Paris Convention for the Protection of Industrial Property,[42] Protocol Relating to Madrid Agreement Concerning International Registration of Marks,[43] and opinions by the European Commission.[44]

35 *Ibid.*, 1027.
36 *Morrison*, 561 US at 266.
37 *Abitron*, 216 L. Ed. 2d 1027 (citing *Kiobel v Royal Dutch Petroleum Co.*, 569 US 108, 115 (2013)).
38 *Abitron*, 216 L. Ed. 2d 1028.
39 *Ibid.*, 2028 (citing *Jesner v Arab Bank, PLC*, 138 S. Ct. 1386, 1412 (2018) (Gorsuch, J., concurring in part and concurring in judgment)).
40 *Ibid.*, 1027.
41 *Ibid.*
42 Under the Paris Convention, a "'mark duly registered in a country of the Union shall be regarded as independent of marks registered in other countries of the Union,' and the seizure of infringing goods is authorised 'on importation' to a country 'where such mark or trade name is entitled to legal protection"'. The Convention also permits trademark holders to secure protections of their marks in other countries "under the domestic law of those countries". *Abitron*, 216 L. Ed. 2d at 1027–1028 (citing Paris Convention for the Protection of Industrial Property, July 14, 1967, 21 U.S.T. 1583, T. I. A. S. No. 6923, Arts. 2(1), 4(1)–(2), 6(3), 9(1), id., at 1639, 1647).
43 This Protocol provides a mechanism through which individuals can extend trademark protections to other jurisdictions under the domestic law of that nation. *Abitron*. 216 L. Ed. 2d at 1027–1028 (citing the Protocol Relating to Madrid Agreement Concerning International Registration of Marks, June 27, 1989, T. I. A. S. No. 03–112, S. Treaty Doc. No. 106–141 (entered into force Dec. 1, 1995)).
44 In its brief, the European Commission warned against applying the Lanham Act extraterritorially "to acts of infringement occurring . . . in the European Union" and outside the territory of the United States. Further, the Brief asserted that to "police allegations of infringement occurring in Germany" would be an "unseemly" act of "meddling in extraterritorial affairs" – noting that this is especially important because there are "international treaty obligations that equally bind the United States." *Abitron*, 216 L. Ed. 2d at 1028 (citing Brief for European Commission on Behalf of the European Union as Amicus Curiae 4).

The Court even cited the Lanham Act itself – noting that it was designed to implement "treaties and conventions respecting trademarks" and that it specifically requires that "registration of a foreign trademark in the United States 'shall be independent of the registration in the country of origin' and that the rights of that mark in the United States are governed by domestic law".[45] The same reasoning applies to patents. The Supreme Court in an earlier opinion observed that "[t]he presumption that United States law governs domestically but does not rule the world applies with particular force in patent law".[46] This traditional understanding that patent law operates only domestically within the United States and does not extend to foreign activities is "embedded in the Patent Act itself, which provides that a patent confers exclusive rights in an invention within the United States".[47] This suggests a greater emphasis on international comity concerns in addition to statutory construction techniques, especially for areas that are considered distinct or inherently local.

3.2 *Federal Securities Regulation*

The United States has exhibited a very volatile trend when determining how and when to apply its federal securities laws extraterritorially. The main federal securities statutes in the United States are the Securities Act of 1933[48] and the Exchange Act of 1934.[49] Traditionally, the purposes of the federal securities laws have been to protect US investors and US capital markets against fraud, misrepresentation, and other forms of deceit to foster a free market system.[50] At the same time, states often see the importance and profitability of attracting foreign capital and foreign companies to their own markets. Logically, such foreign companies wishing to operate in the United States will be subject to certain US securities laws.[51]

In the mid-twentieth century, US courts developed standards for determining when and under what circumstances it can apply the federal securities laws extraterritorially to foreign activities and foreign conduct. The conduct and

45 *Abitron*, 216 L. Ed. 2d at 1027–1028 (citing The Lanham Act, §1127, §1126(f)).

46 *Microsoft Corp. v AT&T Corp.*, 550 US 437, 454–455 (2007).

47 35 USC § 154(a)(1) (stating that a patentee's rights over their invention apply to manufacture, use, or sale "throughout the United States" and to importation "into the United States").

48 15 USC § 77a et seq.

49 15 USC § 78a et seq.

50 Stephen Choi and Andrew Guzman, "The Dangerous Extraterritoriality of American Securities Law," *Northwestern Journal of International Law & Business* 17(1) (1996): 222.

51 Jennifer A. Zerk, "Extraterritorial Jurisdiction: Lessons for the Business and Human Rights Sphere from Six Regulatory Areas," *A Working Paper of the: Corporate Social Responsibility Initiative* (2010), 65.

effects tests were articulated,[52] followed by further refinements such as mandating that more than "merely preparatory conduct in the United States" be required but that actually "perpetrat[ing] fraudulent acts" is sufficient.[53] The effects test has been particularly controversial because it permits extraterritorial jurisdiction without necessarily any conduct by the foreign company for effects that may be arguably unintentional.[54] The ability to extend the securities laws abroad in connection to foreign conduct and foreign companies was magnified when private litigants began to rely on the private right of action in Rule 10b-5 (the antifraud provision), which was judicially created.[55] This allowed for private enforcement of securities violations for damages by non-US nationals against foreign entities.[56] Over the years, the US courts continued to define and refine multiple versions of the conduct and effects tests.[57]

In 1975, the Second Circuit pronounced a multi-level test for extraterritoriality depending on the claimant's citizenship and location of the alleged fraudulent conduct: (1) US citizens in the United States can allege losses from the sale of securities regardless of whether the acts of material importance occurred in the United States; (2) US citizens in a foreign country must allege acts of "material importance" that occurred in the United States which "significantly contributed" to the fraud; and (3) non-US citizens must allege fraudulent acts that "directly caused" their financial losses.[58] The Circuit refused to promulgate a bright-line rule, instead opting for a sliding scale approach based on the closeness or connections to the United States. With

52 *Leasco Data Processing Equipment Corp. v Maxwell*, 468 F.2d 1326, 1334–1337 (2d Cir. 1972). The conduct test permitted extraterritorial jurisdiction in cases where the conduct that took place within the United States was the "essential link" in the securities fraud scheme, such as in instances where "substantial misrepresentations" were made in US territory. *Schoenbaum v Firstbrook*, 405 F.2d 200, 206 (2d Cir. 1968). The effects test permitted extraterritorial jurisdiction in cases where the foreign conduct caused some kind of injury to, or effect, US investors and capital markets, such that extraterritorial extension was "necessary to protect American investors".

53 *Bersch v Drexel Firestone, Inc.*, 519 F.2d 974, 991 (2d Cir. 1975); *IIT v Vencap, Ltd.*, 519 F.2d 1001, 1018 (2d Cir. 1975).

54 Zerk, "Extraterritorial Jurisdiction," 65 (citing Howard M. Friedman and Eric. C. Chaffee, *Securities Regulation in Cyberspace* (New York: Wolters Kluwer, 2018), 13–49).

55 17 C.F.R. 240.10b-5, promulgated under section 10(b) of the Securities Exchange Act of 1934. (In brief, Rule 10b-5 makes it unlawful for any person to make a statement that is untrue or otherwise misleading in connection with the purchase or sale of securities).

56 Zerk, "Extraterritorial Jurisdiction," 69.

57 Fifth Circuit cases have determined that issues of extraterritorial jurisdiction in cross-border securities cases "turns on the facts" at issue in the case, with facts considered to be the "key events" in the case tending to support jurisdiction. As another example, the Seventh Circuit adopted a "balancing approach" where the conduct in the United States had to be a "substantial part" of the fraudulent securities scheme and "material to [the scheme's] success." See *Kauthar SDN BHD v Sternberg*, 149 F.3d 659, 667 (7th Cir. 1998); *Robinson v TCI/US W. Cable Communications Inc.*, 117 F.3d 900, 907 (5th Cir. 1997); *MCG, Inc. v Great W. Energy Corp.*, 896 F.2d 170, 173 (5th Cir. 1990).

58 *Bersch*, 519 F.2d at 993.

respect to the first situation, there is no issue of jurisdiction because the effect occurs within the United States. However, additional confirmation from Congress was needed before the court would apply this law to cases involving one or more foreign elements, such as those seen in the second and third situations. The court observed that Congress likely did not intend for US citizens in a foreign country to obtain damages for violations of the securities laws if there are no defendants who engaged in significant activities within the United States.[59]

The court also qualified its opinion by noting that there is no language in the statutes that expressly provides for this multi-part test. The federal securities were passed "in the midst of the depression", and the Congress that passed such legislation in the early 1930s "could hardly have been expected to foresee the development of off-shore funds thirty years later".[60] This approach was also based on the court's "best judgment as to what Congress would have wished if these problems had occurred to it".[61] As a result, this sliding scale approach gave the US courts more discretion to determine whether the facts presented and the present realities of trading permit extraterritorial application.

Thus, before the 1990s, there were multiple "judicially-created versions" of the conduct and effects tests.[62] The increase in extraterritorial application in this area was justified as a necessary and "immediate response" to the "increased potential for transnational criminal securities fraud".[63] Further, the way securities markets operate is constantly changing due to "technological developments, market liberalisation, the rise of developing country economies and the consequent changes in patterns of supply and demand of capital", all of which contributed to the "*internationalisation* of the financial services industry".[64] In 2010, the Supreme Court decided *Morrison*.[65] *Morrison* involved a class action lawsuit brought by foreign (Australian) investors against an Australian bank for shares purchased on the Australian and other foreign exchanges.[66] Because this was, in essence, a foreign party suing a foreign defendant in connection with foreign conduct, it was classified as a *foreign-cubed transaction*.[67] The Australian bank had purchased a mortgage service company headquartered in Florida before the cause of action arose.[68]

59 *Bersch*, at 992.
60 *Ibid.*, 993.
61 *Ibid.*
62 Veneziano, "A New Era," 84.
63 Edgardo Rotman, "Extraterritorial Criminal Enforcement of Securities Fraud Regulations after *United States v Vilar*," *University of Miami Law Review* 70(1) (2015): 59.
64 Zerk, "Extraterritorial Jurisdiction," 73.
65 *Morrison v Nat'l Austl. Bank Ltd.*, 561 US 247 (2010).
66 *Ibid.*, 251–253.
67 *Morrison v. Nat'l Austl. Bank Ltd.*, 547 F.3d 167, 172 (2d Cir. 2008), *aff'd*, 561 US 247 (2010).
68 *Morrison*, 561 US at 251.

This was the only US link. The complaint alleged that officers in this Florida company misrepresented financial models to the detriment of investors and that the Australian bank was aware of this and did nothing.[69]

Morrison was a significant holding because it promulgated two very radical holdings in the securities laws' context. First, the Court determined that extraterritoriality is a merits question and not one of subject matter jurisdiction. Traditionally, courts have treated the extraterritorial reach of the federal securities laws as questions of subject matter jurisdiction, not a question of prescriptive jurisdiction; the former refers to the courts' power to hear a case, while the latter refers to Congress' authority to make a rule applicable to conduct and/or persons.[70] The Court noted that to ask about what conduct the statute reaches is to ask what conduct the statute prohibits, "which is a merits question".[71] The relevant statute must indicate that Congress intended to apply its provisions extraterritorially. Thus, congressional intent and statutory interpretation should be the only guiding principles for the courts. The Supreme Court firmly held that "[w]hen a statute gives no clear indication of an extraterritorial application, it has none".[72]

Second, the decision abandoned the former conduct/effects tests and articulated the new transactional test for cross-border securities cases. The Court described the prior tests as "judicial-speculation-made-law" of trying to determine what Congress had intended; instead, the better approach, the Court continued, is to "apply the presumption in all cases" regardless of any conflict between foreign law and an American statute.[73] It noted that "it is a rare case of prohibited extraterritorial application that lacks *all* contact with the territory of the United States".[74] Thus, the Supreme Court said that courts must determine the "focus" of the statute; in other words, it must determine what Congress is seeking to regulate.[75] For Section 10(b) of the Exchange Act – which was the provision of the federal securities law at issue in *Morrison* – the Court determined the focus was on the "purchases and sales of securities in the United States". Considering this, the Supreme Court formulated the "transactional test", which holds that Section 10(b) applies only to "securities listed on domestic exchanges, and domestic transactions in other securities".[76] Because the plaintiffs did not fit under a category, their claim was dismissed.[77]

When the Supreme Court articulates a holding that Congress does not agree with, Congress has the power to legislate to the contrary. That is exactly

69 *Ibid.*, 252.
70 Restatement (Fourth) of Foreign Relations Law: Jurisdiction § 201 cmt. a, pt. II, ch. 1.
71 *Morrison*, 561 US at 254.
72 *Ibid.*, 254–255.
73 *Ibid.*, 255, 261.
74 *Morrison*, 561 US at 266.
75 *Ibid.*, 267.
76 *Ibid.*, 266–267.
77 *Ibid.*, 273.

what happened here. One month after *Morrison* was decided, Congress passed the Wall Street Reform and Consumer Protection Act – Dodd-Frank.[78] Section 929P(b) of the Act specifically allowed for extraterritorial applications if either the conduct or effects tests from the prior trends were satisfied, but only if the Securities and Exchange Commission (SEC)[79] or the United States' Department of Justice (DOJ)[80] brings the case; it does not mention the private right of action (*i.e.*, lawsuits brought by individual claimants).[81] Thus, it is not the citizenship of the plaintiff or even the location of the conduct that matters; it is whether the 'focus' is deemed to be inside or outside the United States unless Congress provides otherwise.

It is clear that Section 929P(b) was Congress' intent to overrule *Morrison* in actions brought by the SEC or DOJ and resurrect the conduct/effects tests that had been used for over four decades prior to *Morrison*. However, a significant debate ensued because the statute was drafted in jurisdictional language even though the Supreme Court had held that extraterritoriality is a merits question – an issue of prescriptive jurisdiction for Congress.[82] As a result, it was unclear whether courts should be applying the transactional test or the conduct/effects tests in actions brought by the SEC or DOJ.[83] Courts have also tried to articulate additional standards such as the "irrevocable liability test", which holds that transactions are "domestic" under *Morrison*'s second prong if "irrevocable liability is incurred or title passes within the United States" – *irrevocability* of which refers to situations where the transaction cannot be undone such as where the purchaser pays for the security or where the seller delivers the security.[84] Courts have also tried to narrow *Morrison*'s holding in subsequent cases, leading to the same confusion that arose pre-*Morrison* regarding the extraterritoriality of the securities laws.[85] These addi-

78 Dodd-Frank Wall Street Reform and Consumer Protection Act, § 929P(b), Pub. L. No. 111–203, 124 Stat. 1376, 1865 (2010).

79 The SEC is a governmental agency in the United States responsible for enforcing laws aimed at preventing market abuse and manipulation, regulating US securities markets, and protecting US investors.

80 The DOJ is an executive department of the government of the United States responsible for enforcing federal law, administering justice, and defending the interests of the United States in various cases for which the United States has an interest.

81 Dodd-Frank, § 929P(b).

82 Andrew Rocks, "Whoops – The Imminent Reconciliation of US Securities Laws with International Comity after *Morrison v National Australia Bank* and the Drafting Error in the Dodd-Frank Act," *Villanova Law Review* 56(1) (2011), 167, 198. Richard Painter, "The Dodd-Frank Extraterritorial Jurisdiction Provision: Was It Effective, Needed or Sufficient?" *Harvard Business Law Review* 1 (2011): 208–209.

83 *United States v Coffman*, 771 F. Supp. 2d 735, 737 (E.D. Ky. 2011); *Cornwell v Credit Suisse Group*, 729 F. Supp. 2d 620, 627 No. 3 (S.D.N.Y. 2010).

84 *Absolute Activist Value Master Fund Ltd. v Ficeto*, 677 F.3d 60, 67–68 (2d Cir. 2012).

85 "Securities Regulation – Securities Exchange Act – Second Circuit Holds That Transactions in Unlisted Securities Are Domestic If Irrevocable Liability Is Incurred or If Title Passes Within the United States. – *Absolute Activist Value Master Fund Ltd. v Ficeto*, 677 F.3d 60 (2d Cir. 2012)." *Harvard Law Review* 126(5) (2013): 1437.

tional standards led to the same dilemma of one branch of government (the US judiciary) disregarding the express intentions of the other (Congress).[86]

The Court in *Morrison* was worried that the conduct and effects tests were too excessive when it came to cross-border securities actions and that the United States has become the "Shangri-La of class-action litigation for lawyers representing those allegedly cheated in foreign securities markets".[87] Courts in the United States cannot be the arbiters of the world for such foreign-cubed transactions initiated by zealous private parties flocking to US courts. Not only does this harm international relations from the fact that the United States is deciding the claims of foreign nationals and foreign securities transactions, but it also consumes the scarce resources associated with investigations and litigation and overload the US district courts. Imposing more restrictive requirements for the private right of action in these cases immediately addressed these concerns. Interestingly, such concerns did not extend to public regulatory authorities in the United States. The SEC and DOJ are regulators for justice and promoters for the protection of markets and investing, so there is an implicit trust placed in these public authorities. They are regarded as detached from the objective of profiting from lawsuits. There is also less of a concern for bringing frivolous lawsuits when the case is initiated by these regulatory authorities.

Even though Congress recognised this distinction between government-initiated, or public, and private party-initiated lawsuits, it nevertheless called for a study on the private right of action as per Dodd-Frank Section 929Y.[88] This Section directed the SEC to solicit public comment to conduct a study on the private right of action in cross-border securities fraud actions involving securities purchased or sold outside the United States and whether this private right of action should be modified or narrowed.[89] In conclusion, presently, public regulators have more latitude via Dodd-Frank to bring cross-border securities cases with one or more foreign elements as long as there is some conduct or effects in the United States. Private litigants must meet the more burdensome and restrictive transactional test of *Morrison*.

3.3 *White Collar Crime*

The Second Circuit in 2013 held that the presumption also applies in the criminal context[90] – embracing many white collar crimes. In 2016, the

86 Alina Veneziano, "Should Extraterritoriality in the Midst of Congressional Silence be a Political Question?" *NYU Journal of International Law and Politics* 51 (2019): 644–645.

87 *Morrison*, 561 US at 270.

88 Dodd-Frank, § 929Y.

89 SEC. Study on the Cross-Border Scope of the Private Right of Action Under Section 10(b) of the Securities Exchange Act of 1934. (2012). https://www.sec.gov/files/929y-study-cross-border-private-rights.pdf.

90 *United States v Vilar*, 729 F.3d 62 (2d Cir. 2013).

Supreme Court in *RJR Nabisco* was faced with a case involving 26 member states of the European Community. Here, the European Community sued RJR Nabisco for operating as an "enterprise" in connection to a pattern of racketeering[91] under RICO.[92] Specifically, the European Community alleged that RJR Nabisco engaged in a global money laundering scheme with several organised crime groups whereby drug traffickers would smuggle narcotics into Europe and sell them – the proceeds of which were used to pay for multiple shipments of RJR cigarettes into Europe.[93]

The issue was whether RICO applied extraterritorially and, if so, the extent of such reach. The Court held that the presumption had been overcome in § 1962 "provided that each of those offenses violates a predicate statute that is itself extraterritorial".[94] The Court observed that even though Congress did not expressly state that RICO applies to patterns of racketeering in foreign countries, it defined "racketeering" and a "pattern" of racketeering activity to include violations of predicate statutes that do themselves expressly apply extraterritorially. Therefore, §1962 of RICO applies extraterritorially only if the underlying statute that has been violated is "itself extraterritorial".[95]

However, RICO's private right of action under § 1964(c) received a strikingly different analysis. Justice Alito's opinion in this case makes various distinctions between public RICO enforcement actions and private RICO actions, the private right of which permits treble damages. Importantly, the Court underscored how private actions raise critical issues, such as the "decision to permit enforcement without the check imposed by prosecutorial discretion".[96] The Court went through an extensive discussion of the dangers of private actions when the conduct occurs in the territory of a

91 RICO defines 'racketeering activity' to include dozens of state and federal offences, known as predicates. These predicates are any act 'indictable' under specified federal statutes, §§1961(1)(B)–(C), (E)–(G), as well as certain crimes 'chargeable' under state law, §1961(1)(A), and any offence involving bankruptcy or securities fraud or drug-related activity that is 'punishable' under federal law, §1961(1)(D). Predicates implicate RICO when part of a 'pattern of racketeering activity'. This pattern requires a series of related predicates that together indicate continued criminal activity, either the existence or threat of such criminal activity. It requires at least two predicates committed within the past ten years. *H. J. Inc. v Northwestern Bell Telephone Co.*, 492 US 229, 239 (1989); see §1961(5).

92 *RJR Nabisco, Inc. v European Cmty.*, 579 US 325 (2016).

93 *Ibid.*, 325.

94 *Ibid.*, 340–341, 346. The Supreme Court also held that the presumption was not overcome for RICO's § 1964(c) private right of action unless the private claimant demonstrates "a domestic injury to its business or property." It provided, in relevant part, the following: "Violations of § 1962 are subject to criminal penalties, and civil proceedings to enforce those prohibitions may be brought by the Attorney General of the United States. Separately, RICO, §§ 1961–1968, create a private civil cause of action permitting any person injured in his business or property from a violation of § 1962 to sue in federal district court and recover treble damages, costs, and attorney's fees. § 1964(c)".

95 *Ibid.*, 340.

96 *Ibid.*, 346–348 (quoting *Sosa* v *Alvarez-Machain*, 542 US 692, 727 (2004)).

foreign sovereign. It noted that, although the presumption applies regardless of the potential for any foreign friction or a conflict between US and foreign law, "where such a risk is evident, the need to enforce the presumption is at its apex".[97] Here, the Court refused to extend civil RICO actions abroad for these "foreign-injury claims" without a clear indication from Congress to the contrary.[98]

The European Community argued that such "international friction" concerns are inapplicable since those bringing the case are not private parties but are instead the "foreign countries themselves".[99] In their brief, the European Community argued that their allegations "comport[] with limitations on prescriptive jurisdiction under international law and respects the dignity of foreign sovereigns".[100] Without opining on the veracity of this claim, the Court noted that not all cases would be limited to foreign sovereigns and that "nongovernmental" parties will "not [be] so sensitive to foreign sovereigns' dignity". As a result, the Court held that it will not adopt a case-by-case standard that looks to the consent of the sovereign affected.[101] Further, the Court noted how other statutes, such as antitrust laws which permit private treble damages for conduct occurring abroad, have led to "considerable controversy" in foreign nations "even when those nations agree with US substantive law".[102] Thus, the Court refused to adopt a standard that looked to the consent or agreement of the foreign nation when deciding whether to use the presumption.

This decision was a recognition by the Supreme Court that a private individual must allege more facts – domestic injury – for courts to provide relief under RICO. To do otherwise would be to allow private claimants to utilise extraterritoriality without regard to comity, or "international friction", as the Court noted.[103] As a result, the private right of action in civil RICO cases was reduced and was similarly reduced with respect to other statutes that do not have the affirmative intent of Congress for extraterritoriality.[104]

3.4 Employment Law

Employment/labour law represents a unique area of law in the United States. Unlike antitrust or securities regulation, for example, employment and

97 *Ibid.*, 348 (citing *Morrison*, 561 US at 255).
98 *Ibid.*
99 *RJR Nabisco*, 579 US at 349.
100 *Ibid.* (*quoting* Brief for Respondents 52–53).
101 *Ibid.*
102 *RJR Nabisco, Inc.*, 347 (*quoting F. Hoffmann-La Roche Ltd v Empagran S. A.*, 542 US 155, 167 (2004)).
103 *Ibid.*, 345–346.
104 Carlos M. Vazquez, "Out-Beale-Ing Beale." *Georgetown Law Faculty Publications and Other Works* (2016): 71.

labour issues are very specific and can be highly dependent on locality, not to mention the fact that many employment issues are governed by unions, collective bargaining agreements, private contracts, and so on. Thus, when it comes to violations and enforcement of remedies, there is a strong private aspect to employment cases. As a result, the extraterritoriality of the US employment laws has been utilised at a much slower rate. This is true regardless of whether the parties in the case are private litigants or whether the employment claim is brought by a governmental agency such as the Equal Employment Opportunity Commission (EEOC)[105] like in *Aramco*. It is often difficult – if not impossible – for courts to apply a federal statute in this area extraterritorially for the benefit of a single employee.

Courts resist applying employment laws extraterritorially because employment regulation is primarily a local matter; that said, employment issues involving more than one state only took force within the past few decades.[106] In other words, courts have taken less interest in resolving purely local employment matters involving cross-border issues.

However, the rise of the gig economy, the prevalence of cross-border employment, remote work opportunities, and the transient nature of certain jobs necessitated a broader approach. This was exacerbated by the possibility of remote working, such as US employees working abroad. To start, anti-discrimination is a core requirement of employment and labour statutes. In the United States, the three most important federal statutes on anti-discrimination are Title VII of the Civil Rights Act of 1964, The Americans with Disabilities Act (ADA), and The Age Discrimination in Employment Act (ADEA) (collectively, the Acts).[107] These statutes were initially all silent on the issue of extraterritoriality.[108] Because these statutes were silent on this issue, courts denied extraterritoriality when the conduct occurred in a foreign country.[109] Courts relied on the Supreme Court's holding in 1949 that "legislation of Congress, unless a contrary intent appears, is meant to apply only within the territorial jurisdiction of the United States".[110] Thus, a US citizen could not maintain a suit against a US employer in connection with conduct covered under the Acts which took place outside the United States.[111] In two

105 The EEOC is a federal agency in the United States established from the Civil Rights Act of 1964; its duties are to enforce civil rights laws and prevent discrimination in the workplace.

106 Alina Veneziano, "The Extraterritoriality of US Employment Laws: A Story of Illusory Borders and the Indeterminate Applications of US Employment Laws Abroad," *Berkeley Journal of Employment and Labor Law* 41(1) (2020): 159–160.

107 42 USCS § 2000e; 42 USCS § 12112; 29 USCS § 623.

108 Robert Stulberg and Amy Shulman, "Representing Americans Employed Abroad: The Extraterritorial Application of Federal and State Anti-Discrimination Laws," *ILSA Journal of International and Comparative Law* 11(2) (2005): 423–426.

109 *Cleary v United States Lines, Inc.*, 555 F. Supp. 1251 (D. NJ. 1983); *Love v Pullman Co.*, 1976 US Dist. LEXIS 13997, 2–5 (1976).

110 *Foley Bros., Inc. v Filardo*, 336 US 281, 285 (1949) (quoting *Blackmer*, 284 US at 437).

111 Veneziano, "The Extraterritoriality of US Employment Laws," 144–147.

critical Supreme Court opinions – *Filardo* and *Aramco* – the Court denied extraterritorial application for the simple reason that Congress did not intend to enforce the anti-discrimination statutes outside the United States.[112] The Court in *Aramco* noted that Congress "may similarly amend Title VII and in doing so will be able to calibrate its provisions in a way that [the Court] cannot",[113] thus providing an invitation for Congress to amend an otherwise unjust consequence perceived by the US judiciary: that US citizens cannot recover when their US employer discriminates against them abroad.

Congress took up this implicit offer for all three of the core anti-discrimination statutes, providing an explicit indication for extraterritorial application. The amendments were inserted to permit extraterritoriality in favour of US citizens with respect to employment by a US employer "in a foreign country".[114] In other words, after the amendments, US employees could turn to US courts for violations of the anti-discriminatory statutes for conduct that occurred either in the United States or abroad as long as they worked for a US employer.[115] However, the statutes carved out an important exception to extraterritoriality – called the *foreign law defence*.[116] It basically allows the employer to claim the defence if compliance with the US anti-discriminatory statute would result in violation of a local law of the foreign country.[117] But, because this is not well-defined in the statutes, courts are left without guidance as to when and under what circumstances an employer can claim this defence and avoid compliance with the Acts. For example, some decisions articulate a strict approach, requiring the employer to demonstrate that compliance with US law will cause it to violate a law of the host country.[118] Other decisions signify that employers need to show more evidence as to why they were qualified to rely on the foreign law defence.[119] The insertion of this *foreign law defence* is another attempt by the United States to consider international concerns and avoid possible foreign friction.

3.5 Defence, Trade Secrets, and Jurisdictional Statutes

In this category, the same recurring principles are used by the courts: the presumption, statutory construction, and discerning congressional intent, and (to a lesser extent) comity. As an example, consider the Defend Trade

112 *Filardo*, 336 US at 284–285; *EEOC v Arabian Am. Oil Co.*, 499 US 244, 248 (*Aramco*).
113 *Aramco*, 499 US at 259.
114 42 USC §2000e-1; 42 USC § 12112(c)(1); 29 USC § 623(f)(1).
115 Sean Bunting, "The Extraterritorial Force of Title VII: Regulating the Conduct of American Employers Overseas," *Hofstra Labor and Employment Law Journal* 9(1) (1991): 257.
116 Nie Carrie, "Extraterritorial Application of US Employment Laws: Clearing the Murky Conflicting Foreign Laws Defence," *International Lawyer* 46(4) (2012): 1039.
117 Veneziano, "The Extraterritoriality of US Employment Laws," 161–162.
118 *Kern v Dynalectron Corp.*, 577 F. Supp. 1196 (N.D. Tex. 1983).
119 *Abrams v Baylor College of Medicine*, 805 F.2d 528 (5th Cir. 1986).

Secrets Act (DTSA).[120] In 2016, the DTSA was supplemented to the Economic Espionage Act[121] and created a private right of action for owners of trade secrets to bring a lawsuit in US federal courts for misappropriation of trade secrets in foreign or interstate commerce.[122] A district court in 2020 held for the first time that private actions for damages under the DTSA apply extraterritorially.[123] First, the district court held that the presumption had been overcome because of clear congressional intent in the statute.[124] Second, the Court observed how the claimant had provided sufficient evidence that the defendant committed the alleged act in the United States even though the misappropriation took place abroad.[125] Thus, the statute supported permissible extraterritorial application.[126]

The court in *Motorola* drew a distinction between the private right of action in the DTSA and the private right of action in RICO claims, as discussed in *RJR Nabisco*. Here, in *Motorola*,[127] the court found that the section on the private right of action was added within a chapter that does not contain any limiting language – the private right of action is broadly inserted and provides that "[a]n owner of a trade secret that is misappropriated may bring a civil action under this subsection if the trade secret is related to a product or service used in, or intended for use in, interstate or foreign commerce".[128] However, in *RJR Nabisco*, the Supreme Court made a distinction between criminal extraterritorial application (which applies extraterritorially if the underlying predicate offence does) and private, civil extraterritorial application. Regarding the private claims in RICO, the Court found limiting language regarding the availability of civil damages – namely, that it had to be damages to business or property.[129] The *Motorola* opinion came at a time when the United States was combating IP theft from China.[130] Many cases

120 18 USC §1836.
121 110 Stat. 3488 (1996).
122 *Ibid.*, at 1836(b).
123 *Motorola Solutions v Hytera Communs. Corp.*, 436 F. Supp. 3d 1150 (N.D. Ill. 2020).
124 *Ibid.*, 12–13, 18–19.
125 *Ibid.*, 27–28.
126 *Ibid.*, 27–28.
127 In this case, Motorola alleged that Hytera had misappropriated its trade secrets when it hired engineers from Motorola's office in Malaysia who subsequently stole a significant number of confidential documents from Motorola. Once Hytera had the confidential information, Motorola alleged that Hytera used these trade secrets to develop radios which were "functionally indistinguishable" from Motorola's radios and then sold them around the world. *Ibid.*, 5–6.
128 18 USC 1836(b); *Motorola Solutions v Hytera Communs. Corp.*, 436 F. Supp. 3d 1150, 1160 (N.D. Ill. 2020).
129 *Ibid.*
130 Alina Veneziano, "The Extraterritorial Application of the Defend Trade Secrets Act," *Notre Dame Journal of International and Comparative Law Online*, 14 July 2020. Accessed 20 September 2024. https://ndjicl.org/online/2020/the-extraterritorial-application-of-the-defend-trade-secrets-act.

were decided at this time that aligned with the broad goal of curbing Chinese theft and misappropriation of US trade secrets. Reflecting a bipartisan consensus, the Department of Justice and the Attorney General made various announcements at this time of their intent to be aggressive in combating IP theft in America perpetrated by the Chinese government. The *Motorola* court simply discerned the clear congressional intent that the private right of action under the DTSA permitted extraterritorial application.

In 2013, the Supreme Court in *Kiobel*[131] had to address the extraterritorial reach of the Alien Tort Statute – a statute which provides that "[t]he district courts shall have original jurisdiction of any civil action by an alien for a tort only, committed in violation of the law of nations or a treaty of the United States".[132] The Court discussed the presumption as a safeguard and held that the presumption "similarly constrain[s] courts considering causes of action that may be brought under the ATS".[133] The issue was not whether courts have jurisdiction but whether courts can recognise such a cause of action at all.[134] The Supreme Court examined the statute and found that the ATS contains no clear indication of extraterritoriality.[135] Going one step further, it held that "even where the claims touch and concern the territory of the United States, they must do so with *sufficient force* to displace the presumption against extraterritorial application".[136] In *Kiobel*, the presumption had not been rebutted, and the plaintiff could not maintain the action in US court for an alleged international law violation that took place abroad.[137]

The Supreme Court in *Kiobel* relied on its earlier opinion in *Sosa* when discussing the private right of action.[138] In *Sosa*, the Court noted that the decision to create a private right of action is best left to Congress. The mere existence of a private right of action involves "a decision to permit enforcement without the check imposed by prosecutorial discretion".[139] Further, the "possible collateral consequences of making international rules privately actionable argue for judicial caution".[140] *Kiobel* was important because it held that although the presumption usually applies to conduct-regulating

131 *Kiobel v Royal Dutch Petro. Co.*, 569 US 108, 111–112 (2013). In *Kiobel*, a group of Nigerian nationals who resided in the United States sued certain Dutch, British, and Nigerian corporations under the Alien Tort Statute, alleging that the corporations violated the statute by aiding and abetting the government of Nigeria in committing violations of the law of nations that took place in Nigeria.
132 28 USCS § 1350.
133 *Kiobel*, 569 US at 116.
134 *Ibid.*, 119.
135 *Ibid.*, 124.
136 *Ibid.*, 124–125.
137 *Ibid.*, 125.
138 *Sosa v Alvarez-Machain*, 542 US 692 (2004).
139 *Ibid.*, 727.
140 *Ibid.*

statutes, it should also apply to jurisdictional statutes, including the ATS, because these statutes could also result in foreign policy implications. The Court noted that "the danger of unwarranted judicial interference in the conduct of foreign policy is magnified in this context, where the question is not what Congress has done but what courts may do".[141]

4 Significant Influences of Extraterritoriality Over Time and Their Emphasis

The United States has progressed from a fledgling nation that adhered to traditional notions of sovereignty to one that slowly recognised the importance of international law as it became a world power. It wasn't long before comity considerations and fact-sensitive interest analysis came into play. As soon as the United States realised that extraterritoriality was more effective than conquest or even treaties, US courts adopted broad approaches in cross-border cases and became major players in the international field. In essence, extraterritoriality was a simple way for a dominant nation such as the United States to project its current ideology, goals, and power across borders in the form of regulations. However, as foreign friction developed and as foreign parties flocked for relief to US courts in connection with foreign conduct, the presumption against extraterritoriality was articulated. The tricky part was whether the congressional intent for extraterritoriality could be inferred or discerned by the courts or whether such intent had to be provided for directly in the statutory provision. Despite congressional statutory revisions to the contrary, courts managed to find ways to articulate additional refinements and distinctions to statutes based on whether they perceived extraterritorial application to be a good or bad idea in the case at hand.

In addition, while factors of consideration such as comity have not completely disappeared in cross-border decision-making by US courts, they have both (1) fluctuated in terms of the importance placed on them throughout the decades and (2) been supplemented with distinctions based on whether a private or public party initiates the lawsuit, whether the case involves civil or criminal matters, whether the statute explicitly references or permits extraterritoriality. These changes stem from nothing more than the realities of the US common law system – an internal battle between the political preferences of Congress as reflected in statutory provisions and the opinions of US courts interpreting those statutes and refining them with additional standards and distinctions (*i.e.*, public vs private; criminal vs civil, etc.).

Let's return for a moment to *Morrison*, *Kiobel*, and *RJR Nabisco*. Private parties, as per *Morrison,* have to allege a domestic transaction/exchange in order to bring a cross-border securities fraud claim. Private parties alleging violations under the Alien Tort Statute as per *Kiobel* must

141 *Kiobel*, 569 US at 109.

show that their claim concerns the United States and that such connection and, even where they do, it must be with "sufficient force" to rebut the presumption – making it harder for this statute to apply to foreign conduct. Lastly, the private right of action under RICO, as per *RJR Nabisco,* requires private parties to allege a domestic injury. The rationale behind these opinions was to prevent the appearance that the United States could regulate the claims of any party and any case – no matter what. Although the presumption has worked in avoiding extraterritorial applications in cases with little US connection or where the policy implications would be too severe,[142] it is still unclear how negative policy implications can be avoided or mitigated in cases where the presumption is rebutted, and the law is applied abroad – a phenomenon which was not present in *Morrison, Kiobel*, or *RJR Nabisco*. Further, the concerns when private litigants bring cases are not present when the government or public authorities deal with cases. For example, the government, as per Dodd-Frank Section 929P(b), can rely on the more flexible, lenient conduct/effects tests when initiating cross-border securities fraud cases. As a society in the United States, there is an implicit assumption that we trust our government to bring legitimate cases based on facts and plausible arguments in a way that does not waste or otherwise consume court time, discovery and investigation tools, or litigation resources. Thus, many conclude that the government is often in a better position to assess foreign implications and concerns compared to private parties.

5 Conclusion

Extraterritoriality is a powerful regulatory tool that has been used by the United States for centuries. Its use of extraterritoriality has changed dramatically from a trend of strict territorialism to one of conducts/effects and finally to an approach of statutory construction and analysis. While extraterritoriality under international law principles is reserved for Congress as a matter of prescriptive jurisdiction, the US judiciary – by virtue of the nation's common law system – has taken a very active role in promulgating standards and applying laws abroad. The willingness and extent of US extraterritoriality have been influenced by technological advancements, globalisation, and even the political context of that time. As US extraterritoriality started to become excessive, the judiciary articulated various judicially-invented tools, or safeguards, to curb such harmful effects. These safeguards included the presumption against extraterritoriality. However, it is sometimes challenging to see the benefits of these safeguards. For instance, the judiciary, via extraterritoriality, is applying statutes abroad and becoming international political actors. Further, once a judicial decision is rendered, Congress retains the authority to amend a statute to overturn a recent

142 *RJR Nabisco*; *Kiobel*; *Morrison*.

decision. While this has led to multiple intra-governmental conflicts within the three branches of government, it has also produced negative consequences on an international level, such as hindered US/foreign relations. Over time, case decisions involving US extraterritorial jurisdiction have shown hostility towards private claimants by increasing the standards for which they must demonstrate to claim US jurisdiction, while case decisions have granted more leniency in actions initiated by public governmental authorities. Many scholars have promoted efforts at multi-lateral negotiations for harmonisation, but this task has proven to be unworkable since each nation's laws are often unique, specialised, and local. As a result, extraterritorial regulation will not fade any time soon. That said, the United States has demonstrated its concern to prevent foreign friction and consider international comity as a part of its legislation and decision-making processes. Where the United States and its use of extraterritoriality go from here remains to be seen.

Bibliography

Barella, Derek. "Checking the 'Trigger-Happy' Congress: The Extraterritorial Extension of Federal Employment Laws Requires Prudence." *Indiana Law Journal* 69(3) (1994): 889–920.

Bradley, Curtis A. *International Law in the US Legal System*. Oxford: Oxford University Press, 3rd edition, 2020.

Bunting, Sean. "The Extraterritorial Force of Title VII: Regulating the Conduct of American Employers Overseas." *Hofstra Labor & Employment Law Journal* 9(1) (1991): 257–288.

Choi, Stephen, and Andrew Guzman. "The Dangerous Extraterritoriality of American Securities Law." *Northwestern Journal of International Law & Business* 17(1) (1996): 207–241.

Dodge, William S. "International Comity in American Law." *Columbia Law Review* 114(8) (2015): 2071–2142.

Friedman, Howard M., and Eric C. Chaffee. *Securities Regulation in Cyberspace*. New York: Wolters Kluwer, 2018.

Neuman, Gerald L. "Extraterritoriality and the Interest of the United States in Regulating Its Own." *Cornell Law Review* 99(6) (2014): 1441–1470.

Nie, Carrie. "Extraterritorial Application of US Employment Laws: Clearing the Murky Conflicting Foreign Laws Defence." *International Lawyer* 46(4) (2012): 1027–1043.

Painter, Richard. "The Dodd-Frank Extraterritorial Jurisdiction Provision: Was It Effective, Needed or Sufficient?" *Harvard Business Law Review* 1 (2011): 195–229.

Putnam, Tonya L. *Courts without Borders: Law, Politics, and US Extraterritoriality*. Cambridge: Cambridge University Press, 2016.

Raustiala, Kal. *Does the Constitution Follow the Flag?: The Evolution of Territoriality in American Law*. Oxford: Oxford University Press, 2009.

Rocks, Andrew. "Whoops – The Imminent Reconciliation of US Securities Laws with International Comity after *Morrison v. National Australia Bank* and the Drafting Error in the Dodd-Frank Act." *Villanova Law Review* 56(1) (2011): 163–198.

Rotman, Edgardo. "Extraterritorial Criminal Enforcement of Securities Fraud Regulations after *United States v. Vilar*." *University of Miami Law Review* 70(1) (2015): 53–95.

Ryngaert, Cedric. *Jurisdiction in International Law*. Oxford: Oxford University Press, 2nd edition, 2015.

"Securities Regulation – Securities Exchange Act – Second Circuit Holds That Transactions in Unlisted Securities Are Domestic If Irrevocable Liability Is Incurred or If Title Passes Within the United States. – *Absolute Activist Value Master Fund Ltd. v. Ficeto*, 677 F.3d 60 (2d Cir. 2012)." *Harvard Law Review* 126(5) (2013): 1430–1437.

Seigmund, Erica. "Extraterritoriality and the Unique Analogy between Multinational Antitrust and Securities Fraud Claims Note." *Virginia Journal of International Law* 51(4) (2011): 1047–1082.

Stulberg, Robert and Amy Shulman. "Representing Americans Employed Abroad: The Extraterritorial Application Of Federal And State Anti-Discrimination Laws." *ILSA Journal of International & Comparative Law* 11(2) (2005): 421–433.

Vazquez, Carlos M. "Out-Beale-Ing Beale." *Georgetown Law Faculty Publications and Other Works* (2016): 68–73.

Veneziano, Alina. "A New Era in the Application of US Securities Law Abroad: Valuing the Presumption Against Extraterritoriality and Managing the Future with the Sustainable-Domestic-Integrity Standard." *Annual Survey of International & Comparative Law* 23(1) (2019): 79–132.

Veneziano, Alina. "Should Extraterritoriality in the Midst of Congressional Silence be a Political Question?" *NYU Journal of International Law and Politics* 51 (2019): 637–650.

Veneziano, Alina. "The Eras of Extraterritoriality in the United States." *University of Bologna Law Review* 5(2) (2020): 240–267.

Veneziano, Alina. "The Extraterritorial Application of the Defend Trade Secrets Act." *Notre Dame Journal of International & Comparative Law* (2020). Accessed 20 September 2024. https://ndjicl.org/online/2020/the-extraterritorial-application-of-the-defend-trade-secrets-act

Veneziano, Alina. "The Extraterritoriality of US Employment Laws: A Story of Illusory Borders and the Indeterminate Applications of US Employment Laws Abroad." *Berkeley Journal of Employment and Labor Law* 41(1) (2020): 121–165.

Zerk, Jennifer A. "Extraterritorial Jurisdiction: Lessons for the Business and Human Rights Sphere from Six Regulatory Areas." *A Working Paper of the: Corporate Social Responsibility Initiative* (2010).

Part III
Progressive Approaches

11 A Progressive Interpretation of Extraterritoriality in Light of Italian Doctrine and Practice

Francesca Capone

1 Introduction

The scope of the present chapter is to provide the reader with an overview of Italy's approach to extraterritorial jurisdiction. So far, the topic has been addressed by the Italian scholarship in a fragmented way, paying attention to one aspect and/or one field at a time. The present work will not be able to offer an exhaustive analysis of Italy's progress in this area. Instead, it will seek to first sketch out the main developments and then delve into some of them. Italian authors have been proactive in reflecting and commenting on noteworthy events in which the scope and degree of exercise of Italy's jurisdiction has played a central role in the international domain. In shaping Italy's approach towards extraterritoriality, it is certainly important to single out the pivotal role of the Court of Cassation (or Italian Supreme Court).

Given the plethora of relevant judicial decisions as well as theoretical input on extraterritorial jurisdiction, it is possible to conclude that Italy certainly represents a compelling case study. Due to the fact that it is simply unfeasible to provide a comprehensive overview of Italy's approach, the present work will limit its scope by focussing on some key issues. The identification of the selected topics stems from Italy's interpretation of the principles enshrined in the Case of the *SS Lotus* (*France v Turkey*), which, albeit controversial, still govern the lawfulness of the exercise of extraterritorial jurisdiction.[1] According to Menno T. Kamminga, in a famous passage of the decision, it is possible to infer three principles related to extraterritorial jurisdiction.[2] Borrowing from his intuition, the present work will rely on these principles to discuss Italy's take on extraterritoriality.[3] The first principle affirms that whether a state may lawfully exercise extraterritorial jurisdiction is a matter of international law. According to the second principle of international law,

1 Menno T. Kamminga, "Extraterritoriality," in *Max Planck Encyclopedia of Public International Law*, ed. Anne Peters (Oxford: Oxford University Press, 2020).
2 *SS Lotus* (*France v Turkey*), Judgment, [1927] PCIJ Rep Series A, No. 10, paras. 18–19.
3 Kamminga, "Extraterritoriality".

DOI: 10.4324/9781003402978-14

generally, prohibits the exercise of extraterritorial enforcement jurisdiction unless this is specifically permitted. From this perspective, the law of state immunity, and in particular Italy's controversial approach, represents an excellent opportunity to test the first two principles, respectively with regard to (1) the so-called "humanitarian exception"[4] carved by Italian courts and the extent to which it is reshaping the applicable legal framework, and (2) the enforcement jurisdiction exercised by Italy through *exequatur* proceedings in state immunity's disputes, notably identified by Italian courts and by the International Court of Justice (ICJ) as an exercise of jurisdictional power.[5] The third principle clarifies that the exercise of extraterritorial prescriptive and adjudicative jurisdictions is permitted only if there is a sufficient connection between the state exercising it and the extraterritorial event. In relation to this principle, the present work will focus on Italy's position vis-à-vis extraterritorial criminal jurisdiction, especially with regard to the notion of a "sufficient connection" to establish jurisdiction[6] and the alternative reading of Article 7(1)(5) of the Italian criminal code, which expresses the principle of a 'mild' universal jurisdiction adopted by the Italian legislator. By relying on timely examples that purport significant developments, this analysis will reflect on Italy's contribution to reinforcing the notion of extraterritoriality under international law.

2 State Immunity and Extraterritoriality: So Far, Yet So Close!

It is blatant to observe that national approaches to extraterritoriality vary, and states differ considerably in their understanding of the extent to which they are entitled to make, apply, and enforce rules of conduct in respect of events that occur outside their own territory. Italy is no exception, and although it is possible to identify some prevailing trends, for instance, the fact that Italy's judicial power might embrace a reading of a given case that

4 *Ferrini v Germany*, Cass. Sez. Unite civili, Appeal decision, 11 March 2004, No. 5044/04. The literature on the case and its ramifications is very rich; see, for instance, Alessandra Gianelli, "Crimini internazionali ed immunità degli Stati dalla giurisdizione nella sentenza Ferrini," *Rivista di Diritto Internazionale* 87 (2004): 643; Massimo Iovane, "The Ferrini Judgment of the Italian Supreme Court: Opening up Domestic Courts to Claims of Reparation for Victims of Serious Violations of Fundamental Human Rights," *The Italian Yearbook of International Law* 14 (2004): 165.

5 Nerina Boschiero, "Jurisdictional Immunities of the State and Exequatur of Foreign Judgments: A Private International Law Evaluation of the Recent ICJ Judgment in Germany v Italy," in *International Courts and the Development of International Law*, eds. Nerina Boschiero et al. (The Hague: T.M.C. Asser Press, 2013), 781.

6 Cass. pen. sez. 6, Ord. 22 October n. 30642. See Claudia Cantone, "Estradizione e limiti all'esercizio della giurisdizione penale extraterritoriale nel diritto internazionale: riflessioni a margine della sentenza della Corte di cassazione n. 30642/2020," *Rivista di diritto internazionale privato e processuale* 3 (2020): 620.

is different from the executive's position,[7] it is difficult to speak of a uniform and consistent outlook on the issue.

Whenever a state attempts to exercise its jurisdiction in the aftermath of events that cause ripples not only in the political and diplomatic circles but also within the international legal community, the risk of giving rise to direct conflict with other states is obviously high. Italy is not new to situations that, willingly or not, placed it at the centre of the international stage. In this author's view, the law of state immunity can be seen as a litmus test to better grasp Italy's approach to the first two of the three principles governing the exercise of extraterritorial jurisdiction, as identified in the *Lotus* case's judgment.[8] In *Lotus*, which remains to these days one of the judgments that has attracted the most attention as well as criticism,[9] the Permanent Court of International Justice (PCIJ) specified a crucial distinction between prescriptive and enforcement jurisdiction. Whereas international law would pose no limits on a state's jurisdiction to prescribe its rules for persons and events outside its borders *absent a prohibitive rule to the contrary*, a state would be precluded from enforcing its laws in another state's territory *absent a permissive rule to the contrary*.[10] This general statement eloquently summarises the first two of the three principles, which together set the basis for the lawful exercise of extraterritorial jurisdiction. In declaring its first principle, the PCIJ famously affirmed that whether a state may lawfully exercise extraterritorial jurisdiction is "a matter of international law", thus subjected to the existing international rules. It would be difficult to qualify this principle as controversial, given the fact that in a community made of sovereign and equal states, none of them can unilaterally set the limits of its own competence to exercise jurisdiction beyond its territory. At the same time, there are undoubtedly instances when the 'matter' is unsolved or subject to changes resulting, for example, from the affirmation of human rights law, the centrality of which has led to second-guessing many tenets attached to the dogma of state sovereignty and thus immunity.

The second *Lotus* principle deals with the exercise of extraterritorial enforcement jurisdiction, which refers to a state's jurisdiction "to enforce or compel compliance or to punish noncompliance with its laws or regulations, whether through the courts or by use of executive, administrative, police, or other nonjudicial action".[11] As noted by Cedric Ryngaert, the

7 Lucia Leontiev, doctoral thesis "Jurisdiction of Territorial Non-State Entities in International Law," 242, on file with author.

8 *SS Lotus* (*France v Turkey*), paras. 18–19.

9 For an excellent overview of the criticism see Máté Csernus, "Might Contain Traces of Lotus: The Limits of Exclusive Flag State Jurisdiction in the Norstar and the Enrica Lexie Cases," *Leiden Journal of International Law* 36 (2023): 947.

10 Cedric Ryngaert, *Jurisdiction in International Law* (Oxford: Oxford University Press, 2nd ed., 2015), 31.

11 *Ibid.*

rules of enforcement jurisdiction are far stricter than the rules of prescriptive jurisdiction,[12] meaning that, as the PCIJ held in the *Lotus case*, states are not entitled to enforce their laws outside their territory, "except by virtue of a permissive rule derived from international custom or from a convention".[13] Extraterritorial enforcement is, therefore, unlawful without the consent of the host state because it violates that state's right to respect its territorial integrity. Translated into practice, this entails that a state cannot, for example, use military force to compel another state to abide by its law. It cannot resort to legal implementation measures such as penalties, fines, seizures, investigations, or demands for information to give extraterritorial effect to its rules.[14] Accordingly, enforcement can only happen through territorial measures, *e.g.*, by arresting a person who is voluntarily present on the territory or by seizing the property of the defendant located in the territory. Both the first and the second principles aim to preserve the coherence of the international legal framework, striving for a balance between what is allowed and what is forbidden, but without shedding light on what happens when new tensions occur and developments inevitably take place.

Indeed, one of the ambits in which the Italian case study appears to be particularly intriguing for the application of the first two *Lotus* principles is that of state immunity, *i.e.*, the immunity that a state enjoys in respect of itself (jurisdictional immunity) and its property (enforcement immunity) from the jurisdiction of the courts of another state.[15] Notably, the Italian case law on jurisdictional immunities of foreign states is at the leading edge in the development of international customary law, pushing the traditional boundaries of immunity and promoting the recognition of the category of *delicta imperii*, *i.e.*, international crimes exempt from the customary prerogative of full state immunity. The well-known and highly scrutinised work of the Italian courts has been the object of heated debate and thorough analysis, but, to this author's knowledge, the extraterritorial elements, in particular in relation to the cases involving Greek nationals, *e.g.*, the victims of the Distomo massacre carried out by Nazis during WW II,[16] have seldomly been placed at the centre of the discussion. This is not surprising, even though it is evident that "a perennial issue in the doctrine of State immunity is the *irreconcilable*

12 *Ibid.*

13 *SS Lotus* (*France v Turkey*), para. 18.

14 Consent to extraterritorial enforcement may be granted through bilateral agreements or through multilateral instruments that foster international cooperation, for instance, to bring about the presence of the presumed perpetrator by means of extradition, or to have a domestic court order enforced against assets located abroad. See Kamminga, "Extraterritoriality".

15 Peter-Tobias Stoll, "State Immunity," in *Max Planck Encyclopedia of Public International Law*, ed. Anne Peters (Oxford: Oxford University Press, 2020).

16 *Prefecture of Voiotia v Federal Republic of Germany*, Case No. 11/2000, Hellenic Supreme Court (Areios Pagos), 4 May 2000 (ILR, Vol. 129, p. 513).

conflict of jurisdiction between two States: the forum and the foreign State".[17] Hopefully, the next paragraphs will contribute to filling this lacuna.

2.1 *Unpacking Italy's Approach to State Immunity Through the Lenses of Extraterritoriality*

Towards the end of the 19th century, through their jurisprudence and an accurate interpretation of the principle *par in parem non habet iurisdictionem*, both Italian and Belgian courts were the first to endorse a significant shift from absolute state immunity to restrictive immunity.[18] According to Italian and Belgian judges, if the aim of this principle was to protect the sovereignty of a state, then immunity should not be granted in cases where the state acted as a private entity. Soon, the courts of other states started to follow the Italian and Belgian lead, developing a general practice able to create a new customary norm, according to which state immunity was limited to the so-called *acta jure imperii*. Moreover, the new trend paved the way for applying the restrictive immunity theory to the jurisdiction to execute.[19] One of the reasons that explains the significance of Italy's contribution can be traced to the absence of state legislation on the matter, which resulted in the direct application of the relevant international norms by Italian judges, who were free to interpret and enact the rules without the filter of national norms.[20] Furthermore, regarding the jurisdiction to execute, a significant step in the direction of restricting immunity was the abolition of the national legislation requiring prior authorisation of the Ministry of Justice to execute the property of a foreign state,[21] which is still a requirement in many countries, including Greece. In relation to the first *Lotus* principle, as the description of the judicial saga we will provide later will show, Italy's approach is relevant in light of the determination of its courts to carve out a so-called "humanitarian exception" to the norms on state immunity[22] The recognition of such an exception could potentially open the floodgates for endless cases concerning the commission of international crimes by states, also beyond the territory of the forum state. Regarding the second principle, its relevance emerges when investigating Italy's attitude

17 Hazel Fox and Philippa Webb, *The Law of State Immunity* (Oxford: Oxford University Press, 3rd ed., 2013), 414.

18 Micaela Frulli, *Immunità e crimini internazionali: l'esercizio della giurisdizione penale e civile nei confronti degli organi statali sospettati di gravi crimini internazionali* (Torino: Giappichelli, 2007), 143; Andrea Atteritano, "Immunity of States and Their Organs: The Contribution of Italian Jurisprudence Over the Past Ten Years," *The Italian Yearbook of International Law* 19 (2009): 31.

19 *Ibid.*, 34.

20 *Ibid.*

21 The authorisation by the Ministry of Justice was established by Law No. 1263 of 15 July 1926 and ultimately declared unconstitutional by the Constitutional Court with decision of 15 July 1992, No. 329.

22 Fox and Webb, *The Law of State Immunity*, 414.

towards immunity from enforcement, considered by the ICJ itself as a separate question from that of jurisdictional immunity.[23]

2.2 *A Close-up on the Ferrini Case and Italy's Exequatur Decisions*

The thoroughly dissected *Ferrini* case, accompanied by many similar proceedings, marks a further step towards the affirmation of Italy's increasingly restrictive approach to state immunity.[24] Mr Ferrini, an Italian citizen who was abducted on 4 August 1944 near Arezzo, Italy, by the German army and deported to Germany to work as a forced labourer for German firms, brought a civil action for liability in tort against the Federal Republic of Germany in relation to war crimes committed against him by Nazi military forces during the Second world war. Following the trials before the lower courts,[25] in ascertaining its jurisdiction over the case, the Italian Court of Cassation abandoned the traditional distinction between *acta jure imperii* and *acta jure gestionis* and denied immunity to Germany since the unlawful acts under consideration resulted in the violation of peremptory norms of international law.[26] As stated in the judgment, since the norms of *jus cogens* prevail over customary rules (*lex superior*), state immunity could not be granted. Subsequent decisions issued by Italian tribunals affirmed that this "humanitarian exception" to the immunity rule is progressively consolidating as customary law. Notably, the reading of the law of state immunity was not confined to cases initiated by Italian citizens before Italian courts, but it also gave rise to the enforcement of foreign judgments following proceedings brought by Greek nationals in Greece, *i.e., exequatur* decisions,[27] notwith-

23 *Jurisdictional Immunities of the State* (*Germany v Italy; Greece Intervening*), paras. 113–114.

24 *Ferrini v Germany*, Cass. Sez. Unite civili, Appeal decision, 11 March 2004, no 5044/04.

25 Carlo Focarelli, "Denying Foreign State Immunity for Commission of International Crimes: The Ferrini Decision," *The International and Comparative Law Quarterly* 54(4) (2005): 955.

26 Riccardo Pavoni and Stephane Beulah, "L'immunité des États et le jus cogens en droit international: étude croisée Italie/Canada (State Immunity and Jus Cogens in International Law: A Comparative Study of Italian and Canadian Practice)," *Revue juridique Thémis* 43 (2009): 491; Micaela Frulli, "The Times They Are A-Changing the Italian Court of Cassation Denies Germany Immunity from Execution to Allow Compensation to War Crimes' Victims," *Journal of International Criminal Justice* 9 (2011): 1129.

27 The facts of the case are well known. In a nutshell, on 10 June 1944, during the German occupation of Greece, German armed forces committed a massacre in the Greek village of Distomo, disrupting the lives of many civilians. In 1995, the relatives of the victims of the Distomo massacre initiated proceedings against Germany before Greek courts and claimed compensation for loss of life and property. The Greek Court of First Instance awarded damages to the successors in title of the victims of the massacre. Germany's appeal of that judgement was dismissed by the Hellenic Supreme Court (Areios Pagos) on 4 May 2000. Despite the unprecedented win in court, the judgment against Germany remained unexecuted in Greece due to the lack of authorisation from the Minister for Justice to enforce a judgment against a foreign state. *Prefecture of Voiotia v Federal Republic of Germany*, Case No. 11/2000, Hellenic Supreme Court (Areios Pagos), 4 May 2000 (ILR, Vol. 129, 513).

standing the negative outcome of the same claim before the European Court of Human Rights (ECtHR)[28] and the German Federal Supreme Court.[29] As is well known, after the Italian *exequatur* proceedings,[30] the Greek claimants were even able to register a legal charge over Villa Vigoni, a cultural centre owned by the German State in Italy.[31]

To oppose the trend initiated before the Italian courts, which could potentially provide a justice venue for all victims of German crimes during WWII, Germany brought a case against Italy before the ICJ, leading to the Court's (in)famous judgment in 2012 (*Germany v Italy No. 1*),[32] which found Italy in breach of customary law on sovereign immunity. The Court was requested to adjudge and declare that Italy has failed to respect the jurisdictional immunity that Germany enjoys under international law, in three different ways: (1) by allowing, before the Italian courts, several civil claims brought by Italian nationals against Germany seeking reparation for damages caused by breaches of international humanitarian law committed by the German Reich during World War II; (2) by taking measures of constraint against a German State property (*i.e.*, Villa Vigoni) used for government non-commercial purposes; and (3) by declaring enforceable in Italy certain Greek judgments against Germany awarding compensation for civil damages to the successors of Greek nationals who had been victims of the Distomo massacre.[33] Without delving into the already widely assessed judgment, what is important to stress here is how the ICJ reasoned in relation to Germany's third submission, dealing with Italy's *exequatur* decision that declared enforceable in Italy the judgments rendered by Greek courts.[34]

It is worth remembering that *exequatur* is a concept that, traditionally, is specific to private international law and refers to a precise procedure by which a national court authorises the enforcement of a foreign judgment in its country. Nonetheless, in the ICJ judgment, enforcement of foreign judgments has been expressly recognised as a topic at the crossroads of

28 *Kalogeropoulou and Others v Greece and Germany*, Application No. 59021/00, ECtHR, decision of 12 December 2002.

29 *Greek Citizens v Federal Republic of Germany*, Case No. III ZR 245/98, German Federal Supreme Court (Bundesgerichtshof).

30 *Federal Republic of Germany v Prefecture of Voiotia*, Cass. Sez. Unite civili, Judgment, 29 May 2008, No. 14199.

31 Boschiero, "Jurisdictional Immunities of the State and Exequatur of Foreign Judgments," 781. See also Olivia Lopes Pegna, "Giù le mani da Villa Vigoni: quale tutela 'effettiva' per le vittime di gravi violazioni dei diritti umani?" *Rivista di Diritto Internazionale* 101(1) (2018): 1237.

32 *Jurisdictional Immunities of the State* (*Germany v Italy; Greece Intervening*), paras 120.

33 Boschiero, "Jurisdictional Immunities of the State and Exequatur of Foreign Judgments," 783.

34 *Jurisdictional Immunities of the State* (*Germany v Italy; Greece Intervening*), paras. 121–133.

public and private international law. Thus, as noted by Nerina Boschiero, the ICJ has openly challenged the "distinction between the law applicable to the rights and obligations of states with respect to other subjects of international law and individuals (public international law) and issues of jurisdiction, applicable law, and the recognition and enforcement of judgments before national courts (private international law)".[35] The Court's thinking focused on the assessment of whether Germany would have been entitled to immunity if the proceedings on the merits had been instituted in Italy, *i.e.*, the state called upon to grant *exequatur*. The Court concluded that Italian courts declaring Greek decisions enforceable had violated Germany's immunity. In the ICJ's view, granting *exequatur* to a foreign judgment had effects comparable to rendering a judgment on the merits. In other words, since Germany would have enjoyed immunity before Italian courts had the compensation claims for the Distomo massacre come before them, the Court found that Italian courts declaring Greek decisions enforceable had violated Germany's immunity.[36]

Despite the ICJ's clear stance on the matter,[37] Italy's approach to state immunity, also with respect to *exequatur* proceedings, continues to question the still prevailing position on the issue. An example that corroborates this statement is provided by the *Angela Stergiopoulos v Iran* case,[38] in which the Italian Court of Cassation reaffirmed that state immunity does not bar *exequatur* proceedings against a foreign state when those proceedings seek the recognition and enforcement of a foreign judicial decision finding the state responsible for serious breaches of human rights law. The Court's order 39391/2021 results from the mass litigation by victims of the 11 September terrorist attack, who initiated a civil lawsuit before the US District Court for the Southern District of New York (SDNY).[39] The SDNY issued a default judgment finding Iran liable for all allegations brought against it and awarded both compensatory and punitive damages to the

35 Boschiero, "Jurisdictional Immunities of the State and Exequatur of Foreign Judgments," 785.

36 Benjamin Nußberger and Victoria Otto, "Jurisdictional Immunities of the State (*Germany v Italy: Greece Intervening*)," in *Max Planck Encyclopedia of Public International Law*, ed. Rüdiger Wolfrum (Oxford: Oxford University Press, 2015).

37 Notably, right after the ICJ decision, the issue seemed to be settled; Italy became party to the not-yet-in-force UN Convention on Jurisdictional Immunities of States and their Property, and the Court of Cassation openly embraced the ICJ's decision.

38 *Stergiopoulos v Islamic Republic of Iran*, Cass. civ. sez. 1, Ord. 10 December 2021, No. 39391.

39 The family members of victims of the September 11 terrorist attacks sued Iran in the Southern District of New York for aiding and abetting Al Qaeda in the perpetration of those events. They proceeded under the terrorism exception to foreign sovereign immunity, which allows plaintiffs to sue foreign nations appearing on the State Department's list of state sponsors of terrorism. See Elliston Perot Bissel V. and Joseph R. Shottenfeld, "Exceptional Judgments: Revising the Terrorism Exception to the Foreign Sovereign Immunities Act," *The Yale Law Journal* 127(7) (2018): 1890–19015.

plaintiffs who later sought to seize Iranian assets in Europe.[40] While other national courts swiftly dismissed the claims, aligning themselves with the approach followed by the ICJ in *Germany v Italy No. 1*, Italy's Court of Cassation provided yet another evidence of "its inclination to champion a human rights limitation to State immunity, in contrast to mainstream transnational case law".[41]

The perils of this strategy have been eloquently highlighted by several commentators. In particular, Daniele Amoroso and Riccardo Pavoni note how, in *Stergiopoulos,* the Italian Supreme Court has missed the opportunity to better outline the exact contours of its efforts to effectively limit state immunity.[42] More in detail, the Court could have specified that the exception applies solely to serious human rights and (humanitarian law) violations that are suffered in the forum state's territory and/or by that state's nationals.[43] Furthermore, in case of *exequatur* decisions, which do not entail a thorough review of the merits of the foreign judgment, there is also the need to make sure that the fair trial concerns triggered by these kinds of proceedings are duly addressed; otherwise, there is a significant risk of watering down Italy's efforts to stand up to the ICJ to enhance the promotion of human rights. In addition to the challenges that are intrinsic to the Court of Cassation's approach, there are also other hurdles that come from the Italian apparatus in general. In fact, as the next paragraph will show, the conclusions reached by the Italian Supreme Court in *Stergiopoulos* might even seem at odds with the most recent developments in the dispute between Germany and Italy.

2.3 *The Constitutional Court's and the Government's View on Germany's Immunity from Enforcement: Finally Shaking Hands or Still Arm Wrestling?*

In 2014, in yet another unexpected turn of events, the Italian Constitutional Court declared that the ICJ interpretation of immunity from foreign civil jurisdiction and Law No.5/2013, adopted to codify the effect of the ICJ judgment in *Germany v Italy No. 1*, were incompatible with Italian constitutional principles.[44] The Constitutional Court, allegedly resorting

40 Notably, the judges awarded the class a default judgment of $1.8 billion in damages.

41 Daniele Amoroso and Riccardo Pavoni, "Stergiopoulos v Iran 315. Italian Supreme Court of Cassation Decision on Human Rights Limitations on Sovereign Immunity in International Law and Italian Constitutional Law," *American Journal of International Law* 117(2) (2023): 305.

42 *Ibid.*, 320–321.

43 Riccardo Pavoni, "Germany versus Italy Reloaded: Whither a Human Rights Limitation to State Immunity?" *Question of international Law Zoom-in* 94 (2022): 19, 21–28.

44 *Judgment No. 238*, Italian Constitutional Court, 22 October 2014 (hereinafter 'Judgment No. 238'). More in detail, the Court affirmed that due to the lack of a judicial alternative remedy available to the victims of Nazi crimes, the Court found that the immunity rule, as interpreted

to the doctrine of "counter-limits",[45] held that state immunity could not result in the absolute sacrifice of individuals' fundamental right to judicial protection.[46] In particular, in the Court's view, there is no jurisdictional immunity if victims have no other way to receive justice for serious violations of the universal values of human rights and dignity, as such atrocities go beyond individual states' interests. From then on, the Court of Cassation consistently confirmed states' lack of jurisdictional immunity and held that enforcement immunity only shields them from execution over properties with a public, institutional, or diplomatic function, while measures of constraint can be applied to foreign properties without public purpose.[47] As the Constitutional Court annulled the law by which the Italian Parliament had sought to prevent civil complaints against Germany, victims or their relatives resumed legal actions or started new ones. A few of them resulted in the attachment of real estate owned by Germany in Rome since the German Government refused to pay court-ordered compensation. Blatantly unpleased with the approach followed by Italian courts in the aftermath of Judgment No. 238, Germany resorted once again to the ICJ in April 2022 (*Germany v Italy No. 2*), seeking Italy's condemnation, assurance of

by the ICJ, is inconsistent with Articles 2 and 24 of the Italian Constitution. Amongst the many comments on the case see Natalino Ronzitti, "La Cour constitutionnelle italienne et l'immunité juridictionnelle des Etats," *Annuaire Français de Droit International* LX (2014): 9; Marco Longobardo, "The Italian Constitutional Court's Ruling Against State Immunity when International Crimes Occur: Thoughts on Decision No. 238 of 2014," *Melbourne Journal of International Law* 16 (2015): 255; Pietro Pustorino, "La sentenza n. 238 del 2014 della Corte costituzionale: limiti e prospettive nell'ottica della giurisprudenza italiana," *Diritti Umani e Diritto Internazionale* 9 (2015): 51, 52–56.

45 The doctrine of counter-limits refers to the need to preserve "a national legal space entirely protected from the influence of [international law], a space in which the State continues to retain full sovereignty . . . and is therefore free to have its own sources". See Fulvio M. Palombino, "Italy's Compliance with ICJ Decisions vs. Constitutional Guarantees: Does the 'Counter-limits' Doctrine Matter?" *Italian Yearbook of International Law* 22 (2013): 187. For a discussion on whether the doctrine has attained the necessary degree of consensus among states, see Massimo Iovane, "The Italian Constitutional Court Judgment No. 238 and the Myth of the 'Constitutionalization' of International Law," *Journal of International Criminal Justice* 14 (2016): 604, 605.

46 For a thorough discussion on the doctrine of "counter-limits" and its developments, see Fulvio M. Palombino, "Compliance with International Judgments: Between Supremacy of International Law and National Fundamental Principles," *Zeitschrift für ausländisches öffentliches Recht und Völkerrecht* 75 (2015): 503.

47 Notably, recognitions include the already discussed *exequatur* of Germany-owned Villa Vigoni in Lake Como based on the judgments from Greek courts condemning Germany for the Distomo massacre of 10 June 1944. Andrea M. Pelliconi, "The Italian Constitutional Court's New Decision on State Immunity and the ICJ Germany vs Italy No. 2," *EJIL: Talk!*, 28 July 2023. Accessed 19 December 2023. https://www.ejiltalk.org/the-italian-constitutional-courts-new-decision-on-state-immunity-and-the-icj-germany-vs-italy-no-2/.

"non-repetition", and, at first, also urgent provisional measures to prevent the sale at public auction of its properties.[48]

The core of the application lies in Germany's claim that Judgment No. 238 of the Italian Constitutional Court was adopted in conscious violation of international law and of Italy's duty to comply with a judgment of the principal judicial organ of the United Nations.[49] Furthermore, since the delivery of Judgment No. 238, "at least 25 new cases have been brought against Germany [before Italian courts]" and "in at least 15 proceedings, Italian domestic courts . . . have entertained and decided upon claims against Germany in relation to conduct of the German Reich during World War II".[50] Since Judgment No. 238 was handed down by the Constitutional Court, the Italian Government has done its best to keep good relationships with Germany while recognising victims' rights to compensation.[51] Therefore, it does not come as a surprise that the day after the 2022 proceedings were instituted before the ICJ, a Decree-Law, later converted into law,[52] was published in the Italian Official Journal, with the aim to address, at least to some extent, the concerns raised by Germany.[53] The Decree-Law was, in the first place, designed to protect Germany from non-recognition of immunity from execution. In fact, through the establishment of a fund for reparations, Italy assumed full responsibility for compensating successful applicants in merit proceedings against Germany.[54] Article 43(3) of the

48 Pietro Franzina, "Jurisdictional Immunities: Germany v. Italy, Again," *The European Association of Private International Law*, 4 May 2022. Accessed 19 December 2023. https://eapil.org/2022/05/04/jurisdictional-immunities-germany-v-italy-again/.

49 Tullio Scovazzi, "Come se non esistesse," *Rivista di diritto internazionale* 104 (2021): 167; Paolo Palchetti, "Right of Access to (Italian) Courts über alles? Legal Implications Beyond Germany's Jurisdictional Immunity," in *Remedies against Immunities? Reconciling International and Domestic Law after the Italian Constitutional Court's Sentenza 238/2014*, eds. Valentina Volpe, Anne Peters and Stefano Battini (Heidelberg: Springer, 2021), 39–54.

50 See Giorgia Berrino, "Plus Ça Change, Plus C'est la Même Chose: State Immunity and International Crimes in Judgment No. 20442/2020 of the Corte di Cassazione Note to: Corte di Cassazione (Sezioni Unite Civili), P.T. v. Federal Republic of Germany and Republic of Italy, 28 September 2020, No. 20442," *The Italian Review of International and Comparative Law* 1 (2022): 374; Chiara Venturini, "Le Sezioni Unite sulle immunità degli Stati (sent. n. 20442 del 2020): un'evoluzione soltanto apparente," *Forum di Quaderni Costituzionali* (2021): 169.

51 Giorgia Berrino, "Il 'ristoro' dei cittadini italiani vittime di crimini di guerra e contro l'umanità commessi dalla Germania durante il secondo conflitto mondiale," *Rivista di diritto internazionale* 105(2) (2022): 827; Roberto Baratta, "Il Fondo 'ristori' tra rispetto del diritto internazionale, controlimiti e ragioni creditorie delle vittime di crimini nazisti: il punto di tenuta dell'ordine costituzionale," *Rivista di diritto internazionale* 106(4) (2023): 1093.

52 Law No. 79 of 29 June 2022.

53 Decree-Law No. 36/2022 of 30 April 2022.

54 Lorenzo Gradoni, "Is the Dispute between Germany and Italy Over State Immunities Coming to an End (Despite Being Back at the ICJ)?" *EJIL: Talk!*, 10 May 2022. Accessed 26 December 2023. https://www.ejiltalk.org/is-the-dispute-between-germany-and-italy-over-state-immunities-coming-to-an-end-despite-being-back-at-the-icj/.

Decree-Law makes judgments awarding compensation unenforceable until they become final,[55] derogating *de facto* from Article 282 of the Italian Code of Civil Procedure, according to which first-instance judgments are provisionally enforceable. The same provision further prevents the initiation of new enforcement proceedings over German assets and automatically extinguishes existing ones. This means that not only may the enforcement proceedings be dismissed, but that the substantive rights to compensation also cease to exist.[56] The law's constitutionality was challenged before the Italian Constitutional Court, which on 21 July 2023 issued a new decision on state immunity restating that, although Germany does not enjoy immunity from jurisdiction as that would prevent victims of international crimes from getting justice, Germany's assets with public purpose enjoy immunity from enforcement. Despite the widespread optimism,[57] the decision did not bring the proceeding between Germany and Italy, currently pending before the ICJ, to a conclusion.

Without examining the Constitutional Court's decision in detail, as it mainly reaffirms Italy's commitment to the recognition of a 'humanitarian' exception and its *animus inducendi consuetudinem*,[58] what is worth noting here, and for the purpose of the present work, is *why* the decision has not been able to quell the dispute between Germany and Italy. In the Constitutional Court's view, as expressed in its decision from July 2023, the establishment of a compensation fund that shifts the economic burden to redress the victims from Germany, the original debtor, to Italy offers an "adequate alternative safeguard" equivalent to judicial execution, which compensates for the automatic extinction of enforcement proceedings. The Constitutional Court, in its reasoning, further stressed that the fund "offers greater protection to claimants", with the exclusion of foreign individuals, also when their claims stem from foreign judgments,[59] as they do not have access to the Italian compensation fund. Indeed, the Constitutional Court did not pronounce itself on the constitutionality of the extinguishment of procedures engaged by foreign claimants, even though the Greek region of Sterea Ellada, a

55 Giorgia Berrino, "The Impact of Article 43 of Decree-Law No 36/2022 on Enforcement Proceedings Regarding German State-Owned Assets," *Questions of International Law Zoom-in* 94 (2022): 59.

56 *Ibid.*, 66.

57 Pelliconi, "The Italian Constitutional Court's New Decision on State Immunity."

58 Berrino, "Plus Ça Change, Plus C'est la Même Chose," 377.

59 Originally, the text of Decree-Law no 36/2022 referred only to enforcement proceedings initiated by foreigners before Italian courts. The revised text in Law No.79 expanded the scope of the exclusion also to *exequatur* in Italy of foreign judgments granted to foreigners. See Giorgia Berrino, "Quale effettività della tutela giurisdizionale nel caso Germania c. Italia? L'art. 43 del d.l. n. 36/2022 come 'rimedio' costituzionalmente legittimo," *Diritti Umani e Diritto Internazionale* 17(1) (2023): 211.

claimant in the Distomo massacre proceeding,[60] intervened in the case, pointing out that while the Italian Law No.79 quashed all enforcement proceedings, including those executing foreign judgments, compensation through the fund was only envisaged for Italian citizens.[61] As noted by Germany in its request to extend until 12 January 2025 the time limit for the filing of its Memorial before the ICJ in *Germany v Italy No. 2*,[62] two sets of proceedings are pending before the Court of Rome, which concern procedures of constraint against German properties. In either of these proceedings, the question of the constitutionality of the Italian compensation fund could (and should) again be referred to the Italian Constitutional Court, considering that the decision issued in July 2023 did not deal with the question of differentiated treatment raised by Sterea Ellada.

To use Giorgia Berrino's words, the key issue "would be to assess whether the fact that the crimes occurred abroad and the fact that the victim is a foreigner provide a sufficient justification for the described difference in treatment"[63] Most likely, the justification would appear to be insufficient and Article 43 of Law No.79 would be declared constitutionally illegitimate at least in so far as it does not provide access to the fund to the foreign victims of German violations committed outside the Italian territory who obtained the *exequatur* of a foreign judgment in Italy and are deprived of the possibility to seize German-owned assets intended for commercial purposes.[64] Law No.79 undeniably gives rise to a blatant asymmetry between the more favourable position of Germany and that of other states, against which enforcement proceedings can still be brought and *exequatur* can still be granted, with the only limit of immunity from measures of constraint on properties used for public, or non-commercial, purposes. As stressed by Donato Greco,

> this asymmetry reflects negatively not only on the principle of sovereign equality of States but also on foreign victims of serious human rights violations, whose legitimate aspiration to reparation for the damage suffered is ultimately conditioned to the identity of the defendant State.[65]

60 See Maria Gavouneli and Ilias Bantekas, "Prefecture of Voiotia v. Federal Republic of Germany. Case No. 11/2000," *The American Journal of International Law* 95(1) (2001): 198.

61 Pelliconi, "The Italian Constitutional Court's New Decision on State Immunity".

62 *Questions of Jurisdictional Immunities of the State and Measures of Constraint against State-Owned Property* (*Germany v Italy*) ICJ Order, 5 December 2023.

63 Berrino, "The Impact of Article 43 of Decree-Law No. 36/2022," 71.

64 *Ibid.*

65 Donato Greco, "Jurisdictional Immunities and Reparation for WWII Crimes: The Impact of the Italian Constitutional Court's Judgment No. 159/2023 on Greek Victims' Claims," *EJIL: Talk!*, 15 August 2023. Accessed 10 January 2024. https://www.ejiltalk.org/jurisdictional-immunities-and-reparation-for-wwii-crimes-the-impact-of-the-italian-constitutional-courts-judgement-no-159-2023-on-greek-victims-claims/.

If Greek nationals are precluded from seeking the *exequatur* in Italy of foreign judgments ordering Germany to compensate WWII damages and can no longer bring enforcement proceedings before Italian courts, a similar obstacle is not encountered, as discussed in the previous paragraph, by US creditors of Iran in cases like *Stergiopoulos*.[66]

In conclusion, it is undeniable that Italy's approach to state immunity challenges the mainstream position on the issue, especially in relation to judicial immunity, and it does so by relying both on its courts' case law and on the unwavering but never uncritical support of the Italian international legal scholarship. While there are some tensions between the Government's desire to put an end to the dispute with Germany and the judiciary's favour towards the affirmation of victims' rights, it is blatant to observe that there is no coming back from Judgment 238 and that the Italian position is no longer isolated. It has even inspired a few courts around the world,[67] leading to the emergence of a still embryonic trend in transnational jurisprudence.[68]

3 Italy's Exercise of Extraterritorial Criminal Jurisdiction and the Third Lotus Principle

The third principle governing extraterritorial jurisdiction outlined by the PCIJ in the *Lotus* case deals with the exercise of extraterritorial prescriptive and adjudicative jurisdictions, which is permitted only if there is a sufficient connection between the state exercising it and the extraterritorial event.[69] States continue to consider territoriality as the most straightforward and certain way of delimiting competencies between them.[70] As a result, jurisdictional analyses remain mainly centred on territorial connections, even where such connections become increasingly volatile, as it happens in the case of essentially non-territorial cyberspace or global climate

66 *Ibid.*

67 For an assessment of this trend, with respect to recent decisions issued by domestic courts in Ukraine, South Korea, and Brazil, see Ielyzaveta Badanova, "Jurisdictional Immunities v Grave Crimes: Reflections on New Developments from Ukraine," *EJIL:Talk!*, 8 September 2022. Accessed 17 January 2024. https://www.ejiltalk.org/jurisdictional-immunities-v-grave-crimes-reflections-on-new-developments-from-ukraine/; Alessandro Bufalini, "Immunità degli Stati dalla giurisdizione e negoziazioni fra Stati: sulla vicenda delle comfort women coreane," *Diritti Umani e Diritto Internazionale* 15(3) (2021): 699; Aziz Tuf Saliba and Lucas C. Lima, "The Law of State Immunity before the Brazilian Supreme Court: What is at Stake with the 'Changri-la' Case?" *Brazilian Journal of International Law* 18(1) (2021): 53.

68 Amoroso and Pavoni, "Stergiopoulos v Iran," 318.

69 Kamminga, "Extraterritoriality."

70 Cedric Ryngaert, "The Concept of Jurisdiction in International Law," in *Research Handbook on Jurisdiction and Immunities in International Law*, ed. Alexander Orakhelashvili (Cheltenham: Edward Elgar 2015), 50–75.

change.[71] What is a 'sufficient connection' may be determined initially by resorting to certain general principles of jurisdiction, territoriality, active nationality principle, passive nationality principle, protective principle, and universality principle. Nonetheless, it should immediately be stressed that these principles must be employed with great caution. It is too simplistic to affirm that any exercise of extraterritorial jurisdiction that is based on one of these principles is automatically lawful under international law. In fact, the principles differ considerably in the degree to which they provide a legitimate basis for exercising jurisdiction.[72]

Moreover, the principles shall not be deemed as exhaustive and ultimately, it is the rule of reason that aims "at identifying the State with the strongest connection, in terms of contacts or interests, with the situation".[73] Some authors have described the application of the rule of reason as a "shift from a focus on power to a focus on interests"[74] in the domain of extraterritorial jurisdiction. However, in practice, a rule of reason can be difficult to objectively apply. First, because reasonableness may "be (only) in the eye of the beholder",[75] and accordingly give rise to pro-forum bias, and second, as noted by Ryngaert, because "non-elected judges and administrative authorities might not be well-situated to carry out an interest-balancing test" that "involves considerations of political economy and impinges on the political branches' prerogative to conduct foreign relations".[76] With these premises in mind, the Italian approach to the exercise of extraterritorial criminal jurisdiction definitely deserves to be further analysed, in light of Italy's judges' understanding of the 'sufficient connection' criterion and, more in general, of the 'expansive' reading of Article 7(1)(5) of the Italian criminal code, which affirms that "it is punishable according to the Italian law the Italian national or the foreigner who commits abroad . . . any other crime for which special norms or *international conventions* establish the application of Italian criminal law".

3.1 *Italy's View on the Existence of a Sufficient Connection*

Recently, the judges of the Italian Supreme Court had the opportunity to reflect on the notion of a sufficient connection to establish jurisdiction, providing an interesting, but not indisputable, approach to the matter. In a pivotal judgment issued on 22 October 2020, the Court of Cassation dealt with the

71 *Ibid.*, 53.
72 Kamminga, "Extraterritoriality."
73 Ryngaert, "The Concept of Jurisdiction in International Law," 62.
74 Anne-Marie Slaughter, "Liberal International Relations Theory and International Economic Law," *American University International Law Review* 10(2) (1995): 717, 735.
75 Ryngaert, "The Concept of Jurisdiction in International Law," 63.
76 *Ibid.*, 64–65.

issue while assessing an extradition case towards the United States of America.[77] The Supreme Court's decision is noteworthy since its focus was, for the first time, on the restrictions imposed by public international law on states in the exercise of criminal jurisdiction outside their territory. To reach the conclusion that the US had the right to exercise jurisdiction and thus request the extradition of the two non-US nationals accused of conspiracy, the Italian Supreme Court reflected on the existence of a 'reasonable connection', which, as stressed previously, could justify the exercise of extraterritorial jurisdiction under international law. The Court first reasoned on the fact that under international law, the exercise of extraterritorial criminal jurisdiction, prescriptive and adjudicative, is not prohibited and, as stated in the third principle stemming from *Lotus*, such exercise is allowed only if there is a sufficient connection between the state exercising it and the extraterritorial event. The Italian judges did not delve into the elements of the sufficient connection since, as noted by the Court of Cassation, the assessment of the existence of said connection in extradition proceedings shall be carried out by the judge that requests the extradition and not by the judge on the receiving end, in the case at stake the Italian one. Nonetheless, in its findings, the Court reflected on the characteristics of the connection by using the adjective 'reasonable' to qualify it. It is difficult, as noted by other commentators,[78] to evaluate the extent to which, by selecting this specific adjective in lieu of 'sufficient' or any other synonyms, the Italian Court of Cassation deliberately decided to weigh in on the theory of jurisdictional reasonableness or rule of reason.[79] If this is true, and the Court intentionally resorted to 'reasonableness' as a criterion to circumscribe the exercise of extraterritorial jurisdiction and contribute to better qualifying the connection, it is possible that the implicit intention was to join the long-lasting debate on the rule of reason.

To provide the reader with a quick overview of how the debate unfolded so far, it suffices to mention that it sees on one side the US arguing for the qualification of the rule of reason as a norm of customary international law, or in any case for the recognition of its role in the legal sphere, and on the other the majority of states, which has distanced itself from this approach.[80] Without consistent state practice applying the reasonableness requirement based on a sense of legal obligation,[81] no such requirement can be said to

77 Cass. pen. sez. 6, Ord. 22 October n. 30642.

78 Cantone, "Estradizione e limiti all'esercizio della giurisdizione penale extraterritoriale," 629.

79 Ryngaert, *Jurisdiction in International Law*, 154; William S. Dodge, "A Modest Approach to the Customary International Law of Jurisdiction," *European Journal of International Law* 32(4) (2021): 1471.

80 Ryngaert, *Jurisdiction in International Law*, 153. See Cedric Ryngaert, "The Restatement and the Law of Jurisdiction: A Commentary," *European Journal of International Law* 32(4) (2021): 1455.

81 Dodge, "A Modest Approach to the Customary International Law of Jurisdiction," 1474.

exist as a matter of customary international law.[82] It will thus depend on the evolution of state practice and *opinio juris* to determine if it will be possible to reach a point where reasonableness will be considered a norm of international law in the field of jurisdiction and beyond. The role of Italian practice in this regard may be pivotal, but only if and when the Court of Cassation confirms its orientation and agrees to further delve into the key elements of the "reasonable" connection, which, if correctly delineated, could be extremely helpful to strike a balance between assertions of extraterritorial jurisdiction and domestic doctrines that rely on a presumption against extraterritoriality.

3.2 *The 'Alternative' Reading of Article 7(1)(5) of the Italian Criminal Code*

The last aspect that deserves to be discussed in the course of the present analysis is the alternative reading of Article 7(1)(5) of the Italian criminal code, which expresses the principle of a 'mild' universal jurisdiction adopted by Italy.[83] In the *Tarek* case, the Court of Cassation took the opportunity to further reflect on the reach of the provision and, in particular, on the exercise of extraterritorial jurisdiction in situations where this is allowed by an international convention.[84] The case is relevant inasmuch as it sets a new development in motion, departing from the previous approach followed by the Supreme Court.[85] In the decision, which deals with the transnational crime of smuggling of migrants, which resulted in the death of 49 people at sea, the Court ruled on some critical aspects related to the application of Article 7(1)(5) and the effectiveness of the international duties on criminalisation that have been incorporated into the Italian legal framework.[86] More in detail, the Court was called to articulate its views on the legitimacy of Italian criminal jurisdiction, reflecting on the scope of Article 15 of the United Nations Convention on Transnational Organized Crime (UNTOC). Article 15 of the UNTOC establishes that a State Party may exercise its jurisdiction against any conduct that is perpetrated "with a view to the commission of a serious crime within its territory" (Article 15(2)(c)), and, in any case, "when the alleged offender is present in its territory and it [the

82 *Ibid.*

83 Tullio Treves, *La giurisdizione penale nel diritto internazionale* (Padova: CEDAM, 1973), 99; Mariangela La Manna, *La giurisdizione penale universale nel diritto internazionale* (Napoli: Edizioni Scientifiche, 2020).

84 *Jomaa Laamami Tarek*, Cass. pen. sez. I., Sent. 2 July 2021 n. 31652. Daniele Mandrioli, "Relationship Between Municipal and International Law: Between the Principle of Legality and the Renvoi to International Treaties: Italian Jurisdiction Over Transnational Crimes Committed Beyond National Territory," *The Italian Yearbook of International Law* 31(1) (2022): 481.

85 *Tartoussi*, Cass. pen. sez. 1, Sent. 17 June 2020 n. 19762.

86 Mandrioli, "Relationship Between Municipal and International Law," 482–483.

State] does not extradite him or her" (Article 15(4)). Since the smuggling of migrants was directed to Italy and the defendants were on Italian territory at the time of the proceedings, the Court assessed jurisdiction by virtue of Article 7(1)(5) of the Italian criminal code read jointly with the previously mentioned UNTOC provisions.[87]

A preliminary caveat is needed to better frame the issue: although the Italian criminal code upholds the principle of territoriality ex Article 6; Articles 7, 8, and 9 provide specific exceptions to the application of this principle. In particular, Article 7(1)(5) explicitly recognises the legitimacy of extraterritorial jurisdiction when international agreements allow this possibility. As explained by Daniele Mandrioli, for a long time, Italian scholars have discussed at length the correct interpretation and, thus, the breadth of the provision enshrined in Article 7(1)(5). It is possible to single out two main theories.[88] According to the first and most widely shared thesis, the extraterritorial expansion of Italian criminal jurisdiction envisaged in Article 7(1)(5) necessarily requires the given international rule to be adequately incorporated into the Italian legal system.[89] This is the approach followed by the Court of Cassation in the *Tartoussi* case when the Italian judges ruled out the applicability of Article 7(1)(5) of the Italian criminal code read jointly with Article 15(4) of the UNTOC. Notably, the decision in *Tartoussi* was based on the assumption that Article 15(4) of the UNTOC was not incorporated into the Italian legal system through the execution order enshrined in Article 2 of the ratification Law No. 146 of 2006.[90] Thus, in the *Tartoussi* case, it is possible to infer that the Italian Supreme Court endorsed the mainstream interpretation of Article 7(1)(5) of the Italian criminal code, namely that the transposition of the duties of criminalisation into national law is an essential condition for the extraterritorial reach of Italian criminal jurisdiction, as allowed by international treaty law.[91]

Departing from its previous position, the Court reached the opposite conclusion in the *Tarek* decision by allegedly endorsing the second possible interpretation of Article 7(1)(5) of the Italian criminal code, namely that the provision provides an "open and mobile" *renvoi* to international treaties

87 *Ibid.*, 483.

88 *Ibid.*, 482.

89 Treves, *La giurisdizione penale nel diritto internazionale*, 99–100.

90 Khrystyna Gavrysh, "La natura obbligatoria del criterio di giurisdizione previsto dall'art. 15, par. 2, della Convenzione di Palermo del 2000, nella sentenza del 17 giugno 2020 della Cassazione italiana," *Diritti Umani e Diritto Internazionale* 15 (2021): 717. Niccolò Zugliani, "In the Matter of Criminal Proceedings against Jomaa Laamami Tarek and Others," Final Appeal Judgment, No 31652/2021, in *Oxford Reports on International Law in Domestic Courts*, 2021; Claudia Cantone, "La giurisdizione penale universale nel diritto internazionale e il 'modello italiano' tra presente e futuro," in *Diritti Umani e Diritto Internazionale* 16(2) (2022): 447.

91 Mandrioli, "Relationship Between Municipal and International Law," 484.

to which Italy is bound.[92] In line with this interpretation, Article 7(1)(5) would allow an extraterritorial expansion of Italian criminal jurisdiction, even if the relevant treaty provisions have not been formally transposed into domestic law. According to the Court's reasoning, Article 7(1)(5) would unfold its effects regardless of the formal internalisation of a given conventional provision within the Italian legal system. By embracing this interpretation, it could, therefore, be possible to overcome the issue of whether Article 15 of the UNTOC is effectively incorporated into Italian law through the execution order in Article 2 of Law No. 146 of 2006. However, the approach of the Court has attracted much criticism from the Italian doctrine. As pointed out by most commentators, once it is recognised that the provisions enshrined in UNTOC, as well as in other treaties, allow states to expand their criminal jurisdiction beyond their territorial borders, referring to those international norms cannot be sufficient to establish any domestic legal effect.[93] As these norms are not self-executing, it would be necessary for a specific regulatory intervention of the state aiming at avoiding normative conflicts and exercising what cannot be regarded as an obligation but simply as a faculty bestowed on state parties by international law.[94] Despite the persuasive, and in this author's view, correct arguments against this reading of Article 7(1)(5) of the Italian criminal code, the Court of Cassation seems prone to stand by the approach inaugurated with *Tarek* and confirmed in subsequent decisions.[95]

Notably, with regard to the crime of smuggling migrants, it is worth stressing that the amendments to the Italian legal system made in the aftermath of the deadly shipwreck that occurred in Cutro, Italy, on 25 February 2023 mark a further and important development. More in detail, the Decree-Law adopted on 10 March 2023 and later converted in Law No. 50 of 5 May

92 Daniele Amoroso, "I rinvii al diritto internazionale e comunitario nelle recenti codificazioni di settore," *Rivista di diritto internazionale privato e processuale* 44(4) (2008): 1029.

93 Lorenzo Acconciamessa and Francesca Tammone, "La diretta applicabilità dei trattati nell'ordinamento italiano: quo vadis?" *Diritti Umani e Diritto Internazionale* 16(1) (2022): 91; Laura Magi, "The Mediterranean Sea between Legend and Crime: The Tricky Question of Jurisdiction for Mediterranean States," *Italian Yearbook of International Law* 31(1) (2022): 117.

94 Luigi Condorelli, *Il giudice italiano e i trattati internazionali: gli accordi self-executing e non self-executing nell'ottica della giurisprudenza* (Padova: CEDAM, 1974); Roberto Baratta, "L'effetto diretto delle disposizioni internazionali self-executing," *Rivista di diritto internazionale* 103(1) (2020): 5; Niccolò Zugliani, "Implementing International Treaties into the Italian Legal Order: Diverging Views on the Identification of Self Executing Provisions," in *Italian Yearbook of International Law* 30(1) (2020): 489; Beatrice I. Bonafè, "Constitutional Judicial Review and International Obligations of Criminalization," *International Criminal Law Review* 21(4) (2021): 660.

95 See Cass. pen. sez. I, Sent. 7 December 2021, no. 15556; Cass. pen. sez. I, Sent. 18 January 2023, no. 432. Daniele Mandrioli, "La giurisdizione penale extra-territoriale e la Convenzione di Palermo: analisi del nuovo orientamento assunto dalla Corte di cassazione a partire dalla sentenza Tarek," *Quaderni di SIDIblog* 1 (2022): 237, 243–246.

2023 has modified Legislative Decree No. 286 of 25 July 1998. Article 8(6) establishes that

> without prejudice to Article 6 of the Italian criminal code (which upholds the territoriality principle), if the conduct is directed to facilitate the illegal entrance into the State's territory, the crime is punished according to Italian law, even when the death or injury has taken place outside Italian territory.[96]

By allowing the judges to resort directly to Italian norms, the amendment overcomes the tensions caused by the Court's recent position as it clearly affirms the extraterritorial reach of Italian jurisdiction when smuggling is committed. The problems briefly sketched here remain, however, in relation to all other transnational criminal conducts for which the Italian Court of Cassation is likely to confirm the extraterritorial expansion of the Italian jurisdiction under Article 7(1)(5) of the Italian criminal code.

4 Conclusion

The present work pursued the difficult task of sketching the main progress of the Italian doctrine and practice in relation to extraterritorial jurisdiction and its application in different ambits. The take-home points that emerge from this inquiry clearly display the tireless engagement of Italian jurists and their willingness to prioritise a reading of international and domestic norms that, first and foremost, privileges the rights of individuals. This is something that cannot be taken for granted, ever, and especially in light of the current global scenario. The analysis, far from being comprehensive, showed the unquestionable proactiveness of Italian scholars and judges alike. This is not unexpected, as Italy's contribution to the development of international law has always been pivotal. Rather than relying on the writings of the most authoritative Italian scholars, whose work is well known and well received also outside Italian borders,[97] this chapter aimed at showcasing the impressive achievements of a younger generation of (Italian) international lawyers, *e.g.*, Giorgia Berrino, Claudia Cantone, Donato Greco, Daniele Mandrioli, Niccolò Zugliani, by referring to their punctual observations and critical input.

Since the reference to the three principles that Kamminga extracted from *Lotus* has guided the whole investigation, it is worth following the same

96 Author's translation.

97 Giulio Bartolini, ed., *A History of International Law in Italy* (Oxford: Oxford University Press, 2020); Francesca Capone, "The Development of the Italian Doctrine in the Words of Antonio Cassese. Towards a More Pragmatic Approach?" *Italian Review of International and Comparative Law* 2(1) (2022): 219.

approach also in this concluding paragraph. Zooming in on the first and second principles concerning, respectively, the lawful exercise of extraterritorial jurisdiction as a matter of international law and the prohibition to exercise extraterritorial enforcement jurisdiction unless this is specifically permitted, this work has discussed Italy's controversial position in the field of state immunity, by delving in particular into the treatment of Greek claimants and their role in the Italian saga vis-à-vis judicial immunity (via *exequatur* proceedings) and immunity from enforcement. In relation to both aspects, the chapter ultimately reflected on the consistency of Italy's position despite unavoidable tensions that surfaced, especially between the Government and the judiciary. The chapter also focussed on the risk of creating asymmetries deriving from the tension between Italy's overarching victim-centred stance that the Court of Cassation has upheld in other contexts and the need to finally quell the international dispute reignited by Germany. Discussing Italy's take on the third *Lotus* principle – according to which the exercise of extraterritorial prescriptive and adjudicative jurisdictions is permitted only if there is a sufficient connection between the state exercising it and the extraterritorial event – the inquiry led to the conclusions that Italian judges are prone not only to promote but also to expand domestic jurisdiction by resorting to the criterion of a 'reasonable connection' and by relying on a far-reaching reading of Article 7(1)(5) of the Italian criminal code. The downside of this route, which has triggered well-founded criticism from the doctrine, is that the Court of Cassation, in its pronouncements, has missed the opportunity to shed light on its reasoning and better outline its views also in the context of the ongoing international debate.

References

Acconciamessa, Lorenzo, and Francesca Tammone. "La diretta applicabilità dei trattati nell'ordinamento italiano: quo vadis?" *Diritti Umani e Diritto Internazionale* 16(1) (2022): 91–102.

Amoroso, Daniele. "I rinvii al diritto internazionale e comunitario nelle recenti codificazioni di settore." *Rivista di diritto internazionale privato e processuale* 44(42) (2008): 1029–1054.

Amoroso, Daniele, and Riccardo Pavoni. "Stergiopoulos v. Iran 315. Italian Supreme Court of Cassation Decision on Human Rights Limitations on Sovereign Immunity in International Law and Italian Constitutional Law." *American Journal of International Law* 117(2) (2023): 305–321.

Atteritano, Andrea. "Immunity of States and Their Organs: The Contribution of Italian Jurisprudence over the Past Ten Years." *The Italian Yearbook of International Law* 19 (2009): 31–56.

Baratta, Roberto. "L'effetto diretto delle disposizioni internazionali self-executing." *Rivista di diritto internazionale* 103(1) (2020): 4–48.

Baratta, Roberto. "Il Fondo 'ristori' tra rispetto del diritto internazionale, controlimiti e ragioni creditorie delle vittime di crimini nazisti: il punto di tenuta dell'ordine costituzionale." *Rivista di diritto internazionale* 106(4) (2023): 1093–1099.

Bartolini, Giulio, ed. *A History of International Law in Italy.* Oxford: Oxford University Press, 2020.

Berrino, Giorgia. "Il 'ristoro' dei cittadini italiani vittime di crimini di guerra e contro l'umanità commessi dalla Germania durante il secondo conflitto mondiale." *Rivista di diritto internazionale* 105(2) (2022): 827–858.

Berrino, Giorgia. "The Impact of Article 43 of Decree-Law no 36/2022 on Enforcement Proceedings Regarding German State-Owned Assets." *Questions of International Law Zoom-in* 94 (2022): 59–72.

Berrino, Giorgia. "Quale effettività della tutela giurisdizionale nel caso Germania c. Italia? L'art. 43 del d.l. n. 36/2022 come 'rimedio' costituzionalmente legittimo." *Diritti Umani e Diritto Internazionale* 17(1) (2023): 211–232.

Bufalini, Alessandro. "Immunità degli Stati dalla giurisdizione e negoziazioni fra Stati: sulla vicenda delle comfort women coreane." *Diritti Umani e Diritto Internazionale* 15(3) (2021): 699–708.

Cantone, Claudia. "Estradizione e limiti all'esercizio della giurisdizione penale extraterritoriale nel diritto internazionale: riflessioni a margine della sentenza della Corte di cassazione n. 30642/2020." *Rivista di diritto internazionale privato e processuale* 3 (2020): 620–639.

Cantone, Claudia. "La giurisdizione penale universale nel diritto internazionale e il 'modello italiano' tra presente e futuro." *Diritti Umani e Diritto Internazionale* 16(2) (2022): 447–476.

Capone, Francesca. "The Development of the Italian Doctrine in the Words of Antonio Cassese. Towards a More Pragmatic Approach?" *Italian Review of International and Comparative Law* 2(1) (2022): 219–226.

Condorelli, Luigi. *Il giudice italiano e i trattati internazionali: gli accordi self-executing e non self-executing nell'ottica della giurisprudenza*. Padova: CEDAM, 1974.

Csernus, Máté. "Might Contain Traces of Lotus: The Limits of Exclusive Flag State Jurisdiction in the Norstar and the Enrico Lexie Cases." *Leiden Journal of International Law* 36 (2023): 947–970.

Dodge, William S. "A Modest Approach to the Customary International Law of Jurisdiction." *European Journal of International Law* 32(4) (2021): 1471–1481.

Focarelli, Carlo. "Denying Foreign State Immunity for Commission of International Crimes: The Ferrini Decision." *The International and Comparative Law Quarterly* 54(4) (2005): 951–958.

Fox, Hazel, and Philippa Webb. *The Law of State Immunity*. Oxford: Oxford University Press, 3rd edition, 2013.

Frulli, Micaela. *Immunità e crimini internazionali: l'esercizio della giurisdizione penale e civile nei confronti degli organi statali sospettati di gravi crimini internazionali*. Torino: Giappichelli, 2007.

Frulli, Micaela. "The Times They are A-Changing: The Italian Court of Cassation Denies Germany Immunity from Execution to Allow Compensation to War Crimes' Victims." *Journal of International Criminal Justice* 9 (2011): 1129–1142.

Gavouneli, Maria, and Ilias Bantekas. "Prefecture of Voiotia v. Federal Republic of Germany. Case No. 11/2000." *The American Journal of International Law* 95(1) (2001): 198–204.

Gavrysh, Khrystyna. "La natura obbligatoria del criterio di giurisdizione previsto dall'art. 15, par. 2, della Convenzione di Palermo del 2000, nella sentenza del 17 giugno 2020 della Cassazione italiana." *Diritti Umani e Diritto Internazionale* 15 (2021): 717–722.

Gianelli, Alessandra. "Crimini internazionali ed immunità degli Stati dalla giurisdizione nella sentenza Ferrini." *Rivista di Diritto Internazionale* 87 (2004): 643–684.

Iovane, Massimo. "The Ferrini Judgment of the Italian Supreme Court: Opening up Domestic Courts to Claims of Reparation for Victims of Serious Violations of Fundamental Human Rights." *The Italian Yearbook of International Law* 14 (2004): 165–193.

Iovane, Massimo. "The Italian Constitutional Court Judgment No. 238 and the Myth of the 'Constitutionalization' of International Law." *Journal of International Criminal Justice* 14 (2016): 596–605.
Kamminga, Menno T. "Extraterritoriality." In *Max Planck Encyclopedia of Public International Law*, edited by Anne Peters. Oxford: Oxford University Press, 2020.
La Manna, Mariangela. *La giurisdizione penale universale nel diritto internazionale.* Napoli: Edizioni Scientifiche, 2020.
Longobardo, Marco. "The Italian Constitutional Court's Ruling Against State Immunity when International Crimes Occur: Thoughts on Decision No 238 of 2014." *Melbourne Journal of International Law* 16 (2015): 255–269.
Lopes Pegna, Olivia. "Giù le mani da Villa Vigoni: quale tutela 'effettiva' per le vittime di gravi violazioni dei diritti umani?" *Rivista di Diritto Internazionale* 101(1) (2018): 1237–1245.
Mandrioli, Daniele. "La giurisdizione penale extra-territoriale e la Convenzione di Palermo: analisi del nuovo orientamento assunto dalla Corte di cassazione a partire dalla sentenza Tarek." *Quaderni di SIDIblog* 1 (2022): 237–247.
Mandrioli, Daniele. "Relationship Between Municipal and International Law: Between the Principle of Legality and the Renvoi to International Treaties: Italian Jurisdiction Over Transnational Crimes Committed Beyond National Territory." *The Italian Yearbook of International Law* 31(1) (2022): 481–486.
Nußberger, Benjamin, and Victoria Otto. "Jurisdictional Immunities of the State (Germany v Italy: Greece Intervening)." In *Max Planck Encyclopedia of Public International Law*, edited by Rüdiger Wolfrum. Oxford: Oxford University Press, 2015.
Palchetti, Paolo. "Right of Access to (Italian) Courts über alles? Legal Implications Beyond Germany's Jurisdictional Immunity." In *Remedies against Immunities? Reconciling International and Domestic Law after the Italian Constitutional Court's Sentenza 238/2014*, edited by Valentina Volpe, Anne Peters, and Stefano Battini, 39–54. Heidelberg: Springer, 2021.
Palombino, Fulvio M. "Italy's Compliance with ICJ Decisions vs. Constitutional Guarantees: Does the 'Counter-Limits' Doctrine Matter?" *The Italian Yearbook of International Law* 22 (2013): 187–206.
Palombino, Fulvio M. "Compliance with International Judgments: Between Supremacy of International Law and National Fundamental Principles." *Zeitschrift für ausländisches öffentliches Recht und Völkerrecht* 75 (2015): 503–530.
Pavoni, Riccardo. "Germany versus Italy Reloaded: Whither a Human Rights Limitation to State Immunity?" *Questions of International Law Zoom-in* 94 (2022): 19–40.
Pavoni, Riccardo, and Stephane Beulah. "L'immunité des États et le jus cogens en droit international: étude croisée Italie/Canada (State Immunity and Jus Cogens in International Law: A Comparative Study of Italian and Canadian Practice)." *Revue juridique Thémis* 43 (2009): 491–529.
Pustorino, Pietro. "La sentenza n. 238 del 2014 della Corte costituzionale: limiti e prospettive nell'ottica della giurisprudenza italiana." *Diritti Umani e Diritto Internazionale* 9 (2015): 51–60.
Ronzitti, Natalino. "La Cour constitutionnelle italienne et l'immunité juridictionnelle des États." *Annuaire Français de Droit International* LX (2014): 3–15.
Ryngaert, Cedric. "The Concept of Jurisdiction in International Law." In *Research Handbook on Jurisdiction and Immunities in International Law*, edited by Alexander Orakhelashvili, 50–75. Cheltenham Glos: Edward Elgar, 2015.
Ryngaert, Cedric. "The Restatement and the Law of Jurisdiction: A Commentary." *European Journal of International Law* 32(4) (2021): 1455–1469.
Ryngaert, Cedric. *Jurisdiction in International Law.* Oxford: Oxford University Press, 2nd edition, 2015.

Scovazzi, Tullio. "Come se non esistesse." *Rivista di diritto internazionale* 104 (2021): 167–181.

Shottenfeld, Joseph R. "Exceptional Judgments: Revising the Terrorism Exception to the Foreign Sovereign Immunities Act." *The Yale Law Journal* 127(7) (2018): 1890–1915.

Slaughter, Anne-Marie. "Liberal International Relations Theory and International Economic Law." *American University International Law Review* 10(2) (1995): 717–743.

Stoll, Peter-Tobias. "State Immunity." In *Max Planck Encyclopedia of Public International Law*, edited by Anne Peters. Oxford: Oxford University Press, 2020.

Treves, Tullio. *La giurisdizione penale nel diritto internazionale*. Padova: CEDAM, 1973.

Venturini, Chiara. "Le Sezioni Unite sulle immunità degli Stati (sent. n. 20442 del 2020): un'evoluzione soltanto apparente." *Forum di Quaderni Costituzionali* (2021): 169–182.

Zugliani, Niccolò. "Implementing International Treaties into the Italian Legal Order: Diverging Views on the Identification of Self Executing Provisions." *Italian Yearbook of International Law* 30(1) (2020): 481–493.

Zugliani, Niccolò. "In the Matter of Criminal Proceedings against Jomaa Laamami Tarek and Others." Final Appeal Judgment, No. 31652/2021. In *Oxford Reports on International Law in Domestic Courts*, 2022.

12 Constitutional Values and Imperatives in South Africa's Approach to Extraterritorial Jurisdiction

Sarah McGibbon

1 Introduction

Extraterritorial jurisdiction, or extraterritoriality,[1] refers to a state's competence – whether prescriptive, adjudicative, or enforcement – to make, apply, and enforce laws beyond its territory.[2] However, competing interpretations of this concept across the international community render a unitary definition elusive, resulting in varied state practices. Despite this ambiguity – or perhaps because of it – extraterritorial jurisdiction remains an important regulatory tool for states in addressing cross-border legal and policy challenges.

Although extraterritoriality appears intrinsic to the concept of 'territory' in international law,[3] jurisdiction itself is not inherently territorial. Rather, the relationship between these two concepts is the result of a series of political, economic, and social decisions made within the international community.[4] Acknowledging this artificial but intentional connection facilitates a deeper understanding of the exercise of extraterritorial jurisdiction and the underlying role of policy and politics.

The intricate legal framework governing extraterritorial jurisdiction[5] both reflects and potentially shapes the broader political community

1 Extraterritoriality also refers to a broader theoretical discussion in law, but, in this chapter, I use it interchangeably with extraterritorial jurisdiction. For an interesting collection of chapters on extraterritoriality in the broader sense, see Daniel S. Margolies et al., eds., *The Extraterritoriality of Law: History, Theory, Politics* (London/New York: Routledge, 2019).

2 Menno T. Kamminga, "Extraterritoriality," in *Max Planck Encyclopedias of International Law* (Oxford University Press, Online ed., 2020), para. 1.

3 See *Banković and Others v Belgium and Others* (2002) 123 ILR 94 in general, but para. 59 in particular. On the conflation of the notions of 'territory' and 'jurisdiction', see Jure Vidmar, *Territorial Status in International Law* (London: Hart Publishing, 2024), 25–29.

4 Sué González Hauck and Max Milas, "Jurisdiction," in *Public International Law: A Multi-Perspective Approach*, eds. Sué González Hauck, Raffaela Kunz and Max Milas (Abingdon/New York: Routledge, 2024), 322.

5 Explained in more detail in Chapter 1 of this book.

DOI: 10.4324/9781003402978-15

constituted and bound by these laws.[6] Thus, the study of jurisdiction is also an inquiry into this political community, positioning jurisdiction as an inherently political and politicised concept.[7] This, in turn, highlights jurisdiction's significance in constitutional law settings,[8] warranting closer examination in one of the most dynamic contemporary constitutional law environments: South Africa.

At first glance, the decision to focus on a national constitution – rather than traditional 'policy drivers' – when assessing extraterritorial jurisdiction in the context of this volume may seem counterintuitive. However, the values enshrined in the South African Constitution[9] are the product of decades of social and political struggle against colonialism and apartheid.[10] As such, they represent a convergence of multiple policy imperatives that influence all legal and political decisions in the country. Indeed, the Constitution embodies an "objective, normative value system".[11] In one of the first judgments handed down by the Constitutional Court, Mohamed J remarked that the Constitution –

> retains from the past only what is defensible and represents a decisive break from, and a ringing rejection of, that part of the past which is disgracefully racist, authoritarian, insular, and repressive and a vigorous identification of and commitment to a democratic, universalistic, caring and aspirationally egalitarian ethos, expressly articulated in the Constitution.[12]

This is further reflected in the Preamble to the Constitution, which states (in part):[13]

6 González Hauck and Milas, "Jurisdiction," 328.

7 Asha Kaushal, "The Politics of Jurisdiction," *Modern Law Review* 78(5) (2015): 760.

8 Ibid.

9 Constitution of the Republic of South Africa (1996). It is worth noting that section 2 prescribes that the Constitution is the supreme law of the land, transforming South Africa's legal system from one of parliamentary supremacy to constitutional supremacy. See also *Du Plessis and Others v De Klerk and Another* 1996 (3) SA 850, para. 128, where the Constitutional Court remarked that "the Constitution is elevated to supremacy over all law, and then all organs of state are enjoined to honour and enforce that supremacy".

10 For a concise but helpful summary of the history and relevant legal developments in this regard, see Letlhokwa George Mpedi, "Law and Social Policy in South Africa: From Untold Suffering and Injustice to a Future Based on Human Rights," in *Law and Social Policy in the Global South: Brazil, China, India, South Africa*, eds. Ulrike Davy and Albert H.Y. Chen (London: Routledge, 2022).

11 *Carmichele v Minister of Safety and Security and Another* 2001 (4) SA 938 (CC) (*Carmichele*), para. 54.

12 *S v Makwanyane and Another* 1995 (3) SA 391 (*Makwanyane*), para. 262.

13 See Ncgobo J's separate concurring opinion in *Bato Star Fishing (Pty) Ltd v Minister of Environmental Affairs and Tourism and Others* 2004 (4) SA 490 (CC) (*Bato Star*), para. 73: South Africa is a country in transition. It is a transition from a society based on inequality to one based on equality. This transition was introduced by the interim Constitution, which was

We, the people of South Africa,
Recognise the injustices of our past;
Honour those who suffered for justice and freedom in our land;
Respect those who have worked to build and develop our country; and
Believe that South Africa belongs to all who live in it, united in our diversity.
We therefore, through our freely elected representatives, adopt this Constitution as the supreme law of the Republic so as to –

Heal the divisions of the past and establish a society based on democratic values, social justice and fundamental human rights.

The Constitution provides a comprehensive framework for a government founded on fundamental human rights, democracy, and judicial independence.[14] Its founding values, articulated in section 1(a), are human dignity, equality, and freedom – principles that must inform all legal conduct in South Africa. Chapter 2 establishes the Bill of Rights as the "cornerstone of democracy in South Africa".[15] Sections 7 and 8 affirm its binding effect on all legal and governmental conduct, with section 8(1) stating that the Bill of Rights "applies to all law, and binds the legislature, the executive, the judiciary, and all organs of state".[16] However, it remains unclear whether these constitutional protections – or indeed any other provisions – extend beyond South Africa's borders.

This chapter examines South Africa's approach to extraterritoriality as developed through case law,[17] with particular emphasis on the constitutional values that drive this approach. It begins with a discussion of key concepts,

---

designed 'to create a new order based on equality in which there is equality between men and women and people of all races so that all citizens should be able to enjoy and exercise their fundamental rights and freedoms.' This commitment to the transformation of our society was affirmed and reinforced in 1997, when the Constitution came into force. The Preamble to the Constitution 'recognises the injustices of our past' and makes a commitment to establishing 'a society based on democratic values, social justice and fundamental rights'. This society is to be built on the foundation of the values entrenched in the very first provision of the Constitution. These values include human dignity, the achievement of equality and the advancement of human rights and freedoms.

14 Here, I am paraphrasing the late US Supreme Court Justice Ruth Bader Ginsburg, speaking in 2012 in a controversial interview where she advised Egypt to look to, among others, the South African Constitution for inspiration, rather than the US Constitution: Al Hayat TV, US Supreme Court Justice Ruth Bader Ginsburg to Egyptians, 30 January 2012. Accessed 6 October 2024. https://www.memri.org/tv/us-supreme-court-justice-ruth-bader-ginsburg-egyptians-look-constitutions-south-africa-or-canada.

15 Constitution of the Republic of South Africa, section 7(1).

16 Section 7(2) obliges the state to "respect, protect, promote and fulfil the rights in the Bill of Rights"; while section 8 contains the general applicability rules.

17 South Africa is a hybrid common law country with a strong system of precedent.

followed by an analysis of South Africa's constitutional framework. The chapter then explores case law relating to two constitutional policy drivers: the protection of human rights and a commitment to justice and accountability. Finally, before concluding, it assesses South Africa's stance on universal jurisdiction as a unique case of jurisdiction unbound from territorial constraints.

2 Clarifying Concepts

Before examining South African law, it is important to clarify that the concept of extraterritoriality addressed in this chapter refers to the international law doctrine outlined – albeit briefly – in the introduction, rather than the two domestic law conceptions that may be relevant in the South African context. These domestic law conceptions include: (i) situations in which the actions of South African public officials within the country cause harm that manifests in another state;[18] and (ii) cases where South Africa exercises effective control over foreign territory such that the Constitution becomes applicable to the conduct of the South African officials in their relations with the foreigners under their control.[19]

3 International Law Under the Constitutional Framework

As was established in Part 1, the Bill of Rights contained in the South African Constitution is made applicable to all public authorities by virtue of sections 7 and 8. The protection of people *within* South African borders is arguably the primary purpose of the Bill of Rights, but it is worth noting that its

18 See, for example, the South African Constitutional Court's decision in *Mohamed v President of the Republic of South Africa* 2001 (3) SA 893 (CC) (*Mohamed*). This case concerns the failure of South African officials to obtain (or even seek) a guarantee that the death sentence would not be sought in relation to an accused (Mr Khalfan Mohamed) subject to extradition proceedings to the US. Mr Mohamed was accused of involvement in the bombing of the US embassies in Nairobi and Dar es Salaam on 7 August 1998. This case is often cited in discussions on South Africa's approach to extraterritoriality. However, Max du Plessis has thoughtfully pointed out that this case does not concern the international law conception of extraterritoriality. See Max Du Plessis, "The Extra-Territorial Application of the South African Constitution," *South African Law Journal* 120(4) (2003): 799. His analysis is supported by John Dugard and Andreas Coutsoudis in John Dugard and Andreas Coutsoudis, "The Place of International Law in South African Municipal Law," in *Dugard's International Law: A South African Perspective*, eds. John Dugard et al. (Cape Town: Juta & Company, Limited, 2019), 123. Cf. Stuart Woolman's discussion arguing the facts are analogous to those in *Kaunda and Others v President of the Republic of South Africa* 2005 (4) SA 235 (CC) (*Kaunda*), which is discussed in detail in this chapter: Stuart Woolman, "Application," in *Constitutional Law of South Africa* (Cape Town: Juta & Company, Limited, 2nd ed., 2002), 31–121.

19 For a detailed discussion of the South African position on these two scenarios, see Du Plessis, "The Extra-Territorial Application of the South African Constitution."

protection is not limited to South African citizens or nationals.[20] Most of the rights within the Bill of Rights are directed at 'everyone';[21] otherwise, they may be denied to 'no one'.[22]

While the Constitution's protection is naturally all-encompassing within South Africa, the position is not as immediately clear in relation to extraterritorial conduct. While there is nothing in sections 7(2) or 8(1) to limit the application of the Constitution to conduct by public authorities committed within South African territory, there is also no indication that the Constitution's protections extend beyond South Africa's territorial borders.[23] Nonetheless, South African courts have been presented with a few opportunities to consider this question. These cases will be discussed in what follows.

For the purpose of the following discussion on the case law, it is also helpful to know that section 39 of the Constitution provides instructions for the interpretation of the Bill of Rights. Of import for the purpose of this chapter is the fact that section 39(1)(b) obliges any court, tribunal, or forum to consider international law when interpreting the Bill of Rights.[24] Similarly, when interpreting legislation or developing the common law, adjudicative bodies must "promote the spirit, purport and objects of the Bill of Rights".[25]

Sections 231 to 233 of the Constitution set out specific provisions pertaining to the application of international law as part of domestic law in South Africa. Section 231(4) provides for international agreements to become law within South Africa once enacted through domestic legislation, while section 232 provides that customary international law is law in South Africa

20 See *Mohamed*; Iain Currie and Johan de Waal, *The Bill of Rights Handbook* (Lansdowne: Juta & Company, Limited, 5th ed., 2005), 35.

21 See, for example, section 9(1) which provides: "Everyone is equal before the law and has the right to equal protection and benefit of the law". The same subject is used in respect of the rights to human dignity (section 10); life (section 11); freedom and security of the person (section 12); privacy (section 14); freedom of religion, belief and opinion (section 15); freedom of expression (section 16); assembly, demonstration, picket and petition (section 17); freedom of association (section 18); freedom of movement and residence (section 21); fair labour practices (section 23); a safe (and protected) environment (section 24); access to adequate housing (section 26); access to health care, food, water and social security; education (section 29); language and culture (section 30); access to information (section 32); just administrative action (section 33); access to courts (section 34); and fair trial and due process (in respect of arrested, detained, and accused persons) (section 35).

22 See, for example, section 25(1) which provides: "No one may be deprived of property except in terms of law of general application, and no law may permit arbitrary deprivation of property". The same term of expression is used in the provision relating to slavery, servitude, and forced labour (section 13).

23 Du Plessis, "The Extra-Territorial Application of the South African Constitution," 799.

24 Section 39(1)(b) reads: "When interpreting the Bill of Rights, a court, tribunal or forum must consider international law". Such adjudicative bodies are not obliged, but may, consider foreign law. See Constitution of the Republic of South Africa, section 39(1)(c).

25 Constitution of the Republic of South Africa, section 39(2).

unless it is inconsistent with the Constitution or an Act of Parliament. Section 233 of the Constitution provides that when "interpreting any legislation, every court must prefer any reasonable interpretation of the legislation that is consistent with international law over any alternative interpretation that is inconsistent with international law". The Constitutional Court has noted that this applies equally to the provisions of the Bill of Rights and the other provisions of the Constitution as a whole.[26]

4 Constitutional Policy Drivers for Extraterritorial Jurisdiction

As will be demonstrated in this section, the South African courts (in particular, the Constitutional Court) have made much of grounding their analysis of international law and extraterritoriality in the Constitution. This commitment to the founding values and principles of the Constitution reveals two primary constitutional policy drivers for South Africa's approach to extraterritoriality: the protection of human rights and a commitment to justice and accountability. Each of these is explored in further detail in what follows.

4.1 Protection of Human Rights

The protection of human rights is a theme that was confronted by the Constitutional Court in the *Kaunda* case in the context of diplomatic protection. The Court was approached by 69 applicants attempting to ensure that their rights to dignity, freedom, personal security, and fair conditions of detention and trial would be consistently respected and protected in both Zimbabwe and Equatorial Guinea following arrest.[27] The facts played out in the context of the 2004 Wonga coup in Equatorial Guinea, in which a group of British financiers attempted to overthrow sitting President Teodoro Obiang and install opposition leader Sevoro Moto.[28] The applicants were detained in Zimbabwe on 7 March 2004, where they were picking up weapons on their way to Equatorial Guinea. Two days later, on 9 March 2004, 15 men were arrested in Malabo, the capital of Equatorial Guinea. They were all accused of being mercenaries involved in the planned coup. Most of those arrested were South African nationals.[29]

26 *Kaunda*, para. 33.
27 *Ibid.*, para. 3–4.
28 For more information on the circumstances surrounding this event involving numerous high-profile individuals, including Mark Thatcher, see Adam Roberts, *The Wonga Coup: Guns, Thugs, and a Ruthless Determination to Create Mayhem in an Oil-Rich Corner of Africa* (Hachette UK, 2007). See also "An African Adventure: Inside Story of the Wonga Coup," *The Independent*, 12 March 2008, sec. News, https://www.independent.co.uk/news/world/africa/an-african-adventure-inside-story-of-the-wonga-coup-794470.html.
29 *Kaunda*, para. 2.

The applicants in *Kaunda* were concerned that they could be extradited from Zimbabwe to Equatorial Guinea, where they would face trial alongside the individuals arrested there. They argued that, if this occurred, they would not receive a fair trial and, if found guilty, they could face the death penalty.[30] At the time of the application to the Constitutional Court, the applicants faced numerous serious charges in Zimbabwe.[31] They were also being detained in Chikurubi Maximum Security Prison, and they had made serious allegations about the conditions in which they were being detained. Their Zimbabwean trial was delayed to allow the South African Constitutional Court to rule on the matter.[32]

The applicants argued that their rights to dignity, life, freedom, and security of the person, including the right not to be treated or punished in a cruel, inhuman, or degrading way, and also the right to a fair trial,[33] were being infringed in Zimbabwe and were likely to be infringed if they are extradited to Equatorial Guinea. They relied on section 7(2) of the Constitution, which requires the state to "respect, protect, promote and fulfil the rights in the Bill of Rights" to argue that South Africa was obliged to protect these rights, and that the only way it could do so in the circumstances of the case was to provide them with diplomatic protection.[34]

One of the most difficult questions before the Court in this case was the proper scope of any right to diplomatic protection.[35] Dire Tladi has noted that *Kaunda* is a significant case because of its role in clarifying the existing case law in relation to the justiciability of state actions in the area of foreign relations[36] rather than establishing new law.[37] However, the scope of any such right is not the concern of this chapter, so my consideration will be limited to the relevant discussions of the judgments on extraterritoriality in establishing whether such a right exists in the first place.

30 *Ibid.*

31 *Ibid.*, para. 12. These included, among others, contraventions of the Zimbabwean Public Order and Safety Act, Firearms Act, and Immigration Act.

32 *Ibid.*, para. 12.

33 Entrenched in sections 10, 11, 12 and 35 of the Constitution.

34 *Kaunda*, para. 31.

35 Mary Coombs, "International Decision: Kaunda v The President of the Republic of South Africa," *American Journal of International Law* 99 (2005): 685.

36 See, for example, *Kolbatschenko v King NO and Another* 2001 4 SA 336 (CC); *Mohamed*; *Geuking v President of the Republic of South Africa* 2003 3 SA 34 (CC).

37 Dire Tladi, "The Right to Diplomatic Protection, the Von Abo Decision, and One Big Can of Worms: Eroding the Clarity of Kaunda," *Stellenbosch Law Review* 1 (2009): 18–19. See further discussion in Dire Tladi and Polina Dlagnekova, "The Act of State Doctrine in South Africa: Has Kaunda Settled a Vexing Question?" *SA Public Law* 22(2) (2007): 444–456.

4.1.1 *Majority Approach: Locating the Obligation in Section 7(2)*[38]

After setting out its understanding of the international law position on diplomatic protection,[39] Chaskalson CJ (writing for the majority) considers whether South African law affords South Africans abroad a right to diplomatic protection. The Chief Justice, in contrast to Ngcobo J and O'Regan J (considered later in this chapter), attempts to locate this right within section 7(2) of the Constitution.[40] He accepts that there is a positive obligation on the state to comply with the rights in the Bill of Rights under this section.[41] In doing so, he cites the numerous cases in which this has previously been confirmed by the Court.[42] However, Chaskalson CJ confirms that this obligation does not mean that nationals' rights under the Constitution attached to them when outside South Africa or that this obligation to "respect, protect, promote, and fulfil" the rights in the Bill of Rights extends beyond South African territory.[43] The judgment acknowledges that although there are instances where domestic law extends beyond national borders, this is only the case where such extension would not interfere with the sovereignty of other states.[44] The Court held:

> For South Africa to assume an obligation that entitles its nationals to demand, and obliges it to take action to ensure, that laws and conduct

38 There were several judgments prepared by members of the bench in this case, with the majority judgment penned by Chaskalson CJ. Although it is this majority judgment that is decisive (and binding in South Africa's system of precedent), the separate judgments are worth considering for the depth they bring, and the distinctions that can be drawn. These separate judgments also remain persuasive in South African courts.

39 All parties before the Court invoked section 232 of the Constitution to introduce international law arguments. The Court considered customary international law (as disclosed in *Barcelona Traction, Light and Power Company, Limited*, Judgement. ICJ Reports 1970, p. 3, para. 78–79) and the report by the International Law Commission, including summaries of debates by the Special Rapporteur on Diplomatic Protection, John Dugard. However, this chapter is not concerned with any particular international law understanding of diplomatic protection or the development thereof. Instead, it is prudent to focus on the South African court's approach to ascertaining and applying the international law position.

40 In taking this approach, Chaskalson CJ separates the consideration of section7(2) (and its interaction with international law) and the more substantive section 3 (citizenship rights, and their interaction with international law). This particular approach to the analysis necessarily has an impact on the overall understanding of South Africa's approach to extraterritoriality, even if it did not impact the case at hand. This is reflected in the separate judgments prepared by Ngcobo J and O'Regan J.

41 *Kaunda*, para. 32.

42 See, for example, some of the stalwarts of South African constitutional law jurisprudence: *Carmichele*, para. 44; *Mohamed*, para. 37; *Government of the Republic of South Africa and Others v Grootboom and Others* 2001 (1) SA 46, para. 20; *S v Baloyi* 2000 (2) SA 425 (CC), para. 11.

43 *Kaunda*, para. 32.

44 *Ibid.*, para. 44.

> of a foreign state and its officials meet not only the requirements of the foreign state's own laws, but also the rights that our nationals have under our Constitution, would be inconsistent with the principle of state sovereignty. Section 7(2) should not be construed as imposing a positive obligation on government to do this.[45]

Chaskalson CJ notes that although the Constitution includes rights which go beyond those recognised by international law and major human rights instruments, it explains those expressly when doing so.[46] He finds that the Bill of Rights is extensive and well thought-out, covering conventional and less conventional rights. Confirming an earlier finding of the Court that the drafters of the Constitution "were well informed regarding provisions in international, regional and domestic human and fundamental rights", he finds that any right to diplomatic protection would have been expressly included.[47] Therefore, the starting point to determine extraterritorial application is the text of the Constitution itself.

The Constitution provides the framework for the governance of South Africa, which necessarily limits its territorial application.[48] Even though the protection offered by the Bill of Rights is expansive and includes foreigners, Chaskalson CJ finds that the latter lose that protection when they leave South African borders. Therefore, for the Constitution's protection to attach to South Africans beyond its territorial borders, section 7(2) would place a more extensive obligation on the state in relation to South African nationals.[49] As mentioned previously, there is no express indication within the text of the Constitution itself that this is the case. Woolman has subsequently criticised this finding of the Court, noting that there is nothing clear about the text of the Constitution in relation to the position of extraterritorial application to foreigners.[50]

Chaskalson CJ considered the international law position that the laws of a state ordinarily only apply within its own territory but that, in certain circumstances, its laws may be binding on nationals regardless of their geographic location.[51] Naturally, conflicts between the applicable laws may arise. As a general rule, a state exercising jurisdiction beyond its borders

45 *Ibid.*

46 *Ibid.*, para. 34. In this case, the Court turned to the Universal Declaration of Human Rights (1948), the International Covenant on Civil and Political Rights (1966), and the African Charter on Human and People's Rights (1986).

47 *Ibid.*, para. 35, citing *Bernstein and Others v Bester and Others* NNO 1996 (2) SA 751 (CC), para. 106. See also *Du Plessis and Others v De Klerk and Another* 1996 (3) SA 850 (CC), para. 45.

48 *Ibid.*, para. 36.

49 *Ibid.*

50 Woolman, "Application," 31–117.

51 *Kaunda*, para. 38. For a discussion on the international law position, see generally González Hauck and Milas, "Jurisdiction."

constitutes an interference with the other state's sovereignty – as much was dealt with in the *Lotus* case.[52] The majority judgment[53] in *Kaunda* accepts this as its starting point[54] and finds that there is no reason why the protection of the Bill of Rights extends to nationals outside South African territory. Chaskalson CJ holds that the Bill of Rights binds the South African government but not other governments.[55] He further finds that if the question was extradition from South Africa, the protections would apply, but not in the case of extradition from foreign territories.[56]

Although the Chief Justice finds that there is no enforceable right to diplomatic protection, the judgment nevertheless confirms that South African citizens are entitled to request diplomatic protection from South Africa against the wrongful acts of a foreign state. While South Africa is under no obligation to take action (except in cases of extreme human rights abuses),[57] it may do so if requested.[58] The majority judgment does make an exception in the case of egregious breaches of international human rights that come to the state's knowledge: in such cases, there may be a duty on the state to act, even where assistance has not been requested (because the victim(s) may not be in a position to make a request).[59]

Woolman has argued that the textual interpretation of Chaskalson CJ ultimately turns on the presence of the preposition 'in' in section 7(1) of the Constitution: "[The Bill of Rights] enshrines the rights of all people *in* our country and affirms the democratic values of human dignity, equality and freedom".[60] He critiques the fact that the majority judgment does not offer any external authority to support its interpretation, as is the fashion in purposive approaches (which the Court ordinarily adopts).[61]

Woolman also argues that the Chief Justice's alleged confusion in this judgment stems from the conflation of the extraterritorial application of the Bill of Rights to the South African state and the extraterritorial application of the Bill of Rights to foreign law.[62] However, this critique lacks rigour, partly because it appears to rely largely on one cherry-picked paragraph from the majority judgment,[63] while failing to appreciate the judgment in

52 *SS Lotus (France v Turkey)* (1927) PCIJ Series A, No. 10, para. 18–19.
53 The majority judgment is referred to interchangeably as the majority judgment and the main judgment.
54 *Kaunda*, para. 40.
55 *Ibid.*, para. 54.
56 *Ibid*, para. 55–56.
57 *Ibid.*, para. 69.
58 *Ibid.*, para. 60–61.
59 *Ibid.*, para. 70.
60 Emphasis added.
61 *Department of Land Affairs and Others v Goedgelegen Tropical Fruits (Pty) Ltd* 2007 (6) SA 199 (CC), para. 51.
62 Woolman, "Application," 31–113 and 31–118.
63 Paragraph 36, to be precise.

its entirety. The majority judgment can certainly be critiqued for lacking some conceptual and argumentative precision,[64] but my understanding of it aligns with Tladi's: that is, the majority judgment rejects the extraterritorial application of the Bill of Rights to foreign law and authorities but confirms it in the case of extraterritorial acts of South African authorities and their conduct. Tladi exemplifies this (roughly using the facts of a subsequent case):

> I do not read *Kaunda* to imply that when in Zimbabwe the South African government can act inconsistently with the Constitution, but rather that in Zimbabwe, it is the Zimbabwean law that applies and therefore one cannot argue that the *Zimbabwean government* has violated a South African national's rights to life, property or a fair trial *under the South African Constitution*.[65]

As Tladi rightly points out, there is an important distinction that applies when dealing with diplomatic protection cases: diplomatic protection flows from international human rights law or internationally wrongful conduct rather than any rights in the South African Constitution directly.[66] Michèle Olivier attributes this mischaracterisation to a general conceptual conflation of the extraterritorial application of the Bill of Rights and the operation of multilateral human rights obligations by South African courts, observing that the *raison d'être* for international law is commonly sought in the Constitution.[67] Legal issues arising in the area of foreign affairs always make it tricky to cognitively disentangle the diplomatic issues from the international law issues, but it is important to do so in order to assess and apply the legal consequences correctly.

4.1.2 *Separate Judgments: Locating the Obligation in Citizens' Rights*

Ngcobo J wrote a compelling separate concurring judgment in which he agreed with the overall outcome but distinguished his approach to the question of extraterritoriality. Ngcobo J's approach differs by his express acknowledgement that section 3(2) (containing certain rights and privileges to which South Africans are entitled) and section 7(2) must be read together as defining the obligations of the South African government towards its citizens.[68] In this sense, the rights are conferred by section 3, and the duty is

64 Although Tladi, "The Right to Diplomatic Protection," 21 disagrees, finding the judgment "coherent and clear".

65 Ibid., 20.

66 *Ibid.*

67 M. E. Olivier, "Diplomatic Protection – Right or Privilege?: South African Judicial Decisions," *South African Yearbook of International Law* 30(1) (2005): 241.

68 *Kaunda*, para. 176.

imposed on South African authorities by section 7(2). Therefore, the analysis must first consider whether citizens' rights include a right to diplomatic protection instead of trying to locate that right in relation to section 7(2), as the majority judgment does.

Ngcobo J also focuses on the founding values of South African democracy and the role of the Constitution in advancing and protecting fundamental rights.[69] He starts by recalling Mohamed J's classification of the Constitution in *Makwanyane* as –

> the shared aspirations of a nation; the values which bind its people, and which discipline its government and its national institutions; the basic premises upon which judicial, legislative and executive power is to be wielded; the constitutional limits and the conditions upon which that power is to be exercised; the national ethos which defines and regulates that exercise; and the moral and ethical direction which that nation has identified for its future.[70]

In this sense, Ngcobo J conceptualises the Constitution as a promissory note.[71]

Unlike Chaskalson CJ in the main judgment, Ngcobo J considers the rights protected in the relevant human rights conventions in more detail and finds that the ratification of the instruments containing these rights (right to a fair trial, fair detention, and the right against torture) –

> is a positive statement by the government to the world and to South African nationals that it will act in accordance with these instruments if any of the fundamental human rights enshrined in the international instruments it has ratified are violated.[72]

He notes that these instruments are binding under the Constitution and should guide foreign policy. Although the provisions of the relevant instruments are permissive (by providing that a state 'may' take action in case of violations), Ncgobo J is of the view that this does not detract from the obligation assumed by South Africa upon ratification to promote and protect these rights. He "venture[s] to suggest" that South Africa is obligated to take 'some steps' when there is an egregious violation of the rights enshrined in those instruments.[73]

69 *Ibid.*, para. 154–156. See the introduction of this chapter for more information. Ncgobo J has generally situated his analysis within what he terms as the 'constitutional context' in his judgments. See also, for example, *Bato Star*.

70 *Makwanyane*, para. 262.

71 *Kaunda*, para. 157.

72 *Ibid.*, para. 162.

73 *Kaunda*, para. 164.

In the earlier case of *De Lange v Smuts*, the Constitutional Court found that the South African state assumes the obligation of assisting citizens and non-citizens with enforcing their rights.[74] Although this finding was made in an entirely different context, Ncgobo J opines that the principle in relation to the positive obligation on a state holds when considering South Africa's obligation to protect South Africans. He finds that the obligation does not cease when South Africans leave the state's territory.[75]

For Ngcobo J, the potential conflict created in foreign relations by this approach is resolved by turning to the scope of the constitutional duty. The conduct of foreign relations is a matter which, under South Africa's rubric of separation of powers, falls within the purview of the executive. Affording states wide discretion on whether and in what manner to grant diplomatic protection (under international law) reflects the idea that states are the best judges of when and how to intervene. However, this does not mean that the exercise of such discretion is immune to judicial scrutiny.[76] Indeed, he holds that the government bears a duty to properly consider the request for diplomatic protection, including by following a fair procedure in processing the request and furnishing reasons for its decision.[77] The exercise of such discretion would be an exercise of a public power subject to review under the administrative justice framework to ensure compliance with section 33 of the Constitution.[78]

Despite finding that the rights of the Constitution are applicable beyond South African borders, Ncgobo J is careful to note that the Constitution only binds the South African government abroad and not foreign governments. It is expressly stated that the South African government cannot require foreign governments to act in accordance with the Constitution.[79] In this sense, the applicants misconceived their claims, and the relief sought could not be granted, and this is why Ncgobo J ultimately agrees with the order made by Chaskalson CJ.

O'Regan J also wrote a separate judgment (Mokgoro J concurring) where she differs with Chaskalson CJ's finding on whether there is an obligation (independent of a request by a citizen) on South Africa to take steps to protect citizens abroad against the conduct of other states that may result in a breach of fundamental rights.[80] As her starting point, O'Regan J asks whether there is a positive constitutional obligation on the state to exercise its international law rights with respect to its nationals.[81]

74 *De Lange v Smuts NO and Others* 1998 (3) SA 785 (CC), para. 31.
75 *Kaunda*, para. 183 and 187.
76 *Ibid.*, para. 189 and 191.
77 *Ibid.*, para. 192.
78 *Ibid.*, para. 193.
79 *Ibid.*, para. 209.
80 Although she concurs with the final order.
81 *Kaunda*, para. 217.

In answering this question, O'Regan J notes that the South African Constitution asserts the promotion and protection of human rights as a foundational value, which acts as both a constitutional injunction and as a boundary for the conduct of the three branches of government.[82] However, although it is clear the Bill of Rights binds the South African executive, there is no evidence that it binds courts or governments in other countries. To this extent, O'Regan J finds that the Bill of Rights has no direct extraterritorial effect.[83] She further finds that the international law right of any state to protect its nationals relates only to breaches of international law; therefore, the issue of extraterritorial effect of the Constitution is not raised in this case.[84]

O'Regan J does go on to remark that the application of the Bill of Rights does not stop at South African borders in relation to the conduct of South African authorities extraterritorially,[85] but that is not the conduct with which this chapter is concerned. Nonetheless, it is worth noting that O'Regan J is particular in clarifying that if the enforcement of the Bill of Rights were to run contrary to international law in any context, this would be impermissible under the Constitution. In this sense, any extraterritorial application of the Bill of Rights is limited by the international law principle that domestic law provisions are only enforceable against other states insofar as they comply with the principle of sovereignty. This determination needs to be made on a case-by-case basis.[86]

In answering the question of whether there is an obligation on the South African government to intervene on behalf of its nationals, O'Regan J (like Ngcobo J) also turns to the content of citizens' rights first and interprets 'diplomatic representations' as a benefit as contemplated by the Bill of Rights under section 3(2)(a), which reads: "All citizens are equally entitled to the rights, privileges and *benefits* of citizenship".[87] She finds that in light of the normative commitment to human rights, it is correct to read section 3 of the Bill of Rights as imposing a positive obligation on the South African government to provide diplomatic protection to citizens to "prevent or repair" *egregious* violations of human rights.[88] Where the violation does not meet this threshold of gravity, the situation may differ.

4.1.3 Sachs J's Judgment

Sachs J also wrote a brief separate concurring opinion, in which he agrees with the majority judgment, as well as the 'texture' added by the separate

82 *Ibid.*, para. 218–221.
83 *Ibid.*, para. 227.
84 *Ibid.*, para 231.
85 *Ibid.*, para. 228.
86 *Ibid.*, para. 229.
87 Emphasis added. *Ibid.*, para. 236.
88 *Ibid.*, para. 238.

opinions of Ngcobo J and O'Regan J. What is worth noting from his judgment is the view that the "values of [the] Constitution and the human rights principles enshrined in international law are mutually reinforcing, interrelated and, where they overlap, indivisible".[89] He is also of the view that the government must act to prevent South Africans abroad from being subjected to egregious human rights violations, although the government has wide discretion on how best to offer diplomatic protection.[90]

4.2 *Commitment to Justice and Accountability*

The second constitutional policy driver – South Africa's commitment to justice and accountability – is also evident in what might be viewed as a correlative to the protection of human rights: prosecution for human rights violations. Although the Constitutional Court has found that there is an obligation on the South African government to intervene on behalf of citizens abroad at risk of *egregious* human rights violations,[91] there is no converse obligation to prosecute citizens who commit crimes abroad.[92] A statute will have to explicitly authorise the exercise of jurisdiction based on (active) nationality, as is the case in the Implementation of the Rome State of the International Criminal Court Act (ICC Act).[93] It is interesting to note that the ICC Act also empowers South African courts to exercise jurisdiction in respect of genocide, crimes against humanity, and war crimes outside of South Africa where such crime is committed against a South African citizen or resident,[94] despite the fact that the Rome Statute itself does not provide for jurisdiction based on passive personality.

4.2.1 *Immunity and Cooperation with Prosecution*

This tricky area of accountability has raised itself before South African courts in the cases concerning the arrest of former Sudanese President Omar al-Bashir.[95] Although these cases do not relate strictly to the extraterritorial

89 *Ibid.*, para. 274.
90 *Ibid.*, para. 275.
91 But, as discussed in the preceding section, not in other cases.
92 John Dugard, Max Du Plessis and Eshed Cohen, "Jurisdiction and International Crimes," in *Dugard's International Law: A South African Perspective*, eds. John Dugard et al. (Cape Town, South Africa: Juta & Company, Limited, 2019), 221.
93 Act 27 of 2002.
94 Section 4(3)(d) of the ICC Act.
95 For an interesting account of these cases from one of the counsel appearing on behalf of the civil society organisation instituting proceedings, as well as some suggestions to resolve some of the conflicting international law norms at play, see Max du Plessis, "The Omar Al-Bashir Case: Exploring Efforts to Resolve the Tension between the African Union and the International Criminal Court," in *In Pursuit of a Brave New World in International Law: Essays in Honour of John Dugard*, eds. Tiyanjana Maluwa, Max Du Plessis and Dire Tladi (Leiden/Boston: Brill, 2017).

application of South African law, immunity is an important area of jurisdiction, and these cases are mentioned briefly to highlight (again) the interaction between South Africa's constitutional values and its general approach to international law issues.

These cases concerned two arrest warrants on charges of war crimes, crimes against humanity, and genocide issued by the International Criminal Court (ICC) in 2009 and 2010 in relation to the conduct of al-Bashir's government and its supporters (such as the Janjaweed militia) primarily in the Darfur region of Sudan since 1 July 2002.[96] In June 2015, al-Bashir travelled to South Africa to attend the African Union (AU) Assembly in Johannesburg, and South African authorities took no steps to arrest him on the grounds that he enjoyed immunity from arrest.[97]

The Southern African Litigation Centre successfully launched an urgent application in the High Court, declaring this failure to be in breach of the Constitution and compelling South African authorities to arrest him and hand him over to the ICC for prosecution.[98] The element of intrigue in this case grew when it emerged that al-Bashir had exited the country, apparently unobserved, via a military base reserved for dignitaries during the course of oral arguments, despite counsel for the state repeatedly assuring the High Court that he remained in the country.[99] Therefore, despite the order of the High Court compelling South African authorities to arrest al-Bashir, it was impossible to do so due to the fact that he was no longer present in the country.

The South African government appealed the order to the Supreme Court of Appeal (SCA), and argued that customary international law and section 4(1) of the Diplomatic Immunities and Privileges Act (DIPA)[100] grant sitting heads of state immunity from arrest and prosecution.[101] The appellants contended that the general immunity that a head of state enjoys under customary international law and section 4(1) of DIPA qualified the obligation of South Africa that would otherwise exist as a state party to the Rome Statute,

96 Warrant of Arrest for Omar Hassan Ahmad Al-Bashir, Al Bashir (ICC-02/05-01/09) (in respect to war crimes and crimes against humanity) and Second Warrant of Arrest for Omar Hassan Ahmad Al-Bashir, Al Bashir (ICC-02/05-01/09) (in respect to genocide).

97 *Minister of Justice and Constitutional Development and Others v Southern African Litigation Centre and Others* 2016 (3) SA 317 (SCA) (*Al-Bashir SCA*), para. 4.

98 *Southern Africa Litigation Centre v Minister of Justice and Constitutional Development and Others* 2015 (5) SA 1 (GP).

99 *Al-Bashir SCA*, para. 7. For an example of news coverage around this event, see Owen Bowcott, "Sudan President Omar Al-Bashir Leaves South Africa as Court Considers Arrest," *The Guardian*, 15 June 2015, sec. World News. Accessed 13 October 2024. https://www.theguardian.com/world/2015/jun/15/south-africa-to-fight-omar-al-bashirs-arrest-warrant-sudan.

100 Act 37 of 2001.

101 *Al-Bashir SCA*, para. 14, 49–50. Section 4(1)(a) of DIPA reads (in relevant part): "A head of state is immune from the criminal and civil jurisdiction of the Courts of the Republic, and enjoys such privileges as heads of state enjoy in accordance with the rules of customary international law".

to arrest and surrender a head of state for whom the ICC has issued an arrest warrant in respect of the commission of international crimes.[102] Therefore, according to the government parties, the High Court was incorrect in ordering the arrest and surrender of al-Bashir, and there was no obligation on South African authorities to arrest him had he remained in the country.

For the purpose of this chapter, it is important that the SCA grounded its analysis in the Constitution in this case.[103] Recalling the Constitutional Court's judgement in *Glenister (II)*,[104] which re-emphasised the constitutional imperative to interpret South African law in compliance with international law, Wallis JA observes that democratic South Africa strives to play a full role as an accepted member of the international community. As part of this aim, it enacted the ICC Act.[105] Wallis JA is careful to note that the role of South African courts is to interpret and apply international law as it is and not to develop it.[106]

The SCA was also careful to distinguish between the potential exception to immunity *ratione personae* established in *Arrest Warrant* (providing that incumbent state officials may be subject to criminal proceedings before international criminal courts with jurisdiction as a matter of prosecution)[107] versus an obligation on national courts to provide assistance to that tribunal not bound by an otherwise ordinary rule of international law.[108] The SCA noted (after thorough consideration) that the position on immunity in such latter cases (as was the case before the SCA) is in a state of flux and found that it could not find conclusive support in customary international law for an obligation to arrest al-Bashir.[109]

However, in this case, the SCA held that the ICC Act removed both uncertainty and the immunity al-Bashir would otherwise enjoy.[110] The Court noted that if the international crimes concerned were committed in South Africa, they would infringe a number of rights guaranteed under the Bill of Rights.[111]

102 *Al-Bashir SCA*, para. 16.
103 *Ibid.*, para. 61.
104 *Glenister v President of the Republic of South Africa and Others* 2011 (3) SA 347 (CC) (*Glenister (II)*), para. 97. *Glenister (II)* dealt with the legality of the dissolution of the Directorate of Special Operations ('Scorpions') and its replacement with the Directorate for Priority Crime Investigation ('Hawks'). The Constitutional Court held that the new unit lacked sufficient independence to combat corruption, violating South Africa's international law obligations, particularly the United Nations Convention Against Corruption and the African Union Convention on Preventing and Combating Corruption (2006).
105 *Al-Bashir SCA*, para. 62–63.
106 *Ibid.*, para. 74.
107 *Arrest Warrant of 11 April 2000 (Democratic Republic of the Congo v Belgium)*, 2002 ICJ Reports 3 (*Arrest Warrant*), para. 61.
108 *Al-Bashir SCA*, para. 77.
109 *Ibid.*, para. 77–84.
110 *Ibid.*, para. 86.
111 *Ibid.*, para. 87.

This is relevant because it illustrates the importance of construing the ICC Act in a way that accords with the Bill of Rights.[112] Ultimately, the Court finds that to afford al-Bashir (or any other incumbent state official subject to an ICC arrest warrant) immunity would be "absurd and non-compliant with [South Africa's] international obligations".[113]

Wallis JA concludes that when South Africa decided to implement its obligations under the Rome Statute by passing the ICC Act, it did so on the basis that all forms of immunity, including head of state immunity, would not constitute a bar to the prosecution of international crimes in South Africa. Nor would such immunity bar South Africa from cooperating with the ICC by way of the arrest and surrender of persons charged with crimes before the ICC, where an arrest warrant had been issued and a request for cooperation made.[114] He notes that this puts South Africa at the forefront of attempts to ensure accountability for international crimes, which is wholly consistent with its commitment to human rights at a national and international level.[115]

Nonetheless, Mia Swart has compellingly criticised the SCA for its failure to engage properly with the *ius cogens* nature of the crimes and the implications this has on immunity.[116] Unfortunately, this case did not proceed to the Constitutional Court, so it was denied the opportunity to make pronouncements on *ius cogens* crimes and South Africa's duty to cooperate in the prosecution of international crimes.[117] The Court has been presented with this opportunity in other cases, but it has not always taken that up.[118]

112 *Ibid.*, para. 88.

113 *Ibid.*, para. 93.

114 *Ibid.*, para. 103. In his separate judgment (para. 115), Ponnan JA contends that this finding renders the consideration of customary international law in the majority judgment unnecessary.

115 *Ibid.*, para. 103.

116 See generally, Mia Swart, "Breaking the Silence: The Treatment of Ius Cogens in Zimbabwe Torture Docket and Al Bashir," *Constitutional Court Review* 9 (2019): 537–558.

117 The state parties filed an appeal to the Constitutional Court, which was set down for hearing, but was later withdrawn. See Michael Masutha, "Media Briefing on International Criminal Court and Sudanese President Omar Al Bashir," *South African Government*, 21 October 2016. Accessed 13 October 2024. https://www.gov.za/speeches/minister-michael-masutha-media-briefing-international-criminal-court-and-sudanese-president. In the same media briefing, incumbent Minister of Justice and Constitutional Development, Michael Masutha, noted that South Africa had delivered its notice of intent to withdraw from the ICC, although that withdrawal was subsequently abandoned following a High Court judgment ordering that Parliament had to approve any withdrawal. See *Democratic Alliance v Minister of International Relations and Cooperation and Others* 2017 (3) SA 212 (GP). The threat of withdrawal continues to rear its head from time to time. See "Lindiwe Sisulu: Debate to Stay in the ICC Reopened," *Mail & Guardian*, 5 July 2018. Accessed 13 October 2024. https://mg.co.za/article/2018-07-05-lindiwe-sisulu-debate-to-stay-in-the-icc-reopened/; Carien Du Plessis, "South Africa to Try to Withdraw from ICC Again – Ramaphosa," *Reuters*, 25 April 2023, sec. Africa. Accessed 13 October 2024. https://www.reuters.com/world/africa/south-africa-try-withdraw-icc-again-ramaphosa-2023-04-25/.

118 Swart, "Breaking the Silence," 539.

4.2.2 *Accountability of South African Representatives Extraterritorially*

In addition to criminal accountability, South African courts have also been faced with the question of administrative justice in relation to extraterritorial conduct by South African state representatives. In *LSSA v President*,[119] the issue of the extraterritorial effect of the Constitution was indirectly raised when challenging the legality of the President's conduct in relation to the Southern African Development Community (SADC) Summit's suspension of the SADC Tribunal in 2011,[120] as well as the President's subsequent signature of the new Protocol on the Tribunal in the Southern African Development Community (2014) (which removed the Tribunal's jurisdiction to consider disputes of individuals against SADC member states).[121]

At the time of the impugned conduct, the President was acting in his capacity as a member of SADC – an international organisation not based in South Africa – and was participating in a consensus decision-making process governed by international law and not domestic law.[122] Despite this, his conduct was ultimately held to be unlawful (for following an impermissible or irregular procedure)[123] and irrational,[124] and therefore unconstitutional.[125] This declaration of unconstitutionality also related to the President's failure to object to the Summit's decision to suspend the Tribunal, even though the Summit was attended by a representative for the President – the High Commissioner to Namibia – and not the President himself.[126]

Dugard and Coutsoudis argue that this judgment may be authority for the proposition that the actions of South African diplomats and representatives in international organisations remain subject to the confines of the Constitution. This means that these officials' decisions must be rational under South African law and must comply with both international law and constitutional law obligations.[127] I find it difficult to disagree with their conclusions in this regard, even if the Court did not give express consideration to this implication in its judgment.

119 *Law Society of South Africa and Others v President of the Republic of South Africa and Others* 2019 (3) SA 30 (CC) (*LSSA v President*).
120 The SADC Summit is SADC's highest policy-making body.
121 *LSSA v President*, para. 7. See also Dugard and Coutsoudis, "The Place of International Law in South African Municipal Law," 124.
122 The Southern African Development Community Treaty (Consolidated Version of 2015) governed the dispute.
123 *LSSA v President*, para. 56.
124 *Ibid.*, para. 70.
125 *Ibid.*, para. 85. The details of the constitutional/administrative non-compliance are not relevant for the purposes of this chapter.
126 Dugard and Coutsoudis, "The Place of International Law in South African Municipal Law," 124.
127 *Ibid.*, 124–125.

5 Universal Jurisdiction

Both of the constitutional policy drivers discussed previously are also demonstrated in South Africa's approach to the special (and somewhat controversial) principle of universal jurisdiction. Universal jurisdiction is a special case of jurisdiction removed from the construct of territory, in which a crime may be prosecuted by a state unconnected to the commission of the crime, the place where it occurred, the accused, or the victim because that crime is of universal concern.[128] It is already evident that South Africa's commitment to being an equal member of the international community has led to its participation in the movement towards international criminal accountability. However, it has gone a step further than implementing the Rome Statute by finding that South Africa is obliged (where appropriate) to exercise universal jurisdiction in relation to the crime of torture.[129]

In the *Zimbabwe Torture Docket* case, the question before the Constitutional Court was whether the South African police had a duty to investigate allegations of torture committed in Zimbabwe by and against Zimbabwean nationals as part of an alleged campaign of pre-election violence and intimidation by the ruling party, Zimbabwe African National Union–Patriotic Front (ZANU-PF) against members of the opposition party, Movement for Democratic Change (MDC).[130] Extensive evidence of the torture (meeting the threshold of crimes against humanity) was collected by the Southern African Human Rights Litigation Centre (SALC, the first respondent) in what was called the 'torture docket'. This, together with a SALC memorandum, was delivered to the South African National Prosecuting Authority (NPA) due to fear for the safety of victims, the possibility that the Zimbabwean courts could not hold perpetrators accountable, and the risk of the collapse of the rule of law in Zimbabwe. The SALC memorandum requested the NPA to investigate the alleged acts of torture under the ICC Act.[131]

The crux of SALC's argument was that the purpose of the ICC Act was to investigate international crimes and hold perpetrators accountable in South African courts[132] and that the South African police and NPA had failed in this duty through their extended delay and ultimate refusal to investigate.[133] The

128 Annalisa Ciampi, Taxiarchis Fiskatoris, and Raghavi Viswanath, "International Criminal Law," in *Public International Law: A Multi-Perspective Approach*, eds. Sué González Hauck, Raffaela Kunz and Max Milas (Abingdon/New York: Routledge, 2024), 641.

129 *National Commissioner of the South African Police Service v Southern African Human Rights Litigation Centre and Another* 2015 (1) SA 315 (CC) (*Zimbabwe Torture Docket*), para. 40.

130 *Zimbabwe Torture Docket*, para. 4, 9.

131 *Ibid.*, para. 11.

132 *Ibid.*, para. 12.

133 *Ibid.*, para. 14.

Court was therefore called upon to consider whether the police have a duty to investigate crimes against humanity committed extraterritorially and, if so, when such a duty is triggered.[134]

By this point in time (2015), the relationship between the Constitution and international law had been fairly concretely addressed in a number of cases, including *Mohamed, Kaunda,* and *Glenister (II).* In considering the matter of jurisdiction, the Court held that limiting investigations and the exercise of adjudicative jurisdiction to the territory of the investigating state is in line with the principles of universal jurisdiction.[135] The Court notes that the Rome Statute places primary responsibility for the investigation and prosecution of international crimes on domestic courts, emphasising the Preamble of the Rome Statute, where it reads "that it is the *duty* of every State to exercise its criminal jurisdiction over those responsible for international crimes".[136]

In addition to the customary international law prohibition of torture being applicable law in South Africa by virtue of section 232 of the Constitution, the Torture Act also criminalises torture.[137] The Court notes that torture is also proscribed as a crime against humanity in South Africa by virtue of section 232 of the Constitution, the Torture Act, and the ICC Act.[138] However, the requirement to investigate (and the limit on universal jurisdiction) lies in understanding the jurisdiction provisions of the ICC Act, which read (in relevant part):

(1) Despite anything to the contrary in any other law of the Republic, any person who commits a crime, is guilty of an offence and is liable on conviction to a fine or imprisonment, including imprisonment for life, or such imprisonment without the option of a fine, or both a fine and such imprisonment.

...

(3) *In order to secure the jurisdiction of a South African court for purposes of this Chapter*, any person who commits a crime contemplated in subsection (1) outside the territory of the Republic, is deemed to have committed that crime in the territory of the Republic if –

  (a) that person is a South African citizen; or
  (b) that person is not a South African citizen but is ordinarily resident in the Republic; or
  (c) *that person, after the commission of the crime, is present in the territory of the Republic*; or

134 *Ibid.*, para. 21.
135 *Ibid.*, para. 29.
136 *Ibid.*, para 30–31.
137 Prevention and Combating of Torture of Persons Act 13 of 2013 (Torture Act).
138 *Zimbabwe Torture Case*, para. 39.

(d) that person has committed the said crime against a South African citizen or against a person who is ordinarily resident in the Republic.[139]

Madjiedt J held that section 4(3) sets jurisdictional limits on the *courts* and not on investigation (as argued by the government parties). The Court further concluded that an investigation of an international crime committed extraterritorially may be conducted without violating the Constitution or international law.[140] Madjiedt J found that to require the presence of the accused would render nugatory the object of combatting crimes against humanity.[141]

The Constitutional Court found that South Africa could assert prescriptive and – to some extent – adjudicative jurisdiction through universal jurisdiction by investigating the torture allegations as a precursor to the possible next step of prosecution or an extradition request.[142] Madjiedt J ruled that South Africa's duty to investigate crimes against humanity must be discharged through its law enforcement agencies,[143] and therefore, the police have a duty to investigate alleged crimes against humanity of torture arising from the Constitution read with the ICC Act.[144] This is in contrast to the NPA, which (under section 179(2) of the Constitution) has a 'power' (and therefore, discretion) to institute criminal proceedings.[145]

However, the universal jurisdiction to investigate identified by the Court is subject to two limitations. First, the principles of subsidiarity (which usually requires a substantial connection between the subject matter and the source of the jurisdiction) and non-intervention, which kick in only once the jurisdiction is properly founded. In respect of the latter, an investigation in another state will only be permissible if that state is unwilling or unable to prosecute and only if the investigation is confined to the territory of the investigating state.[146] Second, the principle of practicability, which is an assessment to be made in light of all relevant circumstances on a case-by-case basis.[147] Foremost amongst these considerations are whether the investigation is likely to lead to a prosecution, and – accordingly – whether the alleged perpetrators are likely to be present in South Africa on their own or through an extradition request; the geographical

139 Emphasis as added by Madjiedt J.
140 *Zimbabwe Torture Case*, para. 43–47.
141 *Ibid.*, para. 48.
142 *Ibid.*, para. 49.
143 Section 205(3) of the Constitution reads: "The objects of the police service are to prevent, combat and *investigate* crime, to maintain public order, to protect and secure the inhabitants of the Republic and their property, and to uphold and enforce the law". (Emphasis added.) Section 16(1) of the South African Police Service Act 68 of 1995, read with its Schedule, defines the crime against humanity of torture as a national priority offence that requires national prevention or investigation.
144 *Zimbabwe Torture Case*, para. 55.
145 *Zimbabwe Torture Docket*, para. 56.
146 *Ibid.*, para. 61.
147 *Ibid.*, para. 63.

proximity of South Africa to the place of the crime and the likelihood of the suspects being arrested for the purpose of prosecution; the prospects of gathering the evidence which is needed to satisfy the elements of a crime; and the nature and the extent of the resources required for an effective investigation.[148]

The Court's version of universal jurisdiction has been characterised as 'robust'.[149] Unlike the *Kaunda* and *Al-Bashir SCA* judgments, which do not give much consideration to *ius cogens* norms, the Court in *Zimbabwe Torture Docket* mentions these norms numerous times. Swart notes that it is a distinct progression from previous cases in this regard and is "the most progressive domestic case on international criminal law not just in South Africa but also arguably in Africa".[150]

6 Conclusion

South Africa's isolation during apartheid means that it has only had a relatively short history of engaging with international law in its domestic courts, meaning that in the past years, many have considered it too 'exotic' to be a reliable framework for legal claims.[151] However, it has still managed to develop an interesting body of jurisprudence, situating its approach within the values enshrined by its Constitution.

These values – in the form of protection of human rights and a commitment to justice and accountability – have also acted as policy drivers in determining South Africa's relatively expansive approach to extraterritoriality. As it stands, foreign governments and foreign law may not be subjected to the demands of the South African Constitution, except in cases of egregious human rights violations, when there is a duty on the South African authorities to intervene. However, South African law enforcement agencies are obliged to investigate (in a geographically limited sense) alleged crimes against humanity on the basis of universal jurisdiction. South African authorities and courts are also compelled to assist the ICC with the prosecution of international crimes by the ICC Act's removal of immunity for incumbent government officials.

South Africa has a clear self-image as one of the great protectors of human rights in the international arena, which is often (although not always)[152] supported by its foreign relations and case law. However, this position in the

148 *Ibid.*, para. 64.

149 Max Du Plessis, "The Zimbabwe Torture Docket Decision and Proactive Complementarity" (Institute for Security Studies, November 2015), 4. Accessed 14 October 2024. https://issafrica.s3.amazonaws.com/site/uploads/PolicyBrief81.pdf.

150 Swart, "Breaking the Silence," 556.

151 Mia Swart, "The Wouter Basson Prosecution: The Closest South Africa Came to Nuremberg?" *Heidelberg Journal of International Law* 68 (2008): 213; Swart, "Breaking the Silence," 556.

152 Here, in particular, I am thinking of the South African government's failure to denounce Russia's invasion of Ukraine in 2022. See, for example, Crystal Orderson, "A 'Russian Love Affair': Why South Africa Stays 'Neutral' on War," *Al Jazeera*. Accessed 16 October 2024. https://www.aljazeera.com/features/2023/6/2/a-russian-love-affair-why-south-africa-stays-neutral-on-war.

vanguard is confirmed in the recent case before the International Court of Justice in which South Africa sought provisional measures against Israel in relation to its conduct in Gaza, alleging violations of the Convention on the Prevention and Punishment of the Crime of Genocide (1948).[153]

This image encapsulates these policy drivers and will likely continue to determine its approach to matters of extraterritoriality while the legal system remains committed to – and guided by – its Bill of Rights. I have no doubt that South Africa will be a country to watch as the international community tries to work out the kinks in international law's own approaches to the balancing act between the protection of human rights and accountability.

References

Ciampi, Annalisa, Taxiarchis Fiskatoris, and Raghavi Viswanath. "International Criminal Law." In *Public International Law: A Multi-Perspective Approach*, edited by Sué González Hauck, Raffaela Kunz, and Max Milas. Abingdon, New York: Routledge, 2024.

Coombs, Mary. "International Decision: Kaunda v The President of the Republic of South Africa." *American Journal of International Law* 99 (2005): 681.

Currie, Iain, and Johan de Waal. *The Bill of Rights Handbook*. Lansdowne: Juta & Company, Limited, 5th edition, 2005.

Du Plessis, Max. "The Extra-Territorial Application of the South African Constitution." *South African Law Journal* 120(4) (2003): 797.

Du Plessis, Max. "The Omar Al-Bashir Case: Exploring Efforts to Resolve the Tension between the African Union and the International Criminal Court." In *The Pursuit of a Brave New World in International Law: Essays in Honour of John Dugard*, edited by Tiyanjana Maluwa, Max Du Plessis, and Dire Tladi. Leiden; Boston: Brill, 2017.

Du Plessis, Max. "The Zimbabwe Torture Docket Decision and Proactive Complementarity." *Institute for Security Studies*, November 2015. Accessed 14 October 2024. https://issafrica.s3.amazonaws.com/site/uploads/PolicyBrief81.pdf.

Dugard, John, and Andreas Coutsoudis. "The Place of International Law in South African Municipal Law." In *Dugard's International Law: A South African Perspective*, edited by John Dugard, Max Du Plessis, Tiyanjana Maluwa, and Dire Tladi. Cape Town: Juta & Company, Limited, 2019.

Dugard, John, Max Du Plessis, and Eshed Cohen. "Jurisdiction and International Crimes." In *Dugard's International Law: A South African Perspective*, edited by John Dugard, Max Du Plessis, Tiyanjana Maluwa, and Dire Tladi. Cape Town, South Africa: Juta & Company, Limited, 2019.

González Hauck, Sué, and Max Milas. "Jurisdiction." In *Public International Law: A Multi-Perspective Approach*, edited by Sué González Hauck, Raffaela Kunz, and Max Milas. Abingdon, New York: Routledge, 2024.

Kamminga, Menno T. "Extraterritoriality." In *Max Planck Encyclopedias of International Law*, Oxford University Press, 1st edition, 2020.

Kaushal, Asha. "The Politics of Jurisdiction." *Modern Law Review* 78(5) (2015): 759–792.

153 Application of the Convention on the Prevention and Punishment of the Crime of Genocide in the Gaza Strip *(South Africa v Israel)*, Order for Provisional Measures, 26 January 2024 (*South Africa v Israel*).

Margolies, Daniel S., Umut Özsu, Maïa Pal, and Ntina Tzouvala, eds. *The Extraterritoriality of Law: History, Theory, Politics*. London, New York: Routledge, 2019.
Mpedi, Letlhokwa George. "Law and Social Policy in South Africa: From Untold Suffering and Injustice to a Future Based on Human Rights." In *Law and Social Policy in the Global South: Brazil, China, India, South Africa*, edited by Ulrike Davy and Albert H.Y. Chen. London: Routledge, 2022.
Olivier, M. E. "Diplomatic Protection – Right or Privilege?: South African Judicial Decisions." *South African Yearbook of International Law* 30(1) (2005): 238–252.
Roberts, Adam. *The Wonga Coup: Guns, Thugs, and a Ruthless Determination to Create Mayhem in an Oil-Rich Corner of Africa*. Hachette UK, 2007.
Swart, Mia. "The Wouter Basson Prosecution: The Closest South Africa Came to Nuremberg?" *Heidelberg Journal of International Law* 68 (2008): 209.
Swart, Mia. "Breaking the Silence: The Treatment of Ius Cogens in Zimbabwe Torture Docket and Al Bashir." *Constitutional Court Review* 9 (2019): 537–558.
Tladi, Dire. "The Right to Diplomatic Protection, The Von Abo Decision, and One Big Can of Worms: Eroding the Clarity of Kaunda." *Stellenbosch Law Review* 1 (2009).
Tladi, Dire, and Polina Dlagnekova. "The Act of State Doctrine in South Africa: Has Kaunda Settled a Vexing Question?" *SA Public Law* 22(2) (2007): 444–456.
Vidmar, Jure. *Territorial Status in International Law*. London: Hart Publishing, 2024.
Woolman, Stuart. "Application." In *Constitutional Law of South Africa*. Cape Town: Juta & Company Limited, 2nd edition, 2002.

13 The Politics of Criminal Universal Jurisdiction in Argentina

Juan Ignacio Stampalija

1 Introduction

In Argentina, extraterritorial jurisdiction has had very different manifestations and implications in numerous areas of the law. However, with some notable exceptions,[1] there is little literature addressing the politics of extraterritoriality in the Argentinian legal system. The purpose of this chapter is to help fill part of that vacuum by studying the politics around universal criminal jurisdiction in the country. The focus on criminal universal jurisdiction is justified by the relevant role that Argentinian courts and human rights organisations have played in this field.

Part 2 of this chapter will introduce the concept of criminal universal jurisdiction. Part 3 will examine the constitutional basis for universal jurisdiction in Argentina and its implications with respect to crimes against humanity. Part 4 will review the practice of universal jurisdiction by Argentinian courts. It will focus on the most paradigmatic cases, including crimes committed in Spain during Franco's regime and the crimes against the Rohingya people in Myanmar. Part 5 will look into the politics of such practice. For this purpose, it analyses the country's experience prosecuting and adjudicating crimes against humanity committed during the government of the military junta (1976–1982). This experience led to a strong human rights tradition in the country and influenced universal jurisdiction. Part 6 will address the role of human rights organisations as supporters of trials for crimes against humanity in Argentina and their participation in universal jurisdiction cases. Part 7 will explore the vast expertise and resources that local prosecutors and courts gained and obtained handling cases related to crimes against humanity. Part 8 will briefly explain the strong support that exists in Argentina with respect to crimes against humanity. Part 9 will consider the reputational gains that local courts obtained from prosecuting these crimes. Part 10 concludes.

1 See, in this respect, Alejandro Chehtman, "Strategic Approaches to Extraterritoriality in Latin America," in *Research Handbook on Extraterritoriality in International Law*, eds. Austin Parrish et al. (Cheltenham: Edward Elgar Publishing, 2023).

DOI: 10.4324/9781003402978-16

2 The Concept of Criminal Universal Jurisdiction

In most cases, a state exercises criminal jurisdiction over acts committed within its territory (territorial principle). Also, extraterritorial jurisdiction can be established by the nationality of the perpetrator or the victim (active or passive personality principle) and also with respect to a specific protected interest of the state (protection principle). In these scenarios, jurisdiction is justified by a link between the state and the act or between the state and any of the persons involved.

The principle of criminal universal jurisdiction is different from the previous jurisdictional grounds. It started to spark great interest at the end of the 1990s with the arrest of General Pinochet in England.[2] Universal jurisdiction "may be exercised by any State over a specific offense, without the offense having any link with the State (except perhaps for the presence of the offender)".[3]

Universal jurisdiction is currently related to the commission of certain international crimes, such as genocide, crimes against humanity, and other crimes the seriousness of which justifies their prosecution and punishment by any state.[4] The objective of asserting this type of jurisdiction is to avoid impunity. International crimes are usually committed by governmental authorities or officials. Given their official character, they may be able to influence or pressure local courts in their countries to avoid prosecution or punishment. They might even benefit themselves with an amnesty. Universal jurisdiction intends to break with safe heavens by assuring that such heinous criminals can be brought to justice in any country.

Universal jurisdiction usually involves two types of rules: legislative, which characterise certain conducts as international crimes, and jurisdictional, which provide national courts jurisdiction to investigate and prosecute international crimes.[5]

Universal jurisdiction can be considered extraterritorial since it exceeds the territoriality principle: it can be established even if the offence in question has no link at all with the state, its territory, its nationals, and its particular interests.

2 Jorge E. Viñuales, "Observaciones sobre la compatibilidad de la jurisdicción universal con la noción de debido proceso," *El Derecho – Revista de Derecho Penal* (2007): 47.

3 Cedric Ryngaert, *Jurisdiction in International Law* (Oxford: Oxford University Press, 2nd ed., 2015), 106.

4 Jorge E. Viñuales, "Aspectos conceptuales de la jurisdicción universal," *Revista de Derecho Penal y Procesal Penal* 1 (2008): 9.

5 Viñuales, "Aspectos conceptuales," 9. As examples of the former, the author mentions Articles 2 and 5 of the International Convention for the Protection of All Persons from Enforced Disappearance; as for the latter, Articles 9, para. 2 and 11, para. 1 of the same Convention serve as examples.

3 Constitutional Basis of Universal Jurisdiction in Argentina

Argentina does not have an express provision in its criminal code or other laws related to universal jurisdiction. As pointed out by Jorge E. Viñuales, the principles that regulate the jurisdiction of courts in criminal matters in Argentina have been deeply influenced by a territorial approach. The territoriality principle is the cornerstone of Argentine criminal jurisdiction. This practice is in line with the international law perspective.[6]

The Argentine Criminal Code limits its application to the national territory.[7] There are three exceptions: (i) those cases in which a conduct carried out outside Argentine jurisdiction produces effects in Argentine territory; (ii) those in which state agents, in the performance of their duties, carry out the incriminated conduct while they are outside the national territory; (iii) those cases of transnational bribery committed abroad by Argentine nationals or companies.[8] These scenarios imply the recognition of the principles of objective territoriality, protection, and active personality.[9] Hence, from the point of view of Argentine criminal legislation, Argentine courts cannot be considered to have jurisdiction over international crimes committed abroad by foreigners and against foreigners if the conduct does not produce an effect in Argentine territory.[10]

However, the Argentine Constitution, already in its original version of 1853, contained a rule that ended up being important in matters of universal jurisdiction. Article 118 of the Argentine Constitution in its current form provides:

> The trial of all ordinary criminal cases not arising from the right to impeach granted to the House of Deputies, shall be decided by jury once this institution is established in the Nation. The trial shall be held in the province where the crime has been committed; *but when committed outside the territory of the Nation against public international law, the trial shall be held at such place as Congress may determine by a special law* (emphasis added).[11]

6 Ryngaert, *Jurisdiction*, 85.
7 Argentina National Criminal Code, Article 1, para. 1 provides that it is applicable to "crimes committed . . . in the territory of the Argentine Nation, or in places subject to its jurisdiction".
8 Argentina National Criminal Code, Article 1, paras. 1, 2, and 3.
9 Viñuales, "Observaciones," 47.
10 *Ibid.*, 47.
11 In Argentina's original Constitution, which was enacted in 1853, this provision was included as Article 102. After the 1994 amendment of the Constitution, it is now Article 118. The text of the provision remained unchanged.

The first part of this article is based on Article III (2), last paragraph of the United States of America Constitution,[12] which is about jury trials and the distribution of jurisdiction among provinces. Therefore, it is not relevant for the purposes of this paper. The second part is the basis on which universal jurisdiction has developed in Argentina; however, there is no agreement as to its source. Some authors refer to the 1789 Judiciary Act of the United States,[13] while others refer to the Constitution of Venezuela of 1811.[14] The first alternative is not convincing since the 1789 Judiciary Act of the United States has no similar provision.[15] Instead, the influence of the 1811 Venezuelan Constitution – sanctioned 42 years earlier than the Argentine Constitution – is clear since it had an almost identical provision. Article 117 of the Venezuelan Constitution provides: "[W]hen the crime is outside the limits of the Confederation against the law of nations, the Congress shall determine by a particular law the place where the trial shall be held".[16]

As pointed out by María A. Gelli, the rule is not sufficiently clear to determine the scenarios in which the provision could be applied. In any case, it supports the idea that, already in 1853, Argentina accepted the principle of extraterritorial criminal jurisdiction for certain cases.[17] Nonetheless, the truth is that the provision remained irrelevant for 150 years.[18] No special law has ever been passed by Congress, and no crimes were prosecuted, or jurisdiction was exercised based on this provision until the 2000s.

In the early 2000s, Argentine courts decided that certain amnesty laws were unconstitutional and, therefore, that crimes against humanity committed in Argentina during the government of the military junta between 1976 and 1982 should be prosecuted.[19] These cases did not involve crimes committed outside the country. However, courts resorted to Article 118 regarding two issues. First, they considered that crimes against humanity were prohibited under international law; hence, they could be prosecuted by Argentine courts. Second, and most importantly for the purpose of this chapter, in certain decisions, judges stated – *obiter dicta* – that Article 118 incorporated the

12 United States Constitution, Article 3, section 2, para. 3: "The Trial of all Crimes, except in Cases of Impeachment, shall be by Jury; and such Trial shall be held in the State where the said Crimes shall have been committed; but when not committed within any State, the Trial shall be at such Place or Places as the Congress may by Law have directed".

13 Carlos E. Colautti, "El artículo 118 de la Constitución Nacional y la jurisdicción extraterritorial," *Revista del Colegio Público de Abogados de la Capital Federal* (1998): 30.

14 Alejandro J. Padilla, "Un aporte al estudio de los antecedentes del art. 113 de la Constitución Nacional," *Boletín Informativo de la Asociación Argentina de Derecho Constitucional* 179 (2001).

15 1789 Judiciary Act of the United States.

16 1811 Federal Constitution of Venezuela.

17 María A. Gelli, *Constitución Comentada. Tomo II* (Buenos Aires: La Ley, 2011), 573.

18 Viñuales, "Observaciones," 47.

19 Argentinian Supreme Court of Justice, "Simón, Julio Héctor y otros s/privación ilegítima de la libertad, etc. (Poblete)," 06/14/2005. This question will be examined in detail in Part 5.

principle of universal jurisdiction for the prosecution of international crimes in Argentine law. For example, the concurring opinion of Justice Boggiano in *Simón* expressed that the seriousness of crimes against humanity

> may provide grounds for universal jurisdiction, as is clear from Article 118 of the National Constitution, which contemplates crimes against the law of nations outside the limits of the Nation . . . . This assumes that such crimes may be tried in the Republic.[20]

This line of reasoning left a propitious field for cases to be brought under the principle of universal jurisdiction. It is no surprise that just six months after the decision of the Supreme Court in the *Simón* case, the first high-profile universal jurisdiction case was filed before Argentine courts, namely, the case against Chinese authorities for crimes against the Falun Dafa followers.[21] In the *Falun Dafa* case, Argentine courts asserted universal jurisdiction to engage in the prosecution of international crimes against humanity (with no effects in Argentina).[22] In 2010, a judge ordered the international arrest of former Chinese leader Jiang Zemin, which never materialised.

From this case onward, courts tried to justify universal jurisdiction by invoking Article 118 of the Constitution. In application of the provision, the Federal Court of Criminal Cassation has affirmed that "the gravity of the conduct denounced could be considered crimes against humanity and, as such, would make universal jurisdiction applicable".[23]

To recap, the idea of universal jurisdiction was present in the Argentine Constitution as early as 1853. Despite being dormant for more than 150 years, Article 118 has provided the constitutional basis of universal jurisdiction in Argentina. Viñuales explains that the interpretation of the provision shows that legal developments do not always derive from the adoption of new rules but also from the 'reinterpretation' of the existing ones.[24]

4 Universal Jurisdiction Cases in Argentina

There is no official public information available regarding the total of universal jurisdiction cases before Argentine courts. According to Alejandro

20 Argentine Supreme Court of Justice, *Simón*, concurring vote of Judge Boggiano, para. 28.

21 The Supreme Court's decision in *Simón* was issued on 06/14/2005, and the complaint in the Falun Dafa case was filed on 12/13/2005.

22 Viñuales, "Aspectos conceptuales," 9.

23 Federal Court of Criminal Cassation, Chambre IV, Case No. 4591/2010/8/CFC1, 06/11/2018.

24 Viñuales, "Aspectos conceptuales," 9.

Chehtman, "Argentina has initiated 96 investigations on grounds of universal jurisdiction".[25]

Universal jurisdiction cases before Argentine courts involve a wide array of countries and defendants. Among the early cases, it is worth mentioning the case against former Chinese authorities for crimes against the Falun Dafa supporters (2005), the case against former Spanish officials for crimes during the Franco dictatorship (2010), and the case against former officials of the Paraguayan government under the Stroessner regime (2013). More recently, cases were initiated against Myanmar authorities for the alleged crimes against the Rohingya (2019), Nicaraguan (2022), and Venezuelan (2023) authorities and officials for crimes against humanity.[26]

The section focuses on the cases against Spanish officials and Myanmar authorities. This choice is justified by the public information available and because they represent both the old and the recent universal jurisdiction cases.

The case regarding the crimes of Franco's regime is one of the first and most high-profile universal jurisdiction cases in Argentina. It started in Spain in 2006, when then Judge Baltasar Garzón opened an investigation into allegations of crimes against humanity committed during the Franco dictatorship. The investigation was closed by the Spanish Supreme Court, which considered that those crimes could not be prosecuted because they were covered by the Amnesty Law passed after democratic elections were held in Spain in 1977.[27]

In 2010, Spanish and Argentinian human rights organisations filed a criminal complaint in Argentina on behalf of Spanish victims against former

25 Chehtman, "Strategic Approaches," 186.

26 The case against Nicaraguan authorities was started by a complaint filed by two Argentine lawyers against Nicaraguan authorities, including President Daniel Ortega. They requested the investigation of extrajudicial killings, illegal detentions, forced disappearances, and torture against political dissidents. For more information, see Almudena Calatrava, "Argentina Judge Launches Probe into Nicaragua Abuse Claims," *The Associated Press*, 6 October 2022. Accessed 20 June 2024. https://apnews.com/article/crime-caribbean-judiciary-argentina-criminal-investigations-25894f039e20680d511a40e809e3b127. The case regarding Venezuela refers to alleged crimes against humanity committed by Venezuela's President, Nicolás Maduro, and the Bolivarian National Guard, which is part of the country's armed forces. The case involved alleged illegal persecutions, detentions, and killings by members of the Venezuelan armed forces. The complaint was filed by victims of the regime, as well as the Clooney Foundation for Justice. For more information, see Nicolas Misculin, "Clooney Foundation Denounces Venezuelan Security Forces for Alleged Human Rights Abuses," *Reuters*, 15 June 2023. Accessed 20 June 2024. https://www.reuters.com/world/americas/clooney-foundation-sues-venezuela-over-alleged-human-rights-abuses-2023-06-14/.

27 Amnesty Law No. 46/1977 from 15 October 1977. The law established amnesty for all acts of politically motivated crimes committed before 15 June 1977. Likewise, it also granted amnesty to authorities, officials, and law enforcement officers who had committed crimes or misdemeanors during the prosecution of political acts or had violated "the rights of individuals".

Spanish officials of the Franco administration for alleged crimes against humanity committed in Spain between 1936 and 1978.

The process was long, and its specific details exceed the scope of this paper. However, it is worth mentioning that the Argentine judge hearing the case sustained a very active prosecutorial role. She issued several arrest warrants against some of the suspects and requested extradition from Spanish authorities. She also asked the Spanish authorities for permission to go to Spain to hear some of the defendants. Nonetheless, all requests, including extradition, were rejected by Spanish courts on more than one occasion. They ruled that Amnesty laws precluded the possibility of any type of prosecution for those cases.

The case regarding crimes against the Rohingya people was initiated in 2019. The Burmese Rohingya Organisation UK, along with Latin American and Argentine human rights groups, filed a claim in Argentine courts for alleged genocide and crimes against humanity committed since 2017. The suspects were several military and civilian leaders of the Myanmar government.

In 2021, the federal courts decided to open the investigation. After an initial dismissal in the first instance, the Court of Appeals opened the case. In its ruling, the majority considered that Argentine courts had jurisdiction based on the principle of universal jurisdiction as incorporated in Article 118 of the Constitution. It was also stated that the "exercise of universal jurisdiction in the country . . . does not require any link with the state where the facts took place".[28]

That same year, six Rohingya women, refugees in Bangladesh, took part in a virtual hearing before the Argentinian court in which they said they had been victims of sexual violence and mentioned the death of family members as a result of state repression.

An interesting question discussed in the case has to do with the interaction between domestic courts and the International Criminal Court in universal jurisdiction cases. In this case, the first instance court refused to hear the case because of the ongoing investigation in the International Criminal Court, among other reasons. However, the Court of Appeals decided that the case should be opened, notwithstanding the ICC's investigation. The Court of Appeals argued that Myanmar was not a member of the ICC and, therefore, that its investigation only dealt with crimes committed against the Rohingya in the territory of Bangladesh, which is a party to the ICC. In the Argentine case, the investigation was meant to be about crimes committed in Myanmar. That is why, according to the Court of Appeals, the scope of both investigations was different.[29]

28 National Criminal and Correctional Court of Appeals, Chamber I, "Burmese Rohingya Organisation," 26 November 2021.

29 The same solution was followed in the case against Venezuelan authorities. The first instance court refused to hear the case due to the ongoing investigation in the International Criminal

It is important to note that no foreign officials were ever arrested and subjected to trial in Argentina in the context of any universal jurisdiction prosecution.[30] Under current Argentine law, it is possible to prosecute absent suspects but not to bring them to trial.[31] This constitutes a fundamental barrier to the effectiveness of the principle of universal justice in Argentina. In this type of case, bringing the suspects to trial requires extradition, which is difficult to obtain in such highly sensitive cases.

5 Argentina's Experience in Prosecuting Crimes Against Humanity

The explanation of this vigorous role in universal jurisdiction cases of Argentine courts is related to the country's human rights tradition. This tradition started after the country's last military junta's government (1976–1982). While the junta was in power, Argentina witnessed widespread human rights abuses, including forced disappearances, torture, and killings. In 1983, Argentina held its first democratic elections in nearly a decade, resulting in the election of President Raúl Alfonsín. The new president pledged to investigate and prosecute those responsible for those human rights abuses.

The trial against the most prominent members of the military junta began in 1985 and was known as the *Trial of the Juntas*. It was a groundbreaking event in many aspects. The trial was held in a civilian court, ensuring due process and transparency. The trial saw high-ranking military officials, including General Jorge Rafael Videla and Admiral Emilio Massera, in the dock. It also featured powerful testimonies from survivors and relatives of the victims, shedding light on the heinous crimes committed under the junta's rule. The court sentenced Videla, Massera, and other military leaders to long prison terms for their roles in the human rights abuses. By doing so, Argentina became (and remains) the only country in the region to have been able to prosecute, bring to trial, and convict the highest-ranking members of a military government for human rights abuses.[32]

Court against Venezuela, namely, the 'Situation in the Bolivarian Republic of Venezuela I'. Once again, the Court of Appeals decided that the case must be prosecuted urgently. Both the majority and concurring opinions focused on the extreme gravity of the alleged crimes and the need to give an immediate response to avoid more damage to the rights involved. They also pointed out that the alleged crimes could be different and, therefore, exceeded those under investigation by the International Criminal Court. Consequently, the Court of Appeals ordered the lower court to urgently move forward with the investigation and to take the formal statements of the accused.

30 Chehtman, "Strategic Approaches," 186–187.

31 Argentine National Criminal Procedure Code, Article 290.

32 It is worth noting that, during the decades 1960 to 1990, several countries in Latin America were subjected to military governments, which took power by force. For example, General Pinochet ruled Chile after a military coup in 1973 until 1990. Similarly, General Bánzer governed Bolivia from 1971 to 1978. In Brazil, a military government held power from 1964 to

Years later, different military insurrections led to amnesties. In 1986 and 1987, two separate laws rendered impossible any new trials for military personnel involved in crimes committed during the military junta's government.[33] In 1990, even those convicted in the *Trial of the Juntas* were amnestied and released from prison.[34] As a consequence, no more trials for violations of human rights during the military government were initiated in more than a decade.

In 2003, Law No. 25779 was passed, annulling the Due Obedience and Full Stop amnesty laws. In 2005, the Supreme Court declared in the *Simón* case that both laws were unconstitutional.[35] As mentioned, one of the concurring opinions in *Simón* expressly admitted the existence of universal jurisdiction under Article 118 of the Argentine Constitution. Six months later, the case against Chinese authorities for crimes against the Falun Dafa supporters was initiated, *i.e.,* the first universal jurisdiction case filed before Argentine courts.

The annulment of amnesty laws and the decision in the *Simón* case allowed the trial of hundreds of persons, civilian and military, whose prosecutions had been interrupted. After these events, almost 300 rulings were issued, and more than 1,000 people were convicted for crimes against humanity.[36]

These trials helped crystallise a very significant human rights tradition. In particular, it is worth mentioning: (i) an active role of human rights organisations; (ii) the resources and experience of courts and prosecutors to deal with cases involving mass atrocities; (iii) a strong popular support for human rights causes; and (iv) certain reputational motivations of federal criminal courts. These aspects have been crucial for the development of universal jurisdiction in Argentina.

1985. Those governments were supposed to fight the rise of revolutionary left-wing governments and guerrillas on the continent, and all kinds of human rights abuses were committed. Once democracy was restored, different amnesty laws were passed, and none of them were held accountable in courts for human rights abuses, as opposed to the Argentine case.

33 The Full Stop Law No. 23.492 was enacted on 24 December 1986. It established the suspension of the judicial proceedings initiated in 1985 against those accused of the crime of forced disappearance of persons during the military dictatorship. The Due Obedience Law No. 23.521 was enacted on 4 June 1987. This law provided a presumption *iuris et de iure* that crimes committed by members of the Armed Forces below the rank of colonel (as long as they had not appropriated children or the property of disappeared persons) were not punishable. It was considered that they had acted by virtue of the so-called 'due obedience', a military concept according to which subordinates are limited to obeying orders issued by their superiors.

34 Decree 2741/90 granted pardon to the members of the military junta who had been convicted for human rights violations in 1985.

35 Argentine Supreme Court of Justice, "Simón, Julio Héctor y otros s/privación ilegítima de la libertad, etc. (Poblete)," 14 June 2005.

36 Procuraduría de Crímenes contra la Humanidad, *Informe estadístico sobre el estado de las causas por delitos de lesa humanidad en Argentina. Diagnóstico* Buenos Aires: 2022. Accessed 20 June 2024. https://www.argentina.gob.ar/sites/default/files/anexo_vi_-_ced.pdf.

6 The Role of Human Rights Organisations

Human rights organisations played a central role in the fight for justice concerning the crimes committed by the military junta. During the years of the military government, human rights organisations led the efforts at home and abroad to denounce the human rights abuses of the junta. The case of the mothers and grandmothers of Plaza de Mayo is paradigmatic in this respect. In 1977, every Thursday, mothers and grandmothers of those disappeared by the military junta started marching in the Plaza de Mayo in front of the House of Government, demanding to know the whereabouts of their missing children and grandchildren.

During the 1978 football World Cup that took place in Argentina, the Mothers of Plaza de Mayo were interviewed by foreign media present in the country. After those interviews, their cause became known internationally, especially in Europe. In 1979, Amnesty International supported a trip of several mothers to European countries to explain the dramatic human rights situation in Argentina. This was the beginning of a long and close relationship between local and foreign human rights organisations. Also, in 1979, the Centre of Legal and Social Studies (*Centro de Estudios Legales y Sociales*) was established. This organisation was meant to assist victims and their families to take legal action seeking justice for human rights violations.[37] These organisations are just two – maybe the most high-profile ones – out of many that led the resistance against the military regime and its human rights abuses.

The work of human rights organisations did not finish with the end of the military junta. Once democracy was restated in the country, human rights organisations were actively involved in the *Trial of the Juntas*. They supported the work of the prosecutors in many ways, such as gathering evidence and testimonies of the victims.[38] The outcome of the trial, and the fact that many of the allegations made by human rights organisations in the previous years were confirmed, increased the prestige of those organisations, both locally and internationally.

Understandably, human rights organisations fiercely opposed the Due Obedience and Full Stop amnesty laws. Before Congress annulled those laws, both Mothers of Plaza de Mayo and the Centre of Legal and Social Studies filed criminal complaints requesting the declaration of unconstitutionality of the amnesty laws and the prosecution of those involved in those crimes.[39] These proceedings became what has been known as the *Simón* case, at the occasion of which those amnesty laws were declared unconstitutional.

Once the amnesty laws were no longer in force, human rights organisations were one of the leading forces involved in the opening of new

37 Larrandart, 25.
38 *Ibid.*, 85–86.
39 *Ibid.*, 112–113.

investigations. As a matter of fact, they were parties to many of the cases that led to convictions.[40]

The work of local and international human rights organisations is relevant to explain universal jurisdiction cases before Argentine courts. If we see the plaintiffs in these cases, most of them are supported, when not directly motivated, by human rights organisations, local or international. For example, the case of the victims of the Franco regime was brought to Argentine courts by several human rights organisations, such as the Mothers of Plaza de Mayo, Grandmothers of Plaza de Mayo, and the Centre for Legal and Social Studies.[41] Similarly, the case against Myanmar authorities for crimes against the Rohingya was filed by the Burmese Rohingya Organisation UK, along with Latin American and Argentine human rights groups, like the Grandmothers of Plaza de Mayo.[42] In addition, Amnesty International, with connections to the Mothers of Plaza de Mayo since 1979, acted – and still acts in universal jurisdiction cases in Argentina – as *amicus curie* in the case against Venezuelan authorities for crimes against humanity.[43]

Finally, it is relevant to remember that some of these human rights organisations, especially the Mothers of Plaza de Mayo, Grandmothers of Plaza de Mayo, and the Centre for Legal and Social Studies, have been extremely close to the political party that ruled Argentina from 2003 to 2015, and from 2019 to 2023. As a matter of fact, some of their principal figures were outright supporters of the administration. This fact increased their political influence, as well as their resources to pursue their goals.

7 Resources and Expertise of Courts and Prosecutors

The investigation and prosecution of crimes against humanity are complex tasks. It is difficult for prosecutors and judges used to deal with ordinary crimes to adapt to the complexities of proceedings involving a mass of highly traumatised victims, powerful perpetrators, forensic evidence difficult to obtain, etc.

40 In Argentinian criminal procedure, those affected by crimes can be parties to the criminal process as "private complainants" (in Spanish, *querellantes*). It is similar to a 'private prosecution', different from public prosecution. In the same case, the prosecutor will be in charge of the public prosecution, whereas private complainants will lead the 'private prosecution'. Both have similar prerogatives.

41 Redacción Canal Abierto, "Querella argentina contra el franquismo, diez años," *Canal Abierto*, 17 April 2020. Accessed 20 June 2024. https://canalabierto.com.ar/2020/04/17/querella-argentina-contra-el-franquismo-diez-anos/.

42 "El caso de jurisdicción universal en Argentina que investiga crímenes contra las personas Rohingya en Myanmar." Accessed 20 June 2024. https://www.globaljusticecenter.net/el-caso-de-jurisdiccion-universal-en-argentina-que-investiga-crimenes-contra-las-personas-rohingya-en-myanmar/.

43 "Argentina: Amicus curiae on crimes against humanity in Venezuela." Accessed 20 June 2024. https://www.amnesty.org/es/documents/amr53/7749/2024/es/.

In this respect, the prosecutors and judges of the *Trial of the Juntas* had to overcome numerous obstacles. The case involved a special team of prosecutors with limited resources and no experience in this kind of case. They had to gather evidence and take testimony from hundreds of victims. Moreover, the armed forces, *i.e.*, the former rulers of the country, were still very powerful and vehemently opposed the trial. Many threats and pressures against the prosecutors put the trial at risk.

Many years later, when new investigations and trials started after 2003, the situation was also challenging for different reasons. The armed forces were less powerful and enjoyed little, if any, popular support, so their ability to affect the investigations was limited. However, there were other difficulties. Contrary to the *Trial of the Juntas*, the new investigations and trials involved more than a thousand defendants and hundreds of separate proceedings.[44] Testimonies and other pieces of evidence were also more difficult to obtain as more than two decades had passed since the crimes under investigation were committed.

This new dynamic seriously delayed the proceedings. In order to cope with the challenges, it was necessary to increase available resources and adapt the existing structures and procedures.

The Public Prosecutor's Office assumed a leading role in this respect. It provided the human and material resources to support the investigations and trials of crimes against humanity. It also issued several instructions to prosecutors to accelerate and avoid unnecessary steps or delays.[45] Even a special unit inside the Public Prosecutor's Office was created to assist and coordinate these cases in 2013. It is called the Office of the Prosecutor for Crimes Against Humanity (*Procuraduría de Crímenes contra la Humanidad*).[46]

Furthermore, the Supreme Court of Justice and the Federal Court of Criminal Cassation, which are the highest tribunals to intervene in cases regarding crimes against humanity, also took measures to speed up procedures. The Supreme Court urged judges to avoid delays and requested more resources in terms of infrastructure for the oral hearings.[47] The Federal Court of Criminal

44 According to official figures, 304 trials were conducted from 2003 to the present. Information available at "Juicios de lesa humanidad en tiempo real." Accessed 20 June 2024. https://www.juiciosdelesahumanidad.ar/.

45 For example, Resolution No. 13/08 of the Public Prosecutor's Office (Ministerio Público Fiscal), 3 August 2008.

46 It was created by Resolution No. 1442/13 of the Public Prosecutor's Office (Ministerio Público Fiscal), 29 July 2013. It succeeded a previous unit, namely, the Prosecutor's Unit for the Coordination and Follow-up of Cases of Human Rights Violations committed during State Terrorism (Unidad Fiscal de Coordinación y Seguimiento de las Causas por Violaciones a los Derechos Humanos cometidas durante el Terrorismo de Estado).

47 Argentinian Supreme Court of Justice Administrative Decision No. 42/08, 29 December 2008, available at "La Corte convoca a los demás poderes para acelerar los juicios de lesa humanidad." Accessed 20 June 2024. https://www.cij.gov.ar/nota-719-La-Corte-convoca-a-los-dem-s-poderes-para-acelerar-juicios-de-lesa-humanidad.html.

Cassation issued a set of 'Practical Rules' aimed at adapting the rules of criminal procedure to crimes against humanity. These rules provided that "unnecessary delays and formalities that hinder the process should be avoided".[48] They also included rules on how to treat victims and witnesses to respect their human rights and safety.[49]

Ultimately, these investigations and trials resulted in a high degree of specialisation of courts and prosecutors concerning crimes against humanity. This capacity proved paramount in handling universal jurisdiction cases in Argentina.

8 Public Support for Human Rights Causes

The whole history of cases related to human rights abuses during the military junta's government resulted in significant popular support for human rights causes in the country. When the *Trials of the Juntas* started in 1985, Argentina's society was somewhat divided between those supporting and opposing the trials. The evidence gathered in the trials, the heart-wrenching testimonies of the victims, as well as the final judgment against some members of the junta, all of which were presented on live TV, helped increase the support for the trials.

In 2003, when the amnesty laws were annulled by Congress, the issue gained momentum again. The newly elected administration of President Néstor Kirchner became very close to human rights organisations and firmly supported the reopening of trials for those crimes against humanity. This approach proved very popular. Even young people, who were born in a democracy, expressed their support for the trials.

A concrete example of such support happened in 2017 as the Supreme Court issued its decision in the *Muiña* case.[50] In short, the majority of the Court considered that those convicted of crimes against humanity could benefit from a special regime that reduced the time to be spent in prison. This decision caused a strong public reaction, which resulted in massive demonstrations against the Court's judgment in all the country.[51] Due

48 Federal Court of Criminal Cassation, Administrative Decision No. 1/12, 28 February 2012. For a deeper analysis of this resolution, Mariano Sicardi, "La aplicación de las reglas prácticas de la Cámara Federal de Casación Penal en las causas por delitos de lesa humanidad." In Gabriel Ignacio Anitua et al., ed., Los juicios por crímenes de lesa humanidad, ediciones Didot, Buenos Aires, 2015, 65–81.

49 Federal Court of Criminal Cassation, Acordada No. 1/12, 28 February 2012.

50 Argentinian Supreme Court of Justice, "Muiña," 3 May 2017, available at "La Corte Suprema, por mayoría, declare aplicable el cómputo del 2x1 para la prisión en un caso de delitos de lesa humanidad." Accessed 20 June 2024. https://www.cij.gov.ar/nota-25746-La-Corte-Suprema-por-mayor-a-declar-aplicable-el-c-mputo-del-2x1-para-la-prisi-n-en-un-caso-de-delitos-de-lesa-humanidad.html.

51 Carlos E. Cué and Ramiro Barreiro, "Masiva marcha en Argentina contra la sentencia favorable a los represores." *El País*, 11 May 2017. Accessed 20 June 2024. https://elpais.com/internacional/2017/05/10/argentina/1494431965_661817.html.

to public pressure, Congress passed Law No. 27362, which declared the inapplicability of such benefit in crimes against humanity. In 2018, the Supreme Court changed its *Muiña* doctrine and aligned itself with Law No. 27362.[52]

The revolt against the *Muiña* decision demonstrates that the prosecution of crimes against humanity is very present in Argentinian society and that it boasts strong public support.

9 Reputational Motivations of Courts

Last but not least, it is worth noting that Argentine courts see domestic and foreign human rights cases as useful for gaining legitimacy and public approval.

In Argentina, prosecutions for crimes against humanity are heard by federal criminal courts. The jurisdiction of these courts is limited to high-profile crimes, such as corruption, drug trafficking, and the like. Generally speaking, the work of these courts is perceived by the public to be deficient. For example, investigations in corruption cases tend to last several years, even decades, and it is extremely rare to find convictions despite corruption being endemic in the country. This has undermined the public's confidence in the federal criminal courts.[53]

These courts have heard cases regarding human rights violations during the government of the last military junta and have received important support from public opinion. Although universal jurisdiction cases do not have the same domestic impact, they help reinforce the idea that federal criminal courts are favourable to human rights. In this way, these courts can regain a part of the legitimacy affected by their less effective work in other fields and notorious cases.

The idea that universal jurisdiction in Argentina is more linked to the interests of courts and human rights organisations than to an actual policy of the political branches of government (executive and legislative) is also reflected in the fact that universal jurisdiction has not been expressly included in any piece of criminal legislation. Even after universal jurisdiction cases started growing in courts in the 2000s, there were no new legal regulations

52 Argentinian Supreme Court of Justice, "Batalla," 4 December 2018, available at "Penal: inaplicabilidad del beneficio del 2x1 para los delitos de lesa humanidad". Accessed 20 June 2024. https://www.cij.gov.ar/nota-32689-PENAL-Inaplicabilidad-del-beneficio-del-2x1-para-los-delitos-de-lesa-humanidad.html.

53 For example, in a national survey carried out in 2023, only 8% said they trusted the judicial brunch, and only 9% said that the work of courts was efficient. See Redacción La Nación, "Según una encuesta, sólo el 8% de los argentinos confía en la Justicia." *La Nación*, 28 November 2023. Accessed 20 June 2024. https://www.lanacion.com.ar/politica/segun-una-encuesta-solo-el-8-de-los-argentinos-confia-en-la-justicia-nid28112023/.

passed by Congress. This is an important difference from other countries, where laws were passed to regulate universal jurisdiction.[54]

One may argue that there was no need for a new regulation, as Article 118 was enough to ensure universal jurisdiction. However, it is difficult to think that leaving courts only with a 170-year-old vague constitutional provision to deal with these cases is a reasonable alternative. In effect, this demonstrates that universal jurisdiction has not been considered a relevant question by political powers. Instead, universal jurisdiction is a development related to the interests of human rights organisations and federal courts to advance their agendas, something that has been tolerated by political actors.

10 Conclusion

Universal criminal jurisdiction allows states to exercise their jurisdiction over specific international crimes without the offence having any link to the state. It can be considered a type of extraterritorial jurisdiction since it exceeds the territoriality principle. As examined in this chapter, Argentina has been actively involved in the development of criminal universal jurisdiction.

The country does not have an express provision in its criminal code or other laws related to universal jurisdiction. However, the idea of universal jurisdiction is present in Article 118 (formerly Article 102) of the Argentine Constitution since 1853. Despite being dormant for more than 150 years, this provision has been the constitutional basis for the exercise of universal jurisdiction in Argentina.

Argentina's active role in universal jurisdiction cases is related to a human rights tradition in the country. This tradition is closely linked to the resistance against the government of the military junta that ruled the country from 1976 to 1982 and perpetrated massive crimes against humanity. The *Trial of the Juntas* in 1985 and the hundreds of procedures started after 2003 were vital for the development of universal jurisdiction in the country.

Relevant aspects of this human rights tradition were essential for the development of universal jurisdiction in the country. The role of human rights organisations, the resources and experience gained by courts and prosecutors to handle cases involving mass atrocities, the substantial popular support for human rights causes, and the reputational motivations of federal criminal courts have been particularly important.

54 For example, France (Article 689 of the French Criminal Procedural Code) and Spain (Article 23, Organic Law of the Judiciary).

References

Amnesty International. "Argentina: Amicus Curiae on Crimes Against Humanity in Venezuela." Accessed 20 June 2024. https://www.amnesty.org/es/documents/amr53/7749/2024/es/.

Calatrava, Almudena. "Argentina Judge Launches Probe into Nicaragua Abuse Claims." *The Associated Press*, 6 October 2022. Accessed 20 June 2024. https://apnews.com/article/crime-caribbean-judiciary-argentina-criminal-investigations-25894f039e20680d511a40e809e3b127.

Centro de Información Judicial. "La Corte convoca a los demás poderes para acelerar los juicios de lesa humanidad." Accessed 20 June 2024. https://www.cij.gov.ar/nota-719-La-Corte-convoca-a-los-dem-s-poderes-para-acelerar-juicios-de-lesa-humanidad.html.

Centro de Información Judicial. "La Corte Suprema, por Mayoría, Declara Aplicable el Cómputo del 2x1 para la Prisión en un Caso de Delitos de Lesa Humanidad." Accessed 20 June 2024. https://www.cij.gov.ar/nota-25746-La-Corte-Suprema--por-mayor-a--declar--aplicable-el-c-mputo-del-2x1-para-la-prisi-n-en-un-caso-de-delitos-de-lesa-humanidad.html.

Centro de Información Judicial. "Penal: Inaplicabilidad del Beneficio del 2x1 para los Delitos de Lesa Humanidad." Accessed 20 June 2024. https://www.cij.gov.ar/nota-32689-PENAL---Inaplicabilidad-del-beneficio-del-2x1-para-los-delitos-de-lesa-humanidad.html.

Chehtman, Alejandro. "Strategic Approaches to Extraterritoriality in Latin America." In *Research Handbook on Extraterritoriality in International Law,* edited by Austen Parrish and Cedric Ryngaert, 180–194. Cheltenham: Edward Elgar Publishing, 2023.

Colautti, Carlos E. "El Artículo 118 de la Constitución Nacional y la Jurisdicción Extraterritorial." *Revista del Colegio Público de Abogados de la Capital Federal* (1998): 30.

Cué, Carlos E., and Ramiro Barreiro. "Masiva Marcha en Argentina Contra la Sentencia Favorable a los Represores." *El País*, 11 May 2017. Accessed 20 June 2024. https://elpais.com/internacional/2017/05/10/argentina/1494431965_661817.html.

Gelli, María A. *Constitución Comentada. Tomo II.* Buenos Aires: La Ley, 2011.

Global Justice Center. "El Caso de Jurisdicción Universal en Argentina Que Investiga crímenes contra las personas Rohingya en Myanmar." Accessed 20 June 2024. https://www.globaljusticecenter.net/el-caso-de-jurisdiccion-universal-en-argentina-que-investiga-crimenes-contra-las-personas-rohingya-en-myanmar/

Juicios de Lesa. "Juicios de Lesa Humanidad en Tiempo Real." Accessed 20 June 2024. https://www.juiciosdelesahumanidad.ar/

Larrandart, Lucila E. *Memoria, Verdad y Justicia.* Buenos Aires: Hammurabi, 2016.

Misculin, Nicolas. "Clooney Foundation Denounces Venezuelan Security Forces for Alleged Human Rights Abuses." *Reuters*, 15 June 2023. Accessed 20 June 2024. https://www.reuters.com/world/americas/clooney-foundation-sues-venezuela-over-alleged-human-rights-abuses-2023-06-14/.

Padilla, Alejandro J. "Un Aporte al Estudio de los Antecedentes del Art. 113 de la Constitución Nacional." *Boletín Informativo de la Asociación Argentina de Derecho Constitucional* 179 (2001).

Redacción Canal Abierto. "Querella argentina contra el franquismo, diez años." *Canal Abierto,* 17 April 2020. Accessed 20 June 2024. https://canalabierto.com.ar/2020/04/17/querella-argentina-contra-el-franquismo-diez-anos/.

Redacción La Nación. "Según una Encuesta, Sólo el 8% de los Argentinos Confía en la Justicia". *La Nación*, 28 November 2023. Accessed 20 June 2024. https://www.lanacion.com.ar/politica/segun-una-encuesta-solo-el-8-de-los-argentinos-confia-en-la-justicia-nid28112023/

Ryngaert, Cedric. *Jurisdiction in International Law*. Oxford: Oxford University Press, 2015.

Sicardi, Mariano. "La Aplicación de las Reglas Prácticas de la Cámara Federal de Casación Penal en las Causas por Delitos de Lesa Humanidad." In *Los Juicios por Crímenes de Lesa Humanidad*, edited by Gabriel Ignacio Anitua, Alexis Álvarez Nakagawa, and Mariano Gaitán, 65–81. Buenos Aires: Ediciones Didot, 2015.

Viñuales, Jorge E. "Observaciones sobre la Compatibilidad de la Jurisdicción Universal con la Noción de Debido Proceso." *El Derecho – Revista de Derecho Penal* (2007): 47.

Viñuales, Jorge E. "Aspectos Conceptuales de la Jurisdicción Universal." *Revista de Derecho Penal y Procesal Penal* 1 (2008): 9.

Index

Note: Page references following "n" refer notes.

FSC
www.fsc.org
MIX
Papier | Fördert gute Waldnutzung
FSC® C083411

Kolibri 360 GmbH
Ferdinand-Jühlke-Straße 7
99095 Erfurt, Deutschland
produktsicherheit@kolibri360.de